PATTERNS
for a
PURPOSE

PATTERNS
for a
PURPOSE

Barbara Fine Clouse

McGraw-Hill, Inc.
New York   St. Louis   San Francisco
Auckland   Bogotá   Caracas   Lisbon   London   Madrid
Mexico City   Milan   Montreal   New Delhi   San Juan
Singapore   Sydney   Tokyo   Toronto

This book was set in Garamond Light by Better Graphics, Inc.
The editors were Tim Julet, Laurie PiSierra, and Jean Akers;
the designer was Karen K. Quigley;
the production supervisor was Louise Karam.
R. R. Donnelley & Sons Company was printer and binder.

Cover photos
Clockwise from top left: Stuart Cohen; Bill Ellzey; Bob Pizaro;
Thomas Wear; Comstock; John Cooke; Bruce Hands; Com-
stock.

PATTERNS *for a* PURPOSE

This book is printed on acid-free paper.

2 3 4 5 6 7 8 9 0 DOC DOC 9 0 9 8 7 6 5

ISBN 0-07-011419-6

Library of Congress Cataloging-in-Publication Data

Clouse, Barbara Fine.
     Patterns for a purpose / Barbara Clouse.
          p.   cm.
     ISBN 0-07-011419-6
     1. College readers.   2. English language—Rhetoric.   I. Title.
PE1417.C6314   1995
808′.0427—dc20   94-13172

For Denny, with love

CONTENTS

Thematic Contents   *xix*
Preface   *xxiii*

CHAPTER 1
THE ELEMENTS OF THE ESSAY   1

The Thesis   1
Purpose   3
Audience   4
The Writer's Role   4
Tone   4
Supporting Details   5
    Adequate Detail   5
    Relevant Detail   6
    The Source and Form of Supporting Details   7
    Organizing Supporting Details into Body Paragraphs   8
    When to Paragraph   8
    Ordering Supporting Details   9
    Transitions   9
The Introduction   11
    Open with an Arresting Statement   12
    Provide Background Information   12
    Tell a Story (Use Narration)   12
    Establish Yourself as Someone Knowledgeable about the Subject   12
    Explain Your Purpose   13
    Describe Something   13
    Define Something   13
    Use an Interesting or Pertinent Quotation   13
The Conclusion   13

Draw a Conclusion from the Information in the Essay 14
Present the Final, Most Important Point 14
Offer a Solution to a Problem Mentioned in the Essay 14
Call Your Readers to Action 15
Look to the Future 15
Leave Your Reader with a Final Impression 15
The Title 15
A Sample Student Essay: Is Today's Athlete a Good Sport? 16

CHAPTER 2
READING AN ESSAY 18

Active Reading 19
How to Be an Active Reader 19
Step 1: Review the Material 19
Step 2: Read the Selection in One Sitting, If Possible 19
Step 3: Read and Study 19
A Sample Marked Essay: Americanization Is Tough on "Macho" 21

CHAPTER 3
WRITING AN ESSAY 26

Idea Generation 26
Finding a Topic 27
Discovering Ideas to Develop Your Topic 29
Establishing Purpose, Audience, Role, and Tone 31
Outlining 31
The Scratch Outline 31
The Informal Outline 33
The Outline Tree 33
The Outline Worksheet 34
The Formal Outline 35
Writing the First Draft 36
Revising the Draft 38
Tips for Revising 38
Revision Checklist 39
Editing the Draft 39
Proofreading the Final Copy 39

CHAPTER 4
DESCRIPTION 41

The Purpose of Description 42
Objective and Expressive Details 43
Descriptive Words 43
Similes and Metaphors 45
Selecting and Ordering Details 46
Suggestions for Writing Description 47
Annotated Student Essay: In Chelsea's Room 48

Dawn Watch *John Ciardi* 49
*Ciardi shares his impression of first light to persuade the reader
that dawn is the best part of the day.*

The Sounds of the City *James Tuite* 54
*Share Tuite's view of Manhattan as a city of sounds and learn
a bit about this complex place.*

Once More to the Lake *E. B. White* 58
*After 40 years, White returns to a family vacation spot with his
son and comes to a startling conclusion. To share with his reader,
White combines description with narration, comparison, and
contrast.*

My Backyard *Mary E. Mebane* 65
*In this excerpt from her autobiography, Mary Mebane describes
the backyard of her childhood to share something of herself with
the reader.*

My Neighborhood *Alfred Kazin* 71
*With vivid images, Kazin shares his response to the Brownsville
tenement that he grew up in.*

The Deer at Providencia *Annie Dillard* 76
*An important contemporary author combines description
with narration to share her experiences with suffering and
her uncertainty about why it exists.*

Additional Essay Assignments 81

CHAPTER 5
NARRATION

82

The Purpose of Narration   83
Supporting Details   83
Selecting and Ordering Details   84
Suggestions for Writing Narration   86
Annotated Student Essay: The Family Reunion, Revisited   87

Salvation *Langston Hughes*   89
    Langston Hughes shares a painful experience: his loss of faith
    at a revival service.

My Mother Never Worked *Bonnie Smith-Yackel*   93
    To persuade the reader that "woman's work" in the home
    should be valued as much as salaried work outside the home,
    the author tells the story of her mother's life of labor.

The Endless Streetcar Ride into the Night, and the Tinfoil Noose
Jean Shepherd   98
    With narration and description, Jean Shepherd shares part of
    his past and entertains the reader. At the same time,
    classification and cause-and-effect analysis help him inform
    the reader about what separates the "movers and shakers"
    from the rest of the population.

A Hanging *George Orwell*   105
    To share, inform, and persuade, Orwell combines narration
    and description in an account of an execution.

By Any Other Name *Santha Rama Rau*   111
    The author shares her experience with discrimination in an
    English school in India and informs the reader about the
    nature and effect of British colonial rule and prejudice.

The Water-Faucet Vision *Gish Jen*   118
    Jen's stories of her childhood allow her to share part of her
    childhood and how it was affected by her family and religious
    beliefs.

Additional Essay Assignments   127

CHAPTER 6
EXEMPLIFICATION 128

The Purpose of Exemplification 129
Supporting Details 130
Selecting and Ordering Details 130
Suggestions for Writing Exemplification 132
Annotated Student Essay: A Man's Game 133

"Why" Is Worse Than "What" *George E. Condon* 135
*In a humorous piece, George Condon illustrates that the
explanation can be as absurd as the event.*

Class Acts *John Berendt* 139
*Examples help define "class act" to inform the reader. You will
be heartened to learn that there is still a lot of class in the
world.*

On Holidays and How to Make Them Work *Nikki Giovanni* 143
*Do Americans know how to celebrate holidays? Prominent
poet and essayist Nikki Giovanni uses examples to persuade
the reader that we don't.*

University Days *James Thurber* 146
*American humorist James Thurber entertains with five
humorous, extended examples of the absurdity and frustration
of college life during the World War I era. Has anything
changed?*

What I've Learned from Men: Lessons for a Full-Grown Feminist
Barbara Ehrenreich 153
*Using exemplification, cause-and-effect analysis, definition,
and contrast, Ehrenreich informs the reader about the ladylike
behavior of women and argues that women should abandon
that behavior.*

Untouchables *Jonathan Kozol* 159
*Combining exemplification with cause-and-effect analysis,
Kozol gives a dramatic account of the real proportions of
homelessness to persuade the reader that government policy
and our own fear are part of the problem.*

Additional Essay Assignments 169

CHAPTER 7
PROCESS ANALYSIS 170

The Purpose of Process Analysis 171
Supporting Details 172
Selecting and Ordering Details 173
Suggestions for Writing a Process Analysis 174
Annotated Student Essay: Your Basic Blast 175

The Unbearable Lightness of Air Travel *Roy Blount, Jr.* 177
  *A popular humorist entertains the reader with an amusing
  process analysis that pokes fun at the airline industry.*

Don't Just Stand There *Diane Cole* 182
  Cole explains how to deal with ethnic, racial, and sexist slurs.

How I'll Become an American *Miklós Vámos* 189
  *Hungarian-born Vámos takes a satiric look at Americans and
  in the process suggests areas for improvement. Perhaps the
  process analysis will also convince you that we Americans
  need to change our ways.*

The Knife *Richard Selzer* 193
  *Selzer combines process analysis with description, comparison,
  and definition to inform the reader about the surgical process
  and to share his attitude about surgery, surgeons, the human
  body, and "the knife." Because his description is so masterful,
  you are likely to be entertained by the author-surgeon's use of
  language.*

Behind the Formaldehyde Curtain *Jessica Mitford* 198
  *Mitford tells you more than you may want to know about the
  processes of embalming and burial. But her purpose goes
  beyond informing the reader to convincing her audience that
  embalming is unnecessary.*

What Sort of Car-Rt-Sort Am I? *Erik Larson* 207
  *In an examination of threats to privacy, the author combines
  process analysis with exemplification and cause-and-effect
  analysis to explain how data about us is compiled and sold.
  The result is entertaining, persuasive, and informational.*

Additional Essay Assignments 218

CHAPTER 8
COMPARISON AND CONTRAST 220

The Purpose of Comparison and Contrast 221
Supporting Details 222
Selecting Details 222
Ordering Details 223
Suggestions for Writing Comparison and Contrast 225
Annotated Student Essay: Opposites Attract 226

Neat People vs. Sloppy People *Suzanne Britt* 228
    Sloppy people are morally superior to neat people, according
    to this entertaining contrast of the neat and the sloppy.

Two Views of the Mississippi *Mark Twain* 232
    Twain shares his experiences on the Mississippi River and
    informs the reader that with familiarity and knowledge come
    loss of romance and beauty.

Grant and Lee: A Study in Contrasts *Bruce Catton* 235
    Historian Bruce Catton compares and contrasts the two most
    important generals of the Civil War to inform the reader that
    each admirably represented a force in American society.

Am I Blue? *Alice Walker* 240
    Walker combines comparison, narration, and description in
    the story of a horse named Blue. The patterns allow the author
    to share part of her experience, to inform the reader about the
    nature of animals, and to persuade the reader that animals
    should be treated better.

Brains and Computers *Robert Jastrow* 246
    By pointing out the similarities and differences in the ways
    they work, Jastrow informs the reader about how both brains
    and computers operate.

Talk in the Intimate Relationship: His and Hers *Deborah Tannen* 252
    With contrast, exemplification, and cause-and-effect analysis,
    the author informs the reader of the different ways men and
    women communicate, how these differences emerge, and what
    their effects are.

Additional Essay Assignments 261

CHAPTER 9
CAUSE-AND-EFFECT ANALYSIS   263

The Purpose of Cause-and-Effect Analysis   264
Supporting Details   264
Selecting and Ordering Details   265
Suggestions for Writing Cause-and-Effect Analysis   266
Annotated Student Essay: Why Athletes Use Steroids   267

American Has Gone on a Trip Out of Tune *Dave Barry*   270
    Humorist Dave Barry's entertaining analysis of the decline of
    group singing may not make the required reading list of our
    greatest social scientists, but it will make most readers chuckle.

Why We Crave Horror Movies *Stephen King*   274
    Who could be better than horror novelist and screenwriter Ste-
    phen King to explain why we love the grisly evil of horror
    movies? And who else could manage to entertain the reader in
    the process?

India: A Widow's Devastating Choice *Juthica Stangl*   278
    Juthica Stangl combines narration and cause-and-effect
    analysis to inform her reader of the brutal social and
    economic reality widows in India face and to persuade the
    reader that change must occur.

Just Walk on By: A Black Man Ponders His Power to Alter Public Space
Brent Staples   285
    To inform the reader, Brent Staples looks at why the black
    man is automatically perceived as a threat. Then he goes on
    to share how that fact affects him.

No Kick from Champagne *Harold Saltzman*   291
    The author informs the reader of the effects of weddings on
    single people and shares his own experiences as a single at
    weddings. The result is an essay that works to persuade the
    reader that singles are the target of discrimination.

Complexion *Richard Rodriguez*   295
    Rodriguez uses contrast, narration, and description to share
    how he was affected by his dark complexion.

Additional Essay Assignments   300

CHAPTER 10
CLASSIFICATION-DIVISION

CHAPTER 10 CLASSIFICATION-DIVISION   301

The Purpose of Classification-Division   302
Selecting a Principle for Classification-Division   303
Selecting Detail   303
Structuring Classification-Division   304
Suggestions for Writing Classification-Division   306
Annotated Student Essay: *Strictly Speaking*   307

Wait Division *Tom Bodett*   309
    Humorist Tom Bodett classifies kinds of waiting with very
    entertaining results.

White Lies *Sissela Bok*   313
    Are white lies really harmless? Bok informs the reader of the
    forms these lies can take and argues that they may not be as
    harmless as we think they are.

Country Codes *Noel Perrin*   317
    If you visit rural New England, you better know the codes
    Perrin informs you of in this essay. Perrin also entertains and
    shares something of his own experience.

College Pressures *William Zinsser*   323
    Zinsser combines classification, exemplification, and cause-
    and-effect analysis to inform the reader of the kinds of
    pressures faced by Yale college students. What's the solution?
    Zinsser argues that it rests with the students themselves.

The Way of Meeting Oppression *Martin Luther King, Jr.*   332
    Civil rights leader Dr. Martin Luther King, Jr. informs his
    reader
    of the ways to respond to oppression, and then he works to
    persuade his audience that the nonviolent way is the best.

Shades of Black *Mary Mebane*   336
    To share her own experiences with discrimination and to
    inform about color discrimination among blacks and its
    effects on black females, Mebane uses classification,
    exemplification, narration, definition, and cause and effect
    analysis.

Additional Essay Assignments   341

CHAPTER 11
DEFINITION
343

The Purpose of Definition 344
Supporting Details 345
Structuring Definition 345
Suggestions for Writing Definition 346
Annotated Student Essay: Autumn 347

What Is Poverty? *Jo Goodwin Parker* 349
*Parker informs the reader of the true nature of poverty in an
effort to persuade her audience to take action against it.*

The Holocaust *Bruno Bettelheim* 355
*Holocaust survivor Bruno Bettelheim combines definition with
cause and effect analysis and process analysis to inform the
reader about Nazi crimes and to argue that the holocaust and
its victims are misnamed.*

Good Souls *Dorothy Parker* 360
*American humorist Dorothy Parker writes an entertaining
definition that attempts to persuade the reader that her subject
is worthy of contempt.*

I Want a Wife *Judy Brady* 366
*Brady's definition explains the difficulty of the traditional
wife's role, and it works to persuade the reader of the
unfairness of that role.*

The View from 80 *Malcolm Cowley* 370
*Malcolm Cowley's definition of old age is combined with
several other patterns to allow the author to share his
experience with old age and inform the reader of what old age
is like.*

Lists *Jeanine Larmoth* 379
*Larmoth's entertaining essay shares the role lists play in her
life.*

Additional Essay Assignments 385

CHAPTER 12
A CASEBOOK FOR ARGUMENTATION
AND PERSUASION:
THE CHANGING FAMILY

CHAPTER 12 A CASEBOOK FOR ARGUMENTATION AND PERSUASION: THE CHANGING FAMILY — 386

The Purpose of Argumentation-Persuasion — 387
Argumentative Detail — 388
Avoiding Errors in Logic — 389
Persuasive Detail — 391
Raising and Countering Objections — 391
Organizing Argumentation-Persuasion — 392
Suggestions for Writing Argumentation-Persuasion — 394
Annotated Student Essay: Who Should Decide? — 395

Marriage Is a Fundamental Right *Thomas Stoddard* — 397
  Stoddard argues in favor of same-sex marriages.

Reserve Marriage for Heterosexuals *Bruce Fein* — 400
  Fein argues against same-sex marriages.

I Wish They'd Do It Right *Jane Doe* — 403
  Her son and his "wife" are not married, but according to Jane Doe, they should be.

Cohousing and the American Dream *Kathryn McCamant and Charles Durrett* — 407
  McCamant and Durrett argue the need for an alternative housing concept.

Families *Jane Howard* — 413
  The author explains the characteristics of good families.

Needed: A Policy for Children When Parents Go to Work *Maxine Phillips* — 423
  Maxine Phillips argues for a national child care policy.

Homemaking *William Raspberry* — 427
  Columnist William Raspberry comments on the low value we place on homemaking and argues that homemaking should be valued more.

Self-Help—A Black Tradition *Dorothy Height* — 431
  Among the strengths of the black family is its tradition of self-help.

Additional Essay Assignments — 438

APPENDIX
WRITING PARAPHRASES, QUOTATIONS,
SUMMARIES, AND SYNTHESES

APPENDIX WRITING PARAPHRASES, QUOTATIONS, SUMMARIES, AND SYNTHESES 440

Paraphrasing 440
Quoting 441
Documenting Borrowed Material 443
Summarizing 445
    The Purpose of Summaries 445
    Suggestions for Writing a Summary 445
    A Sample Summary 446
Synthesizing 448
    The Purpose of Synthesis 448
    Detail in a Synthesis 448
    Suggestions for Synthesizing Information 449
    A Sample Synthesis 450

Index 453

THEMATIC CONTENTS

Rituals and Celebrations
Dawn Watch 49
On Holidays and How to Make Them Work 143
Behind the Formaldehyde Curtain 198
America Has Gone on a Trip Out of Tune 270
The View from 80 370
Marriage Is a Fundamental Right 397
Reserve Marriage for Heterosexuals 400
I Wish They'd Do it Right 403

Bias and Discrimination
My Mother Never Worked 93
A Hanging 105
By Any Other Name 111
What I've Learned from Men 153
Untouchables 159
Don't Just Stand There 182
How I'll Become an American 189
Am I Blue? 240
India: A Widow's Devastating Choice 278
Just Walk on By 285
The Way of Meeting Oppression 332
Shades of Black 336
The Holocaust 355
I Want a Wife 366
Marriage Is a Fundamental Right 397
Reserve Marriage for Heterosexuals 400
Homemaking 427
Self-Help—A Black Tradition 431

Education
By Any Other Name   111
The Water-Faucet Vision   118
University Days   142
College Pressures   323
Shades of Black   336

Health and Medicine
The Deer at Providencia   76
The Knife   193
Behind the Formaldehyde Curtain   198
Two Views of the Mississippi   232

Change
The Sounds of the City   54
Once More to the Lake   58
The Water-Faucet Vision   118
Two Views of the Mississippi   232
The View from 80   370
Cohousing and the American Dream   407

Memories
Once More to the Lake   58
My Backyard   65
My Neighborhood   71
Salvation   89
The Endless Streetcar Ride into the Night and the Tinfoil Noose   98
The Water-Faucet Vision   118
Complexion   295
Shades of Black   336

Modern Problems
"Why" Is Worse Than "What"   135
Untouchables   159
The Unbearable Lightness of Air Travel   177
What Sort of Car-Rt-Sort Am I?   207
No Kick from Champagne   291
What Is Poverty?   349
I Wish They'd Do It Right   403
Families   413
Needed: A Policy for Children When Parents Go to Work   423

Relationships with Animals
The Deer at Providencia   76
Am I Blue?   240

Places
Dawn Watch 49
The Sounds of the City 54
Once More to the Lake 58
My Backyard 65
My Neighborhood 71

Childhood, Adolescence, and Old Age
Once More to the Lake 58
My Backyard 65
My Neighborhood 71
Salvation 89
The Endless Streetcar Ride into the Night and the Tinfoil Noose 98
The Water-Faucet Vision 118
Behind the Formaldehyde Curtain 198
Complexion 295
The View from 80 370

Day-to-Day Living
Dawn Watch 49
The Sounds of the City 54
"Why" Is Worse Than "What" 135
Class Acts 139
How I'll Become an American 189
Wait Division 309
White Lies 313
Country Codes 317
Lists 379

Interactions
My Backyard 65
My Neighborhood 71
The Endless Streetcar Ride into the Night and the Tinfoil Noose 98
A Hanging 105
By Any Other Name 111
The Water-Faucet Vision 118
Class Acts 139
Why We Crave Horror Movies 274
No Kick from Champagne 291
White Lies 313
The Holocaust 355
Good Souls 360
I Wish They'd Do It Right 403
Cohousing and the American Dream 4077

Men and Women
The Endless Streetcar Ride into the Night and the Tinfoil Noose 98
The Water-Faucet Vision 118
What I Learned from Men 153
Talk in the Intimate Relationship 252

India: A Widow's Devastating Choice 278
No Kick from Champagne 291
Shades of Black 336
I Want a Wife 366
Homemaking 427

Marriage and Family
My Backyard 65
My Mother Never Worked 93
The Water-Faucet Vision 118
Untouchables 159
Am I Blue? 240
India: A Widow's Devastating Choice 278
Complexion 295
What Is Poverty? 349
I Want a Wife 366
Marriage Is a Fundamental Right 397
Reserve Marriage for Heterosexuals 400
I Wish They'd Do It Right 403
Cohousing and the American Dream 407
Families 413
Needed: A Policy for Children When Parents Go to Work 423
Homemaking 427
Self-Help—A Black Tradition 431

Technology
What Sort of Cart-Rt-Sort Am I? 207
Brains and Computers 246

Humor and Satire
"Why" Is Worse Than "What" 135
University Days 146
The Unbearable Lightness of Air Travel 177
How I'll Become an American 189
Neat People vs. Sloppy People 228
America Has Gone on a Trip out of Tune 270
Wait Division 309
Good Souls 360

PREFACE

The wealth of rhetorical readers on the market would seem to offer considerable choice, but their reading selections, apparatus, and underlying philosophy vary so little that the books are almost interchangeable. *Patterns for a Purpose*, however, is a rhetorical reader with several important differences. While it retains all the features proven effective—the ones that recur from rhetorical reader to rhetorical reader—it makes a number of refinements that enhance teachability and connect instruction in the modes to "real-world writing." Thus, instructors who favor rhetorical readers will find everything they have come to expect of the genre—and a bit more.

First, rather than present the rhetorical patterns as ends unto themselves, the text focuses on the patterns as ways to fulfill the writer's purpose. To this end, the readings in each rhetorical chapter are identified in terms of how they help the author share, entertain, inform, and/or persuade. In addition, *Patterns for a Purpose* acknowledges that rhetorical patterns often appear in combination, so each of the essay chapters includes two readings that show how two or more patterns can be combined to achieve a variety of purposes.

Another distinguishing feature of *Patterns for a Purpose* is its treatment of argumentation-persuasion. Other rhetorical readers treat argumentation-persuasion as a rhetorical pattern, and thus they gather argumentative-persuasive essays together in a separate chapter, perhaps after classification or cause and effect analysis. Yet persuasion is a purpose, not a pattern, so in *Patterns for a Purpose* argumentative or persuasive essays appear in every chapter of readings. That is, since every pattern can be used to a persuasive end, every pattern is illustrated in the service of that end. The chapter on cause and effect analysis, for example, will include a cause and effect analysis meant to persuade the reader, the chapter on description will include a descriptive essay meant to persuade the reader, and so forth.

However, because of the importance of argumentation-persuasion and the level of sophistication it demands of students, it is worthy of singular focus in its own chapter. For this reason, Chapter 12 focuses on argumentation-persuasion in a unique way. Called "A Casebook for Argumentation and Persuasion: The Changing Family," the chapter includes explanation of the principles of argumentation-persuasion along with eight argumentation-persuasion essays that focus on the changing character of the family. This chapter conforms to the pattern of the earlier ones by following each reading with questions on ideas and techniques, a collaborative activity, a prompt for a journal entry, and two or more argumentation or persuasive writing assignments. The chapter closes with additional argumentation-persuasive writing assignments related to the changing family, assignments which give students an opportunity to respond to multiple essays. Also, by focusing on a single issue, the chapter gives students the satisfaction of exploring one topic in some depth as they increase their proficiency with argumentation and persuasion.

Because one purpose of a reader is to provide ideas both to stimulate writing and help students backup their points, students are expected to draw on some of the essays for their own writings. For this reason, *Patterns for a Purpose* treats paraphrasing, quoting, summarizing, synthesizing, and documenting borrowed material, so students can learn how to handle borrowed material responsibly and according to prevailing academic conventions. This material is gathered in the appendix to ensure flexibility. Thus, at any point in the term or text that instructors want to bring up the incorporation of borrowed material, they can turn to this section. Furthermore, because paraphrasing, quoting, summarizing, and synthesizing are such important academic skills, the appendix is a particularly helpful part of the text.

 ## THE COMPONENTS OF *PATTERNS FOR A PURPOSE*

■ *Chapter 1, "The Elements of the Essay,"* explains and illustrates the points students—as both readers and writers of essays—need to know about the thesis, introduction, supporting details, conclusion, and title. In addition, the chapter treats audience, purpose, role and tone. To illustrate the points made in this chapter, a student essay appears with helpful marginal annotations to point out key features.

■ *Chapter 2, "Reading an Essay,"* describes and illustrates the active reading process. Emphasis is on showing students how to interact with a text rather than just letting the words wash over them. To help them appreciate how an active reader can mark a text, a sample marked text is provided.

■ *Chapter 3, "Writing an Essay,"* describes a range of procedures for idea generation (finding a topic, generating ideas, establishing audience, purpose, role, and tone), outlining, drafting, revising, and editing. By presenting a variety of techniques, the chapter helps students develop successful writing processes by sampling procedures until they find the ones that work the best for them. A helpful revision checklist also appears.

■ *Chapters 4–11,* which focus on rhetorical patterns, all have the same features:

1. There are six readings in the pattern under consideration, two of which illustrate the pattern in combination with one or more other patterns. Because the essence of any reader is the readings, care was taken to select

high-interest readings with good representation of women, minority, and multicultural authors. The readings, a mix of old favorites and newer selections that treat both contemporary and timeless issues, represent a modest range of length and difficulty.

2. An opening page lists the essays in the chapter and notes to what purpose the pattern in each essay is put.

3. Introductory material explains the purposes the pattern can serve, characteristics of the supporting details, considerations for selecting and ordering details, and suggestions for topic selection, generating ideas, and revising.

4. A student essay illustrates the features discussed in the introductory material. The essay is annotated to serve as a study aid. (Care was taken to select typical student essays that represent realistic models. Too many readers discourage students by using heavily revised student essays barely distinguishable from the professional pieces.)

5. A headnote before each essay explains something about the author, the purpose the pattern is put to, and one or more features students should look for when they read; the significance of these features is reinforced in the apparatus following the reading.

6. After each reading, the following apparatus exists:
   —two sets of study questions, one on content and one on technique
   —an assignment for group consideration or collaborative learning
   —a topic for a journal entry
   —3-4 essay assignments in the pattern under consideration
   —2 essay assignments on thematic issues, 1 that focuses on a theme in the essay under consideration, and 1 that draws on that essay and at least 1 other essay, usually from a different chapter

7. Each chapter ends with 20 additional essay topics in the pattern under consideration.

■ *Chapter 12, "A Casebook for Argumentation and Persuasion: The Changing Family,"* has the following features:

1. There is detailed explanation of purpose, supporting detail, avoiding errors in logic, and organizing argumentation-persuasion.

2. An annotated student essay illustrates the points emphasized in the chapter.

3. There are eight argumentative-persuasive essays on the subject of the changing family. The single-issue focus of the chapter allows students to explore a topic in some depth, and it allows students to draw on and respond to more than one essay when they write. If this chapter is combined with the appendix on paraphrasing, quoting, summarizing, and synthesizing, the chapter can be used for controlled research assignments, which makes for an excellent bridge into the research paper course that is often the second-term freshman composition requirement.

4. After each reading, the following apparatus exists:
   —two sets of study questions, one on content and one on technique
   —an assignment for group consideration or collaborative learning
   —a topic for a journal entry
   —two or more argumentative-persuasive essay assignments

5. The chapter ends with ten additional argumentative-persuasive essay assignments, some of which require students to consider two or more readings.

■ *The Appendix, "Writing Paraphrases, Quotations, Summaries, and Syntheses,"* focuses on handling borrowed material responsibly. Since one purpose of a reader is to provide departure points for writing and ideas to back-up assertions, students need to learn how to handle source material. In addition to explanations of paraphrasing, quoting, summarizing, and synthesizing, the appendix also includes an annotated summary and an annotated synthesis for study aids and information on documentation. By combining this appendix with Chapter 12, instructors can create controlled research assignments that serve as a bridge into a research course. Otherwise, the appendix material can be introduced whenever the instructor finds it appropriate to do so.

 ## ACKNOWLEDGMENTS

It is a pleasure to work with the editorial and production teams at McGraw-Hill because their enthusiasm, support, generosity, and good humor are unflagging. In particular, I thank Lesley Denton, whose early support and guidance got the project started, and Jean Akers, a gracious, elegant editorial supervisor, who makes all the problems go away—there is none better. My debt to Laurie PiSierra is especially profound. As the manuscript was written and rewritten, she was editor, advisor, psychiatrist, and friend—and she executed all those roles to perfection.

I am also grateful to the following reviewers who read the manuscript so thoughtfully and offered sound advice, helpful criticism, and the wisdom born of their classroom experience. They helped shape the manuscript in significant ways, and I am truly appreciative: Alan Brown, Livingston University; Mitzi Brunsdale, Maryville State University; Marian Davis, Jacksonville State University; Mary Ann McCandless, Butler County Community College; Patrick McMahon, Tallahassee Community College; Walden Madsen, City University of New York–Brooklyn; Carol Newell, Northern Virginia Community College; Christopher Picard, San Juan College; Douglas Roycraft, Erie Community College; Merritt Stark, Henderson State University; Vivian Thomlinson, Cameron University; Lawrence Watson, University of Wisconsin–Steven's Point; and Gary Zacharias, Palomar College.

Finally, my debt to my ever-indulgent, understanding husband and children is beyond expression. Nonetheless, my heartfelt thanks goes to Denny, who always understands and who always clears a path, and to Greg and Jeff, who lower the boom box so I can think.

Barbara Fine Clouse

THE ELEMENTS OF THE ESSAY

If you are reading this page, you have made your way into a college writing class, and you will spend the coming weeks reading and writing essays. To help you get the most from the experience, the early chapters of this book explain procedures for reading and writing efficiently and effectively. This particular chapter will explain the characteristics of successful essays.

 ## THE THESIS

A successful essay has a central point—a main message the writer wants to convey. This central point is the thesis, the idea that everything else in the essay relates to.

Very often, the thesis has two parts. One part expresses the subject of the essay; the other part expresses the author's position on that subject.

Thesis	Subject	Writer's Position on Subject
Parents should limit their children's exposure to MTV.	MTV	Parents should limit their children's exposure to it.
Careful observation reveals three kinds of practical jokers.	practical jokers	There are three kinds.
My father was a strict disciplinarian.	the author's father	He was a strict disciplinarian.

A thesis can do more than indicate the subject and the writer's position on the subject. It can also note the main points the writer will make in the essay, like this:

thesis:	Parents should limit their children's exposure to MTV because the channel contains sexually explicit material, and it demeans people.
subject:	MTV
writer's position:	Parents should limit their children's exposure to it.
points to be made:	MTV contains sexually explicit material. It demeans people.

An essay's thesis is one or two sentences that often appear in the essay's introduction, frequently at the end of that section. However, a thesis can also be in the middle of an essay or at the end, in the conclusion. Sometimes the thesis is not stated at all. Instead, it is strongly implied by the information in the essay. As a student writer, you may find it easiest to state the thesis and place it at the end of the introduction, where it can stand as a reference point for everything that follows.

Regardless of where a writer places the thesis, some guidelines apply:

1. The thesis should not be a formal announcement.

no:	This paper will discuss the reasons the United States needs election reform.
yes:	The United States would benefit from election reform.
no:	The following essay will explain how to behave during a job interview.
yes:	If you want to land that dream job, follow my advice during the job interview.
no:	I want to tell you the characteristics of a nurturing family.
yes:	All nurturing families share the same characteristics.

2. The thesis should present something arguable or in need of explanation, rather than a statement of fact.

no:	Drunk drivers are a menace to everyone. (No one will disagree with this statement of fact, so why construct an essay around it?)
yes:	To make the roads safer for everyone, we should suspend the driver's license of anyone convicted of drunk driving. (This thesis presents an arguable point.)
no:	During the depression my grandmother raised four children by herself. (This is a statement of fact.)
yes:	I have always admired my grandmother's strength and courage during difficult times. (This thesis allows for explanation.)

3. The thesis should present a manageable topic; it should not take in too much.

> no: Our system of education is in need of a complete overhaul. (An essay that discusses changes in every aspect of the educational system will be much longer than the standard college essay. If the essay is a reasonable length, the discussion will be superficial.)
>
> yes: To be competitive with the rest of the world, we must change the way we teach mathematics. (This thesis presents a topic that can be treated in adequate detail in a manageable length.)

4. The thesis should be written in specific language; avoid using such vague words as *nice, interesting, good, bad,* and *great.*

> no: Playing high school football was a great experience.
>
> yes: Playing high school football taught me self-confidence and the importance of teamwork.

 PURPOSE

A successful essay is written for one or more of these purposes:

- To entertain the reader
- To share the writer's experience and/or feelings with the reader
- To inform the reader about something interesting or important
- To persuade the reader to think or act a particular way

Purpose is an important element of the essay because it influences the writer's approach. Let's say, for example, that you are a single parent who wants to write about the child care problems in this country. If you want to entertain your reader, you can write a funny piece about what you went through the day you had to take final examinations and the babysitter canceled. If you want to share with your reader, you can describe how much you worry about whether your children get quality care while you are at work. If you want to inform your reader, you can explain what the child care options are for a single working parent of preschool children. If you want to persuade your reader, you can argue for a federally funded child care program. Of course, you can also combine purposes. For example, you can share your own experiences and then go on to argue that a federally funded program would make life easier for you and others. Obviously, each of these essays would have a different character because the content would be shaped by the writer's purpose.

 ## AUDIENCE

The writer of a successful essay will have a clear sense of audience—that is, a clear sense of who the reader is and what that reader is like. A sense of audience is important if the writer is going to fulfill his or her purpose. Suppose you want to write an essay about the pollution in a local river. If the essay were written for your biology class, it might include a great deal of technical information about specific chemical pollutants. However, if the essay were for a letter to your local newspaper, such technical information might overwhelm the average reader. Now let's say that you are writing to convince your reader to support a school levy that would raise property taxes. If your reader has school-age children, you could argue that the quality of their education will improve if the levy passes. However, if your reader has no children, you may do better to argue that good schools will increase the value of the reader's property.

In some writing classrooms, you can establish any audience for your writing, but in others you must consider your classmates and teacher to be your audience. Regardless of the situation in your particular writing class, be sure you have a clear sense of who your reader is and what your audience's particular characteristics and needs are.

 ## THE WRITER'S ROLE

In addition to audience and purpose, the writer's role influences the character of an essay. For example, a student writing for a teacher will be careful to conform to all the terms of the assignment. An employee writing for a supervisor will adopt the appropriate respectful tone. A friend writing to another friend may be casual and use slang, but a student writing an essay as part of a scholarship competition will not include slang.

To appreciate the significance of the writer's role, consider a report on how to select the right college. A person in the role of a high school counselor will provide an objective set of procedures, but a person in the role of a college admissions counselor may slant detail to favor his or her school. A person in the role of a student may express the frustrations that are part of the process, but a person in the role of a parent may stress financial concerns.

 ## TONE

The tone of an essay is set by the writer's attitude. Thus, a piece can be angry, sarcastic, serious, preachy, argumentative, conciliatory, hurtful, earnest, scornful, hostile, enthusiastic, neutral, and so on. The clue to tone is word choice. Notice, for example, how word choice creates the different tones in the following sentences on the same subject.

angry tone: Many so-called citizens who are too tight-fisted to invest in the future of our children refuse to vote for the school levy.

neutral tone: A significant number of citizens hesitate to pass the school levy and thereby increase their taxes.

 ## SUPPORTING DETAILS

The supporting details are all the points made to prove or explain the thesis. It is impossible to overestimate the importance of the supporting details because they are the heart of an essay. In fact, the supporting details are so important that an essay's success or failure rests on them. To be successful, supporting details must be adequate and relevant.

Adequate Detail

Each main point you offer in your essay is a generalization. To have adequate detail, you must back up every generalization with enough detail to prove or explain it to your reader's satisfaction. If, for instance, you say your roommate is a practical joker, you've made a generalization. You then must prove that generalization with examples of your roommate's practical jokes. If you say that Chez Paris is the most beautiful restaurant in town, you are making a generalization and must support it with descriptive details, showing why you find it beautiful, so your reader appreciates your point. If you say that schoolchildren should not be grouped by ability because such grouping discourages achievement, you must explain that generalization by showing how ability grouping discourages achievement. In short, you cannot expect a reader to accept what you say just because you say it—you must explain and prove your generalizations. A good way to remember the need to provide adequate detail is to remind yourself that a writer must "show and not just tell."

You can show and not just tell by carefully moving from the general to the specific. To do this, first state a generalization; then go on to give specific points to prove or support that generalization.

To appreciate the need to show and not just tell, and to see how a writer can move from the general to the specific, contrast the following two drafts. Draft A does not support generalizations, but draft B does—by moving from the general to the specific. The specific points appear underscored as a study aid.

DRAFT A

Dr. Garcia is a dedicated teacher. She is concerned about students and always willing to give a struggling young scholar extra attention. In addition, she takes pains to include everyone in class discussions, even the shy students who ordinarily do not participate. Particularly impressive is the personal interest she

takes in each of her students. No wonder her class is always one of the first to fill up every semester.

DRAFT B

Dr. Garcia is a dedicated teacher. She is concerned about students and always willing to give a struggling young scholar extra attention. Last week, for example, two students were having trouble finding topics for their research papers, so Dr. Garcia met them at the library and helped them explore the possibilities. In addition, she takes pains to include everyone in class discussions, even the shy students who ordinarily do not participate. One way she does this is to ask people their opinions on subjects under discussion. That way, they do not have to worry about giving a wrong answer. Another way she brings students into discussions is to plan group work so students can talk to each other in more comfortable, smaller groups.

Particularly impressive is the personal interest Dr. Garcia takes in each of her students. Everyone writes a journal, and from the journals Dr. Garcia learns about her students' interests, successes, problems, and family life. Because she comes to know her students so well, she can talk to them about things important to them, which creates a bond between student and teacher. As a result, all her students come to understand that Dr. Garcia cares about them. No wonder her class is always one of the first to fill up every semester.

Relevant Detail

Supporting details must be relevant, which means they must be clearly related to the thesis. Most readers will grow annoyed when details are not related to the matter at hand. Thus, if you want to argue for the elimination of the physical education requirement at your school, you would not mention that it would also be a good idea to eliminate the foreign language requirement. In the following draft, one sentence presents irrelevant detail. When you read, you will notice the annoying distraction created by that sentence.

> Many universities are altering their teacher education curricula to require prospective teachers to get into the classroom as soon as possible, even in the freshman year. These future teachers observe, tutor, and in general get the feel of a teacher's responsibilities. The plan is a good one because students can decide early on if they are suited to teaching and change their majors if necessary. In the more traditional curriculum, an education major waits until the junior or senior year to get into the classroom, when it can be too late to change majors without serious inconvenience and expense. Many students in all programs change majors and problems are to be expected. Certainly it makes sense to move prospective teachers into the classroom as early as possible, so the plan should catch on.

You probably found the next to last sentence annoying and distracting because it is not closely enough related to the matter at hand. To avoid such irrelevant detail in your own writing, outline carefully to be sure everything is related to the thesis. (See page 31 for a discussion of outlining.)

The Source and Form of Supporting Details

Now that you understand the need to provide adequate, relevant detail, you may be wondering where all these details will come from. For the most part, your supporting details will come from your own experience and observation. In addition, you may draw details from what you learn in the classroom and as a result of reading, watching television, or listening to the radio. If you need to go beyond these sources for supporting details, you may rely on the facts, statistics, and opinions of experts, some of which you may find in this book and some of which you can research in the library. If you do use such borrowed material, however, be sure to check the appendix for information on paraphrasing, quoting, summarizing, synthesizing, and documenting source material.

Most of the rest of this book helps you learn about the forms your supporting details can take. These forms are called *patterns of development*. Specifically, there are chapters on these patterns of development: description, narration, exemplification, process analysis, comparison and contrast, cause-and-effect analysis, definition, and classification-division. Of course, you can combine two or more of these patterns to form your supporting detail.

Each pattern of development is treated in its own chapter; however, the inside covers of this book also give a brief explanation of each pattern. Take a look now at that information on the inside covers and refer to it whenever a particular pattern is mentioned and you are unsure of its nature.

So you can see how the patterns of development can help you back up your points and achieve your purpose, here are examples of how they support the thesis used earlier in the chapter: Dr. Garcia is a dedicated teacher.

description:	give details that show how Dr. Garcia looks and acts
narration:	tell a story about a time Dr. Garcia helped a student
exemplification:	give examples of ways Dr. Garcia shows interest in students
process analysis:	explain Dr. Garcia's process for using groups to help students learn
comparison and contrast:	compare and/or contrast Dr. Garcia with other teachers to show how good she is
cause-and-effect analysis:	explain the effects of one or more of Dr. Garcia's teaching methods
definition:	define a "good teacher" and show how Dr. Garcia conforms to that definition
classification-division:	classify all the ways Dr. Garcia helps students

Of course, you would not use all these patterns in a single essay, but they do provide options to consider as you develop your supporting details.

Organizing Supporting Details into Body Paragraphs

The supporting details of an essay are arranged in central paragraphs called *body paragraphs*. Typically, each body paragraph focuses on one aspect of the thesis and develops that aspect with adequate, relevant supporting details. (An aspect of the thesis that requires considerable explanation can be the focus of more than one body paragraph, however.) The focus of each body paragraph can be stated in a sentence or two known as the *topic sentence*, which can come at the beginning, in the middle, or at the end of the body paragraph. At times, the topic sentence can be strongly implied by the detail in the paragraph rather than expressly stated.

Student writers often find it easiest to compose a body paragraph that begins with a topic sentence followed by the supporting details meant to explain or prove the idea in that topic sentence. Thus, if you were writing an essay with the thesis "Dr. Garcia is a dedicated teacher," your essay might have three body paragraphs, each beginning with a version of one of these topic sentences:

Dr. Garcia makes sure every student is relaxed in class.

Dr. Garcia is always willing to give students extra help.

Dr. Garcia takes a personal interest in each of her students.

Notice that each of these topic sentences is relevant to the thesis. Similarly, the supporting detail in each body paragraph should be relevant to the topic sentence of that paragraph. Thus, the first body paragraph would include only details about helping students relax, the second only details about providing students with extra help, and the third only details about taking a personal interest in students.

When to Paragraph

Typically, writers begin a new body paragraph each time they move to a new idea to support the thesis. However, other considerations can dictate when to paragraph. For example, if you have a great deal to say about one point, you can break up the discussion into two or more paragraphs. If you have a point that deserves special emphasis, you can place it in its own paragraph, or if you have an extended example or narration (a story), you can set it off by placing it in its own paragraph.

Ordering Supporting Details

A reader who cannot follow the progression of a writer's ideas will become confused and frustrated. Thus, a writer must order ideas logically to keep the reader engaged in the essay. In general, a writer has three possibilities for ordering details:

1. Chronological order

2. Spatial order

3. Progressive order

Details in *chronological order* are arranged across time. The event that occurred first is written first; the event that occurred second is written second, and so on. Obviously, this technique is useful for storytelling (narration). However, it is also helpful for giving the details of a process, when it is necessary to explain what is done first, second, third, and so on.

Spatial order involves arranging details as they appear across space—front to back, near to far, top to bottom, left to right. This order is often used to describe a place or scene.

Another arrangement for details is *progressive order*. With this order, you arrange details from the least to the most important, compelling, interesting, representative, surprising, and so forth. A progressive order allows for a big finish because the most significant detail comes at the end. A variation of progressive order is to begin and end with the strongest points and sandwich everything else in the middle for the strongest possible beginning and ending. Progressive order is often used in argumentation-persuasion because a strong final point helps convince a reader.

Because the pattern of development often determines the order of details, the introductions to chapters that discuss patterns of development (Chapters 4 through 11) also discuss ordering details. In addition, since you will often find yourself combining patterns, you will also combine orders. An essay that combines narration and description, for example, may use both chronological and spatial orders.

Transitions

Arranging details in a logical order is not always enough. A writer may also have to signal how ideas relate to each other with devices called *transitions*.

1. Transitional Words and Phrases.   A number of words and phrases can signal the relationship between ideas. The accompanying chart (p. 10) notes some of them.

TRANSITION CHART

Relationship	Transitions	Example
addition	also, and, too, in addition, furthermore, first, further	The apartment has all the features I want. In addition, the rent is low.
time	now, then, before, after, earlier, later, soon, finally, next	First, measure the flour. Then add it to the butter and eggs.
space	near, next to, away from, beside, inside, to the left, alongside, behind	Go two blocks west to the light. On the right is the park.
comparison	similarly, likewise, in the same way, in like manner	The mayor will recommend some layoffs. Similarly, she will not approve any new hirings.
contrast	however, in contrast, but, still, on the contrary, nevertheless, yet	The House will pass the jobs bill. However, the Senate will vote it down.
cause and effect	since, because, so, as a result, consequently, thus, therefore, hence	Half the students are sick with the flu. Thus, school will be closed.
emphasis	indeed, in fact, surely, certainly, without a doubt	Everyone enjoys Dr. Hill's class. In fact, it is always the first to close.
illustration	for example, for instance, specifically, in particular	Counting fat grams is a good way to diet. Dana, for example, lost a pound a week that way.
summary or clarification	in summary, in conclusion, in brief, in short, in other words, all in all	The President has vetoed the spending bill. In short, he will not raise taxes.

2. *Repetition of Words or Ideas.* Repeating key words or ideas can help a writer achieve transition and improve the flow of writing. Here are two examples:

repeating a word: Chronic fatigue <u>syndrome</u> is becoming more widely recognized in the medical community and therefore more frequently diagnosed. This <u>syndrome</u> is so debilitating that its sufferers often cannot work.

repeating an idea: <u>A group of volunteer parents is now working cooperatively with school authorities</u> to introduce more extracurricular activities into the schools and to begin a drug awareness program. <u>These worthy efforts</u> will no doubt improve the quality of education in our township.

3. *Synonyms.* Another way to achieve transition is to use a synonym for a word or idea mentioned earlier, like this:

The workers expressed their <u>dissatisfaction</u> with management's latest wage offer. Their <u>discontent</u> may well lead to a strike.

4. *Topic Sentences That Look Backward and Forward.* A good way to achieve transition between paragraphs is to write a topic sentence that looks back to something in the previous paragraph and forward to something in the paragraph coming up. Assume, for example, that you have just written a paragraph about the fact that Dr. Garcia gives students extra help, and you are about to write a paragraph about how she makes students feel comfortable in class. You could write one of these topic sentences for the new paragraph and achieve transition by looking back to the previous paragraph and forward to the one coming up:

looking back   looking forward
[In addition to giving students extra help,] [Dr. Garcia always makes them feel comfortable in class.]

looking back
[Dr. Garcia does more than provide extra help to those in need.] [She also
looking forward
makes sure that everyone feels comfortable in class.]

 THE INTRODUCTION

Because first impressions are important, a successful essay will begin well. In general, that beginning will be a one- or two-paragraph introduction aimed at stimulating the reader's interest and presenting the thesis. A writer can approach the introduction many ways, some of which are illustrated in the examples that follow. (Notice that the thesis, underlined as a study aid, appears as the last sentence of each introduction. Student writers often find this placement convenient.)

Open with an Arresting Statement

Parents don't want to be parents anymore. That's what Ann Landers discovered after asking her readers whether they would have children if they had it to do over again. An overwhelming majority responded no. <u>I can only conclude from this that too many of us become parents for the wrong reasons.</u>

Provide Background Information

Five percent of the population is afflicted with attention deficit disorder, a neurological condition that makes people distractible, hyperactive, and unable to concentrate. At one time, we thought ADD was a childhood disorder that was outgrown by the age of eighteen. Now we know differently. <u>Thus, colleges should make special provision for the significant number of students who have attention deficit disorder.</u>

Tell a Story (Use Narration)

The new kid walked into fourth-period English with his head down. He handed a slip to Mrs. Kuhlins, who announced, "Frankie is our new student, class. I trust that you will make him welcome." With that, Frankie brushed a stray hair out of his eyes and shuffled to a seat in the back. His clothes were hopelessly out of date, and his hair was a mess. But as he passed my desk, our eyes met, and I saw something there. <u>At that moment, I knew there was something special about this new kid.</u>

Establish Yourself as Someone Knowledgeable about the Subject

When I was six, I joined a T-ball league and spent a glorious summer at third base. When I was ten, I began playing intramural basketball and learned the pleasures of rebounding and making foul shots. In junior high school, I began running middle distances for the track team and learned the joy of crossing the finish line in one last burst of speed. In high school, I lettered in three sports. <u>As a result of all these years of playing team sports, I have come to realize that there are three kinds of coaches.</u>

Explain Your Purpose

If you are planning to buy a used car, you run the risk of making a very costly mistake. For this reason, you should know what to look for when you examine and test drive an automobile.

Describe Something

His belly swelled over his belt line and cascaded toward the bony knees that poked out between the white knee socks and navy blue polyester stretch shorts. His face was twisted into a permanent scowl, and his eyes squinted against the sun until they formed slits. To call roll, he barked each boy's name and checked it off on the clipboard that was never more than arm's reach away. I was only five minutes into seventh-grade gym, but I could tell Mr. Winnikee deserved his reputation as the gym teacher from hell.

Define Something

A grandmother is supposed to be a white-haired, chubby woman who rolls her stockings below the knee and spends her days knitting scarves and baking cookies for her grandchildren. However, someone forgot to tell my mother's mother all this because, believe me, she is not the typical grandmother.

Use an Interesting or Pertinent Quotation

Last week at his press conference, the governor said, "It is with regret that I announce a 20 percent subsidy cut to higher education. I believe, however, that this cut is the least painful way to balance the state budget." The governor is wrong; these cuts will have a catastrophic effect on the people of this state.

◆ *Note:* Avoid quotations such as "The early bird gets the worm" or "Better late than never." These are clichés more likely to bore than interest a reader.

For additional ways to handle the introduction, you can consult the openings to Chapters 4 through 11.

 ## THE CONCLUSION

The conclusion is a very important part of a successful essay because it influences the reader's final, lasting impression. No matter how strong your introduction and body paragraphs are, if your ending is weak, your reader will come away from the essay feeling let down.

An effective conclusion can be a sentence or two, or it can be a full paragraph. Either way, many approaches are available to the writer. If your essay is long, with many ideas, you can summarize your main points as a helpful reminder to your reader. However, if your essay is brief and the ideas are easily remembered, summarizing is not a good idea because it will bore rather than help a reader.

Sometimes an effective conclusion comes from repeating the thesis or another important idea. Typically, this approach works when the repetition provides emphasis for dramatic effect. Other times, writers delay the statement of their thesis until the conclusion because they want to build up to it.

Another common technique is to introduce a new but related idea in the conclusion. The idea must be clearly related to the rest of the essay, though, or the reader will feel confused by the mention of something that seems unconnected to the topic. Finally, a writer often crafts an effective conclusion by combining approaches.

Other approaches to the conclusion are illustrated below. In addition, the openings to Chapters 4 through 11 suggest ways to handle conclusions.

Draw a Conclusion from the Information in the Essay

Recent evidence suggests that the children of divorced parents suffer a number of difficulties, regardless of their age at the time of the divorce. For this reason, parents who stay together "for the sake of the children" may be doing the right thing.

Present the Final, Most Important Point

The most compelling reason to oppose censorship is the threat it poses to our First Amendment rights. Once we limit free speech, we establish a climate that permits the chipping away at our freedoms until our rights are severely curtailed.

Offer a Solution to a Problem Mentioned in the Essay

College athletics will remain controversial until we reform the system dramatically. Perhaps the most honest thing to do is to hire the athletes to play and pay them salaries. If they want to use their paychecks to pay for tuition, fine. If not, they can just be university employees. The fans will still turn out to see the teams, regardless of whether the players are student athletes or professional athletes.

Call Your Readers to Action

To improve the quality of education, we must increase teachers' salaries to make them compatible with those in business and industry. Only then will we attract the best people to the profession. Thus, we must support school levies that fund pay increases and lobby boards of education to do whatever it takes to increase teachers' salaries.

Look to the Future

Once the Route 8 bypass is built, our area will become a major crossroads. In ten years, our economy will be flourishing from the business and commerce that will result from our strategic location, and our tax base will broaden to the benefit of our schools and infrastructure.

Leave Your Reader with a Final Impression

Our society discriminates against overweight people, and it's a shame. Many capable people never get a chance to show what they can do because of our narrow-mindedness.

 THE TITLE

Although the title is the first thing a reader sees, many people develop it last because a good title often suggests itself after the supporting details are written. There are many ways to approach the title. Sometimes a clever or funny title is a good way to pique your reader's interest. However, not everyone can be clever or funny, so it's fine to write a title that suggests the content of the essay, like "Homemaking" or "Lists," which are in this book. Sometimes an intriguing title like "What Sort of Car-Rt-Sort Am I?" (which also appears in this book) can stimulate a reader's interest. Usually, you should avoid a title that presents your thesis. If your title is "Capital Punishment Is Inhumane," you will tip your hand too soon. Also, avoid very broad titles that do not suggest your content. "Television" is too broad, but "The Effects of Television Violence" is fine.

 A SAMPLE STUDENT ESSAY

The essay that follows was written by a student. It was prompted by the examples of good sportsmanship in "Class Acts" (page 139). The notes in the margin call your attention to some of the points made in this chapter. If you would like a brief explanation of the patterns of development mentioned in the marginal notes, refer to the inside covers. If you would like to see the student's idea generation material, see pages 27 and 30. For the student's outline, see page 36; for the student's rough draft, see page 37.

<table>
<tr><td>

Title suggests content of essay.

Paragraph 1
The introduction establishes the author as knowledgeable and gives background.

"In short" is a transition to the thesis, which gives the essay's focus as the dual personality of the athlete.

</td><td>

Is Today's Athlete a Good Sport?

1   I have been playing soccer for almost fifteen years, and over those years I've noticed a change in the way people play: they have gone from playing assertively but fairly to playing aggressively and unfairly. Today's athletes will do anything to win, even violent, immoral things they would not do outside sports. In short, today's athlete is one person on the playing field and another person off the playing field.

</td></tr>
</table>

Paragraph 2
Topic sentence is first sentence. It gives first aspect of thesis under consideration.

Topic sentence is relevant to thesis, and supporting detail is relevant to topic sentence.

An example from personal experience helps support topic sentence generalization.

Transitions include "for example," "then," and repetition of "hurt" and main idea ("inflicting punishment").

2   People who cannot justify violence outside sports feel that hurting someone during competition is all right because that is "just part of the game." My roommate, for example, plays basketball. He's a gentle guy until he gets on the court. Then he uses his elbows as weapons and thinks nothing of taking all the cheap shots he can under the boards. He would never think of using his elbows to get through a crowd on the street, but he will do anything to win a basketball game, including hurting an opposing player. If he were not willing to hurt someone—if he didn't have that "killer instinct"—then the coach would bench him and put in someone who *was* willing to inflict punishment.

Paragraph 3
Topic sentence is first sentence. It presents next aspect of thesis under consideration.

Detail is adequate and relevant.

Supporting detail includes narration from personal experience and cause-and-effect analysis.

Transitions include "then," "for example," and "this illegal shot."

3   Many players justify their violence by claiming that they have to play rough to beat the other players. Then as long as they come out on top, they don't feel they've done anything wrong. In one of my soccer games, for example, the score was tied, and there was time for one last play. An opposing player was near our goal; our sweeper was guarding him. Jumping up for a shot, the opposing player intentionally spiked the sweeper in the calf and then hit the ball into the goal with his hands instead of with his head. Because of some confusion, the referees didn't see this illegal shot, and we lost the game. After the game, I asked that player why he did what he did,

and he replied, "It's all part of the game. You know you would have done the same thing if you had the chance." The only thing athletes have on their minds during competition is getting the other guys before the other guys get them.

Paragraph 4

Topic sentence is first sentence. It presents next aspect of thesis and is relevant to thesis.

Supporting detail is relevant and adequate.

Examples and cause-and-effect analysis are used to support generalization that sports behavior does count.

Transition into paragraph is achieved with "oftentimes" and repetition of ideas "aggression" and "violence."

4   Oftentimes, players justify their aggression and violence by saying "it's only a game." The obvious implication is that the sport isn't reality, so the behavior exhibited doesn't really count. Well, it may be only a game, but the behavior counts, all right. During another one of my soccer games, an opposing player who was trying to score slid into our goalie and knocked him back into the goal. Our goalie ended up with a severe concussion and a broken leg. He missed a month of school while recuperating, and even today, if he exerts himself too much, sharp pains shoot through his leg. I'm sure the opposing player didn't think twice about the consequences of his action because it was only a game, but if he had hurt someone like that off the soccer field, he would probably feel terrible. Either way, however, the consequences are real and lasting.

Paragraph 5

Topic sentence is first sentence. The words "biggest reason" indicate a progressive order for details.

5   Probably the biggest reason athletes turn violent is that fans want it that way. The more violent the game, the more they cheer. In fact, a player who isn't willing to do whatever it takes is considered a wimp and won't last very long. The violence is even spreading to the stands, as more and more stories are reported about injury and death because of fan riots.

Paragraph 6

Conclusion brings essay to a satisfying finish by calling the reader to action and by suggesting a solution to the problem.

6   It is time to put an end to the violence in sports. Fans should demand a return to good sportsmanship. Players should be penalized for undue aggression, cheap shots, and a "winning at any cost" attitude. Sure, the level of play may be less intense as a result, but that's a small price to pay for reducing injuries and returning to reason.

READING AN ESSAY

When you read to relax, you can grab a well-plotted novel, put your feet up, and lose yourself in the story as the words wash over you and the tensions of the day melt away. This kind of reading is one of life's pleasures.

College reading, however, demands more involvement from you. It requires you to stay focused on the material, actively considering and evaluating it. It requires you to think of the material in light of what you already know and to judge the importance of what you read. College reading requires you to question, draw conclusions, make associations, develop opinions, and support those opinions. In short, college reading requires you to interact with the text. The process of interacting with a text is active reading, and this chapter will suggest procedures for helping you become an active reader.

 ACTIVE READING

Many people believe that reading involves studying a text until it yields up the writer's message. Yes, readers discover meaning when they read, but they also help make that meaning. Thus, when you read an essay in this book, you will bring to it all your previous experience, observations, and awareness, and these will affect your interpretation of what you read. Active reading, then, is a process of bringing something to a text as well as taking something away from it—and what you take away is influenced by what you bring. This fact helps explain why different people get different meanings from what they read.

Because you bring a great deal to your reading, you should come to trust your reactions. If a thoughtful reading leads you to a conclusion different from that of your classmates, that's fine. You are entitled to your own judgments and conclusions. You will, of course, be expected to explain why you react the way you do, but that's all part of the active reading process. You will also be required to decide what you think the author's position is.

You are, however, allowed to be uncertain about an essay, and you are allowed to change your mind. If you are puzzled, just say so and question other readers, and ask questions in class. If today you think one thing about an essay but yesterday you thought another, that's all right too, because you were a different person yesterday. In short, reading is an ongoing process. Your reactions and views may change upon further reflection—but active readers *always* engage in further reflection.

 ## HOW TO BE AN ACTIVE READER

Active reading requires time and energy. The longer and more complex the piece, the more time and energy you must invest. The procedures described below will help you. While they are suitable for most college reading, feel free to vary them to suit yourself and the material you encounter.

Step 1: Preview the Material

Before you read, you should preview the material for clues about its content, author, purpose, audience, and tone. These five procedures can help.

1. Consider the author and title and what they suggest about the piece. Do you know the author's politics or usual subject matter? Is the author a newspaper columnist, a humorist, or a political commentator? Think about the title and what hints it gives you. Of course, some titles will tell you more than others. In this book, for example, the title "College Pressures" tells you much more than the title "What Sort of Car-Rt-Sort Am I?"

2. Check out the publication information (in this book, see the acknowledgments page). When and where the essay first appeared will suggest how current the information is and who the original audience was.

3. Read the headnote before the essay for information about the essay and its author.

4. Read headings, charts, bold type, and lists for clues to content.

5. Read the first paragraph or two and the first sentence of each paragraph to learn a little about the tone, subject matter, and organization.

Step 2: Read the Selection in One Sitting, If Possible

Once you have previewed the material, you will have formed some expectations about the selection. Next, you should quickly read the material through in one sitting, without pausing or laboring over anything. Just relax and get whatever you can from the piece, and don't worry about what you don't get. If you encounter words you do not know, circle them to check later. (If the piece is too long to read in one sitting, read it as quickly as you can in as few sittings as possible.)

As you read quickly, form whatever impressions you can about the thesis, content, purpose, intended audience, tone, organization, and quality of the piece. If you keep a journal, write down your impressions in the journal after you have finished this first reading. Otherwise, note your impressions at the end of the essay or on a separate sheet of paper.

Step 3: Read and Study

After your quick reading of the selection, read and study the material closely to discover as much as you can. Shorter, simpler selections may take only one additional reading, but longer, more complex pieces may require several more readings. You should read and study with a pen in your hand so you can make notes in the margin, in a journal, or on a separate sheet. You may find the following procedures helpful as you read and study.

1. Look up the words you circled earlier and write their meanings in the margin as a study aid.

2. Identify the thesis. If it is stated, place brackets around it; if it is implied, write out the thesis in the margin or at the end of the piece.

3. Underline the main points made to support the thesis. Often these can be found in the topic sentences. Be careful not to underline too much or the selection will have more sentences underlined than not.

4. Talk to the author by making notations in the margin. If you like a passage, place an exclamation point next to it. If you disagree, write "no." If a point is well made or unproven, say so. If you don't understand something, write a question mark. In addition, write any other responses that you have, responses like "clever," "reminds me of Bob," "seems silly," and so forth. For an example of a marked essay, see "Americanization Is Tough on 'Macho' " on pages 21 through 24.

Before considering your active reading complete, you should try to answer these questions about the selection in your journal, on a separate sheet of paper, or in the margins:

a. What is the source of the author's ideas: experience, observation, or research?
b. Is the author expressing facts, opinions, or both?
c. Is the author's detail adequate and convincing? Does the author support generalizations by showing and not just telling?
d. What are the author's purpose, tone, and intended audience?
e. What patterns of development does the author use? What approach does the author take to the introduction and conclusion?
f. Do you agree or disagree with the author? Do you like or dislike the selection? What does it make you think of? Does it arouse any strong feelings?

To see what a marked essay can look like, review the following selection marked by a student. Following the essay, also look at the questions the student answered in her journal.

 A SAMPLE MARKED ESSAY

AMERICANIZATION IS TOUGH ON "MACHO"
Rose Del Castillo Guibault

1   What is *macho*? That depends which side of the border you come from.

2   Although it's not unusual for words and expressions to lose their subtlety in translation [the negative connotations of *macho* in this country are troublesome to Hispanics.]   *closest thing to a stated thesis*

who is this?   3   Take the newspaper descriptions of alleged mass murderer Ramon Salcido. That an insensitive, insanely jealous, hard-drinking, violent Latin male is referred to as *macho* makes Hispanics cringe.

4   *"Es muy macho,"* the women in my family nod approvingly, describing a man they respect. But in the United States, when women say, "He's so macho," it's with disdain.

5   The Hispanic *macho* is manly, responsible, hardworking, a man in charge, a patriarch. A man who expresses strength through silence. What the Yiddish language would call a *mensch*.

male head of family

sounds like my dad

6   The American *macho* is a chauvinist, a brute, uncouth, selfish, loud, abrasive, capable of inflicting pain, and sexually promiscuous.

good description

crude

7   Quintessential *macho* models in this country are Sylvester Stallone, Arnold Schwarzenegger, and Charles Bronson. In their movies, they exude toughness, independence, masculinity. But a closer look reveals their machismo is really violence masquerading as courage, sullenness disguised as silence, and irresponsibility camouflaged as independence.

pure

Interesting— never thought of this before.

8   If the Hispanic ideal of *macho* were translated to American screen roles, they might be Jimmy Stewart, Sean Connery, and Laurence Olivier.

9   In Spanish, *macho* enobles Latin males. In English, it devalues them. This pattern seems consistent with the conflicts ethnic minority males experience in this country. Typically the cultural traits other societies value don't translate as desirable characteristics in America.

I could use some examples from other cultures.

10   I watched my own father struggle with these cultural ambiguities. He worked on a farm for twenty years. He laid down miles of irrigation pipe, carefully plowed long, neat rows in fields, hacked away at recalcitrant weeds and drove tractors through whirlpools of dust. He stoically worked twenty-hour days during harvest season, accepting the long hours as part of agricultural work. When the boss complained or upbraided him for minor mistakes, he kept quiet, even when it was obvious the boss had erred.

hard to handle

Is not complaining a strength or a weakness?

11   He handled the most menial tasks with pride. At home he was a good provider, helped out my mother's family in Mexico without complaint, and was indulgent with me. Arguments between my mother and him generally had to do with money, or with his stubborn reluctance to share his troubles. He tried to work them out in his own silence. He didn't want to trouble my mother—a course that backfired, because the imagined is always worse than the reality.

this is my idea of macho—males never share worries & fears

12   Americans regarded my father as decidedly un-*macho*. His character was interpreted as nonassertive, his loyalty nonambition, and his quietness ignorance. I once overheard the boss's son blame him for plowing crooked rows in a field. My father merely smiled at the lie, knowing the boy had done it, but didn't refute it, confident his good work was well known. But the boss instead ridiculed him for being "stupid" and letting a kid get away with a lie. Seeing my embarrassment, my father dismissed the incident, saying, "They're the dumb ones. Imagine, me fighting with a kid."

why unions are needed!

well put

13   I tried not to look at him with American eyes because sometimes the reflection hurt.

14   Listening to my aunts' clucks of approval, my vision focused on the qualities America overlooked. "He's such a hard worker. So serious, so responsible." My aunts would secretly compliment my mother. The unspoken comparison was that he was not like some of their husbands, who drank and womanized. My uncles represented the darker side of *macho*.

Father is meek but strong?

the thing to do, but not the macho thing.

15   In a patriarchal society, few challenge their roles. If men drink, it's because it's the manly thing to do. If they gamble, it's because it's how men relax. And if they fool around, well, it's because a man simply can't hold back so much man! My aunts didn't exactly meekly sit back, but they put up with these transgressions because Mexican society dictated this was their lot in life.

I don't get this.

16   In the United States, I believe it was the feminist movement of the early '70s that changed *macho*'s meaning. Perhaps my generation of Latin women was in part responsible. I recall Chicanos complaining about the chauvinistic nature of Latin men and the notion they wanted their women barefoot, pregnant, and in the kitchen. The generalization that Latin men embodied chauvinistic traits led to this interesting twist of semantics. Suddenly a word that represented something positive in one culture became a negative (prototype) in another.

model

This essay really makes me sad for all the men who show strength every day but are seen in a negative light.

17   The problem with the use of *macho* today is that it's become an accepted stereotype of the Latin male. And like all stereotypes, it distorts truth.

18   The impact of language in our society is undeniable. And the misuse of *macho* hints at a deeper cultural misunderstanding that extends beyond mere word definitions.

this is interesting; I wish she had explored this more.

QUESTIONS ANSWERED IN JOURNAL

1. What is the source of the author's ideas: experience, observation, or research? *The author's ideas came from personal experience and observation.*

2. Is the author expressing facts, opinions, or both? *The points about the connotation of macho are facts, as are the examples about the father and other relatives. The rest is opinion.*

3. Is the author's detail adequate and convincing? Does the author support generalizations by showing and not just telling? *More detail is needed to prove the point in paragraph 9. At the end, the author needs to explain more about the cultural misunderstandings.*

4. What are the author's purpose, tone, and intended audience? *Her purpose is to correct misunderstandings about the meaning of macho and the nature of Latin males. The tone is serious and controlled. The audience is non-Hispanics.*

5. What patterns of development does the author use? What approach does the author take to the introduction and conclusion? *The patterns are cause and effect, narration, and exemplification; the introduction gives background information; the ending draws a conclusion from the details.*

6. Do you agree or disagree with the author? Do you like or dislike the selection? What does it make you think of? Does it arouse any strong feelings? *I don't have enough experience around Hispanic males to agree or disagree, but I see little evidence of the stereotyped Hispanic male in the media. I like the essay, especially the parts about the author's family, but I wish there were more details. It makes me sad for a group of men who are very strong but viewed as weak.*

C H A P T E R

WRITING AN ESSAY

The best way to become a better writer is to improve the procedures you use when you write. Unfortunately, no one can tell you that certain procedures will guarantee successful writing. Instead, you must experiment a little to discover the procedures that work best for you. This chapter can help with that experimentation. It describes the areas that all writers must turn their attention to (idea generation, ordering ideas, drafting, revising, and editing) and several procedures for tending to each of these areas. If you keep sampling these procedures until you find the ones that work well for you, your writing is bound to improve. Keep in mind, though, that different writers function in different ways, and the procedures that work well for some of your classmates will not necessarily be successful for you. Your goal is to find your own effective procedures.

As you come to develop your own process by discovering effective procedures for handling the stages of writing, keep in mind that writing rarely moves in a straight line from idea generation through editing. You will frequently find yourself doubling back before going forward. For example, while you are checking your draft for spelling errors (part of editing), you may think of a better way to handle your introduction (idea generation). By all means, go back and rewrite; never consider something "done," just because you first turned your attention to it during an earlier phase.

IDEA GENERATION

The earliest phase of writing is idea generation, the time when writers settle on a writing topic and determine what they will say about that topic. People who think that ideas are the product of inspiration believe that idea generation involves staring at a blank page until thoughts come to them in a brilliant flash.

However, this is a surefire prescription for frustration. Successful writers know not to depend on inspiration because it is unreliable. Instead, they use some of the idea generation techniques described below to go after ideas in the absence of inspiration. (If you sample all of these techniques and still have trouble generating ideas, speak to other writers, including your classmates and instructor, to learn what techniques they use to come up with ideas.)

Finding a Topic

If you are developing your own writing topic, the following procedures may help.

1.   Review the Journal Entries and Marginal Notes You Made during Active Reading. The comments, questions, and areas of disagreement and agreement may suggest a topic. For example, the marginal note in response to paragraph 7 of "Americanization Is Tough on 'Macho'" (page 21) could prompt an essay about the image of males presented in action movies.

2.   Use a Provocative Quotation as a Topic Source. For example, in paragraph 16 of "Americanization Is Tough on 'Macho'" the author says, "I believe it was the feminist movement of the early '70s that changed *macho's* meaning." This quotation could prompt an essay about the changing meaning of *macho.*

3.   Pick a Subject Treated in a Reading and Brainstorm. To brainstorm, make a list of every idea that occurs to you and then examine the list for possible topics. For best results, you should not censor yourself. Just list everything that occurs to you without evaluating the worth of the ideas. The student who wrote "Is Today's Athlete a Good Sport?" (page 16) developed his topic after writing the following brainstorming list:

fan violence	why athletes are violent
player violence	Are athletes too violent?
causes of violence	Is it violence or aggression?
effects of violence	How can we make sports less violent?
Is the violence justified?	Fans love it.
violence = part of the game	Players think it's okay.
It's expected.	Are players violent off the field?
Is society sick if it likes violence?	fans getting hurt
players getting hurt	

The student drew his topic from the question in his list "Are players violent off the field?" That question prompted him to write about players being violent on the playing field and nonviolent off the field.

4. Freewrite for about Ten Minutes on a Subject Found in a Reading.

To freewrite, write nonstop without censoring yourself. Simply record everything that occurs to you without worrying about its quality or about spelling, grammar, or neatness. Do not stop writing for any reason. If you run out of ideas, just write anything: the alphabet, names of family members—anything. Soon new ideas will occur to you and you can record those.

The following freewriting was done by a student in response to "Homemaking" on page 422 (an essay that argues that female homemakers should not be financially dependent on their husbands). As you review the freewriting, notice that the author did not worry about correctness. Also notice that she allowed herself to write even silly things as she waited for better ideas to surface.

William Raspberry says women who are homemakers shouldn't be considered as dependant on male breadwinners. Well that's true but aren't male breadwinners dependant on the homemaker too? Could they cope if the woman walked out? I bet not, theird be hell to pay. Let's see what to write, oh the guy would have to pay sommeone to come in and clean and cook and take care of the kiddies. That would be hard and expensive. Let's see what do I think now? Maybe we should pay homemakers a salary. Could that be done? Maybe. Or maybe a giant PR campaign to upgrade the image of homemakers—yeah bring Madison Avenue into the act. I agree with Raspberry that women shouldn't be dependant financially if they are homemakers but I know a lot of women who don't mind so I doubt anything will change.

The student's freewriting suggests at least three topics:

■ the need to upgrade the image of homemakers
■ paying homemakers for the jobs they do
■ why some women don't mind depending on males

Your freewriting may not yield as many topics, but it is likely to suggest at least one.

5. Examine the Subject of a Reading from Different Angles. Answering these questions will help:

a. Can I describe something related to the subject?

b. Can I compare and/or contrast the subject with something?
c. Does the subject make me think of something else?
d. Why is the subject important?
e. Do I agree or disagree with the author?
f. What interests me about the subject?
g. Can I give the author's ideas a broader or different application?
h. Can I explain the causes and effects of something in the reading?
i. Can I relate the subject to my own experience?

Discovering Ideas to Develop Your Topic

Once you have a topic, whether it is one you developed yourself or one that was assigned to you by your instructor, you will need to discover ideas for developing that topic. Some of the following procedures may help.

1.   Write a Discovery Draft. A discovery draft is not really a first draft. It's more a preliminary effort to identify what you already know about your topic and what you can think of along the way. To write a discovery draft, simply start jotting down anything that comes to mind about your topic. Don't worry about anything except getting down everything you can think of. If you cannot think of much, you may not know enough about your topic, or you may need to try some other idea generation techniques.

2.   Review the Journal Entries and Marginal Notes You Made during Active Reading. They may include ideas for developing your topic.

3.   Write a Brainstorming List that Focuses on Your Subject. Like brainstorming for a topic, brainstorming for ideas to develop a topic involves listing every idea that occurs to you. Remember, do not evaluate the worth of your ideas; just write down everything you can think of. Later, you can reject anything unusable.

4.   Consider the Patterns of Development. If you ask yourself the following questions, you may discover specific patterns and ideas for developing your topic.

a. What can I describe about my topic?
b. What story can I tell about my topic?
c. What examples illustrate my points?
d. What process or procedures relate to my topic?
e. What can I compare or contrast my topic to?
f. What are the causes or effects of my topic?
g. Is there anything about my topic that can be classified into groups?
h. Are there any terms or concepts that I can define?

5.   *Try Clustering.* Clustering is a technique that helps you generate ideas and see how those ideas relate to each other. To cluster, first write your topic in the center of the page and draw a circle around it. As ideas to develop your topic occur to you, write them down, circle them, and draw lines attaching them to the circled ideas they relate to. As with all idea generation techniques, do not censor yourself. Write down everything, regardless of its quality. The following sample clustering was done as a form of idea generation for "Is Today's Athlete a Good Sport?" on page 16.

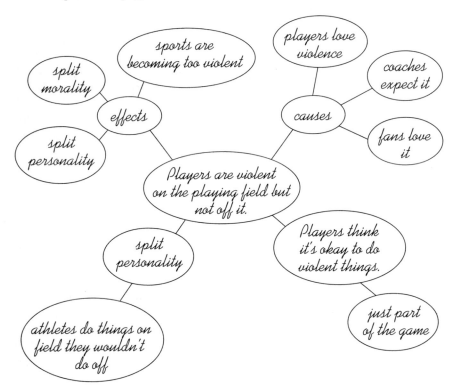

If you read the final version of the student's essay on page 16, you will notice that the writer did not use all of the ideas in his clustering; also, he used some ideas that do not appear in the clustering. That's all fine because nothing about idea generation is set in stone. Also notice that the writer placed "split personality" in two spots on the clustering. That's also fine. If you are unsure what an idea relates to, jot it down in more than one spot and solve the problem later.

6.   *Talk to Other People about Your Topic.* Your classmates, in particular, can suggest ideas for developing your topic.

7. *Consult Library Sources and Other Materials for Ideas on Your Topic.* However, check the Appendix on ways to handle material you take from other sources.

Establishing Purpose, Audience, Role, and Tone

In Chapter 1, you learned about the importance of the writer's purpose, audience, role, and tone. Because these factors affect the detail in an essay, you should consider them carefully early on in the writing process. Of course, all of the decisions you make about purpose, audience, role, and tone can be changed later, but preliminary decisions are important so you can make wise choices about what to include in your essay. (If you need to review purpose, audience, role, and tone, see the discussion beginning on page 3).

To be sure you do not overlook any of these important considerations, you can use the Worksheet on page 32. Once you have completed the worksheet, review your ideas and see whether they help fulfill your stated purpose and whether they are compatible with your audience, role, and tone.

 OUTLINING

Outlining can help you find the best order for your details so you do not ramble and thereby confuse your reader. Many people resist outlining because they are only familiar with the formal outline that involves numbered and lettered lists and subcategories. This kind of outline can be very helpful, but if it is not for you, alternatives are available. To learn which kind of outlining is best for you, try one or more of the techniques described in this chapter.

Regardless of the kind of outline you write, some guidelines apply. First, write a preliminary version of your thesis. (See page 1 on the qualities of an effective thesis.) Although this thesis is subject to change, it can serve as a guide for your work. As you outline, check your details against this early version of your thesis to be sure they are relevant. Also, consider your details in light of your purpose, audience, role, and tone to be sure your points are compatible with them. Finally, as you outline, feel free to add and delete details. Idea generation is ongoing, so you should remain receptive to ideas as they occur to you.

The Scratch Outline

The scratch outline is the least detailed outline. It is simply a list of the main ideas you plan to include in your first draft, written in the order you plan to cover them. Typically, the scratch outline just covers main points with no

WORKSHEET FOR ESTABLISHING PURPOSE, AUDIENCE, ROLE, AND TONE

1. The purpose of my essay is _____.
   If you have trouble establishing your purpose, ask yourself these questions:

   a. What feelings, ideas, or experiences can I share with my reader?
   b. Of what can I inform my reader?
   c. Of what can I persuade my reader?
   d. In what way can I entertain my reader?

2. The audience for my essay is _____.
   If you have trouble establishing your audience, ask yourself these questions:

   a. Who could learn something from my essay?
   b. Who would enjoy reading about my topic?
   c. Who could be influenced to think or act a certain way?
   d. Who is interested in my topic or would find it important?
   e. Who needs to hear what I have to say?

3. The role I will assume is _____.
   If you have trouble establishing your role, try one of the following:

student	friend	authority
employee	citizen	neutral party
woman or man	average, general reader	teenager
parent	child	consumer

4. The tone of my essay will be _____.
   If you have trouble deciding on a tone, consider one of the following:

angry	serious	sarcastic	annoyed
neutral	scornful	preachy	enthusiastic
hostile	concerned	argumentative	playful
silly	ironic	pessimistic	hopeful

mention of details for developing those points, so it is not well suited for complicated essays or for writers who must plan carefully before drafting. A scratch outline for "Is Today's Athlete a Good Sport?" on page 16 might look like this:

preliminary thesis: *Even nonviolent people are often violent on the playing field.*

Violence is okay because it's part of the game. A player has to be violent to compete with other players.

Sports is different from the real world, so violence is justified. Fans want the violence.

The Informal Outline

The informal outline is more detailed than the scratch outline. It includes some details for developing main points and it groups related ideas together, so the writer has a sense of which details will appear together in the same paragraph. Although more detailed than the scratch outline, the informal outline still may not be suitable for complex papers or writers who need a fair amount of structure before they draft. An informal outline for "Is Today's Athlete a Good Sport?" might look like this:

preliminary thesis: *Even nonviolent people are often violent on the playing field.*

<u>Violence is okay because it's part of the game.</u>
     Use roommate as example.
     Coaches only play people with killer instinct.

<u>A player has to be violent to compete with other players.</u>
     Get other guys before they get you.
     If everyone else is violent, you have to be, too.
     Violence is okay if you win the game.

<u>Sports is different from the real world, so violence is justified.</u>
     It's only a game and not part of reality, so it's okay to be violent.
     But the injuries are real.

<u>Fans want the violence.</u>
     Fans cheer for violence.
     They even act violently themselves in the stands.

The Outline Tree

An outline tree, which can be moderately to heavily detailed, allows a writer to see how ideas relate to each other. Many writers appreciate the visual representation the tree provides. To construct an outline tree, write your preliminary

thesis at the top of a page and connect ideas with "branches," the way the following student example illustrates:

Even nonviolent people are often violent on the playing field.

Violence is okay because it's part of the game.

A player has to be violent to compete with other players.

Sports is different from the real world, so violence is justified.

Fans want the violence.

Roommate as example

Get other guy before he gets you.

Violence is okay if you win.

Fans cheer violence

Fans are violent in the stands.

Coaches only play people with killer instinct

If everyone is violent, you have to be, too.

It's only a game and not part of reality.

Violent on court but not off

But the injuries are real

Use soccer example

The Outline Worksheet

With an outline worksheet, you can plan your draft in detail by filling in the blanks with words and phrases that indicate the points you will make in your draft:

Paragraph 1

1. Opening comments to arouse reader's interest:_____

_____

_____

2. Preliminary thesis:_____

_____

Paragraph 2

1. Main point (topic sentence idea):———————————
———————————————————————————

2. Supporting details to develop main point:——————
———————————————————————————
———————————————————————————

Paragraph 3

1. Main point (topic sentence idea):———————————
———————————————————————————

2. Supporting details to develop main point:——————
———————————————————————————
———————————————————————————

[*Note*: Continue this way until all your main points are discussed.]

Final Paragraph

Ideas to bring essay to a satisfying finish:———————
———————————————————————————

The Formal Outline

The formal outline allows you to plan your essay in considerable detail. To construct a formal outline, write your preliminary thesis at the top of the page. Then represent your main points with roman numerals and your supporting details with capital letters. Details that explain or illustrate supporting details are given numbers. You are probably familiar with the formal outline, which looks something like this:

Preliminary thesis:———————————

I.
  A.
  B.
  C.
II. A.
  B.
      1.
      2.

III. A.
    1.
    2.
    3.
  B.
    1.
    2.
  C.

So you can see how a formal outline plots a draft, here is a formal outline for "Is Today's Athlete a Good Sport?"

<u>preliminary thesis:</u>   Nonviolent people can be violent on the playing field.

I. Hurting people is part of the game.
  A. My roommate is gentle off the basketball court and hurtful on the court.
  B. If he didn't hurt others, the coach would bench him.
II. Violence is necessary for winning.
  A. Players feel violence is okay if they win.
    1. In my soccer game, an opposing player intentionally hurt one of our players.
    2. He did it to win.
  B. Players injure others so they don't get hurt themselves.
III. Players think violence is okay because sports are games.
  A. But the violence is real.
  B. The injuries are lasting.
    1. Our soccer goalie missed a month of school.
    2. He still has effects from a violent play.
IV. Fans like violence.
  A. Fans encourage player violence.
  B. Fans are violent themselves.

 ## WRITING THE FIRST DRAFT

The first draft is nothing more than an initial attempt to get ideas down in essay form. Because it is a first attempt, it will be very rough—and that's fine. First drafts are supposed to be rough, which is why they are often called rough drafts. Later, during revising, you can make all the necessary improvements.

When you draft, the following tips may be helpful:

1. ***Use your outline as a guide,*** but do not be a slave to it. Add and delete ideas as you judge necessary. Remember, idea generation continues through all stages of writing.

2. **Push through from beginning to end** in one sitting so you maintain momentum.

3. **Skip troublesome parts.** If you cannot think of a word or a way to express something or a way to develop a point, leave a blank space and go on. If you want, leave a note about what needs to be done later: "Explain this," "Add an example," "Find word," and so on.

4. **Skip your introduction** if it is keeping you from progressing. But write out your preliminary thesis so you do not lose sight of it.

5. **Try returning to idea generation and outlining** if a reasonable amount of time passes and you cannot get the draft down. You may not yet have enough ideas for a draft.

To see how rough a first draft can be and how much it can vary from the final, revised version of an essay, look at the first draft below and compare it to the final version on page 16.

Is Today's Athlete a Good Sport

I have been playing soccer for a long time and I can see that players are playing much more violently now than they used to. Players will do anything to win, even stuff they would never consider doing off the field. I think that today's athlete is one person on the field and another person off the field.

Players think that hurting someone is okay because it's just part of the game. My roommate, for example, is a real gentle guy until he gets on the basketball court, then he's rough and ready and violent. [Find better words.] If he didn't play that way, the coach would keep him on the bench. [Add details about what Jeff does on the court.]

Many players say they have to be violent to beat the other players. They don't feel they've done anything wrong as long as they win. In one of my soccer games, for example, an opposing player intentionally spiked the sweeper and cheated to get the goal. [Give more details.]

A lot of times, players justify violence by saying "it's only a game" and not reality. Yes, it's a game but the injuries are real and can cause a lot of problems and pain. For example, a player on my soccer team missed a month of school as a result of an opposing player who knocked him into the goal. I'm sure the player didn't think twice about the consequences of his actions.

Unfortunately, fans love the violence. The more violence, the more cheering. They're violent in the stands, too. [This needs more.]

The violence must stop and players should be penalized for it. Otherwise, people will get hurt more and more.

REVISING THE DRAFT

Experienced writers will tell you that the real heart of any writing process is revision, the process of shaping and refining the first draft until it is ready for the reader. Revision is a difficult, time-consuming process; it is *not* a matter of making a few word changes, adding a comma here and there, correcting spellings, then typing up the essay. It is a complete rethinking of the essay to be sure everything is suited to the writer's purpose, audience, role, and tone. Thus, revising involves changing words, reordering details, adding and deleting ideas, reshaping sentences, and so on. It does not, however, involve matters of correctness such as grammar, spelling, punctuation, and capitalization. These concerns are dealt with later, during editing. To be sure you consider all that you should when you revise, you may want to use the Checklist on page 39.

Tips for Revising

*1. **Leave your work for at least a day*** to clear your head and gain objectivity about your draft. This way, you stand a better chance of identifying changes that should be made.

*2. **Allow plenty of time,*** because revising is time-consuming. Plan your work to allow revising over a period of several days.

*3. **Revise in stages*** by considering one or two of the revision concerns at a time. As an alternative, revise one or two paragraphs at a time. Be sure to take a break whenever you get tired.

*4. **Read your draft aloud*** to hear problems you overlook visually.

*5. **Revise typed copy*** because you are less likely to overlook problems in type than in your own handwriting.

*6. **Trust your instincts*** if you have a nagging feeling that a problem exists. It probably does, even if you can't give the problem a name or figure out a solution at the moment.

*7. **Avoid editing,*** which comes later. If you deal with spelling, grammar, and such, you will be distracted and not focus on revision concerns.

*8. **Ask reliable readers to react to your draft,*** but be sure you use people who know the qualities of effective writing and who will not hesitate to offer constructive criticism. (Praise makes a writer feel good, but it does not help with revision.) Also, evaluate your readers' reactions carefully and accept or reject them thoughtfully.

9.   *Be prepared to write multiple drafts.* Writers often go from first draft to second, third, and fourth before reaching final copy.

Revision Checklist

Thesis (see page 1)
1. Be sure your essay has a clearly stated or strongly implied thesis.
2. Be sure your thesis is not a statement of fact.
3. Be sure your thesis can be treated in a manageable length.
4. If stated, be sure your thesis is not a formal announcement and that it is expressed in specific language.

Introduction (see page 11)
1. Be sure your introduction makes a good first impression.
2. Be sure your introduction is suited to your purpose, audience, tone, and role.

Supporting Details (see page 5)
1. Be sure all your details are suited to your purpose, audience, tone, and role.
2. Be sure your details are in a logical order and arranged in body paragraphs.
3. Be sure each body paragraph has a clearly stated or strongly implied topic sentence.
4. Be sure all your details are relevant to the thesis and appropriate topic sentence.
5. Be sure you have enough details to support the thesis, each topic sentence, and each generalization.
6. Be sure you use transitions to move smoothly from idea to idea and from paragraph to paragraph.

Conclusion (see page 13)
1. Be sure your essay comes to a satisfying finish.
2. Be sure your conclusion is appropriate to your purpose, audience, tone, and role.

Expression
1. Eliminate unnecessary words.
2. Be sure all your ideas are clearly expressed.
3. Substitute specific words for vague ones.
4. Change any words not compatible with your tone.
5. Rewrite tired expressions (clichés) such as "cold as ice."

EDITING THE DRAFT

Before typing the essay into its final form, the successful writer carefully checks for mistakes in grammar, spelling, punctuation, capitalization, and usage. This check is editing. Editing is very important because a reader will lose confidence in the writer if the essay has too many errors. When you edit, consider the following points.

1. *Leave your draft for a day* before editing to clear your head and improve your chances of finding mistakes.

2. *Know the kinds of mistakes you typically make* and be on the lookout for them. For example, if spelling is a problem for you, pay particular attention to this feature of your draft.

3. *Edit more than once,* each time checking for one kind of mistake that you have a tendency to make.

4. *Point to each word with a pen* and linger over it for a second or two. This will prevent you from building speed and overlooking errors.

5. *Place a ruler under each line as you edit* to block out other material and prevent it from distracting you.

6. *Read your work aloud* to listen for mistakes. Be careful, though, to read *exactly* what is on the page, not what you intended to write.

7. *Trust your instincts.* If you have a feeling that something is wrong, the odds are good that a problem exists.

8. *Learn the rules.* You cannot edit effectively if you do not know the rules, so buy a handbook in your campus book store, check it on matters of grammar and usage, and learn any rules you are unfamiliar with.

 PROOFREADING THE FINAL COPY

After editing, use your typewriter or word processor to type your essay into the proper form for your reader. However, your work is not complete until you check carefully for typing errors. Read very slowly, lingering over each word and punctuation mark, so you do not build up too much speed and miss something. If your instructor permits, neatly ink in corrections; otherwise, retype the page or print out a new copy.

DESCRIPTION

The Purpose of Description
Objective and Expressive Details
Descriptive Words
Similes and Metaphors
Selecting and Ordering Details
Suggestions for Writing Description
Annotated Student Essay: In Chelsea's Room

Dawn Watch—John Ciardi (*description to share and per-suade*)
The Sounds of the City—James Tuite (*description to share, entertain, and inform*)
*Once More to the Lake—E. B. White (*description to share*)
My Backyard—Mary E. Mebane (*description to share*)
My Neighborhood—Alfred Kazin (*description to share and inform*)
*The Deer at Providencia—Annie Dillard (*description to share*)

Additional Essay Assignments

*To fulfill the author's purpose, description is combined with one or more other patterns.

This sentence is from a newspaper description of Tennessee's Reelfoot Lake:

Shaggy cypress trees jut from dark waters where white waterlilies as big as dinner plates bloom.

Can you picture that scene? Probably more clearly than you would with this less descriptive sentence:

Trees grow out of the lake at the point where large waterlilies bloom.

The first sentence shows the power of words to create mental pictures, and that is what description is all about: using words to help your reader mentally see, hear, smell, taste, and touch in a particular way.

 ## THE PURPOSE OF DESCRIPTION

People write description to share, to entertain, to inform, and to persuade. For example, on vacation, you might write description on a postcard to *share* the breathtaking view from your hotel balcony with someone back home. Newspaper columnist Russell Baker once wrote a humorous description of a local shopping mall to *entertain* his readers. Someone in the public relations department of your university might draft a description of the campus for inclusion in the school catalog in order to *inform* prospective students about what the campus is like. A travel agent can describe a Caribbean beach resort to *persuade* people to book a tour to that spot.

Because description helps the reader form mental pictures, writers often rely on it to add interest and vividness. That is, description helps writers do more than just *tell* that something is true; it allows them to *show* that something is true. For this reason, writers often combine description with other patterns of development. For example, suppose you are writing an explanation of how to make the perfect spaghetti sauce (this would be *process analysis,* an explanation of how something is made). If you tell your reader to pick only the best tomatoes, you might go on to describe what these tomatoes look, feel, and smell like so your reader knows how to select them. Now suppose you are telling a story about the time you wrecked your uncle's '57 Chevy (this would be *narration*). You might describe what the car looked like after the wreck to add vividness and to help your reader appreciate what kind of shape the car was in.

OBJECTIVE AND EXPRESSIVE DETAILS

Objective details give a factual, impartial, unemotional account, while *expressive details* present a more personal or emotional view. A bank appraiser describing a piece of property would use objective details because his or her personal opinion about the property is not relevant. However, an advertising executive writing a description of a new car would use expressive detail to create an emotional appeal and move the consumer to buy the car. Notice the difference between objective and expressive details in these examples, taken from the readings in this chapter.

objective details:	The Rock Pile, full of weeds and tall trees, was a place of mystery. It had so many rocks and some of them were so large that it was left uncleared with just a path through it. Behind me I could overhear voices coming from the back porch and kitchen. (From "My Backyard," page 65.)
expressive details:	Our cardinals know what time it is. They drop pure tones from the hemlock tops. The black gang of grackles that makes a slum of the pine oak also knows the time but can only grate at it. They sound like a convention of broken universal joints grating uphill. The grackles creak and squeak, and the cardinals form tones that only occasionally sound through the noise. (From "Dawn Watch," page 49.)

Whether expressive or objective, descriptive details are *sensory details* (details that pertain to the senses: sight, sound, taste, smell, and touch). Sometimes a writer uses only one sense, as James Tuite does in "The Sounds of the City" (page 54). Other times, a writer may appeal to several senses, the way E. B. White does in "Once More to the Lake" (page 58).

DESCRIPTIVE WORDS

The writer of both objective and expressive description chooses words carefully. Unfortunately, some writers think that choosing the right words means dashing to the dictionary and thesaurus to find as many big words as possible. The unpleasant result of the word hunt can be something like this:

The pulchritudinous daisy imparted delightful olfactory sensations upon me.

This sentence illustrates two problems that can occur when writers abandon their own natural styles and pile on words taken from the thesaurus and dictionary: the writing becomes stiff, pretentious, and unnatural, and the reader has a hard time understanding.

Of course, you can turn to the dictionary and thesaurus when you are stuck, but usually you can write effective description with words you already know. The key is to use *specific* nouns, verbs, and modifiers rather than general ones because specific words are more descriptive. The following list will help you see the difference between general and specific words.

General nouns	Specific nouns
car	Ford Taurus
sweater	cardigan
shoe	Nike
class	Physics 103
meat	filet mignon
magazine	*Newsweek*

General verbs	Specific verbs
walk	stroll
spoke	shouted
look	glance
went	raced

General modifiers	Specific modifiers
nice	elegant
awesome	overwhelming
terrible	frightening
bad	gaudy

The more expressive you want your description to be, the more specific your word choice should be. Consider the following sentence, which could be well suited to objective description:

The shopper picked up every item on the sale table, looked it over carefully, and dropped it back on the table.

However, for expressive description, more specific word choice is called for:

The bargain hunter seized a neatly folded sweater, scrutinized every inch, then dropped it in an unfolded heap in the middle of the table.

To develop effective descriptive language, expect to work through a series of refinements, something like this:

first draft: The house stood in the shadow of the huge tree.

revision 1:   The huge tree cast a shadow over the house.

revision 2:   The enormous poplar cast a shadow over the house.

revision 3:   The enormous poplar cast an eerie shadow over the house.

Because a little description can go a long way, be careful not to overwhelm your reader by stringing together too many modifiers, like this:

The emaciated, spindly, waxen old man stared vacantly into the barren, colorless hallway as his bony, arthritic, pale fingers played absently with the beige fringes of the faded blue bedspread.

When you do have highly descriptive sentences, balance them with less descriptive ones so your reader is not overwhelmed. For example, consider this passage from "The Sounds of the City," where a highly descriptive sentence is preceded by a less descriptive one:

A bottle shatters against concrete. The whine of a police siren slices through the night, moving ever closer, until an eerie Doppler effect brings it to a guttural halt.

 ## SIMILES AND METAPHORS

Similes and metaphors are often part of description because they help create mental images. A simile uses the words *like* or *as* to compare two things that are not usually seen as similar. Here is an example of a simile taken from "My Backyard":

The water below looked like quicksilver in the sun. (Water is compared to quicksilver with the word *like*.)

A metaphor also compares two things not usually seen as similar, but without *like* or *as*. Here is an example from "The Sounds of the City":

Metallic jaws on sanitation trucks gulp and masticate the residue of daily living, then digest it with a satisfied groan of gears. (The sanitation trucks are compared to an animal or monster with jaws.)

SELECTING AND ORDERING DETAILS

If you describe something small and uncomplicated, such as a chair, you can probably describe all its features. However, if you are describing something larger or more complex, including all the features would be difficult for you and overwhelming for your reader. With more complex descriptions, writers can settle on a *dominant impression* of what they are describing, then select only those details that convey that impression. For example, let's say you want to describe the house you grew up in. Describing all aspects of that house is a formidable task, but one you can cut to manageable size by choosing only those details that convey how you feel about the house or how you view the house. Thus, if the house had warmth, describe only the features that show warmth and ignore everything else. If the house was rundown, describe only the rundown features; if the house was cheerful, describe the cheerful features; if the house was an architect's nightmare, then describe the architectural problems, and so on.

To shape a thesis, write a sentence that expresses what you are describing and your dominant impression. Here are some examples:

I was always embarrassed by the rundown house I grew up in. (The house will be described; the dominant impression is "rundown.")

At noon, the park comes alive with businesspeople taking a midday respite from the pressures of work. (The park at noon will be described; the dominant impression is that it is alive with the activity of businesspeople.)

To order your descriptive details, a number of arrangements are possible. Often a *spatial* arrangement makes sense. In this arrangement, you order details across space, from front to back, near to far, left to right, and so on. Sometimes a *progressive* order is effective. This way, you order details from the least to the most important or telling. For example, if you were describing your rundown house, you would begin with the least rundown features and move gradually to the most rundown, saving the most telling description for a big finish. If you are moving through a place, a *chronological* order is possible. This way, you describe what you see first, second, third, and so on across time.

To help your reader recognize how you are grouping and ordering ideas, topic sentences can present the focus of some or all of your paragraphs. For example, in "Dawn Watch" John Ciardi uses these topic sentences to guide the reader:

There is an old mountain laurel on the island of the driveway turn-around. (The details in the paragraph with this topic sentence focus on the mountain laurel and the area around it.)

The damned crabgrass is wrestling with the zinnias, and I stop to weed it out. (The details in the paragraph with this topic sentence focus on the crab-grass.)

SUGGESTIONS FOR WRITING DESCRIPTION

1. Describe something you can go to and observe, so selecting details is easier. If you describe something from memory, be sure the memory is fresh enough to allow for vivid, specific details.
2. If you have trouble settling on a dominant impression, make a list of all the emotions your subject arouses in you and all the reactions you have to the subject; then choose one of those feelings or reactions as your dominant impression.
3. Make a list of all the details of what you are describing (observe your subject, if possible). Do not worry about being descriptive at this point. Just get down ideas the best way you can. Then review your list and circle the points you will include in your first draft.
4. When you write your first draft, be as descriptive as you comfortably can be, but do not labor over anything. Descriptive language does not come easily; choosing specific nouns, verbs, and modifiers takes time and often involves a series of revisions, so do not expect too much too soon. When you revise after writing your draft, you can get your descriptions just right.
5. If you use a dictionary or thesaurus for help, be aware of the connotations of words you take from these sources, and be sure you use words that are natural for you. Otherwise your style will be inflated, and your meaning may be unclear.

ANNOTATED STUDENT ESSAY

Student author Julie Cummins uses expressive detail to describe the soothing quality of her daughter's bedroom. As you read, notice how the simple, specific words create effective description.

IN CHELSEA'S ROOM

Paragraph 1
Thesis (last sentence) says what is being described (Chelsea's room) and gives dominant impression (soothing atmosphere). Thesis includes a simile ("like a fluttering moth").

Paragraph 2
Topic sentence (sentence 1) gives focus. Supporting details are expressive details of sight. "Silent sentinels" is a simile. Descriptive words are simple and specific (*pastel, haven, silken hair, tangled,* etc.)

Paragraph 3
Second sentence is the topic sentence. Details are of sound. Note specific words like *muffles, din,* and *filtered. Cathedral* is used as a metaphor.

Paragraph 4
Expressive detail and specific words convey the sense of a soothing atmosphere.

Paragraph 5
Conclusion provides closure by noting the effect of the room on the writer.

1   My baby's bedroom provides shelter and rest, and so it is special. Everything in the room is designed to soothe and comfort a newborn, making it a sanctuary from the rest of the world. Just to enter the room is to leave all problems and stress behind, so whenever my day has been particularly hectic or rushed, the soothing atmosphere of my daughter Chelsea's room draws me like a fluttering moth to a gentle flame.

2   Chelsea's room is at its most relaxing late at night when everything is quiet. Even though the rest of the house may be dark, Chelsea's room has its own special glow. In addition to the dimly shining nightlight, the soft light from the street casts muted shadows on the walls. These shadows move slowly and quietly, tiptoeing past Chelsea like silent sentinels. In her crib, the baby sleeps in a pastel haven, her silken hair tangled by a chubby fist. Around her, softening all the corners, the stuffed animals smile, offering their unconditional love.

3   The sights are not the only comforting features in Chelsea's room. All sounds are lulling and soothing. The deep carpet muffles any noise, so even the din from the street seems filtered and more pure. Her room has the hushed ambience of a cathedral. Listening closely, I can hear Chelsea's soft breathing as she sleeps. It sounds like a whisper, calming and relaxing my jangled nerves. Even the soft tinkle of the mobile calms me. There is nothing jarring in Chelsea's room.

4   From the corner, the softly padded rocking chair beckons, inviting me with arms outstretched to sit on its lap. I ease in, and it relaxes me with a warm hug and a lulling movement. The muffled creak of the chair rocks in gentle time with the mobile. Chelsea stirs in her sleep, nestling further under the thick comforter. It is easy to rest in such a sanctuary of softness.

5   Everybody's life gets complicated sometimes. Whenever I feel my life closing in, Chelsea's room is always waiting. It reminds me that life can be slower, more innocent, more pure. Chelsea's room always makes me feel better.

DAWN WATCH
John Ciardi

◆

John Ciardi (1916–1986) was a poet, essayist, and translator whose work captured the small details of daily life. "Dawn Watch" is no exception, for its rich detail focuses on a daily occurrence: sunrise. As Ciardi shares his impressions of this event, he works to persuade the reader that it is the best part of the day. As you read, notice the playful, down-to-earth quality of Ciardi's writing.

◆

1   Unless a man is up for the dawn and for the half hour or so of first light, he has missed the best of the day.

2   The traffic has just started, not yet a roar and a stink. One car at a time goes by, the tires humming almost like the sound of a brook a half mile down in the crease of a mountain I know—a sound that carries not because it is loud but because everybody else is still.

3   It isn't exactly a mist that hangs in the thickets but more nearly the ghost of a mist—a phenomenon like side vision. Look hard and it isn't there, but glance without focusing and something registers, an exhalation that will be gone three minutes after the sun comes over the treetops.

4   The lawns shine with a dew not exactly dew. There is a rabbit bobbing about on the lawn and then freezing. If it were truly a dew, his tracks would shine black on the grass, and he leaves no visible track. Yet, there is something on the grass that makes it glow a depth of green it will not show again all day. Or is that something in the dawn air?

5   Our cardinals know what time it is. They drop pure tones from the hemlock tops. The black gang of grackles that makes a slum of the pine oak also knows the time but can only grate at it. They sound like a convention of broken universal joints grating uphill. The grackles creak and squeak, and the cardinals form tones that occasionally sound through the noise. I scatter sunflower seeds by the birdbath for the cardinals and hope the grackles won't find them.

6   My neighbor's tomcat comes across the lawn, probably on his way home from passion, or only acting as if he had had a big night. I suspect him of being one of those poolroom braggarts who can't get next to a girl but who likes to let on that he is a hot stud. This one is too can-fed and too lazy to hunt for anything. Here he comes now, ignoring the rabbit. And there he goes.

7   As soon as he has hopped the fence, I let my dog out. The dog charges the rabbit, watches it jump the fence, shakes himself in a self-satisfied way, then trots dutifully into the thicket for his morning service, stopping to sniff everything on the way back.

8   There is an old mountain laurel on the island of the driveway turn-around. From somewhere on the wind a white morning-glory rooted next to it and has climbed it. Now the laurel is woven full of white bells tinged pink by the first rays through the not quite mist. Only in earliest morning can they be seen. Come out two hours from now and there will be no morning-glories.

9   Dawn, too, is the hour of a weed I know only as a day flower—a bright blue button that closes in full sunlight. I have weeded bales of it out of my flower beds, its one daytime virtue being the shallowness of its root system that allows it to be pulled out effortlessly in great handfuls. Yet, now it shines. Had it a few more hours of such shining in its cycle, I would cultivate it as a ground cover, but dawn is its one hour, and a garden is for whole days.

10   There is another blue morning weed whose name I do not know. This one grows from a bulb to pulpy stems and a bedraggled daytime sprawl. Only a shovel will dig it out. Try weeding it by hand and the stems will break off to be replaced by new ones and to sprawl over the chosen plants in the flower bed. Yet, now and for another hour it outshines its betters, its flowers about the size of a quarter and paler than those of the day flower but somehow more brilliant, perhaps because of the contrast of its paler foliage.

11   And now the sun is slanting in full. It is bright enough to make the leaves of the Japanese red maple seem a transparent red bronze when the tree is between me and the light. There must be others, but this is the only tree I know whose leaves let the sun through in this way—except, that is, when the fall colors start. Aspen leaves, when they first yellow and before they dry, are transparent in this way. I tell myself it must have something to do with the red-yellow range of the spectrum. Green takes sunlight and holds it, but red and yellow let it through.

12   The damned crabgrass is wrestling with the zinnias, and I stop to weed it out. The stuff weaves too close to the zinnias to make the iron claw usable. And it won't do to pull at the stalks. Crabgrass (at least in a mulched bed) can be weeded only with dirty fingers. Thumb and forefinger have to pincer into the dirt and grab the root-center. Weeding, of course, is an illusion of hope. Pulling out the root only stirs the soil and brings new crabgrass seeds into germinating position. Take a walk around the block and a new clump will have sprouted by the time you get back. But I am not ready to walk around the block. I fill a small basket with the plucked clumps, and for the instant I look at them, the zinnias are weedless.

13   Don't look back. I dump the weeds in the thicket where they will be smothered by the grass clippings I will pile on at the next cutting. On the way back I see the cardinals come down for the sunflower seeds, and the jays join them, and then the grackles start ganging in, gate-crashing the buffet and clattering all over it. The dog stops chewing his rawhide and makes a dash into the puddle of birds, which splashes away from it.

14   I hear a brake-squeak I have been waiting for and know the paper has arrived. As usual, the news turns out to be another disaster count. The function

of the wire services is to bring us tragedies faster than we can pity. In the end we shall all be inured, numb, and ready for emotionless programming. I sit on the patio and read until the sun grows too bright on the page. The cardinals have stopped singing, and the grackles have flown off. It's the end of birdsong again.

15   Then suddenly—better than song for its instant—a hummingbird the color of green crushed velvet hovers in the throat of my favorite lily, a lovely high-bloomer I got the bulbs for but not the name. The lily is a crest of white horns with red dots and red velvet tongues along the insides of the petals and with an odor that drowns the patio. The hummingbird darts in and out of each horn in turn, then hovers an instant, and disappears.

16   Even without the sun, I have had enough of the paper. I'll take that hummingbird as my news for this dawn. It is over now. I smoke one more cigarette too many and decide that, if I go to bed now, no one in the family need know I have stayed up for it again. Why do they insist on shaking their heads when they find me still up for breakfast, after having scribbled through the dark hours? They always do. They seem compelled to express pity for an old loony who can't find his own way to bed. Why won't they understand that this is the one hour of any day that must not be missed, as it is the one hour I couldn't imagine getting up for, though I can still get to it by staying up? It makes sense to me. There comes a time when the windows lighten and the twittering starts. I look up and know it's time to leave the papers in their mess. I could slip quietly into bed and avoid the family's headshakes, but this stroll-around first hour is too good to miss. Even my dog, still sniffing and circling, knows what hour this is.

17   Come on, boy. It's time to go in. The rabbit won't come back till to-morrow, and the birds have work to do. The dawn's over. It's time to call it a day.

Considering Ideas

1. Why do you think Ciardi enjoys dawn so much?
2. How does Ciardi's family view his habit of staying up to enjoy first light?
3. What can you tell about Ciardi's work habits and lifestyle as a result of reading the essay?
4. What do you think Ciardi means when he says in paragraph 12 that "weeding . . . is an illusion of hope"?
5. Ciardi opens by saying, "Unless a man is up for the dawn and for the half hour or so of first light, he has missed the best of the day." How do you react to the use of "man" and "he"? Do you think Ciardi is excluding women? Does the fact that the essay was published in 1972 affect your view?
6. *Irony* is the contrast between what is stated or what occurs and what is expected by the reader. What irony occurs at the end of the essay?

Considering Technique

1. Which sentence presents the thesis of "Dawn Watch"? What does that thesis say is being described, and what does it note as the author's dominant impression?
2. In what order does Ciardi arrange most of his details? Why does he use this order?
3. Ciardi makes frequent use of topic sentences to present the focus of his paragraphs. Cite two examples of such topic sentences.
4. Ciardi's description includes similes and metaphors (see page 45). Cite an example of each. What do you think the similes and metaphors contribute to the essay?
5. Ciardi describes some sounds along with the sights of dawn. What are these sounds?
6. Is Ciardi's description primarily objective or expressive (see page 43)? Mention a description or two that you particularly enjoy. Why do you like this description? What specific nouns, verbs, and modifiers do these descriptions include?
7. Consult a dictionary if you are unsure of the meaning of any of these words: *grackles* (paragraph 5), *universal joints* (paragraph 5), *braggarts* (paragraph 6), *bedraggled* (paragraph 10), *spectrum* (paragraph 11), *pincer* (paragraph 12), *wire services* (paragraph 14), *inured* (paragraph 14).

For Group Consideration

Ciardi works all night and goes to sleep after sunrise. What are the advantages and disadvantages of such a schedule? Consider this question with two or three classmates.

Journal Entry

What is the best part of the day for you? Explain why this part of the day is your favorite.

Essay Assignments

1. Use descriptive detail to share your impressions of a particular time of day (dawn, dusk, noon, midnight, and so on) at a particular place.
2. Ciardi includes descriptions of both plant and animal life in "Dawn Watch." For example, he describes a tomcat, a hummingbird, weeds, and leaves. Select some form of plant or animal life that you can observe closely and describe both its features and how you react to those features.
3. Ciardi describes dawn as the "best of the day." Describe what you think is the "worst of the day": rush hour, supper time, the first hour you are awake, and so on. Be sure your description conveys why this time is so unpleasant.

Considering Thematic Issues

1. In paragraph 14, Ciardi raises an important issue about newspapers. Explain his opinion and then go on to agree or disagree with him, using examples from newspapers, your own experience, and your own observation to make your point. If you like, you can also explain whether you think Ciardi's opinion holds true for television news.
2. What similarities and/or differences do you notice between the view Ciardi has of his surroundings and the view Mary Mebane has of her surroundings in "My Backyard" (page 65)? Explain what you think accounts for these similarities and/or differences.

THE SOUNDS OF THE CITY
James Tuite

James Tuite, a longtime sportswriter and former sports editor for the New York Times, *shares his unique perceptions of Manhattan and entertains the reader in the process. In addition, the reader who is unfamiliar with Manhattan is likely to learn something about the city. Although writers of description usually rely heavily on visual detail, James Tuite creates his mental pictures of midtown Manhattan with sensory detail of sound. Nonetheless, the images of sound conjure up vivid visual images. As you read, notice this sound/sight connection.*

◆

1   New York is a city of sounds: muted sounds and shrill sounds; shattering sounds and soothing sounds; urgent sounds and aimless sounds. The cliff dwellers of Manhattan—who would be racked by the silence of the lonely woods—do not hear these sounds because they are constant and eternally urban.

2   The visitor to the city can hear them, though, just as some animals can hear a high-pitched whistle inaudible to humans. To the casual caller to Manhattan, lying restive and sleepless in a hotel twenty or thirty floors above the street, they tell a story as fascinating as life itself. And back of the sounds broods the silence.

3   Night in midtown is the noise of tinseled honky-tonk and violence. Thin strains of music, usually the firm beat of rock 'n' roll or the frenzied outbursts of the discotheque, rise from ground level. This is the cacophony, the discordance of youth, and it comes on strongest when nights are hot and young blood restless.

4   Somewhere in the canyons below there is shrill laughter or raucous shouting. A bottle shatters against concrete. The whine of a police siren slices through the night, moving ever closer, until an eerie Doppler effect* brings it to a guttural halt.

5   There are few sounds so exciting in Manhattan as those of fire apparatus dashing through the night. At the outset there is the tentative hint of the first-due company bullying his way through midtown traffic. Now a fire whistle from the opposite direction affirms that trouble is, indeed, afoot. In seconds, other sirens converging from other streets help the skytop listener focus on the scene of excitement.

6   But he can only hear and not see, and imagination takes flight. Are the flames and smoke gushing from windows not far away? Are victims trapped

---

* The drop in pitch that occurs as a source of sound quickly passes by a listener.

there, crying out for help? Is it a conflagration, or only a trash-basket fire? Or, perhaps, it is merely a false alarm.

7   The questions go unanswered and the urgency of the moment dissolves. Now the mind and the ear detect the snarling, arrogant bickering of automobile horns. People in a hurry. Taxicabs blaring, insisting on their checkered priority.

8   Even the taxi horns dwindle down to a precocious few in the gray and pink moments of dawn. Suddenly there is another sound, a morning sound that taunts the memory for recognition. The growl of a predatory monster? No, just garbage trucks that have begun a day of scavenging.

9   Trash cans rattle outside restaurants. Metallic jaws on sanitation trucks gulp and masticate the residue of daily living, then digest it with a satisfied groan of gears. The sounds of the new day are businesslike. The growl of buses, so scattered and distant at night, becomes a demanding part of the traffic bedlam. An occasional jet or helicopter injects an exclamation point from an unexpected quarter. When the wind is right, the vibrant bellow of an ocean liner can be heard.

10   The sounds of the day are as jarring as the glare of a sun that outlines the canyons of midtown in drab relief. A pneumatic drill frays countless nerves with its rat-a-tat-tat, for dig they must to perpetuate the city's dizzy motion. After each screech of brakes there is a moment of suspension, of waiting for the thud or crash that never seems to follow.

11   The whistles of traffic policemen and hotel doormen chirp from all sides, like birds calling for their mates across a frenzied aviary. And all of these sounds are adult sounds, for childish laughter has no place in these canyons.

12   Night falls again, the cycle is complete, but there is no surcease from sound. For the beautiful dreamers, perhaps, the "sounds of the rude world heard in the day, lulled by the moonlight have all passed away," but this is not so in the city.

13   Too many New Yorkers accept the sounds about them as bland parts of everyday existence. They seldom stop to listen to the sounds, to think about them, to be appalled or enchanted by them. In the big city, sounds are life.

Considering Ideas

1. Who are the "cliff dwellers of Manhattan" (paragraph 1), and why do they not hear the sounds of the city?
2. Tuite says, "New York is a city of sounds." To prove his point, he describes a wide range of things that can be heard. What do all the diverse sounds have in common?
3. Why do you think that Tuite chose to describe New York using sound rather than sight?
4. Does Tuite's description make you want to visit Manhattan? Why or why not?

Considering Technique

1. What is Tuite describing, and what is his dominant impression of what he is describing? In which paragraphs do you find this information?
2. Is Tuite's description objective or expressive?
3. In what order does Tuite arrange his descriptive details? What are the clues to this arrangement?
4. One reason Tuite's description is effective is that he uses specific nouns ("arrogant *bickering* of automobile horns"), specific verbs ("a police siren *slices* through the night"), and specific modifiers ("*frenzied* outbursts of the discotheque"). Give two examples of specific nouns, three of specific verbs, and four of specific modifiers.
5. Record one or two descriptions in "The Sounds of the City" that you particularly enjoy. Why do these descriptions appeal to you?
6. What approach does Tuite take to the conclusion of his essay? (See page 13 on approaches to the conclusion.)
7. Consult a dictionary if you are unsure of the meaning of any of these words: *inaudible* (paragraph 2), *restive* (paragraph 2), *raucous* (paragraph 4), *tentative* (paragraph 5), *precocious* (paragraph 8), *vibrant* (paragraph 9), *perpetuate* (paragraph 10).

For Group Consideration

With three or four classmates, consider this question and report your conclusions to the rest of the class: Is a reader who has visited Manhattan likely to react differently to "The Sounds of the City" than a reader who has not visited Manhattan? Explain why or why not. If your answer is yes, go on to tell about some of the differences in the reactions.

Journal Entry

Reread "The Sounds of the City" and then in your journal note how the essay makes you feel about life in the big city. Does it seem vital and exciting or intimidating and frightening? How do you think Tuite feels about life in Manhattan? Is there any specific evidence in the essay to support your view?

Essay Assignments

1. Like Tuite, write a descriptive essay that relies heavily on sensory detail of sound. You might describe the sounds in your campus library, the student union, your dormitory, a dining hall, a dentist's office, a shopping mall, or a park. Title your essay "The Sounds of _____." (Fill in the blank with the place you are describing.)

2. If you have spent time in the country, write an essay called "The Sounds of the Country." Settle on a dominant impression and use sensory detail of sound to show why you have formed that dominant impression.

3. Pick one of the mental pictures created in Tuite's essay (the discotheque, the fire emergency, the taxis on the street, the garbage collection, the traffic police, etc.) and expand the image to essay proportions using whatever sensory details you wish.

4. Rewrite "The Sounds of the City" so that the description is objective rather than expressive.

Considering Thematic Issues

1. Record the sounds in a familiar place (your residence hall, a campus spot, the mall, etc.), then play back the tape. Based on what you hear, write an essay that explains what the sounds tell you about the place. Also explain whether there are any sounds on the tape that you had not noticed before because familiarity had numbed you to them.

2. Look closely at "The Sounds of the City" and "Dawn Watch" (page 49). Use the information in these essays, along with your own experience and observation, to explain how people are affected by their environment.

ONCE MORE TO THE LAKE
E. B. White

◆

*A superb essayist whose literary accom-
plishments won him the Presidential Medal of Freedom, Elwyn Brooks White
(1899–1985) wrote for* The New Yorker *and helped establish its reputation for
excellence. He also wrote the popular children's book* Charlotte's Web. *In "Once
More to the Lake," White uses description to share his past and present visits to a
family vacation spot. As you read, notice that White's description leads him to a
disarming conclusion.*

◆

1   One summer, along about 1904, my father rented a camp on a lake in
Maine and took us all there for the month of August. We all got ringworm from
some kittens and had to rub Pond's Extract on our arms and legs night and
morning, and my father rolled over in a canoe with all his clothes on; but
outside of that the vacation was a success and from then on none of us ever
thought there was any place in the world like that lake in Maine. We returned
summer after summer—always on August 1 for one month. I have since
become a salt-water man, but sometimes in summer there are days when the
restlessness of the tides and the fearful cold of the sea water and the incessant
wind that blows across the afternoon and into the evening make me wish for
the placidity of a lake in the woods. A few weeks ago this feeling got so strong I
bought myself a couple of bass hooks and a spinner and returned to the lake
where we used to go, for a week's fishing and to revisit old haunts.

2   I took along my son, who had never had any fresh water up his nose and
who had seen lily pads only from train windows. On the journey over to the
lake I began to wonder what it would be like. I wondered how time would have
marred this unique, this holy spot—the coves and streams, the hills that the sun
set behind, the camps and the paths behind the camps. I was sure that the tarred
road would have found it out, and I wondered in what other ways it would be
desolated. It is strange how much you can remember about places like that
once you allow your mind to return into the grooves that lead back. You
remember one thing, and that suddenly reminds you of another thing. I guess I
remembered clearest of all the early mornings, when the lake was cool and
motionless, remembered how the bedroom smelled of the lumber it was made
of and of the wet woods whose scent entered through the screen. The partitions
in the camp were thin and did not extend clear to the top of the rooms, and as I
was always the first up I would dress softly so as not to wake the others, and
sneak out into the sweet outdoors and start out in the canoe, keeping close
along the shore in the long shadows of the pines. I remembered being very
careful never to rub my paddle against the gunwale for fear of disturbing the
stillness of the cathedral.

3   The lake had never been what you would call a wild lake. There were cottages sprinkled around the shores, and it was in farming country although the shores of the lake were quite heavily wooded. Some of the cottages were owned by nearby farmers, and you would live at the shore and eat your meals at the farmhouse. That's what our family did. But although it wasn't wild, it was a fairly large and undisturbed lake and there were places in it that, to a child at least, seemed infinitely remote and primeval.

4   I was right about the tar: It led to within half a mile of the shore. But when I got back there, with my boy, and we settled into a camp near a farmhouse and into the kind of summertime I had known, I could tell that it was going to be pretty much the same as it had been before—I knew it, lying in bed the first morning smelling the bedroom and hearing the boy sneak quietly out and go off along the shore in a boat. I began to sustain the illusion that he was I, and therefore, by simple transposition, that I was my father. This sensation persisted, kept cropping up all the time we were there. It was not an entirely new feeling, but in this setting it grew much stronger. I seemed to be living a dual existence. I would be in the middle of some simple act, I would be picking up a bait box or laying down a table fork, or I would be saying something and suddenly it would be not I but my father who was saying the words or making the gesture. It gave me a creepy sensation.

5   We went fishing the first morning. I felt the same damp moss covering the worms in the bait can, and saw the dragonfly alight on the tip of my rod as it hovered a few inches from the surface of the water. It was the arrival of this fly that convinced me beyond any doubt that everything was as it always had been, that the years were a mirage and that there had been no years. The small waves were the same, chucking the rowboat under the chin as we fished at anchor, and the boat was the same boat, the same color green and the ribs broken in the same places, and under the floorboards the same fresh water leavings and debris—the dead hellgrammite, the wisps of moss, the rusty discarded fishhook, the dried blood from yesterday's catch. We stared silently at the tips of our rods, at the dragonflies that came and went. I lowered the tip of mine into the water, tentatively, pensively dislodging the fly, which darted two feet away, poised, darted two feet back, and came to rest again a little farther up the rod. There had been no years between the ducking of this dragonfly and the other one—the one that was part of memory. I looked at the boy, who was silently watching his fly, and it was my hands that held his rod, my eyes watching. I felt dizzy and didn't know which rod I was at the end of.

6   We caught two bass, hauling them in briskly as though they were mackerel, pulling them over the side of the boat in a businesslike manner without any landing net, and stunning them with a blow on the back of the head. When we got back for a swim before lunch, the lake was exactly where we had left it, the same number of inches from the dock, and there was only the merest suggestion of a breeze. This seemed an utterly enchanted sea, this lake you could leave to its own devices for a few hours and come back to, and find that it

had not stirred, this constant and trustworthy body of water. In the shallows, the dark, water-soaked sticks and twigs, smooth and old, were undulating in clusters on the bottom against the clean ribbed sand, and the track of the mussel was plain. A school of minnows swam by, each minnow with its small individual shadow, doubling the attendance, so clear and sharp in the sunlight. Some of the other campers were in swimming, along the shore, one of them with a cake of soap, and the water felt thin and clear and unsubstantial. Over the years there had been this person with the cake of soap, this cultist, and here he was. There had been no years.

7   Up to the farmhouse to dinner through the teeming dusty field, the road under our sneakers was only a two-track road. The middle track was missing, the one with the marks of the hooves and the splotches of dried, flaky manure. There had always been three tracks to choose from in choosing which track to walk in; now the choice was narrowed down to two. For a moment I missed terribly the middle alternative. But the way led past the tennis court, and something about the way it lay there in the sun reassured me; the tape had loosened along the backline, the alleys were green with plantains and other weeds, and the net (installed in June and removed in September) sagged in the dry noon, and the whole place steamed with midday heat and hunger and emptiness. There was a choice of pie for dessert, and one was blueberry and one was apple, and the waitresses were the same country girls, there having been no passage of time, only the illusion of it as in a dropped curtain—the waitresses were still fifteen; their hair had been washed, that was the only difference—they had been to the movies and seen the pretty girls with the clean hair.

8   Summertime, oh, summertime, pattern of life indelible with fade-proof lake, the wood unshatterable, the pasture with the sweetfern and the juniper forever and ever, summer without end; this was the background, and the life along the shore was the design, the cottages with their innocent and tranquil design, their tiny docks with the flagpole and the American flag floating against the white clouds in the blue sky, the little paths over the roots of the trees leading from camp to camp and the paths leading back to the outhouses and the can of lime for sprinkling, and at the souvenir counters at the store the miniature birchbark canoes and the postcards that showed things looking a little better than they looked. This was the American family at play, escaping the city heat, wondering whether the newcomers in the camp at the head of the cove were "common" or "nice," wondering whether it was true that the people who drove up for Sunday dinner at the farmhouse were turned away because there wasn't enough chicken.

9   It seemed to me, as I kept remembering all this, that those times and those summers had been infinitely precious and worth saving. There had been jollity and peace and goodness. The arriving (at the beginning of August) had been so big a business in itself, at the railway station the farm wagon drawn up, the first smell of the pine-laden air, the first glimpse of the smiling farmer, and the great

importance of the trunks and your father's enormous authority in such matters, and the feel of the wagon under you for the long ten-mile haul, and at the top of the last long hill catching the first view of the lake after eleven months of not seeing this cherished body of water. The shouts and cries of the other campers when they saw you, and the trunks to be unpacked, to give up their rich burden. (Arriving was less exciting nowadays, when you sneaked up in your car and parked it under a tree near the camp and took out the bags and in five minutes it was all over, no fuss, no loud wonderful fuss about trunks.)

10   Peace and goodness and jollity. The only thing that was wrong now, really, was the sound of the place, an unfamiliar nervous sound of the outboard motors. This was the note that jarred, the one thing that would sometimes break the illusion and set the years moving. In those other summertimes all motors were inboard; and when they were at a little distance, the noise they made was a sedative, an ingredient of summer sleep. They were one-cylinder and two-cylinder engines, and some were make-and-break and some were jump-spark, but they all made a sleepy sound across the lake. The one-lungers throbbed and fluttered, and the twin-cylinder ones purred and purred, and that was a quiet sound, too. But now the campers all had outboards. In the daytime, in the hot mornings, these motors made a petulant, irritable sound; at night in the still evening when the afterglow lit the water, they whined about one's ears like mosquitoes. My boy loved our rented outboard, and his great desire was to achieve single-handed mastery over it, and authority, and he soon learned the trick of choking it a little (but not too much), and the adjustment of the needle valve. Watching him I would remember the things you could do with the old one-cylinder engine with the heavy flywheel, how you could have it eating out of your hand if you got really close to it spiritually. Motorboats in those days didn't have clutches, and you would make a landing by shutting off the motor at the proper time and coasting in with a dead rudder. But there was a way of reversing them, if you learned the trick, by cutting the switch and putting it on again exactly on the final dying revolution of the flywheel, so that it would kick back against compression and begin reversing. Approaching a dock in a strong following breeze, it was difficult to slow up sufficiently by the ordinary coasting method, and if a boy felt he had complete mastery over his motor, he was tempted to keep it running beyond its time and then reverse it a few feet from the dock. It took a cool nerve, because if you threw the switch a twentieth of a second too soon you would catch the flywheel when it still had speed enough to go up past center, and the boat would leap ahead, charging bull-fashion at the dock.

11   We had a good week at the camp. The bass were biting well and the sun shone endlessly, day after day. We would be tired at night and lie down in the accumulated heat of the little bedrooms after the long hot day and the breeze would stir almost imperceptibly outside and the smell of the swamp drift in through the rusty screens. Sleep would come easily and in the morning the red squirrel would be on the roof, tapping out his gay routine. I kept remembering

everything, lying in bed in the mornings—the small steamboat that had a long rounded stern like the lip of a Ubangi, and how quietly she ran on the moonlight sails, when the older boys played their mandolins and the girls sang and we ate doughnuts dipped in sugar, and how sweet the music was on the water in the shining night, and what it had felt like to think about girls then. After breakfast we would go up to the store and the things were in the same place—the minnows in a bottle, the plugs and spinners disarranged and pawed over by the youngsters from the boys' camp, the Fig Newtons and the Beeman's gum. Outside, the road was tarred and cars stood in front of the store. Inside, all was just as it had always been, except there was more Coca-Cola and not so much Moxie and root beer and birch beer and sarsaparilla. We would walk out with the bottle of pop apiece and sometimes the pop would backfire up our noses and hurt. We explored the streams, quietly, where the turtles slid off the sunny logs and dug their way into the soft bottom; and we lay on the town wharf and fed worms to the tame bass. Everywhere we went I had trouble making out which was I, the one walking at my side, the one walking in my pants.

12   One afternoon while we were at that lake a thunderstorm came up. It was like the revival of an old melodrama that I had seen long ago with childish awe. The second-act climax of the drama of the electrical disturbance over a lake in America had not changed in any important respect. This was the big scene, still the big scene. The whole thing was so familiar, the first feeling of oppression and heat and a general air around camp of not wanting to go very far away. In midafternoon (it was all the same) a curious darkening of the sky, and a lull in everything that had made life tick; and then the way the boats suddenly swung the other way at their moorings with the coming of a breeze out of the new quarter, and the premonitory rumble. Then the kettle drum, then the snare, then the bass drum and cymbals, then crackling light against the dark, and the gods grinning and licking their chops in the hills. Afterward the calm, the rain steadily rustling in the calm lake, the return of light and hope and spirits, and the campers running out in joy and relief to go swimming in the rain, their bright cries perpetuating the deathless joke about how they were getting simply drenched, and the children screaming with delight at the new sensation of bathing in the rain, and the joke about getting drenched linking the generations in a strong indestructible chain. And the comedian who waded in carrying an umbrella.

13   When the others went swimming my son said he was going in, too. He pulled his dripping trunks from the line where they had hung all through the shower and wrung them out. Languidly, and with no thought of going in, I watched him, his hard little body, skinny and bare, saw him wince slightly as he pulled up around his vitals the small, soggy, icy garment. As he buckled the swollen belt, suddenly my groin felt the chill of death.

Considering Ideas

1. Why do you think White returns to the lake after a 40-year absence?
2. White mentions several times that he has trouble distinguishing himself from his son, and that he has trouble distinguishing the present from the past. Why do you think he experiences this blurring of identities and time?
3. Why do you think White believes that his past summers at the lake were "infinitely precious and worth saving" (paragraph 9)?
4. White is a little unnerved because the road to the farmhouse has been reduced from three to two tracks. Why is he unnerved?
5. What conclusion does White draw about the passage of time? Where is that conclusion best expressed?
6. Do you find "Once More to the Lake" an upbeat or depressing essay? Why?

Considering Technique

1. What do you think White's dominant impression of the lake is as an adult?
2. White appeals to the senses of smell, touch, and sound in addition to the sense of sight. Cite one example each of description that appeals to smell, touch, and sound. Underline the specific words.
3. What metaphor does White include in paragraph 2? In paragraph 12? What do these metaphors contribute?
4. Cite two examples of descriptive language that you find particularly appealing. Underline the specific words.
5. *Narration* is storytelling. What narration does White include?
6. *Comparison and contrast* shows similarities and differences. In what way does White compare and contrast?
7. Consult a dictionary if you are unsure of the meaning of any of these words: *incessant* (paragraph 1), *placidity* (paragraph 1), *haunts* (paragraph 1), *marred* (paragraph 2), *gunwale* (paragraph 2), *primeval* (paragraph 3), *hellgrammite* (paragraph 5), *pensively* (paragraph 5), *indelible* (paragraph 8), *petulant* (paragraph 10), *imperceptibly* (paragraph 11), *Ubangi* (paragraph 11), *premonitory* (paragraph 12), *languidly* (paragraph 13).

For Group Consideration

Who do you think is more likely to appreciate "Once More to the Lake," a young adult reader or a middle-aged reader? Why? Discuss these questions with two or three classmates and share your conclusions with the rest of the class.

Journal Entry

In paragraph 12, when he writes of the thunderstorm, White notes that "the joke about getting drenched [links] the generations in a strong indestructible chain."

What events, experiences, and circumstances link the generations in your family or in your locale? Explain in a page or two of your journal.

Essay Assignments

1. White says, "It is strange how much you can remember about places like [the lake] once you allow your mind to return into the grooves that lead back." Allow your mind "to return into the grooves" and lead you back to a place you enjoyed as a child. Describe that place in a way that conveys why you enjoyed it.
2. If you have ever returned to a place after being away for a while, describe the ways the place changed and the ways it stayed the same. You could, for example, describe your first trip home after being away at school for several months.
3. In paragraph 9, White describes the excitement of arriving at the lake. Write a description of your arrival someplace special or important. For example, you could describe your arrival at college, the site of your wedding, your graduation ceremony, an annual vacation spot, or the hospital for an operation.
4. Paragraph 12 describes a thunderstorm. Write your own description of a thunderstorm or write a description of another kind of weather: a spring shower, a blizzard, an ice storm, a tornado, a hurricane, or a windstorm, for example. If you like, you can use one or more metaphors.

Considering Thematic Issues

1. In "Once More to the Lake," White comes to recognize his own mortality. Tell about some event that caused you to recognize or think about your mortality. Explain what happened, how you were affected, and why you were affected that way.
2. In "Two Views of the Mississippi" (page 232), Mark Twain, like White, considers his youthful and adult views of a significant place. Explain the conclusions each author reaches about the passage of time and to what extent the authors agree or disagree. Also, include your own view about how the passage of time affects a person's opinion of a place.

MY BACKYARD
Mary E. Mebane

Mary Mebane is an English professor who has written two autobiographies. In this excerpt from one of them, she describes her childhood surroundings to share part of her experience with her reader. As you read, notice the early signs that Mebane was to become a writer.

◆

1   My name is Mary.

2   When I first opened my eyes to the world, on June 26, 1933, in the Wildwood community in Durham County, North Carolina, the world was a green Eden—and it was magic. My favorite place in the whole world was a big rock in the backyard that looked like the back of a buried elephant. I spent a lot of time squatting on that rock. I realize now that I probably selected it because it was in the *center* of our yard, and from it, by shifting ever so slightly, this way and that, I could see *everything*. I liked to look. Mama must have told me several thousand times that I was going to die with my eyes open, looking.

3   When I sat on the rock with my back to the house, the fields were in front of me. On the left was another lot that we called the Rock Pile, and to the right was an untended strip of land, strewn with rocks but cleared enough to be plowed sometimes. The Rock Pile, full of weeds and tall trees, was a place of mystery. It had so many rocks and some of them were so large that it was left uncleared with just a path through it. Behind me I could overhear voices coming from the back porch and kitchen. I could see who was chopping or picking something in the garden and I could see who was coming through the Rock Pile.

4   The road in front of our house was a dirty strip swirling with the thick red dust of state trucks going to and from the rock quarry. I saw the quarry once. To me it was one of the Seven Wonders of the World—a very wide hole, dug deep in the ground. The trucks around it looked like little toys. It was a mountain going in the wrong direction, with me standing at the top. Good-looking Edmund, the one with the limp from polio, died at the rock quarry. Explosives. They didn't want anyone to see his body. Someone said that they found only pieces. He was a grown man and I was a child at the time, but I remember him. He came down from Virginia to stay with his sister and find work. Like his sisters, he was very light-skinned and had thick, curly brown hair. I used to wonder about his hair. Did they find a lock of curly brown hair after the explosion?

5   Then there was the rich white contractor who lived on the highway. His oldest son had died as a young man, in another part of the state, backing a truck too near such an opening. The truck had started to slide and he couldn't stop it.

I saw his picture once, when I went as a teenager to baby-sit at their house. His brother, then a grown man and my employer for the evening, told me about the accident. In the photograph the dead heir was still a child, about nine years old, sitting on a horse, smiling at the camera.

6   The world consisted of me at first; then, when Ruf Junior, the baby, was big enough to walk, he joined me on the rock. My older brother, Jesse, was a boy who came dashing by to or from some adventure, and he might say something or he might not. My mother, Nonnie, and my father, Rufus, were the grown people who called me to dinner, to bed, or to do chores.

7   One day a car came up to the house and a lady got out, while a man put suitcases on the porch. The lady was Aunt Jo, and she stayed with us for several years. Sometimes other people came, but they were visitors, and unless they had someone my age for me to play with, they didn't affect me one way or the other.

8   I would squat on that rock, my stick legs poking through the openings of my dirt-stained bloomers, my birdlike head turning from side to side, my gaze, unblinking, focusing up, down, in front of me, in back of me, now zooming in on the lower yard, then penetrating deeper into the garden, then rising up ever so slightly to where the corn was planted on the hill. I was in the center of life and I didn't miss a thing; nothing slipped by unobserved or unnoted. My problems started when I began to comment on what I saw. I insisted on being accurate. But the world I was born into didn't want that. Indeed, its very survival depended on not knowing, not seeing—and, certainly, not saying anything at all about what it was really like.

9   The whole backyard slanted down. It started at the well and sloped down to the lettuce patch. When it rained, water ran in gullies clear down to a ditch Daddy had dug parallel to the flow to make the water run off. Later he decided to stop the flow up higher, and Ruf Junior and Jesse and I toted rocks and formed a little dam between the big sloping rock and the two less-big rocks that lay on either side of it.

10   The rock on the left was big, but it looked like a rock, not like the back of a buried elephant. I could see all around it, but it was big. My brothers and I couldn't move it, not even when we all pushed together. The one on the right of the big sloping rock looked like its brother. You couldn't see where it started or stopped. Its back was like the back of a smaller gray buried elephant—the younger brother of the large gray sloping elephant that was buried in the middle.

11   The little dam, built up with sticks and rocks, held fast; later, when it rained, the running dirt stopped there and backed up and covered some of the hundreds of rocks that studded the backyard and on which we stubbed innu-merable bare toes in the May-to-September, school-is-out summer.

12   The well was in the upper part of the backyard, before the slope started. The wooden box that was the superstructure of the well was partly rotted; there

were wide spaces between the boards, and my brothers and I had been warned not to lean too hard on them when we pulled the bucket up or we would fall in. The bucket was beaten up from banging on the rocks that lined the narrow well, and when the bucket came out, water sloshed over the side and spurted out of the little holes in it. The rocks in the well had wet green moss on them as far down as the eye could see. The well was about the width of a giant inner tube, but rough where the rocks stuck out all the way down. When you looked over the boards, the water below looked like quicksilver in the sun. I would look into the well and think deep thoughts and smell the wet moss and rotting wood.

13   Hanging on a nail on the well was a gourd to drink out of. This was full and round at one end and tubular at the other, and had tiny ridges in its mud-brown interior. A drink of cool well water from a sweet-tasting gourd when you're thirsty is the best drink in the world.

14   Sometimes I liked to lean over the edge of the well and look past the box where the wood had rotted and splintered from the water, past the moss lining the bottom of the wood and the rocks paving the well. I thought that under-neath the moving water was China. I read a story in the second grade that said that if you dug a deep, deep hole down from where you were and put your eye down, clear through the hole on the other side you would see China.

15   I believed stories like that. Just as once I read a story about Mexico and was struck by the bold designs on the pottery. That night I dreamed that I was in heaven and God looked like the father of a Mexican family, dark, with black hair and a long, colorful robe, with his wife and child by his side. They were standing in front of a clay house, and nearby were enormous pottery jars with bright designs on them.

16   Our well wasn't as deep as it should have been, and a couple of summers it went dry, so we would go to one of the springs. The nearest, at the bottom of a little slope, bubbled clear water up out of clean sand. The shallow encircling wall was about three hands high and a child could curl up and hold his feet with his hands around its circumference. The water there bubbled up endlessly, clear and sweet, shaded by tall North Carolina pines. The other spring was farther away. It was larger, more conventional, and not nearly so romantic.

17   In the morning the sun glistened on the long grass in the vacant lot that was never mowed. The cow ate the grass and kept it low, all except the spot where I emptied the peepots. She wouldn't eat there unless Mama sprinkled a lot of salt on it to fool her. Then sometimes she would eat it and sometimes she wouldn't. This grass was on the lot next to the main yard. Daddy sometimes plowed it all up and harrowed it and sowed it with grain and got mad when Mr. Jake's chickens came over from next door and ate it all up. But it was dry, hard, cracked land and never grew much of anything.

18   On the left side of the main yard was the Rock Pile, where I picked blackberries. Aunt Jo made purple dye from the pokeberries that also grew

there, and sometimes she cooked poke salad, which I hated; it tasted like cooked leaves. But I liked the dye. When Aunt Jo dipped a white gunnysack in the dark water and it came up a beautiful purple, I was filled with wonder.

19   Sometimes my brothers and I played jumping from rock to rock. If you stepped off a rock you were "out." Sometimes snakes slid out of the Rock Pile. My brothers and I couldn't run through it; the briars tore too bad. But we had a path and as long as I stayed in the path I felt safe. One step either to the right or the left of the patch and I felt scared. Not only of snakes and other natural dangers but of something else. I didn't know what.

20   At the bottom of the yard there was a vegetable garden with green growing things: lettuce and cabbage and cucumbers and squash. Little sticks held up the vines of tomatoes and string beans and butter beans. Beyond it, the field ran up a little hill from the garden a long way and then down to some pines. After the rows of pines, the Bottom started. It was low there and wet most of the time, but I liked it; my father worked hard there with Suki, the mule, plowing. I followed him there all the time, but I liked mainly to play near the creek in the Bottom and on the pine-straw-covered mounds, where I slid down into the gullies.

Considering Ideas

1. From Mebane's description of her backyard and her activities, what can you conclude about her childhood? Was she happy? How do you know?
2. From the clues in the essay, what can you tell about the world the author grew up in?
3. Using the evidence in the essay as clues, what early indications were there that Mebane had a writer's sensibilities?
4. When Mebane says in her second sentence that "the world was a green Eden—and it was magic," she leads the reader to expect an upbeat description. Yet her essay has many dark notes: people died prematurely; her surroundings were stark; her family was poor. Given the essay's opening, are these dark notes a problem? Why do you think Mebane mentions the darker side of her life?
5. In paragraph 8, Mebane says, "My problems started when I began to comment on what I saw. I insisted on being accurate. But the world I was born into didn't want that. Indeed, its very survival depended on not knowing, not seeing—and, certainly, not saying anything at all about what it was really like." What do you think Mebane means? Does her essay conform to the ideas she is expressing here?
6. Do you think that Mebane feels deprived because her childhood was spent in poverty? Explain.

Considering Technique

1. Mebane uses both objective and expressive description. Cite examples of each. Which does she rely on more heavily?
2. Mebane's description includes metaphors and similes. Cite an example of each.
3. Mebane's description extends beyond her backyard. Is this a problem? Explain.
4. In your own words, write a thesis that conveys the subject and dominant impression of the essay.
5. Consult a dictionary if you are unsure of the meaning of any of these words: *quarry* (paragraph 4), *Seven Wonders of the World* (paragraph 4), *toted* (paragraph 9), *quicksilver* (paragraph 12), *gourd* (paragraph 13).

For Group Consideration

As a child, Mebane had no video games, Barbie dolls, swing sets, and other expensive toys that many children have. Do you think she had less fun than children who had more toys? Do you think she had an advantage over children with more toys? Consider these questions with two or three classmates.

Journal Entry

In about two pages, tell about your childhood. In what ways was it similar to Mebane's, and in what ways was it different?

Essay Assignment

1. In paragraph 3, Mebane says that the Rock Pile next door "was a place of mystery." Using expressive and/or objective detail, describe a place from your youth that "was a place of mystery."
2. For Mebane, the rock quarry was a special place of wonderment: "it was one of the Seven Wonders of the World." Using expressive and/or objective detail, describe a place from your youth that was full of wonderment. If you like, you can also tell what you did there.
3. Write a description of the backyard of your childhood home. Like Mebane, convey a sense of your surroundings, the people in your world, and your activities. Also like Mebane, try to convey what life was like in the world that included your backyard.

Considering Thematic Issues

1. Think back to some aspect of your own childhood world (your house, your backyard, your neighborhood, your school, and so forth). Explain how that part of your world influenced you then and whether its influence continues into the present.

2. "Shades of Black" on page 337 was also written by Mebane, but it deals with adult concerns. Read that selection and refer to "My Backyard" to explain what aspects of Mebane's thinking and personality as an adult were evident when she was a child.

MY NEIGHBORHOOD
Alfred Kazin

◆

A prolific writer of literary criticism and autobiographical works, Alfred Kazin is a masterful wordsmith. In "My Neighborhood," he paints a vivid portrait of the harsh reality of the Brownsville, Brooklyn, N.Y., tenement that he grew up in. As you read, notice that Kazin does more than share the particulars of his childhood neighborhood; he also shares the conflicting feelings he had about the block he grew up on and the world beyond it.

◆

1   The block: *my* block. It was on the Chester Street side of our house, between the grocery and the back wall of the old drugstore, that I was hammered into the shape of the streets. Everything beginning at Blake Avenue would always wear for me some delightful strangeness and mildness, simply because it was not of my block, *the* block, where the clang of your head sounded against the pavement when you fell in a fist fight, and the rows of storelights on each side were pitiless, watching you. Anything away from the block was good: even a school you never went to, two blocks away: there were vegetable gardens in the park across the street. Returning from "New York," I would take the longest routes home from the subway, get off a station ahead of our own, only for the unexpectedness of walking through Betsy Head Park and hearing the gravel crunch under my feet as I went beyond the vegetable gardens, smelling the sweaty sweet dampness from the pool in summer and the dust on the leaves as I passed under the ailanthus trees. On the block itself everything rose up only to test me.

2   We worked every inch of it, from the cellars and the backyards to the sickening space between the roofs. Any wall, any stoop, any curving metal edge on a billboard sign made a place against which to knock a ball; any bottom rung of a fire escape ladder a goal in basketball; any sewer cover a base; any crack in the pavement a "net" for the tense sharp tennis that we played by beating a soft ball back and forth with our hands between the squares. Betsy Head Park two blocks away would always feel slightly foreign, for it belonged to the Amboys and the Bristols and the Hopkinsons as much as it did to us. *Our* life every day was fought out on the pavement and in the gutter, up against the walls of the houses and the glass fronts of the drugstore and the grocery, in and out of the fresh steaming piles of horse manure, the wheels of passing carts and automobiles, along the iron spikes of the stairway to the cellar, the jagged edge of the open garbage cans, the crumbly steps of the old farmhouses still left on one side of the street.

3   As I go back to the block now, and for a moment fold my body up again in its narrow arena—there, just there, between the black of the asphalt and the old

women in their kerchiefs and flowered housedresses sitting on the tawny kitchen chairs—the back wall of the drugstore still rises up to test me. Every day we smashed a small black viciously hard regulation handball against it with fanatical cuts and drives and slams, beating and slashing at it almost in hatred for the blind strength of the wall itself. I was never good enough at handball, was always practicing some trick shot that might earn me esteem, and when I was weary of trying, would often bat a ball down Chester Street just to get myself to Blake Avenue. I have this memory of playing one-o'-cat by myself in the sleepy twilight, at a moment when everyone else had left the block. The sparrows floated down from the telephone wires to peck at every fresh pile of horse manure, and there was a smell of brine from the delicatessen store, of egg crates and of the milk scum left in the great metal cans outside the grocery, of the thick white paste oozing out from behind the fresh Hecker's Flour ad on the metal signboard. I would throw the ball in the air, hit it with my bat, then with perfect satisfaction drop the bat to the ground and run to the next sewer cover. Over and over I did this, from sewer cover to sewer cover, until I had worked my way to Blake Avenue and could see the park.

4   With each clean triumphant ring of my bat against the gutter leading me on, I did the whole length of our block up and down, and never knew how happy I was just watching the asphalt rise and fall, the curve of the steps up to an old farmhouse. The farmhouses themselves were streaked red on one side, brown on the other, but the steps themselves were always gray. There was a tremor of pleasure at one place; I held my breath in nausea at another. As I ran after my ball with the bat heavy in my hand, the odd successiveness of things in myself almost choked me, the world was so full as I ran—past the cobblestoned yards into the old farmhouses, where stray chickens still waddled along the stones; past the little candy store where we went only if the big one on our side of the block was out of Eskimo Pies; past the three neighboring tenements where the last of the old women sat on their kitchen chairs yawning before they went up to make supper. Then came Mrs. Rosenwasser's house, the place on the block I first identified with what was farthest from home, and strangest, because it was a "private" house; then the fences around the monument works, where black cranes rose up above the yard and you could see the smooth gray slabs that would be cut and carved into tombstones, some of them already engraved with the names and dates and family virtues of the dead.

5   Beyond Blake Avenue was the pool parlor outside which we waited all through the tense September afternoons of the World's Series to hear the latest scores called off the ticker tape—and where as we waited, banging a ball against the bottom of the wall and drinking water out of empty coke bottles, I breathed the chalk off the cues and listened to the clocks ringing in the fire station across the street. There was an old warehouse next to the pool parlor; the oil on the barrels and the iron staves had the same rusty smell. A block away was the park, thick with the dusty gravel I liked to hear my shoes crunch in as I ran round and round the track; then a great open pavilion, the inside myste-

riously dark, chill even in summer; there I would wait in the sweaty coolness before pushing on to the wading ring where they put up a shower on the hottest days.

6   Beyond the park the "fields" began, all those still unused lots where we could still play hard ball in perfect peace—first shooing away the goats and then tearing up goldenrod before laying our bases. The smell and touch of those "fields," with their wild compost under the billboards of weeds, goldenrod, bricks, goat droppings, rusty cans, empty beer bottles, fresh new lumber, and damp cement, lives in my mind as Brownsville's great open door, the wastes that took us through to the west. I used to go round them in summer with my cousins selling near-beer to the carpenters, but always in a daze, would stare so long at the fibrous stalks of the goldenrod as I felt their harshness in my hand that I would forget to make a sale, and usually go off sick on the beer I drank up myself. Beyond! Beyond! Only to see something new, to get away from each day's narrow battleground between the grocery and the back wall of the drugstore! Even the other end of our block, when you got to Mrs. Rosenwasser's house and the monument works, was dear to me for the contrast. On summer nights, when we played Indian trail, running away from each other on prearranged signals, the greatest moment came when I could plunge into the darkness down the block for myself and hide behind the slabs in the monument works. I remember the air whistling around me as I ran, the panicky thud of my bones in my sneakers, and then the slabs rising in the light from the street lamps as I sped past the little candy store and crept under the fence.

7   In the darkness you could never see where the crane began. We liked to trap the enemy between the slabs and sometimes jumped them from great mounds of rock just in from the quarry. A boy once fell to his death that way, and they put a watchman there to keep us out. This made the slabs all the more impressive to me, and I always aimed first for that yard whenever we played follow-the-leader. Day after day the monument works became oppressively more mysterious and remote, though it was only just down the block; I stood in front of it every afternoon on my way back from school, filling it with my fears. It was not death I felt there—the slabs were usually faceless. It was the darkness itself, and the wind howling around me whenever I stood poised on the edge of a high slab waiting to jump. Then I would take in, along with the fear, some amazement of joy that I had found my way out that far.

Considering Ideas

1. In the opening sentence, Kazin says that he "was hammered into the shape of the streets." What do you think he means?
2. Kazin says, "We worked every inch of it [his block]." What do you think he means?
3. Contrast Kazin's feelings about his neighborhood with his feelings about the territory beyond his neighborhood.

4. Describe the conflicting feelings Kazin had about his neighborhood. Describe the conflicting feelings Kazin had about the world beyond his neighborhood.
5. Since it is at the edge of the neighborhood, the monument works can be taken as the bridge from Kazin's neighborhood to the outside, a bridge from the known to the unknown. With this in mind, how do you interpret the last two sentences of this selection?

Considering Technique

1. Very early in the essay—in the first two paragraphs, in fact—Kazin conveys the idea that his neighborhood was a harsh, difficult place. Cite three or four examples of word choice that help convey this idea.
2. Kazin uses both objective and expressive description. Cite an example of each.
3. To which of the five senses does Kazin's description appeal? Cite an example of description that appeals to each sense you name.
4. Which paragraphs begin with topic sentences?
5. Cite a description that you particularly like and try to explain why it appeals to you.
6. Consult a dictionary if you are unsure of the meaning of any of these words: *tawny* (paragraph 3), *fanatical* (paragraph 3), *brine* (paragraph 3), *ticker tape* (paragraph 5), *near-beer* (paragraph 6).

For Group Consideration

Although Kazin enjoyed aspects of his neighborhood, he found life on the block harsh, difficult, and confining. Although he longed for the world beyond because he found it milder, he feared the uncertainty of the outside. How do you explain Kazin's ambivalent feelings? Are they normal? Do young people commonly experience such conflicting feelings regardless of where they are raised? With three or four classmates, consider the answers to these questions.

Journal Entry

Write out the most vivid memory of your childhood neighborhood and the positive and/or negative emotions this memory stirs in you. Also, try to explain why you feel the way you do.

Essay Assignment

1. Like Kazin, share a part of your past by describing the neighborhood where you grew up. Your description should convey whether you liked the neighborhood, disliked the neighborhood, or had conflicting feelings about it.

2. Describe any place that raises conflicting emotions in you—your house or apartment, a doctor's office, a hospital, or your parents' home, for example. Select details that help you convey these conflicting emotions.

3. Part of Kazin's description focuses on the games he played as a child. Describe one or more of your childhood games. You can include the place where you played and the people you played with if you like. Try to convey what the game(s) meant to you or what you learned as a result of playing.

4. Kazin's neighborhood had a significant impact on him. In fact, he says that he "was hammered into the shape of the streets." Select a place that had a significant impact on you (for example, your grandparents' farm, your best friend's house, or the Little League fields) and describe it, being sure to express how the place affected you.

Considering Thematic Issues

1. The monument works were a source of both fear and attraction for Kazin. Tell about something from your childhood that both attracted and frightened you. What do you think caused the conflicting emotions? As an alternative, tell about some vivid childhood memory and the emotions the memory stirs. (Consult your previous journal entry for ideas for this essay.)

2. Explain how Kazin viewed his childhood surroundings and how Mary Mebane viewed hers (see "My Backyard," page 65). Then go on to draw one or more conclusions about how children are affected by their surroundings.

THE DEER AT PROVIDENCIA
Annie Dillard

A writer and a teacher of writing, Annie Dillard won a Pulitzer Prize in 1975 for her first book of prose, Pilgrim at Tinker Creek. *The following description of the torment of a deer is a powerful component of a narration (story) about the suffering of humans and animals. As you read, notice Dillard's seamless weaving of descriptive and narrative elements as she shares her experience and her uncertainty with readers who probably have the same question she has: "What is going on?"*

1   There were four of us North Americans in the jungle, in the Ecuadorian jungle on the banks of the Napo River in the Amazon watershed. The other three North Americans were metropolitan men. We stayed in tents in one riverside village, and visited others. At the village called Providencia we saw a sight which moved us, and which shocked the men.

2   The first thing we saw when we climbed the riverbank to the village of Providencia was the deer. It was roped to a tree on the grass clearing near the thatch shelter where we would eat lunch.

3   The deer was small, about the size of a whitetail fawn, but apparently full-grown. It had a rope around its neck and three feet caught in the rope. Someone said that the dogs had caught it that morning and the villagers were going to cook and eat it that night.

4   This clearing lay at the edge of the little thatched-hut village. We could see the villagers going about their business, scattering feed corn for hens about their houses, and wandering down paths to the river to bathe. The village headman was our host; he stood beside us as we watched the deer struggle. Several village boys were interested in the deer; they formed part of the circle we made around it in the clearing. So also did four businessmen from Quito who were attempting to guide us around the jungle. Few of the very different people standing in this circle had a common language. We watched the deer, and no one said much.

5   The deer lay on its side at the rope's very end, so the rope lacked slack to let it rest its head in the dust. It was "pretty," delicate of bone like all deer, and thin-skinned for the tropics. Its skin looked virtually hairless, in fact, and almost translucent, like a membrane. Its neck was no thicker than my wrist; it was rubbed open on the rope, and gashed. Trying to paw itself free of the rope, the deer had scratched its own neck with its hooves. The raw underside of its neck showed red stripes and some bruises bleeding inside the muscles. Now three of its feet were hooked in the rope under its jaw. It could not stand, of course, on

one leg, so it could not move to slacken the rope and ease the pull on its throat and enable it to rest its head.

6   Repeatedly the deer paused, motionless, its eyes veiled, with only its rib cage in motion, and its breaths the only sound. Then, after I would think, "It has given up; now it will die," it would heave. The rope twanged; the tree leaves clattered; the deer's free foot beat the ground. We stepped back and held our breaths. It thrashed, kicking, but only one leg moved; the other three legs tightened inside the rope's loop. Its hip jerked; its spine shook. Its eyes rolled; its tongue, thick with spittle, pushed in and out. Then it would rest again. We watched this for fifteen minutes.

7   Once three young native boys charged in, released its trapped legs, and jumped back to the circle of people. But instantly the deer scratched up its neck with its hooves and snared its forelegs in the rope again. It was easy to imagine a third and then a fourth leg soon stuck, like Brer Rabbit and the Tar Baby.

8   We watched the deer from the circle, and then we drifted on to lunch. Our palm-roofed shelter stood on a grassy promontory from which we would see the deer tied to the tree, pigs and hens walking under village houses, and black-and-white cattle standing in the river. There was even a breeze.

9   Lunch, which was the second and better lunch we had that day, was hot and fried. There was a big fish called *doncella,* a kind of catfish, dipped whole in corn flour and beaten egg, then deep fried. With our fingers we pulled soft fragments of it from its sides to our plates, and ate; it was delicate fish-flesh, fresh and mild. Someone found the roe, and I ate of that too—it was fat and stronger, like egg yolk, naturally enough, and warm.

10   There was also a stew of meat in shreds with rice and pale brown gravy. I had asked what kind of deer it was tied to the tree; Pepe had answered in Spanish, *"Gama."* Now they told us this was *gama* too, stewed. I suspect the word means merely game or venison. At any rate, I heard that the village dogs had cornered another deer just yesterday, and it was this deer which we were now eating in full sight of the whole article. It was good. I was surprised at its tenderness. But it is a fact that high levels of lactic acid, which builds up in muscle tissues during exertion, tenderizes.

11   After the fish and meat we ate bananas fried in chunks and served on a tray; they were sweet and full of flavor. I felt terrific. My shirt was wet and cool from swimming; I had had a night's sleep, two decent walks, three meals, and a swim—everything tasted good. From time to time each one of us, separately, would look beyond our shaded roof to the sunny spot where the deer was still convulsing in the dust. Our meal completed, we walked around the deer and back to the boats.

12   That night I learned that while we were watching the deer, the others were watching me.

13   We four North Americans grew close in the jungle in a way that was not the usual artificial intimacy of travelers. We liked each other. We stayed up all that night talking, murmuring, as though we rocked on hammocks slung above time. The others were from big cities: New York, Washington, Boston. They all said that I had no expression on my face when I was watching the deer—or at any rate, not the expression they expected.

14   They had looked to see how I, the only woman, and the youngest, was taking the sight of the deer's struggles. I looked detached, apparently, or hard, or calm, or focused, still. I don't know. I was thinking. I remember feeling very old and energetic. I could say like Thoreau that I have traveled widely in Roanoke, Virginia. I have thought a great deal about carnivorousness; I eat meat. These things are not issues; they are mysteries.

15   Gentlemen of the city, what surprises you? That there is suffering here, or that I know it?

16   We lay in the tent and talked. "If it had been my wife," one man said with special vigor, amazed, "she wouldn't have cared *what* was going on; she would have dropped *everything* right at that moment and gone in the village from here to there to there, she would not have *stopped* until that animal was out of its suffering one way or another. She couldn't *bear* to see a creature in agony like that."

17   I nodded.

18   Now I am home. When I wake I comb my hair before the mirror above my dresser. Every morning for the past two years I have seen in that mirror, beside my sleep-softened face, the blacked face of a burnt man. It is a wire-service photograph clipped from a newspaper and taped to my mirror. The caption reads: "Alan McDonald in Miami hospital bed." All you can see in the photograph is a smudged triangle of face from his eyelids to his lower lip; the rest is bandages. You cannot see the expression in his eyes; the bandages shade them.

19   The story, headed MAN BURNED FOR SECOND TIME, begins:

> "Why does God hate me?" Alan McDonald asked from his hospital bed.
> "When the gunpowder went off, I couldn't believe it," he said. "I just couldn't believe it. I said, 'No, God couldn't do this to me again."

He was in a burn ward in Miami, in serious condition. I do not even know if he lived. I wrote him a letter at the time, cringing.

20   He had been burned before, thirteen years previously, by flaming gasoline. For years he had been having his body restored and his face remade in dozens of operations. He had been a boy, and then a burnt boy. He had already been stunned by what could happen, by how life could veer.

21   Once I read that people who survive bad burns tend to go crazy; they have a very high suicide rate. Medicine cannot ease their pain; drugs just leak away, soaking the sheets, because there is no skin to hold them in. The people just lie there and weep. Later they kill themselves. They had not known, before

they were burned, that the world included such suffering, that life could permit them personally such pain.

22   This time a bowl of gunpowder had exploded on McDonald.

> "I didn't realize what had happened at first," he recounted. "And then I heard that sound from 13 years ago. I was burning. I rolled to put the fire out and I thought, 'Oh God, not again.'
>
> "If my friend hadn't been there, I would have jumped into a canal with a rock around my neck."

His wife concludes the piece, "Man, it just isn't fair."

23   I read the whole clipping again every morning. This is the Big Time here, every minute of it. Will someone please explain to Alan McDonald in his dignity, to the deer at Providencia in his dignity, what is going on? And mail me the carbon.

24   When we walked by the deer at Providencia for the last time, I said to Pepe, with a pitying glance at the deer, *"Pobrecito"*—"poor little thing." But I was trying out Spanish. I knew at the time it was a ridiculous thing to say.

Considering Ideas

1. Why does Dillard note (in paragraph 10) that high levels of lactic acid tenderize meat?
2. What view of women is referred to in paragraphs 15 and 16?
3. How would you describe Dillard's reaction to suffering?
4. Do you agree with Dillard that *"Pobrecito"* ("poor little thing") was a ridiculous thing for her to say as she walked by the deer? Explain.
5. Why do you think that Dillard kept the picture and article about Alan McDonald?

Considering Technique

1. What approach does Dillard take to her introduction (see page 11)?
2. Dillard writes of the deer at Providencia and Alan McDonald. What do these two have in common? That is, how is it possible to discuss both in the same essay?
3. In your own words, write a sentence or two that expresses the thesis of "The Deer at Providencia."
4. Which paragraphs are developed primarily with description, and which with narration (storytelling)? See page 83 for an explanation of narration.
5. Which of the descriptive paragraphs are developed primarily with objective detail, and which with expressive detail (see page 43)?
6. Consult a dictionary if you are unsure of the meaning of any of these words: *watershed* (paragraph 1), *thatch* (paragraph 2), *translucent* (paragraph 5), *spittle* (paragraph 6), *promontory* (paragraph 8), *carnivorousness* (paragraph 14).

For Group Consideration

With three or four classmates, consider this question: Do you see a difference between the suffering of the deer and the suffering of Alan McDonald? If so, explain what that difference is. If not, explain why.

Journal Entry

At one time, killing animals for food was a necessity, but many people claim that we no longer need to do so, that vegetarianism is a solution to animal killing and suffering. Attack or defend the killing of animals for food.

Essay Assignments

1. Like Dillard, describe an animal engaged in some activity. For example, you could describe a kitten at play, a cat washing itself, a dog chasing a ball, or fish swimming in a tank. If possible, use expressive detail to convey the animal's level of comfort or contentment.
2. If you have ever experienced pain, write a description of what you went through. You can describe, for instance, having a broken leg, the chicken pox, a migraine headache, or a sports injury.
3. Like Dillard, share an experience by telling a story that includes description. If possible, pick an experience that teaches something about life.

Considering Thematic Issues

1. What kind of world allows the suffering the deer and McDonald endured? That is, answer the question that Dillard poses in paragraph 23.
2. Read "Untouchables" on page 159 and "What Is Poverty?" on page 350. Using the information in those essays, the information in "The Deer at Providencia," and your own ideas, explain the degree and kinds of suffering in the world and/or how people cope with that suffering.

Additional Essay Assignments

1. Describe a place you go to relax and convey why the place helps you unwind.
2. Describe a favorite nightspot, someplace people go to have fun. Try to convey the sense that people are enjoying themselves.
3. Describe a view from a window, using expressive detail to convey a dominant impression.
4. Describe a store you frequently shop at, using objective detail to convey to what extent the store's features meet the needs of its customers.
5. Describe a place where you enjoy spending leisure time: a bowling alley, the student union, a shopping mall, a porch, a theater, or a basketball court, for example. Use expressive detail to convey why the place appeals to you.
6. Describe the room you liked best in the house you grew up in. Your dominant impression will be how the room made you feel.
7. Describe a place during a holiday celebration. For example, you could describe your parents' dining room at Thanksgiving, Main Street during the Christmas season, or a park on Independence Day.
8. Describe your favorite vacation spot, using expressive detail to convey why you enjoy this place.
9. Describe a winter scene, a fall scene, a spring scene, or a summer scene.
10. Describe one of your classrooms.
11. Describe your bedroom. Use expressive detail to reveal what the bedroom says about you.
12. Describe your favorite campus spot, using expressive detail to convince a prospective freshman to attend your school.
13. Describe a room after a party has been held there.
14. Using objective detail, describe the place where you work to show whether or not your work environment is pleasant.
15. Describe an amusement park midway.
16. Describe your favorite restaurant to convince other people to try it.
17. Describe the neighborhood you grew up in to share a portion of your past with your reader.
18. Describe a scene that shocked you.
19. Describe a rock concert for someone who has never been to one.
20. Describe MTV for someone who has never seen it.

NARRATION

The Purpose of Narration
Supporting Details
Selecting and Ordering Details
Suggestions for Writing Narration
Annotated Student Essay: The Family Reunion, Revisited

Salvation—Langston Hughes *(narration to share)*
My Mother Never Worked—Bonnie Smith-Yackel *(narration to persuade)*
*The Endless Streetcar Ride into the Night, and the Tinfoil Noose—Jean Shepherd *(narration to entertain, share, and inform)*
*A Hanging—George Orwell *(narration to share, inform, and persuade)*
By Any Other Name—Santha Rama Rau *(narration to share and inform)*
The Water-Faucet Vision—Gish Jen *(narration to share)*

Additional Essay Assignments

* To fulfill the author's purpose, narration is combined with one or more other patterns.

Everyone likes a good story. We go to movies for good stories, we read books for good stories, and we gravitate toward people at parties who tell good stories. So taken are we by stories that we tell them to our children before they go to sleep. In writing, a story is called a narration, and this chapter will explain the techniques of effective narration.

 ## THE PURPOSE OF NARRATION

Obviously, a narration can *entertain* because a good story can amuse us and help us lose ourselves for a time. This helps explain the popularity of romance novels: they are loaded with pure, escapist entertainment value. But narrations can do more than entertain, and the selections in this chapter demonstrate the range of narrative purpose. In "By Any Other Name," Santha Rama Rau tells a story that *informs* her audience about the nature of racial discrimination; in "Salvation," Langston Hughes narrates a story to *share* a moment of disappointment and loss of faith; in "The Endless Streetcar Ride into the Night," Jean Shepherd narrates a humorous story to *entertain* the reader; and in "My Mother Never Worked," Bonnie Smith-Yackel tells the story of her mother's life in order to *persuade* the reader of the value and importance of "woman's work."

 ## SUPPORTING DETAILS

A narration usually includes the answers to the journalist's questions who, what, when, where, why, and how. That is, the story explains *who* was involved, *what* happened, *when* it happened, *where* it happened, *why* it happened, and *how* it happened. Of course, some answers may not be appropriate for some narrations, but they are a good starting point for generating ideas. Also, different answers may be emphasized in different narrations. Thus, in some stories *who* was involved may get a great deal of attention, but in other stories, *when* it happened may be more significant and thus treated with more detail.

In addition to the answers to the journalist's questions, narration often includes descriptive detail. When a person's appearance is important to the story, that person will be described; when locale is important, a place will be described. For example, in "The Endless Streetcar Ride into the Night" (page 98), Jean Shepherd uses description to set the scene for his narration:

> I will never forget that particular Saturday as long as I live. The air was as soft as the finest of spun silk. The scent of lilacs hung heavy. The catalpa trees rustled in the early evening breeze from off the Lake. The inner Me itched in that nameless way, that indescribable way that only the fourteen-year-old Male fully knows.

◆ *Note:* Now would be a good time to review the information on using specific words for description on page 44.

To advance the story and add vividness, narrations often include conversation. To appreciate what conversation can add to a story, consider the difference between these two approaches:

1. Katie yelled to her mother and asked if she remembered to pick them up. Louise responded that she had, as she reached for the shoebox with the new tap shoes in it.
2. "Hi, Mom," Katie yelled. "Did you remember to pick them up?" "Yes, darlin'," Louise responded, reaching for the shoebox with the new tap shoes in it.

The second example is more vivid and interesting because of the use of conversation. (When you use conversation, be sure to check a handbook for correct capitalization and punctuation.)

If the reader needs additional information to appreciate the story, an author can provide background information or an explanation of something. For example, in "By Any Other Name" (page 111), the author provides this explanation to help the reader understand why she and her sister attended the school that figures significantly into the narration:

> We had been sent to that school because my father, among his responsibilities as an officer of the civil service, had a tour of duty to perform in the villages around that steamy little provincial town, where he had his headquarters at that time. He used to make his shorter inspection tours on horseback, and a week before, in the stale heat of a typically postmonsoon day, we had waved good-by to him and a little procession. . . .

Finally, since stories are often told because they make a particular point, a narration can include a statement of the significance of the story. For example, in "Salvation" (page 89), Langston Hughes tells a story about attending a revival service when he was twelve. He concludes his narration with a statement of the story's significance, which reads, in part:

> I didn't believe there was a Jesus any more, since he didn't come to help me.

 ## SELECTING AND ORDERING DETAILS

If you've ever listened to someone tell a story and drone on and on, you know how important it is to select narrative details carefully to avoid boring your reader with unnecessary information. This means you must choose carefully which *who, what, when, where, why,* and *how* questions to answer. It also means you must be careful not to include insignificant details, and you must not emphasize minor points, or your reader will think, "Get on with it, already." In other words, the key to a successful narration is pacing.

Arranging narrative details usually involves placing the events in chronological order. Most often this means beginning with the first event, moving to the second, on to the third, and so on. Variations of this pattern are possible, however. For some stories, you may want to begin at the end or in the middle, then flash back to the beginning.

Let's say, for example, you want to narrate an account of a car accident you were involved in. You could begin with the first event and move forward to the last event, like this:

> A year ago, I was on my way to pick up my girlfriend, looking forward to a pleasant dinner. As I approached the intersection at Fifth and Grove, the light turned yellow, but I figured I had plenty of time to slide through.

After this opening, you would narrate an account of the accident and then go on to tell about its aftermath.

You could also begin at the end and flash back to the beginning, like this:

> As I walked out of my last physical therapy session, I thought about how remarkable it is that I can walk at all. The accident nine months earlier had left me in critical condition with a smashed pelvis.

From here, you would flash back to the beginning and narrate an account of the accident and all the events up to the time you walked out of your last physical therapy session.

You could also begin in the middle of the chronology, like this:

> I remember waking up in the hospital with my parents and sister at my side. Mom was crying and Dad looked worried. In an instant the pain overwhelmed me and I could not remember what happened. Then all at once I remembered the accident.

From this point in the middle, you would flash back to the beginning and narrate an account of the accident. You would then move chronologically through the events until you reached the last event, walking out of your last physical therapy session.

To signal chronological order and help your reader follow the events, you can use transitions like the following:

meanwhile	later	next
soon	at first	in the meantime
second	the next day	at the same time

If you want to explain something, do so at the point in the narration where the explanation is called for. If you want to state the point your narration makes, doing so in the conclusion or in the thesis can be effective.

Many times writers omit the introduction and thesis in a narration and begin instead with the first event in the story. However, if your reader needs background information to appreciate the story, the introduction is an excellent place to supply it. Your thesis can mention the story you will tell and the significance of that story, like this:

> When my younger brother and I got lost in the woods, I learned the real meaning of responsibility. (The story is about the time the writer got lost in the woods, and the significance is that the writer learned the meaning of responsibility.)

Because a story is told in chronological order, writers often omit topic sentences. The time sequence provides a clear structure, so the reader often does not need the organizational signposts provided by topic sentences.

Formal conclusions, too, may be omitted in narrations, particularly if the last event in the narration provides sufficient closure. However, if you want to state the significance of the story and you have not already done so, the conclusion can be an excellent spot for this information.

SUGGESTIONS FOR WRITING NARRATION

1. Pick a story for a reason. Rather than just tell a story for the sake of telling a story, have a purpose in mind: to entertain your reader, to inform or persuade your audience of something, and/or to share something with your audience. If you have a purpose in mind, your story will be more interesting because it will have a point.

2. To generate ideas, make a list with the answers to the *who, what, when, where, why,* and *how* questions. Decide which of these should be emphasized.

3. Identify important features about people and places and note them as points in the narration where you may want to add descriptive details.

4. Write out a statement of the significance of your narration.

5. Write your draft in one sitting; do not worry about anything except getting all the events down and answering all the appropriate journalist's questions.

6. When you revise, consider the following:
   a. Will my reader need an introduction with background information?
   b. Is the significance of the narration clear, or should I state it in a thesis, introduction, or conclusion?
   c. Will my reader need an explanation of any of the events?
   d. Can I describe a person or scene?
   e. Will conversation move the narrative along and add interest?
   f. Have I omitted insignificant details?
   g. Does the last event provide sufficient closure, or do I need a formal conclusion?

ANNOTATED STUDENT ESSAY

Student writer Robbie Warnock shares an account of the annual family reunion and comes to see the event differently now than in the past. As you read, notice the important role description plays in this narration.

THE FAMILY REUNION, REVISITED

Paragraph 1
The introduction provides background and tells *what* and *when*. The thesis is the last sentence; it gives the subject as the annual reunion and the writer's position that the reunion was dreaded. Note the descriptive language.

1   Once a year, with the regularity of Old Faithful, scores of people claiming to be my kin stormed my hometown. The brood did not appear gradually, but as a veritable deluge of eccentricity, and often senility. The family's elders in their twenty-year-old gas guzzlers circled the town like vultures, finally "nesting" at the community center. As the rusty doors squeaked open in protest, I could almost hear John Williams's "Imperial March" blasting dirgelike through my mind. It was time for the annual family reunion, and I dreaded it as much as a trip to the dentist because to a youngster like me, everyone was as old as Methuselah and as quirky as Larry, Moe, and Curly.

Paragraph 2
This paragraph centers on *who* by describing the people involved.

2   Every woman present was clad in a floral spring dress, each with a distinct pattern. Most of the botanical togs reeked of mothballs. This pungent aroma was the only thing that held the bees attracted by the dress at bay. The men, on the other hand, looked like reject golfers or court jesters in their mismatched clothes of many colors. After each example of Henry Ford's worst nightmare had ejected the people crammed inside, the center's double doors were opened, and the celebration commenced.

Paragraph 3
Description and specific word choice add interest and vitality.

3   Food is a major love for my family, which explains why portliness is the status quo. At the reunion, long wooden tables, like those in Hrothgar's Meadhall, were laden with all types of dishes. However, an elderly matriarch of the clan became discontented with the same old food served every year. To ease the monotony, she created the "Annual Odd Recipe Contest," the goal of which was to create the most appetizing dish from the most bizarre ingredients.

Paragraph 4
This paragraph flashes back to the more distant past.

4   I was present at the inception of this contest, albeit reluctantly. Along with the down-home staples, fried chicken and chocolate layer cake, I sampled a curious-looking green and purple casserole. Immediately, I fell victim to Aunt Frankie's infamous "Eggplant and Kudzu Surprise." Upon tasting the foul abomination, I fled to the nearest McDonald's and vowed never to consume another bite even remotely connected with the old crone.

Paragraphs 5 and 6
Details are in chronological order, and each paragraph begins with a transitional phrase. Details emphasize *who* and *what*. The vivid description continues.

5   After the wonderful meal of poultry and vegetation, the family would seek amusement. Refusing to simply converse the evening away, the motley crew would begin to square dance. Recovering from whatever odd recipe I had unwittingly subjected myself to, I would glance inside to view a plethora of octogenarians tramping and stomping in a futile attempt at dancing. Then the entertainment took a nosedive. Uncle Oliver produced a set of bagpipes and unleashed a sonic aberration akin to the sound produced when a few dozen cats are run over slowly by a bulldozer.

6   After the musical torture, the group underwent a schism. The men ditched their wives and each group would nestle in a separate corner and settle down enough to actually begin conversations unrelated to food. Now the talk focused on the past. At just the right moment, Uncle Oliver presented a hundred or so bags, each sealed, labeled, and containing a piece of debris from the family homeplace. As he presented these heirlooms, he recited a stentorian lecture on the "sacred domicile." Each member of the family then received a fragment of the house.

Paragraph 7
The conclusion presents the last event and the significance of the narration (the reunion served an important purpose). The last paragraph also answers *why*.

7   Stomach churning, ears smarting, and bearing a Ziploc bag containing a burnt bit of shingle, I returned home at the end of the day, praising God for deliverance. Today, I see things differently, however. Rather than eccentricity, I see love and a memorial to past times. The would-be Scotsman Oliver wanted the kids to cherish their heritage. I now regret my impatience and impudence because I realize that the reunion was an annual link between the past and the present. I now realize that the past is a treasure and the key to the future. For one more chance to remember and relive those times, I would square dance, listen to bagpipes, and even choke down kudzu.

SALVATION
Langston Hughes

◆

Poet, playwright, critic, and fiction writer, Langston Hughes (1902–1967) was an important figure in the 1920s' blossoming of literature and music known as the Harlem Renaissance. The following selection is from Hughes's autobiographical The Big Sea. *In the essay, Hughes shares a time of youthful disillusionment. As you read, ask yourself what pressures led Hughes to take the action that he did.*

◆

1   I was saved from sin when I was going on thirteen. But not really saved. It happened like this. There was a big revival at my Auntie Reed's church. Every night for weeks there had been much preaching, singing, praying, and shouting, and some very hardened sinners had been brought to Christ, and the membership of the church had grown by leaps and bounds. Then just before the revival ended, they held a special meeting for children, "to bring the young lambs to the fold." My aunt spoke of it for days ahead. That night, I was escorted to the front row and placed on the mourner's bench with all other young sinners, who had not yet been brought to Jesus.

2   My aunt told me that when you were saved you saw a light, and something happened to you inside! And Jesus came into your life! And God was with you from then on! She said you could see and hear and feel Jesus in your soul. I believed her. I have heard a great many old people say the same thing and it seemed to me they ought to know. So I sat there calmly in the hot, crowded church, waiting for Jesus to come to me.

3   The preacher preached a wonderful rhythmical sermon, all moans and shouts and lonely cries and dire pictures of hell, and then he sang a song about the ninety and nine safe in the fold, but one little lamb was left out in the cold. Then he said: "Won't you come? Won't you come to Jesus? Young lambs, won't you come?" And he held out his arms to all us young sinners there on the mourner's bench. And the little girls cried. And some of them jumped up and went to Jesus right away. But most of us just sat there.

4   A great many old people came and knelt around us and prayed, old women with jet-black faces and braided hair, old men with work-gnarled hands. And the church sang a song about the lower lights are burning, some poor sinners to be saved. And the whole building rocked with prayer and song.

5   Still I kept waiting to *see* Jesus.

6   Finally all the young people had gone to the altar and were saved, but one boy and me. He was a rounder's son named Westley. Westley and I were surrounded by sisters and deacons praying. It was very hot in the church, and getting late now. Finally Westley said to me in a whisper: "God damn! I'm tired o' sitting here. Let's get up and be saved." So he got up and was saved.

7 Then I was left all alone on the mourner's bench. My aunt came and knelt at my knees and cried, while prayers and songs swirled all around me in the little church. The whole congregation prayed for me alone, in a mighty wail of moans and voices. And I kept waiting serenely for Jesus, waiting, waiting—but he didn't come. I wanted to see him, but nothing happened to me. Nothing! I wanted something to happen to me, but nothing happened.

8 I heard the songs and the minister saying: "Why don't you come? My dear child, why don't you come to Jesus? Jesus is waiting for you. He wants you. Why don't you come? Sister Reed, what is this child's name?"

9 "Langston," my aunt sobbed.

10 "Langston, why don't you come? Why don't you come and be saved? Oh, Lamb of God! Why don't you come?"

11 Now it was really getting late. I began to be ashamed of myself, holding everything up so long. I began to wonder what God thought about Westley, who certainly hadn't seen Jesus either, but who was now sitting proudly on the platform, swinging his knickerbockered legs and grinning down at me, surrounded by deacons and old women on their knees praying. God had not struck Westley dead for taking his name in vain or for lying in the temple. So I decided that maybe to save further trouble, I'd better lie, too, and say that Jesus had come, and get up and be saved.

12 So I got up.

13 Suddenly the whole room broke into a sea of shouting, as they saw me rise. Waves of rejoicing swept the place. Women leaped in the air. My aunt threw her arms around me. The minister took me by the hand and led me to the platform.

14 When things quieted down, in a hushed silence, punctuated by a few ecstatic "Amens," all the new young lambs were blessed in the name of God. Then joyous singing filled the room.

15 That night, for the last time in my life but one—for I was a big boy twelve years old—I cried. I cried, in bed alone, and couldn't stop. I buried my head under the quilts, but my aunt heard me. She woke up and told my uncle I was crying because the Holy Ghost had come into my life, and because I had seen Jesus. But I was really crying because I couldn't bear to tell her that I had lied, that I had deceived everybody in the church, that I hadn't seen Jesus, and that now I didn't believe there was a Jesus any more, since he didn't come to help me.

Considering Ideas

1. What does young Langston Hughes expect will happen at the revival? What happens instead?
2. Why does young Langston pretend to see Jesus and be saved?
3. How was Hughes affected by what happened at the revival?
4. What do you think Hughes means in the first two sentences?

5. Do you think that at the time he wrote "Salvation" Hughes still "didn't believe there was a Jesus"? Explain.

Considering Technique

1. Do the first two sentences of "Salvation" make an effective opening? Explain why or why not.
2. Where does Hughes explain the significance of the narration?
3. Hughes includes description of people and events in his narration. Cite two examples of this description and explain what it contributes to the narration. What metaphor appears in paragraph 13 (see page 45 on metaphors)? What does this metaphor contribute to the description?
4. Which of the *who, what, when, where, why,* and *how* questions does Hughes emphasize the most?
5. To help the reader recognize and follow the chronological order, Hughes opens several of his paragraphs with transitions that signal time order (see page 85). Which paragraphs open with transitions, and what are those transitions?
6. In addition to telling his story, Hughes offers some explanation. What is explained and where does this explanation occur?
7. Consult a dictionary if you are unsure of the meaning of any of these words: *revival* (paragraph 1), *dire* (paragraph 3), *rounder* (paragraph 6), *deacons* (paragraph 6), *knickerbockered* (paragraph 11), *ecstatic* (paragraph 14).

For Group Consideration

With two or three classmates, consider the following questions: What do you think would have happened if young Langston had not pretended to see Jesus and be saved? How would his aunt have reacted? How would Westley have reacted?

Journal Entry

In about a page, explain whether your own religious experiences more closely parallel the experiences of the young Langston Hughes or the experiences of his aunt. Also provide an example to illustrate.

Essay Assignments

1. In paragraph 2, Hughes explains that he believed his aunt when she described what it was like to be saved. However, his experience did not conform to his aunt's description. Tell a story about a time when you were led to expect something, but it did not happen. If you like, explain how you reacted.

2. Like Hughes, narrate a story about some traumatic experience you had when you were young. Also like Hughes, explain the impact the event had on you.
3. Hughes says he pretended to see Jesus "to save further trouble." Narrate an account of a time you or someone you know did something to avoid trouble or inconvenience. Explain the outcome.
4. Hughes felt pressured to see Jesus and be saved. Narrate an account of a time you or someone you know was pressured to think or behave a particular way. Explain how you or the other person responded to the pressure.

Considering Thematic Issues

1. The religious community and a family member pressured twelve-year-old Hughes to see Jesus and be saved. Pick one organization, institution, or group—religion, school, the family, the community, a peer group, and so on—and explain one or more of the pressures it exerts on us. Explain whether the pressure is a positive or negative influence.
2. Read "White Lies" (page 313) and explain whether or not you think Hughes's deception is a form of white lie. If so, explain whether or not the lie was justified under the circumstances. If you do not think the deception was a white lie, explain what you would call Hughes's behavior and why.

MY MOTHER NEVER WORKED
Bonnie Smith-Yackel

◆

Bonnie Smith-Yackel has a definition of "work" that differs from the government's definition. In "My Mother Never Worked," which first appeared in Women: A Journal of Liberation *and later in* Ms., *she tells a story to persuade the reader that her definition is the more appropriate one, while the government's is symptomatic of society's devaluation of "woman's work." As you read, notice what objective description contributes to the narration and to its persuasive quality.*

◆

1   "Social Security Office." (The voice answering the telephone sounds very self-assured.)

2   "I'm calling about . . . I . . . my mother just died . . . I was told to call you and see about a . . . death-benefit check, I think they call it. . . ."

3   "I see. Was your mother on Social Security? How old was she?"

4   "Yes . . . she was seventy-eight. . . ."

5   "Do you know her number?"

6   "No . . . I, ah . . . don't you have a record?"

7   "Certainly. I'll look it up. Her name?"

8   "Smith. Martha Smith. Or maybe she used Martha Ruth Smith. . . . Sometimes she used her maiden name . . . Martha Jerabek Smith."

9   "If you'd care to hold on, I'll check our records   it'll be a few minutes."

10   "Yes. . . ."

11   Her love letters—to and from Daddy—were in an old box, tied with ribbons and stiff, rigid-with-age leather thongs: 1918 through 1920; hers written on stationery from the general store she had worked in full-time and managed, single-handed, after her graduation from high school in 1913; and his, at first, on YMCA or Soldiers and Sailors Club stationery dispensed to the fighting men of World War I. He wooed her thoroughly and persistently by mail, and though she reciprocated all his feelings for her, she dreaded marriage. . . .

12   "It's so hard for me to decide when to have my wedding day—that's all I've thought about these last two days. I have told you dozens of times that I won't be afraid of married life, but when it comes down to setting the date and then picturing myself a married woman with half a dozen or more kids to look after, it just makes me sick. . . . I am weeping right now—I hope that some day I can look back and say how foolish I was to dread it all."

13   They married in February, 1921, and began farming. Their first baby, a daughter, was born in January, 1922, when my mother was 26 years old. The second baby, a son, was born in March, 1923. They were renting farms; my father, besides working his own fields, also was a hired man for two other farmers. They had no capital initially, and had to gain it slowly, working from

dawn until midnight every day. My town-bred mother learned to set hens and raise chickens, feed pigs, milk cows, plant and harvest a garden, and can every fruit and vegetable she could scrounge. She carried water nearly a quarter of a mile from the well to fill her wash boilers in order to do her laundry on a scrub board. She learned to shuck grain, feed threshers, shock and husk corn, feed corn pickers. In September, 1925, the third baby came, and in June, 1927, the fourth child—both daughters. In 1930, my parents had enough money to buy their own farm, and that March they moved all their livestock and belongings themselves, 55 miles over rutted, muddy roads.

14   In the summer of 1930 my mother and her two eldest children reclaimed a 40-acre field from Canadian thistles, by chopping them all out with a hoe. In the other fields, when the oats and flax began to head out, the green and blue of the crops were hidden by the bright yellow of wild mustard. My mother walked the fields day after day, pulling each mustard plant. She raised a new flock of baby chicks—500—and she spaded up, planted, hoed, and harvested a half-acre garden.

15   During the next spring their hogs caught cholera and died. No cash that fall.

16   And in the next year the drought hit. My mother and father trudged from the well to the chickens, the well to the calf pasture, the well to the barn, and from the well to the garden. The sun came out hot and bright, endlessly, day after day. The crops shriveled and died. They harvested half the corn, and ground the other half, stalks and all, and fed it to the cattle as fodder. With the price at four cents a bushel for the harvested crop, they couldn't afford to haul it into town. They burned it in the furnace for fuel that winter.

17   In 1934, in February, when the dust was still so thick in the Minnesota air that my parents couldn't always see from the house to the barn, their fifth child—a fourth daughter—was born. My father hunted rabbits daily, and my mother stewed them, fried them, canned them, and wished out loud that she could taste hamburger once more. In the fall the shotgun brought prairie chickens, ducks, pheasant, and grouse. My mother plucked each bird, carefully reserving the breast feathers for pillows.

18   In the winter she sewed night after night, endlessly, begging cast-off clothing from relatives, ripping apart coats, dresses, blouses, and trousers to remake them to fit her four daughters and son. Every morning and every evening she milked cows, fed pigs and calves, cared for chickens, picked eggs, cooked meals, washed dishes, scrubbed floors, and tended and loved her children. In the spring she planted a garden once more, dragging pails of water to nourish and sustain the vegetables for the family. In 1936 she lost a baby in her sixth month.

19   In 1937 her fifth daughter was born. She was 42 years old. In 1939 a second son, and in 1941 her eighth child—and third son.

20   But the war had come, and prosperity of a sort. The herd of cattle had grown to 30 head; she still milked morning and evening. Her garden was more

than a half acre—the rains had come, and by now the Rural Electricity Administration and indoor plumbing. Still she sewed—dresses and jackets for the children, housedresses and aprons for herself, weekly patching of jeans, overalls, and denim shirts. Still she made pillows, using the feathers she had plucked, and quilts every year—intricate patterns as well as patchwork, stitched as well as tied—all necessary bedding for her family. Every scrap of cloth too small to be used in quilts was carefully saved and painstakingly sewed together in strips to make rugs. She still went out in the fields to help with the haying whenever there was a threat of rain.

21   In 1959 my mother's last child graduated from high school. A year later the cows were sold. She still raised chickens and ducks, plucked feathers, made pillows, baked her own bread, and every year made a new quilt—now for a married child or for a grandchild. And her garden, that huge, undying symbol of sustenance, was as large and cared for as in all the years before. The canning, and now freezing, continued.

22   In 1969, on a June afternoon, mother and father started out for town so that she could buy sugar to make rhubarb jam for a daughter who lived in Texas. The car crashed into a ditch. She was paralyzed from the waist down.

23   In 1970 her husband, my father, died. My mother struggled to regain some competence and dignity and order in her life. At the rehabilitation institute, where they gave her physical therapy and trained her to live usefully in a wheelchair, the therapist told me: "She did fifteen pushups today—fifteen! She's almost seventy-five years old! I've never known a woman so strong!"

24   From her wheelchair she canned pickles, baked bread, ironed clothes, wrote dozens of letters weekly to her friends and her "half dozen or more kids," and made three patchwork housecoats and one quilt. She made balls and balls of carpet rags—enough for five rugs. And kept all her love letters.

25   "I think I've found your mother's records—Martha Ruth Smith; married to Ben F. Smith?"

26   "Yes, that's right."

27   "Well, I see that she was getting a widow's pension. . . ."

28   "Yes, that's right."

29   "Well, your mother isn't entitled to our $255 death benefit."

30   "Not entitled! But why?"

31   The voice on the telephone explains patiently:

32   "Well, you see—your mother never worked."

Considering Ideas

1. What point do you think the narration makes?

2. What do you think the significance of the essay's title is?

3. Write a list of words that describe the author's mother.

4. What is the difference between the way the government defines "work" and the way Smith-Yackel defines it?

5. Why did the author's mother work so hard at her rehabilitation?
6. What kind of reader do you think Smith-Yackel is trying to reach?

Considering Technique

1. The thesis of "My Mother Never Worked" is not stated, but it is strongly implied. In a sentence or two, write out that thesis in your own words.
2. Smith-Yackel arranges her details in chronological order with a flashback technique. In what paragraph does she flash back from the present of the essay to the past? In what paragraph does she return to the present of the essay?
3. Smith-Yackel uses a considerable amount of objective description in her narration (see page 43), particularly to indicate the nature and extent of her mother's labor. What does this description contribute to the essay?
4. Cite four examples of specific word choice to create a mental picture.
5. Are all the *who, what, when, where, why,* and *how* questions answered? Which answers are emphasized the most?
6. Would the narration be as effective if Smith-Yackel had left out the telephone conversation? Explain.
7. "My Mother Never Worked" does not have a formal conclusion. Is this a problem? Explain.
8. Consult a dictionary if you are unsure of the meaning of any of these words: *reciprocated* (paragraph 11), *scrounge* (paragraph 13), *cholera* (paragraph 15), *fodder* (paragraph 16), *sustenance* (paragraph 21).

For Group Consideration

"My Mother Never Worked" was written in 1975. Is there still disparity between the value placed on paid work done *outside* the home and on uncompensated work done *in* the home? Do many people still believe there is "women's work" and "men's work" and that the former is not as important as the latter? With three or four classmates, consider these questions and give examples to support your view.

Journal Entry

Based on what you know about Bonnie Smith-Yackel's mother, write a page or two in your journal telling whether you admire the woman for everything she was or pity her for the kind of life she led. Be sure to explain why you feel the way you do.

Essay Assignments

1. Tell a story that reveals something about your mother, your father, or another caregiver. Your purpose is to inform your reader about what this person is or was like. Be sure that the significance of your narration is clear.
2. Tell your own story to reveal how hard someone works. For example, you can narrate an account of the work of a basketball player, a sales clerk, a gas station attendant, a teacher, or a student. Your purpose is to convince your reader that the individual works harder than most people realize. If possible, include objective description (see p. 43), the way Smith-Yackel does, to help your reader appreciate the nature and extent of the individual's work.
3. Tell a story about some kind of injustice you experienced or witnessed. For example, you can tell the story about an injustice that occurred in the classroom, on the playing field, or where you work. Your purpose is to share and/or to inform.

Considering Thematic Issues

1. Using the clues in the essay, describe the personality of Bonnie Smith-Yackel's mother. Then go on to explain whether or not she is a person you admire and why or why not.
2. Both "My Mother Never Worked" and "India: A Widow's Devastating Choice" (page 278) tell something about traditional views of women. The first essay describes traditional views in the United States and the second describes traditional views in India. Discuss the similarities and differences in these views.

THE ENDLESS STREETCAR RIDE INTO THE NIGHT, AND THE TINFOIL NOOSE
Jean Shepherd

◆

Author, actor, and radio and television personality Jean Shepherd treats growing up in America's heartland with humor and insight. In "The Endless Streetcar Ride into the Night, and the Tinfoil Noose," he shares the pain of a blind date gone awry. However, the narration does more than allow the author to share; it explains what determines the path a person's life will take. In addition, the essay entertains the reader with its tale of an adolescent's moment of truth. As you read, notice that in addition to using narration and description, the author explains the cause and effect of an event.

◆

1   Mewling, puking babes. That's the way we all start. Damply clinging to someone's shoulder, burping weakly, clawing our way into life. *All* of us. Then gradually, surely, we begin to divide into two streams, all marching together up that long yellow brick road of life, but on opposite sides of the street. One crowd goes on to become the Official people, peering out at us from television screens; magazine covers. They are forever appearing in newsreels, carrying attaché cases, surrounded by banks of microphones while the world waits for their decisions and statements. And the rest of us go on to become . . . just us.

2   They are the Prime Ministers, the Presidents, Cabinet members, Stars, dynamic molders of the Universe, while we remain forever the onlookers, the applauders of their real lives.

3   Forever down in the dark dungeons of our souls we ask ourselves:

4   "How did they get away from me? When did I make that first misstep that took me forever to the wrong side of the street, to become eternally part of the accursed, anonymous Audience?"

5   It seems like one minute we're all playing around back of the garage, kicking tin cans and yelling at girls, and the next instant you find yourself doomed to exist as an office boy in the Mail Room of Life, while another ex-mewling, puking babe sends down Dicta, says, "No comment" to the Press, and lives a real, genuine *Life* on the screen of the world.

6   Countless sufferers at this hour are spending billions of dollars and endless man hours lying on analysts' couches, trying to pinpoint the exact moment that they stepped off the track and into the bushes forever.

7   It all hinges on one sinister reality that is rarely mentioned, no doubt due to its implacable, irreversible inevitability. These decisions cannot be changed, no matter how many brightly cheerful, buoyantly optimistic books on HOW TO ACHIEVE A RICHER, FULLER, MORE BOUNTIFUL LIFE or SEVEN MAGIC GOLDEN KEYS TO INSTANT DYNAMIC SUCCESS or THE SECRET OF HOW TO BECOME A BILLIONAIRE we

read, or how many classes are attended for instruction in handshaking, back-slapping, grinning, and making After-Dinner speeches. Joseph Stalin was not a Dale Carnegie graduate. He went all the way. It is an unpleasant truth that is swallowed, if at all, like a rancid, bitter pill. A star is a star; a numberless cipher is a numberless cipher.

8 Even more eerie a fact is that the Great Divide is rarely a matter of talent or personality. Or even luck. Adolf Hitler had a notoriously weak handshake. His smile was, if anything, a vapid mockery. But inevitably his star zoomed higher and higher. Cinema luminaries of the first order are rarely blessed with even the modicum of Talent, and often their physical beauty leaves much to be desired. What is the difference between Us and Them, We and They, the Big Ones and the great, teeming rabble?

9 There are about four times in a man's life, or a woman's, too, for that matter, when unexpectedly, from out of the darkness, the blazing carbon lamp, the cosmic searchlight of Truth shines full upon them. It is how we react to those moments that forever seals our fate. One crowd simply puts on its sunglasses, lights another cigar, and heads for the nearest plush French restaurant in the jazziest section of town, sits down and orders a drink, and ignores the whole thing. While we, the Doomed, caught in the brilliant glare of illumination, see ourselves inescapably for what we are, and from that day on skulk in the weeds, hoping no one else will spot us.

10 Those moments happen when we are least able to fend them off. I caught the first one full in the face when I was fourteen. The fourteenth summer is a magic one for all kids. You have just slid out of the pupa stage, leaving your old baby skin behind, and have not yet become a grizzled, hardened, tax-paying beetle. At fourteen you are made of cellophane. You curl easily and everyone can see through you.

11 When I was fourteen, Life was flowing through me in a deep, rich torrent of Castoria. How did I know that the first rocks were just ahead, and I was about to have my keel ripped out on the reef? Sometimes you feel as though you are alone in a rented rowboat, bailing like mad in the darkness with a leaky bailing can. It is important to know that there are at least two billion other ciphers in the same boat, bailing with the same leaky can. They all think they are alone and are crossed with an evil star. They are right.

12 I'm fourteen years old, in my sophomore year at high school. One day Schwartz, my purported best friend, sidled up to me edgily outside of school while we were waiting on the steps to come in after lunch. He proceeded to outline his plan:

13 "Helen's old man won't let me take her out on a date on Saturday night unless I get a date for her girlfriend. A double date. The old coot figures, I guess, that if there are four of us there won't be no monkey business. Well, how about it? Do you want to go on a blind date with this chick? I never seen her."

14 Well. For years I had this principle—absolutely *no* blind dates. I was a man of perception and taste, and life was short. But there is a time in your life

when you have to stop taking and begin to give just a little. For the first time the warmth of sweet Human Charity brought the roses to my cheeks. After all, Schwartz was my friend. It was little enough to do, have a blind date with some no doubt skinny, pimply girl for your best friend. I would do it for Schwartz. He would do as much for me.

15   "Okay. Okay, Schwartz."

16   Then followed the usual ribald remarks, feckless boasting, and dirty jokes about dates in general and girls in particular. It was decided that next Saturday we would go all the way. I had a morning paper route at the time, and my life savings stood at about $1.80. I was all set to blow it on one big night.

17   I will never forget that particular Saturday as long as I live. The air was soft as the finest of spun silk. The scent of lilacs hung heavy. The catalpa trees rustled in the early evening breeze from off the Lake. The inner Me itched in that nameless way, that indescribable way that only the fourteen-year-old Male fully knows.

18   All that afternoon I had carefully gone over my wardrobe to select the proper symphony of sartorial brilliance. That night I set out wearing my magnificent electric blue sport coat, whose shoulders were so wide that they hung out over my frame like vast, drooping eaves, so wide I had difficulty going through an ordinary door head-on. The electric blue sport coat that draped voluminously almost to my knees, its wide lapels flapping soundlessly in the slightest breeze. My pleated gray flannel slacks began just below my breastbone and indeed chafed my armpits. High-belted, cascading down finally to grasp my ankles in a vise-like grip. My tie, indeed one of my most prized possessions, had been a gift from my Aunt Glenn upon the state occasion of graduation from eighth grade. It was of a beautiful silky fabric, silvery pearly colored, four inches wide at the fulcrum, and of such a length to endanger occasionally my zipper in moments of haste. Hand-painted upon it was a magnificent blood-red snail.

19   I had spent fully two hours carefully arranging and rearranging my great mop of wavy hair, into which I had rubbed fully a pound and a half of Greasy Kid Stuff.

20   Helen and Schwartz waited on the corner under the streetlight at the streetcar stop near Junie Jo's home. Her name was Junie Jo Prewitt. I won't forget it quickly, although she has, no doubt, forgotten mine. I walked down the dark street alone, past houses set back off the street, through the darkness, past privet hedges, under elm trees, through air rich and ripe with promise. Her house stood back from the street even farther than the others. It sort of crouched in the darkness, looking out at me, kneeling. Pregnant with Girldom. A real Girlfriend house.

21   The first faint touch of nervousness filtered through the marrow of my skullbone as I knocked on the door of the screen-enclosed porch. No answer. I knocked again, louder. Through the murky screens I could see faint lights in the house itself. Still no answer. Then I found a small doorbell button buried in the

sash. I pressed. From far off in the bowels of the house I heard two chimes "Bong" politely. It sure didn't sound like our doorbell. We had a real ripper that went off like a broken buzz saw, more of a BRRRAAAAKKK than a muffled Bong. This was a rich people's doorbell.

22   The door opened, and there stood a real, genuine, gold-plated Father: potbelly, underwear shirt, suspenders, and all.

23   "Well?" he asked.

24   For one blinding moment of embarrassment I couldn't remember her name. After all, she was a blind date. I couldn't just say:

25   "I'm here to pick up some girl."

26   He turned back into the house and hollered:

27   "JUNIE JO! SOME KID'S HERE!"

28   "Heh, heh . . ." I countered.

29   He led me into the living room. It was an itchy house, sticky stucco walls of a dull orange color, and all over the floor this Oriental rug with the design crawling around, making loops and sworls. I sat on an overstuffed chair covered in green mohair that scratched even through my slacks. Little twisty bridge lamps stood everywhere. I instantly began to sweat down the back of my clean white shirt. Like I said, it was a very itchy house. It had little lamps sticking out of the walls that looked like phony candles, with phony glass orange flames. The rug started moaning to itself.

30   I sat on the edge of the chair and tried to talk to this Father. He was a Cub fan. We struggled under water for what seemed like an hour and a half, when suddenly I heard someone coming down the stairs. First the feet; then those legs, and there she was. She was magnificent! The greatest-looking girl I ever saw in my life! I have hit the double jackpot! And on a blind date! Great Scot!

31   My senses actually reeled as I clutched the arm of that bilge-green chair for support. Junie Jo Prewitt made Cleopatra look like a Girl Scout!

32   Five minutes later we are sitting in the streetcar, heading toward the bowling alley. I am sitting next to the most fantastic creation in the Feminine department known to Western man. There are four of us in that long, yellow-lit streetcar. No one else was aboard; just us four. I, naturally, being a trained gentleman, sat on the aisle to protect her from candy wrappers and cigar butts and such. Directly ahead of me, also on the aisle, sat Schwartz, his arm already flung affectionately in a death grip around Helen's neck as we boomed and rattled through the night.

33   I casually flung my right foot up onto my left knee so that she could see my crepe-soled, perforated, wing-toed, Scotch bluchers with the two-toned laces. I started to work my famous charm on her. Casually, with my practiced offhand, cynical, cutting, sardonic humor I told her about how my Old Man had cracked the block in the Oldsmobile, how the White Sox were going to have a good year this year, how my kid brother wet his pants when he saw a snake, how I figured it was going to rain, what a great guy Schwartz was, what a good

second baseman I was, how I figured I might go out for football. On and on I rolled, like Old Man River, pausing significantly for her to pick up the conversation. Nothing.

34   Ahead of us Schwartz and Helen were almost indistinguishable one from the other. They giggled, bit each other's ears, whispered, clasped hands, and in general made me itch even more.

35   From time to time Junie Jo would bend forward stiffly from the waist and say something I could never quite catch into Helen's right ear.

36   I told her my great story of the time that Uncle Carl lost his false teeth down the airshaft. Still nothing. Out of the corner of my eye I could see that she had her coat collar turned up, hiding most of her face as she sat silently, looking forward past Helen Weathers into nothingness.

37   I told her about this old lady on my paper route who chews tobacco, and roller skates in the backyard every morning. I still couldn't get through to her. Casually I inched my right arm up over the back of the seat behind her shoulders. The acid test. She leaned forward, avoiding my arm, and stayed that way.

38   "Heh, heh, heh . . ."

39   As nonchalantly as I could, I retrieved it, battling a giant cramp in my right shoulder blade. I sat in silence for a few seconds, sweating heavily as ahead Schwartz and Helen are going at it hot and heavy.

40   I was then that I became aware of someone saying something to me. It was an empty car. There was no one else but us. I glanced around, and there it was. Above us a line of car cards looked down on the empty streetcar. One was speaking directly to me, to me alone.

Do You Offend?

41   Do I *offend?!*

42   With no warning, from up near the front of the car where the motorman is steering I see this thing coming down the aisle directly toward *me*. It's coming closer and closer. I can't escape it. It's this blinding, fantastic, brilliant, screaming blue light. I am spread-eagled in it. There's a pin sticking through my thorax. I see it all now.

43   *I* AM THE BLIND DATE!

44   *ME!!*

45   *I'm* the one they're being nice to!

46   I'm suddenly getting fatter, more itchy. My new shoes are like bowling balls with laces; thick, rubber-crepe bowling balls. My great tie that Aunt Glenn gave me is two feet wide, hanging down to the floor like some crinkly tinfoil noose. My beautiful hand-painted snail is seven feet high, sitting up on my shoulder, burping. Great Scot! It is all clear to me in the searing white light of Truth. My friend Schwartz, I can see him saying to Junie Jo:

47   "I got this crummy fat friend who never has a date. Let's give him a break and . . ."

48   *I AM THE BLIND DATE!*

49   They are being nice to *me!* She is the one who is out on a Blind Date. A Blind Date that didn't make it.

50   In the seat ahead, the merriment rose to a crescendo. Helen tittered; Schwartz cackled. The marble statue next to me stared gloomily out into the darkness as our streetcar rattled on. The ride went on and on.

51   *I AM THE BLIND DATE!*

52   I didn't say much the rest of the night. There wasn't much to be said.

Considering Ideas

1. In paragraphs 1 through 9, Shepherd groups people into two types. What are these types? What are the characteristics of each type?
2. If he were one of the "Big Ones," how would Shepherd have reacted when he realized that he was the blind date?
3. What is the significance of the narration?
4. If he were one of the "Big Ones," how would Shepherd have reacted when he realized he was the blind date?
5. Would you consider Shepherd to be an optimist or a pessimist? Cite evidence in the text to support your view.

Considering Technique

1. Does the opening paragraph engage your interest? Why or why not?
2. In what paragraph does the actual narration begin?
3. Which paragraph presents Shepherd's thesis?
4. What does the conversation contribute to the narration?
5. Which paragraphs in the narration are predominantly description? What does this description contribute?
6. Select two descriptions that appeal to you. Write them out and underline the specific words.
7. Are all the journalist's questions answered? Which answers are emphasized the most?
8. Cause-and-effect analysis, which is discussed in Chapter 9, explains the causes and effects of something. What does Shepherd present as the cause of something? What does he give as the effect of that cause?
9. Consult a dictionary if you are unsure of the meaning of any of these words: *mewling* (paragraph 1), *rancid* (paragraph 7), *vapid* (paragraph 8), *modicum* (paragraph 8), *Castoria* (paragraph 11), *purported* (paragraph 12), *ribald* (paragraph 16), *feckless* (paragraph 16), *sartorial* (paragraph 18).

For Group Consideration

With three or four classmates, list the characteristics of the "Big Ones" and the characteristics of everyone else ("just us"). Draw on the information in the essay and your own experience and observation. Is it possible for someone who is "just us" to join the ranks of the "Big Ones"? If so, how is this accomplished? If not, why not?

Journal Entry

Shepherd says that those who ignore moments of truth become the "Big Ones," while those who don't become "the great, teeming rabble." In a page or so, explain what you think Shepherd means. Do you agree with Shepherd, or do you think that to be a "Big One" a person must face moments of truth? Explain.

Essay Assignments

1. If you have had a moment of truth, tell a story that shares it with your reader. If possible, include description and conversation. Be sure to indicate what you learned.
2. Like Shepherd, tell a story about a date you have had in order to share with or entertain your reader. Try to include description and conversation.
3. Shepherd tells a story about an event that had a significant impact on him. Tell your own story about an event that had a significant impact on you. Make clear what that impact was or is.
4. When Shepherd realized that *he* was the blind date, he recognized that things were not as he at first thought they were. Tell a story about a time when things were not as you thought they were.

Considering Thematic Issues

1. Shepherd is exaggerating when he suggests that his blind date set him on a course that would keep him from being a "Big One." Yet the circumstances and events of adolescence can influence us dramatically. Explain the importance of adolescence and the impact it has on us into adulthood. If you like, explain whether the significance of adolescence suggests that any changes should be made in our child-rearing or education practices.
2. How happy we are can often be determined by the way we choose to look at things: we can see a glass as half empty or half full. Using your own experience and observation along with examples from "Two Views of the Mississippi" (page 232) and "The Water-Faucet Vision" (page 118), illustrate the fact that how we view things influences our level of happiness.

A HANGING
George Orwell

♦

George Orwell (1903–1950), the pen name of Eric Arthur Blair, was born in India, where his father was in the British civil service. The author of Animal Farm *and* 1984, *Orwell served as a police officer in Burma, after being educated in England. "A Hanging" shares Orwell's experience at the hanging of a prisoner. It also informs the reader of what the hanging was like and thereby works to persuade the reader that capital punishment is wrong. As you read, notice the description and decide what it contributes.*

♦

1   It was in Burma, a sodden morning of the rains. A sickly light, like yellow tinfoil, was slanting over the high walls into the jail yard. We were waiting outside the condemned cells, a row of sheds fronted with double bars, like small animal cages. Each cell measured about ten feet by ten and was quite bare within except for a plank bed and a pot for drinking water. In some of them brown, silent men were squatting at the inner bars, with their blankets draped round them. These were the condemned men, due to be hanged within the next week or two.

2   One prisoner had been brought out of his cell. He was a Hindu, a puny wisp of a man, with a shaven head and vague liquid eyes. He had a thick, sprouting mustache, absurdly too big for his body, rather like the mustache of a comic man on the films. Six tall Indian warders were guarding him and getting him ready for the gallows. Two of them stood by with rifles and fixed bayonets, while the others handcuffed him, passed a chain through his handcuffs and fixed it to their belts, and lashed his arms tight to his sides. They crowded very close about him, with their hands always on him in a careful, caressing grip, as though all the while feeling him to make sure he was there. It was like men handling a fish which is still alive and may jump back into the water. But he stood quite unresisting, yielding his arms limply to the ropes, as though he hardly noticed what was happening.

3   Eight o'clock struck and a bugle call, desolately thin in the wet air, floated from the distant barracks. The superintendent of the jail, who was standing apart from the rest of us, moodily prodding the gravel with his stick, raised his head at the sound. He was an army doctor, with a gray toothbrush mustache and a gruff voice. "For God's sake, hurry up, Francis," he said irritably. "The man ought to have been dead by this time. Aren't you ready yet?"

4   Francis, the head jailer, a fat Dravidian[1] in a white drill suit and gold

---

[1] A native speaker of one of the southern Indian languages.

spectacles, waved his black hand. "Yes sir, yes sir," he bubbled. "All iss satisfactorily prepared. The hangman iss waiting. We shall proceed."

5   "Well, quick march, then. The prisoners can't get their breakfast until this job's over."

6   We set out for the gallows. Two warders marched on either side of the prisoner, with their rifles at the slope; two others marched close against him, gripping him by the arm and shoulder, as though at once pushing and supporting him. The rest of us, magistrates and the like, followed behind. Suddenly, when we had gone ten yards, the procession stopped short without any order or warning. A dreadful thing had happened—a dog, come goodness knows whence, had appeared in the yard. It came bounding among us with a loud volley of barks and leapt round us wagging its whole body, wild with glee at finding so many human beings together. It was a large woolly dog, half Airedale, half pariah. For a moment it pranced around us, and then, before anyone could stop it, it had made a dash for the prisoner, and jumping up tried to lick his face. Everybody stood aghast, too taken aback even to grab the dog.

7   "Who let that bloody brute in here?" said the superintendent angrily. "Catch it, someone!"

8   A warder detached from the escort, charged clumsily after the dog, but it danced and gamboled just out of his reach, taking everything as part of the game. A young Eurasian jailer picked up a handful of gravel and tried to stone the dog away, but it dodged the stones and came after us again. Its yaps echoed from the jail walls. The prisoner, in the grasp of the two warders, looked on incuriously, as though this was another formality of the hanging. It was several minutes before someone managed to catch the dog. Then we put my handkerchief through its collar and moved off once more, with the dog still straining and whimpering.

9   It was about forty yards to the gallows. I watched the bare brown back of the prisoner marching in front of me. He walked clumsily with his bound arms, but quite steadily, with that bobbing gait of the Indian who never straightens his knees. At each step his muscles slid neatly into place, the lock of hair on his scalp danced up and down, his feet printed themselves on the wet gravel. And once, in spite of the men who gripped him by each shoulder, he stepped lightly aside to avoid a puddle on the path.

10   It is curious; but till that moment I had never realized what it means to destroy a healthy, conscious man. When I saw the prisoner step aside to avoid the puddle, I saw the mystery, the unspeakable wrongness, of cutting a life short when it is in full tide. This man was not dying, he was alive just as we are alive. All the organs of his body were working—bowels digesting food, skin renewing itself, nails growing, tissues forming—all toiling away in solemn foolery. His nails would still be growing when he stood on the drop, when he was falling through the air with a tenth-of-a-second to live. His eyes saw the yellow gravel and the gray walls, and his brain still remembered, foresaw, reasoned—even about puddles. He and we were a party of men walking

together, seeing, hearing, feeling, understanding the same world; and in two minutes, with a sudden snap, one of us would be gone—one mind less, one world less.

11   The gallows stood in a small yard, separate from the main grounds of the prison, and overgrown with tall prickly weeds. It was a brick erection like three sides of a shed, with planking on top, and above that two beams and a crossbar with the rope dangling. The hangman, a gray-haired convict in the white uniform of the prison, was waiting beside his machine. He greeted us with a servile crouch as we entered. At a word from Francis the two warders, gripping the prisoner more closely than ever, half led, half pushed him to the gallows and helped him clumsily up the ladder. Then the hangman climbed up and fixed the rope round the prisoner's neck.

12   We stood waiting, five yards away. The warders had formed in a rough circle round the gallows. And then, when the noose was fixed, the prisoner began crying out to his god. It was a high, reiterated cry of "Ram! Ram! Ram! Ram!"[2] not urgent and fearful like a prayer or cry for help, but steady, rhythmical, almost like the tolling of a bell. The dog answered the sound with a whine. The hangman, still standing on the gallows, produced a small cotton bag like a flour bag and drew it down over the prisoner's face. But the sound, muffled by the cloth, still persisted, over and over again: "Ram! Ram! Ram! Ram! Ram!"

13   The hangman climbed down and stood ready, holding the lever. Minutes seemed to pass. The steady, muffled crying from the prisoner went on and on, "Ram! Ram! Ram!" never faltering for an instant. The superintendent, his head on his chest, was slowly poking the ground with his stick; perhaps he was counting the cries, allowing the prisoner a fixed number—fifty, perhaps, or a hundred. Everyone had changed color. The Indians had gone gray like bad coffee, and one or two of the bayonets were wavering. We looked at the lashed, hooded man on the drop, and listened to his cries—each cry another second of life; the same thought was in all our minds; oh, kill him quickly, get it over, stop that abominable noise!

14   Suddenly the superintendent made up his mind. Throwing up his head he made a swift motion with his stick. "Chalo!"[3] he shouted almost fiercely.

15   There was a clanking noise, and then dead silence. The prisoner had vanished, and the rope was twisting on itself. I let go of the dog, and it galloped immediately to the back of the gallows; but when it got there it stopped short, barked, and then retreated into a corner of the yard, where it stood among the weeds, looking timorously out at us. We went round the gallows to inspect the prisoner's body. He was dangling with his toes pointed straight downwards, very slowly revolving, as dead as a stone.

---

[2] The prisoner calls upon Rama, Hindu god who sustains and preserves.
[3] (Hindi) "Hurry up!"

16   The superintendent reached out with his stick and poked the bare brown body; it oscillated slightly. *"He's* all right," said the superintendent. He backed out from under the gallows, and blew out a deep breath. The moody look had gone out of his face quite suddenly. He glanced at his wristwatch. "Eight minutes past eight. Well, that's all for this morning, thank God."

17   The warders unfixed bayonets and marched away. The dog, sobered and conscious of having misbehaved itself, slipped after them. We walked out of the gallows yard, past the condemned cells with their waiting prisoners, into the big central yard of the prison. The convicts, under the command of warders armed with lathis,[4] were already receiving their breakfast. They squatted in long rows, each man holding a tin pannikin,[5] while two warders with buckets marched around ladling out rice; it seemed quite a homely, jolly scene, after the hanging. An enormous relief had come upon us now that the job was done. One felt an impulse to sing, to break into a run, to snigger. All at once everyone began chattering gaily.

18   The Eurasian boy walking beside me nodded toward the way we had come, with a knowing smile: "Do you know, sir, our friend" (he meant the dead man) "when he heard his appeal had been dismissed, he pissed on the floor of his cell. From fright. Kindly take one of my cigarettes, sir. Do you not admire my new silver case, sir? From the boxwallah, two rupees eight annas. Classy European style."

19   Several people laughed—at what, nobody seemed certain.

20   Francis was walking by the superintendent, talking garrulously: "Well, sir, all has passed off with the utmost satisfactoriness. It was all finished—flick! Like that. It iss not always so—oah, no! I have known cases where the doctor wass obliged to go beneath the gallows and pull the prissoner's legs to ensure decease. Most disagreeable!"

21   "Wriggling about, eh? That's bad," said the superintendent.

22   "Ach, sir, it iss worse when they become refractory! One man, I recall, clung to the bars of his cage when we went to take him out. You will scarcely credit, sir, that it took six warders to dislodge him, three pulling at each leg. We reasoned with him, 'My dear fellow,' we said, 'think of the all the pain and trouble you are causing to us!' But no, he would not listen! Ach, he wass very troublesome!"

23   I found that I was laughing quite loudly. Everyone was laughing. Even the superintendent grinned in a tolerant way. "You'd better all come out and have a drink," he said quite genially. "I've got a bottle of whiskey in the car. We could do with it."

24   We went through the big double gates of the prison into the road. "Pulling at his legs!" exclaimed a Burmese magistrate suddenly, and burst into a loud chuckling. We all began laughing again. At that moment Francis' anecdote

[4] Policemen's wooden clubs.
[5] Small pan.

seemed extraordinarily funny. We all had a drink together, native and European alike, quite amicably. The dead man was a hundred yards away.

Considering Ideas

1. What is Orwell's attitude toward capital punishment? Which paragraph best expresses that attitude?
2. What is Orwell's attitude toward the condemned prisoners? How can you tell what his attitude is?
3. Why do you think Orwell calls the appearance of the dog "a dreadful thing"?
4. How would you describe the superintendent's attitude toward the prisoner and the execution?
5. What is the significance of the condemned man stepping aside "to avoid the puddle" (paragraph 10)?
6. How do you explain the behavior of the men after the hanging?
7. What do you see as the significance of the fact that natives and Europeans had a drink together after the hanging (paragraph 24)?
8. What do you see as the significance of the narration?

Considering Technique

1. Orwell uses a considerable amount of description in his essay. Cite an example and explain what the description contributes.
2. Paragraph 1 includes two similes (see page 45 on similes): the light is "like yellow tinfoil," and the cells are "like small animal cages." What do these similes contribute?
3. Orwell often uses conversation in the essay. What purpose does this conversation serve?
4. How would you describe the tone of "A Hanging"? (See page 4 on tone.)
5. What is the effect of the last two sentences of the essay? Do you think they help Orwell fulfill his persuasive purpose? Explain.
6. Consult a dictionary if you are unsure of the meaning of any of these words: *sodden* (paragraph 1), *puny* (paragraph 2), *magistrates* (paragraph 6), *volley* (paragraph 6), *pariah* (paragraph 6), *gamboled* (paragraph 8), *incuriously* (paragraph 8), *gait* (paragraph 9), *servile* (paragraph 11), *reiterated* (paragraph 12), *timorously* (paragraph 15), *oscillated* (paragraph 16), *garrulously* (paragraph 20), *refractory* (paragraph 22), *amicably* (paragraph 24).

For Group Consideration

Orwell never mentions the crime for which the prisoner has been condemned to hang. Why do you think the author fails to mention the crime? Would it make a difference if the crime were mentioned? Discuss these questions with two or three classmates and report your conclusions to the rest of the class.

Journal Entry

Do you believe in the death penalty? Explain why or why not in a page of your journal. As an alternative, explain whether your opinion about the death penalty has changed as a result of reading "A Hanging."

Essay Assignments

1. "A Hanging" is a narration meant to persuade the reader that capital punishment is wrong. Tell a story of your own to persuade the reader of the injustice of something: cheating, grades, final exams, college admission procedures, Little League tryouts, student council elections, hazing, and so on.
2. The men who witnessed and supervised the hanging were clearly uncomfortable, which helps explain their behavior before, during, and after the execution. Tell a story about an event to which witnesses had a strong reaction (an accident, a death, an embarrassing moment, an argument, for example) and show how the people witnessing the event behaved.
3. Orwell's narration tells of oppression. If you have witnessed or experienced oppression or discrimination, tell a story that reveals what you witnessed or experienced.
4. In "A Hanging," Orwell comes to a realization: he recognizes that capital punishment is wrong. Narrate an account of a time you came to realize something important.

Considering Thematic Issues

1. Using the evidence in the essay, explain Orwell's attitude toward capital punishment. Then go on to agree or disagree with him, making clear why you hold your view. (Your preceding journal entry may give you ideas.)
2. What do "A Hanging" and "By Any Other Name" (page 111) reveal about the attitude of the British toward the native populations they ruled? Why do you think the British felt and behaved the way they did? Have you seen a similar attitude in anyone you know? Explain.

BY ANY OTHER NAME
Santha Rama Rau

Born in India and educated in the United States and England, Santha Rama Rau writes of the Eastern experience. In "By Any Other Name," which takes place during the period of British colonial rule in India, Rau tells the story of her first and last days as an Indian child in a British school. She shares her experience and informs the reader about the nature of discrimination. As you read, notice the description and try to determine what it contributes to the essay.

1   At the Anglo-Indian day school in Zorinabad to which my sister and I were sent when she was eight and I was five and a half, they changed our names. On the first day of school, a hot, windless morning of a north Indian September, we stood in the headmistress's study and she said, "Now you're the *new* girls. What are your names?"

2   My sister answered for us. "I am Premila, and she"—nodding in my direction—"is Santha."

3   The headmistress had been in India, I suppose, fifteen years or so, but she still smiled her helpless inability to cope with Indian names. Her rimless half-glasses glittered, and the precarious bun on top of her head trembled as she shook her head. "Oh, my dears, those are much too hard for me. Suppose we give you pretty English names. Wouldn't that be more jolly? Let's see, now— Pamela for you, I think." She shrugged in a baffled way at my sister. "That's as close as I can get. And for *you*," she said to me, "how about Cynthia? Isn't that nice?"

4   My sister was always less easily intimidated than I was, and while she kept a stubborn silence, I said, "Thank you," in a very tiny voice.

5   We had been sent to that school because my father, among his responsibilities as an officer of the civil service, had a tour of duty to perform in the villages around that steamy little provincial town, where he had his headquarters at that time. He used to make his shorter inspection tours on horseback, and a week before, in the stale heat of a typically postmonsoon day, we had waved good-by to him and a little procession—an assistant, a secretary, two bearers, and the man to look after the bedding rolls and luggage. They rode away through our large garden, still bright green from the rains, and we turned back into the twilight of the house and the sound of fans whispering in every room.

6   Up to then, my mother had refused to send Premila to school in the British-run establishments of that time, because, she used to say, "you can bury a dog's tail for seven years and it still comes out curly, and you can take a Britisher away from his home for a lifetime, and he still remains insular." The examinations and degrees from entirely Indian schools were not, in those days,

considered valid. In my case, the question had never come up, and probably never would have come up if Mother's extraordinary good health had not broken down. For the first time in my life, she was not able to continue the lessons she had been giving us every morning. So our Hindi books were put away, the stories of the Lord Krishna as a little boy were left in midair, and we were sent to the Anglo-Indian school.

7   That first day at school is still, when I think of it, a remarkable one. At that age, if one's name is changed, one develops a curious form of dual personality. I remember having a certain detached and disbelieving concern in the actions of "Cynthia," but certainly no responsibility. Accordingly, I followed the thin, erect back of the headmistress down the veranda to my classroom feeling, at most, a passing interest in what was going to happen to me in this strange, new atmosphere of School.

8   The building was Indian in design, with wide verandas opening onto a central courtyard, but Indian verandas are usually whitewashed, with stone floors. These, in the tradition of British schools, were painted dark brown and had matting on the floors. It gave a feeling of extra intensity to the heat.

9   I suppose there were about a dozen Indian children in the school—which contained perhaps forty children in all—and four of them were in my class. They were all sitting at the back of the room, and I went to join them. I sat next to a small, solemn girl who didn't smile at me. She had long, glossy-black braids and wore a cotton dress, but she still kept on her Indian jewelry—a gold chain around her neck, thin gold bracelets, and tiny ruby studs in her ears. Like most Indian children, she had a rim of black kohl around her eyes. The cotton dress should have looked strange, but all I could think of was that I should ask my mother if I couldn't wear a dress to school, too, instead of my Indian clothes.

10   I can't remember too much about the proceedings in class that day, except for the beginning. The teacher pointed to me and asked me to stand up. "Now, dear, tell the class your name."

11   I said nothing.

12   "Come along," she said frowning slightly. "What's your name, dear?"

13   "I don't know," I said finally.

14   The English children in the front of the class—there were about eight or ten of them—giggled and twisted around in their chairs to look at me. I sat down quickly, and opened my eyes very wide, hoping in that way to dry them off. The little girl with the braids put out her hand and very lightly touched my arm. She still didn't smile.

15   Most of that morning I was rather bored. I looked briefly at the children's drawings pinned to the wall, and then concentrated on a lizard clinging to the ledge of the high, barred window behind the teacher's head. Occasionally it would shoot out its long yellow tongue for a fly, and then it would rest, with its eyes closed and its belly palpitating, as though it were swallowing several times quickly. The lessons were mostly concerned with reading and writing and simple numbers—things that my mother had already taught me—and I paid

very little attention. The teacher wrote on the easel blackboard words like "bat" and "cat," which seemed babyish to me; only "apple" was new and incomprehensible.

16 When it was time for the lunch recess, I followed the girl with braids out onto the veranda. There the children from the other classes were assembled. I saw Premila at once and ran over to her, as she had charge of our lunchbox. The children were all opening packages and sitting down to eat sandwiches. Premila and I were the only ones who had Indian food—thin wheat chapatties, some vegetable curry, and a bottle of buttermilk. Premila thrust half of it into my hand and whispered fiercely that I should go and sit with my class, because that was what the others seemed to be doing.

17 The enormous black eyes of the little Indian girl from my class looked at my food longingly, so I offered her some. But she only shook her head and plowed her way solemnly through her sandwiches.

18 I was very sleepy after lunch, because at home we always took a siesta. It was usually a pleasant time of day, with the bedroom darkened against the harsh afternoon sun, the drifting off into sleep with the sound of Mother's voice reading a story in one's mind, and, finally, the shrill, fussy voice of the ayah waking one for tea.

19 At school, we rested for a short time on low, folding cots on the veranda, and then we were expected to play games. During the hot part of the afternoon we played indoors, and after the shadows had begun to lengthen and the slight breeze of the evening had come up we moved outside to the wide courtyard.

20 I had never really grasped the system of competitive games. At home, whenever we played tag or guessing games, I was always allowed to "win"—"because," Mother used to tell Premila, "she is the youngest, and we have to allow for that." I had often heard her say it, and it seemed quite reasonable to me, but the result was that I had no clear idea of what "winning" meant.

21 When we played twos-and-threes that afternoon at school, in accordance with my training, I let one of the small English boys catch me, but was naturally rather puzzled when the other children did not return the courtesy. I ran about for what seemed like hours without ever catching anyone, until it was time for school to close. Much later I learned that my attitude was called "not being a good sport," and I stopped allowing myself to be caught, but it was not for years that I really learned the spirit of the thing.

22 When I saw our car come up to the school gate, I broke away from my classmates and rushed toward it yelling, "Ayah! Ayah!" It seemed like an eternity since I had seen her that morning—a wizened, affectionate figure in her white cotton sari, giving me dozens of urgent and useless instructions on how to be a good girl at school. Premila followed more sedately, and she told me on the way home never to do that again in front of the other children.

23 When we got home we went straight to Mother's high, white room to have tea with her, and I immediately climbed onto the bed and bounced gently up and down on the springs. Mother asked how we had liked our first day in

school. I was so pleased to be home and to have left that peculiar Cynthia behind that I had nothing whatever to say about school, except to ask what "apple" meant. But Premila told Mother about the classes, and added that in her class they had weekly tests to see if they learned their lessons well.

24   I asked, "What's a test?"

25   Premila said, "You're too small to have them. You won't have them in your class for donkey's years." She had learned the expression that day and was using it for the first time. We all laughed enormously at her wit. She also told Mother, in an aside, that we should take sandwiches to school the next day. Not, she said, that *she* minded. But they would be simpler for me to handle.

26   That whole lovely evening I didn't think about school at all. I sprinted barefoot across the lawns with my favorite playmate, the cook's son, to the stream at the end of the garden. We quarreled in our usual way, waded in the tepid water under the lime trees, and waited for the night to bring out the smell of the jasmine. I listened with fascination to his stories of ghosts and demons, until I was too frightened to cross the garden alone in the semidarkness. The ayah found me, shouted at the cook's son, scolded me, hurried me into supper—it was an entirely usual, wonderful evening.

27   It was a week later, the day of Premila's first test, that our lives changed rather abruptly. I was sitting at the back of my class, in my usual inattentive way, only half listening to the teacher. I had started a rather guarded friendship with the girl with the braids, whose name turned out to be Nalini (Nancy, in school). The three other Indian children were already fast friends. Even at that age it was apparent to all of us that friendship with the English or Anglo-Indian children was out of the question. Occasionally, during the class, my new friend and I would draw pictures and show them to each other secretly.

28   The door opened sharply and Premila marched in. At first, the teacher smiled at her in a kindly and encouraging way and said, "Now, you're little Cynthia's sister?"

29   Premila didn't even look at her. She stood with her feet planted firmly apart and her shoulders rigid, and addressed herself directly to me. "Get up," she said. "We're going home."

30   I didn't know what had happened, but I was aware that it was a crisis of some sort. I rose obediently and started to walk toward my sister.

31   "Bring your pencils and your notebook," she said.

32   I went back for them, and together we left the room. The teacher started to say something just as Premila closed the door, but we didn't wait to hear what it was.

33   In complete silence we left the school grounds and started to walk home. Then I asked Premila what the matter was. All she would say was "We're going home for good."

34   It was a very tiring walk for a child of five and a half, and I dragged along behind Premila with my pencils growing sticky in my hand. I can still remember looking at the dusty hedges, and the tangles of thorns in the ditches by the side of the road, smelling the faint fragrance from the eucalyptus trees and wonder-

ing whether we would ever reach home. Occasionally a horse-drawn tonga passed us, and the women, in their pink or green silks, stared at Premila and me trudging along on the side of the road. A few coolies and a line of women carrying baskets of vegetables on their heads smiled at us. But it was nearing the hottest time of day, and the road was almost deserted. I walked more and more slowly, and shouted to Premila, from time to time, "Wait for me!" with increasing peevishness. She spoke to me only once, and that was to tell me to carry my notebook on my head, because of the sun.

35   When we got to our house the ayah was just taking a tray of lunch into Mother's room. She immediately started a long, worried questioning about what are you children doing back here at this hour of the day.

36   Mother looked very startled and very concerned, and asked Premila what had happened.

37   Premila said, "We had our test today, and she made me and the other Indians sit at the back of the room, with a desk between each one."

38   Mother said, "Why was that, darling?"

39   "She said it was because Indians cheat," Premila added. "So I don't think we should go back to that school."

40   Mother looked very distant, and was silent a long time. At last she said, "Of course not, darling." She sounded displeased.

41   We all shared the curry she was having for lunch, and afterward I was sent off to the beautifully familiar bedroom for my siesta. I could hear Mother and Premila talking through the open door.

42   Mother said, "Do you suppose she understood all that?"

43   Premila said, "I shouldn't think so. She's a baby."

44   Mother said, "Well, I hope it won't bother her."

45   Of course, they were both wrong. I understood it perfectly, and I remember it all very clearly. But I put it happily away, because it had all happened to a girl called Cynthia, and I never was really particularly interested in her.

Considering Ideas

1. What is the significance of the narration? Where is that significance mentioned?
2. What differences in temperament and personality are there between Santha and Premila?
3. What are the cultural differences between the way the Indian and British students approach games?
4. In paragraph 13, Santha says that she didn't know her name. How do you account for this lapse?
5. In paragraph 27, Rau says that friendship with the English or Anglo-Indian children was out of the question. Explain why.
6. Do you think the sisters were right to leave school? Was there another way to handle the discrimination encountered there? Explain.

Considering Technique

1. What purpose does the first sentence of the essay serve?
2. At what point does the narration begin?
3. Several paragraphs give the reader background information and helpful explanations. Cite three such paragraphs and explain how they help the reader.
4. A considerable amount of description appears in the essay. Which paragraphs include description? Select one of the descriptive passages and tell what it contributes to the essay.
5. What does the conversation contribute to the essay?
6. Paragraphs 16, 26, and 27 contain topic sentences. What are those topic sentences and what purpose do they serve?
7. Which answers to the *who, what, when, where, why,* and *how* questions are emphasized? That is, which journalist's questions are answered in the most detail?
8. What approach does Rau take to her conclusion?
9. Consult a dictionary if you are unsure of the meaning of these words: *precarious* (paragraph 3), *intimidated* (paragraph 4), *insular* (paragraph 6), *veranda* (paragraph 7), *kohl* (paragraph 9), *ayah* (paragraph 18).

For Group Consideration

Santha and Premila each coped with discrimination in her own way. With three or four of your classmates, discuss how each girl dealt with the discrimination at school. Then go on to consider the advantages and disadvantages of each coping strategy. Report your conclusions to the rest of the class.

Journal Entry

In paragraph 6, Santha mentions that her mother at first did not send Premila to British schools, saying "you can bury a dog's tail for seven years and it still comes out curly, and you can take a Britisher away from his home for a lifetime, and he still remains insular." In your journal, explain what you think the mother's comment means.

Essay Assignments

1. Like Rau, tell a story about a school event that had a significant impact on you. Be sure to make clear what the significance of your narration is by mentioning the impact.
2. Narrate a story about a time a teacher showed a lack of interest or disregard for students. If possible, use conversation and description for vividness. Your purpose is to share with your reader.

3. If you have experienced or witnessed prejudice, narrate an account of how you or others responded to the prejudice.

4. Was there ever a time when, like Santha and Premila, you felt isolated, as if you didn't fit in? If so, narrate a story that shares the experience with your reader or informs your reader of what it is like to be isolated.

Considering Thematic Issues

1. The school in "By Any Other Name" is a reflection of the larger society in India at the time. Thus, the intolerance and insensitivity of the teacher reflect the same features in the world outside the school. Look back on the school system you were in and write an essay that shows in what ways that system reflected the attitudes and values of society. Be sure to back up your points with specific examples.

2. Using the information in "By Any Other Name," and "Shades of Black" (page 336), along with your own experience and observation, explain what school is like for students who are different in some way from the majority of the class.

THE WATER-FAUCET VISION
Gish Jen

◆

In February 1990, the Atlantic Monthly *magazine honored Gish Jen by naming her one of the new generation's most prominent writers. In "The Water-Faucet Vision," Jen narrates several childhood memories centered on family and religion. As you read, consider how your own religious beliefs (or lack of them) have influenced you.*

◆

1   To protect my sister Mona and me from the pains—or, as they pronounced it, the "pins"—of life, my parents did their fighting in Shanghai dialect, which we didn't understand; and when my father one day pitched a brass vase through the kitchen window, my mother told us he had done it by accident.

2   "By accident?" said Mona.

3   My mother chopped the foot off a mushroom.

4   "By accident?" said Mona. "By *accident?*"

5   Later I tried to explain to her that she shouldn't have persisted like that, but it was hopeless.

6   "What's the matter with throwing things?" She shrugged. "He was *mad.*"

7   That was the difference between Mona and me: fighting was just fighting to her. If she worried about anything, it was only that she might turn out too short to become a ballerina, in which case she was going to be a piano player.

8   I, on the other hand, was going to be a martyr. I was in fifth grade then, and the hyperimaginative sort—the kind of girl who grows morbid in Catholic school, who longs to be chopped or frozen to death but then has nightmares about it from which she wakes up screaming and clutching a stuffed bear. It was not a bear that I clutched, though, but a string of three malachite beads that I had found in the marsh by the old aqueduct one day. Apparently once part of a necklace, they were each wonderfully striated and swirled, and slightly humped toward the center, like a jellyfish; so that if I squeezed one, it would slip smoothly away, with a grace that altogether enthralled and—one those dream-harrowed nights—soothed me, soothed me as nothing had before or has since. Not that I've lacked occasion for soothing: though it's been four months since my mother died, there are still nights when sleep stands away from me, stiff as a well-paid sentry. But that is another story. Back then I had my malachite beads, and if I worried them long and patiently enough, I was sure to start feeling better, more awake, even a little special—imagining, as I liked to, that my nightmares were communications from the Almighty Himself, preparation for my painful destiny. Discussing them with Patty Creamer, who had also promised her life to God, I called them "almost visions"; and Patty, her mouth wadded with the three or four sticks of Doublemint she always seemed to have going at once, said, "I bet you'll be doin' miracleth by seventh grade."

9   Miracles. Today Patty laughs to think she ever spent good time stewing on such matters, her attention having long turned to rugs, and artwork, and antique Japanese bureaus—things she believes in.

10   "A good bureau's more than just a bureau," she explained last time we had lunch. "It's a hedge against life. I tell you: if there's one thing I believe, it's that cheap stuff's just money out the window. Nice stuff, on the other hand— now that you can always cash out, if life gets rough. *That* you can count on."

11   In fifth grade, though, she counted on different things.

12   "You'll be doing miracles too," I told her, but she shook her shaggy head and looked doleful.

13   "Na' me," she chomped. "Buzzit's okay. The kin' things I like, prayers work okay on."

14   "Like?"

15   "Like you 'member the dreth I liked?"

16   She meant the yellow one, with the crisscross straps.

17   "Well gueth what."

18   "Your mom got it for you."

19   She smiled. "And I only jutht prayed for it for a week," she said.

20   As for myself, though, I definitely wanted to be able to perform a wonder or two. Miracle-working! It was the carrot of carrots: it kept me doing my homework, taking the sacraments; it kept me mournfully on key in music hour, while my classmates hiccuped and squealed their carefree hearts away. Yet I couldn't have said what I wanted such powers *for,* exactly. That is, I thought of them the way one might think of, say, an ornamental sword—as a kind of collectible, which also happened to be a means of defense.

21   But then Patty's father walked out on her mother, and for the first time, there was a miracle I wanted to do. I wanted it so much I could see it: Mr. Creamer made into a spitball; Mr. Creamer shot through a straw into the sky; Mr. Creamer unrolled and replumped, plop back on Patty's doorstep. I would've cleaned out his mind and given him a shave en route. I would've given him a box of peanut fudge, tied up with a ribbon, to present to Patty with a kiss.

22   But instead all I could do was try to tell her he'd come back.

23   "He will not, he will not!" she sobbed. "He went on a boat to Rio Deniro. To Rio Deniro!"

24   I tried to offer her a stick of gum, but she wouldn't take it.

25   "He said he would rather look at water than at my mom's fat face. He said he would rather look at water than at me." Now she was really wailing, and holding her ribs so tightly that she almost seemed to be hurting herself—so tightly that just looking at her arms wound around her like snakes made my heart feel squeezed.

26   I patted her on the arm. A one-winged pigeon waddled by.

27   "He said I wasn't even his kid, he said I came from Uncle Johnny. He said I was garbage, just like my mom and Uncle Johnny. He said I wasn't even his kid, he said I wasn't his Patty, he said I came from Uncle Johnny!"

28   "From your Uncle Johnny?" I asked stupidly.

29   "From Uncle Johnny," she cried. "From Uncle Johnny!"

30   "He said that?" I said. Then, wanting to go on, to say *something,* I said, "Oh Patty, don't cry."

31   She kept crying.

32   I tried again. "Oh Patty, don't cry," I said. Then I said, "Your dad was a jerk anyway."

33   The pigeon produced a large runny dropping.

34   It was a good twenty minutes before Patty was calm enough for me just to run to the girls' room to get her some toilet paper; and by the time I came back she was sobbing again, saying "to Rio Deniro, to Rio Deniro" over and over again, as though the words had stuck in her and couldn't be gotten out. As we had missed the regular bus home and the late bus too, I had to leave her a second time to go call my mother, who was mad only until she heard what had happened. Then she came and picked us up, and bought us each a Fudgsicle.

35   Some days later, Patty and I started a program to work on getting her father home. It was a serious business. We said extra prayers, and lit votive candles; I tied my malachite beads to my uniform belt, fondling them as though they were a rosary, I a nun. We even took to walking about the school halls with our hands folded—a sight so ludicrous that our wheeze of a principal personally took us aside one day.

36   "I must tell you," she said, using her nose as a speaking tube, "that there is really no need for such peee-ity."

37   But we persisted, promising to marry God and praying to every saint we could think of. We gave up gum, then gum and Slim Jims both, then gum and Slim Jims and ice cream—and when even that didn't work, we started on more innovative things. The first was looking at flowers. We held our hands beside our eyes like blinders as we hurried by the violets by the flagpole, the window box full of tulips outside the nurse's office. Next it was looking at boys: Patty gave up angel-eyed Jamie Halloran and I, gymnastic Anthony Rossi. It was hard, but in the end our efforts paid off. Mr. Creamer came back a month later, and though he brought with him nothing but dysentery, he was at least too sick to have all that much to say.

38   Then, in the course of a fight with my father, my mother somehow fell out of their bedroom window.

39   Recently—thinking a mountain vacation might cheer me—I sublet my apartment to a handsome but somber newlywed couple, who turned out to be every bit as responsible as I'd hoped. They cleaned out even the eggshell chips I'd sprinkled around the base of my plants as fertilizer, leaving behind only a shiny silverplate cake server and a list of their hopes and goals for the summer. The list, tacked precariously to the back of the kitchen door, began with a fervent appeal to God to help them get their wedding thank-yous written in three weeks or less. (You could see they had originally written "two weeks" but scratched it out—no miracles being demanded here.) It went on:

Please help us, Almighty Father in Heaven Above, to get Ann a teaching job within a half-hour drive of here in a nice neighborhood.

Please help us, Almighty Father in Heaven Above, to get John a job doing anything where he won't strain his back and that is within a half-hour drive of here.

Please help us, Almighty Father in Heaven Above, to get us a car.

Please help us, A.F. in H.A., to learn French.

Please help us, A.F. in H.A., to find seven dinner recipes that cost less than 60 cents a serving and can be made in a half-hour. And that don't have tomatoes, since You in Your Heavenly Wisdom made John allergic.

Please help us, A.F. in H.A., to avoid books in this apartment such as You in Your Heavenly Wisdom allowed John, for Your Heavenly Reasons, to find three nights ago (June 2nd).

Et cetera. In the left-hand margin they kept score of how they had fared with their requests, and it was heartening to see that nearly all of them were marked "Yes! Praise the Lord" (sometimes shortened to PTL), with the sole exception of learning French, which was mysteriously marked "No! PTL to the Highest."

40   That note touched me. Strange and familiar both, it seemed like it had been written by some cousin of mine—some cousin who had stayed home to grow up, say, while I went abroad and learned what I had to, though the learning was painful. This, of course, is just a manner of speaking; in fact I did my growing up at home, like anybody else.

41   But the learning *was* painful: I never knew exactly how it happened that my mother went hurtling through the air that night years ago, only that the wind had been chopping at the house, and that the argument had started about the state of the roof. Someone had been up to fix it the year before, but it wasn't a roofer, it was some man my father insisted could do just as good a job for a quarter of the price. And maybe he could have, had he not somehow managed to step through a knot in the wood under the shingles and break his uninsured ankle. Now the shingles were coming loose again, and the attic insulation was mildewing besides, and my father was wanting to sell the house altogether, which he said my mother had wanted to buy so she could send pictures of it home to her family in China.

42   "The Americans have a saying," he said. "They saying, 'You have to keep up with the Jones family,' I'm saying if Jones family in Shanghai, you can send any picture you want, *an-y* picture. Go take picture of those rich guys' house. You want to act like rich guys, right? Go take picture of those rich guys' house."

43   At that point my mother sent Mona and me to wash up, and started speaking Shanghaiese. They argued for some time in the kitchen while we listened from the top of the stairs, our faces wedged between the bumpy Spanish scrolls of the wrought-iron railing. First my mother ranted, then my father, then they both ranted at once until finally there was a thump, followed by a long quiet.

44   "Do you think they're kissing now?" said Mona. "I bet they're kissing, like this." She pursed her lips like a fish and was about to put them to the railing when we heard my mother locking the back door. We hightailed it into bed; my parents creaked up the stairs. Everything at that point seemed fine. Once in their bedroom, though, they started up again, first softly, then louder and louder, until my mother turned on a radio to try to disguise the noise. A door slammed; they began shouting at one another; another door slammed; a shoe or something banged the wall behind Mona's bed.

45   "How're we supposed to *sleep?*" said Mona, sitting up.

46   There was another thud, more yelling in Shanghaiese, and then my mother's voice pierced the wall, in English. "So what you want I should do? Go to work like Theresa Lee?"

47   My father rumbled something back.

48   "You think you're big shot because you have job, right? You're big shot, but you never get promotion, you never get raise. All I do is spend money, right? So what do you do, you tell me. So what do you do!"

49   Something hit the floor so hard that our room shook.

50   "So kill me," screamed my mother. "You know what you are? You are failure. Failure! You are failure!"

51   Then there was a sudden, terrific bursting crash—and after it, as if on a bungled clue, the serene blare of an a cappella soprano, picking her way down a scale.

52   By the time Mona and I knew to look out the window, a neighbor's pet beagle was already on the scene, sniffing and barking at my mother's body, his tail crazy with excitement; then he was barking at my stunned and trembling father, at the shrieking ambulance, the police, at crying Mona in her bun-nyfooted pajamas, and at me, barefoot in the cold grass, squeezing her shoulder with one hand and clutching my malachite beads with the other.

53   My mother wasn't dead, only unconscious, the paramedics figured that out right away, but there was blood everywhere, and though they were reassuring about her head wounds as they strapped her to the stretcher, commenting also on how small she was, how delicate, how light, my father kept saying, "I killed her, I killed her" as the ambulance screeched and screeched headlong, forever, to the hospital. I was afraid to touch her, and glad of the metal rail between us, even though its sturdiness made her seem even frailer than she was; I wished she was bigger, somehow, and noticed, with a pang, that the new red slippers we had given her for Mother's Day had been lost somewhere along the way. How much she seemed to be leaving behind as we careened along— still not there, still not there—Mona and Dad and the medic and I taking up the whole ambulance, all the room, so there was no room for anything else; no room even for my mother's real self, the one who should have been pinching the color back to my father's grey face, the one who should have been calming Mona's cowlick—the one who should have been bending over us, to help us to be strong, to help us get through, even as we bent over her.

54   Then suddenly we were there, the glowing square of the emergency room entrance opening like the gates of heaven; and immediately the talk of miracles began. Alive, a miracle. No bones broken, a miracle. A miracle that the hemlocks cushioned her fall, a miracle that they hadn't been trimmed in a year and a half. It was a miracle that all that blood, the blood that had seemed that night to be everywhere, was from one shard of glass, a single shard, can you imagine, and as for the gash in her head, the scar would be covered by hair. The next day my mother cheerfully described just how she would part it so that nothing would show at all.

55   "You're a lucky duck-duck," agreed Mona, helping herself, with a little *pirouette,* to the cherry atop my mother's chocolate pudding.

56   That wasn't enough for me, though. I was relieved, yes, but what I wanted by then was a real miracle, not for her simply to have survived, but for the whole thing never to have happened—for my mother's head never to have had to be shaved and bandaged like that, for her high, proud forehead never to have been swollen down over her eyes, for her face and neck and hands never to have been painted so many shades of blue-black, and violet, and chartreuse. I still want those things—for my parents not to have had to live with this affair like a prickle bush between them, for my father to have been able to look my mother in her swollen eyes and curse the madman, the monster that could have dared do this to the woman he loved. I wanted to be able to touch my mother without shuddering, to be able to console my father, to be able to get that crash out of my head, the sound of that soprano—so many things that I didn't know how to pray for them, that I wouldn't have known where to start even if I had the power to work miracles, right there, right then.

57   A week later, when my mother was home, and her head beginning to bristle with new hairs, I lost my malachite beads. I had been carrying them in a white cloth pouch that Patty had given me, and was swinging the pouch on my pinky on my way home from school, when I swung just a bit too hard, and it went sailing in a long arc through the air, whooshing like a perfectly thrown basketball through one of the holes of a nearby sewer. There was no chance of fishing it out: I looked and looked, crouching on the sticky pavement until the asphalt had crazed the skin of my hands and knees, but all I could discern was an evil-smelling musk, glassy and smug and impenetrable.

58   My loss didn't quite hit me until I was home, but then it produced an agony all out of proportion to my string of pretty beads. I hadn't cried at all during my mother's accident, and now I was crying all afternoon, all through dinner, and then after dinner too, crying past the point where I knew what I was crying for, wishing dimly that I had my beads to hold, wishing dimly that I could pray but refusing, refusing, I didn't know why, until I finally fell into an exhausted sleep on the couch, where my parents left me for the night—glad, no doubt, that one of the more tedious of my childhood crises seemed to be finally winding off the reel of life, onto the reel of memory. They covered me, and somehow grew a pillow under my head, and, with uncharacteristic disregard

for the living room rug, left some milk and pecan sandies on the coffee table, in case I woke up hungry. Their thoughtfulness was prescient: I did wake up in the early part of the night; and it was then, amid the unfamiliar sounds and shadows of the living room, that I had what I was sure was a true vision.

59   Even now what I saw retains an odd clarity: the requisite strange light flooding the room, first orange, and then a bright yellow-green, then a crackling bright burst like a Roman candle going off near the piano. There was a distinct smell of coffee, and a long silence. The room seemed to be getting colder. Nothing. A creak; the light starting to wane, then waxing again, brilliant pink now. Still nothing. Then, as the pink started to go a little purple, a perfectly normal middle-aged man's voice, speaking something very like pig Latin, told me quietly not to despair, not to despair, my beads would be returned to me.

60   That was all. I sat a moment in the dark, then turned on the light, gobbled down the cookies—and in a happy flash understood I was so good, really, so near to being a saint that my malachite beads would come back through the town water system. All I had to do was turn on all the faucets in the house, which I did, one by one, stealing quietly into the bathroom and kitchen and basement. The old spigot by the washing machine was too gunked up to be coaxed very far open, but that didn't matter. The water didn't have to be full blast, I understood that. Then I gathered together my pillow and blanket and trundled up to my bed to sleep.

61   By the time I woke up in the morning I knew that my beads hadn't shown up, but when I knew it for certain, I was still disappointed; and as if that weren't enough, I had to face my parents and sister, who were all abuzz with the mystery of the faucets. Not knowing what else to do, I, like a puddlebrain, told them the truth. The results were predictably painful.

62   "Callie had a *vision*," Mona told everyone at the bus stop. "A vision with lights, and sinks in it!"

63   Sinks, visions. I got it all day, from my parents, from my classmates, even some sixth and seventh graders. Someone drew a cartoon of me with a halo over my head in one of the girls' room stalls; Anthony Rossi made gurgling noises as he walked on his hands at recess. Only Patty tried not to laugh, though even she was something less than unalloyed understanding.

64   "I don' think miracles are thupposed to happen in *thewers*," she said.

65   Such was the end of my saintly ambitions. It wasn't the end of all holiness; the ideas of purity and goodness still tippled my brain, and over the years I came slowly to grasp of what grit true faith was made. Last night, though, when my father called to say that he couldn't go on living in our old house, that he was going to move to a smaller place, another place, maybe a condo—he didn't know how, or where—I found myself still wistful for the time religion seemed all I wanted it to be. Back then the world was a place that could be set right: one had only to direct the hand of the Almighty and say, just here, Lord, we hurt here—and here, and here, and here.

Considering Ideas

1. As a child, how was Jen affected by her religion and Catholic school education?
2. How did Jen's religious attitudes as an adult differ from her attitudes as a child?
3. What view of family life is presented in "The Water-Faucet Vision"?
4. In paragraph 41, Jen says that "learning *was* painful." What did she learn that caused her pain?
5. What does the list of requests on the refrigerator door tell you about the view of God held by the tenants to whom Jen rented her apartment?
6. What do you judge to be the significance of the narration?

Considering Technique

1. Does Jen tell one story or more than one? Explain.
2. Jen uses descriptions of people, scenes, and events in her narration. Cite two examples and explain what the descriptions contribute to the essay.
3. In which paragraph does Jen provide the most information about the significance of the narration?
4. Jen uses a flashback technique (see page 85). What does this technique contribute to the piece?
5. Which paragraphs open with transitions that help the reader follow the time sequence? (See page 85 on transitions.)
6. Consult a dictionary if you are unsure of the meaning of any of these words: *Shanghai* (paragraph 1), *martyr* (paragraph 8), *morbid* (paragraph 8), *malachite* (paragraph 8), *aqueduct* (paragraph 8), *striated* (paragraph 8), *doleful* (paragraph 12), *sacraments* (paragraph 20), *votive* (paragraph 35), *rosary* (paragraph 35), *a capella* (paragraph 51), *prescient* (paragraph 58), *trundled* (paragraph 60), *wistful* (paragraph 65).

For Group Consideration

In her last paragraph, Jen says that she came "to grasp of what grit true faith was made." Decide what you think Jen's statement means and then give some examples of the "grit" of true faith.

Journal Entry

Religious belief is an important part of Jen's life. Explain what role religious belief plays in your life and whether that role has changed over the years.

Essay Assignments

1. Tell a story about a time when your parents or other caregivers had a fight that you overheard. Use conversation to provide some or all of what was said. If you like, explain how the argument affected you.
2. Tell a story about a time you lost something important to you, as when Jen lost her malachite beads. Tell how you lost the item and what happened afterwards. Also, be sure to explain why the item was important to you.
3. The children in "The Water-Faucet Vision" learn that parents are far from perfect. Tell a story about a time you learned a parent or some other adult important to you was not perfect. As an alternative, tell about a time when a parent or other adult disappointed you.
4. Tell a story about some religious experience you had or about a time you lost or redefined your faith in something. As an alternative, tell about a time when you became disillusioned with someone or something.

Considering Thematic Issues

1. Some would say that Jen's youthful view of religion and God matured after her vision. Explain the differences between Jen's youthful and mature views. Then go on to explain whether her youthful views are better suited to a child and whether her mature views are better suited to an adult.
2. As we mature, changes occur in our thinking, in our emotions, in our relationships, and in our circumstances. Often this change means that we gain something but lose something else. For example, when Jen lost her belief in a God who finds beads, she gained an understanding of the true nature of religious faith. Give examples of change as a series of gains and losses using ideas from "The Water-Faucet Vision," your own experience and observation, and one or both of the following essays: "Two Views of the Mississippi" (page 232) and "The View from 80" (page 370).

Additional Essay Assignments

1. Narrate an account of an event that caused you to change your view of someone or something.
2. Narrate an account of an embarrassing moment suffered by you or someone you know. If you wish, make the narration humorous.
3. Narrate an account of a childhood memory. If possible, include description and conversation.
4. Tell the story of a time when things did not go as you expected them to. Be sure to indicate the significance of the narration.
5. Tell the story of an event that marked a turning point in your life. Be sure to indicate how you were affected by this event.
6. Narrate an account of your best birthday or holiday celebration. Try to include conversation and description.
7. Tell the story of a time when you displayed or witnessed courage.
8. Tell the story of an athletic event in which you were involved. Be sure to indicate the significance of the narration.
9. Tell the story of a disappointment experienced by someone you know. Be sure to indicate the significance of the narration.
10. Narrate an account of a first-time experience: the first time you drove a car, a first kiss, your first day of college, your first job, your first time away from home, and so on. Indicate the effect this experience had on you. If you want, you can make the narration humorous.
11. Tell a story that shows that people can be cruel (or kind).
12. Tell a story that shows that ignorance is bliss.
13. Tell the story of a time that you or someone you know overcame an obstacle. Be sure to indicate the significance of the narration.
14. Tell the story of a time when hard work did (or did not) pay off.
15. Tell a story to persuade your reader that the public school system is in better shape than many people think it is.
16. Tell a story that reveals a personality trait of someone. For example, if you have a friend who is reckless, tell a story that illustrates that recklessness. Try to use description and conversation.
17. Tell a story that shows that things are not always what they seem.
18. Tell a story that shows that some modern device (the car, the VCR, the computer, the microwave, for example) is more trouble than it is worth. If you like, you can make the narration humorous.
19. Tell a story that shows we should be careful of what we wish for because we may get it.
20. Narrate an account of a difficult decision that you had to make. Be sure to indicate the effect the decision had on you.

C H A P T E R

6

EXEMPLIFICATION

The Purpose of Exemplification
Supporting Details
Selecting and Ordering Details
Suggestions for Writing Exemplification
Annotated Student Essay: A Man's Game

"Why" Is Worse than "What"—George E. Condon *(exemplification to entertain)*
Class Acts—John Berendt *(exemplification to inform)*
On Holidays and How to Make Them Work—Nikki Giovanni *(exemplification to persuade)*
University Days—James Thurber *(exemplification to entertain and inform)*
* *What I've Learned from Men: Lessons for a Full-Grown Feminist*—Barbara Ehrenreich *(exemplification to inform and persuade)*
* *Untouchables*—Jonathan Kozol *(exemplification to inform and persuade)*

Additional Essay Assignments

* To fulfill the author's purpose, exemplification is combined with one or more other patterns.

How many times have you said, "Can you give me an example?" Like most of us, you probably ask for examples often—and for good reason, because nothing clarifies better. Usually, examples clarify by making the general more specific or by showing that something is true. To understand how examples work to clarify, consider this statement:

Living in a high-tech society has its drawbacks.

To clarify that general statement, examples can be added for specificity, like this:

Living in a high-tech society has its drawbacks. For example, our devices have become so complicated that many people can no longer operate them. I don't know anyone who can program a VCR or figure out how to get the message light to stop blinking on an answering machine after a power outage.

Now consider this statement:

There's a great deal to do in Las Vegas besides gamble.

To clarify the statement, examples can be added to show that the statement is true, like this:

There's a great deal to do in Las Vegas besides gamble. On my last trip, I visited Hoover Dam, which was an exciting excursion. In the past, I have also experienced the beauty of the desert, visited the Ethel M chocolate factory, enjoyed a cactus garden, seen the Liberace Museum, gone to a huge water park, and played golf on championship courses.

Because examples are so important for clarification, writers rely on them all the time, even when they use other patterns of development. Thus, you are likely to see examples in essays developed largely with description, narration, cause-and-effect analysis, process analysis, and any other pattern or combination of patterns.

 ## THE PURPOSE OF EXEMPLIFICATION

In addition to forming part of an essay developed with any pattern of development or combination of patterns, exemplification can form the primary pattern of development to help the writer entertain, share, inform, and/or persuade. For instance, humorous examples of why things happen in "'Why' Is Worse than 'What'" (page 135) allow George Condon to *entertain* his audience. An example taken from personal experience allows Barbara Ehrenreich to *share* a difficult moment of sexual harassment in "What I've Learned from Men" (page 153). Examples can also help a writer *inform* the reader. For instance, in "Class Acts" (page 139) Berendt provides examples to help the reader understand what a "class act" is. Finally, examples can *persuade*. This is the case in "On Holidays and How to Make Them Work" (page 143), in which Nikki Giovanni lets examples of how poorly Americans celebrate holidays prove that we really do not celebrate very well.

 ## SUPPORTING DETAILS

Sometimes an example is a simple explanation. For example, John Berendt makes this statement in "Class Acts":

> By "class act," I mean any behavior so virtuous that it puts normal behavior to shame.

His clarifying example, which follows the statement, is a simple explanation:

> By "class act," I mean any behavior so virtuous that it puts normal behavior to shame. It was a class act, for instance, when Alexander Hamilton aimed high and fired over Aaron Burr's head.

An example can also take the form of a narration (a story). In "Untouchables" (page 159), Jonathan Kozol tells the story of how relatively secure Richard Lazarus became homeless. This story illustrates that even middle-class people can suffer reversals that lead to the loss of their homes.

Sometimes examples take the form of description. Let's say that you wanted to show that people do not really care about cleaning up the planet. As an example, you could describe the litter and pollution in a public park near your home.

Examples can be both brief and extended. In general, the longer each example is, the fewer you need. For instance, in "'Why' Is Worse than 'What'" George Condon provides only two examples, but each is well detailed. In "Class Acts," on the other hand, many examples are given, but no single example is of substantial length. Sometimes, too, writers combine highly detailed and less-detailed examples. The important thing is not how many examples you provide; it is that you provide enough examples in enough detail to clarify adequately and make your point.

 ## SELECTING AND ORDERING DETAILS

Examples can come from a variety of sources: personal experience, observation, general knowledge, and reading or research. In "Untouchables" Jonathan Kozol's examples come from research—he interviewed many homeless people to get his information. In "University Days" (page 146) James Thurber notes the absurdity of college life with examples taken from his personal experiences at Ohio State University. In "Class Acts" John Berendt's knowledge of history is the source of his example about Alexander Hamilton. If you wanted to illustrate that people behave badly at football games, you could provide examples of poor behavior that you have observed.

In an exemplification essay, the thesis should embody the generalization that your examples will clarify. For example, in "Class Acts" John Berendt writes this thesis:

> By "class act," I mean any behavior so virtuous that it puts normal behavior to shame.

The rest of the essay provides examples of virtuous behaviors that qualify as class acts.

For clarity you can introduce your examples with topic sentences. In " 'Why' Is Worse than 'What,' " for instance, George Condon introduces an example with this topic sentence:

> Take the experience of the couple from Lorain [Ohio] who bought a house trailer and went on a vacation trip to Florida.

Following this topic sentence, Condon tells the story of the couple, a story that serves as an example.

To provide smooth movement into an example, two transitions are helpful: "for example" and "for instance." Notice how smoothly the example is introduced with the help of the transition:

> When I know I must make a good impression, I become so nervous that I make a terrible impression instead. *For example*, when I first met my future mother-in-law I was so tense that I spilled coffee on her lap.

Another helpful transition is *such as*. However, avoid opening sentences with this transition, or you will create a problem called a *sentence fragment*. Although a sentence fragment has a period and a capital letter, it is not a sentence and should not be punctuated as such.

no: Exercise has many benefits. *Such as* improved cardiovascular fitness, reduction of stress, and increased muscle mass.

yes: Exercise has many benefits, *such as* improved cardiovascular fitness, reduction of stress, and increased muscle mass.

Sometimes it does not matter in what order you arrange your examples, but more often the order should be carefully considered. For a *progressive order*, arrange your examples from the least to the most compelling. Or place your two strongest examples first and last, with the less telling ones in between. Progressive order is particularly effective for a persuasive purpose because it provides a strong final impression with the most telling example.

Sometimes *chronological* (or time) *order* makes sense. If you want to illustrate the fact that registration is a problem at your school, for instance, you could give examples in the order they occur in the registration process.

On occasion, a spatial order is also possible. If, for instance, you want to show that your campus was not designed with the physically disabled in mind, you could move across space (maybe north to south), giving examples of structural barriers.

SUGGESTIONS FOR WRITING EXEMPLIFICATION

1. If you have trouble finding a generalization to clarify with examples, fill in the blanks in one of these sentences:

   _____ is the best (worst) _____ I know.

   _____ is the most (least) _____ I know.

   You may end up with generalizations like these:

   Lee is the wackiest person I know.

   Television advertising is the most manipulative form of communication I know.

   Nurses are the least appreciated professionals I know.

   These sentences provide generalizations you can clarify with examples: you can give examples of Lee's wacky behavior, examples of manipulative television ads, and examples of ways nurses are underappreciated.
2. Decide early on whether you want to share, inform, entertain, and/or persuade your reader, because your purpose will influence the examples you use.
3. To generate examples for supporting details, you can ask yourself these questions:
   a. What have I experienced that illustrates my generalization?
   b. What have I observed that illustrates my generalization?
   c. What have I read that illustrates my generalization?
   d. What have I learned in school that illustrates my generalization?
   e. What stories can I tell to illustrate my generalization?
   f. What can I describe to illustrate my generalization?
4. List all the examples you will use and number them in the order you will present them.
5. Write your draft using your numbered list as a scratch outline. Do not worry about polished prose now. Just get your ideas down any way you can; you can refine later.

6. When you revise, consider the following:
   a. Do I have a thesis that presents the generalization I am clarifying?
   b. Do I need topic sentences to present my examples?
   c. Do I have enough examples in enough detail to clarify my generalization to my reader's satisfaction?
   d. Are my examples arranged in a logical order?

 ## ANNOTATED STUDENT ESSAY

In the following piece, the student author uses exemplification to persuade the reader that female athletes can be as tough as male athletes. To make his point, the student draws on examples taken from his own experience.

A MAN'S GAME

Paragraph 1
The introduction is an anecdote that arouses interest. The thesis (the last sentence) presents the generalization to be proven and indicates that examples will come from experience.

1   A tall blonde wearing purple gym shorts and a Youngstown State sweatshirt nervously stands in the corner of the volleyball court. The score is twenty to sixteen, and her team is behind two games to one. She already has one fault, and if they lose the serve, they will surely lose the game. She hits the ball, but it does not get enough height and crashes into the net. An angry voice from the crowd yells, "That's what you get when you let a woman play a man's game." All too often I have heard thoughtless fans criticize quality women players because of their sex. In my experience with coeducational sports, I have found that, pound for pound, women are just as tough as men.

Paragraph 2
This paragraph gives the first example to support the generalization. The example comes from personal experience. The first two sentences introduce the example.

2   I can remember when I was younger and played football in the sandlot next to my house. The only thing unusual about the games was that one of our players was named Sally, and happened to be a girl. Sally was no more a tomboy than any of the other girls in the neighborhood and really only played to escape boredom. She relied on her quickness and agility instead of trying to use brute force, which proved that she was more intelligent than the rest of us. I can remember the other teams laughing at her until she streaked by them for a touchdown; then it was her turn to laugh. Sally proved that she was as good an athlete as any of us.

Paragraph 3
This paragraph presents the second example from personal experience. Specific words keep the example lively.

3   Last summer I further learned how formidable a female opponent can be. I was playing tennis with my sister-in-law, who happens to be ten years older than I am. After a relaxed volley, we played a set in earnest. Her first serve was a bomb to my backhand. She aced me. Every shot she made was a powerhouse. Left, right, net, baseline—she ran me ragged and beat me handily, 6-2. Frankly, I think she gave me two games to salvage my male ego.

Paragraph 4
The topic sentence introduces an extended example, which is a narration. "Another example" acts as a transition.

Examples are in chronological order.

4   Another example of women athletes performing well is still fresh in my mind because it happened this winter. I was captain of an intramural volleyball team and we needed some practice, so we were looking for a team to scrimmage. After about a week, a friend found a team that was willing to play us. The name of the team was the Bruisers, so we were expecting a mean game. However, when we entered the gym, we saw six cute girls practicing serves and doing warmups. They were wearing black and blue shirts with the name "Bruisers" printed across the chest, and we thought for sure someone was playing a joke on us. When we told them we thought it was a joke, they became furious and said that by the end of the game, an ambulance would have to carry us away. Laughingly, we accepted the challenge. I told the guys to take it easy on them because they were only girls. What a mistake! By the end of the game, we were fighting for our lives. When the final bell sounded, they had beaten us three games to two. The most embarrassing play of the game occurred when Lisa showed me just how tough she was. The ball was just above the net, and we both went for it; before I knew what was happening, the ball bounced off my face and sent me reeling to the ground. Even though my nose felt broken, my ego was damaged more.

Paragraph 5
The conclusion reaffirms author's position.

5   Ever since that day I have never underestimated a female opponent. Playing with and against females has taught me to admire and respect them. The idea of women as the weaker sex is a figment of some man's imagination.

"WHY" IS WORSE THAN "WHAT"
George E. Condon

◆

We all have our embarrassing moments,
but as George E. Condon points out in this entertaining piece, the causes of these
moments can be stranger than the moments themselves. As you read this 1975
article from the Cleveland, Ohio, Plain Dealer, *notice the specific word choice.*

◆

1   To quote one of the comforting clichés that puzzled people have been falling back on for many, many years, "There's an explanation for everything." Truer aphorism was never circulated. It is also true that sometimes the explanation is just as incredible as the actual happening.

2   Take the experience of the couple from Lorain [Ohio] who bought a house trailer and went on a vacation trip to Florida. All went well until the return trip home. The husband grew weary after many hours at the wheel and finally abdicated the driver's seat in favor of his wife, while he went back to the trailer and feel asleep.

3   It was a nervous sleep, to be sure. He had never before trusted his wife at the wheel, and he was naturally uneasy over the risks involved. When the vehicle suddenly came to an abrupt screeching stop, he immediately assumed the worst and leaped out the back of the house trailer to see what had gone wrong.

4   All that had happened, actually, was that a traffic signal suddenly had turned red and the wife had found it necessary to slam on the brake. By the time the husband, dressed only in his underwear, made his exit to the street and in his slow, sleep-fogged way sized up the situation, the light had turned green and the wife blithely drove away, leaving him in the middle of the intersection in his underdrawers. That's where a police cruiser came upon him a few minutes later.

5   "I can explain it all, officer!" said the husband to the policeman as his shivering shanks were hustled into the cop car. No doubt he did, in time, but the explanation could not possibly have been an easy one.

6   Which brings us around to a related dilemma that faced a woman in Clearwater, Fla., a few weeks ago when she drove her new luxury car with less than 1,000 miles on it to Sarasota, not far away.

7   Sarasota is the permanent home of the Ringling Circus, of course, and she parked her car in a lot near circus headquarters while she visited an art show. When she returned to her car it immediately occurred to her that there was something different about her new automobile. The roof, so to speak, had caved in.

8   But the mystery was quickly cleared up by a man who had come upon the scene.

9   "This your car, lady? Ah, you're probably wondering what happened to the old buggy to flatten it that way, eh? Well, you see, we were moving some elephants through the lot and one of them decided to sit down."

10   On top of her car, of course.

11   But the representative of the parking lot hastened to assure her that the Ringling people would repair the car. He noted that while the car looked rather bad, most of the damage was in the rear and it could be driven. He gave her instructions on the repair procedure to follow and she got in the battered new car and swung it towards its Clearwater home.

12   On the way, however, a bad traffic accident caused considerable congestion at an intersection, and the woman decided on a short cut through a shopping center's parking lot. She was making this shrewd move when a police car cornered her and an officer leaped out and approached.

13   "Why are you leaving the scene of that accident?" he demanded to know.

14   "I'm not trying to leave an accident," she replied. "I'm trying to drive around one."

15   The policeman nodded. He was a reasonable man.

16   "Uh-huh," he said agreeably, "then you wouldn't mind telling me how that car of yours got smashed flat, would you?"

17   Now, then, all she had to do was tell the copper that an elephant had come by and sat on her car. A simple enough explanation, surely, but one that would take a bit of telling. "It was this way, officer. You see, an elephant came along and . . ."

18   There's an explanation for everything, it's true, but some explanations are more readily acceptable than others. That's the way it is.

Considering Ideas

1. Condon wrote "'Why' Is Worse than 'What'" for a large daily newspaper. Do you think his examples are well suited to his audience? Explain.
2. Do you find Condon's examples amusing? Why or why not?
3. Can you relate to one of the examples more than the other? Explain why or why not.
4. Explain the meaning of the title.
5. Why do you think that newspapers include lighthearted pieces like Condon's?

Considering Technique

1. Which sentence is the thesis, because it presents a generalization that the author will clarify with examples?
2. Condon uses topic sentences to introduce his examples. What are those topic sentences?
3. What method of development does the author use for his examples?

4. Why do you think the author presents his examples in the order that he does?
5. What approach does the author take to his introduction? To his conclusion? Why do you think his introduction and conclusion are so brief?
6. Consult a dictionary if you are unsure of the meaning of any of these words: *aphorism* (paragraph 1), *abdicated* (paragraph 2), *blithely* (paragraph 4), *shanks* (paragraph 5).

For Group Consideration

Much of the interest and liveliness of "'Why' Is Worse than 'What'" comes from Condon's use of specific word choice. With two or three classmates reread the essay and identify examples of specific nouns, verbs, and modifiers. (See page 44 if you need to review specific word choice.)

Journal Entry

In a page or two of your journal, write about your most embarrassing moment. Tell what happened and how you reacted.

Essay Assignments

1. Condon's examples, especially the first one, point out life's embarrassing moments. To entertain and/or to share with your reader, use examples to show that we all have our own embarrassing moments. You can limit yourself to embarrassments you have experienced, or you can include embarrassments others have suffered. Your journal entry may help you with this assignment.
2. Both of Condon's examples focus on problems people experience with their vehicles. Write an essay that illustrates the problems a car or some other modern convenience can cause. Your purpose can be to share, inform, and/or entertain.
3. Write your own lighthearted piece suitable for a newspaper, one that uses examples to illustrate the absurdity of life.

Considering Thematic Issues

1. "'Why' Is Worse than 'What'" calls attention to the fact that unexpected events can cause problems. Although Condon's essay is humorous, the unexpected can also have serious consequences. Tell about a time you were surprised by the unexpected. Tell what happened, how you reacted, and how you were affected.

2. Condon points to the absurdities caused by cars and travel. Examine your own experience and that of your classmates to discover some absurdities related to college life. You can also draw on "University Days" (page 146) and "College Pressures" (page 323) for ideas. Your purpose can be to entertain or to inform your reader about what college students must put up with.

CLASS ACTS
John Berendt

◆

You probably know what a "class act" is, but if asked to define it, could you? In the next essay, which originally appeared in Esquire, *John Berendt lends an informative hand with examples that help clarify the term. As you read, notice that Berendt writes an opening paragraph that serves two purposes.*

◆

1   One day in 1957, the songwriter Johnny Mercer received a letter from Sadie Vimmerstedt, a widowed grandmother who worked behind a cosmetics counter in Youngstown, Ohio. Mrs. Vimmerstedt suggested Mercer write a song called "I Want to Be Around to Pick Up the Pieces When Somebody Breaks Your Heart." Five years later, Mercer got in touch to say he'd written the song and that Tony Bennett would record it. Today, if you look at the label on any recording of "I Wanna Be Around," you'll notice that the credits for words and music are shared by Johnny Mercer and Sadie Vimmerstedt. The royalties were split fifty-fifty, too, thanks to which Mrs. Vimmerstedt and her heirs have earned more than $100,000. In my opinion, Mercer's generosity was a class act.

2   By *class act*, I mean any behavior that is virtuous beyond the call of duty and that puts normal behavior to shame. It was a class act, for instance, when Alexander Hamilton intentionally aimed high and fired over Aaron Burr's head. Benjamin Guggenheim performed a class act on the *Titanic* when he gave his life jacket to a lady passenger and then put on white tie and tails so he could die "like a gentleman." That same year, 1912, Captain Lawrence Oates became frostbitten and lame on Scott's ill-fated expedition to the South Pole; rather than delay the others, he went to the opening of the tent one night and said, "I am just going outside and may be some time." He thereupon walked to his death in a blizzard. Certainly a class act.

3   It was a class act of a different order, but a class act nonetheless, for the writer Laurence Housman (brother of the poet A. E.) to take off his jacket at a proper English tea party so that a man who had just arrived in shirt-sleeves would not feel embarrassed at being underdressed. And it was likewise a class act for King Christian X of Denmark to wear a yellow armband in a show of solidarity with Danish Jews during the Nazi occupation.

4   In politics, class acts do happen, though not very often. I count Ben Bagert's withdrawal from last fall's four-way U.S. Senate race in Louisiana as a class act. Bagert was the Republican who bowed out in order to ensure that David Duke, a former grand wizard of the Ku Klux Klan, would not win and defile the Senate with his presence. You could argue that Bagert never had a chance of winning anyhow and that anyone in his position would have done the same thing but you'd be wrong. I cite as proof the 1980 Senate race in New

York, in which Jacob Javits, having lost the Republican nomination, ran on the Liberal Party line and refused to drop out so that Elizabeth Holtzman could beat the repugnant Alfonse D'Amato. Javits took 11 percent of the vote, which was enough to install D'Amato in the Senate, where he remains to this day, a living memorial to Javit's devotion to himself over principle, party, and country.

5   Simple good sportsmanship can rise to the level of class act, as it did when tennis player Mats Wilander won the 1982 French Open. At match point in the semifinals, the umpire ruled that a shot by Wilander's opponent was out. Wilander walked over to the umpire and said, "I can't win like this. The ball was good." The point was played over, and Wilander won fair and square. (Compare that with the insufferable bellyaching of John McEnroe.) Of course, the concept of good sportsmanship does change over time. In 1940, Cornell conceded a football game to Dartmouth when films showed that Cornell's game-ending, game-winning touchdown had been made on a fifth down. When the very same thing happened last fall between Colorado and Missouri, not only did Colorado *not* offer to forfeit the win, its coach was singularly ungracious in refusing.

6   On the stage, the tradition that the show must go on has produced a number of class acts. Katharine Hepburn, Orson Welles, and Carol Channing have all performed in wheelchairs. During the run of *The King and I*, Gertrude Lawrence was dying of cancer but told no one. When she missed a series of performances, the producers wrote her lawyers, suggesting she was faking illness. They warned that if this continued, she would forfeit her share of the profits. The letter arrived on a Monday; Gertrude Lawrence had died over the weekend.

7   But heartless producers and all the others who do not measure up deserve to be forgiven. Forgiveness is, after all, a class act in its own right. Which brings to mind Queen Elizabeth I and an incident recorded by John Aubrey, the seventeenth-century historian. According to Aubrey, the Earl of Oxford approached the queen one day and made a deep bow during which he "happened to let a fart." The man was so ashamed he fled the country and traveled for seven years. Upon his return, Queen Elizabeth welcomed him home with the words, "My lord, I have forgot the fart."

Considering Ideas

1. Why does Berendt consider Johnny Mercer's royalty arrangement with Sadie Vimmerstedt a "class act"?
2. Of the class acts referred to in the essay, which do you think are the "classiest"? Why?
3. Write your own one- or two-sentence definition of "class act," one that applies to all the examples in the essay.
4. Why does Berendt call Housman's action (paragraph 3) a class act "of a different order"?

5. Do you think that Colorado should have forfeited its win when it was discovered that its game-winning touchdown had been made on a fifth down? Why or why not?

Considering Technique

1. Which sentence serves as Berendt's thesis? That is, which sentence includes the generalization that the author will clarify?
2. Berendt's opening paragraph is his introduction. In addition to stimulating reader interest, this paragraph serves another function. What is that function?
3. Which of Berendt's examples take the form of narration?
4. Which paragraphs have a topic sentence to introduce an example?
5. Do the examples clarify a generalization by showing that something is true, by making the general more specific, or both?
6. "Class Acts" lacks a formal conclusion; instead, it ends with the last example. Do you find the lack of a conclusion to be a problem? Why or why not?
7. What is the source of Berendt's examples?
8. Consult a dictionary if you are unsure of the meaning of any of these words: *Titanic* (paragraph 2), *solidarity* (paragraph 3), *defile* (paragraph 4), *repugnant* (paragraph 4), *insufferable* (paragraph 5), *bellyaching* (paragraph 5).

For Group Consideration

"Class Acts" lacks a formal conclusion. With two or three classmates, draft a suitable conclusion. Then assume you are the members of a magazine editorial board and decide whether the essay should be published with the addition of your conclusion or in its original form.

Journal Entry

Many athletes would say that Mats Wilander's refusal to accept the line judge's call was stupid because good breaks and bad breaks are a part of competition, and both should be accepted. In particular, good breaks—like the one Wilander refused—compensate for the bad breaks every competitor experiences along the way. What do you think? Should Wilander have refused to take the point? Was his action a "class act" or a foolish act?

Essay Assignments

1. Explain what you think a class act is, using examples from your own experience, observation, and knowledge. Like Berendt, open with a paragraph that will stimulate interest and serve as an example.

2. Explain "tackiness" and illustrate it with examples from your own experience, observation, and knowledge. If possible, open with a paragraph that will stimulate interest and serve as an example.
3. Explain "good sportsmanship" (or "bad sportsmanship") and illustrate its meaning with examples. Try to make at least one of your examples a narration.
4. Use examples to explain an ethnic term you are familiar with (for example, *chutzpah* or *gringo*). Your purpose is to inform readers who may not be familiar with the term.

Considering Thematic Issues

1. Do the values apparent in middle-class American society encourage or discourage the performance of class acts? Consider the business world, our education system, the sports arena, and/or the media when you respond. What, if anything, do you think we can do to encourage more class acts?
2. Read "White Lies" (page 313), then explain whether or not telling a white lie can ever be a class act. Be sure to explain why you believe as you do. You can use your own experience and observation as well as the information in the essays to support your view.

ON HOLIDAYS AND HOW TO MAKE
THEM WORK
Nikki Giovanni

◆

Nikki Giovanni, one of the most widely read African-American poets and essayists, was named Woman of the Year by Ebony *magazine. In "On Holidays and How to Make Them Work," Giovanni has a persuasive purpose. Written at the time of the first Martin Luther King Day observance, the essay argues that Americans do not know the appropriate way to celebrate their holidays. As a result, King's day could become as commercial and meaningless as other U.S. holidays. As you read, try to determine why Giovanni takes exception to these celebrations.*

◆

1   A proper holiday, coming from the medieval "holy day," is supposed to be a time of reflection on great men, great deeds, great people. Things like that. Somehow in America this didn't quite catch on. Take Labor Day. On Labor Day you take the day off, then go to the Labor Day sales and spend your devalued money with a clerk who is working. And organized labor doesn't understand why it suffers declining membership? Pshaw. Who wants to join an organization that makes you work on the day it designates as a day off? Plus, no matter how hidden the agenda, who wants a day off if they make you march in a parade and listen to some politicians talk on and on about nothing.

2   Hey. I'm a laborer. I used to work in Walgreen's on Linn Street. We were open every holiday and I, being among the junior people, always "got" to work the time-and-a-half holidays. I hated those people who came in. Every fool in the Western world, and probably in this universe, knows that Christmas is December 25. Has been that way for over a thousand years, yet there they'd be, standing outside the door, cold, bleary-eyed, waiting for us to open so they could purchase a present. Memorial Day, which used to be Armistice Day until we got into this situation of continuous war, was the official start of summer. We would want to be out with our boyfriends barbecuing . . . or something, but there we were behind the counter waiting to see who forgot that in order to barbecue you need: (1) a grill, (2) charcoal, (3) charcoal starter. My heart goes out to the twenty-four-hour grocery people, who are probably selling meat!

3   But hey. It's the American way. The big Fourth of July sales probably reduced the number of fatal injuries as people spent the entire day sober in malls, fighting over markdowns. Minor cuts and bruises were way up, though, I'll bet. And forget the great nonholiday, Presidents' Day. The damned thing could at least have a real name. What does that mean—Presidents' Day? Mostly that we don't care enough to take the time to say to Washington and Lincoln: Well done. But for sure, as a Black American I've got to go for it. Martin Luther King, Jr.'s birthday has come up for the first time as a national holiday. If we are

serious about celebrating it, Steinberg's will be our first indication: GHETTO BLASTERS 30% OFF! FREE TAPE OF "I HAVE A DREAM" WITH EVERY VCR PURCHASED AT THE ALL-NEW GIGANTIC MARTY'S BIRTHDAY SALE. Then Wendy's will, just maybe, for Black patrons (and their liberal sympathizers) Burn-A-Burger to celebrate the special day. Procter & Gamble will withhold Clorox for the day, respectfully requesting that those Black spots be examined for their liberating influence. But what we really want, where we can know we have succeeded, is that every Federated department store offers 50 percent off to every colored patron who can prove he or she is Black in recognition of the days when colored citizens who were Black were not accorded all the privileges of other shoppers. That will be a big help because everybody will want to be Black for a Day. Sun tanneries will make fortunes during the week preceding MLK Day. Wig salons will reap great benefits. Dentists will have to hire extra help to put that distinctive gap between the middle front teeth. MLK Day will be accepted. And isn't that the heart of the American dream?

4   I really love a good holiday—it takes the people off the streets and puts them safely in the shopping malls. Now think about it. Aren't you proud to be with Uncle Sam?

Considering Ideas

1. What is Giovanni's chief objection to the way Americans celebrate holidays?
2. What is the significance of the title of the essay? Explain the wordplay in the title.
3. Giovanni's description of potential Martin Luther King Day celebrations is the most extensive and the most satiric example in the essay. Why do you think that this is so?
4. Do you think that Giovanni expects to change the way Americans celebrate holidays? If not, what is her goal?

Considering Technique

1. Which paragraph contains Giovanni's thesis idea? That is, which paragraph includes the generalization that the author will clarify? In your own words, write a sentence that expresses this thesis/generalization.
2. Do Giovanni's examples clarify by showing that something is true, by making the general specific, or both?
3. What examples does Giovanni provide to clarify her generalization? Are these examples brief or extended?
4. What is the source of Giovanni's examples?
5. What approach does Giovanni take to her conclusion?
6. Consult a dictionary if you are unsure of the meaning of this word: *pshaw* (paragraph 1).

For Group Consideration

With two or three classmates, choose a holiday celebrated in this country (Martin Luther King Day, Memorial Day, Labor Day, Thanksgiving, Presidents' Day) and decide how the holiday should be celebrated. How different is that from the way the holiday actually *is* celebrated?

Journal Entry

In paragraph 3, Giovanni mentions the *American dream* and the *American way*. Reread that paragraph; then write a page or two that explains what you think Giovanni means by one of these terms. Provide your own explanation of the same term if your meaning differs from Giovanni's.

Essay Assignments

1. Select a holiday observed in the United States and provide your own examples to explain to the reader why you think it is celebrated in an inappropriate fashion.
2. Use examples to show how a particular holiday should be celebrated so that it is, according to Giovanni, "a time of reflection on great men, great deeds, great people" (paragraph 1). (The preceding group activity may give you ideas for this essay.)
3. To share with your reader, provide examples to show how a particular holiday is celebrated in your family.
4. If you have ever worked on a holiday, write a generalization to describe what it was like. Then provide examples to clarify the generalization.

Considering Thematic Issues

1. If you agree with Nikki Giovanni that Americans do not know how to celebrate their holidays, explain why you think Americans have this problem and what the effects of it are. If you disagree with Giovanni, argue that there is nothing wrong with the way Americans celebrate their holidays.
2. Read "The Ways of Meeting Oppression" (page 332), "Shades of Black" (page 336), and "Just Walk on By" (page 285), then describe the activities that you think should take place in schools to observe Martin Luther King Day.

UNIVERSITY DAYS
James Thurber

◆

The American humorist James Thurber (1894–1961) wrote essays and cartoons for the New Yorker. *He also wrote several humorous books, including* My Life and Hard Times, *from which "University Days" is taken. In this essay, which includes five extended examples of the absurdity and frustration of college life during the era of World War I, Thurber entertains his reader. Although his examples are exaggerated, ask yourself if they point to truths still in evidence today.*

◆

1   I passed all the other courses that I took at my university, but I could never pass botany. This was because all botany students had to spend several hours a week in a laboratory looking through a microscope at plant cells, and I could never see through a microscope. I never once saw a cell through a microscope. This used to enrage my instructor. He would wander around the laboratory pleased with the progress all the students were making in drawing the involved and, so I am told, interesting structure of flower cells, until he came to me. I would just be standing there. "I can't see anything," I would say. He would begin patiently enough, explaining how anybody can see through a microscope, but he would always end up in a fury, claiming that I could *too* see through a microscope but just pretended that I couldn't. "It takes away from the beauty of flowers anyway," I used to tell him. "We are not concerned with beauty in this course," he would say. "We are concerned solely with what I may call the *mechanics* of flars." "Well," I'd say, "I can't see anything." "Try it just once again," he'd say, and I would put my eye to the microscope and see nothing at all, except now and again a nebulous milky substance—a phenomenon of maladjustment. You were supposed to see a vivid, restless clockwork of sharply defined plant cells. "I see what looks like a lot of milk," I would tell him. This, he claimed, was the result of my not having adjusted the microscope properly, so he would readjust it for me, or rather, for himself. And I would look again and see milk.

2   I finally took a deferred pass, as they called it, and waited a year and tried again. (You had to pass one of the biological sciences or you couldn't graduate.) The professor had come back from vacation brown as a berry, bright-eyed, and eager to explain cell-structure again to his classes. "Well," he said to me, cheerily, when we met in the first laboratory hour of the semester, "we're going to see cells this time, aren't we?" "Yes, sir," I said. Students to right of me and to left of me and in front of me were seeing cells; what's more, they were quietly drawing pictures of them in their notebooks. Of course, I didn't see anything.

3   "We'll try it," the professor said to me, grimly, "with every adjustment of the microscope known to man. As God is my witness, I'll arrange this glass so

that you see cells through it or I'll give up teaching. In twenty-two years of botany, I—" He cut off abruptly for he was beginning to quiver all over, like Lionel Barrymore, and he genuinely wished to hold onto his temper: his scenes with me had taken a great deal out of him.

4   So we tried it with every adjustment of the microscope known to man. With only one of them did I see anything but blackness or the familiar lacteal opacity, and that time I saw, to my pleasure and amazement, a variegated constellation of flecks, specks, and dots. These I hastily drew. The instructor, noting my activity, came back from an adjoining desk, a smile on his lips and his eyebrows high in hope. He looked at my cell drawing. "What's that?" he demanded, with a hint of a squeal in his voice. "That's what I saw," I said. "You didn't, you didn't, you *didn't!*" he screamed, losing control of his temper instantly, and he bent over and squinted into the microscope. His head snapped up. "That's your eye!" he shouted. "You've fixed the lens so that it reflects! You've drawn your eye!"

5   Another course that I didn't like, but somehow managed to pass, was economics. I went to that class straight from the botany class, which didn't help me any in understanding either subject. I used to get them mixed up. But not as mixed up as another student in my economics class who came there direct from a physics laboratory. He was a tackle on the football team, named Bolencie-cwcz. At that time Ohio State University had one of the best football teams in the country, and Bolenciecwcz was one of its outstanding stars. In order to be eligible to play it was necessary for him to keep up in his studies, a very difficult matter, for while he was not dumber than an ox he was not any smarter. Most of his professors were lenient and helped him along. None gave him more hints in answering questions or asked him simpler ones than the economics professor, a thin, timid man named Bassum. One day when we were on the subject of transportation and distribution, it came Bolenciecwcz's turn to answer a question. "Name one means of transportation," the professor said to him. No light came into the big tackle's eyes. "Just any means of transportation," said the professor. Bolenciecwcz sat staring at him. "That is," pursued the professor, "any medium, agency, or method of going from one place to another." Bolen-ciecwcz had the look of a man who is being led into a trap. "You may choose among steam, horse-drawn, or electrically propelled vehicles," said the instruc-tor. "I might suggest the one which we commonly take in making long journeys across land." There was a profound silence in which everybody stirred uneasily, including Bolenciecwcz and Mr. Bassum. Mr. Bassum abruptly broke this silence in an amazing manner. "Choo-choo-choo," he said, in a low voice, and turned instantly scarlet. He glanced appealingly around the room. All of us, of course, shared Mr. Bassum's desire that Bolenciecwcz should stay abreast of the class in economics, for the Illinois game, one of the hardest and most important of the season, was only a week off. "Toot, toot, too-toooooooot!" some student with a deep voice moaned, and we all looked encouragingly at Bolenciecwcz. Somebody else gave a fine imitation of a locomotive letting off steam. Mr.

Bassum himself rounded off the little show. "Ding, dong, ding, dong," he said, hopefully. Bolenciecwcz was staring at the floor now, trying to think, his great brow furrowed, his huge hands rubbing together, his face red.

6   "How did you come to college this year, Mr. Bolenciecwcz?" asked the professor. "*Chuffa* chuffa, *chuffa* chuffa."

7   "M'father sent me," said the football player.

8   "What on?" asked Bassum.

9   "I git an 'lowance," said the tackle, in a low, husky voice, obviously embarrassed.

10   No, no," said Bassum. "Name a means of transportation. What did you *ride* here on?"

11   "Train," said Bolenciecwcz.

12   "Quite right," said the professor. "Now, Mr. Nugent, will you tell us—"

13   If I went through anguish in botany and economics—for different reasons—gymnasium work was even worse. I don't even like to think about it. They wouldn't let you play games or join in the exercises with your glasses on and I couldn't see with mine off. I bumped into professors, horizontal bars, agricultural students, and swinging iron rings. Not being able to see, I could take it but I couldn't dish it out. Also, in order to pass gymnasium (and you had to pass it to graduate) you had to learn to swim if you didn't know how. I didn't like the swimming pool, I didn't like swimming, and I didn't like the swimming instructor, and after all these years I still don't. I never swam but I passed my gym work anyway, by having another student give my gymnasium number (978) and swim across the pool in my place. He was a quiet, amiable blond youth, number 473, and he would have seen through a microscope for me if we could have got away with it, but we couldn't get away with it. Another thing I didn't like about gymnasium work was that they made you strip the day you registered. It is impossible for me to be happy when I am stripped and being asked a lot of questions. Still, I did better than a lanky agricultural student who was cross-examined just before I was. They asked each student what college he was in—that is, whether Arts, Engineering, Commerce, or Agriculture. "What college are you in?" the instructor snapped at the youth in front of me. "Ohio State University," he said promptly.

14   It wasn't that agricultural student but it was another a whole lot like him who decided to take up journalism, possibly on the ground that when farming went to hell he could fall back on newspaper work. He didn't realize, of course, that that would be very much like falling back full-length on a kit of carpenter's tools. Haskins didn't seem cut out for journalism, being too embarrassed to talk to anybody and unable to use a typewriter, but the editor of the college paper assigned him to the cow barns, the sheep house, the horse pavilion, and the animal husbandry department generally. This was a genuinely big "beat," for it took up five times as much ground and got ten times as great a legislative appropriation as the College of Liberal Arts. The agricultural student knew animals, but nevertheless his stories were dull and colorlessly written. He took

all afternoon on each of them, on account of having to hunt for each letter on the typewriter. Once in a while he had to ask somebody to help him hunt. "C" and "L," in particular, were hard letters for him to find. His editor finally got pretty much annoyed at the farmer-journalist because his pieces were so uninteresting. "See here, Haskins," he snapped at him one day, "why is it we never have anything hot from you on the horse pavilion?" Here we have two hundred head of horses on this campus—more than any other university in the Western Conference except Purdue—and yet you never get any real lowdown on them. Now shoot over to the horse barns and dig up something lively." Haskins shambled out and came back in about an hour; he said he had something. "Well, start it off snappily," said the editor. "Something people will read." Haskins set to work and in a couple of hours brought a sheet of typewritten paper to the desk; it was a two-hundred-word story about some disease that had broken out among the horses. Its opening sentence was simple but arresting. It read: "Who has noticed the sores on the tops of the horses in the animal husbandry building?"

15   Ohio State was a land grant university and therefore two years of military drill was compulsory. We drilled with old Springfield rifles and studied the tactics of the Civil War even though the World War was going on at the time. At 11 o'clock each morning thousands of freshmen and sophomores used to deploy over the campus, moodily creeping up on the old chemistry building. It was good training for the kind of warfare that was waged at Shiloh but it had no connection with what was going on in Europe. Some people used to think there was German money behind it, but they didn't dare say so or they would have been thrown in jail as German spies. It was a period of muddy thought and marked, I believe, the decline of higher education in the Middle West.

16   As a soldier I was never any good at all. Most of the cadets were glumly indifferent soldiers, but I was no good at all. Once General Littlefield, who was commandant of the cadet corps, popped up in front of me during regimental drill and snapped, "You are the main trouble with this university!" I think he meant that my type was the main trouble with the university but he may have meant me individually. I was mediocre at drill, certainly—that is, until my senior year. By that time I had drilled longer than anybody else in the Western Conference, having failed at military at the end of each preceding year so that I had to do it all over again. I was the only senior still in uniform. The uniform which, when new, had made me look like an interurban railway conductor, now that it had become faded and too tight made me look like Bert Williams in his bellboy act. This had a definitely bad effect on my morale. Even so, I had become by sheer practice little short of wonderful at squad maneuvers.

17   One day General Littlefield picked our company out of the whole regiment and tried to get it mixed up by putting it through one movement after another as fast as we could execute them: squads right, squads left, squads on right into line, squads right about, squads left front into line, etc. In about three minutes one hundred and nine men were marching in one direction and I was

marching away from them at an angle of forty degrees, all alone. "Company, halt!" shouted General Littlefield. "That man is the only man who has it right!" I was made a corporal for my achievement.

18   The next day General Littlefield summoned me to his office. He was swatting flies when I went in. I was swatting flies when I went in. I was silent and he was silent too, for a long time. I don't think he remembered me or why he had sent for me, but he didn't want to admit it. He swatted some more flies, keeping his eyes on them narrowly before he let go with the swatter. "Button up your coat!" he snapped. Looking back on it now I can see that he meant me although he was looking at a fly, but I just stood there. Another fly came to rest on a paper in front of the general and began rubbing its hind legs together. The general lifted the swatter cautiously. I moved restlessly and the fly flew away. "You startled him!" barked General Littlefield, looking at me severely. I said I was sorry. "That won't help the situation!" snapped the General, with cold military logic. I didn't see what I could do except offer to chase some more flies toward his desk, but I didn't say anything. He stared out the window at the faraway figures of co-eds crossing the campus toward the library. Finally, he told me I could go. So I went. He either didn't know which cadet I was or else he forgot what he wanted to see me about. It may have been that he wished to apologize for having called me the main trouble with the university; or maybe he had decided to compliment me on my brilliant drilling of the day before and then at the last minute decided not to. I don't know. I don't think about it much any more.

Considering Ideas

1. What absurdities and frustrations of college life does Thurber point out with his examples?
2. Note two or three specific passages that you find amusing. Why are these passages funny? If you do not find anything amusing, explain why not.
3. Thurber probably stretches the truth in his examples. Does the fact that the examples are not strictly factual create a problem for you? Explain why or why not.
4. Thurber's essay is about college life during World War I. Is his essay still relevant today? Why or why not?
5. In order to enjoy Thurber's essay, must the reader have attended college? Explain.

Considering Technique

1. Thurber has no stated thesis and, therefore, no specifically stated generalization for his examples to clarify. In your own words, then, write out Thurber's thesis/generalization.

2. Are Thurber's examples brief or extended? What pattern of development is used for the examples?
3. Thurber's examples are introduced with topic sentences. What are those topic sentences?
4. Do you think that Thurber's closing sentence makes a suitable conclusion for the essay? Explain.
5. Cite three examples of specific word choice.
6. How does Thurber use exaggeration?
7. Consult a dictionary if you are unsure of the meaning of any of these words: *nebulous* (paragraph 1), *Lionel Barrymore* (paragraph 3), *lacteal opacity* (paragraph 4), *variegated* (paragraph 4), *land grant university* (paragraph 15).

For Group Consideration

Are the instructors and students in Thurber's examples unfair stereotypes, or are their characters rooted in fact? Discuss this question with two or three classmates and report your findings to the rest of the class.

Journal Entry

In two or three pages, write about your own "university days." You can consider some or all of these questions: What have your chief high and low points been? Who are your best and worst instructors? Your best and worst classes? Who are the best and worst students you know? What frustrations and absurdities have you faced? What joys have you known?

Essay Assignments

1. Use your own examples—extended or brief—to illustrate the frustrations of life on your college campus. (Your journal entry may give you some ideas.)
2. Use examples to illustrate a generalization about your own university days. (Your journal entry may give you some ideas.)
3. Write a generalization about instructors you have had (use fictional names) and illustrate that generalization with two or three extended, narrative examples. If possible, use exaggeration for humorous effect.
4. Use examples to illustrate a generalization about some past experience: membership in the Boy or Girl Scouts, a job, your elementary school days, marching band, religious school, sports, and so on.

Considering Thematic Issues

1. Write an essay that presents and describes the characteristics of higher education as Thurber sees them in "University Days." Then explain which aspects of Thurber's view you agree with and/or which you disagree with, and why.

2. In "College Pressures," (page 323) William Zinsser classifies the causes of pressure on college students. Identify the sources of pressure apparent in "University Days" and note which of Zinsser's groupings they fall into. If they do not fall into any of his groupings, create your own classifications. Also classify any sources of pressure you are familiar with that are not treated in either essay.

WHAT I'VE LEARNED FROM MEN: LESSONS FOR A FULL-GROWN FEMINIST

Barbara Ehrenreich

◆

Barbara Ehrenreich is the author of several books. She has also been a college professor, reporter, magazine editor, and regular contributor to Ms. *and* Mother Jones. *In the following essay, which first appeared in* Ms. *in 1985, Ehrenreich combines several patterns of development with exemplification to inform the reader of a problem she thinks women have: they are too ladylike. Enrenreich goes on to argue that women should become assertive. As you read, notice where in the essay this persuasive purpose becomes apparent.*

◆

1   For many years I believed that women had only one thing to learn from men: how to get the attention of a waiter by some means short of kicking over the table and shrieking. Never in my life have I gotten the attention of a waiter, unless it was an off-duty waiter whose car I'd accidentally scraped in a parking lot somewhere. Men, however, can summon a maître d' just by thinking the word "coffee," and this is a power women would be well-advised to study. What else would we possibly want to learn from them? How to interrupt someone in mid-sentence as if you were performing an act of conversational euthanasia? How to drop a pair of socks three feet from an open hamper and keep right on walking? How to make those weird guttural gargling sounds in the bathroom?

2   But now, at mid-life, I am willing to admit that there are some real and useful things to learn from men. Not from all men—in fact, we may have the most to learn from some of the men we like the least. This realization does not mean that my feminist principles have gone soft with age: what I think women could learn from men is how to get *tough*. After more than a decade of consciousness-raising, assertiveness training, and hand-to-hand combat in the battle of the sexes, we're still too ladylike. Let me try that again—we're just too *damn* ladylike.

3   Here is an example from my own experience, a story that I blush to recount. A few years ago, at an international conference held in an exotic and luxurious setting, a prestigious professor invited me to his room for what he said would be an intellectual discussion on matters of theoretical importance. So far, so good. I showed up promptly. But only minutes into the conversation—held in all-too-adjacent chairs—it emerged that he was interested in something more substantial than a meeting of minds. I was disgusted, but not enough to overcome 30-odd years of programming in ladylikeness. Every time his comments took a lecherous turn, I chattered distractingly; every time his hand found

its way to my knee, I returned it as if it were something he had misplaced. This went on for an unconscionable period (as much as 20 minutes); then there was a minor scuffle, a dash for the door, and I was out—with nothing violated but my self-esteem. I, a full-grown feminist, conversant with such matters as rape crisis counseling and sexual harassment at the workplace, had behaved like a ninny—or, as I now understand it, like a lady.

4   The essence of ladylikeness is a persistent servility masked as "niceness." For example, we (women) tend to assume that it is our responsibility to keep everything "nice" even when the person we are with is rude, aggressive, or emotionally AWOL. (In the above example, I was so busy taking responsibility for preserving the veneer of "niceness" that I almost forgot to take responsibility for myself.) In conversations with men, we do almost all the work: sociologists have observed that in male-female social interactions it's the woman who throws out leading questions and verbal encouragements ("So how did you *feel* about that?" and so on) while the man, typically, says "Hmmmm." Wherever we go, we're perpetually smiling—the on-cue smile, like the now-outmoded curtsy, being one of our culture's little rituals of submission. We're trained to feel embarrassed if we're praised, but if we see a criticism coming at us from miles down the road, we rush to acknowledge it. And when we're feeling aggressive or angry or resentful, we just tighten up our smiles or turn them into rueful little moues. In short, we spend a great deal of time acting like wimps.

5   For contrast, think of the macho stars we love to watch. Think, for example, of Mel Gibson facing down punk marauders in "The Road Warrior" . . . John Travolta swaggering his way through the early scenes of "Saturday Night Fever" . . . or Marlon Brando shrugging off the local law in "The Wild One." Would they simper their way through tight spots? Chatter aimlessly to keep the conversation going? Get all clutched up whenever they think they might—just might—have hurt someone's feelings? No, of course not, and therein, I think, lies their fascination for us.

6   The attraction of the "tough guy" is that he has—or at least seems to have—what most of us lack, and that is an aura of power and control. In an article, feminist psychiatrist Jean Baker Miller writes that "a woman's using self-determined power for herself is equivalent to selfishness [and] destructiveness"—an equation that makes us want to avoid even the appearance of power. Miller cites cases of women who get depressed just when they're on the verge of success—and of women who do succeed and then bury their achievement in self-deprecation. As an example, she describes one company's periodic meetings to recognize outstanding salespeople: when a woman is asked to say a few words about her achievement, she tends to say something like, "Well, I really don't know how it happened. I guess I was just lucky this time." In contrast, the men will cheerfully own up to the hard work, intelligence, and so on, to which they owe their success. By putting herself down, a woman avoids feeling brazenly powerful and potentially "selfish"; she also

does the traditional lady's work of trying to make everyone else feel better ("She's not really so smart, after all, just lucky").

7   So we might as well get a little tougher. And a good place to start is by cutting back on the small acts of deference that we've been programmed to perform since girlhood. Like unnecessary smiling. For many women—waitresses, flight attendants, receptionists—smiling is an occupational require-ment, but there's no reason for anyone to go around grinning when she's not being paid for it. I'd suggest that we save our off-duty smiles for when we truly feel like sharing them, and if you're not sure what to do with your face in the meantime, study Clint Eastwood's expressions—both of them.

8   Along the same lines, I think women should stop taking responsibility for every human interaction we engage in. In a social encounter with a woman, the average man can go 25 minutes saying nothing more than "You don't say?" "Izzat so?" and, of course, "Hmmmm." Why should we do all the work? By taking so much responsibility for making conversations go well, we act as if we had much more at stake in the encounter than the other party—and that gives him (or her) the power advantage. Every now and then, we deserve to get more out of a conversation than we put into it: I'd suggest not offering information you'd rather not share ("I'm really terrified that my sales plan won't work") and not, out of sheer politeness, soliciting information you don't really want ("Wher-ever did you get that lovely tie?"). There will be pauses, but they don't have to be awkward for *you*.

9   It is true that some, perhaps most, men will interpret any decrease in female deference as a deliberate act of hostility. Omit the free smiles and perky conversation-boosters and someone is bound to ask, "Well, what's come over *you* today?" For most of us, the first impulse is to stare at our feet and make vague references to a terminally ill aunt in Atlanta, but we should have as much right to be taciturn as the average (male) taxi driver. If you're taking a vacation from smiles and small talk and some fellow is moved to inquire about what's "bothering" you, just stare back levelly and say, the international debt crisis, the arms race, or the death of God.

10   There are all kinds of ways to toughen up—and potentially move up—at work, and I leave the details to the purveyors of assertiveness training. But Jean Baker Miller's study underscores a fundamental principle that anyone can master on her own. We can stop acting less capable than we actually are. For example, in the matter of taking credit when credit is due, there's a key difference between saying "I was just lucky" and saying "I had a plan and it worked." If you take the credit you deserve, you're letting people know that you were confident you'd succeed all along, and that you fully intend to do so again.

11   Finally, we may be able to learn something from men about what to do with anger. As a general rule, women get irritated; men get *mad*. We make tight little smiles of ladylike exasperation; they pound on desks and roar. I wouldn't

recommend emulating the full basso profundo male tantrum, but women do need ways of expressing justified anger clearly, colorfully, and, when necessary, crudely. If you're not just irritated, but *pissed off*, it might help to say so.

12   I, for example, have rerun the scene with the prestigious professor many times in my mind. And in my mind, I play it like Bogart. I start by moving my chair over to where I can look the professor full in the face. I let him do the chattering, and when it becomes evident that he has nothing serious to say, I lean back and cross my arms, just to let him know that he's wasting my time. I do not smile, neither do I nod encouragement. Nor, of course, do I respond to his blandishments with apologetic shrugs and blushes. Then, at the first flicker of lechery, I stand up and announce coolly, "All right, I've had enough of this crap." Then I walk out—slowly, deliberately, confidently. Just like a man.

13   Or—now that I think of it—just like a woman.

Considering Ideas

1. What three things has Barbara Ehrenreich learned from men?

2. Why did Ehrenreich behave as she did in the company of the lecherous professor?

3. Why do you think some women get depressed when "they're on the verge of success," and why do others "bury their achievement in self-deprecation" (see paragraph 6)?

4. Using the evidence in the essay, write a one- or two-sentence definition of "lady" or "ladylike" that reflects Ehrenreich's meaning of one of these terms.

5. Ehrenreich's essay was first published in 1985. Is her message still timely today? Explain.

Considering Technique

1. Ehrenreich's thesis is delayed until paragraph 2. Which sentence presents that thesis?

2. The material before the thesis is humorous. What purpose does the humor serve? Do you think that the author was wise to begin her discussion of a serious topic in an amusing way?

3. What is the function of the narrative example in paragraph 3? Does this example clarify by showing that something is true, by making the general specific, or both?

4. Brief examples appear in paragraphs 4, 5, 6, 7, 8, and 10. What purpose do these examples serve?

5. The narrative example in paragraph 3 sets up a contrast. What is that contrast? Which other paragraphs include contrast? (Contrast, discussed in Chapter 8, points out differences.)

6. Which paragraph provides a definition of "ladylikeness" and "lady"? What is the purpose of that definition? (Definition, which explains the meaning of something, is discussed in Chapter 11.)

7. Paragraphs 6, 9, and 10 include cause-and-effect analysis. (Cause-and-effect analysis, which explains the causes and/or effects of something, is explained in Chapter 9.) What purpose does this analysis serve?

8. What paragraph marks Ehrenreich's move from an informative to a persuasive purpose?

9. The last two paragraphs form the essay's conclusion. What approach does Ehrenreich take to this conclusion?

10. Consult a dictionary if you are unsure of the meaning of any of these words: *maître d'* (paragraph 1), *euthanasia* (paragraph 1), *guttural* (paragraph 1), *lecherous* (paragraph 3), *unconscionable* (paragraph 3), *veneer* (paragraph 4), *rueful* (paragraph 4), *moues* (paragraph 4), *taciturn* (paragraph 9), *purveyors* (paragraph 10), *basso profundo* (paragraph 11), *blandishments* (paragraph 12).

For Group Consideration

In paragraph 12, Ehrenreich writes a narration to illustrate what she should have done when she was in the company of the lecherous professor. With two or three classmates, write your own narration to illustrate behavior that Ehrenreich could or should have displayed.

Journal Entry

Do you agree or disagree with Ehrenreich? How do you think women should behave? Should men be assertive while women are more passive? Respond to these questions in about two pages, being sure to explain why you believe what you do.

Essay Assignments

1. Spend some time observing the way male and female students behave in the classroom. Pay attention to how often they speak, what they say, how many questions they ask, where they sit, how they interact with the instructor, how they interact with other students, and so on. If you notice a difference, explain and illustrate that difference. If you like, write an essay about what female students can learn from males or about what male students can learn from females.

2. Write an essay with the title "What I've Learned from _____." Fill in the blank with the name of a teacher, a boss, a coach, a minister, a relative, or

anyone you like. Give examples to illustrate the person's desirable behavior. Your purpose is to share with your reader.

3. Do you agree with Ehrenreich? Write an essay to persuade your reader that Ehrenreich is right (or wrong). Use examples to help prove your point. (Your journal entry may give you ideas.)

Considering Thematic Issues

1. Ehrenreich recommends that women "get a little tougher" (paragraph 7). If women followed this advice, how do you think their behavior would change? How do you think such changed behavior would affect men and how they behave?

2. Ehrenreich attacks the cultural conditioning that disposes women toward niceness. Using the information in "Class Acts" (page 139), along with your own thinking, experience, and observation, defend "niceness."

UNTOUCHABLES
Jonathan Kozol

◆

Jonathan Kozol, a two-time winner of the National Book Award, writes extensively about social problems. "Untouchables" is an excerpt from Rachel and Her Children, *a book based on Kozol's interviews with the homeless. In this excerpt, Kozol combines graphic examples with an explanation of the causes and effects of homelessness to inform his reader about the plight of the homeless. In addition, Kozol works to persuade the reader that government officials and the general public are part of the problem. As you read, try to determine why.*

◆

1   Richard Lazarus, an educated, thirty-six-year-old Vietnam veteran I met two days after Thanksgiving in the subway underneath [New York's] Grand Central Station, tells me he had never been without a job until the recent summer. In July he underwent the loss of job, children and wife, all in a single stroke. As in almost all these situations, it was the simultaneous occurrence of a number of emergencies, any one of which he might sustain alone but not all at the same time, that suddenly removed him from his home.

2   "Always, up until last summer, I have found a job that paid at least $300. Now I couldn't find a job that paid $200. When I found an opening at a department store they said that I was overqualified. If someone had asked me a year ago who are the homeless, I would not have known what to reply. Now I know the answer. They are people like myself. I went to Catholic elementary school. I had my secondary education in a private military school. I joined the service and was sent to Thailand as an airman." He has a trade. It's known as "inventory data processing." He had held a single job in data processing for seven years until last summer when the company shut down, without a warning, and moved out of state.

3   "When the company left I could find nothing. I looked everywhere. I got one job for two months in the summer. Part-time, as a security guard in one of the hotels for homeless families."

4   When I ask which one it was, he says the Martinique. "I clocked the floors for fire check. From the top floor to the lobby I swore to myself: rat infested, roach infested, drug infested, filth infested, garbage everywhere, and little children playing in the stairs. Innocent people, women, children, boxed in by their misery. Most people are permitted to make more than one mistake. Not when you're poor."

5   In September he was sick. "I was guarding homeless people and I didn't have a home. I slept in Washington Square and Central Park." He's living now in a run-down hotel operated in conjunction with the Third Street Shelter on the

Bowery. "When you come in at night the guards wear gloves. They check you with a metal detector. They're afraid to touch me."

6   While we talk we watch an old man nearby who is standing flat and motionless against the wall, surrounded by two dozen bright red shopping bags from Macy's. Every so often, someone stops to put a coin into his hand. I notice the care with which the people drop their coins, in order that their hands do not touch his. When I pass that spot some hours later he will still be there. I'll do the same. I'll look at his hand—the fingers worn and swollen and the nails curled in like claws—and I will drop a quarter and extract my hand and move off quickly. . . .

7   Many homeless people, unable to get into shelters, frightened of disease or violence, or else intimidated by the regulations, look for refuge in such public places as train stations and church doorways.

8   Scores of people sleep in the active subway tunnels of Manhattan, inches from 600-volt live rails. Many more sleep on the ramps and station platforms. Go into the subway station under Herald Square on a December night at twelve o'clock and you will see what scarce accommodations mean at the rockbottom. Emerging from the subway, walk on Thirty-second Street to Penn Station. There you will see another form of scarce accommodations: Hot-air grates in the area are highly prized. Homeless people who arrive late often find there is no vacancy, even in a cardboard box over a grate.

9   A man who's taken shelter from the wind that sweeps Fifth Avenue by sleeping beneath the outstretched arms of Jesus on the bronze doors of St. Patrick's Cathedral tells a reporter he can't sleep there anymore because shop-keepers feel that he is hurting business. He moves to the south side of the church where he will be less visible.

10   Stories like these are heard in every state and city of the nation. A twenty-year-old man in Florida tells me that he ran away when he was nine years old from a juvenile detention home in Michigan. He found that he was small enough to slip his body through the deposit slot of a Good Will box. Getting in was easy, he explains, and it was warm because of the clothes and quilts and other gifts that people dropped into the box. "Getting out," he says, "was not so easy. I had to reach my arms above my head, grab hold of the metal edge, twist my body into an *S*, and pull myself out slowly through the slot. When I was fourteen I was too big to fit into the slot. I believe I am the only person in America who has lived for five years in a Good Will box."

11   Thousands of American people live in dumpsters behind restaurants, hotels, and groceries. A woman describes the unimaginable experience of being awakened in the middle of a winter's night by several late-arriving garbage trucks. She nearly drowned beneath two tons of rotting vegetables and fruit.

12   A thirty-four-year-old man in Chicago found his sanctuary in a broken trash compactor. This offered perhaps the ultimate concealment, and the rotting food which generated heat may have protected him against the freezing

weather of Chicago. One night, not knowing that the trash compactor had in his absence been repaired, he fell asleep. When the engine was turned on, he was compressed into a cube of refuse.

13   People in many cities speak of spending nights in phone booths. I have seen this only in New York. Public telephones in Grand Central Station are aligned in recessed areas outside the main concourse. On almost any night before one-thirty, visitors will see a score of people stuffed into these booths with their belongings. Even phone-booth vacancies are scarce in New York City. As in public housing, people are sometimes obliged to double up. One night I stood for an hour and observed three people—man, woman, and child—jammed into a single booth. All three were asleep.

14   Officials have tried a number of times to drive the homeless from Grand Central Station. In order to make conditions less attractive, benches have been removed throughout the terminal. One set of benches has been left there, I am told, because they have been judged "historic landmarks." The terminal's 300 lockers, used in former times by homeless people to secure their few belongings, were removed in 1986. Authorities were forced to justify this action by declaring them, in the words of the city council, "a threat to public safety." Shaving, cleaning of clothes, and other forms of hygiene are prohibited in the men's room of Grand Central. A fast-food chain that wanted to distribute unsold donuts in the terminal was denied the right to do so on the grounds that this would draw more hungry people.

15   At one-thirty every morning, homeless people are ejected from Grand Central. Many have attempted to take refuge on the ramp that leads to Forty-second Street. The ramp initially provided a degree of warmth because it was protected from the street by wooden doors. The station management responded to this challenge in two ways. First, the ramp was mopped with a strong mixture of ammonia to produce a noxious smell. When the people sleeping there brought cardboard boxes and newspapers to protect them from the fumes, the entrance doors were chained wide open. Temperatures dropped some nights to ten degrees.

16   In a case that won brief press attention in December 1985, an elderly woman who had been living in Grand Central on one of the few remaining benches was removed night after night during the weeks preceding Christmas. On Christmas Eve she became ill. No ambulance was called. At one-thirty the police compelled her to move to the ramp outside. At dawn she came inside, climbed back on bench number 9 to sleep, and died that morning of pneumonia.

17   At Penn Station, fifteen blocks away, homeless women are denied use of the bathroom. Amtrak police come by and herd them off each hour on the hour. In June of 1985, Amtrak officials issued this directive to police: "It is the policy of Amtrak to not allow the homeless and undesirables to remain. . . . Officers are encouraged to eject all undesirables. . . . Now is the time to train and educate them that their presence will not be tolerated as cold weather sets in."

In an internal memo, according to CBS, an Amtrak official later went beyond this language and asked flatly: "Can't we get rid of this trash?"

18   In a surprising action, the union representing the police resisted this directive and brought suit against Penn Station's management in 1986. Nonetheless, as temperatures plunged during the nights after Thanksgiving, homeless men and women were ejected from the station. At 2:00 A.M. I watched a man about my age carry his cardboard box outside the station and try to construct a barricade against the wind that tore across Eighth Avenue. The man was so cold his fingers shook and, when I spoke to him, he tried but could not answer.

19   Driving women from the toilets in a railroad station raises questions that go far beyond the issue of "deterrence." It may surprise the readers to be told that many of these women are quite young. Few are dressed in the familiar rags that are suggested by the term "bag ladies." Some are dressed so neatly and conceal their packages and bags so skillfully that one finds it hard to differentiate them from commuters waiting for a train. Given the denial of hygienic opportunities, it is difficult to know how they are able to remain presentable. The sight of clusters of police officials, mostly male, guarding a women's toilet from its use by homeless females does not speak well for the public conscience of New York.

20   Where do these women defecate? How do they bathe? What will we do when, in her physical distress, a woman finally disrobes in public and begins to urinate right on the floor? We may regard her as an animal. She may by then begin to view herself in the same way.

21   Several cities have devised unusual measures to assure that homeless people will learn quickly that they are not welcome. In Laramie, Wyoming, they are given one night's shelter. On the next morning, an organization called "The Good Samaritan Fund" gives them one-way tickets to another town. The college town of Lancaster, Ohio, offers homeless families one-way tickets to Columbus.

22   In a number of states and cities, homeless people have been murdered, knifed, or set on fire. Two high school students in California have been tried for the knife murder of a homeless man whom they found sleeping in a park. The man, an unemployed house painter, was stabbed seventeen times before his throat was slashed.

23   In Chicago a man was set ablaze while sleeping on a bench in early morning, opposite a popular restaurant. Rush-hour commuters passed him and his charred possessions for four hours before someone called police at noon. A man who watched him burning from a third-floor room above the bench refused to notify police. The purpose was "to get him out," according to a local record-store employee. A resident told reporters that the problem of the homeless was akin to that of "nuclear waste."

24   In Tucson, where police use German shepherds to hunt for the homeless in the skid-row neighborhoods, a mayor was recently elected on the promise

that he'd drive the homeless out of town. "We're tired of it. Tired of feeling guilty about these people," said an anti-homeless activist in Phoenix.

25   In several cities it is a crime to sleep in public; in some, armrests have been inserted in the middle of park benches to make it impossible for homeless people to lie down. In others, trash has been defined as "public property," making it a felony to forage in the rotted food.

26   Grocers in Santa Barbara sprinkled bleach on food discarded in their dumpsters. In Portland, Oregon, owners of some shops in redeveloped Old Town have designed slow-dripping gutters (they are known as "drip lines") to prevent the homeless from attempting to take shelter underneath their awnings.

27   Harsher tactics have been recommended in Fort Lauderdale. A city council member offered a proposal to spray trash containers with rat poison to discourage foraging by homeless families. The way to "get rid of vermin," he observed, is to cut their food supply. Some of these policies have been defeated, but the inclination to sequester, punish and conceal the homeless has attracted wide support.

28   "We are the rejected waste of the society," said Lazarus. "They use us, if they think we have some use, maybe for sweeping leaves or scrubbing off graffiti in the subway stations. They don't object if we donate our blood. I've given plasma. That's one way that even worthless people can do something for democracy. We may serve another function too. Perhaps we help to scare the people who still have a home—even a place that's got no heat, that's rat infested, filthy. If they see us in the streets, maybe they are scared enough so they will learn not to complain. If they were thinking about asking for a better heater or a better stove, they're going to think twice. It's like farmers posting scarecrows in the fields. People see these terrifying figures in Penn Station and they know, with one false step, that they could be here too. They think: 'I better not complain.'

29   "The problem comes, however, when they try to find a place to hide us. So it comes to be an engineering question: waste disposal. Store owners certainly regard us in that way. We ruin business and lower the value of good buildings. People fear that we are carriers of illness. Many times we are. So they wear those plastic gloves if they are forced to touch us. It reminds me of the workers in the nuclear reactors. They have to wear protective clothing if they come in contact with the waste. Then you have state governors all over the United States refusing to allow this stuff to be deposited within their borders. Now you hear them talking about dumping toxic waste into the ocean in steel cans. Could they find an island someplace for the homeless?"

30   His question brings back a strange memory for me. In Boston, for years before the homeless were identified as a distinguishable category of the dispossessed, a de facto caste of homeless people dwelt in a vast public housing project built on a virtual island made, in part, of landfill and linked only by one access road to the United States. Columbia Point, adjacent to a camp for

prisoners of war in World War II, was so crowded, violent and ugly that social workers were reluctant to pay visits there, few shop owners would operate a business, and even activists and organizers were afraid to venture there at night. From the highway to Cape Cod, one could see the distant profile of those high-rise structures. A friend from California asked me if it was a prison. He told me that it looked like Alcatraz. I answered that it was a housing project. The notion of shoving these people as far out into the ocean as we can does bring to mind the way that waste-disposal problems sometimes are resolved.

31 New York has many habitable islands. One of those islands has already earned a place in history as the initial stopping point for millions of European refugees who came to the United States in search of freedom. One reason for their temporary isolation was the fear that they might carry dangerous infection. New York's permanent refugees are carriers of every possible infection; most, moreover, have no prospering relatives to vouch for them, as earlier generations sometimes did, in order to assure that they will not become a burden to the state. They are already regarded as a burden. An island that served once as quarantine for aliens who crowded to our shore might serve this time as quarantine for those who huddle in train stations and in Herald Square.

32 Lazarus may not be paranoid in speaking of himself as human waste; he may simply read the headlines in the press. "I just can't accommodate them," says the owner of a building in midtown Manhattan. The mayor of Newark, where a number of homeless families have been sent from New York City, speaks of his fear that displaced families from New York might be "permanently dumped in Newark." He announces a deadline after which they will presumably be dumped back in New York.

33 New Yorkers, according to the *New York Times*, "are increasingly opposing [city] attempts to open jails, shelters for the homeless, garbage incinerators" in their neighborhoods. The *Times* reports the city has begun to "compensate communities" that will accept "homeless shelters and garbage-burning generating plants."

34 Do homeless children have some sense of this equation?

35 "Be not forgetful to entertain strangers," wrote Saint Paul, "for thereby some have entertained angels unawares." But the demonology that now accrues to homeless people, and the filth with which their bodies soon become encrusted, seem to reassure us that few of these strangers will turn out to have been angels in disguise.

36 When homeless infants die in New York City, some are buried not in New York itself but on an island in an unmarked grave. Homeless mothers therefore live with realistic fears that they may lose their infants to anonymous interment. Another fear is that their child may be taken from them at the hour of birth if they should be homeless at the time. Hundreds of babies taken by the state for this and other reasons—often they are very ill and sometimes drug addicted—remain in hospitals, sometimes for months or even years, before a foster home

is found. Some of these "boarder babies," as they are described, have been kept so long that they have learned to walk and, for this reason, must be tethered in their cribs. Infants held in hospitals so long, physicians tell us, are likely to grow retarded. Some, even after many months, have not been given names. Like their homeless parents in the city's shelters, they remain bed numbers.

37   Many of these children do in time find homes, though most end up in dismal institutions where conditions are no better and often a great deal worse than those they would have faced had they been left with their own parents. Mayor Koch attempted in 1986 to establish a group home for six or seven of these babies in a small house on a quiet street in Queens. Unknown vandals set the house on fire. "Afraid of Babies in Queens," the *New York Times* headlined its editorial response.

38   It seems we *are* afraid of homeless children, not only in Queens but everywhere in the United States. It is hard to know exactly what it is we fear (the children themselves, the sickness they may carry, the adolescents they will soon become if they survive, or the goad to our own conscience that they represent when they are visible, nearby); but the fear is very real. Our treatment of these children reaffirms the distancing that now has taken place. They are not of us. They are "the Other."

39   What startles most observers is not simply that such tragedies persist in the United States, but that almost all have been well documented and that even the most solid documentation does not bring about corrective action. Instead of action, a common response in New York, as elsewhere, is the forming of a "task force" to investigate. This is frequently the last we hear of it. Another substitute for action is a press event at which a city official seems to overleap immediate concerns by the unveiling of a plan to build a thousand, or a hundred thousand, homes over the course of ten or twenty years at an expense of several billion dollars. The sweep of these announcements tends to dwarf the urgency of the initial issue. When, after a year or so, we learn that little has been done and that the problem has grown worse, we tend to feel not outrage but exhaustion. Exhaustion, however, as we have seen, turns easily to a less generous reaction.

40   "I am about to be heartless," wrote a columnist in *Newsweek* in December 1986. "There are people living on the streets . . . turning sidewalks into dormitories. They are called the homeless. . . . Often they are called worse. They are America's living nightmare. . . . They have got to go."

41   The author notes that it is his taxes which pay for the paving and the cleaning of the streets they call their home. "That makes me their landlord. I want to evict them."

42   A senior at Boston University sees homeless people on the streets not far from where he goes to class. He complains that measures taken recently to drive them from the area have not been sufficiently aggressive: "I would very much like to see actions more severe. . . ." Perhaps, he admits, it isn't possible to have them all arrested, though this notion seems to hold appeal for him;

perhaps "a more suitable middle ground" may be arrived at to prevent this "nauseating . . . element" from being permitted to "run free so close to my home."

43 "Our response," says one Bostonian, "has gone from indifference to pitying . . . to hatred." I think this is coming to be true and that it marks an incremental stage in our capacity to view the frail, the ill, the dispossessed, the unsuccessful not as people who have certain human qualities we share but as an outcaste entity. From harsh deterrence to punitive incarceration to the willful cutting off of life supports is an increasingly short journey. "I am proposing triage of a sort, triage by self-selection," writes Charles Murray. "The patient always has the right to fail. Society always has the right to let him."

44 Why is it that writings which present these hardened attitudes seem to prevail so easily in public policy? It maybe that kindly voices are more easily derided. Callous attitudes are never subject to the charge of being sentimental. It is a recurrent theme in *King Lear*, writes Ignatieff,* that "there is a truth in the brutal simplicities of the merciless which the more complicated truth of the merciful is helpless to refute." A rich man, he observes, "never lacks for arguments to deny the poor his charity. 'Basest beggars' can always be found to be 'in the poorest things superfluous.'"

45 "They are a nightmare. I evict them. They will have to go."

46 So from pity we graduate to weariness; from weariness to impatience; from impatience to annoyance; from annoyance to dislike and sometimes to contempt.

* A noted scholar who has written on the homeless.

Considering Ideas

1. According to Kozol, what are the prevailing attitudes toward the homeless?
2. Explain the significance of the title. Which paragraphs illustrate why the title is appropriate?
3. To what extent are government officials and the general public part of the problem of homelessness?
4. In paragraph 38, Kozol says that we are afraid of homeless children. What do you think we are afraid of?
5. Do you find any examples particularly moving? Which ones? Why do you think they affect you the way they do?
6. Has your perception of the homeless changed as a result of reading "Untouchables"? Explain.

Considering Technique

1. "Untouchables" lacks a stated thesis, but you can still identify the central point of the piece. In your own words, write out that central point.

2. The opening five paragraphs are an extended example. What pattern of development is used for the example? What purposes does the example serve?

3. In addition to the opening paragraphs, much of the essay illustrates the plight of the homeless. Cite at least five paragraphs that serve this purpose.

4. Which paragraphs illustrate government indifference to the homeless?

5. Which paragraphs illustrate the public's indifference or fear of the homeless?

6. From paragraph 17 to the end of the essay, examples appear with cause-and-effect analysis. (Cause and effect analysis explains the causes or effects of something; see Chapter 9.) According to these paragraphs, what causes people to treat the homeless the way they do?

7. Consult a dictionary if you are unsure of the meaning of any of these words: *Bowery* (paragraph 5), *sanctuary* (paragraph 12), *refuse* (paragraph 12), *concourse* (paragraph 13), *noxious* (paragraph 15), *deterrence* (paragraph 19), *skid-row* (paragraph 24), *foraging* (paragraph 27), *vermin* (paragraph 27), *de facto* (paragraph 30), *caste* (paragraph 30), *Alcatraz* (paragraph 30), *demonology* (paragraph 35), *interment* (paragraph 36), *goad* (paragraph 38), *triage* (paragraph 43).

For Group Consideration

After reading "Untouchables," draw some conclusions with three or four classmates about the kind of people we are as a society. What do homelessness and our reaction to the homeless say about us? Why do we fear and scorn the homeless?

Journal Entry

Lazarus says that the homeless are "the rejected waste of the society" (paragraph 28). In a page or so, explain what you think Lazarus means and go on to note whether you think his assessment is correct.

Essay Assignments

1. Pick a particular group of people on campus (for example, athletes, international students, nontraditional students, or minorities) and use examples to illustrate what life is like for that group. If you like, explain why that group's situation is what it is. (If you need ideas, do what Kozol did: interview people for information.)

2. Some of Kozol's examples illustrate government indifference to the homeless, and others illustrate the general public's indifference. Kozol also explains the effect the indifference has on the homeless. In a similar fashion, write an essay that gives examples of perceived government and public indifference to another group, AIDS victims for example. Then explain the effects of this indifference. If necessary, you can check newspaper and magazine articles in your campus library for information. (The *New York Times Index* and the *Reader's Guide to Periodical Literature* can be good places to start.) Be sure to check the appendix to learn how to document material you take from sources.

3. The homeless are not the only "untouchables" in our society. Pick another group that is often feared or scorned and give examples to illustrate our treatment of this group. If you like, explain why the group is treated the way it is and the effects of that treatment.

4. Were there any "untouchables" in your high school (any people feared or scorned)? If so, pick one of these groups or one of these people and use examples to illustrate how they were treated. If you like, explain why the person or people were treated a particular way and the effects of that treatment.

Considering Thematic Issues

1. Solving the problem of homelessness will require creative thinking. Consider the problem as you understand it from reading "Untouchables" and from any other reading, television viewing, and classwork you have done. Explain a step or steps society can take to begin addressing the problem. Think about what the government, private business, individual citizens, or schools can do.

2. Using "What Is Poverty?" (page 349) and "Untouchables" to stimulate your thinking, describe our attitudes toward the poor and explain why you think we have those attitudes. If you like, go on to explain how our attitudes contribute to the growing problem of poverty and homelessness.

Additional Essay Assignments

1. Use extended and/or brief examples to show that the life of a teenager is not an easy one.
2. Use brief examples to prove that advertisements cause people to want things that they do not really need.
3. Use extended examples to show that life has its surprising moments.
4. Use humorous examples to show that people often make fools of themselves.
5. Use examples to illustrate the effects of some aspect of your life (being the only, youngest, oldest, or middle child; living in the city or country; being tall or short; being the child of divorced parents; being part of a large or small family, and so on).
6. Form a generalization about the way some group is depicted on television (women, police officers, the elderly, teenagers, or fathers, for instance) and provide examples to illustrate that generalization.
7. Provide two or three extended examples to illustrate the fact that appearances can be deceiving.
8. Form a generalization about your relationship with one of your parents or caregivers and illustrate that generalization with examples.
9. Use illustrations to persuade your reader that television has negative (or positive) effects on people.
10. Use illustrations to persuade your reader that sometimes a lie is better than the truth.
11. Provide humorous examples to illustrate Murphy's First Law ("What *can* go wrong, *will* go wrong").
12. Provide examples to show that people are at their worst when they are behind the wheels of their cars.
13. Use examples to persuade your reader that athletics have (or have not) assumed excessive importance in this country.
14. Use examples to persuade your reader that a student athlete is not a "dumb jock."
15. Use examples to persuade your reader that the U.S. education system is in need of a major overhaul.
16. Use examples to illustrate the best characteristics of your favorite teacher.
17. Use examples to illustrate the fact that sometimes people can surprise you.
18. To share with your reader, use examples to illustrate some aspect of the relationship you had with your best friend when you were growing up.
19. Provide brief and/or extended examples to illustrate the fact that jealousy is a destructive emotion.
20. Provide examples to illustrate the fact that people make their own luck.

C H A P T E R

7

PROCESS ANALYSIS

The Purpose of Process Analysis
Supporting Details
Selecting and Ordering Details
Suggestions for Writing a Process Analysis
Annotated Student Essay: Your Basic Blast

The Unbearable Lightness of Air Travel—Roy Blount, Jr.
   (process analysis to entertain)
Don't Just Stand There—Diane Cole *(process analysis to
   inform)*
How I'll Become an American—Miklós Vámos *(process
   analysis to inform, entertain, and persuade)*
*The Knife—Richard Selzer *(process analysis to share,
   inform, and persuade)*
Behind the Formaldehyde Curtain—Jessica Mitford *(process
   analysis to inform and persuade)*
*What Sort of Car-Rt-Sort Am I?—Erik Larson *(process analysis to inform, persuade, and share)*

Additional Essay Assignments

* To fulfill the author's purpose, process analysis is combined with one or more other patterns.

A process analysis explains how something is made or done. You encounter process analysis all the time. For example, when you buy a digital watch, the accompanying instruction booklet includes explanations of how to set the time, how to change the battery, how to work the alarm, and so on. Each of these explanations is a process analysis. When you read a recipe to prepare a new dish, you are following a process analysis. When you apply for a scholarship, the instructions that explain the application procedure are a process analysis. Even your textbooks include process analysis. For example, in your biology text, the explanation about how photosynthesis works is a process analysis.

 ## THE PURPOSE OF PROCESS ANALYSIS

A process analysis can inform the reader in a number of ways. First, it can tell how something is made or done so the reader can perform the process. For example, a process analysis that explains how to program a VCR serves this informational purpose. A process analysis can also inform the reader of a better way to do something. For example, you already know how to study, but you still might be interested in a process analysis with the title "Six Steps to More Efficient Studying" because the essay may save you time and improve your grades by showing you a better way to do something.

Sometimes a process analysis informs by explaining how something is made or done, even when the author knows that the reader will never perform the process. This is the case with "Behind the Formaldehyde Curtain" (page 198), which explains how a body is prepared for burial. The author knows you are not reading her essay because you want to go out and embalm a body. You are reading it because you are curious about how this process is performed and you want to learn about it.

Finally, a process analysis can inform a reader about the beauty, difficulty, or complexity of a process so the reader can better appreciate it. For example, let's say that you are a distance runner. If you want your reader to appreciate the rigor and discipline that go into running a cross-country race, you can describe the process of running that race to impress the reader with its difficulty.

In addition to informing a reader, a process analysis can entertain. In "The Unbearable Lightness of Air Travel" (page 177), for example, Roy Blount, Jr., entertains with a humorous account of how airplane passengers should handle themselves.

A process analysis can also be a vehicle for sharing. For example, a writer who wants to share a portion of his childhood could describe a process whereby he and his grandfather prepared for their annual fishing trips.

Finally, a process analysis can be written to persuade a reader. If you want to convince your reader that your way of performing a process is the best way, you will have to tell how your process is performed. If you want to convince your reader that a particular process is harmful, you will need to detail that process. In "What Sort of Car-Rt-Sort Am I?" (page 207), for example, Erik Larson explains how companies compile information about us. Larson's purpose is to show that this process is dangerous because it invades our privacy.

 ## SUPPORTING DETAILS

Because a process analysis explains how something is made or done, the primary detail will be the steps in the process. Sometimes, you will find it necessary to go on to explain how a particular step is performed. For example, in "Don't Just Stand There" (page 182), Diane Cole describes how to deal with racial, ethnic, and sexist remarks. At one point she tells what to do when the remark occurs at a large meeting or public talk, and then she goes on to explain how to perform the step:

> At a large meeting or public talk, you might consider passing the speaker a note. . . . You could write, "You may not realize it, but your remarks were offensive because. . . ."

At times, you may want to explain why a step is performed so your reader appreciates the importance of the step. For example, let's say you are explaining the best job application procedure, and you mention that you should follow every interview with a letter of thanks that also reaffirms your interest in the position. To help your reader appreciate the importance of this step, you can explain that the letter marks you as someone who is courteous and as someone who follows through—two qualities that can help you land the job.

If you need to clarify a step to be sure your reader understands, an example may be in order. In this excerpt from "Don't Just Stand There," notice how the author uses an example to clarify how the host of a gathering can control the behavior of guests:

> If you, yourself, are the host, you can exercise more control; you are, after all, the one who sets the rules and the tone of behavior in your home. Once, when Professor Kahn's party guests began singing offensive, racist songs, for instance, he kicked them all out, saying, "You don't sing songs like that in my house!" And, he adds, "they never did again."

If you think your reader might perform a step incorrectly or might perform an unnecessary step, you can explain what not to do and why. For example, in "Don't Just Stand There," the author cautions the reader not to deal with offensive remarks by embarrassing a person publicly:

> But in general, psychologists say, shaming a person in public may have the opposite effect of the one you want: The speaker may deny his offense all the more strongly in order to save face.

If a particular part of the process can be troublesome, you can point that out to the reader, as Mitford does in "Behind the Formaldehyde Curtain":

> Proper placement of the body requires a delicate sense of balance. It should lie as high as possible in the casket, yet not so high that the lid, when lowered, will hit the nose. On the other hand, we are cautioned, placing the body too low creates the impression that the body is in a box.

If you use any specialized vocabulary in your process analysis, your reader may need a definition. Notice how Erik Larson handles this in "What Sort of Car-Rt-Sort Am I?":

> Next time you see "car-rt-sort" on your bulk-rate mail, know this: Whoever sent it got a postal discount by sorting it by carrier route, a hunk of postal geography smaller than a zipcode zone.

If completing the process requires particular materials, make note of that fact early on, perhaps even in the first paragraph. If, for example, you are explaining how to build a bookcase, note the lumber sizes, tools, and other materials needed.

Finally, description can be part of a process analysis, particularly if you want to help your reader appreciate the beauty or complexity of the process. Notice, for example, how Richard Selzer uses description in "The Knife" (page 193) when he explains the process of cutting into a body during surgery:

> It is an entry into the body that is nothing like a caress; still, it is among the gentlest of acts. Then stroke and stroke again, and we are joined by other instruments, hemostats and forceps, until the wound blooms with strange flowers whose looped handles fall to the sides in steely array.

 ## SELECTING AND ORDERING DETAILS

The thesis for a process analysis can mention the process to be explained, something like this:

> A person should take great care when choosing a personal physician. (Thesis indicates that the essay will explain how to choose a personal physician.)

In addition to mentioning the process, the thesis can also explain why it is important to understand the process:

> To be sure you do not make a costly mistake, follow this procedure when you shop for a car. (Thesis indicates that the process is important because it can save the reader money.)

If you do not mention the importance of the process in the thesis, you can do so elsewhere in the essay, perhaps in your introduction or conclusion. In "Don't Just Stand There," Diane Cole uses her fourth paragraph to explain why it is important to know the process for dealing with racial and ethnic insults:

> But left unchecked, racial slurs and offensive ethnic jokes "can poison the atmosphere," says Michael McQuillan, adviser for racial/ethnic affairs for the Brooklyn borough president's office. "Hearing these remarks conditions us to accept them; and if we accept these, we can become accepting of other acts."

If it is important to explain why you are qualified to describe the process, you can do so in your introduction. For example, if you are explaining an efficient note-taking system you have devised, you can explain that you have made the dean's list every term since you started using the system.

When the steps in the process must be performed in a particular order, details are arranged in a chronological (or time) order. To help your reader follow the chronological order, transitions like these can help:

First, you must . . .

Next, be careful to . . .

Now, you can . . .

After that, try . . .

Finally, you should . . .

If you need to mention what *not* to do so your reader does not make a mistake or misunderstand a step, include this information at the point in the process when the confusion can occur. If you need to define a term, do so the first time the term is used. Finally, if you need to explain why a step is performed, do so when the step is given.

SUGGESTIONS FOR WRITING A PROCESS ANALYSIS

1. Be sure to pick a process you know well so you are not struggling for details or presenting the process incompletely.
2. List every step in the process in the order it is performed.
3. With your list of steps as a guide, write out your process in one sitting, without worrying about grammar, punctuation, or anything else. You can revise later.
4. When you revise, answer these questions to determine if you need additional details:

a. Do I need to explain how any steps are performed?
b. Do I need to mention what not to do?
c. Do I need to explain why any steps are performed?
d. Do I need any clarifying examples?
e. Do I need to describe anything?
f. Do I need to define any terms?
g. Do I need to point out any troublesome aspects?

5. If you do not have a thesis that mentions the process, check to be sure the essay can manage without it.

6. Does your essay indicate the importance of understanding the process? If not, you can include this information in your thesis, introduction, or conclusion.

 ## ANNOTATED STUDENT ESSAY

Student author Rhonda Ware uses process analysis to entertain her reader. Notice how her specific word choice, amusing detail, and lighthearted tone contribute to the essay's humor.

YOUR BASIC BLAST

Paragraphs 1–3
These are the introduction. Interest is created with humor and specific word choice. Some benefits are listed to establish the importance of understanding the process. Paragraph 3 includes description.

1   For those of you would-be surfing fanatics who live in the boondocks of Nebraska and South Dakota, there is finally a sport you can engage in right near home that allows you to experience the thrill of riding the waves. It is a lot harder than skydiving or hang gliding, and a lot more strenuous than parasailing. It requires strength, balance, and tough knees.

2   Windsurfing is an ideal water sport for those who live near reservoirs, catfish-filled lakes, or muddy rivers and fantasize about curling the wave in California's increasingly polluted surf. Because a fiberglass windboard is cheaper than a sailboat and much easier to transport, it is convenient to haul around on the top of your car or in the back of your truck. You can even windsurf during spring or fall when the water is like ice. All you have to do is squeeze into one of those sexy wet suits.

3   Actually if your real goal is to look cool and attract brawns or broads, all you need to do when you drive through the cornfields of Kansas is to have a board on your roof, Gargoyles over your eyes, and those iridescent rubber shoes on your feet. You might wish to put a streak of blue or yellow suntan cream under your eyes for effect.

Paragraph 4
The thesis is the first sentence. It indicates that the process of wind surfing will be explained. First step in process is given.

4   If you really want to windsurf and look like an athlete, let me give you a few steps to follow to ensure that you do not destroy the image you want to create or that thrill you wish to enjoy. First, you

need to make sure you have securely tied your board to the roof of your car. It does not do to drag your mast on the pavement or let the board slip off onto the interstate.

Paragraph 5
This paragraph gives the materials needed and why they are needed. The humor is sustained.

5   Next, be sure to bring everything you will need, including the number to call for a medical emergency in case you are clobbered with the mast your first time out. You may want to bring a knife for cutting ropes or for slicing the throat of the person who sold you the board but forgot to include directions for assembly. (It all seemed so easy when he put it together in his backyard; you were sure you could remember the steps.) For the neophyte, rigging a windboard can be like setting the sails on an ocean schooner.

Paragraph 6
This paragraph explains what not to do.

6   With directions in hand, attach the sail to the mast with the right ropes. Remember not to get frustrated and do not curse when you cannot put the frayed ropes through the small holes. (Since I bought cheap ropes, I ended up sticking them in my mouth and then trying to twist the ends together.)

Paragraph 7
Transitions like *next* and *now* indicate the chronological order. The paragraph explains how to perform steps.

7   Next, attach the boom to the mast and sail. (Be sure to refer to the instruction manual so you can use the right lingo if you need to ask someone for help.) Now attach the mast and sail to the board. Be sure the mast is securely attached.

8   You are now ready to drag the whole contraption into the water. Before you try and climb up, you will need to check that the dagger board and rudder are in place.

Paragraph 9
This paragraph gives steps in process, how to perform steps, and what not to do. A troublesome aspect of process is pointed out.

9   The next step is the hardest. Climb on the wind board and try to stand up with one foot slightly in front of the mast and one a couple of feet behind it. Now you have to pull the sail and mast upright, move to the side of the board, hold on to the boom, and sail off. Watch out that you do not lose your balance and have the mast fall and hit you in the head. It is advisable not to let your friends try and help you. The falling mast might konk them instead.

Paragraph 10
Humor is sustained here.

10   If you catch a puff of wind and start to move, scream at all those kids swimming nearby and motion to their moms and dads on floats to get out of the way. Fall gracefully, and do not look discouraged after your fiftieth fall. It took my friend ten hours of practice before he could do it. I'm still trying.

11   Until you get the hang of it, sail near the edge of the shore. It is not easy to paddle the wind board back to shore, particularly if the bay where you are sailing is filled with stinging jellyfish.

Paragraph 12
This is the conclusion. The last step provides closure.

12   Finally, when you are completely exhausted but still determined, pull the board to shore. Put your "Off the Lip" T-shirt back on, pack up all your gear, and head for home where you can watch a videotape of the world windsurfing championship on ESPN.

THE UNBEARABLE LIGHTNESS
OF AIR TRAVEL
Roy Blount, Jr.

◆

Humorist Roy Blount, Jr., has written for
Atlantic, Sports Illustrated, *and* Esquire, *among other publications. The following entertaining process analysis, from his book* Now, Where Were We? *(1989),
takes several swipes at the airline industry. As you read, try to determine how
Blount creates his comic effects.*

◆

1   Okay. You are somewhere, at least in theory, between Butte and Mobile,
going 600 miles an hour in a long metal container that is not in physical contact
with anything. A slight jiggling sensation at your prostate (if you have one) is,
essentially, all that is holding you up 30,000 feet above something that looks
like a badly distressed suede jacket but is in fact the surface of the earth. You
have been served a brown puddle with a lump in it, a rectangle of pale-yellow
congealment, and some kind of mineral-based salad. There is a *wheee-
eengneeeenngn* noise. The jiggle-at-the-prostate feeling gives way to a kind of
giving-way sensation. You are swallowed by a cloud.
2   Rule One: Maintain perspective. You don't *know* what it's like to travel
from Butte to Mobile by camel. Especially these days. If camel travel has gone as
far downhill as air travel, it may not be appreciably more salubrious than flying.
3   I will say this, though. In a moment I am going to give you the other seven
rules for staying physically and mentally sound while hurtling through the air in
a fifth-rate diner, but first I want to say this:
4   If man had been meant to fly, he would not have been given the Eastern
shuttle.
5   I single out the Eastern shuttle only because no other service has ever
flown me from Boston's Logan Airport to Boston's Logan Airport in six hours.
6   On November 13, 1986, I boarded the 7 P.M. Eastern shuttle, whose stated
purpose is to transport people from Boston to New York. I was, I thought, at the
end of a book-promotion tour. The fog of publicity had permeated every fiber
of my self-concept. My blood was two thirds radio-station coffee. My sinuses felt
just on the verge of giving birth to alien beings larger—certainly *thicker*—than
myself. I had set foot in an average of 1.78 airports per day over the preceding
three weeks. But soon I would be in a bed I could call my own. I thought.
7   Logan to New York's La Guardia is supposed to take thirty-five minutes.
We sat on the ground for two hours. We took off and headed south and then
circled La Guardia for a while. Then we landed in Providence, Rhode Island,
and sat on the ground there—too far from the terminal for disembarking—for a
couple of hours. From time to time our pilot offered us a terse explanation:
8   "There is only one runway open in La Guardia, and that one has a crane
on it."

9   "New York has turned to worms."

10   "We don't like this any better than you do."

11   We flew back to Boston. There, at 1 A.M., we were free to sit in the airport until 7 A.M., when we would have an opportunity to try the shuttle again. Or else we could go out into the rain and find ourselves a hotel room (nearest available ones were in Cambridge) at our expense. There were some two hundred of us. If we wanted our tickets back, we had to wait for a single agent to read out each passenger's name in a soft, disconsolate, unamplified voice: "Farquarharson . . . Farquarharson . . ." Sigh. "Van Wilderwiesel? . . . Van Wilder . . . *mie*sel? . . ." Sigh.

12   My point is that you, the passenger, cannot count on the airlines to keep air travel from running you into the ground. You must follow the Eight Rules of Self-Preservation. Here are the other seven:

13   Two: Remember that flight stress may cause the human body to implode. The best way to prevent this is to put the considerable likelihood of it out of your mind. If you have already used a nasal spray and yet you can feel the clog in your sinuses growing denser and more expansive, try not to think about it. Thinking about it causes brain matter to merge with the clog to form a lavalike compound that is even more dangerous to think about than the clog alone. Your entire shoulder-and-upper-back area may be drawn up into your eustachian tubes. If this happens, try not to think about it. In any event, don't resort to the nasal spray again. If you're going to become addicted to something, it might as well be something more glamorous, like glue.

14   Three: Don't listen to anything airline personnel tell you. Particularly "We don't like this any better than you do." Fury only heightens flight symptoms. *No one knows* what is meant by "There is only one runway open, and that one has a crane on it."

15   Four: Don't make eye contact with other people's children. Other people's children in flight are not like small human beings as we know them on earth. They are more like indefatigably flopping, vividly inedible-looking rough fish that are too large to be in the boat with you and too profoundly entangled in your gear to be thrown back. If one tiny speck of glop from an airline meal gets on the elbow of a belted-down flying child, that glop will inevitably be transferred onto every surface and down into every crevice within a radius of six to seven feet. Children in aisles are like shadowy figures in dark alleys.

16   Five: Do not accept any food from an airline that you would not accept from a vendor in Calcutta. If it's bottled or if you peel it yourself, it may be all right. Otherwise it may stay with you for the rest of your life.

17   Six: Breathe a lot before you board. The air on airplanes (air air) is not oxygen but $D_2PE_3FG_4UN_x$: two parts dread, one plastic, three exhalant, four frustrated gravity, and an unknown amount of unknown. Make every effort to keep it away from your lungs.

18   Seven: When traveling by air, try not to bring anything with you. If you

check it, it falls into the hands of people who may send it to Puerto Rico (unless you are going to Puerto Rico), or may subject it to certain pressures that make it look like New York Mayor Ed Koch's body, or may play the Carousel Game with it.

19   Here, briefly, is how the Carousel Game is played. Handlers unload baggage from the plane to a holding area, where they sit on the luggage and peer through tiny peepholes at the crowds forming in the baggage-claim area. The players try to match up—mentally—various bags with people waiting. Then they place bets. Then they break for lunch. When they return one will say, "Wanna toss something on the carousel?" Discussions follow. What the handlers want to avoid is for the first bags on the carousel to be those belonging to the persons who have jostled their way closest to the carousel. The game proceeds at its own pace.

20   If you try to carry items on, then you run into problems. Airplanes themselves have developed intense sinus congestion. If there were room for a comfortable majority of passengers to carry items on and tuck them away, the Carousel Game would suffer and the airlines would have union problems. So today's leaner, meaner aircraft has fewer closets; overhead compartments are half filled with luggage from last month; and, in many cases, flights are canceled so that they may be combined with other flights to produce cabin areas that are tight as ticks. If, an hour or so after scheduled lift-off, some interstices remain uncrammed, then airline employees' relatives, dressed in two or three overcoats each and carrying prostheses to be inserted into pockets of leg room, are hastily summoned and wedged in. (Unavoidably, this may occasion slight delays, since some of these relatives live a couple of hours from the airport.)

21   Eight: Don't let yourself be frustrated. Frustration is bad for the traveler's system. Frustration *is* the airlines' system. When you set out on an aerial voyage, always have a *realistic goal* in mind. Tell yourself firmly and briskly, "Well, if I actually spend some time in the air headed in the right direction during the next twenty-four hours, I'll consider it a day well spent." As you take off from Butte on the first leg of your passage to Mobile, relax. Sit back in your seat, think how much more nearly fitted to the human body this seat is than a camel, and reflect: "By golly, it won't be long now before I find myself magically transported to Mobile. Or Butte. Or someplace that may well lie in between."

Considering Ideas

1. How would you describe Blount's attitude toward air travel?
2. What qualifies Blount to write about air travel? Where are his credentials given?
3. What kind of audience is most likely to appreciate "The Unbearable Lightness of Air Travel"?
4. What aspects of air travel does Blount attack?

Considering Technique

1. Which sentence best expresses Blount's thesis because it presents the process to be explained?
2. Where does Blount explain why it is important to understand the process? What does he say?
3. Which paragraphs include description? What purpose does that description serve?
4. Which paragraph explains how to perform a step, why to perform it, and what not to do? Which paragraph explains a troublesome aspect of the process?
5. Which paragraphs explain what not to do and why not to do it?
6. Which paragraphs form a narration used as a clarifying example? What point does that narrative example illustrate?
7. Consult a dictionary if you are unsure of the meaning of any of these words: *distressed* (paragraph 1), *salubrious* (paragraph 2), *permeated* (paragraph 6), *terse* (paragraph 7), *disconsolate* (paragraph 11), *implode* (paragraph 13), *indefatigably* (paragraph 15), *interstices* (paragraph 20), *prostheses* (paragraph 20).

For Group Consideration

To achieve his humorous effects, Blount relies on a number of techniques. For example, he uses description to comic ends in paragraph 1. With three or four classmates, decide what other techniques the author employs for humorous effect and cite examples of these techniques.

Journal Entry

Do you think a reader who has never flown would react to Blount's essay differently from a reader who has flown? If so, how would the reactions differ? If not, why not? Respond in about a page.

Essay Assignments

1. In paragraph 3, Blount says that he is giving rules "for staying physically and mentally sound while hurtling through the air." Write your own humorous process analysis that shows how to stay "physically and mentally sound while _____." Fill in the blank with some activity.
2. If you have flown, write your own process analysis to explain how to cope with air travel. Like Blount, indicate what not to do. Your piece can be humorous or not, as you prefer.

3. Write a humorous process analysis to explain how to cope with some aspect of campus life: registration, dorm life, examinations, or parking, for example. Try to use some of the techniques Blount uses to achieve a humorous effect.

4. Write a humorous process analysis about some routine fact of life: highway driving, grocery shopping, or last-minute Christmas shopping, for example. Try to use some of the techniques Blount uses to achieve a humorous effect.

Considering Thematic Issues

1. Blount concludes with the satirical (ridiculing) suggestion that when we fly, we should settle for small gains and be grateful. To what extent do we find ourselves forced to settle for less than we deserve because our institutions, businesses, industries, educational system, politicians, and so on have let us down? Cite examples to illustrate your view.

2. Using the information in "The Unbearable Lightness of Air Travel" and "Wait Divisions" (page 309), along with your own experience and observation, discuss the role waiting plays in our lives. You may consider some or all of these questions or any other aspects of the issue that you care to:

    a. How much waiting do we do routinely?

    b. How much of our waiting is justifiable?

    c. How are we affected by waiting?

DON'T JUST STAND THERE
Diane Cole

◆

In addition to serving as a contributing editor to Psychology Today, *Diane Cole has written for the* Wall Street Journal, *the* Washington Post, *the* New York Times, Newsweek, Ms., *and* Glamour. *"Don't Just Stand There" was first published in a* New York Times *supplement called* A World of Difference *(April 16, 1989), which was part of a campaign against bigotry. In her essay, Cole informs the reader how to respond to bigoted remarks and jokes. In addition, she makes the reader more sensitive to the hurtful nature of such slurs. As you read, notice Cole's liberal use of quotations, and ask yourself what they contribute.*

◆

1   It was my office farewell party, and colleagues at the job I was about to leave were wishing me well. My mood was one of ebullience tinged with regret, and it was in this spirit that I spoke to the office neighbor to whom I had waved hello every morning for the past two years. He smiled broadly as he launched into a long, rambling story, pausing only after he delivered the punch line. It was a very long pause because, although he laughed, I did not: This joke was unmistakably anti-Semitic.

2   I froze. Everyone in the office knew I was Jewish; what could he have possibly meant? Shaken and hurt, not knowing what else to do, I turned in stunned silence to the next well-wisher. Later, still angry, I wondered, what else should I—could I—have done?

3   Prejudice can make its presence felt in any setting, but hearing its nasty voice in this way can be particularly unnerving. We do not know what to do and often we feel another form of paralysis as well: We think, "Nothing I say or do will change this person's attitude, so why bother?"

4   But left unchecked, racial slurs and offensive ethnic jokes "can poison the atmosphere," says Michael McQuillan, adviser for racial/ethnic affairs for the Brooklyn borough president's office. "Hearing these remarks conditions us to accept them; and if we accept these, we can become accepting of other acts."

5   Speaking up may not magically change a biased attitude, but it can change a person's behavior by putting a strong message across. And the more messages there are, the more likely a person is to change that behavior, says Arnold Kahn, professor of psychology at James Madison University, Harrisonburg, Va., who makes this analogy: "You can't keep people from smoking in *their* house, but you can ask them not to smoke in *your* house."

6   At the same time, "Even if the other party ignores or discounts what you say, people always reflect on how others perceive them. Speaking up always counts," says LeNorman Strong, director of campus life at George Washington University, Washington, D.C.

7   Finally, learning to respond effectively also helps people feel better about themselves, asserts Cherie Brown, executive director of the National Coalition Building Institute, a Boston-based training organization. "We've found that, when people felt they could at least in this small way make a difference, that made them more eager to take on other activities on a larger scale," she says. Although there is no "cookbook approach" to confronting such remarks— every situation is different, experts stress—these are some effective strategies.

8   *When the "joke" turns on who you are—as a member of an ethnic or religious group, a person of color, a woman, a gay or lesbian, an elderly person, or someone with a physical handicap—shocked paralysis is often the first response. Then, wounded and vulnerable, on some level you want to strike back.*

9   Lashing out or responding in kind is seldom the most effective response, however. "That can give you momentary satisfaction, but you also feel as if you've lowered yourself to that other person's level," Mr. McQuillan explains. Such a response may further label you in the speaker's mind as thin-skinned, someone not to be taken seriously. Or it may up the ante, making the speaker, and then you, reach for new insults—or physical blows.

10   "If you don't laugh at the joke, or fight, or respond in kind to the slur," says Mr. McQuillan, "that will take the person by surprise, and that can give you more control over the situation." Therefore, in situations like the one in which I found myself—a private conversation in which I knew the person making the remark—he suggests voicing your anger calmly but pointedly: "I don't know if you realize what that sounded like to me. If that's what you meant, it really hurt me."

11   State how *you* feel, rather than making an abstract statement like, "Not everyone who hears that joke might find it funny." Counsels Mr. Strong: "Personalize the sense of 'this is how I feel when you say this.' That makes it very concrete"—and harder to dismiss.

12   Make sure you heard the words and their intent correctly by repeating or rephrasing the statement: "This is what I heard you say. Is that what you meant?" It's important to give the other person the benefit of the doubt because, in fact, he may *not* have realized that the comment was offensive and, if you had not spoken up, would have had no idea of its impact on you.

13   For instance, Professor Kahn relates that he used to include in his exams multiple-choice questions that occasionally contained "incorrect funny answers." After one exam, a student came up to him in private and said, "I don't think you intended this, but I found a number of those jokes offensive to me as a woman." She explained why. "What she said made immediate sense to me," he says. "I apologized at the next class, and I never did it again."

14   But what if the speaker dismisses your objection, saying, "Oh, you're just being sensitive. Can't you take a joke?" In that case, you might say, "I'm not so

sure about that, let's talk about that a little more." The key, Mr. Strong says, is to continue the dialogue, hear the other person's concerns, and point out your own. "There are times when you're just going to have to admit defeat and end it," he adds, "but I have to feel that I did the best I could."

15   When the offending remark is made in the presence of others—at a staff meeting, for example—it can be even more distressing than an insult made privately.

16   "You have two options," says William Newlin, director of field services for the Community Relations division of the New York City Commission on Human Rights. "You can respond immediately at the meeting, or you can delay your response until afterward in private. But a response has to come."

17   Some remarks or actions may be so outrageous that they cannot go unnoted at the moment, regardless of the speaker or the setting. But in general, psychologists say, shaming a person in public may have the opposite effect of the one you want: The speaker will deny his offense all the more strongly in order to save face. Further, few people enjoy being put on the spot, and if the remark really was not intended to be offensive, publicly embarrassing the person who made it may cause an unnecessary rift or further misunderstanding. Finally, most people just don't react as well or thoughtfully under a public spotlight as they would in private.

18   Keeping that in mind, an excellent alternative is to take the offender aside afterward: "Could we talk for a minute in private?" Then use the strategies suggested above for calmly stating how you feel, giving the speaker the benefit of the doubt, and proceeding from there.

19   At a large meeting or public talk, you might consider passing the speaker a note, says David Wertheimer, executive director of the New York City Gay and Lesbian Anti-Violence Project: You could write, "You may not realize it, but your remarks were offensive because. . . ."

20   "Think of your role as that of an educator," suggests James M. Jones, Ph.D., executive director for public interest at the American Psychological Association. "You have to be controlled."

21   Regardless of the setting or situation, speaking up always raises the risk of rocking the boat. If the person who made the offending remark is your boss, there may be an even bigger risk to consider: How will this affect my job? Several things can help minimize the risk, however. First, know what other resources you may have at work, suggests Caryl Stern, director of the A World of Difference—New York City campaign: Does your personnel office handle discrimination complaints? Are other grievance procedures in place?

22   You won't necessarily need to use any of these procedures, Ms. Stern stresses. In fact, she advises, "It's usually better to try a one-on-one approach first." But simply knowing a formal system exists can make you feel secure enough to set up that meeting.

23   You can also raise the issue with other colleagues who heard the remark:

Did they feel the same way you did? The more support you have, the less alone you will feel. Your point will also carry more validity and be more difficult to shrug off. Finally, give your boss credit—and the benefit of the doubt: "I know you've worked hard for the company's affirmative action programs, so I'm sure you didn't realize what those remarks sounded like to me as well as the others at the meeting last week. . . ."

24   If, even after this discussion, the problem persists, go back for another meeting, Ms. Stern advises. And if that, too, fails, you'll know what other options are available to you.

25   *It's a spirited dinner party, and everyone's having a good time, until one guest starts reciting a racist joke. Everyone at the table is white, including you. The others are still laughing, as you wonder what to say or do.*

26   No one likes being seen as a party-pooper, but before deciding that you'd prefer not to take on this role, you might remember that the person who told the offensive joke has already ruined your good time.

27   If it's a group that you feel comfortable in—a family gathering, for instance—you will feel freer to speak up. Still, shaming the person by shouting, 'You're wrong!" or "That's not funny!" probably won't get your point across as effectively as other strategies. "If you interrupt people to condemn then, it just makes it harder," says Cherie Brown. She suggests trying instead to get at the resentments that lie beneath the joke by asking open-ended questions: "Grandpa, I know you always treat everyone with such respect. Why do people in our family talk that way about black people?" The key, Ms. Brown says, "is to listen to them first, so they will be more likely to listen to you."

28   If you don't know your fellow guests well, before speaking up you could turn discreetly to your neighbors (or excuse yourself to help the host or hostess in the kitchen) to get a reading on how they felt, and whether or not you'll find support for speaking up: "I know you probably didn't mean anything by that joke, Jim, but it really offended me. . . ." "It's important to say that *you* were offended—not state how the group that is the butt of the joke would feel. "Otherwise," LeNorman Strong says, "you risk coming off as a goody two-shoes."

29   If you yourself are the host, you can exercise more control; you are, after all, the one who sets the rules and the tone of behavior in your home. Once, when Professor Kahn's party guests began singing offensive, racist songs, for instance, he kicked them all out, saying, "You don't sing songs like that in my house!" And, he adds, "they never did again."

30   *At school one day, a friend comes over and says, "Who do you think you are, hanging out with Joe? If you can be friends with those people, I'm through with you!"*

31   Peer pressure can weigh heavily on kids. They feel vulnerable and, because they are kids, they aren't as able to control the urge to fight. "But if you learn to handle these situations as kids, you'll be better able to handle them as an adult," William Newlin points out.

32   Begin by redefining to yourself what a friend is and examining what friendship means, advises Amy Lee, a human relations specialist at Panel of Americans, an intergroup-relations training and educational organization. If that person from a different group fits your requirement for a friend, ask, "Why shouldn't I be friends with Joe? We have a lot in common." Try to get more information about whatever stereotypes or resentments lie beneath your friend's statement. Ms. Lee suggests: "What makes you think they're so different from us? Where did you get that information?" She explains: "People are learning these stereotypes from somewhere, and they cannot be blamed for that. So examine where these ideas came from." Then talk about how your own experience rebuts them.

33   Kids, like adults, should also be aware of other resources to back them up: Does the school offer special programs for fighting prejudice? How supportive will the principal, the teachers, or other students be? If the school atmosphere is volatile, experts warn, make sure that taking a stand at that moment won't put you in physical danger. If that is the case, it's better to look for other alternatives.

34   These can include programs or organizations that bring kids from different backgrounds together. "When kids work together across race lines, that is how you break down the barriers and see that the stereotypes are not true," says Laurie Meadoff, president of CityKids Foundation, a nonprofit group whose programs attempt to do just that. Such programs can also provide what Cherie Brown calls a "safe place" to express the anger and pain that slurs and other offenses cause, whether the bigotry is directed against you or others.

35   In learning to speak up, everyone will develop a different style and a slightly different message to get across, experts agree. But it would be hard to do better than these two messages suggested by teenagers at CityKids: "Everyone on the face of the earth has the same intestines," said one. Another added, "Cross over the bridge. There's a lot of love on the streets."

Considering Ideas

1. According to Cole, why is it important to respond to racial, ethnic, and sexist slurs?
2. Why does Cole think it is best not to laugh at racial slurs and offensive ethnic jokes?
3. When a person makes an offensive remark, why does Cole think it is best not to shame that person publicly?
4. Cole offers procedures to help children deal with bigotry. Why do you think she includes information for children?

5. Did you learn anything as a result of reading "Don't Just Stand There"? If so, explain what you learned.

Considering Technique

1. Which sentence is Cole's thesis because it presents the process under consideration?
2. What does the narration in paragraphs 1 and 2 contribute?
3. Cole makes frequent use of examples. Cite at least three such examples and explain their purpose in the essay.
4. Cite three paragraphs that explain what not to do and why. Which paragraph presents a troublesome aspect of the process?
5. Cole includes a considerable number of quotations. What do you think these quotations contribute?
6. Consult a dictionary if you are unsure of the meaning of any of these words: *ebullience* (paragraph 1), *tinged* (paragraph 1), *anti Semitic* (paragraph 1), *rift* (paragraph 17), *volatile* (paragraph 33).

For Group Consideration

Insulting jokes are told all the time. With three or four classmates, discuss why you think people tell these jokes and report your conclusions to the rest of the class.

Journal Entry

Write about one or more times when you have overheard a racial, sexist, or ethnic slur. How did you respond and why did you respond that way? After reading Cole's essay, do you think you should have handled yourself differently? Explain. As an alternative, write about a time when you made an insulting remark or told an insulting joke. Explain your motivation and how the people around you responded.

Essay Assignments

1. Like Cole, select a hurtful behavior (for example, classroom cheating, lying, or teenage drinking) and describe a process for dealing with it. Also, like Cole, briefly explain why the behavior is a problem. If possible, explain what not to do, and provide a narration that illustrates the problem.
2. Select a bothersome behavior that is not hurtful (for example, talking in theaters, rudeness by salespeople, channel-switching by the person with the remote control, or inattentive table servers) and describe a process for dealing with it. Like Cole, try to explain what not to do, and try to illustrate the steps in the process.

3. Research your university's procedure and policy for handling discrimination and harassment on campus. Then write a process analysis that explains what students or employees should do if they are victims of discrimination or harassment.

4. If you think Cole's process for dealing with insulting remarks can be improved upon, write your own procedure for dealing with ethnic, sexist, and racial slurs. Like Cole, use examples to illustrate the steps in the process.

Considering Thematic Issues

1. Racial, ethnic, gender, and sexual bias are current facts of life. Explain how you think bias originates in people, what it is about people and society that allows the bias to persist, and what you think can be done to address the problem.

2. Cole asserts that when confronted with bigotry, we must speak up. She further maintains that we can do so in a graceful manner, one calculated to achieve maximum results. How do you think Harold Saltzman (see "No Kick from Champagne" on page 291) could apply the principles Cole describes to deal with the discrimination he faces as a single male?

HOW I'LL BECOME AN AMERICAN
Miklós Vámos

◆

Born in Hungary, Miklós Vámos writes short stories, essays, novels, and screenplays. In "How I'll Become an American," he uses process analysis to take a look at Americans, and the resulting portrait is not very attractive. Although entertaining, the essay also informs the reader about the character of Americans, and it works to convince the reader that Americans should change their ways. As you read, think about how much of Vámos's characterization you agree with.

◆

1   I have been Hungarian for 38 years. I'll try something else for the next 38. I'll try to be American, for instance. North American, I mean. As an American, I'll speak English fluently. I'll make American mistakes instead of Hungarian mistakes and I'll call them slang.

2   As an American, I'll have a credit card. Or two. I'll use and misuse them and have to pay the fees. I'll apply for other cards right away. Golden Visa. Golden American. Golden Gate. And I'll buy a car, a great American car. Then I'll sell my car and buy a smaller West German car because it's reliable and doesn't use so much gasoline. Later, I'll sell it and buy a smaller Japanese car with a computer aboard. Then I'll sell it and buy a camper. When I sell the camper I'll buy a bicycle.

3   As an American, I'll buy a dog. And a cat. And a goat. And a white whale. And also some big stones as pets.[*]

4   I'll live in my own house. It will be mine, except for the 99 percent mortgage. I'll sell my house and buy a condo. I'll sell my condo and buy a mobile home. I'll sell my mobile home and buy an igloo. I'll sell my igloo and buy a tent. As an American, I'll be clever: I'll sell my igloo and buy a tent when I move to Florida from Alaska.

5   Anyway, I'll move a lot. And I'll buy the best dishwasher, microwave, dryer and hi-fi in the world—that is, the U.S.A. I'll have warranty for all—or my money back. I'll use automatic toothbrushes, egg boilers and garage doors. I'll call every single phone number starting 1-800.

6   I'll buy the fastest food I can get and I'll eat it very slowly because I'll watch TV during the meals. Of course, I'll buy a VCR. I'll watch the taped programs and then retape. Sometimes I'll retape first.

7   As an American, I'll have an answering machine, too. The outgoing message will promise that I'll call you back as soon as possible, but it won't be possible soon.

[*] A reference to pet rocks, which were novelty items popular for a time in the 1980s.

8   If I answer the phone as an exception, I'll tell you that I can't talk now because I have a long-distance call on the other line, but I'll call you back as soon as possible (see above).

9   And I'll get a job. I'll always be looking for a better job, but I won't get the job I want. I'll work really hard since as an American I wanna be rich. I'll be always in a hurry: Time Is Money. Unfortunately, my time won't be worth as much money as my bosses' time. Sometimes I will have some time and I still won't have enough money. Then I'll start to hate the wisdom of this saying.

10   As an American, sometimes I'll be badly depressed. I'll be the patient of 12 psychiatrists, and I'll be disappointed with all of them. I'll try to change my life a little bit. I'll try to exchange my wives, my cars, my lovers, my houses, my children, my jobs and my pets.

11   Sometimes, I'll exchange a few dollars into other currencies and I'll travel to Europe, Hawaii, Tunisia, Martinique and Japan. I'll be happy to see that people all over the world are jealous of us Americans.

12   I'll take at least 2,000 snapshots on each trip. I'll also buy a video camera and shoot everywhere. I'll look at the tapes, photos and slides, and I'll try to remember my experiences when I have time and am in the mood. But I won't have time or be in the mood because I'll get depressed again and again.

13   I'll smoke cigarettes. Then I'll be afraid of cancer and I'll stop. I'll smoke cigars. And opium. I'll take a breather and then try LSD and heroin and cocaine and marijuana. To top it all off: crack. I'll try to stop then but I won't be able.

14   I'll call 1-800-222-HELP. If nothing helps, I'll have some gay experiences. And swing. And if I am still unhappy I'll make a final effort: I'll try to read a book. I'll buy some best sellers. I'll prefer James A. Michener. My second favorite will be the "How to Be Rich in Seven Weeks." I'll try to follow this advice in seven years.

15   I'll always be concerned about my health as an American. I won't eat anything but health food until I get ill. From time to time, I'll read in the paper that I should stop eating meat, sugar, bread, fiber, grains, iron, toothpaste, and that I should stop drinking milk, soda, water, acid rain. I'll try to follow this advice, but then I'll read in the paper that I should do it the other way around.

16   I'll be puzzled. "Hey, I don't even know what cholesterol is!" Yet I'll stick to decaf coffee, sugar-free cookies, salt-free butter and lead-free gasoline. I'll believe that proper diet and exercise make life longer. I'll go jogging every day until I am mugged twice and knocked down three times. Then I'll just exercise in my room, but it will also increase my appetite. I'll go on several diets, and little by little I'll reach 200 pounds.

17   As an American, I'll buy a new TV every time a larger screen appears on the market. In the end, the screen will be larger than the room. It will be difficult to put this enormous TV into my living room; thus, I will put my living room into the TV. Anyway, my living room will look very much like the living rooms you

can see on the screen. My life won't differ from the lives you can see in the soaps: nobody will complain. I won't complain either. I'll always smile.

18   After all, we are Americans, aren't we?

Considering Ideas

1. What do you think Vámos is saying about the American attitude toward possessions?
2. Does Vámos believe that Americans are typically content with their lot? Explain.
3. How does Vámos evaluate the mental health of Americans?
4. What do you think the author is saying about the American attitude toward fitness?
5. Make a list of words that describe Americans as Vámos sees them.

Considering Technique

1. "How I'll Become an American" lacks a stated thesis. In your own words, write out what you think the thesis is. Why doesn't the author write a thesis early on in the essay?
2. Why doesn't Vámos present the steps in the process in chronological order?
3. At what points does Vámos tell why a step is performed?
4. At what points does Vámos tell how a step is performed?
5. What effect does Vámos create with the repetition of "As an American"?
6. Vámos uses a great deal of exaggeration in the essay. Cite an example of that exaggeration. What purpose does it serve?

For Group Consideration

This essay originally appeared in the *New York Times*. With two or three classmates, consider whether or not the author's audience was likely to be offended by a foreign-born writer criticizing Americans. Report and explain your conclusion to the class.

Journal Entry

In a page or two, explain how much of Vámos's characterization you agree with and how much you disagree with. Explain why you believe as you do.

Essay Assignments

1. Write a process analysis with the title "How to Become an American," but make your portrait of the American a flattering one. If you like, you can create emphasis by repeating "As an American. . . ."
2. Write an essay that gives the process for becoming a student, an instructor, an athlete, a sorority woman, a fraternity man, or some other campus "type." Your purpose is to entertain your reader.
3. Write an essay with the title "How to Become a/an _____." (You fill in the blank.) Use a serious tone to inform your reader of the process involved.

Considering Thematic Issues

1. Do you think that Americans are as materialistic and unattractive as Vámos says in "How I'll Become an American"? Attack or defend Vámos's portrait, drawing on your own experience and observation for support. (Your journal entry may give you some ideas.)
2. Explain how the characteristics of Americans pointed out in "How I'll Become an American" account for the celebrations of holidays as they are described in "On Holidays and How to Make Them Work (page 143).

THE KNIFE
Richard Selzer

◆

*Richard Selzer is a surgeon whose arti-
cles on medicine have appeared in* Esquire, Harper's, *and* Redbook. *"The
Knife" is taken from his book* Mortal Lessons *(1977). In the essay, Selzer informs
the reader about the nature of the surgical process. He combines a number of
patterns with process analysis, but you may be most taken by his masterful
description, which entertains the reader and allows the author to share his
feelings about his profession.*

◆

1   One holds the knife as one holds the bow of a cello or a tulip—by the
stem. Not palmed nor gripped nor grasped, but lightly, with the tips of the
fingers. The knife is not for pressing. It is for drawing across the field of skin.
Like a slender fish, it waits, at the ready, then, go! It darts, followed by a fine
wake of red. The flesh parts, falling away to yellow globules of fat. Even now,
after so many times, I still marvel at its power—cold, gleaming, silent. More, I
am still struck with a kind of dread that it is I in whose hand the blade travels,
that my hand is its vehicle, that yet again this terrible steel-bellied thing and I
have conspired for a most unnatural purpose, the laying open of the body of a
human being.

2   A stillness settles in my heart and is carried to my hand. It is the quietude
of resolve layered over fear. And it is this resolve that lowers us, my knife and
me, deeper and deeper into the person beneath. It is an entry into the body that
is nothing like a caress; still, it is among the gentlest of acts. Then stroke and
stroke again, and we are joined by other instruments, hemostats and forceps,
until the wound blooms with strange flowers whose looped handles fall to the
sides in steely array.

3   There is sound, the tight click of clamps fixing teeth into severed blood
vessels, the snuffle and gargle of the suction machine clearing the field of blood
for the next stroke, the litany of monosyllables with which one prays his way
down and in: *clamp, sponge, suture, tie, cut.* And there is color. The green of
the cloth, the white of the sponges, the red and yellow of the body. Beneath the
fat lies the fascia, the tough fibrous sheet encasing the muscles. It must be sliced
and the red beef of the muscles separated. Now there are retractors to hold
apart the wound. Hands move together, part, weave. We are fully engaged, like
children absorbed in a game or the craftsmen of some place like Damascus.

4   Deeper still. The peritoneum, pink and gleaming and membranous,
bulges into the wound. It is grasped with forceps, and opened. For the first time
we can see into the cavity of the abdomen. Such a primitive place. One expects
to find drawings of buffalo on the walls. The sense of trespassing is keener now,

heightened by the world's light illuminating the organs, their secret colors revealed—maroon and salmon and yellow. The vista is sweetly vulnerable at this moment, a kind of welcoming. An arc of the liver shines high and on the right, like a dark sun. It laps over the pink sweep of the stomach, from whose lower border the gauzy omentum is draped, and through which veil one sees, sinuous, slow as just-fed snakes, the indolent coils of the intestine.

5   You turn aside to wash your gloves. It is a ritual cleansing. One enters this temple doubly washed. Here is man as microcosm, representing in all his parts the earth, perhaps the universe.

6   I must confess that the priestliness of my profession has ever been impressed on me. In the beginning there are vows, taken with all solemnity. Then there is the endless harsh novitiate of training, much fatigue, much sacrifice. At last one emerges as celebrant, standing close to the truth lying curtained in the Ark of the body. Not surplice and cassock but mask and gown are your regalia. You hold no chalice, but a knife. There is no wine, no wafer. There are only the facts of blood and flesh.

7   And if the surgeon is like a poet, then the scars you have made on countless bodies are like verses into the fashioning of which you have poured your soul. I think that if years later I were to see the trace from an old incision of mine, I should know it at once, as one recognizes his pet expressions.

8   But mostly you are a traveler in a dangerous country, advancing into the moist and jungly cleft your hands have made. Eyes and ears are shuttered from the land you left behind; mind empties itself of all other thought. You are the root of groping fingers. It is a fine hour for the fingers, their sense of touch so enhanced. The blind must know this feeling. Oh, there is risk everywhere. One goes lightly. The spleen. No! No! Do not touch the spleen that lurks below the left leaf of the diaphragm, a manta ray in a coral cave, its bloody tongue protruding. One poke and it might rupture, exploding with sudden hemorrhage. The filmy omentum must not be torn, the intestine scraped or denuded. The hand finds the liver, palms it, fingers running along its sharp lower edge, admiring. Here are the twin mounds of the kidneys, the apron of the omentum hanging in front of the intestinal coils. One lifts it aside and the fingers dip among the loops, searching, mapping territory, establishing boundaries. Deeper still, and the womb is touched, then held like a small muscular bottle—the womb and its earlike appendages, the ovaries. How they do nestle in the cup of a man's hand, their power all dormant. They are frailty itself.

9   There is a hush in the room. Speech stops. The hands of the others, assistants and nurses, are still. Only the voice of the patient's respiration remains. It is the rhythm of a quiet sea, the sound of waiting. Then you speak slowly, the terse entries of a Himalayan climber reporting back.

10   "The stomach is okay. Greater curvature clean. No sign of ulcer. Pylorus, duodenum fine. Now comes the gallbladder. No stones. Right kidney, left, all right. Liver . . . uh-oh."

11   Your speech lowers to a whisper, falters, stops for a long, long moment, then picks up again at the end of a sigh that comes through your mask like a last exhalation.

12   "Three big hard ones in the left lobe, one on the right. Metastatic deposits. Bad, bad. Where's the primary? Got to be coming from somewhere."

13   The arm shifts direction and the fingers drop lower and lower into the pelvis—the body impaled now upon the arm of the surgeon to the hilt of the elbow.

14   "Here it is."

15   The voice goes flat, all business now.

16   "Tumor, in the sigmoid colon, wrapped all around it pretty tight. We'll take out a sleeve of the bowel. No colostomy. Not that, anyway. But, God, there's a lot of it down there. Here, you take a feel."

17   You step back from the table, and lean into a sterile basin of water, resting on stiff arms, while the others locate the cancer. . . .

18   What is it, then, this thing, the knife, whose shape is virtually the same as it was three thousand years ago, but now with its head grown detachable? Before steel, it was bronze. Before bronze, stone—then back into unremembered time. Did man invent it or did the knife precede him here, hidden under ages of vegetation and hoofprints, lying in wait to be discovered, picked up, used?

19   The scalpel is in two parts, the handle and the blade. Joined, it is six inches from tip to tip. At one end of the handle is a narrow notched prong upon which the blade is slid, then snapped into place. Without the blade, the handle has a blind, decapitated look. It is helpless as a trussed maniac. But slide on the blade, click it home, and the knife springs instantly to life. It is headed now, edgy, leaping to mount the fingers for the gallop to its feast.

20   Now is the moment from which you have turned aside, from which you have averted your gaze, yet toward which you have been hastened. Now the scalpel sings along the flesh again, its brute run unimpeded by germs or other frictions. It is a slick slide home, a barracuda spurt, a rip of embedded talon. One listens, and almost hears the whine—nasal, high, delivered through that gleaming metallic snout. The flesh splits with its own kind of moan. It is like the penetration of rape.

21   The breasts of women are cut off, arms and legs sliced to the bone to make ready for the saw, eyes freed from sockets, intestines lopped. The hand of the surgeon rebels. Tension boils through his pores, like sweat. The flesh of the patient retaliates with hemorrhage, and the blood chases the knife wherever it is withdrawn.

22   Within the belly a tumor squats, toadish, fungoid. A gray mother and her brood. The only thing it does not do is croak. It too is hacked from its bed as the carnivore knife lips the blood, turning in it in a kind of ecstasy of plenty, a gluttony after the long fast. It is just for this that the knife was created, tempered, heated, its violence beaten into paper-thin force.

23   At last a little thread is passed into the wound and tied. The monstrous booming fury is stilled by a tiny thread. The tempest is silenced. The operation is over. On the table, the knife lies spent, on its side, the bloody meal smear-dried upon its flanks. The knife rests.

24   And waits.

Considering Ideas

1. Although Selzer has been a surgeon for many years, he has not become complacent about what he does. How does he feel about his role? What is his attitude toward his principal tool, the knife?
2. What can you tell about Selzer's view of the knife from the fact that in paragraph 1 he compares holding it to holding the bow of a cello or holding a tulip?
3. In paragraph 1, how does Selzer establish his conflicting attitudes toward the knife? What are those conflicting attitudes? How do you explain the conflict?
4. In paragraph 4, Selzer describes the abdominal cavity as a "primitive place." What do you think he means by this?
5. Using Selzer's description for your clues, what would you judge to be the author's attitude toward the human body?
6. Who would you judge to be the intended audience for "The Knife"?

Considering Technique

1. Paragraph 1 is Selzer's introduction. What approach does he take to the introduction? Which words qualify as the thesis because they present the process under consideration?
2. What process is being explained?
3. Much of "The Knife" is vivid, expressive description. What purpose does this description serve? To which senses does the descriptive detail appeal?
4. Cite two or three descriptions that you find particularly appealing or skillful.
5. Paragraphs 18 and 19 describe the knife. Is this description expressive or objective? (See page 43 on expressive and objective details.)
6. Throughout the essay, Selzer uses comparison to clarify the surgical process. For example, in paragraph 1, he compares the knife to a slender fish. What other comparisons appear in the essay? (See Chapter 8 on comparison.)
7. Part of "The Knife" is developed with definition. Which paragraphs define *surgeon*? (Definition, discussed in Chapter 11, gives the characteristics of something.)
8. The conclusion is given in the last two paragraphs. What approach does Selzer take to the conclusion?
9. Consult a dictionary if you are unsure of the meaning of any of these words: *litany* (paragraph 3), *fascia* (paragraph 3), *peritoneum* (paragraph 4), *sin-*

uous (paragraph 4), *omentum* (paragraph 4), *microcosm* (paragraph 5), *novitiate* (paragraph 6), *celebrant* (paragraph 6), *impaled* (paragraph 13), *colostomy* (paragraph 16), *trussed* (paragraph 19).

For Group Consideration

In paragraph 8, Selzer says that the ovaries are "frailty itself"; in paragraph 20, he says that the incision is "like the penetration of rape"; in paragraph 21, he refers to cutting off the breasts of women; in paragraph 22, he compares a tumor to a "gray mother." With three or four classmates, consider these phrasings and discuss whether or not you think Selzer's essay has sexist elements. Report your findings to the rest of the class.

Journal Entry

What attitudes toward surgeons are held by the general public? Does "The Knife" confirm or dispel these conceptions? Explain in a page or so.

Essay Assignments

1. Like Selzer, describe a process you perform that is mysterious, intimidating, or confusing to others (for example, changing the oil in a car, programming a VCR, competing in an athletic event, or driving a motorcycle). Use vivid, expressive description to convey your attitude toward the process.
2. Pick a process you perform that involves a tool or object of some kind (for example, cutting wood with an ax, writing with a word processor, driving a car or truck, or cooking with an electric mixer). Like Selzer, describe the process with an emphasis on a description of the tool or object and its function. If possible, convey your attitude toward the tool or object.
3. If you have ever had surgery or some other medical procedure, explain the process from the patient's point of view. Try to convey your attitude toward what was happening to you.

Considering Thematic Issues

1. Selzer uses metaphors, which are comparisons, (see page 45) to describe his profession. In paragraph 6, surgeons are compared to priests; in paragraph 7, they are compared to poets; and in paragraph 8, they are compared to travelers in a dangerous country. Explain which of these metaphors you think is the most apt and why. Also explain in what ways this metaphor conforms to and/or departs from the common stereotype of the surgeon.
2. Explain the similarities and differences in the views of the human body presented in "Behind the Formaldehyde Curtain" (page 198) and in "The Knife." Also note what you think accounts for those similarities and differences.

BEHIND THE FORMALDEHYDE CURTAIN
Jessica Mitford

Jessica Mitford is an investigative journalist whose 1963 book The American Way of Death *is an exposé of the funeral business. "Behind the Formaldehyde Curtain" is taken from this book. In this selection, Mitford claims that the funeral industry extracts money for unnecessary services. She argues her point by explaining the process of embalming. As you read, notice how Mitford reveals her attitude toward her subject.*

◆

1   The drama begins to unfold with the arrival of the corpse at the mortuary.

2   Alas, poor Yorick.[*] How surprised he would be to see how his counterpart of today is whisked off to a funeral parlor and is in short order sprayed, sliced, pierced, pickled, trussed, trimmed, creamed, waxed, painted, rouged, and neatly dressed—transformed from a common corpse into a Beautiful Memory Picture. This process is known in the trade as embalming and restorative art, and is so universally employed in the United States and Canada that the funeral director does it routinely, without consulting corpse or kin.[†] He regards as eccentric those few who are hardy enough to suggest that it might be dispensed with. Yet no law requires embalming, no religious doctrine commends it, nor is it dictated by considerations of health, sanitation, or even of personal daintiness. In no part of the world but in Northern America is it widely used. The purpose of embalming is to make the corpse presentable for viewing in a suitably costly container; and here too the funeral director routinely, without first consulting the family, prepares the body for public display.

3   Is all this legal? The processes to which a dead body may be subjected are after all to some extent circumscribed by law. In most states, for instance, the signature of next of kin must be obtained before an autopsy may be performed, before the deceased may be cremated, before the body may be turned over to a medical school for research purposes; or such provision must be made in the decedent's will. In the case of embalming, no such permission is required nor is it ever sought. A textbook, *The Principles and Practices of Embalming*, comments on this: "There is some question regarding the legality of much that is done within the preparation room." The author points out that it would be most unusual for a responsible member of a bereaved family to instruct the mortician, in so many words, to "embalm" the body of a deceased relative. The very term

[*] The reference is to Hamlet's graveyard speech to Horatio about Yorick, who was buried but not embalmed.

[†] The Federal Trade Commission now requires that families be informed that embalming is optional.

embalming is so seldom used that the mortician must rely upon custom in the matter. The author concludes that unless the family specifies otherwise, the act of entrusting the body to the care of a funeral establishment carries with it an implied permission to go ahead and embalm.

4   Embalming is indeed a most extraordinary procedure, and one must wonder at the docility of Americans who each year pay hundreds of millions of dollars for its perpetuation, blissfully ignorant of what it is all about, what is done, how it is done. Not one in ten thousand has any idea of what actually takes place. Books on the subject are extremely hard to come by. They are not to be found in most libraries or bookshops.

5   In an era when huge television audiences watch surgical operations in the comfort of their living rooms, when, thanks to the animated cartoon, the geography of the digestive system has become familiar territory even to the nursery school set, in a land where the satisfaction of curiosity about almost all matters is a national pastime, the secrecy surrounding embalming can, surely, hardly be attributed to the inherent gruesomeness of the subject. Custom in this regard has within this century suffered a complete reversal. In the early days of American embalming, when it was performed in the home of the deceased, it was almost mandatory for some relative to stay by the embalmer's side and witness the procedure. Today, family members who might wish to be in attendance would certainly be dissuaded by the funeral director. All others, except apprentices, are excluded by law from the preparation room.

6   A close look at what does actually take place may explain in large measure the undertaker's intractable reticence concerning a procedure that has become his major *raison d'être*. Is it possible he fears that public information about embalming might lead patrons to wonder if they really want this service? If the funeral men are loath to discuss the subject outside the trade, the reader may, understandably, be equally loath to go on reading at this point. For those who have the stomach for it, let us part the formaldehyde curtain. . . .

7   The body is first laid out in the undertaker's morgue—or rather, Mr. Jones is reposing in the preparation room—to be readied to bid the world farewell.

8   The preparation room in any of the better funeral establishments has the tiled and sterile look of a surgery, and indeed the embalmer-restorative artist who does his chores there is beginning to adopt the term *dermasurgeon* (appropriately corrupted by some mortician-writers as "demi-surgeon") to describe his calling. His equipment, consisting of scalpels, scissors, augers, forceps, clamps, needles, pumps, tubes, bowls, and basins, is crudely imitative of the surgeon's, as is his technique, acquired in a nine- or twelve-month post-high-school course in an embalming school. He is supplied by an advanced chemical industry with a bewildering array of fluids, sprays, pastes, oils, pow-ders, creams, to fix or soften tissue, shrink or distend it as needed, dry it here, restore the moisture there. There are cosmetics, waxes, and paints to fill and cover features, even plaster of Paris to replace entire limbs. There are ingenious aids to prop and stabilize the cadaver: a Vari-Pose Head Rest, the Edwards Arm

and Hand Positioner, the Repose Block (to support the shoulders during the embalming), and the Throop Foot Positioner, which resembles an old-fashioned stocks.

9   Mr. John H. Eckels, president of the Eckels College of Mortuary Science, thus describes the first part of the embalming procedure: "In the hands of a skilled practitioner, this work may be done in a comparatively short time and without mutilating the body other than by slight incision—so slight that it scarcely would cause serious inconvenience if made upon a living person. It is necessary to remove the blood, and doing this not only helps in the disinfecting, but removes the principal cause of disfigurements due to discoloration."

10   Another textbook discusses the all-important time element: "The earlier this is done, the better, for every hour that elapses between death and embalming will add to the problems and complications encountered. . . ." Just how soon should one get going on the embalming? The author tells us, "On the basis of such scanty information made available to this profession through its rudimentary and haphazard system of technical research, we must conclude that the best results are to be obtained if the subject is embalmed before life is completely extinct—that is, before cellular death has occurred. In the average case, this would mean within an hour after somatic death." For those who feel that there is something a little rudimentary, not to say haphazard, about this advice, a comforting thought is offered by another writer. Speaking of fears entertained in early days of premature burial, he points out, "One of the effects of embalming by chemical injection, however, has been to dispel fears of live burial." How true; once the blood is removed, chances of live burial are indeed remote.

11   To return to Mr. Jones, the blood is drained out through the veins and replaced by embalming fluid pumped in through the arteries. As noted in *The Principles and Practices of Embalming,* "every operator has a favorite injection and drainage point—a fact which becomes a handicap only if he fails or refuses to forsake his favorites when conditions demand it." Typical favorites are the carotid artery, femoral artery, jugular vein, subclavian vein. There are various choices of embalming fluid. If Flextone is used, it will produce a "mild, flexibility rigidity. The skin retains a velvety softness, the tissues are rubbery and pliable. Ideal for women and children." It may be blended with B. and G. Products Company's Lyf-Lyk tint, which is guaranteed to reproduce "nature's own skin texture . . . the velvety appearance of living tissue." Suntone comes in three separate tints: Suntan; Special Cosmetic Tint, a pink shade "especially indicated for female subjects"; and Regular Cosmetic Tint, moderately pink.

12   About three to six gallons of a dyed and perfumed solution of formaldehyde, glycerin, borax, phenol, alcohol, and water is soon circulated through Mr. Jones, whose mouth has been sewn together with a "needle directed upward between the upper lip and gum and brought out through the left nostril," with the corners raised slightly "for a more pleasant expression." If he should be bucktoothed, his teeth are cleaned with Bon Ami and coated with

colorless nail polish. His eyes, meanwhile, are closed with flesh-tinted eye caps and eye cement.

13   The next step is to have at Mr. Jones with a thing called a trocar. This is a long, hollow needle attached to a tube. It is jabbed into the abdomen, poked around the entrails and chest cavity, the contents of which are pumped out and replaced with "cavity fluid." This done, and the hole in the abdomen sewn up, Mr. Jones's face is heavily creamed (to protect the skin from burns which may be caused by leakage of the chemicals), and he is covered with a sheet and left unmolested for a while. But not for long—there is more, much more, in store for him. He has been embalmed, but not yet restored, and the best time to start the restorative work is eight to ten hours after embalming, when the tissues have become firm and dry.

14   The object of all this attention to the corpse, it must be remembered, is to make it presentable for viewing in an attitude of healthy repose. "Our customs require the presentation of our dead in the semblance of normality . . . unmarred by the ravages of illness, disease, or mutilation," says Mr. J. Sheridan Mayer in his *Restorative Art*. This is rather a large order since few people die in the full bloom of health, unravaged by illness and unmarked by some disfigure-ment. The funeral industry is equal to the challenge: "In some cases the gruesome appearance of a mutilated or disease-ridden subject may be quite discouraging. The task of restoration may seem impossible and shake the confidence of the embalmer. This is the time for intestinal fortitude and deter-mination. Once the formative work is begun and affected tissues are cleaned or removed, all doubts of success vanish. It is surprising and gratifying to discover the results which may be obtained."

15   The embalmer, having allowed an appropriate interval to elapse, returns to the attack, but now he brings into play the skill and equipment of sculptor and cosmetician. Is a hand missing? Casting one in plaster of Paris is a simple matter. "For replacement purposes, only a cast of the back of the hand is necessary; this is within the ability of the average operator and is quite ade-quate." If a lip or two, a nose, or an ear should be missing, the embalmer has at hand a variety of restorative waxes with which to model replacements. Pores and skin textures are simulated by stippling with a little brush, and over this cosmetics are laid on. Head off? Decapitation cases are rather routinely handled. Ragged edges are trimmed, and head joined to torso with a series of splints, wires, and sutures. It is a good idea to have a little something at the neck—a scarf or a high collar—when time for viewing comes. Swollen mouth? Cut out tissue as needed from inside the lips. If too much is removed, the surface contour can easily be restored by padding with cotton. Swollen necks and cheeks are reduced by removing tissue through vertical incisions made down each side of the neck. "When the deceased is casketed, the pillow will hide the suture incisions . . . as an extra precaution against leakage, the suture may be painted with liquid sealer."

16 The opposite condition is more likely to present itself—that of emacia-tion. His hypodermic syringe now loaded with massage cream, the embalmer seeks out and fills the hollowed and sunken areas by injection. In this pro-cedure the backs of the hands and fingers and the under-chin area should not be neglected.

17 Positioning the lips is a problem that recurrently challenges the ingenuity of the embalmer. Closed too tightly, they tend to give a stern, even disapproving expression. Ideally, embalmers feel, the lips should give the impression of being ever so slightly parted, the upper lip protruding slightly for a more youthful appearance. This takes some engineering, however, as the lips tend to drift apart. Lip drift can sometimes be remedied by pushing one or two straight pins through the inner margin of the lower lip and then inserting them between the two front upper teeth. If Mr. Jones happens to have no teeth, the pins can just as easily be anchored in his Armstrong Face Former and Denture Replacer. Another method to maintain lip closure is to dislocate the lower jaw, which is then held in its new position by a wire run through holes which have been drilled through the upper and lower jaws at the midline. As the French are fond of saying, *il faut souffrir pour être belle.*[*]

18 If Mr. Jones has died of jaundice, the embalming fluid will very likely turn him green. Does this deter the embalmer? Not if he has intestinal fortitude. Masking pastes and cosmetics are heavily laid on, burial garments and casket interiors are color-correlated with particular care, and Jones is displayed beneath rose-colored lights. Friends will say "How *well* he looks." Death by carbon monoxide, on the other hand, can be rather a good thing from the embalmer's viewpoint: "One advantage is the fact that this type of discoloration is an exaggerated form of a natural pink coloration." This is nice because the healthy glow is already present and needs but little attention.

19 The patching and filling completed, Mr. Jones is now shaved, washed, and dressed. Cream-based cosmetic, available in pink, flesh, suntan, brunette, and blond, is applied to his hands and face, his hair is shampooed and combed (and, in the case of Mrs. Jones, set), his hands manicured. For the horny-handed son of toil special care must be taken; cream should be applied to remove ingrained grime, and the nails cleaned. "If he were not in the habit of having them manicured in life, trimming and shaping is advised for better appearance—never questioned by kin."

20 Jones is now ready for casketing (this is the present participle of the verb "to casket"). In this operation his right shoulder should be depressed slightly "to turn the body a bit to the right and soften the appearance of lying flat on the back." Positioning the hands is a matter of importance, and special rubber positioning blocks may be used. The hands should be cupped slightly for a more lifelike, relaxed appearance. Proper placement of the body requires a delicate sense of balance. It should lie as high as possible in the casket, yet not so high that the lid, when lowered, will hit the nose. On the other hand, we are

[*] You have to suffer to be beautiful.

cautioned, placing the body too low "creates the impression that the body is in a box."

21   Jones is next wheeled into the appointed slumber room where a few last touches may be added—his favorite pipe placed in his hand or, if he was a great reader, a book propped into position. (In the case of little Master Jones a Teddy bear may be clutched.) Here he will hold open house for a few days, visiting hours 10 A.M. to 9 P.M.

22   All now being in readiness, the funeral director calls a staff conference to make sure that each assistant knows his precise duties. Mr. Wilber Kriege writes: "This makes your staff feel that they are a part of the team, with a definite assignment that must be properly carried out if the whole plan is to succeed. You never heard of a football coach who failed to talk to his entire team before they go on the field. They have drilled on the plays they are to execute for hours and days, and yet the successful coach knows the importance of making even the benchwarming third-string substitute feel that he is important if the game is to be won." The winning of *this* game is predicated upon glass-smooth handling of the logistics. The funeral director has notified the pallbearers whose names were furnished by the family, has arranged for the presence of clergyman, organist, and soloist, has provided transportation for everybody, has organized and listed the flowers sent by friends. In *Psychology of Funeral Service* Mr. Edward A. Martin points out, "He may not always do as much as the family thinks he is doing, but it is his helpful guidance that they appreciate in knowing they are proceeding as they should. . . . The important thing is how well his services can be used to make the family believe they are giving unlimited expression to their own sentiment."

23   The religious service may be held in a church or in a chapel of the funeral home; the funeral director vastly prefers the latter arrangement, for not only is it more convenient for him but it affords him the opportunity to show off his beautiful facilities to the gathered mourners. After the clergyman has had his say, the mourners queue up to file past the casket for a last look at the deceased. The family is *never* asked whether they want an open-casket ceremony; in the absence of their instruction to the contrary, this is taken for granted. Consequently well over 90 percent of all American funerals feature the open casket—a custom unknown in other parts of the world. Foreigners are astonished by it. An English woman living in San Francisco described her reaction in a letter to the writer:

> I myself have attended only one funeral here—that of an elderly fellow worker of mine. After the service I could not understand why everyone was walking towards the coffin (sorry, I mean casket), but thought I had better follow the crowd. It shook me rigid to get there and find the casket open and poor old Oscar lying there in his brown tweed suit, wearing a suntan makeup and just the wrong shade of lipstick. If I had not been extremely fond of the old boy, I have a horrible feeling that I might have giggled. Then and there I decided that I could never face another American funeral—even dead.

24 The casket (which has been resting throughout the service on a Classic Beauty Ultra Metal Casket Bier) is now transferred by a hydraulically operated device called Porto-Life to a balloon-tired, Glide Easy casket carriage which will wheel it to yet another conveyance, the Cadillac Funeral Coach. This may be lavender, cream, light green—anything but black. Interiors, of course, are color-correlated, "for the man who cannot stop short of perfection."

25 At graveside, the casket is lowered into the earth. This office, once the prerogative of friends of the deceased, is now performed by a patented mechanical lowering device. A "Lifetime Green" artificial grass mat is at the ready to conceal the sere earth, and overhead, to conceal the sky, is a portable Steril Chapel Tent ("resists the intense heat and humidity of summer and the terrific storms of winter . . . available in Silver Gray, Rose, or Evergreen"). Now is the time for the ritual scattering of earth over the coffin, as the solemn words "earth to earth, ashes to ashes, dust to dust" are pronounced by the officiating cleric. This can today be accomplished "with a mere flick of the wrist with the Gordon Leak-Proof Earth Dispenser. No grasping of a handful of dirt, no soiled fingers. Simple, dignified, beautiful, reverent! The modern way!" The Gordon Earth Dispenser (at $5) is of nickel-plated brass construction. It is not only "attractive to the eye and long wearing"; it is also "one of the 'tools' for building better public relations" if presented as "an appropriate non-commercial gift" to the clergyman. It is shaped something like a saltshaker.

26 Untouched by human hand, the coffin and the earth are now united.

27 It is in the function of directing the participants through this maze of gadgetry that the funeral director has assigned to himself his relatively new role of "grief therapist." He has relieved the family of every detail, he has revamped the corpse to look like a living doll, he has arranged for it to nap for a few days in a slumber room, he has put on a well-oiled performance in which the concept of *death* has played no part whatsoever—unless it was inconsiderately mentioned by the clergyman who conducted the religious service. He has done everything in his power to make the funeral a real pleasure for everybody concerned. He and his team have given their all to score an upset victory over death.

Considering Ideas

1. In paragraph 6, Mitford says that her essay will "part the formaldehyde curtain." What do you think she means? Is the phrase a good one? Explain.
2. According to Mitford, what is the real purpose of embalming? What is the ostensible purpose?
3. What are the steps in the embalming process?
4. Why do you think Mitford names the corpse "Mr. Jones"?
5. How would you describe Mitford's attitude toward the mortuary business?
6. Who would you judge to be the original, intended audience for Mitford's exposé?

7. According to Mitford, why do morticians keep the embalming process secret?

Considering Technique

1. What is the thesis of "Behind the Formaldehyde Curtain"?

2. What process does Mitford describe?

3. Mitford begins her explanation of a process in paragraph 7. What is the purpose of the first six paragraphs?

4. Mitford employs a considerable amount of verbal irony (saying one thing but suggesting another). For example, in paragraph 2 she refers to the casket as "a suitably costly container," but she does not really think the cost is appropriate. Cite two or three other examples of verbal irony. What purpose does the irony serve?

5. The description in "Behind the Formaldehyde Curtain" is graphic and, at times, shocking. What purpose does this graphic description serve?

6. Mitford opens with a reference to burial and its preparation as a "drama." In what ways is the metaphor of the drama sustained in the essay? (See page 45 on metaphors.)

7. Consult a dictionary if you are unsure of the meaning of any of these words: *circumscribed* (paragraph 3), *decedent* (paragraph 3), *bereaved* (paragraph 3), *docility* (paragraph 4), *perpetuation* (paragraph 4), *intractable* (paragraph 6), *reticence* (paragraph 6), *raison d'être* (paragraph 6), *augers* (paragraph 8), *somatic* (paragraph 10), *pliable* (paragraph 11), *entrails* (paragraph 13), *stippling* (paragraph 15), *sutures* (paragraph 15), *emaciation* (paragraph 16), *jaundice* (paragraph 18), *queue* (paragraph 23), *hydraulically* (paragraph 24), *cleric* (paragraph 25).

For Group Consideration

A *euphemism* is a polite or indirect substitute for an unpleasant expression. Mitford notes a number of euphemisms employed by the funeral industry. For example, in paragraph 7, she refers to a body "reposing in the preparation room" rather than "dead on a slab in the embalming chamber." With two or three classmates, go through the essay and list other euphemisms that appear. Decide what effect these euphemisms have on an individual's perception of the realities of death and burial, and share your conclusions with the rest of the class.

Journal Entry

Have your views of death and the funeral industry changed after reading "Behind the Formaldehyde Curtain"? Were your views influenced at all by the graphic description in the essay? Explain in a page or two.

Essay Assignments

1. Explain the funeral process for a particular religion or culture. If possible, explain the reasons for the various steps in the process.
2. Like Mitford, provide a graphic description of a grisly process (for example, baiting a hook, cleaning a fish, or dissecting an animal).
3. Select a process that you think is unnecessary or faulty and explain how that process works. Like Mitford, use verbal irony and description to convey your attitude toward the process.

Considering Thematic Issues

1. If you have experienced some of the rituals surrounding death because someone you knew died, describe the rituals and your reaction to them. Explain whether you found them comforting, depressing, confusing, frightening, and so on. Also, explain why you think you reacted the way you did. If you like, you can also describe the reactions of other people. As an alternative, describe the rituals that you think should surround funerals and burials. Explain why you recommend these rituals.
2. A euphemism tries to make a harsh reality less distressing by substituting a pleasant expression for an unpleasant one. Consider the euphemisms in "Behind the Formaldehyde Curtain" and any others you can think of. (For example, a *waiting room* in a doctor's office is a *reception area;* a dentist does not *pull a tooth* but *performs an extraction*.) Then decide if you think Sissela Bok should add the category of euphemisms to her classification of white lies in "White Lies" on page 313. Explain why or why not. (The preceding "For Group Consideration" activity may help you with this assignment.)

WHAT SORT OF CAR-RT-SORT AM I?
Erik Larson

◆

In an essay that originally appeared in Harper's, freelance writer Erik Larson explains several processes to inform the reader about how companies compile and sell information about us. He combines this process analysis with examples and an explanation of the effects of data compilation. He writes to convince the reader to be wary because data compilation can be harmful, but as you read, notice that there are elements of humor to entertain the reader.

◆

1   I get a lot of junk mail. Like most of my friends, I throw most of the letters away unopened. I do save the catalogs, however: I pass them to my wife, who no doubt is one of the mainstays of the $21 billion junk mail industry—"direct mail," as its practitioners prefer. My wife brings catalogs to bed with her at night. She is also a doctor, and people with causes to advance and gadgets to sell like doctors. For every piece of mail I get, she gets ten. Somewhere, I imagine a mountain has been deforested just for her.

2   Together, she and I have been rented, matched, merged, purged, "deduped," stockpiled, downloaded, parsed, and sorted—by zip, carrier route, carrier walk, and zip-plus-four. (Next time you see "car-rt-sort" on your bulk-rate mail, know this: Whoever sent it got a postal discount by sorting it by carrier route, a hunk of postal geography smaller than a zipcode zone.) We've been scavenged by data pickers who sifted through our driving records and auto registrations, our deed and our mortgage, in search of what direct mailers see as the keys to our identities: our sexes, ages, the ages of our cars, the equity we hold in our home. The scavengers record this data in central computers, which, in turn, merge it with other streams of revelatory data collected from other sources—the types of magazines we subscribe to, the organizations we support, how much credit we've got left—and then spit it all out (for a price) to virtually anyone who wants it. The information eventually makes its way to the country's dozen or so largest data banks, electromagnetic colossi maintained by companies that serve the direct-mail industry.

3   I feel so cheap, so used.

4   The direct-mail industry in America has quietly built itself an immense, private intelligence network in which nearly each and every one of us now resides. The biggest companies know a lot about us, and they're getting to know us even better. Lists are the raw materials. There are "compiled" lists built of records bought wholesale from state governments or built piece by piece by the scavengers. There are "response" lists created whenever people subscribe to magazines, order products through the mail, or answer consumer surveys.

Advertisers can rent lists that tell what car you bought, whether you like dried fruit and nuts, whether you have a kid, whether you or your wife is pregnant.

5   Individually, these lists are mostly harmless. So what if strangers know I subscribe to *Country Living?* Within the last five years, however, advanced "merge/purge" software has given the data collectors the power to layer list upon list, cheaply and quickly, and thereby—if they wish—to turn lists into thick dossiers. Suppose my name appears on 100 lists (a conservative estimate, by the way). The data on these lists, if merged, would form a kind of "me," a character with opinions, traits, an entire personality defined by what I've registered, signed—and especially what I've purchased.

6   Moreover, a recent surge of mergers among data companies and their databases is yielding still richer profiles of consumers. Last summer, for example, R. L. Polk & Co., a huge data compiler in Detroit, acquired National Demographics & Lifestyles of Denver—a company that, with the help of the brief questionnaires that come along with the warranty materials in new radios, TVs, and other so-called consumer durables, has built a database listing the hobbies and passions of 20 million American consumers. More disquieting, however, is the entry of TRW and Equifax, the nation's largest credit bureaus, into direct mail. They provide the mailers with lists derived form credit files— files previously available only for purposes of evaluating a consumer's credit-worthiness.

7   The number of people now collected and processed is staggering. TRW keeps monthly tabs on 143 million consumers, or roughly 80 percent of all consumers over the age of eighteen. Donnelley Marketing of Stamford, Connecticut, tracks 80 million households—90 percent of all households in the country. Donnelley enriches this database by mailing marketing surveys to 30 million households at a time, ten times a year. The survey questions can get personal. One example from a recent mailing: "How many times, if any, did you medicate for diarrhea in the past year?"

8   The keepers of big data say they do it for the consumer's benefit. But data have a way of being used for purposes other than originally intended. in 1984— I mean, really, of all years—the Selective Service System used a Farrell's Ice Cream list it had rented to contact young men as they came of draft age. (The list was made up of the names of children who, in registering for an ice cream promotion, had written down their birth dates.) Also in 1984, the IRS tried using mailing lists to track down tax evaders. It approached Donnelley Marketing and two other data giants, but they refused, arguing such use would invade people's privacy. (An IRS official, however, told me one loyal American list broker, Dunhill of Washington, did supply the names and whereabouts of 2 million people.)

9   Could darker scenarios develop? Or could I just be paranoid? Did you know that advertisers can rent lists of names of men who are gay? That there are lists that single out blacks and Hispanics? And what is your first reaction when I tell you that A. B. Data Ltd., in Milwaukee, specializes in collecting the names of

Jews? Two or three times a year it runs the entire population through a program it devised that selects the surnames of people statistically most likely to be Jews. Anyone named Aaroni has a 100 percent chance of being Jewish; anyone named Ronald Reagan, only a 1 percent chance. A. B. does a brisk commerce in Jewish names. Avram Lyon, A. B.'s vice president, noted when I spoke with him that Jews read books; have tended to be generous to charitable causes; and, he added, "they're well-to-do, highly assimilated. They have a lot of disposable cash." I asked if A. B. had ever received inquiries from fundamentalist types bent on direct-mail evangelism. Yes, Lyon said, there had been inquiries, but the company turned them down.

10   My uneasiness about the magnitude of information collected by direct mailers led me to this question: Who wants *me?* On whose lists do I reside? I set out recently to find out, to collect the tiles of my personal mosaic from far-flung computers, trace my direct mail to its sources, have myself profiled, mapped, and clustered. Just who—out there, in the universe of direct mail—do they think I am?

11   I began the search for my direct-mail self on the top floor of the Clarence Mitchell, Jr., Courthouse, in Baltimore. Here, in a mundane room of ochre walls and brown tile, my mail life begins. In microfilm files 1611-278 and 1611-281, there are details stored that I would not tell a friend, let alone a stranger—what I paid for my house, the amount I borrowed to buy it, and how much I was able to scrape together for the down payment. If this information simply remained at the courthouse, it would be one thing. It doesn't. Anyone can collect it and sell it. One day last year data prospectors from Rufus S. Lusk & Son got their hands on it.

12   Lusk operates primarily in Maryland, Virginia, and Washington, D.C., collecting exact home-equity and property-tax information, indexing it, then selling it to realtors, landscapers, interior decorators—anyone who stands to profit when someone buys a home. If you work for Lusk, you spend lots of time in rooms with ochre walls.

13   "It's all public information," Carol Stewart assured me. She is vice president in charge of Lusk's branch in Timonium, Maryland, where I visited with her (her office happens to have ochre walls). To test her conviction, I asked to see the real estate records of Kurt L. Schmoke, Baltimore's mayor. No doubt it would have taken me hours of prodding to get the mayor's address from his press office, let alone the amount of his mortgage. But there it all was, right on the screen of Stewart's microfiche viewer: 3320 Sequoia Avenue, zip 21215. Owner-occupied. Single-family dwelling. Acquired November 1983 for $125,000, with a $112,500 mortgage from Yorkridge-Calvert Savings and Loan. He pays $3,553.36 in annual state and local property taxes.

14   My heart leapt.

15   I asked to see the records on my own home, and these too appeared. Of far more interest to me, however, were the adjacent entries, the homes of my

neighbors. Ah, Richard and Carol, Fred and Betsy, Nancy, Margaret! I know a few things you don't know I know.

16   Seeing my name there, toiling in its own small way to help Lusk make a profit, gave me an odd feeling. My affairs were being monitored, yet I knew nothing about it. Who else was watching?

17   That afternoon, I called the Maryland Motor Vehicle Administration, to see what it might have on me. I was steered to Ed Seidel, a public-information officer who was happy to be of help, and who is himself fed up with the amount of information one has to give up these days. (When paying with a credit card, he won't give out his phone number!) The states keeps two "headers" on me, he said: one containing my registration and title information, the other my license and driving record. Both are available to anyone who wants to see them, and both are collected routinely in national sweeps by private companies (for example, by R. L. Polk). Both headers, of course, were available to me as well. Seidel told me to give him my license number. As I read each digit, he called it out to a woman somewhere nearby. A printer whined at me through the earpiece of my phone. "I hope there's nothing embarrassing there," I said.

18   "Embarrassing?" Seidel said. He chuckled. "You don't know embarrassing. Sometimes the list is as tall as my boss."

19   What can be gleaned from this? My address, of course. And the vital statistics of me and my car; I am thirty-five years old, stand six one, and weigh 185 pounds. I drive a 1984—that year again!—Honda Civic Sedan, plate number WGN103. My car weighs 3,700 pounds.

20   "It also includes an indication if anything's been flagged," Seidel said. "Which yours has."

21   He paused for effect. "You've got a little parking ticket for 12/15/88, city of Baltimore."

22   "I paid that," I said, perhaps too quickly.

23   Not only am I on file, of course; I'm on lists, countless lists. So are you. These lists, in turn, are sold or swapped to others who want to reach you through the mail. You subscribe, give, buy—and your name is put on the lists of those you've subscribed to, given to, bought from. These lists can tell worlds about your hopes and fears. An outfit called the Bureau of Protective Analysis markets the names of its 22,000 members. These people pay an annual fee, send off their urine, and in return get quarterly urinalysis reports so they can keep tabs on what the bureau calls the "eighteen potential trouble spots."

24   No one is spared a list life, not even subscribers to *The New Yorker*. The magazine began marketing its readers for the first time last year. Catalog companies, magazines, causes, and concerns can rent the list for $90 per 1,000 names. The magazine expressly bars its use, however, for such crass endeavors as sweepstakes, real estate offers, politics, and fund-raising. (*Harper's* magazine, too, rents its subscriber list.)

25   We get listed at earlier and earlier ages. *Sesame Street* magazine rents its subscriber list. So do *Snoopy Magazine* and *Mickey Mouse* magazine. Hasbro

Toys peddles the 454,427 names of individuals who sent in proof-of-purchase labels to get a rebate on My Little Pony games, Jem Doll cassettes, and G. I. Joe Figurines. Recently, the mail brought the Right Start Catalog, a kind of Sharper Image for babies. It beat the baby home by a month.

26   Often list owners are reluctant to say how they acquired the names on their lists. I phoned Globe Life and Accident Insurance Co., in Oklahoma City, and asked Cynthia Cooke, list manager there, how she got my name—and, for that matter, how she knew I was a father. (I had received one of the 50 million direct-mail solicitations Globe posts every year.)

27   "I can't give that to you," she said.

28   I was ready with an argument of awesome, primitive power. "Why not?" I asked. "It's my name."

29   She laughed. "We have agreements with other people that we won't disclose that. And even if we didn't, we look upon that as proprietary information. We paid for the use of it, and—it's hard to be delicate about this—it's our business."

30   I was able to piece together a few trails, however. Here's my favorite—involving not me but my wife. Although she's a voracious consumer, she generally shuns politics. Little did she know she'd wind up in the thick of it—just by ordering, by mail, a package of frozen beef from Omaha Steaks. Omaha Steaks rented her to the G.O.P. Victory Fund of the National Republican Congressional Committee and on a separate occasion to the National Security Political Action Committee. Each committee tapped the list on its own, without first trading notes. Is there some affinity then between Republicans and red meat? "I think that's an absurd statement," said Elizabeth Fediay, chair of the National Security PAC, when I phoned her. "At some point someone probably assessed that this list has been successful with political fund-raising and political activism."

31   "The moment of truth," Doug Anderson, a vice president of Claritas Corporation, in Alexandria, Virginia, was saying. Anderson and I were sitting at a computer in a glass-enclosed room just off the company's sleek blue-gray lobby. Claritas, Latin for "clarity," is a target-marketing company, and Anderson had just entered my current zip code into the computer. I also entrusted him with two other chunks of my life—the zip I had when I lived in San Francisco and the zip I grew up with on Long Island. I was about to learn what kind of guy I am, what kind of guy I've been.

32   Claritas was founded by Jonathan Robbin, a man who delights in discovering correlations between seemingly unrelated behaviors—for example, he now knows that people who listen to religious radio don't eat salted nuts. Robbin pioneered the technique of blending census data, market research, and millions of other survey and statistical records, and then analyzing the result to predict consumer behavior. Claritas broke the country into forty neighborhood types, gave each a catchy, evocative name ("Blue-Blood Estates," "Shotguns and Pickups," and "Tobacco Roads"), ranked them in order of affluence, and

dubbed the system PRIZM, for Potential Rating Index for Zip Markets. The theory is that the Blue Bloods of California behave much like the Blue Bloods of New Jersey, although the former may have better tans.

33   "The whole idea is that you can now assign every neighborhood in the United States to one of these forty types," Robbin said. "There are enclaves where people live at one phase of their lives, or are living because they share the same interests and needs as everybody else." In theory, a direct-mail company can divide a list of its best customers into PRIZM clusters, determine which clusters yield the best response rates, and then target those clusters throughout the country.

34   Other companies have followed Claritas's lead. Donnelley, for example, offers ClusterPLUS. CACI International, a defense contractor and information-services company based in Arlington, Virginia, offers ACORN: A Classification of Residential Neighborhoods. ACORN can provide the longitude and latitude of a given residential area. Mine is latitude 39°20'15" and longitude 76°35'40". Now even the Soviets can target my neighborhood.

35   But back to Doug Anderson at his terminal.

36   "All right," he said. My current zip had bared itself on the screen. "You've got a big mix of people here." The cluster most heavily represented in my zip is "Downtown Dixie-Style," downscale souls ranked fifth from last in terms of affluence. About 15 percent occupy cluster 32, "Public Assistance." The bottom rung. (The number assigned to each cluster does not correspond to its affluence rank.)

37   This was just the first step. For target markets, the zip is obsolete. Too broad. Indeed, my zip showed elements of thirteen different clusters. We needed to get closer, so Anderson types in the number of my block group, the smallest census division, consisting of an average of 340 households. Not every household in America gets assigned to a block group. In more rural areas, the Census Bureau tucks people into "minor civil divisions."

38   In census-speak, I live in state 24, county 510, census tract 902, block group 4. In PRIZM, that makes me a member of cluster 27, "Levittown, U.S.A."

39   The thrill of self-discovery. There are things here I never knew about myself: *I am an ice-hockey fan. I buy a lottery ticket one or more times each week. I went bowling more than twenty-five times last year. I belong to a union, install my own faucets, most often frequent pancake houses and doughnut shops. I am not at all likely to chew tobacco or buy comedy tapes and records.*

40   Anderson now began to type in the block groups of my past. How far I've fallen! In San Francisco, I belonged to cluster 37, "Bohemian Mix," one notch higher on the affluence scale than Levittown. Those were heady times: *I traveled by railroad and bought disco tapes. I drank malt liquor and imported brandy. I visited Europe and went to four or more movies every ninety days. I drank Pepsi Light. I did not own a chain saw, drive a pickup, or panel my own walls.*

41   Now, to the deep past—Take me back, Doug! State 36, county 59, census tract 4143.02, block group 5, Freeport, Long Island.

42   Cluster 27. Again. Levittown redux.

43   "You've really come full circle," Robbin said. "From a family back to a family, I mean, that's what I would suppose. Are you married with children?"

44   "Yes."

45   "That's it. You want your kids to live in a house. Do you live in a house?"

46   "Yes."

47   "But when you were in 'Bohemian Mix' you probably lived in an apartment, right?"

48   "Yes."

49   "I mean, look," Robbin said. "Is that easy to say, or is it not? I went through the same damn thing. I hated suburbia. I was brought up in a suburban area of New Jersey, a nice manicured little town called Summit. I *hated* it. I think I was assigned *Madame Bovary* about twenty times. I couldn't even find that book in a bookstore in Summit, New Jersey. Now, of course, it's different. It's upscale. Back then everybody was a troglodyte. And it was *dull*. It's odd that I now live in something very similar. I live in *Bethesda*. I've come full circle back to suburbia. I've never been able to escape it."

50   Here, set out in print for the first time, because I just made it up, is the First Law of Data Coalescence: Data must seek out and merge with other data. The shrinking cost of electronic computing and the advent of powerful list-enhancement software has triggered a wave of electromagnetic mergers. Data companies, and the data they collect, have merged in unprecedented volume over the past several years. The really momentous change, however, has been the entry of TRW and Equifax into target marketing. In 1985, both companies set up formal marketing divisions. Since then, both have aggressively acquired data and data companies, thereby enriching their already robust files. They've brought a powerful new tool to marketing—the ability to track monthly changes in virtually every consumer's financial behavior. But in transforming themselves from simple reporters to avid marketers, they've shaken a fragile compact between themselves and consumers.

51   I acquired my credit report from TRW for $5. I'd always imagined my report to be some kind of Deathstar in high elliptical orbit, periodically casting its shadow over my life.

52   What a letdown.

53   My report was a bland printout of credit lines, credit limits, and account balances, with columns of coded information telling whether I've paid my bills on time. The report did, however, give me a sense of the unfolding of my consumer life—there was my John Wanamaker's department store account from my two-year stay in Philadelphia; my account at Emporium Capwell in my "Bohemian Mix" days; and my account at Granat Brothers' San Francisco

branch, the jewelry store where I paced the soft carpets for hours, agonizing over the right diamond for my wife's engagement ring.

54   Innocuous enough. But misleadingly innocuous. It's *how* the credit bureaus now use this information that gives it life, and gives one pause.

55   Neither TRW nor Equifax directly provides a marketer with credit reports. They instead compile lists of consumer names that reflect the credit data. L. L. Bean, for example, could request a list of all consumers who possess a bank card with $5,000 or more of available credit. (Neither company allows a search by specific brand of card.) TRW then searches its files and pulls a few million names. The company, however, won't return that list directly to Bean, but rather to a third-party printer, ostensibly to protect the privacy of consumers who fit the search criteria.

56   TRW also uses its credit files to build statistical models of consumers. Say L. L. Bean wants to know if those who do not respond to its catalogs have something in common. Bean gives TRW a list of those who did not respond; TRW finds those people in its files, pulls up all the credit, demographic, and auto-registration information it can on each one, and then tries to find the common thread that makes these people so recalcitrant.

57   TRW and Equifax don't need to scavenge for their credit data. It comes to them in a monthly monsoon, unbeckoned, from creditors who by agreement report to them every thirty days. This in turn allows the bureaus to detect when a consumer gets more credit, a new mortgage, or experiences some other changes in status—change being the stuff of marketers' dreams. Change rejuvenates us consumers. The new house we purchase needs down comforters from the Company Store, an armoire from Conran's, a set of chairs from Williams-Sonoma. Word that some lucky soul just got a new credit card can set the direct-mail world aflame. A newsletter sent to me by Listworld, a broker of credit-related lists in Huntsville, Alabama, put it this way: "The holder of a new credit card is a perfect target for just about everything."

58   When my mortgage company searched deep into my past, I resented the intrusion but considered it the company's right. No law required that the company lend me $100,000. My wife and I allowed ourselves to be evaluated because we stood to get something valuable in return.

59   Now, however, without any agreement from me, marketing companies can gain access to my credit history—not to provide me with credit, but to sell me something. TRW, for example, turned my wife and me over to CPC Associates, a list company in Bala Cynwyd, Pennsylvania, which in turn rented us to American Mailing Co-op in Plymouth, Minnesota, which decided we were a "special" family and offered us a peek at Wilderness Resort, fifty-four miles outside Washington, D.C. This special family didn't want a peek at Wilderness Resort. We threw the mail out.

60   Is that what it all comes down to: I simply don't like to open junk mail? I hear some of you: Hey, you don't like it, you throw it away. What's the harm?

And you might even find something you want to buy, or subscribe to, or support.

61   Well, then, if all this is so good for us consumers, why don't Equifax, TRW, and the other data keepers drop us a little note candidly explaining the true extent to which they use our names: "We and a thousand other companies are going to appropriate your name, match it, store it, rent it, swap it; we'll evaluate your geo-demographic profile, determine your ethnic heritage, calculate your propensity to consume. We'll track you for the rest of your consuming life—pitch you baby toys when you're pregnant, condos when you're fifty."

62   Perhaps we could demand they get our permission first, and insist on royalties tied to the number of names in a given database. We could negotiate exclusive licensing agreements and insist on lifelong retainers. Think of it: Some of these envelopes with checks peeking from those little plastic windows would actually contain real checks, not worthless look-alikes designed only to lure us inside.

63   The data keepers say we have nothing to fear, that they are scrupulous about protecting our records. They insist, too, that they have no use for dossiers on individuals, and use the detail available only to help target broad markets and to know the "hot buttons" that make those markets respond.

64   Yes. But the world changes. Events occur and movements swell that cause people to sacrifice the rights of their peers. "The true danger," Edmund Burke wrote, "is when liberty is nibbled away, for expedience and by parts." It is an interesting exercise to imagine the big marketing databases put to use in other times, other places, by less trustworthy souls. What, for instance, might health insurers do with the subscription lists of gay publications such as *The Advocate* and the *New York Native?*

65   If I am only uneasy, and not panicked, it is because I continue to harbor faith that the direct mailers and name harvesters don't really know what they're doing—at least not yet. Some still can't tell that my wife, who goes by her maiden name, Gleason, is indeed my wife—we get two copies of most of our direct mail. And there is an ever growing list of catalog companies that insist that one of us is Gleason Larson. I take comfort, too, in knowing that *Mother Jones* and the conservative National Security PAC *both* seemed to feel my wife was worthy of their attention.

66   What delights me most, however, is that the folks at Victoria's Secret still send me their catalogue, that zesty album of gorgeous babes in skimpy lingerie; they still believe I'm a woman named Laura Lange.

Considering Ideas

1. Larson says, "Individually, [mailing] lists are harmless." What, then, does he see that is so dangerous?
2. Those who compile mailing lists say that the data they amass is for "the consumer's benefit." How does Larson respond to that claim?

3. What particular danger is Larson pointing out in paragraph 9?
4. In the course of describing what information was compiled on him, and who compiled it, Larson asks, "Who else was watching?" What is the significance of this question?
5. Just how concerned is Larson? How can you tell?
6. Do you think that Larson is serious when he suggests in paragraph 62 that we should be paid for the use of our names?

Considering Technique

1. Larson does not begin making his case until paragraph 5. What purpose do paragraphs 1 through 4 serve?
2. Where does the author begin developing his point with process analysis?
3. Larson really explains several processes in his essay. What are those processes?
4. In general, Larson's process analyses show the nature and extent of the information compiled about us, how this information is gathered, and the uses to which it is put. For what purpose does Larson present all this information?
5. The author uses examples to support his points. For instance, in paragraph 6, he cites R. L. Polk & Co.'s acquisition of National Demographics & Lifestyles of Denver as an example of the merger of data companies and databases. Cite three other examples in the essay and indicate what purpose each example serves.
6. In addition to describing a process and providing examples, Larson explains the effects of something. What effects does he explain? (Cause-and-effect analysis is discussed in Chapter 9.)
7. Describe the audience you think is appropriate for "What Kind of Car-Rt-Sort Am I?"
8. Consult a dictionary if you are unsure of the meaning of any of these words: *equity* (paragraph 2), *colossi* (paragraph 2), *dossiers* (paragraph 5), *disquieting* (paragraph 6), *mundane* (paragraph 11), *ochre* (paragraph 11), *proprietary* (paragraph 29), *troglodyte* (paragraph 49), *coalescence* (paragraph 50), *innocuous* (paragraph 54), *armoire* (paragraph 57), *propensity* (paragraph 61).

For Group Consideration

Larson deals with a serious issue: the threat to privacy. However, throughout the essay, elements of humor give the piece a lighthearted tone. With three or four classmates, cite the instances of humor in the essay. Then discuss whether or not this humor undermines Larson's serious purpose.

Journal Entry

Do you feel threatened by the compilation of databases and mailing lists? If so, explain what you think the danger is. If you do not feel threatened, explain why not. Do you think that the threat to privacy will be more an issue in the future? Why or why not?

Essay Assignments

1. Identify a process you perform on your campus that is troublesome (for example, registering, buying books, or selecting an adviser) and write an essay to convince the appropriate administrator that the process is a problem. Like Larson, explain the process and use examples to persuade your reader.
2. Identify a troublesome process that is part of academic life (for example, renewing your driver's license, correcting an incorrect bank card statement, or getting a health insurance company to pay a medical bill). Write an essay that explains the process and use examples to show how troublesome the process is. If you like, you can employ humor and a lighthearted tone.
3. Pick a process you have been involved in, one that affects people's lives significantly (for example, applying for college admission, trying out for a high school athletic team, or applying for a job). Describe the process and use examples to show the effects it has on people.

Considering Thematic Issues

1. Write a draft of a piece of legislation meant to protect the general public by restricting the extent to which information can be collected, stored, shared, and sold. Explain the details of the legislation, including specifically what it will and will not allow, and argue for its passage.
2. If Miklós Vámos were to do everything he mentions in "How I'll Become an American" (page 189), the computers in this country will have volumes of information on him to compile, store, and share. Based on what you can learn from "What Sort of Car-Rt-Sort Am I?" and "How I'll Become an American," explain what information companies will compile on Vámos, how they will get it, with whom they will share it, and how Vámos will be affected as a result.

Additional Essay Assignments

1. Explain a process that people should know so they can cope with an emergency: how to administer CPR, how to administer first aid to someone badly cut, what to do if a tornado strikes, what to do if fire breaks out in the home, or how to rescue a drowning person, for instance. Your purpose is to inform your reader.

2. Select a process you perform well (for example, making pizza, wrapping gifts, throwing a surprise party, or planting a garden) and describe it so that your reader can learn how to do it.

3. Explain a successful process for quitting smoking, losing weight, or giving up a particular bad habit so your reader can try it as part of a self-improvement program.

4. Explain a process that will help your reader save money: how to buy a used car, how to save money on groceries, how to buy clothes at a thrift shop, how to find bargains at flea markets, how to buy presents for less, and so on.

5. If you have a hobby, explain some process associated with that hobby: evaluating the worth of a baseball card, putting together a tropical fish tank, and so on. Your purpose is to share with your reader, so let your pleasure at performing the process show.

6. If you play a sport well, explain some process associated with that sport: shooting a foul shot, sliding into home plate, and so on. Your purpose is to share with your reader, so let your pleasure at performing the process show.

7. To inform your reader, explain some scientific or natural process: photosynthesis, nuclear fission, nuclear fusion, a lightning strike, hurricane formation, or cell division, for instance.

8. To entertain your reader, write a humorous explanation of a process: how to flunk a test, how to make a bad impression on a date, how to irritate a teacher, how to make a bad impression on a job interview, or how to be a slob, for instance.

9. Explain how some mechanical device works: a VCR, a cordless telephone, a compact disc, a computer, and so on.

10. To inform your reader, explain how something is made: paper, decaffeinated coffee, a baseball, and so on. If necessary, do some research to learn about the process. (Consult the appendix on how to handle material taken from sources.)

11. To convince your reader that women suffer unfairly, explain the process they go through to conform to society's concept of beauty.

12. To share and inform, explain the wedding ritual for the religious, ethnic, or cultural group you belong to. Try to use description to make aspects of the process as vivid as possible. As an alternative, explain the ritual for some other life cycle event.

13. Explain some process for improving relationships between people: how to fight fairly, how to communicate better, how to respect differences, how to offer constructive criticism, and so on.

14. To entertain your reader, write a humorous explanation of how to procrastinate.
15. To help a student who is away from home for the first time, explain how to do laundry. Use examples and keep the tone lighthearted.
16. Explain a way to perform a process to convince your reader that your procedures are better. For example, you can explain a better way to study, a better way to clean a room, a better way to shop, a better way to choose an adviser, or a better way to plan a party.
17. To inform college students, explain a process for coping with stress. As an alternative, explain how to relax.
18. To entertain your reader, explain how to survive adolescence. You may write from a parent's or child's point of view.
19. If you believe the system for electing a president in the United States should be changed, explain the current process and what is wrong with it to convince your reader that change is needed.
20. Describe an important academic survival skill: taking notes, taking an exam, getting along with a difficult roommate, reading a textbook, and so on.

C H A P T E R

8

COMPARISON AND CONTRAST

The Purpose of Comparison and Contrast
Supporting Details
Selecting Details
Ordering Details
Suggestions for Writing Comparison and Contrast
Annotated Student Essay: Opposites Attract

Neat People vs. Sloppy People—Suzanne Britt *(contrast to entertain)*
Two Views of the Mississippi—Mark Twain *(contrast to share and inform)*
Grant and Lee: A Study in Contrasts—Bruce Catton *(comparison and contrast to inform)*
* *Am I Blue?*—Alice Walker *(comparison and contrast to inform, share, and persuade)*
Brains and Computers—Robert Jastrow *(comparison and contrast to inform)*
* *Talk in the Intimate Relationship: His and Hers*—Deborah Tannen *(contrast to inform)*

Additional Essay Assignments

* To fulfill the author's purpose, comparison and contrast are combined with one or more other patterns.

Comparison examines similarities; contrast examines differences. Because comparison and contrast let us examine the features of two or more subjects, it is often an important part of decision making. For example, if you want to buy a CD player, you may visit several stores to compare and contrast the features of a number of models so you can make a wise purchase. When you chose a college, you probably compared and contrasted schools before deciding on the one best for you. In this chapter, we will look at how writers use comparison and contrast to achieve a variety of purposes.

THE PURPOSE OF COMPARISON AND CONTRAST

As noted, comparison and contrast can help us make decisions because when we set things side by side and look at their similarities and differences, we are better able to choose between the items. Comparison and contrast can serve a range of other informational purposes as well.

A writer can inform a reader about the nature of something that is not very well understood by comparing and/or contrasting it with something that is better understood. For example, if you wanted to explain how rugby is played, you could compare and contrast it with the better-known football.

Comparison and contrast can also clarify the nature of the subjects under consideration. In "Brains and Computers" (page 246), for example, Robert Jastrow compares how computers function with how the human brain functions, and, as a result, the reader better understands how both operate.

Comparison and contrast can also inform a reader by providing a fresh insight into something already understood. In this case, the comparison and contrast serve to sharpen the reader's awareness. For example, you may think you know about horses and people, but Alice Walker's comparison of the two in "Am I Blue?" (page 240) may give you fresh insight into the nature of both.

In addition to informing, comparison and contrast can entertain a reader, especially if it is humorous. You will probably be entertained when you read the amusing "Neat People vs. Sloppy People" on page 228.

Comparison and contrast can also allow an author to share something with the reader. If you wanted to share the effects of your parents' divorce, for example, you could contrast your life before and after the divorce to communicate the impact that event had on your life.

Finally, by showing that one subject is better than the other, comparison and contrast can persuade a reader to think or act a particular way. For instance, if you wanted to convince your reader to vote for a particular political candidate, you could contrast that candidate with the opposition to show that your choice is better.

SUPPORTING DETAILS

Comparison and contrast may include other patterns of development. For example, if you wanted to compare and contrast two beach vacation spots, you would probably describe the beach in each place.

Examples are also a frequent component of comparison and contrast, particularly when a point of comparison or contrast requires clarification. For instance, if you were comparing two political candidates, and you stated that they both supported progressive legislation, you could clarify and support that point of comparison with an example. You could note that both candidates voted for a bill that would provide tax credits for working parents with children in day care centers.

Because a story can serve as an example, narration can be a part of comparison and contrast. For example, let's say that you want to compare and contrast your relationship with two friends. To show the differences in the way you interact with each person, you can tell the story of the time the three of you went away for the weekend.

Process analysis, too, can form part of comparison and contrast. For example, in "Brains and Computers," Robert Jastrow points to similarities between brains and computers by showing the way each one functions.

SELECTING DETAILS

Rather than mention every point of comparison and contrast, select your details with regard to your purpose for writing. Let's say, for instance, that you are comparing and contrasting public and private schools. If your purpose is to convince your reader that public schools are better, then you might mention that the ethnic diversity often found in these schools can teach students more about people and their cultural heritage. If your purpose is to share your experiences in these schools, you can tell which school you were happier in and why. If your purpose is to inform, you might tell about the academic programs in each kind of school so parents can make up their own minds about which is better for their children. If your purpose is to entertain, you can give humorous portraits of the students and teachers in each kind of school.

In addition to purpose, a sense of balance will influence your detail selection. In general, any point you make about one of your subjects should also be made about the other subject. Thus, if you are comparing and contrasting public and private schools and you discuss the teachers in public school, you should also discuss the teachers in private school; if you discuss course offerings in public school, you should also discuss course offerings in private school, and so on. (You may notice that the authors in this chapter do not always adhere to this principle of balance. An author can depart from this principle only if the essay does not become a random collection of points about the subjects.)

Although you are likely to discuss the same points about each of your subjects, you need not do so in equal detail. A point can be discussed in more detail for one subject than for the other. For example, assume you are contrasting the way you celebrated your birthday as a child and the way you celebrate it now. If you used to have a big birthday dinner with lots of relatives, you could describe the dinner in a full paragraph or more. If you do not have such a dinner now, then you might mention in just a sentence or two that you have dinner just as if it were any other day.

 ## ORDERING DETAILS

The thesis for a comparison and contrast essay can present the subjects under consideration and indicate whether these subjects will be compared, contrasted, or both compared and contrasted. Consider, for example, this thesis from "Brains and Computers":

Brains work in very much the same way as computers.

This thesis notes that the subjects under consideration are brains and computers, and it also indicates that the subjects will be compared. Now consider these two thesis statements:

Although I had been anticipating my first day of college for a full year, it was not what I expected.

Smith and Jones share the same political philosophy, but they differ markedly in the ways they would implement that philosophy.

The first thesis indicates that the essay will contrast the author's expectation for the first day of college with the reality of that day; the second thesis indicates that politicians Smith and Jones will be both compared and contrasted.

The ordering of detail in a comparison and contrast essay requires some thought. One possible arrangement is the block method, whereby all the points about one subject are made (in a block), then all the points about the other subject are made (in a second block.) To appreciate how the block arrangement works, look at the following outline for an essay contrasting political candidates Smith and Jones. Notice that balance is achieved by discussing the same points for both subjects.

I. Smith
  A. Believes in states funding their own health care plans
  B. Believes in supporting education with a state income tax
  C. Wants to form a task force to study lake pollution
II. Jones
  A. Believes the federal government should fund health care
  B. Believes in supporting education with a property tax
  C. Believes lake pollution is not a priority

A second possible arrangement for comparison and contrast detail is the alternating pattern, whereby a point is made for one subject, then for the other. A second point is made for the first subject, then for the other. This alternating pattern continues until all the points are made for both subjects. An outline for an essay contrasting Smith and Jones could look like this if the alternating pattern were used:

I. View on financing health care
  A. Smith believes states should fund their own plans
  B. Jones believes the federal government should fund a plan
II. View on financing education
  A. Smith believes in a state income tax
  B. Jones believes in a property tax
III. View on lake pollution
  A. Smith wants to form a task force to study pollution
  B. Jones believes pollution is not a priority

In general, the block method works better for shorter essays with fewer points because the reader is not forced to remember many ideas about the first subject while reading about the second. If your essay is long or if the ideas are complex, the alternating method may be better.

If you are both comparing and contrasting, you can organize by treating similarities first and differences next. Or you can reverse this order.

To move smoothly from point to point, the following transitions are helpful:

To show similarity: similarly, likewise, in similar fashion, in like manner, in the same way

Smith believes in tax reform. *Similarly*, Jones wants to close tax loopholes.

To show contrast: however, on the other hand, conversely, in contrast

Smith favors tax reform. *However*, Jones believes current tax laws are adequate.

As you can tell, ordering detail for comparison and contrast requires careful planning. For this reason, you may want to outline, even if you do not typically do so for other kinds of essays.

SUGGESTIONS FOR WRITING COMPARISON AND CONTRAST

1. If you need help with a topic, try explaining the similarities between two things usually considered different, or try noting the differences between two things thought of as alike. For example, love and hate are often thought of as opposites, but you could point out key similarities; or you could point out the differences between getting married and having a wedding—two things often thought of as the same.
2. To generate ideas, make two lists—one of every similarity you can think of and one of every difference you can think of. Study your lists and circle the most significant comparisons and contrasts. Then decide if you want to compare, contrast, or both.
3. If you need more ideas, ask yourself these questions:
   a. Do I want to share, inform, entertain, and/or persuade? What details will help me achieve my purpose?
   b. Can I describe anything?
   c. Can I tell a story?
   d. Can I explain a process?
   e. Can I use examples to illustrate anything?
4. Draw up an outline using either the block or alternating method. If you are unsure which is better, try outlining both ways before deciding.
5. Write your draft from your outline the best way you can without laboring over anything.
6. When you revise, consider the following:
   a. Do you have a thesis that presents your subjects and notes whether they will be compared, contrasted, or both?
   b. Have you discussed the same points for both subjects? If not, is this a problem?
   c. Have you avoided stating obvious comparisons and contrasts?

ANNOTATED STUDENT ESSAY

A student author uses contrast to share information about her parents and to inform the reader about what these people are like. Her candid detail helps the writer form a bond with her reader.

OPPOSITES ATTRACT

Paragraph 1
The introduction gives background information. The thesis (the last sentence) indicates that the subjects are the parents and that differences will be treated.

The pattern is alternating.

Paragraph 2
The first sentence is the topic sentence. It presents the first point of contrast (personality). Points discussed for one parent are also discussed for the other.

Paragraph 3
The first sentence is the topic sentence. It presents the next point of contrast (how free time is spent). Points are developed with examples. The transition *on the other hand* moves the reader from one subject to the next.

Paragraph 4
The topic sentence is the first sentence. It presents the next point of contrast (religious differences). The transition *however* moves the reader from one subject to the next.

1   My parents have been married forty-seven years. Many of their friends refer to them as the "perfect couple" because they get along together so well. They have worked together to build a successful business. My father is the manager of a small hardware store, and my mother is the bookkeeper. They spend almost all of their days and nights together. However, despite their outward appearance of compatibility, my parents are two very different individuals.

2   First of all, their personalities are very different. My father shows very little emotion. He seldom says "I love you," and he believes strongly that real men don't cry. In fact, I have only seen him cry on five occasions. When I was growing up, he seldom hugged me or kissed me. He is also very short-tempered. His temper will flare up immediately if something is said or done that he doesn't agree with. He always thinks that he's right, and he is totally self-absorbed. He enjoys his own company more than anyone else's. Thus, he is his own best friend. My mother, however, is just the opposite. She shows her emotions very well, and very frequently. She is always telling me how much she loves me. She often hugs me for no apparent reason. She is very tolerant, so she will take a great deal before she becomes angry. Even when she becomes angry, she never yells or loses control. She will only firmly explain why she is upset. She loves to have other people around. She has many friends whom she constantly goes to for advice.

3   The way they spend their free time is also very different. My father likes to live dangerously. For instance, although he is sixty years old, he continues to drive a sporty car. He has an ultra-light airplane that he flies for fun. Even after he crashed the ultra-light, he continued to savor this dangerous lifestyle. My mother, on the other hand, is a home-centered person. She prefers a quiet night at home with a good book or a walk in the park to help her relax. She enjoys camping in the Great Smoky Mountains or just sitting with her family or friends.

4   Their religious differences have often kept them going in different directions. My father is a man who does not subscribe to traditional religious beliefs and morality. He believes that adultery is fine for the male, and he has proved this with his many affairs. He will "cuss like a sailor" for no reason and "drink like a fish." He is a serious alcoholic. He never attends church and says, "Get what you can while you can." He does not believe it matters who gets hurt as long as he gets what he wants. However, my mother is very religious and has high moral standards. She believes in a one-man marriage. She has always been faithful to my father. She

Paragraph 5
The concluding paragraph restates the thesis (the parents are different) and draws a conclusion (love and God have kept them together).

attends church twice on Sunday and once more during the week. I have never heard her utter a single profane word or seen her take a drink. She believes in helping others as much as possible and proves this by giving to several charities and buying gifts frequently for her grandchildren.

5   I have often wondered what has kept my parents together for so many years. It must be true love and the help of God because, while the differences between them are great, the love they feel for each other appears to be greater.

NEAT PEOPLE VS. SLOPPY PEOPLE
Suzanne Britt

◆

In addition to writing a regular column for North Carolina Gardens and Homes *and* Dickens Dispatch, *Suzanne Britt has written for the* New York Times, Newsweek, *and the* Boston Globe. *A part-time English teacher, Britt has also published two textbooks and several collections of her essays. In "Neat People vs. Sloppy People," an entertaining contrast piece, she describes neat people as "lazier and meaner than sloppy people." Is there any truth to what she says, or does she play it all for laughs? Try to decide as you read.*

◆

1   I've finally figured out the difference between neat people and sloppy people. The distinction is, as always, moral. Neat people are lazier and meaner than sloppy people.

2   Sloppy people, you see, are not really sloppy. Their sloppiness is merely the unfortunate consequence of their extreme moral rectitude. Sloppy people carry in their mind's eye a heavenly vision, a precise plan, that is so stupendous, so perfect, it can't be achieved in this world or the next.

3   Sloppy people live in Never-Never Land. Someday is their métier. Someday they are planning to alphabetize all their books and set up home catalogs. Someday they will go through their wardrobes and mark certain items for tentative mending and certain items for passing on to relatives of similar shape and size. Someday sloppy people will make family scrapbooks into which they will put newspaper clippings, postcards, locks of hair, and the dried corsage from their senior prom. Someday they will file everything on the surface of their desks, including the cash receipts from coffee purchases at the snack shop. Someday they will sit down and read all the back issues of *The New Yorker*.

4   For all these noble reasons and more, sloppy people never get neat. They aim too high and wide. They save everything, planning someday to file, order, and straighten out the world. But while these ambitious plans take clearer and clearer shape in their heads, the books spill from the shelves onto the floor, the clothes pile up in the hamper and closet, the family mementos accumulate in every drawer, the surface of the desk is buried under mounds of paper and the unread magazines threaten to reach the ceiling.

5   Sloppy people can't bear to part with anything. They give loving attention to every detail. When sloppy people say they're going to tackle the surface of the desk, they really mean it. Not a paper will go unturned; not a rubber band will go unboxed. Four hours or two weeks into the excavation, the desk looks exactly the same, primarily because the sloppy person is meticulously creating

new piles of papers with new headings and scrupulously stopping to read all the old book catalogs before he throws them away. A neat person would just bulldoze the desk.

6   Neat people are bums and clods at heart. They have cavalier attitudes toward possessions, including family heirlooms. Everything is just another dust-catcher to them. If anything collects dust, it's got to go and that's that. Neat people will toy with the idea of throwing the children out of the house just to cut down on the clutter.

7   Neat people don't care about process. They like results. What they want to do is get the whole thing over with so they can sit down and watch the rasslin' on TV. Neat people operate on two unvarying principles: Never handle any item twice, and throw everything away.

8   The only thing messy in a neat person's house is the trash can. The minute something comes to a neat person's hand, he will look at it, try to decide if it has immediate use and, finding none, throw it in the trash.

9   Neat people are especially vicious with mail. They never go through their mail unless they are standing directly over a trash can. If the trash can is beside the mailbox, even better. All ads, catalogs, pleas for charitable contributions, church bulletins and money-saving coupons go straight into the trash can without being opened. All letters from home, postcards from Europe, bills and paychecks are opened, immediately responded to, then dropped in the trash can. Neat people keep their receipts only for tax purposes. That's it. No sentimental salvaging of birthday cards or the last letter a dying relative ever wrote. Into the trash it goes.

10   Neat people place neatness above everything, even economics. They are incredibly wasteful. Neat people throw away several toys every time they walk through the den. I knew a neat person once who threw away a perfectly good dish drainer because it had mold on it. The drainer was too much trouble to wash. And neat people sell their furniture when they move. They will sell a La-Z-Boy recliner while you are reclining in it.

11   Neat people are no good to borrow from. Neat people buy everything in expensive little single portions. They get their flour and sugar in two-pound bags. They wouldn't consider clipping a coupon, saving a leftover, reusing plastic nondairy whipped cream containers or rinsing off tin foil and draping it over the unmoldy dish drainer. You can never borrow a neat person's news-paper to see what's playing at the movies. Neat people have the paper all wadded up and in the trash by 7:05 A.M.

12   Neat people cut a clean swath through the organic as well as the inorganic world. People, animals, and things are all one to them. They are so insensitive. After they've finished with the pantry, the medicine cabinet, and the attic, they will throw out the red geranium (too many leaves), sell the dog (too many fleas), and send the children off to boarding school (too many scuffmarks on the hardwood floors).

Considering Ideas

1. Is Britt serious when she claims, in paragraph 1, that the distinction between neat and sloppy people is a moral one? Explain.
2. Britt says that neat people are insensitive, that they are bums and clods. How serious is she in this assessment? If she cannot be taken literally, then how would you describe her attitude toward neat people?
3. Cite two or three humorous passages that appeal to you. Why do you find them funny?
4. Do you think that Britt is being fair to neat people? To sloppy people? Explain.

Considering Technique

1. Which sentence functions as the thesis because it indicates the subjects under consideration and the fact that the subjects will be contrasted?
2. In which paragraphs does Britt use examples to clarify a point of contrast?
3. Does Britt use an alternating or block pattern to organize her details?
4. Does Britt achieve balance by treating the same points about both of her subjects? If not, is the lack of balance a problem? Explain.
5. Three paragraphs describe sloppy people and seven paragraphs describe neat people. Why is there more detail about neat people?
6. Why do you think Britt waits until the end of her essay to discuss how neat people treat living things?
7. Consult a dictionary if you are unsure of the meaning of any of these words: *rectitude* (paragraph 2), *métier* (paragraph 3), *meticulously* (paragraph 5), *scrupulously* (paragraph 5), *cavalier* (paragraph 6), *swath* (paragraph 12).

For Group Consideration

With two of your classmates analyze the humor in "Neat People vs. Sloppy People." Look at word choice, use of examples, and detail selection to determine how Britt achieves her humorous effects.

Journal Entry

Are you a neat or sloppy person? Identify yourself as one or the other and go on to explain whether any of Britt's characterizations are true of you.

Essay Assignments

1. Turn the tables on Britt and write a humorous contrast essay that proclaims the superiority of neat people.

2. Using humor if you wish, contrast one of the following: those who plan ahead and those who are impulsive, those who procrastinate and those who do not put things off, sports fans and those who pay little attention to sports, the athletic and the nonathletic, the lazy and the energetic, or the worriers and the fun-loving.
3. Write a humorous contrast of any of these campus types:
   a. students and teachers
   b. professors and deans
   c. older college students and younger college students
   d. commuter students and residential students
   e. brainy students and average students
   f. jocks and nonathletes

Considering Thematic Issues

1. Explain whether or not you think Britt's sentiments about neat and sloppy people are rooted in fact. To support your view, use the neat and sloppy people that you know as examples, including yourself, if you wish.
2. Read "Lists" on page 379, then write a humorous explanation of the kinds of lists you think neat people and sloppy people make and to what purpose the lists are put.

TWO VIEWS OF THE MISSISSIPPI
Mark Twain

◆

Samuel Clemens, better known as Mark Twain (1835–1910), is an important figure in American literature. His most famous work is the adventure tale Huckleberry Finn *(1884). The following selection is from Twain's autobiographical book* Life on the Mississippi *(1883). In this excerpt, he shares his contrasting views of the Mississippi River—that of a young apprentice riverboat pilot and that of a seasoned pilot. In addition, he informs the reader that when we gain knowledge, we also lose something. As you read, notice Twain's descriptive language and how this language changes with each view.*

◆

1   Now when I had mastered the language of this water, and had come to know every trifling feature that bordered the great river as familiarly as I knew the letters of the alphabet, I had made a valuable acquisition. But I had lost something, too, I had lost something which could never be restored to me while I lived. All the grace, the beauty, the poetry, had gone out of the majestic river! I still keep in mind a certain wonderful sunset which I witnessed when steamboating was new to me. A broad expanse of the river was turned to blood; in the middle distance the red hue brightened into gold, through which a solitary log came floating black and conspicuous; in one place a long, slanting mark lay sparkling upon the water; in another the surface was broken by boiling, tumbling rings, that were as many-tinted as an opal; where the ruddy flush was faintest, was a smooth spot that was covered with graceful circles and radiating lines, ever so delicately traced; the shore on our left was densely wooded, and the somber shadow that fell from this forest was broken in one place by a long, ruffled trail that shone like silver; and high above the forest wall a clean-stemmed dead tree waved a single leafy bough that glowed like a flame in the unobstructed splendor that was flowing from the sun. There were graceful curves, reflected images, woody heights, soft distances; and over the whole scene, far and near, the dissolving lights drifted steadily, enriching it every passing moment with new marvels of coloring.

2   I stood like one bewitched. I drank it in, in a speechless rapture. The world was new to me, and I had never seen anything like this at home. But as I have said, a day came when I began to cease from noting the glories and the charms which the moon and the sun and the twilight wrought upon the river's face; another day came when I ceased altogether to note them. Then, if that sunset scene had been repeated, I should have looked upon it without rapture, and should have commented upon it, inwardly, after this fashion: "This sun means that we are going to have wind to-morrow; that floating log means that the river is rising, small thanks to it; that slanting mark on the water refers to a bluff reef which is going to kill somebody's steamboat one of these nights, if it

keeps on stretching out like that; those tumbling 'boils' show a dissolving bar and a changing channel there; the lines and circles in the slick water over yonder are a warning that that troublesome place is shoaling up dangerously; that silver streak in the shadow of the forest is the 'break' from a new snag, and he has located himself in the very best place he could have found to fish for steamboats; that tall dead tree, with a single living branch, is not going to last long, and then how is a body ever going to get through this blind place at night without the friendly old landmark?"

3   No, the romance and beauty were all gone from the river. All the value any feature of it had for me now was the amount of usefulness it could furnish toward compassing the safe piloting of a steamboat. Since those days, I have pitied doctors from my heart. What does the lovely flush in a beauty's cheek mean to a doctor but a "break" that ripples above some deadly disease? Are not all her visible charms sown thick with what are to him the signs and symbols of hidden decay? Does he ever see her beauty at all, or doesn't he simply view her professionally, and comment upon her unwholesome condition all to himself? And doesn't he sometimes wonder whether he has gained most or lost most by learning his trade?

Considering Ideas

1. What subjects is Twain contrasting?
2. What are Twain's two views of the Mississippi River? What influenced each of these views?
3. As a result of mastering the river, Twain has gained something, but has lost something as well. What has he gained and lost?
4. Although essentially a contrast piece, the selection also includes the comparison of two subjects. What subjects are compared? What are the similarities between these subjects?
5. What point do you think Twain is making about maturity? Do you agree with that point?
6. What kind of reader do you think would make the best audience for the piece? Explain your view.

Considering Technique

1. From which sentences can the thesis be taken?
2. Are Twain's supporting details balanced? Explain.
3. What is the main difference between the word choice in paragraph 1 and paragraph 2? (See the discussion of description in Chapter 4.) How does the word choice in each paragraph help Twain achieve his purpose?
4. Cite two or three descriptions that you find particularly appealing. Why do you like them?
5. Why does Twain close by mentioning doctors? How is this discussion relevant to the rest of the piece?

6. Consult a dictionary if you are unsure of the meaning of any of these words: *trifling* (paragraph 1), *acquisition* (paragraph 1), *wrought* (paragraph 2), *sown* (paragraph 3).

For Group Consideration

Twain closes by asking whether the doctor "has gained most or lost most by learning his trade." With two or three classmates, consider this question and decide what the doctor gains and loses. As an alternative, consider the same issues for another professional: the journalist, the television star, the rock musician, the pilot, or the teacher, for example.

Journal Entry

Tell about a time when becoming more knowledgeable changed your view of something or someone. Overall, do you think you won more than you lost? Explain.

Essay Assignments

1. Contrast how you viewed a person or event when you were innocent and lacking in knowledge with how you viewed the person or event when you were more experienced and knowledgeable. For example, you could contrast your views of a parent, a holiday, a teacher, or your parents' divorce. Indicate whether you lost something as a result of gaining more knowledge about the person or event. (Your journal entry may help you with ideas.)

2. Drawing heavily on description, compare and/or contrast your current view of a particular place and the view you held as a child. For example, you could compare and/or contrast your views of your elementary school, a family vacation spot, your old bedroom, or your old neighborhood.

3. Compare and/or contrast the attitudes of youth and maturity. Use examples to clarify your points. Also indicate which of the attitudes is better and why.

Considering Thematic Issues

1. Twain makes the point that with maturity and knowledge comes a loss of romanticism. As a result, we view things more in terms of their usefulness and their significance than in terms of their beauty and capacity to inspire joy. Explain how this phenomenon contributes to conflicts between young people and their parents.

2. Read "The Knife" on page 193. Then explain to what extent Selzer does and does not conform to the image of the doctor described at the end of "Two Views of the Mississippi." Also, using the clues in "The Knife," answer one or more of the questions Twain poses at the end of his piece.

GRANT AND LEE: A STUDY IN CONTRASTS
Bruce Catton

Historian Bruce Catton, pronounced "Cayton" (1899–1978), was a newspaper reporter in Boston and Cleveland before becoming the editor of American Heritage *magazine. An authority on the Civil War, Catton published extensively on the subject, including the Pulitzer Prize–winning book* A Stillness at Appomattox *(1953). In "Grant and Lee: A Study in Contrasts," Catton compares and contrasts the Civil War's greatest generals to inform the reader that each man's personality reflected the side he represented. As you read, notice how the author organizes his details.*

1   When Ulysses S. Grant and Robert E. Lee met in the parlor of a modest house at Appomattox Court House, Virginia, on April 9, 1865, to work out the terms for the surrender of Lee's Army of Northern Virginia, a great chapter in American life came to a close, and a great new chapter began.

2   These men were bringing the Civil War to its virtual finish. To be sure, other armies had yet to surrender, and for a few days the fugitive Confederate government would struggle desperately and vainly, trying to find some way to go on living now that its chief support was gone. But in effect it was all over when Grant and Lee signed the papers. And the little room where they wrote out the terms was the scene of one of the poignant, dramatic contrasts in American history.

3   They were two strong men, these oddly different generals, and they represented the strengths of two conflicting currents that, through them, had come into final collision.

4   Back of Robert E. Lee was the notion that the old aristocratic concept might somehow survive and be dominant in American life.

5   Lee was tidewater Virginia, and in his background were family, culture, and tradition . . . the age of chivalry transplanted to a New World which was making its own legends and its own myths. He embodied a way of life that had come down through the age of knighthood and the English country squire. America was a land that was beginning all over again, dedicated to nothing much more complicated than the rather hazy belief that all men had equal rights and should have an equal chance in the world. In such a land Lee stood for the feeling that it was somehow of advantage to human society to have a pronounced inequality in the social structure. There should be a leisure class, backed by ownership of land; in turn, society itself should be keyed to the land as the chief source of wealth and influence. It would bring forth (according to this ideal) a class of men with a strong sense of obligation to the community;

men who lived not to gain advantage for themselves, but to meet the solemn obligations which had been laid on them by the very fact that they were privileged. From them the country would get its leadership; to them it could look for the higher values—of thought, of conduct, of personal deportment—to give it strength and virtue.

6   Lee embodied the noblest elements of this aristocratic ideal. Through him, the landed nobility justified itself. For four years, the Southern states had fought a desperate war to uphold the ideals for which Lee stood. In the end, it almost seemed as if the Confederacy fought for Lee; as if he himself was the Confederacy . . . the best thing that the way of life for which the Confederacy stood could ever have to offer. He had passed into legend before Appomattox. Thousands of tired, underfed, poorly clothed Confederate soldiers, long since past the simple enthusiasm of the early days of the struggle, somehow considered Lee the symbol of everything for which they had been willing to die. But they could not quite put this feeling into words. If the Lost Cause, sanctified by so much heroism and so many deaths, had a living justification, its justification was General Lee.

7   Grant, the son of a tanner on the Western frontier, was everything Lee was not. He had come up the hard way and embodied nothing in particular except the eternal toughness and sinewy fiber of the men who grew up beyond the mountains. He was one of a body of men who owed reverence and obeisance to no one, who were self-reliant to a fault, who cared hardly anything for the past but who had a sharp eye for the future.

8   These frontier men were the precise opposite of the tidewater aristocrats. Back of them, in the great surge that had taken people over the Alleghenies and into the opening Western country, there was a deep, implicit dissatisfaction with a past that had settled into grooves. They stood for democracy, not from any reasoned conclusion about the proper ordering of human society, but simply because they had grown up in the middle of democracy and knew how it worked. Their society might have privileges, but they would be privileges each man had won for himself. Forms and patterns meant nothing. No man was born to anything, except perhaps to a chance to show how far he could rise. Life was competition.

9   Yet along with this feeling had come a deep sense of belonging to a national community. The Westerner who developed a farm, opened a shop, or set up in business as a trader, could hope to prosper only as his own community prospered—and his community ran from the Atlantic to the Pacific and from Canada down to Mexico. If the land was settled, with towns and highways and accessible markets, he could better himself. He saw his fate in terms of the nation's own destiny. As its horizons expanded, so did his. He had, in other words, an acute dollars-and-cents stake in the continued growth and development of his country.

10   And that, perhaps, is where the contrast between Grant and Lee becomes most striking. The Virginia aristocrat, inevitably, saw himself in relation to his

own region. He lived in a static society which could endure almost anything except change. Instinctively, his first loyalty would go to the locality in which that society existed. He would fight to the limit of endurance to defend it, because in defending it he was defending everything that gave his own life its deepest meaning.

11   The Westerner, on the other hand, would fight with an equal tenacity for the broader concept of society. He fought so because everything he lived by was tied to growth, expansion, and a constantly widening horizon. What he lived by would survive or fall with the nation itself. He could not possibly stand by unmoved in the face of an attempt to destroy the Union. He would combat it with everything he had, because he could only see it as an effort to cut the ground out from under his feet.

12   So Grant and Lee were in complete contrast, representing two diametrically opposed elements in American life. Grant was the modern man emerging; beyond him, ready to come on the stage, was the great age of steel and machinery, of crowded cities and a restless burgeoning vitality. Lee might have ridden down from the old age of chivalry, lance in hand, silken banner fluttering over his head. Each man was the perfect champion of his cause, drawing both his strengths and his weaknesses from the people he led.

13   Yet it was not all contrast, after all. Different as they were—in background, in personality, in underlying aspiration—these two great soldiers had much in common. Under everything else, they were marvelous fighters. Furthermore, their fighting qualities were really very much alike.

14   Each man had, to begin with, the great virtue of utter tenacity and fidelity. Grant fought his way down the Mississippi Valley in spite of acute personal discouragement and profound military handicaps. Lee hung on in the trenches of Petersburg after hope itself had died. In each man there was an indomitable quality . . . the born fighter's refusal to give up as long as he can still remain on his feet and lift his two fists.

15   Daring and resourcefulness they had, too; the ability to think faster and move faster than the enemy. These were the qualities which gave Lee the dazzling campaigns of Second Manassas and Chancellorsville and won Vicksburg for Grant.

16   Lastly, and perhaps greatest of all, there was the ability, at the end, to turn quickly from war to peace once the fighting was over. Out of the way these two men behaved at Appomattox came the possibility of a peace of reconciliation. It was a possibility not wholly realized, in the years to come, but which did, in the end, help the two sections to become one nation again . . . after a war whose bitterness might have seemed to make such a reunion wholly impossible. No part of either man's life became him more than the part he played in their brief meeting in the McLean house at Appomattox. Their behavior there put all succeeding generations of Americans in their debt. Two great Americans, Grant and Lee—very different, yet under everything very much alike. Their encounter at Appomattox was one of the great moments of American history.

Considering Ideas

1. In what ways were Grant and Lee different? According to Catton, what is the most significant contrast between the generals?
2. In what ways were Grant and Lee similar? What is the most significant similarity?
3. According to Catton, why do Americans owe a debt to Grant and Lee?
4. Catton says that Grant and Lee represented conflicting forces in American society. What were those forces?
5. What do you think the author's attitude toward the two generals is? Does he admire one more than the other?
6. Catton does not specifically mention the two generals' differing views on slavery. Do you think he should have? Explain.

Considering Technique

1. Which paragraphs form the introduction of "Grant and Lee: A Study in Contrasts"? What approach does Catton take to that introduction?
2. Which sentence forms Catton's thesis? Which words in the thesis indicate that Catton will compare and contrast his subjects?
3. Catton combines block and alternating patterns for organizing his details. Which paragraphs include the block pattern, and which include the alternating pattern?
4. Why do you think Catton discusses the differences between Grant and Lee before he discusses the similarities?
5. To what extent does Catton use a progressive order for his details?
6. The author makes frequent use of topic sentences. Which paragraphs open with topic sentences? What purpose do these topics sentences serve?
7. Consult a dictionary if you are unsure of the meaning of any of these words: *poignant* (paragraph 2), *aristocratic* (paragraph 4), *tidewater* (paragraph 5), *chivalry* (paragraph 5), *squire* (paragraph 5), *deportment* (paragraph 5), *sinewy* (paragraph 7), *obeisance* (paragraph 7), *static* (paragraph 10), *diametrically* (paragraph 12), *burgeoning* (paragraph 12), *tenacity* (paragraph 14), *fidelity* (paragraph 14), *indomitable* (paragraph 14).

For Group Consideration

Catton closes his essay by saying that Grant and Lee's "encounter at Appomattox was one of the great moments of American history." With three or four classmates, compile a list of three other "great moments of American history" and explain why they are great.

Journal Entry

In one or two pages, explain what you learned about Grant, Lee, the Civil War, and the Civil War era as a result of reading "Grant and Lee: A Study in Contrasts."

Essay Assignments

1. Catton compares and contrasts two Civil War generals. Compare and/or contrast two people who do the same thing: two teachers, two musicians, two actors, two students, two ball players, and so on.
2. Compare and/or contrast two people who represent different value systems, philosophies of life, or ways of doing things. For example, you can compare and/or contrast a coach who believes that winning is everything with a coach who doesn't, a strict parent and a permissive parent, a liberal and conservative politician, and so on.
3. Like Catton, write a comparison and contrast of two people, one who is tied to the past and one who looks to the future. These people can be acquaintances of yours, historical figures, sports figures, educators, and so on.
4. Do you know two people who are "very different, yet under everything very much alike"? If so, compare and contrast these two people. If you wish, combine block and alternating patterns, as Catton does.

Considering Thematic Issues

1. Catton makes it clear that Grant and Lee each represented a force in American society. Pick someone who represents a force in contemporary society (for example, Madonna, Gloria Steinem, Jesse Jackson, or Rush Limbaugh) and explain what the force is and how the person's traits and behavior represent that force.
2. Explain whether you think the forces at work in today's society are more like those represented by Grant or by Lee. You can draw on your own experience and observation, as well as on one or more of the following essays: "Untouchables" (page 159), "How I'll Become an American" (page 189), "Shades of Black" (page 336), "What Is Poverty?" (page 349), and "Self-Help: A Black Tradition (page 425)".

AM I BLUE?
Alice Walker

Alice Walker is a poet, essayist, and nov-elist. She won a Pulitzer Prize and the American Book Award for fiction for her most famous novel, The Color Purple *(1982). In "Am I Blue?" which first appeared in* Ms. *(July 1986), Walker tells a story that includes both description and comparison and contrast to achieve three purposes: to share a bit of her experience, to inform the reader about the oneness of animals and humans, and to convince the reader to treat animals well. The title of the essay is the same as a great, old blues song. As you read, ask yourself why that title is particularly appropriate.*

◆

1
> *"Ain't these tears in these
> eyes tellin' you?"* *

2   For about three years my companion and I rented a small house in the country that stood on the edge of a large meadow that appeared to run from the end of our deck straight into the mountains. The mountains, however, were quite far away, and between us and them there was, in fact, a town. It was one of the many pleasant aspects of the house that you never really were aware of this.

3   It was a house of many windows, low, wide, nearly floor to ceiling in the living room, which faced the meadow, and it was from one of these that I first saw our closest neighbor, a large white horse, cropping grass, flipping its mane, and ambling about—not over the entire meadow, which stretched well out of sight of the house, but over the five or so fenced-in acres that were next to the twenty-odd that we had rented. I soon learned that the horse, whose name was Blue, belonged to a man who lived in another town, but was boarded by our neighbors next door. Occasionally, one of the children, usually a stocky teen-ager, but sometimes a much younger girl or boy, could be seen riding Blue. They would appear in the meadow, climb up on his back, ride furiously for ten or fifteen minutes, then get off, slap Blue on the flanks, and not be seen again for a month or more.

4   There were many apple trees in our yard, and one by the fence that Blue could almost reach. We were soon in the habit of feeding him apples, which he relished, especially because by the middle of summer the meadow grasses—so green and succulent since January—had dried out from lack of rain, and Blue

---

* From "Am I Blue?" by Grant Clarke and Harry Akst. Copyright 1929 Warner Bros. Inc. (renewed). Used by permission. All rights reserved.

stumbled about munching the dried stalks halfheartedly. Sometimes he would stand very still just by the apple tree, and when one of us came out he would whinny, snort loudly, or stamp the ground. This meant, of course: I want an apple.

5   It was quite wonderful to pick a few apples, or collect those that had fallen to the ground overnight, and patiently hold them, one by one, up to his large, toothy mouth. I remained as thrilled as a child by his flexible dark lips, huge, cubelike teeth that crunched the apples, core and all, with such finality, and his high, broad-breasted *enormity*; beside which, I felt small indeed. When I was a child, I used to ride horses, and was especially friendly with one named Nan until the day I was riding and my brother deliberately spooked her and I was thrown, head first, against the trunk of a tree. When I came to, I was in bed and my mother was bending worriedly over me; we silently agreed that perhaps horseback riding was not the safest sport for me. Since then I have walked, and prefer walking to horseback riding—but I had forgotten the depth of feeling one could see in horses' eyes.

6   I was therefore unprepared for the expression in Blue's. Blue was lonely. Blue was horribly lonely and bored. I was not shocked that this should be the case; five acres to tramp by yourself, endlessly, even in the most beautiful of meadows—and his was—cannot provide many interesting events, and once rainy season turned to dry that was about it. No, I was shocked that I had forgotten that human animals and nonhuman animals can communicate quite well; if we are brought up around animals as children we take this for granted. By the time we are adults we no longer remember. However, the animals have not changed. They are in fact *completed* creations (at least they seem to be, so much more than we) who are not likely *to* change; it is their nature to express themselves. What else are they going to express? And they do. And, generally speaking, they are ignored.

7   After giving Blue the applies, I would wander back to the house, aware that he was observing me. Were more apples not forthcoming then? Was that to be his sole entertainment for the day? My partner's small son had decided he wanted to learn how to piece a quilt; we worked in silence on our respective squares as I thought . . .

8   Well, about slavery: about white children, who were raised by black people, who knew their first all-accepting love from black women, and then, when they were twelve or so, were told they must "forget" the deep levels of communication between themselves and "mammy" that they knew. Later they would be able to relate quite calmly, "My old mammy was sold to another good family." "My old mammy was _____." Fill in the blank. Many more years later a white woman would say: "I can't understand these Negroes, these blacks. What do they want? They're so different from us."

9   And about the Indians, considered to be "like animals" by the "settlers" (a very benign euphemism for what they actually were), who did not understand their description as a compliment.

10 And about the thousands of American men who marry Japanese, Korean, Filipina, and other non-English-speaking women and of how happy they report they are, "*blissfully*," until their brides learn to speak English, at which point the marriages tend to fall apart. What then did the men see, when they looked into the eyes of the women they married, before they could speak English? Apparently only their own reflections.

11 I thought of society's impatience with the young. "Why are they playing the music so loud?" Perhaps the children have listened to much of the music of oppressed people their parents danced to before they were born, with its passionate but soft cries for acceptance and love, and they have wondered why their parents failed to hear.

12 I do not know how long Blue had inhabited his five beautiful, boring acres before we moved into our house; a year after we had arrived—and had also traveled to other valleys, other cities, other worlds—he was still there.

13 But then, in our second year at the house, something happened in Blue's life. One morning, looking out the window at the fog that lay like a ribbon over the meadow, I saw another horse, a brown one, at the other end of Blue's field. Blue appeared to be afraid of it, and for several days made no attempt to go near. We went away for week. When he returned, Blue had decided to make friends and the two horses ambled or galloped along together, and Blue did not come nearly as often to the fence underneath the apple tree.

14 When he did, bringing his new friend with him, there was a different look in his eyes. A look of independence, of self-possession, of inalienable *horse-ness*. His friend eventually became pregnant. For months and months there was, it seemed to me, a mutual feeling between me and the horses of justice, of peace. I fed apples to them both. The look in Blue's eyes was one of unabashed "this is *it*ness."

15 It did not, however, last forever. One day, after a visit to the city, I went out to give Blue some apples. He stood waiting, or so I thought, though not beneath the tree. When I shook the tree and jumped back from the shower of apples, he made no move. I carried some over to him. He managed to half-crunch one. The rest he let fall to the ground. I dreaded looking into his eyes— because I had of course noticed that Brown, his partner, had gone—but I did look. If I had been born into slavery, and my partner had been sold or killed, my eyes would have looked like that. The children next door explained that Blue's partner had been "put with him" (the same expression that old people used, I had noticed, when speaking of an ancestor during slavery who had been impregnated by her owner) so that they would mate and she conceive. Since that was accomplished, she had been taken back by her owner, who lived somewhere else.

16 Will she be back? I asked.

17 They didn't know.

18 Blue was like a crazed person. Blue *was*, to me, a crazed person. He galloped furiously, as if he were being ridden, around and around his five

beautiful acres. He whinnied until he couldn't. He tore at the ground with his hooves. he butted himself against his single shade tree. He looked always and always toward the road down which his partner had gone. And then, occasionally, when he came up for apples, or I took apples to him, he looked at me. It was a look so piercing, so full of grief, a look so *human*, I almost laughed (I felt too sad to cry) to think there are people who do not know that animals suffer. People like me who have forgotten, and daily forget, all that animals try to tell us. "Everything you do to us will happen to you; we are your teachers, as you are ours. We are one lesson" is essentially it, I think. There are those who never once have even considered animals' rights: those who have been taught that animals actually want to be used and abused by us, as small children "love" to be frightened, or women "love" to be mutilated and raped. . . . They are the great-grandchildren of those who honestly thought, because someone taught them this: "Women can't think," and "niggers can't faint." But most disturbing of all, in Blue's large brown eyes was a new look, more painful than the look of despair: the look of disgust with human beings, with life; the look of hatred. And it was odd what the look of hatred did. It gave him, for the first time, the look of a beast. And what that meant was that he had put up a barrier within to protect himself from further violence; all the apples in the world wouldn't change that fact.

19   And so Blue remained, a beautiful part of our landscape, very peaceful to look at from the window, white against the grass. Once a friend came to visit and said, looking out on the soothing view: "And it *would* have to be a *white* horse; the very image of freedom." And I thought, yes, the animals are forced to become for us merely "images" of what they once so beautifully expressed. And we are used to drinking milk from containers showing "contented" cows, whose real lives we want to hear nothing about, eating eggs and drumsticks from "happy" hens, and munching hamburgers advertised by bulls of integrity who seem to command their fate.

20   As we talked of freedom and justice one day for all, we sat down to steaks. I am eating misery, I thought, as I took the first bite. And spit it out.

Considering Ideas

1. Walker compares Blue to a human being. In what ways are the horse and a person similar?
2. In paragraphs 8 through 11, Blue's relationship with people is compared to a number of other human relationships. What are those relationships? What is the common element in each of these comparisons?
3. Specifically, what messages do you think Walker is trying to communicate to her reader?
4. Blue is given human qualities throughout most of the essay. However, in paragraph 18, he becomes a "beast." Why? When he becomes beastlike, is he less like a human and more like an animal? Explain.

5. Walker says that Blue has feelings and the ability to communicate those feelings. Do you agree? Explain.

Considering Technique

1. Which paragraph best presents Walker's focus and the ideas she wants to convey to her reader? Why does she wait so long to present her focus?
2. Which paragraphs include description? What purpose does the description serve?
3. To what extent is "Am I Blue?" a narrative essay (an essay that tells a story)?
4. Do you think Walker's title is a good one? Why or why not?
5. "Am I Blue?" appeared in *Ms.* in 1986. What kind of audience was Walker reaching? Is the essay suited to that kind of audience? Explain.
6. Walker has a persuasive purpose to some extent. Of what is she trying to persuade her reader?
7. Consult a dictionary if you are unsure of the meaning of any of these words from the essay: *succulent* (paragraph 3), *respective* (paragraph 6), *euphemism* (paragraph 8), *ambled* (paragraph 12), *inalienable* (paragraph 13), *unabashed* (paragraph 13).

For Group Consideration

In paragraph 18, Walker indicates that animals say to people, "Everything you do to us will happen to you; we are your teachers, as you are ours. We are one lesson." With three or four classmates, discuss what this quote means and indicate whether you agree or disagree with it. Share your conclusions with the rest of the class.

Journal Entry

What do you think of vegetarianism? Should people show respect for animals by not eating meat? What about wearing leather and fur? Should people wear only materials not made from animals? Explore your feelings on these matters.

Essay Assignments

1. Walker compares Blue to a human being because he can feel and express his emotions. If you have a pet and believe that the pet shares something in common with humans, write a comparison of the pet and human beings. If possible, use some narration and description with your comparison. (Be careful to avoid obvious statements, such as "My cat, like people, must eat and drink every day.")
2. In paragraph 19, Walker contrasts the images of animals in advertising with the reality of these animals' existence. Expand the idea in paragraph 19 into

a full essay that contrasts our images of happy animals (in advertising, in children's stories, in movies, and on television, for example) and the real existence of these animals. For example, you could contrast the image of Elsie, the Borden cow, with the reality of life for dairy cows that are kept as "milking machines."

3. Compare our treatment of animals (as pets, as parts of lab experiments, as sources of income, as helpers, as companions, as beasts of burden, and as sources of entertainment) to our treatment of each other. Your purpose is to persuade your reader that we treat animals the same way we treat human beings.

4. Compare and contrast your view of animals before and after reading "Am I Blue?" to explain the impact the essay had on you.

Considering Thematic Issues

1. Summarize Walker's view of how humans treat animals, and then argue that we should or should not alter our treatment of them. (See the appendix on how to write a summary.)

2. Describe the view of human nature that is presented in "Am I Blue?", "By Any Other Name" (page 111), and "Untouchables" (page 159). Do you subscribe to that view of human nature? Explain why or why not, drawing on examples to illustrate your view.

BRAINS AND COMPUTERS
Robert Jastrow

◆

A physicist with a specialty in astron-omy, Robert Jastrow directed NASA's Goddard Space Flight Center. In "Brains and Computers," he informs the reader about the workings of two complex items: the human brain and the computer. When you are through reading, ask yourself how "intelligent" computers (those capable of learning) can alter our lives.

◆

1   Circuits, wires and computing are strange terms to use for a biological organ like the brain, made largely of water, and without electronic parts. Nonetheless, they are accurate terms because brains work in very much the same way as computers. Brains think; computers add and subtract; but both devices seem to work on the basis of the same fundamental steps in logical reasoning.

2.   All arithmetic and mathematics can be broken down into these fundamental steps. Most kinds of thinking can also be broken down into such steps. Only the highest realms of creative activity seem to defy this analysis, but it is possible that even creative thinking could be broken down in this way, if the subconscious mind could be penetrated to examine the processes that appear at the conscious level as the flash of insight, or the stroke of genius.

3   The basic logical steps that underlie all mathematics and all reasoning are surprisingly simple. The most important ones are called AND and OR. AND is a code name for the reasoning that says, "If 'a' is true *and* 'b' is true, then 'c' is true." OR is a code name for the reasoning that says, "IF 'a' is true *or* 'b' is true, then 'c' is true." These lines of reasoning are converted into electrical circuits by means of devices called "gates." In a computer the gates are made out of electronic parts—diodes or transistors. In the brain of an animal or a human, the gates are neurons or nerve cells. A gate—in a computer or in a brain—is an electrical pathway that opens up and allows electricity to pass through when certain conditions are satisfied. Normally, two wires go into one side of the gate, and another wire emerges from the other side of the gate. The two wires coming into the gate on one side represent the two ideas "a" *and* "b." The wire going out the other side of the gate represents the conclusion "c" based on these ideas. When a gate is wired up to be an AND gate, it works in such a way that if electrical signals flow into it from both the "a" and "b" wires, an electrical signal then flows out the other side through the "c" wire. From an electrical point of view, this is the same as saying, "If 'a' *and* 'b' are true, then 'c' is true."

4   When the gate is wired as an OR gate, on the other hand, it permits electricity to pass through the outgoing, or "c," wire if an electrical signal comes

into the other side through either the "a" wire *or* the "b" wire. Electrically, this is the same as saying, "If 'a' *or* 'b' is true, then 'c' is true."

5   How do these two kinds of gates do arithmetic? How do they carry on a line of reasoning? Suppose a computer is about to add "1" and "1" to make "2"; this means that inside the computer a gate has two wires coming into it on one side, representing "1" and "1," and a wire coming out on the other side, representing "2." If the gate is wired as an AND gate, then, when electrical signals come into it through both of the "1" wires, it sends a signal out the other side through the "2" wire. This gate has added "1" and "1" electrically to make "2."

6   Slightly different kinds of gates, but based on the same idea, can subtract, multiply and divide. Thousands of such gates, wired together in different combinations, can do income tax returns, algebra problems and higher mathematics. They can also be connected together to do the kinds of thinking and reasoning that enter into everyday life. Suppose, for example, that a company distributes several different lines of goods, and its management assigns a computer the task of keeping a continuous check on the inventories in these various product lines. Inside that computer certain gates will be wired as AND gates to work in the following way: two wires coming into one side of the gate carry signals that indicate "stock depleted" and "sales volume heavy." If the stock is depleted *and* the sales are brisk, the gate opens, and a decision comes through: Order more goods!

7   OR gates are just as important in reasoning. Suppose that the same company also relies on its computer for guidance in setting prices. That means that a certain gate inside the computer is wired as an OR gate; coming into one side of this gate is a wire that indicates cash flow, another wire that indicates prices charged by a competitor for similar products, and a third wire that indicates the inventory in this particular product. If the company needs cash, *or* it is being undersold by its competitors, *or* it has an excess inventory, then the decision gate opens and a command comes through: Cut prices!

8   In a simple computer, the gates are wired together permanently, so that the computer can only do the same tasks over and over again. This kind of computer comes into the world wired to do one set of things, and can never depart from its fixed repertoire. A computer that solves the same problems in the same way, over and over again, is like a frog that can only snap at dark, moving spots; if either kind of brain is presented with a novel situation, it will react stupidly, or not react at all, because it lacks the wiring necessary for a new response to a new challenge. Such brains are unintelligent.

9   Larger, more complex computers have greater flexibility. In these computers, the connections between the gates can be changed, and they can be wired up to do different kinds of things at different times; their repertoire is variable. The instructions for connecting the gates to do each particular kind of problem are stored in the computer's memory banks. These instructions are

called the computer's "program." When a computer expert wants his machine to stop one kind of task and start another, he inserts a new program into the computer's memory. The new program automatically erases the old one, takes command of the machine, and sets about doing its appointed task.

10 However, this computer is still not intelligent; it has no innate flexibility. The flexibility and intelligence reside in its programmer. But if the memory banks of the computer are extremely large a great advance in computer design becomes possible, that marks a highlight in the evolution of computers comparable to the first appearance of the mammals on the earth. A computer with a very large memory can store a set of instructions lengthy enough to permit it to learn by experience, just like an intelligent animal. Learning by experience requires a large memory and a very long set of instructions, i.e., a complicated program, because it is a much more elaborate way of solving problems than a stereotyped response would be. When a brain—electronic or animal—learns by experience, it goes through the following steps: first, it tries an approach; then it compares its result with the desired result, i.e., the goal; then, if it succeeds in achieving its goal, it sends an instruction to its memory to use the same approach next time; in the case of failure, it searches through its reasoning or computations to pinpoint the main source of error; finally, the brain adjusts the faulty part of its program to bring the result into line with its desires. Every time the same problem arises, the brain repeats the sequence and makes new adjustments to its program. A large computer has programs that work in just that fashion. Like a brain, it modifies its reasoning as its experience develops. In this way, the computer gradually improves its performance. It is learning.

11 A brain that can learn possesses the beginnings of intelligence. The requirements for this invaluable trait are, first, a good-sized memory, and, second, a wiring inside the brain that permits the circuits connecting the gates to be changed by the experience of life. In fact, in the best brains—judging brain quality entirely by intelligence—many circuits are unwired initially; that is, the animal is born with a large number of the gates in its brain more or less unconnected with one another. The gates become connected gradually, as the animal learns the best strategies for its survival. In man, the part of the brain filled with blank circuits at birth is greater than in any other animal; that is what is meant by the plasticity of human behavior.

12 Large computers have some essential attributes of an intelligent brain: they have large memories, and they have gates whose connections can be modified by experience. However, the thinking of these computers tends to be narrow. The richness of human thought depends to a considerable degree on the enormous number of wires, or nerve fibers, coming into each gate in the human brain. A gate in a computer has two, or three, or at most four wires entering on one side, and one wire coming out the other side. In the brain of an animal, the gates may have thousands of wires entering one side, instead of two

or three. In the human brain, a gate may have as many as 100,000 wires entering it. Each wire comes from another gate or nerve cell. This means that every gate in the human brain is connected to as many as 100,000 other gates in other parts of the brain. During the process of thinking innumerable gates open and close throughout the brain. When one of these gates "decides" to open, the decision is the result of a complicated assessment involving inputs from thousands of other gates. This circumstance explains much of the difference between human thinking and computer thinking.

13   Furthermore, the gates in the brains of an animal or a human do not work on an "all-or-nothing" basis. The AND gate in a computer, for example, will only open if *all* the wires coming into it carry electrical signals. If one wire entering a computer gate fails to carry a signal, the gate remains shut. If every one of the 100,000 pathways into a gate in a human brain had to transmit an electrical signal before that gate could open, the brain would be paralyzed. Instead, most gates in the brain work on the principle of ALMOST, rather than AND or OR. The ALMOST gate makes human thought so imprecise, but so powerful. Suppose that 50,000 wires enter one side of a gate in a human brain; if this were an AND gate in a computer, all 50,000 things would have to be true simultaneously before that gate opened and let a signal through. In real life, 50,000 things are rarely true at the same time, and any brain that waited for such a high degree of assurance before it acted would be an exceedingly slow brain. It would hardly ever reach a decision, and the possessor of a brain like that would not be likely to pass its genes on to the next generation.

14   Real brains work very differently. Wired largely out of ALMOST gates, they only require that, say, 10,000 or 15,000 things out of 50,000 shall be true about a situation before they act, or perhaps an even smaller number than that. As a consequence, they are inaccurate; they make mistakes sometimes; but they are very fast. In the struggle for survival, the value to the individual of the speed of such a brain more than offsets the disadvantages in its imprecision.

Considering Ideas

1. Why do brains and computers operate similarly?
2. Despite their fundamental similarity, brains and computers are different. What are the chief differences between them?
3. What is the chief difference between simple and complex computers?
4. In paragraph 11, Jastrow refers to "the plasticity of human behavior." What do you think this phrase means? What accounts for the plasticity Jastrow refers to?
5. What specific informational purposes does Jastrow have?
6. For what kind of reader do you think the essay is suited?

Considering Technique

1. What is the thesis of "Brains and Computers"? What information does the thesis provide about the essay?
2. Are Jastrow's details arranged in a block or alternating pattern?
3. In which paragraphs does the author use examples to help clarify his points? What role does process analysis play in the essay? (Process analysis, explained in Chapter 7, shows how something is made or done.)
4. What elements of contrast appear in the essay?
5. What approach does Jastrow take to his conclusion?
6. Consult a dictionary if you are unsure of the meaning of these words: *repertoire* (paragraph 8), *plasticity* (paragraph 11).

For Group Consideration

In paragraphs 10 and 11, Jastrow explains that a large computer can learn by experience, and thus it "possesses the beginnings of intelligence." With three or four classmates, consider the implications of "intelligent" computers. What are the chief advantages and drawbacks of a thinking machine? What might "intelligent" computers be capable of in the future? If you need help considering this issue, speak to a student or faculty member in computer science or electrical engineering.

Journal Entry

Write a page or two about computers, focusing on any one or more of these questions: Do you understand how computers work? To what extent do computers figure in your day-to-day living? Have you had any positive or negative experiences with computers? If so, tell about them. Are computers a positive or negative force in society?

Essay Assignments

1. Like Jastrow, compare and/or contrast the way two things work. Select subjects that perform similar functions (for example, eyeglasses and contact lenses, compact disc players and tape players, air conditioners and fans). Your purpose is to clarify something that is not well understood or provide fresh insight into something familiar. If necessary, do some research to gather any information you need.
2. Jastrow compares and contrasts a part of human anatomy (the brain) and a mechanical device (the computer). Do the same thing by comparing and contrasting the human eye and a camera or by comparing and contrasting the human ear and a tape recorder. If necessary, do some research to gather information.

3. Compare and/or contrast life with and without computers to help your reader understand the role computers play in modern life. Be sure to use examples to clarify your points.
4. Compare and/or contrast two versions of the same device: two kinds of cars, two brands of stereos, two kinds of bicycles, and so on.

Considering Thematic Issues

1. Explain to what extent computers figure into your day-to-day living and in what ways they enhance or detract from the quality of your life. (Your journal entry may give you some ideas.)
2. Using the information in "Brains and Computers" and "What Sort of Cart-Rt-Sort Am I?" (page 207), along with your own experience and observation, explain whether computers are a positive or negative force. Do you think people should fear computers? Explain why or why not.

TALK IN THE INTIMATE
RELATIONSHIP:
HIS AND HERS
Deborah Tannen

◆

*Deborah Tannen, a linguistics professor
at Georgetown University, has researched communication between the sexes
and shared her findings on television, in newspapers, and in two books. The
following selection is from her first book,* That's Not What I Meant: How
Conversational Style Makes or Breaks Relationships. *The excerpt explains how
differences between men and women affect the way we communicate. Tannen
says that the sexes have "different expectations about the role of talk in relationships." As you read, ask yourself whether your experience bears out the points
Tannen makes.*

◆

1   Male-female conversation is cross-cultural communication. Culture is simply a network of habits and patterns gleaned from past experience, and women
and men have different past experiences. From the time they're born, they're
treated differently, talked to differently, and talk differently as a result. Boys and
girls grow up in different worlds, even if they grow up in the same house. And
as adults they travel in different worlds, reinforcing patterns established in
childhood. These cultural differences include different expectations about the
role of talk in relationships and how it fulfills that role. . . .

2   **He Said/She Said: His and Her Conversational Styles.**   Everyone
knows that as a relationship becomes long-term, its terms change. But women
and men often differ in how they expect them to change. Many women feel,
"After all this time, you should know what I want without my telling you." Many
men feel, "After all this time, we should be able to tell each other what we
want."

3   These incongruent expectations capture one of the key differences
between men and women. . . . Communication is always a matter of balancing
conflicting needs for involvement and independence. Though everyone has
both these needs, women often have a relatively greater need for involvement,
and men a relatively greater need for independence. Being understood without
saying what you mean gives a payoff in involvement, and that is why women
value it so highly.

4   If you want to be understood without saying what you mean explicitly in
words, you must convey meaning somewhere else—in how words are spoken,
or by metamessages. Thus it stands to reason that women are often more
attuned than men to the metamessages of talk. When women surmise meaning
in this way, it seems mysterious to men, who call it "women's intuition" (if they

think it's right) or "reading things in" (if they think it's wrong). Indeed, it could be wrong, since metamessages are not on record. And even if it is right, there is still the question of scale: How significant are the metamessages that are there? 5   . . . Metamessages are a form of indirectness. Women are more likely to be indirect, and to try to reach agreement by negotiation. Another way to understand this preference is that negotiation allows a display of solidarity, which women prefer to the display of power (even though . . . the aim may be the same—getting what you want). Unfortunately, power and solidarity are bought with the same currency: Ways of talking intended to create solidarity have the simultaneous effect of framing power differences. When they think they're being nice, women often end up appearing deferential and unsure of themselves or of what they want.

6   When styles differ, misunderstandings are always rife. As their differing styles create misunderstandings, women and men try to clear them up by talking things out. These pitfalls are compounded in talks between men and women because they have different ways of going about talking things out, and different assumptions about the significance of going about it.

7   The rest of this [discussion] illustrates these differences, explains their origins in children's patterns of play, and shows the effects when women and men talk to each other in the context of intimate relationships in our culture.

8   **Women Listen for Metamessages.**   Sylvia and Harry celebrated their fiftieth wedding anniversary at a mountain resort. Some of the guests were at the resort for the whole weekend, others just for the evening of the celebration: a cocktail party followed by a sitdown dinner. The manager of the dining room approached Sylvia during dinner. "Since there's so much food tonight," he said, "and the hotel prepared a fancy dessert and everyone already ate at the cocktail party anyway, how about cutting and serving the anniversary cake at lunch tomorrow?" Sylvia asked the advice of the others at her table. All the men agreed: "Sure, that makes sense. Save the cake for tomorrow." All the women disagreed: "No, the party is tonight. Serve the cake tonight." The men were focusing on the message: the cake as food. The women were thinking of the metamessage: Serving a special cake frames an occasion as a celebration.

9   Why are women more attuned to metamessages? Because they are more focused on involvement, that is, on relationships among people, and it is through metamessages that relationships among people are established and maintained. If you want to take the temperature and check the vital signs of a relationship, the barometers to check are its metamessages: what is said and how.

10   Everyone can see these signals, but whether or not we pay attention to them is another matter—a matter of being sensitized. Once you are sensitized, you can't roll your antennae back in; they're stuck in the extended position.

11   When interpreting meaning, it is possible to pick up signals that weren't intentionally sent out, like an innocent flock of birds on a radar screen. The

birds are there—and the signals women pick up are there—but they may not mean what the interpreter thinks they mean. For example, Maryellen looks at Larry and asks, "What's wrong?" because his brow is furrowed. Since he was only thinking about lunch, her expression of concern makes him feel under scrutiny.

12   The difference in focus on messages and metamessages can give men and women different points of view on almost any comment. Harriet complains to Morton, "Why don't you ask me how my day was?" He replies, "If you have something to tell me, tell me. Why do you have to be invited?" The reason is that she wants the metamessage of interest: evidence that he cares how her day was, regardless of whether or not she has something to tell.

13   A lot of trouble is caused between women and men by, of all things, pronouns. Women often feel hurt when their partners use "I" or "me" in a situation in which they would use "we" or "us." When Morton announces, "I think I'll go for a walk," Harriet feels specifically uninvited, though Morton later claims she would have been welcome to join him. She felt locked out by his use of "I" and his omission of an invitation: "Would you like to come?" Meta-messages can be seen in what is not said as well as what is said.

14   It's difficult to straighten out such misunderstandings because each one feels convinced of the logic of his or her position and the illogic—or irresponsibility—of the other's. Harriet knows that she always asks Morton how his day was, and that she'd never announce, "I'm going for a walk," without inviting him to join her. If he talks differently to her, it must be that he feels differently. But Morton wouldn't feel unloved if Harriet didn't ask about his day, and he would feel free to ask, "Can I come along?," if she announced she was taking a walk. So he can't believe she is justified in feeling responses he knows he wouldn't have.

15   **Messages and Metamessages in Talk between . . . Grown Ups?** These processes are dramatized with chilling yet absurdly amusing authenticity in Jules Feiffer's play *Grown Ups*. To get a closer look at what happens when men and women focus on different levels of talk in talking things out, let's look at what happens in this play.

16   Jake criticizes Louise for not responding when their daughter, Edie, called her. His comment leads to a fight even though they're both aware that this one incident is not in itself important.

17   JAKE: Look, I don't care if it's important or not, when a kid calls its mother
             the mother should answer.
    LOUISE: Now I'm a bad mother.
      JAKE: I didn't say that.
    LOUISE: It's in your stare.
      JAKE: Is that another thing you know? My stare?

Louis ignores Jake's message—the question of whether or not she responded when Edie called—and goes for the metamessage: his implication that she's a bad mother, which Jake insistently disclaims. When Louise explains the signals she's reacting to, Jake not only discounts them but is angered at being held accountable not for what he said but for how he looked—his stare.

18   As the play goes on, Jake and Louise replay and intensify these patterns:

> LOUISE: If I'm such a terrible mother, do you want a divorce?
>
> JAKE: I do not think you're a terrible mother and no, thank you, I do not want a divorce. Why is it that whenever I bring up any difference between us you ask me if I want a divorce?

The more he denies any meaning beyond the message, the more she blows it up, the more adamantly he denies it, and so on:

> JAKE: I have brought up one thing that you do with Edie that I don't think you notice that I have noticed for some time but which I have deliberately not brought up before because I had hoped you would notice it for yourself and stop doing it and also—frankly, baby, I have to say this—I knew if I brought it up we'd get into exactly the kind of circular argument we're in right now. And I wanted to avoid it. But I haven't and we're in it, so now, with your permission, I'd like to talk about it.
>
> LOUISE: You don't see how that puts me down?
>
> JAKE: What?
>
> LOUISE: If you think I'm so stupid why do you go on living with me?
>
> JAKE: *Dammit! Why can't anything ever be simple around here?!*

It can't be simple because Louise and Jake are responding to different levels of communication. As in Bateson's example of the dual-control electric blanket with crossed wires, each one intensifies the energy going to a different aspect of the problem. Jake tries to clarify his point by overelaborating it, which gives Louise further evidence that he's condescending to her, making it even less likely that she will address his point rather than his condescension.

19   What pushes Jake and Louise beyond anger to rage is their different perspectives on metamessages. His refusal to admit that his statements have implications and overtones denies her authority over her own feelings. Her attempts to interpret what he didn't say and put the metamessage into the message makes him feel she's putting words into his mouth—denying his authority over his own meaning.

20   The same thing happens when Louise tells Jake that he is being manipulated by Edie:

> LOUISE: Why don't you ever make her come to see you? Why do you always go to her?

> JAKE: You want me to play power games with a nine year old? I want her to know I'm interested in her. Someone around here has to show interest in her.
>
> LOUISE: You love her more than I do.
>
> JAKE: I didn't say that.
>
> LOUISE: Yes, you did.
>
> JAKE: You don't know how to listen. You have never learned how to listen. It's as if listening to you is a foreign language.

Again, Louise responds to his implication—this time, that he loves Edie more because he runs when she calls. And yet again, Jake cries literal meaning, denying he meant any more than he said.

21   Throughout their argument, the point to Louise is her feelings—that Jake makes her feel put down—but to him the point is her actions—that she doesn't always respond when Edie calls:

> LOUISE: You talk about what I do to Edie, what do you think you do to me?
>
> JAKE: This is not the time to go into what we do to each other.

Since she will talk only about the metamessage, and he will talk only about the message, neither can get satisfaction from their talk, and they end up where they started—only angrier:

> JAKE: That's not the point!
>
> LOUISE: It's *my* point.
>
> JAKE: It's hopeless!
>
> LOUISE: Then get a divorce.

American conventional wisdom (and many of our parents and English teachers) tell us that meaning is conveyed by words, so men who tend to be literal about words are supported by conventional wisdom. They may not simply deny but actually miss the cues that are sent by how words are spoken. If they sense something about it, they may nonetheless discount what they sense. After all, it wasn't said. Sometimes that's a dodge—a plausible defense rather than a gut feeling. But sometimes it is a sincere conviction. Women are also likely to doubt the reality of what they sense. If they don't doubt it in their guts, they nonetheless may lack the arguments to support their position and thus are reduced to repeating, "You said it. You did so." Knowing that metamessages are a real and fundamental part of communication makes it easier to understand and justify what they feel.

22   **"Talk to Me."**   An article in a popular newspaper reports that one of the five most common complaints of wives about their husbands is "He doesn't listen to me anymore." Another is "He doesn't talk to me anymore." Political scientist Andrew Hacker noted that lack of communication, while high on women's lists of reasons for divorce, is much less often mentioned by men.

Since couples are parties to the same conversations, why are women more dissatisfied with them than men? Because what they expect is different, as well as what they see as the significance of talk itself.

23   First, let's consider the complaint "He doesn't talk to me."

24   **The Strong Silent Type.**   One of the most common stereotypes of American men is the strong silent type. Jack Kroll, writing about Henry Fonda on the occasion of his death, used the phrases "quiet power," "abashed silences," "combustible catatonia," and "sense of power held in check." He explained that Fonda's goal was not to let anyone see "the wheels go around," not to let the "machinery" show. According to Kroll, the resulting silence was effective on stage but devastating to Fonda's family.

25   The image of a silent father is common and is often the model for the lover or husband. But what attracts us can become flypaper to which we are unhappily stuck. Many women find the strong silent type to be a lure as a lover but a lug as a husband. Nancy Schoenberger begins a poem with the lines "It was your silence that hooked me,/ so like my father's." Adrienne Rich refers in a poem to the "husband who is frustratingly mute." Despite the initial attraction of such quintessentially male silence, it may begin to feel, to a woman in a long-term relationship, like a brick wall against which she is banging her head.

26   In addition to these images of male and female behavior—both the result and the cause of them—are differences in how women and men view the role of talk in relationships as well as how talk accomplishes its purpose. These differences have their roots in the settings in which men and women learn to have conversations: among their peers, growing up.

27   **Growing up Male and Female.**   Children whose parents have foreign accents don't speak with accents. They learn to talk like their peers. Little girls and little boys learn how to have conversations as they learn how to pronounce words: from their playmates. Between the ages of five and fifteen, when children are learning to have conversations, they play mostly with friends of their own sex. So it's not surprising that they learn different ways of having and using conversations.

28   Anthropologists Daniel Maltz and Ruth Borker point out that boys and girls socialize differently. Little girls tend to play in small groups or, even more common, in pairs. Their social life usually centers around a best friend, and friendships are made, maintained, and broken by talk—especially "secrets." If a little girl tells her friend's secret to another little girl, she may find herself with a new best friend. The secrets themselves may or may not be important, but the fact of telling them is all-important. It's hard for newcomers to get into these tight groups, but anyone who is admitted is treated as an equal. Girls like to play cooperatively; if they can't cooperate, the group breaks up.

29   Little boys tend to play in larger groups, often outdoors, and they spend more time doing things than talking. It's easy for boys to get into the group, but

not everyone is accepted as an equal. Once in the group, boys must jockey for their status in it. One of the most important ways they do this is through talk: verbal display such as telling stories and jokes, challenging and sidetracking the verbal displays of other boys, and withstanding other boys' challenges in order to maintain their own story—and status. Their talk is often competitive talk about who is best at what.

30   **From Children to Grown Ups.** Feiffer's play is ironically named *Grown Ups* because adult men and women struggling to communicate often sound like children: "You said so!" "I did not!" The reason is that when they grow up, women and men keep the divergent attitudes and habits they learned as children—which they don't recognize as attitudes and habits but simply take for granted as ways of talking.

31   Women want their partners to be a new and improved version of a best friend. This gives them a soft spot for men who tell them secrets. As Jack Nicholson once advised a guy in a movie: "Tell her about your troubled childhood—that always gets 'em." Men expect to *do* things together and don't feel anything is missing if they don't have heart-to-heart talks all the time.

32   If they do have heart-to-heart talks, the meaning of those talks may be opposite for men and women. To many women, the relationship is working as long as they can talk things out. To many men, the relationship isn't working out if they have to keep working it over. If she keeps trying to get talks going to save the relationship, and he keeps trying to avoid them because he sees them as weakening it, then each one's efforts to preserve the relationship appear to the other as reckless endangerment.

Considering Ideas

1. Why does Tannen believe that men and women are from different cultures?
2. Tannen says that cultural differences mean that men and women in long-term relationships each have a different expectation for talk. What are those different expectations?
3. What are "metamessages"? Tannen says that women are more attuned to them than men. Why? Do you agree with Tannen?
4. According to Tannen, how do their different styles of talking affect communication between men and women?
5. In general, how do you think the communication style of women affects them in the workplace?
6. How do women often react to "the strong silent type"?
7. According to the author, why do men and women communicate differently?

Considering Technique

1. In a sentence of your own, state the thesis of "Talk in the Intimate Relationship: His and Hers."

2. How do paragraphs 1 through 7 function in the essay? You may have found these paragraphs more difficult to read than the rest of the essay. Why are they more difficult?

3. What purpose do the examples in paragraphs 8 through 14 serve? The ones in paragraphs 15 through 21? The ones in paragraph 24?

4. Where does cause-and-effect analysis appear in the essay? (Cause-and-effect analysis, discussed in Chapter 9, explains the causes and/or effects of something.) What purpose does the analysis serve?

5. Tannen's essay has no formal conclusion. Instead, the author ends with her last point. Is this a problem for the reader? Explain.

6. Consult a dictionary if you are unsure of the meaning of any of these words: *incongruent* (paragraph 3), *attuned* (paragraph 4), *deferential* (paragraph 5), *rife* (paragraph 6), *adamantly* (paragraph 18), *plausible* (paragraph 21), *abashed* (paragraph 24), *catatonia* (paragraph 24), *lug* (paragraph 25), *quintessentially* (paragraph 25), *divergent* (paragraph 30).

For Group Consideration

Tannen's essay includes a number of generalizations about women and men. For example, in paragraph 9, she says that women are more attuned to meta-messages than men. With three or four classmates, cite two or three more of these generalizations and discuss whether or not you agree with them. Also discuss whether different communication styles can be solely attributed to sex, or whether other factors (age, economic status, ethnic background, and level of education, for instance) are contributing factors. Report your conclusions and areas of disagreement to the rest of the class.

Journal Entry

How much of what Tannen says is confirmed by your own experience? How much of it is not? Does Tannen say anything that surprises you? Does she say anything that bothers you? Does she say anything that makes sense? Respond to one or more of these questions in about two pages.

Essay Assignments

1. Like Tannen, select two groups of people and contrast their communication styles. Your subjects, for example, could be teens and adults, physicians and patients, teachers and students, advertisers and the general public, or North-erners and Southerners. Use examples to illustrate the different styles, and, if possible, explain why the groups communicate the way they do and/or the effects of the communication styles.

2. Contrast the behavior of men and women, using something other than their communication styles as subjects. For example, you can contrast their dating

behavior, their behavior with friends, their behavior in competitive situations, or their management styles.

3. Compare and/or contrast the ways men are portrayed on television with the ways women are portrayed. Use specific examples from shows and commercials to clarify and support your points. If possible, explain the effects these portrayals have on the viewer.

4. For three or four days, observe the communication styles of men and women as you go about your routine. Take note of any similarities and differences you observe. Then write your own essay that compares and/or contrasts the way men and women talk. If you like, you can limit yourself to the way men and women talk in the classroom. Use examples from your observation to clarify and support your points. If you wish, explain the reasons for the similarities or differences and/or explain the effects of these similarities or differences.

Considering Thematic Issues

1. Tannen says, "Boys and girls grow up in different worlds, even if they grow up in the same house. And as adults they travel in different worlds, reinforcing patterns established in childhood." Explain to what extent you agree or disagree with this assessment, citing your own experience and observation to support your view.

2. Using the information in "Country Codes" (page 317) and "Talk in the Intimate Relationship," explain the potential for talk to facilitate and hinder relationships among rural New Englanders.

Additional Essay Assignments

1. Compare and/or contrast some place on campus at two different times of the day. For example, you can compare and/or contrast a campus eating spot at the noon rush hour and again at the 3:00 lull, the football stadium during and after a game, or the library before and after finals week. Use description for vividness. Your purpose is to share, inform, and/or entertain.

2. Compare and contrast two people who play the same sport: two basketball players, two runners, two football players, and so on. Your purpose is to help your reader appreciate the playing style of each athlete or to persuade your reader that one athlete is better than the other.

3. Compare and/or contrast two close friends, illustrating their traits with example or narration. Your purpose is to inform or share.

4. Compare and/or contrast two similar television shows (two situation comedies, two news broadcasts, two police dramas, and so on) to persuade your reader that one is better than the other.

5. Contrast two celebrations of the same holiday: Christmas before and after children, Independence Day as a child and as an adult, Thanksgiving at different grandparents' houses, and so on.

6. Compare and contrast two magazine advertisements for the same kind of product to inform your reader about how advertisers work to persuade the consumer. You can use ads for two shampoos, two mouthwashes, two makes of cars, and so on.

7. Contrast the way some group of people (for example, mothers, police officers, fathers, or teens) are portrayed on television with the way they are in real life.

8. Contrast two ways to do something (for example, diet, study, give a dinner party, discipline children, or ask for a date) to persuade your reader that one way is better than the other.

9. Consider your circumstances before and after some change in your life: getting married, having children, going to college, getting a job, or joining an athletic team, for example. Your purpose is to share with your reader. As an alternative, make your details humorous and entertain your reader.

10. In your campus library, look up advertisements in *Life* and *Look* magazines from the 1950s and compare and contrast one or two of these ads with ones in contemporary magazines to inform your reader of the changes. Use cause-and-effect analysis to explain the cause and/or the effects of the changes.

11. Contrast two similar restaurants in your area to persuade your reader that one is better than the other. Use description for vividness.

12. Compare and contrast the movie and book versions of the same story (*Gone with the Wind, The Firm, Jurassic Park, Presumed Innocent, The*

Prince of Tides, and so on) to persuade your reader that one version is better than the other.

13. Contrast the right and wrong ways to do something (for example choose a major, study for an exam, write an essay, select an adviser, buy a car, or plan a first date). Make your details humorous and entertain your reader.

14. Compare and contrast the styles of two comedians, actors, or musicians to inform your reader about the characteristics of each one.

15. Compare and contrast the chief arguments on both sides of a controversial issue (for example, abortion, capital punishment, euthanasia, animal rights, distributing condoms in schools, or bilingual education) to inform your reader of the thinking on both sides. If necessary, research the issue in your campus library.

16. Compare and contrast two fictional characters: Batman and Superman, Captain Kirk and Captain Picard, Indiana Jones and Han Solo, and so on.

17. Contrast two kinds of students, teachers, coaches, parents, or clergy.

18. Compare and/or contrast the toys of your youth with those that are popular today. Try to draw a conclusion about what those similarities and/or differences mean.

19. If you have lived in more than one place, compare and contrast life in two of those places in an effort to share with your reader.

20. If you or someone close to you has lived with chronic illness, contrast life as a healthy and sick person to heighten your reader's awareness of what it is like to be ill.

C H A P T E R

9

CAUSE-AND-EFFECT ANALYSIS

The Purpose of Cause-and-Effect Analysis
Supporting Details
Selecting and Ordering Details
Suggestions for Writing Cause-and-Effect Analysis
Annotated Student Essay: Why Athletes Use Steroids

America Has Gone on a Trip Out of Tune—Dave Barry
   (cause-and-effect analysis to entertain)
Why We Crave Horror Movies—Stephen King *(analysis of
   cause to inform and entertain)*
* *India: A Widow's Devastating Choice*—Juthica Stangl
   (cause-and-effect analysis to inform and persuade)
*Just Walk on By: A Black Man Ponders His Power to Alter
   Public Space*—Brent Staples *(cause-and-effect analysis to
   share and inform)*
No Kick from Champagne—Harold Saltzman *(analysis of
   effects to persuade, share, and inform)*
* *Complexion*—Richard Rodriguez *(analysis of effects to
   inform and share)*

Additional Essay Assignments

*To fulfill the author's purpose, cause-and-effect analysis is combined with one or more other patterns.

To make sense of the world, we try to understand what causes things to happen and how events affect us. We examine the causes of earthquakes, try to determine how a particular presidential candidate's victory will change the economy, work to figure out why the car won't get the gas mileage it should, struggle to understand why our best friend suddenly seems distant, and so on. An understanding of causes and effects is important to our sense of security and our feeling that we can successfully deal with people, objects, and events. Thus, it is no surprise that writing often examines the causes of something, the effects of something, or both.

THE PURPOSE OF CAUSE-AND-EFFECT ANALYSIS

Cause-and-effect analysis can entertain, share, inform, and/or persuade. In "America Has Gone on a Trip Out of Tune" (page 270), for example, Dave Barry *entertains* his reader with a funny account of the causes and effects of Americans' inability to sing. An explanation of the causes of heat lightning or the effects of inflation on the economy could be written to *inform* the reader. You could explain the causes of your breakup with your best friend or the effects of your decision to change your major if you wanted to *share* with your reader. Cause-and-effect analysis can also have a *persuasive purpose*, as when you explain the consequences of not funding schools in order to convince your reader to pass a school levy or when you explain the causes of math anxiety to convince your reader that women are often conditioned by our culture to steer away from math.

SUPPORTING DETAILS

To clarify causes and effects, many patterns can be helpful, particularly narration, exemplification, description, and process analysis. For example, let's say you mention that you broke up with your best friend because he or she could not keep a secret. You can establish this point by telling the story of the time your friend betrayed a confidence. You could also give several examples of times your friend shared your secrets with others. Description can also contribute to cause-and-effect analysis. For example, if you want to explain the effects of littering, you can clarify by describing a section of roadside that has been heavily littered. Sometimes, process analysis helps make a point. For example, if you want to explain the effects of tax reduction, you can note the process whereby lower taxes means more disposable income, which leads to increased spending, which spurs manufacturing, which creates jobs, and so forth.

Sometimes cause-and-effect detail includes an explanation of causal chains. In a *causal chain*, a cause leads to an effect; that effect becomes a cause that leads to another effect; then that effect becomes a cause, and so on. For example, if you wanted to explain the effects of being very tall, you might reproduce a causal chain that looks like this: being tall made you feel awkward (effect); feeling awkward (cause) reduced your self-confidence (effect); your reduced self-confidence (cause) made it hard for you to date (effect); not dating (cause) made you depressed (effect).

In addition to reproducing causal chains, you may want to point out something that is not a cause or an effect, especially if you need to correct your reader's understanding. For example, assume that you are explaining the effects of sex education in the schools, and you think your reader mistakenly believes that sex education leads to increased sexual activity. Then you may want to note that increased sexual activity has not been proven to be an effect of sex education.

 ## SELECTING AND ORDERING DETAILS

To develop detail, you can ask the questions "Why?" and "Then what?" For example, let's say you are explaining the causes of your shyness, and you give one reason as the fact that you don't feel comfortable around people. If you ask why you don't feel comfortable, you may get the answer that your family moved so frequently that you never got to know anyone very well—that gives you another cause. Now let's say that you are explaining the effects of your parents' divorce on you, and you indicate that the divorce meant you saw less of your father. Ask "Then what?" and you might answer that you and your father drifted apart, so you never got to know him well—that's another effect you can write about.

When you decide on detail, do not assume that something that happens before or after an event is necessarily the cause or effect of that event. For example, if you buy a new car, then get a date with the person of your dreams, you cannot assume the car led to the date; it could well have been your charm and wit.

Sometimes, any order is suitable for a cause-and-effect analysis, but other times, particular orders are called for. If your purpose is persuasive, you may want a progressive order so you can save your most dramatic, compelling, or significant cause or effect for the end. If you are reproducing causal chains, chronological order is needed, so you can cite the causes and effects in the order they occur. Chronological order is also called for when you are discussing causes and effects as they occurred across time. For example, a discussion of the effects of your musical talent could deal with your childhood, then your adolescence, then your adulthood. At times, you may want to arrange your details in categories. If, for example, you are explaining the effects of the passage of a school levy, you can discuss together all the effects on teachers, then the effects on students, and finally the effects on curriculum.

To focus the essay, the thesis usually indicates the topic and whether causes, effects, or both will be discussed. Your topic sentences, then, can introduce your discussion of each cause or effect. Here are a sample thesis and topic sentences that could be used for an essay about the causes of drug abuse among athletes.

thesis: It is certainly wrong for athletes to use drugs, but the reasons they do so are understandable. (Thesis notes the essay will explain the causes of drug use among athletes.)

topic sentence: The pressure for professional athletes to justify their huge salaries is so great that they often see performance-enhancing drugs as the answer. (Topic sentence presents the first cause: pressure on professional athletes.)

topic sentence: Furthermore, athletes may feel that they must take the drugs in order to be competitive, since so many other athletes are taking them. (Topic sentence presents second cause: others take drugs.)

topic sentence: Finally, many athletes get hooked on drugs because their coaches and trainers administer them. (Topic sentence presents third reason: coaches and trainers give out the drugs.)

Two kinds of transitions can help you signal cause-and-effect relationships to your reader. First, the following transitions signal that one thing is the effect of another: *as a result, consequently, thus, hence, therefore,* and *for this reason.* Here are two examples:

The midterm grades were very low. *For this reason,* Professor Werner reviewed the material with the class.

The storm damage was extensive. *As a result,* the tourist trade in the coastal town declined.

Transitions of addition (*also, in addition, additionally, furthermore,* and *another*) can also signal cause-and-effect analysis, like this:

Another effect of MTV is. . . .

In addition, stress fractures can be caused by. . . .

SUGGESTIONS FOR WRITING CAUSE-AND-EFFECT ANALYSIS

1. If you need help with a topic, try writing about the causes and/or effects of some aspect of your life or personality: shyness, math anxiety, being tall or short, being the first or last born, playing football, fearing heights, your parents' divorce, the loss of a loved one, a special talent or ability, and so on.

2. To generate ideas, list every cause and/or effect that you can think of, without pausing to evaluate whether your ideas are good or not.

3. Ask "Why?" and/or "Then what?" of every item on your list to explore additional causes and effects.

4. Study your ideas and determine which you will use. Then, for each idea note whether you can tell a story, provide an example, describe, or explain a process to help clarify.

5. Add to your list anything you should mention that is not a cause or effect.

6. Number your ideas in the order you will treat them; then write your first draft from this numbered list. At this point, just write things out as best you can without worrying about grammar, spelling, punctuation, or anything else. You can revise later.

7. When you revise, consider the following:

    a. Does your thesis indicate whether you are discussing causes, effects, or both?

    b. Do your topic sentences introduce your discussion of each cause and/or effect?

    c. Have you clarified all causes and effects with explanation, description, narration, examples, and process analysis, as needed?

    d. Have you reproduced causal chains where appropriate?

 ANNOTATED STUDENT ESSAY

Student author Carl Benedict informs his reader by explaining the causes of steroid use among athletes. As you read, notice how carefully each cause is presented and explained.

WHY ATHLETES USE STEROIDS

Paragraph 1
The introduction gives background information. The thesis (the last sentence) indicates that the subject is steroid use and the essay will present causes.

Paragraph 2
Sentence 1 is the topic sentence. It begins with a transition of addition and

1   One of the most heated controversies in athletics centers on the use of anabolic steroids. Behind the dispute is the evidence that steroids pose a health hazard. They are linked to cardiovascular disease, liver disorders, and cancerous tumors. In addition, there is evidence that they cause personality aberrations. Still, an alarming number of athletes are willing to risk their health for the enhanced performance steroids provide—and it is not hard to understand why.

2   First of all, many athletes are so blinded by the obvious benefits of steroid use that they fail to note their adverse effects. They are so focused on the increased strength, stamina, and size that result from steroid use, they may overlook the abuse their bodies are sustaining—often until it is too late. That is, athletes who are delighting in turning in the best performances of their

presents the first cause under consideration.

Paragraph 3
The second cause is presented in the first two sentences. The paragraph also presents an effect: contact sports become more dangerous.

Paragraph 4
This paragraph explains something that is not a cause, then goes on to give a real cause. Note the transition *in addition.*

Paragraph 5
The first sentence is the topic sentence. It begins with a transition and presents the next cause.

Paragraph 6
The first sentence is the topic sentence. "The biggest reason" notes that detail is in a progressive order. The paragraph presents a causal chain.

Paragraph 7
This paragraph presents a cause that is an extension of the one given in the previous paragraph.

lives are not likely to think about future deleterious effects. This is the same psychology that keeps the nicotine addict smoking three packs a day, until the x-ray shows the lung cancer is so advanced that nothing can be done.

3   Some athletes rationalize steroid use another way. They claim that anabolic steroids pose no greater health hazard than participation in such contact sports as football, boxing, and wrestling. However, these athletes fail to understand that in addition to harming the body, steroids also heighten the danger of contact sports by making the participants larger and stronger, thereby increasing their momentum and impact.

4   Some people think steroid use continues despite the life-threatening effects because athletes are just "dumb jocks" who are not smart enough to appreciate the risks. I don't accept that explanation. Instead, I suspect that steroid use continues partly because most athletes are young, and young people never feel threatened. Part of being young is feeling invulnerable. That is why young people drive too fast, drink too much, and bungee jump. They just do not believe that anything can happen to them. The same psychology is at work with athletes. They are young people who feel they will live forever.

5   In addition, athletes assume that because their bodies are so physically conditioned they can withstand more punishment than the average person, so they feel even less at risk by steroid use. They think, "The average person should not do this, but I can because my body is finely tuned."

6   Perhaps the biggest reason athletes use steroids can be explained by the spirit that lies at the heart of all athletics: competition. Once a handful of athletes enhance their performance artificially, then others follow in order to stay competitive. Eventually, steroid users dominate a sport, and anyone who wants to compete at the highest levels is forced to use steroids or lose out. This fact explains why unscrupulous coaches and trainers who want to win at any cost have contributed to the problem by offering steroids to their players and urging them to use them. Sadly, this practice has even filtered down to the high school level in some cases.

7   Competition for the thrill of winning is only part of the explanation, however. Big-time athletics means big-time money. As the financial rewards rise in a given sport, so does the pressure to win at any cost. Huge salaries, enormous purses, big bonuses, and incredibly lucrative commercial endorsements all tempt athletes to enhance their performances any way they can.

Paragraph 8
The conclusion
summarizes the
main causes.

8   Despite drug testing before competitions and dissemination
of information about the dangers of anabolic steroids, athletes still
use steroids because the pressures to do so are so compelling. The
truth is, too many athletes think steroids only hurt the other person,
or else they think using steroids is worth the risk.

AMERICA HAS GONE ON A TRIP
OUT OF TUNE
Dave Barry

◆

Syndicated humor columnist Dave Barry writes for the Miami Herald. *In the following essay, he uses cause-and-effect analysis to entertain his audience. As you read, try to identify the specific techniques he employs to amuse the reader.*

◆

1   Recently, there was a story in *The New York Times* (motto: "Our Motto Alone Is Longer Than An Entire Edition Of *USA Today*") reporting that Americans are no longer any good at singing. This is the latest in a series of alarming news stories about things that Americans are no longer any good at, including reading, writing, arithmetic, and manufacturing any consumer product more technologically sophisticated than pizza.

2   According to the *Times*, Americans used to do a lot of group singing, dating back to the days when hardy pioneers crossing the prairie would entertain themselves by sitting around the campfire and singing folk songs such as:

    "Home, home on the range
    Where the deer
    and the antelope plAAAAACK"

3   "AAAACK" was the musical sound that the hardy pioneers made when their larynxes were punctured by arrows shot by prairie-dwelling Native Americans, who couldn't *stand* that song. Another one they hated was "Mister Froggy Went A-Courting," which inspired them to invent the Ant Hill Torture.

4   **Problems.** Nevertheless, public group singing remained popular until modern times, when it has been hurt by two factors:

5   **The Elimination of Religion from Public Schools.** At one time, most public schools held Christmas Programs, wherein the children sang Christmas carols. Eventually this was viewed, correctly, as unfair to other religious groups, so the schools started holding Winter Programs and including songs from other religions, starting with Judaism and gradually expanding, as society got more sensitive, to include Islam, Buddhism, Confucianism, Scientology and The Cult Of The Big Lizard.

6   Finally, to avoid offending anybody, the schools dropped religion altogether and started singing about the weather. At my son's school, they now hold the Winter Program in February and sing increasingly nonmemorable songs such as "Winter Wonderland," "Frosty the Snowman," and—this is a real

song—"Suzy Snowflake," all of which is pretty funny, because we live in Miami. A visitor from another planet would assume that the children belonged to the Church of Meteorology.

7   **The Rise of Rock and Roll.**   Let's face it, this is not the ideal music for group singing. The family is not going to gather 'round the old upright piano and belt out a hearty chorus of "Shake Your Groove Thing."

8   The result is that fewer and fewer Americans can sing. I have seen stark evidence of this in my own office. One of my co-workers, John Dorschner, has a song stuck in his head and can't get it out. You've probably had this happen to you. Your brain, which is easily the most overrated organ in your body when it comes to intelligence, suddenly decides to devote an entire lobe to a certain song. Sometimes it's a song you don't even like, but your brain plays it over and over and over, especially when you're trying to sleep. You're lying in bed, thinking to yourself, "Big day tomorrow! Got to make a major presentation to top management. Got to get some shut-eye." And just as you're about to lose consciousness, your brain shrieks:

"It's my party, and I'll cry if I want to!
CRY if I want to! CRY if I want to!"

9   You try reasoning with your brain, then speaking sternly to it, then pounding on its door and threatening to strangle it, but it continues shrieking this song until 4:30 A.M., when you finally fall into a fitful sleep, marred by a recurring nightmare wherein you inform the entire board of directors, using audiovisual aids, that they would cry, too, if it happened to them.

10   **Get It Out.**   Leading physicians agree that the only way to cure this condition is to go up to another person and say: "I can't get this darned song out of my head!" Then you sing the song, and suddenly, boom, it's gone from your head, because *now it's stuck in the other person's head.*

11   John has been trying to infect me with his song for several months, but, like an increasing number of Americans, he can't sing. About once a week he sticks his head into my office and says: "Are you sure you don't know this song?" And then he makes a series of noises that, if you didn't know they were supposed to be a song, you would assume were the desperate moans of a woodland creature that has somehow become lodged in John's trachea.

12   "Unnhh unnh unhh," moans the creature.

13   "The chorus goes 'Keep a-rolling',"' adds John, looking at me hopefully.

14   "Don't know it!" I say. "Sorry!" Although of course I am actually happy. Shoulders slumped, John wanders off, looking for another potential victim to infect. According to *The New York Times*, we're going to see more and more unfortunate victims like John unless we, as a nation, start singing together again. So come on! Put your ear next to the newspaper and join in with me now!

"Oh I come from Alabama
With a banjo on my knAAAACK"

Considering Ideas

1. In "America Has Gone on a Trip Out of Tune," Dave Barry pokes fun at aspects of American life. For example, in paragraph 1, he makes fun of the frequently appearing news articles that claim Americans can't do something. What else does Barry poke fun at?
2. According to Barry, what has caused the decline in public singing?
3. According to Barry, what are the effects of people not singing together?
4. Many times, writers use humor to make a serious point. Do you think that Barry is making a serious point? Explain.

Considering Technique

1. Much of Barry's humor comes from positioning something silly next to something plausible. Look, for example, at the list at the end of paragraph 1. Here Barry positions the silly "manufacturing any consumer product more technologically sophisticated than pizza" after the plausible "reading, writing, arithmetic." Cite two other examples of such positioning for humorous effect.
2. Part of Barry's humor comes from the mock serious tone achieved by citing authority. For example, in paragraph 1, he cites *The New York Times* as his source. Note two other examples of this technique.
3. Barry's specific detail adds humor and interest. For example, in paragraph 3, he refers to a specific song title, "Mister Froggy Went A-Courting." Cite two other examples of specific detail.
4. In which paragraph does Barry use exemplification to help explain his cause-and-effect relationship?
5. What approach does Barry take to his introduction?
6. What causal chain does Barry reproduce in his essay?
7. Consult a dictionary if you are unsure of the meaning of *Scientology* (paragraph 5).

For Group Consideration

Dave Barry writes a syndicated humor column that appears in newspapers across the country, and "America Has Gone on a Trip Out of Tune" is representative of his work. Why do you think the typical reader of a large metropolitan newspaper finds Dave Barry funny?

Journal Entry

Do you think Barry performs a service by writing humorous newspaper columns about the little things in life, like the decline of group singing and the irritation of having a song stuck in one's head? Or is his column pointless? Explain your view.

Essay Assignments

1. Like Barry, select something inconsequential that "Americans are no longer any good at" (cooking without a microwave, walking places, changing channels without a remote control, and so on). Then write a humorous account of the causes and effects of the "problem."

2. Take a serious problem (the deficit, the economy, declining knowledge of geography, rising tuition costs, and so on) and write about its humorous effects. For example, if you want to write about the effects of declining math skills, you can include a humorous description of the congestion in grocery store aisles as people stand around trying to figure out how much they can save if they buy the big can of soup rather than the small one.

3. In paragraphs 5 and 6, Barry explains the causes and effects of the elimination of religion from public schools. Select some other change in our education system (inclusion, busing, dress codes, collaborative learning, team teaching, and so on), and explain the causes and/or effects of that change. Your essay can be humorous or not, as you prefer.

4. When Barry explains the causes and effects of the inability to get a song out of one's head, he is poking fun at a harmless human characteristic. Pick another harmless human behavior or characteristic (for example, checking the alarm even though we know it is set, habitually choosing the wrong bank or supermarket line, losing car keys, or buying clothes we look bad in). Then write a humorous essay that explains the causes and/or effects of this behavior.

Considering Thematic Issues

1. In paragraph 5, Barry refers to the fact that because the Constitution calls for the separation of church and state, many public schools have eliminated school programs that refer to or celebrate religious holidays. The reasoning is that celebrating any religious holiday violates that separation because public schools are funded by the government to a large extent. Agree or disagree with the policy of eliminating holiday celebrations from public schools, being sure to supply reasons for your stand.

2. Barry refers to "things that Americans are no longer any good at, including reading, writing, arithmetic . . ." (paragraph 1). In truth, the U.S. education system has been repeatedly criticized for not teaching such basics as reading, writing, and arithmetic effectively. Based on what you know and the facts presented in "College Pressures" (page 323), argue that schools do or do not do a good job of preparing students for college.

WHY WE CRAVE HORROR MOVIES
Stephen King

◆

If anyone should know about horror, it's Stephen King, whose horror novels Misery, Christine, Pet Sematery, *and* Firestarter *(among others) have been made into movies. In "Why We Crave Horror Movies," King analyzes causes to inform his audience. However, notice that the master of horror is not without a sense of humor and that the essay entertains as a result.*

◆

1   I think that we're all mentally ill; those of us outside the asylums only hide it a little better—and maybe not all that much better, after all. We've all known people who talk to themselves, people who sometimes squinch their faces into horrible grimaces when they believe no one is watching, people who have some hysterical fear—of snakes, the dark, the tight place, the long drop . . . and, of course, those final worms and grubs that are waiting so patiently underground.

2   When we pay our four or five bucks and seat ourselves at tenth-row center in a theater showing a horror movie, we are daring the nightmare.

3   Why? Some of the reasons are simple and obvious. To show that we can, that we are not afraid, that we can ride this roller coaster. Which is not to say that a really good horror movie may not surprise a scream out of us at some point, the way we may scream when the roller coaster twists through a complete 360 or plows through a lake at the bottom of the drop. And horror movies, like roller coasters, have always been the special province of the young; by the time one turns 40 or 50, one's appetite for double twists or 360-degree loops may be considerably depleted.

4   We also go to re-establish our feelings of essential normality; the horror movie is innately conservative, even reactionary. Freda Jackson as the horrible melting woman in *Die, Monster, Die!* confirms for us that no matter how far we may be removed from the beauty of a Robert Redford or a Diana Ross, we are still light-years from true ugliness.

5   And we go to have fun.

6   Ah, but this is where the ground starts to slope away, isn't it? Because this is a very peculiar sort of fun, indeed. The fun comes from seeing others menaced—sometimes killed. One critic has suggested that if pro football has become the voyeur's version of combat, then the horror film has become the modern version of the public lynching.

7   It is true that the mythic, "fairy-tale" horror film intends to take away the shades of gray. . . . It urges us to put away our more civilized and adult penchant for analysis and to become children again, seeing things in pure blacks and whites. It may be that horror movies provide psychic relief on this

level because this invitation to lapse into simplicity, irrationality and even outright madness is extended so rarely. We are told we may allow our emotions a free rein . . . or no rein at all.

8   If we are all insane, then sanity becomes a matter of degree. If your insanity leads you to carve up women like Jack the Ripper or the Cleveland Torso Murderer, we clap you away in the funny farm (but neither of those two amateur-night surgeons was ever caught, heh-heh-heh); if, on the other hand, your insanity leads you only to talk to yourself when you're under stress or to pick your nose on your morning bus, then you are left alone to go about your business . . . though it is doubtful that you will ever be invited to the best parties.

9   The potential lyncher is in almost all of us (excluding saints, past and present; but then, most saints have been crazy in their own ways), and every now and then, he has to be let loose to scream and roll around in the grass. Our emotions and our fears form their own body, and we recognize that it demands its own exercise to maintain proper muscle tone. Certain of these emotional muscles are accepted—even exalted—in civilized society; they are, of course, the emotions that tend to maintain the status quo of civilization itself. Love, friendship, loyalty, kindness—these are all the emotions that we applaud, emotions that have been immortalized in the couplets of Hallmark cards and in the verses (I don't dare call it poetry) of Leonard Nimoy.*

10   When we exhibit these emotions, society showers us with positive reinforcement; we learn this even before we get out of diapers. When, as children, we hug our rotten little puke of a sister and give her a kiss, all the aunts and uncles smile and twit and cry, "Isn't he the sweetest little thing?" Such coveted treats as chocolate-covered graham crackers often follow. But if we deliberately slam the rotten little puke of a sister's fingers in the door, sanctions follow—angry remonstrance from parents, aunts and uncles; instead of a chocolate-covered graham cracker, a spanking.

11   But anticivilization emotions don't go away, and they demand periodic exercise. We have such "sick" jokes as, "What's the difference between a truckload of bowling balls and truckload of dead babies?" (You can't unload a truckload of bowling balls with a pitchfork . . . a joke, by the way, that I heard originally from a ten-year-old). Such a joke may surprise a laugh or a grin out of us even as we recoil, a possibility that confirms the thesis: If we share a brotherhood of man, then we also share an insanity of man. None of which is intended as a defense of either the sick joke or insanity but merely as an explanation of why the best horror films, like the best fairy tales, manage to be reactionary, anarchistic, and revolutionary all at the same time.

12   The mythic horror movie, like the sick joke, has a dirty job to do. It deliberately appeals to all that is worst in us. It is morbidity unchained, our most

---

*Actor who portrayed Mr. Spock in the "Star Trek" series. He has also written poetry.

base instincts let free, our nastiest fantasies realized . . . and it all happens, fittingly enough, in the dark. For those reasons, good liberals often shy away from horror films. For myself, I like to see the most aggressive of them—*Dawn of the Dead*, for instance—as lifting a trap door in the civilized forebrain and throwing a basket of raw meat to the hungry alligators swimming around in that subterranean river beneath.

13   Why bother? Because it keeps them from getting out, man. It keeps them down there and me up here. It was Lennon and McCartney who said that all you need is love, and I would agree with that.

14   As long as you keep the gators fed.

Considering Ideas

1. According to King, why do people watch horror movies?
2. King says that watching a horror movie is like "lifting a trap door in the civilized forebrain and throwing a basket of raw meat to the hungry alligators swimming around in that subterranean river beneath." What do you think this comment means?
3. In paragraph 3, King compares watching a horror movie to riding a roller coaster. Do you think this is a good comparison? Explain.
4. In paragraph 11, King refers to "anticivilization emotions" that need periodic exercise. What are these emotions, and why must they be exercised?
5. According to the author, what do sick jokes and horror movies have in common?

Considering Technique

1. At what point in the essay does the reader learn that causes will be dealt with?
2. King uses topic sentences to introduce some of his causes. What are these topic sentences?
3. In what order does King arrange the causes he discusses?
4. What elements of humor appear in the essay, and what does the humor contribute to the piece?
5. An *analogy* is a form of comparison. For example, in paragraph 3, King uses analogy to compare the horror movie to a roller coaster. What other analogy appears in the essay? What purpose do you think it serves?
6. Consult a dictionary if you are unsure of the meaning of any of these words: *grimaces* (paragraph 1), *depleted* (paragraph 3), *voyeur* (paragraph 6), *penchant* (paragraph 7), *status quo* (paragraph 9), *sanctions* (paragraph 10), *remonstrance* (paragraph 10), *recoil* (paragraph 11), *anarchistic* (paragraph 11), *morbidity* (paragraph 12), *subterranean* (paragraph 12).

For Group Consideration

With three or four classmates, discuss the answers to these questions:

1. Why does King say that we are all mentally ill?
2. What is the nature of the insanity we share?
3. How does King maintain the insanity theme in the essay?

After considering these questions, decide whether or not you agree with King that we are all mentally ill, that we have "anticivilization emotions [that] don't go away."

Journal Entry

If you enjoy horror movies, explain why you like to watch them and how you react when you view them. If you do not enjoy horror movies, explain why they do not appeal to you. Respond in about a page.

Essay Assignments

1. Write an essay with the title "Why Teenagers Crave MTV," to explain why teens enjoy watching MTV.
2. Write an analysis of causes to explain why people watch violent movies. If you like, include humor and/or analogy the way King does.
3. Why do people tell ethnic jokes? Consider our motivation, and write an analysis of causes. If you like, you can also explain the effects of this kind of humor.
4. Pick a popular television show and write an analysis that explains why people like to watch the program.

Considering Thematic Issues

1. King believes that horror movies perform a service: they help us keep our baser instincts in check. In what other ways is our dark side kept in control? You can consider one or more of the following: religion, family, school, laws, and anything else you think is relevant. Also, explain how these elements perform the function that they do.
2. Agree or disagree with King's assertion that people have "anticivilization emotions that don't go away" (paragraph 11). For supporting detail, you can use your own experience and observation, as well as the ideas in any one of the following essays: "The Deer at Providencia" (page 76), "Class Acts" (page 139), "Untouchables" (page 159), "Don't Just Stand There" (page 182), and "Country Codes" (page 317).

INDIA: A WIDOW'S DEVASTATING CHOICE
Juthica Stangl

◆

In India, suttee is an ancient ritual whereby widows commit suicide in order to follow their husbands into death. In "India: A Widow's Devastating Choice," Juthica Stangl combines narration with cause-and-effect analysis to inform her reader that because of the difficult social and economic plight of widows in India, suttee is still relevant. Her purpose is persuasive as well: she works to convince her audience that change must occur. As you read, try to view the events from the cultural perspective of Anjali, the author's widowed friend.

◆

1   On October 26, 1981, while Delhi prepared for Deevali, the festival of lights, Anjali Banerji* and her 14-year-old son Ashok each swallowed a lethal handful of sleeping pills. They had already fed a dose to the family dog, Tepi.

2   Anjali Banerji died four days later; Ashok and Tepi survived, thanks to police officers who pumped their stomachs after the attempt.

3   A November issue of *India Today* magazine reported the suicide. Anjali Banerji's husband, Rajib, a doctor at the Hindu Rao Hospital, had been hit by a car and, after a lengthy hospitalization, had died the previous January. In time, the widow began searching for work. She had a degree in social work and 14 years' experience in West Bengal, but no job came her way. She received little sympathy from her family and from friends—only the advice to move in with relatives. After 10 frustrating months, she decided to follow her husband in death, and to take the rest of the family with her.

4   The reporter noted her meticulous preparations—notes written to the police and her brother, the refrigerator emptied and defrosted, kitchen stocked with food for relatives or whoever came to take care of the possessions left behind.

5   Two weeks after her death, friends sent the clipping to me in California.

6   Anjali had been very special to me. We were both about 16 when we met outside a classroom on the first day of college at the University of Calcutta. I still remember it clearly. I was standing alone in an archway, watching a crow feed her little ones. Suddenly I heard footsteps and there was a tall, slender girl with two short braids, wearing a well-starched white sari. Like me, she wore no jewelry, not even the customary thin gold bracelets every middle-class girl wore like a uniform. I had not met anyone before who also rebelled against the

*The names have been fictionalized.

prescribed dress code. What we were wearing would be considered a widow's garb. I felt close to her instantly.

7   I smiled and asked if she was also waiting for room three. She nodded with a smile and said, "Yes, and am I glad to find someone to talk to. None of my friends got into this college. I was so nervous when my father dropped me off at the gate that I didn't sleep all night."

8   "I can understand that, since I have no old friends here either. My name is Juthica, but everyone calls me Julie."

9   She stared at me for a few seconds, then told me her name and that she had attended a large school. She hadn't really expected to get into such a good college. She also asked where I had gone to high school. I was sure she had never heard of my school, so I told her it was a small, British missionary boarding school. My graduating class had only 13 students.

10   "You must be Christian with a name like Julie," she said.

11   I found myself apologizing: "It is only my nickname. I do have a real, honest-to-goodness Bengali name, too."

12   She laughed and said, "Oh, it doesn't bother me a bit that you are Christian. As a matter of fact, many people think I'm one too, because of the way I dress."

13   I tried to explain that I wasn't wearing white because of my religion, but simply because I liked it. I realized we both had many misconceptions about each other's communities. She came from a Hindu Brahmin family, the highest caste, I from a Christian middle-class one. We spoke the same language, but our cultures were very different.

14   From then on, for four years, we were inseparable. We took the same classes, joined the National Cadet Corps, helped each other learn to ride bikes, and visited each other after school. I always invited her home for Christmas dinner, and spent Hindu feasts at hers. We covered for each other, telling little white lies when doing something or going somewhere our families wouldn't approve. We comforted each other through difficult times, and teased and poked fun at each other. She was quiet and sensible, with an irresistible sense of humor. I was wild, impulsive, and boisterous—we complemented each other well.

15   Now she is dead.

16   All those times when I felt that the world had come to an end, that my great love was over, or that I would surely flunk the final, she would patiently listen to my stories, then put her arm around me and reassure me. Even now, 30 years later, the memory of her strength pulls me through difficult times. What could have happened to her strength, her confidence, her optimism?

17   As I read through the clipping, I found I couldn't help blaming myself that I wasn't there when she really needed someone. I began to feel angry at her family.

18   Traditionally, the extended Indian family comes to the rescue in times of trouble. What had happened to them? Her father was a scholarly gentleman

who taught high school. She had two older brothers, one an army doctor, the other an engineer, and an older sister, who was already married and out of the house by the time I met her. Anytime I was visiting I was always struck by how quiet and peaceful the household was. They all spoke in gentle voices. It seemed unnatural to me, being used to seven children playing, laughing, fighting, and loving in my family. When I commented once on this, she said it was true, nothing much was ever going on. Her father spent most of the time in his study, her mother kept the house. I had an image of trees in the forest, growing near, but never touching, except in a big storm, when the contact results in a broken limb.

19   Anjali did produce a storm when she married Rajib. She went against her family's expectations by finding her own future husband, rather than waiting for her match to be arranged. What's more, he was from a lower caste.

20   Rajib's family was even more resentful. Even though Anjali was higher caste, which on one level meant a social achievement, the family missed out on a potentially major dowry. Had Rajib married within his own caste, the family would have been offered clothes, jewelry, and money, and considering that he was a doctor, perhaps even a car or house. His family counted on this; it would have helped with providing Rajib's sisters' dowries. The loss was significant.

21   In the wake of the storm, both Anjali and Rajib ended up as limbs broken off family trees. They established themselves on their own. Except for a few sticks of furniture they had nothing, but seemed very happy. By then I was living in California; I visited her each time I was in India, sometimes really going out of my way to do so to catch up with their frequent moves. Each time I saw them I was impressed with the intimacy of their relationship. They were two people who genuinely enjoyed and respected each other, who truly shared their life in the best sense of the word. I kept up with her every way I could.

22   She was overjoyed when her son was born. Her family, at last, showed some interest in the new grandson. However, Rajib's family did not respond even then. She was determined, with or without the families' support, to continue providing a happy home. From everything I saw, she succeeded. But underneath it, I could tell that she was hurt by her isolation from her family, a feeling of sadness remained for not being accepted by her in-laws.

23   The last time I saw her was in a hotel room in Delhi. Rajib, Anjali, and Ashok lived outside of town at that point; they took a long bus drive to come to see me and my family. She brought some fried fish, my favorite kind, which she remembered from our college days. Her son by this time was about 12, very bright and friendly. I fantasized about our children developing the kind of friendship Anjali and I had, knowing full well that with the distance between us that would not be possible. The relationship I had been impressed with over the years between Anjali and Rajib obviously was still there, and now included their son. I was particularly happy to see that our children and Ashok got along well.

24   We parted with the promise of writing more often. We even talked about her sending Ashok to the United States for a year, when he would stay with us.

25   Is it possible that the article in my hand was about the same Anjali? Suddenly I was furious with her. How could this wonderful woman, this pillar of strength, this model friend and mother, simply do away with herself? What about the promises? How could she just abandon everything, including me?

26   When I was still in India with my family, I got a letter from her about her husband's car accident. I left India knowing only that he was seriously injured and in the hospital. For months I had had no news, despite my many letters to Anjali. I would have called, but they could never afford a telephone. I felt helpless, but not knowing anyone in the area where they were living at the time, there was nothing I could do.

27   The next news came in the form of an invitation to a memorial service for Rajib. It was signed by Ashok, as is the custom. The eldest son takes matters into his hands on the father's death. At this time he was barely 14. I could not imagine my own son, three years younger—having to—or being able to do this. But knowing Anjali I knew that if Ashok was anything like his mother, he would perform his duty admirably.

28   All I could do was to write, offering my help and whatever support I could, long distance. I felt I had failed her completely; I was never there when I might have been able to help.

29   I never heard from her again. I wrote to all our common acquaintances trying to get news. No one seemed to be in touch with her.

30   But the *India Today* reporter described the last nine months of her life in great detail. The family had had a comfortable existence, but their modest savings were used up quickly during Rajib's hospitalization after the hit-and-run accident.

31   In India, of course, accident insurance is uncommon. The application for his life insurance benefit was lost by the company. After months, the company had not responded to the duplicate application. The promised assistance from her husband's employer had not come through despite her repeated appeals. Within weeks she was totally without funds.

32   Given India's unemployment problem, there were few jobs available even to experienced and highly educated men. It is not surprising then that a woman, out of the job market as long as Anjali had been, was not seriously considered by most employers. Further, she did not have the necessary personal connections, or the know-how to pay bribes to secure a job.

33   The prospect of being destitute, with no source of support for herself, her son, or even the dog, must have been devastating to her. India is, of course, best known for its poverty. But perhaps just because of this, extreme poverty is even more unthinkable for someone like Anjali who had never before had to worry about it.

34   The article told of her difficulties with the bureaucratic maze and her resulting depression and loneliness. Her family, whom, according to the article, she had abandoned to marry the man she chose, did not come to her. Her parents had died by now, only her brothers and sisters remained. It is less

surprising that her in-laws did not respond either. They considered their son dead once he had married against their wishes.

35   A reporter interviewed Anjali's brother after the tragedy, and he claimed the family never knew what kind of difficulty she was in. Perhaps her pride kept her from turning to them. Rejected once, she did not want to risk it again.

36   Anjali's whole life had revolved around her husband and son. She simply couldn't imagine leaving Ashok to other people's mercy. Once she decided to end her life she saw no other way but to take her son with her.

37   I suddenly realized that, as I was reading on, the image the article conjured up was not of Anjali, but of a women's demonstration I had seen in Delhi during my last trip to India. Hundreds of angry women, mostly villagers, marched with banners, demanding the reinstatement of suttee, the ancient custom in which a widow is to throw herself onto her husband's funeral pyre. The British had outlawed suttee in 1829.

38   The custom is a testimony to the fact that the life of a widow is superfluous. Once the man is dead, there is no further purpose for the woman. Her role is to bear children; with her husband's death that job is done. Religious tradition holds that her sacrifice helps her husband atone for his sins and for this she becomes a saint.

39   Despite the established tradition, not all widows had always willingly killed themselves in this way. Village elders and family members often had to force a young wife to follow her husband into death. They would do so not just for religious or traditional reasons, but because the burden of supporting the surviving wife was usually too much for the family.

40   When I saw that demonstration, I could hardly believe my eyes. How could women, in this day and age, especially in a country where the prime minister is a woman, actually campaign for the right to commit suicide just because their husbands had died?

41   The demonstration dramatized the fact that the ancient custom still has social and economic relevance today. The marching women realized that by outlawing the custom, the British had succeeded only in making it illegal, not in removing its significance. Even today, India's society has no mechanism to help a woman in a traditional role develop her own identity and avoid becoming a burden. The women were making a statement that suicide is the easier alternative to a life of dependency on unwilling families.

42   Anjali was an educated and sophisticated woman, with a background and social circle totally different from that of the demonstrators. For her, living in 20th-century Delhi, suttee, in its traditional form, was unthinkable. But, in the end, didn't she find herself forced onto her husband's funeral pyre anyway?

Considering Ideas

1. What caused Anjali to kill herself? In which paragraphs are the causes presented?

2. What effects did Anjali's suicide have on the author?

3. What were the effects of Anjali and Rajib's marrying outside their castes?
4. Why did Anjali try to take her son's life? Is it possible to understand or defend her action?
5. Using the information in the essay as a clue, state whether Anjali's Hindu view of suicide is similar to the author's Judeo-Christian view. Explain.
6. Why do you think the author tells about the demonstration to reinstate suttee? How does the mention of the demonstration relate to the rest of the essay?

Considering Technique

1. Does the opening paragraph arouse your interest and make you want to read further? Explain why or why not.
2. Paragraphs 1 through 3 and 6 through 13 are narrative. What do these narrations (stories) contribute to the essay?
3. An *analogy* is a form of comparison. What analogy appears in paragraphs 18 and 21? What does this analogy contribute to the essay?
4. A *rhetorical question* is a question for which no answer is expected. A writer can use a rhetorical question to emphasize a point or to get a reader to think about something. To what use does Stangl put the rhetorical question that closes the essay? Do you think this question provides an effective conclusion? Explain.
5. Construct a causal chain that describes the events beginning with Anjali and Rajib's marrying and ending with Anjali's suicide. (See page 264 on causal chains.)
6. Consult a dictionary if you are unsure of the meaning of any of these words: *Delhi* (paragraph 1), *meticulous* (paragraph 4), *sari* (paragraph 6), *garb* (paragraph 6), *Bengali* (paragraph 11), *Hindu* (paragraph 13), *Brahmin* (paragraph 13), *caste* (paragraph 13), *boisterous* (paragraph 14), *dowry* (paragraph 20), *destitute* (paragraph 33), *funeral pyre* (paragraph 37), *superfluous* (paragraph 38), *atone* (paragraph 38).

For Group Consideration

"India: A Widow's Devastating Choice" tells something about the social and economic reality of life for women in India. With two or three classmates, decide if any of the points Stangl makes about Indian women are also true for women in the United States. Try to illustrate your conclusions with examples you can report to the rest of the class.

Journal Entry

Can you understand why Anjali killed herself? Do you think she had an alternative to suicide? Is suicide ever justifiable? Explain your answers to these questions in a page or two.

Essay Assignments

1. If you have ever lost a friend through death or a parting of the ways, write an essay that explains what happened and the effects of the loss on you. If appropriate, explain what caused the end of the friendship. Also, like Stangl, use narration to reveal something about the nature and extent of the friendship.
2. If you have suffered the loss of a loved one, write about the short- and long-term effects of this loss.
3. If you have ever done something against your family's wishes or expectations, tell what you did, what caused you to do it, and what the effects were. As an alternative, write about someone you know who did something against his or her family's wishes or expectations.
4. Anjali felt that she had no choice but to kill herself. Use narration to tell about a time you felt forced to do something. Then use cause-and-effect analysis to explain why you had no choice and the effects of your action.

Considering Thematic Issues

1. Explain the view of women depicted in "India: A Widow's Devastating Choice." Is that view to any extent shared in the United States? Explain.
2. Using the information in "India: A Widow's Devastating Choice" and "What Is Poverty?" on page 349, discuss to what extent the United States and India share similar social and economic problems. If there are differences pointed out in the selections, note these as well. What conclusion can you draw from the similarities and differences? (The preceding "For Group Consideration" activity may give you some ideas for this activity.)

JUST WALK ON BY:
A BLACK MAN PONDERS HIS POWER
TO ALTER PUBLIC SPACE
Brent Staples

◆

Brent Staples, a member of the New York Times *editorial board, has written for the* New York Times Magazine, Harpers, *and* New York Woman. *The following essay appeared in* Ms. *(September 1986) and in a revised form in* Harper's *(December 1987). In it, Staples uses cause-and-effect analysis to inform his reader about why some people view black men as a threat. He also shares the effects this perception has on him and informs the reader that "being perceived as dangerous" puts the black man at risk. As you read, think about how you react to the appearance of people.*

1   My first victim was a woman—white, well dressed, probably in her early twenties. I came upon her late one evening on a deserted street in Hyde Park, a relatively affluent neighborhood in an otherwise mean, impoverished section of Chicago. As I swung onto the avenue behind her, there seemed to be a discreet uninflammatory distance between us. Not so. She cast back a worried glance. To her, the youngish black man—a broad six feet two inches with a beard and billowing hair, both hands shoved into the pockets of a bulky military jacket—seemed menacingly close. After a few more quick glimpses, she picked up her pace and was soon running in earnest. Within seconds she disappeared into a cross street.

2   That was more than a decade ago. I was 22 years old, a graduate student newly arrived at the University of Chicago. It was in the echo of that terrified woman's footfalls that I first began to know the unwieldy inheritance I'd come into—the ability to alter public space in ugly ways. It was clear that she thought herself the quarry of a mugger, a rapist, or worse. Suffering a bout of insomnia, however, I was stalking sleep, not defenseless wayfarers. As a softy who is scarcely able to take a knife to a raw chicken—let alone hold it to a person's throat—I was surprised, embarrassed, and dismayed all at once. Her flight made me feel like an accomplice in tyranny. It also made it clear that I was indistinguishable from the muggers who occasionally seeped into the area from the surrounding ghetto. That first encounter, and those that followed, signified that a vast, unnerving gulf lay between nighttime pedestrians—particularly women—and me. And I soon gathered that being perceived as dangerous is a hazard in itself. I only needed to turn a corner into a dicey situation, or crowd some frightened, armed person in a foyer somewhere, or make an errant move after being pulled over by a policeman. Where fear and weapons meet—and they often do in urban America—there is always the possibility of death.

3   In that first year, my first away from my hometown, I was to become thoroughly familiar with the language of fear. At dark, shadowy intersections in Chicago, I could cross in front of a car stopped at a traffic light and elicit the *thunk, thunk, thunk, thunk* of the driver—black, white, male, or female— hammering down the door locks. On less traveled streets after dark, I grew accustomed to but never comfortable with people who crossed to the other side of the street rather than pass me. Then there were the standard unpleasantries with police, doormen, bouncers, cab drivers, and others whose business it is to screen out troublesome individuals *before* there is any nastiness.

4   I moved to New York nearly two years ago and I have remained an avid night walker. In central Manhattan, the near-constant crowd cover minimizes tense one-on-one street encounters. Elsewhere—visiting friends in SoHo, where sidewalks are narrow and tightly spaced buildings shut out the sky— things can get very taut indeed.

5   Black men have a firm place in New York mugging literature. Norman Podhoretz in his famed (or infamous) 1963 essay, "My Negro Problem—And Ours," recalls growing up in terror of black males; they "were tougher than we were, more ruthless," he writes—and as an adult on the Upper West Side of Manhattan, he continues, he cannot constrain his nervousness when he meets black men on certain streets. Similarly, a decade later, the essayist and novelist Edward Hoagland extols a New York where once "Negro bitterness bore down mainly on other Negroes." Where some see mere panhandlers, Hoagland sees "a mugger who is clearly screwing up his nerve to do more than just *ask* for money." But Hoagland has "the New Yorker's quick-hunch posture for broken-field maneuvering," and the bad guy swerves away.

6   I often witness that "hunch posture," from women after dark on the warrenlike streets of Brooklyn where I live. They seem to set their faces on neutral and, with their purse straps strung across their chests bandolier style, they forge ahead as though bracing themselves against being tackled. I under-stand, of course, that the danger they perceive is not a hallucination. Women are particularly vulnerable to street violence, and young black males are dras-tically overrepresented among the perpetrators of that violence. Yet these truths are no solace against the kind of alienation that comes of being ever the suspect, against being set apart, a fearsome entity with whom pedestrians avoid making eye contact.

7   It is not altogether clear to me how I reached the ripe old age of 22 without being conscious of the lethality nighttime pedestrians attributed to me. Perhaps it was because in Chester, Pennsylvania, the small angry industrial town where I came of age in the 1960s, I was scarcely noticeable against a backdrop of gang warfare, street knifings, and murders. I grew up one of the good boys, had perhaps a half-dozen fist fights. In retrospect, my shyness of combat has clear sources.

8   Many things go into the making of a young thug. One of those things is the consummation of the male romance with the power to intimidate. An infant

discovers that random flailings send the baby bottle flying out of the crib and crashing to the floor. Delighted, the joyful babe repeats those motions again and again, seeking to duplicate the feat. Just so, I recall the points at which some of my boyhood friends were finally seduced by the perception of themselves as tough guys. When a mark cowered and surrendered his money without resistance, myth and reality merged—and paid off. It is, after all, only manly to embrace the power to frighten and intimidate. We, as men, are not supposed to give an inch of our lane on the highway; we are to seize the fighter's edge in work and in play and even in love; we are to be valiant in the face of hostile forces.

9   Unfortunately, poor and powerless young men seem to take all this nonsense literally. As a boy, I saw countless tough guys locked away; I have since buried several, too. They were babies, really—a teenage cousin, a brother of 22, a childhood friend in his mid-twenties—all gone down in episodes of bravado played out in the streets. I came to doubt the virtues of intimidation early on. I chose, perhaps even unconsciously, to remain a shadow—timid, but a survivor.

10   The fearsomeness mistakenly attributed to me in public places often has a perilous flavor. The most frightening of these confusions occurred in the late 1970s and early 1980s when I worked as a journalist in Chicago. One day, rushing into the office of a magazine I was writing for with a deadline story in hand, I was mistaken for a burglar. The office manager called security and, with an ad hoc posse, pursued me through the labyrinthine halls, nearly to my editor's door. I had no way of proving who I was. I could only move briskly toward the company of someone who knew me.

11   Another time I was on assignment for a local paper and killing time before an interview. I entered a jewelry store on the city's affluent Near North Side. The proprietor excused herself and returned with an enormous red Doberman pinscher straining at the end of a leash. She stood, the dog extended toward me, silent to my questions, her eyes bulging nearly out of her head. I took a cursory look around, nodded, and bade her good night. Relatively speaking, however, I never fared as badly as another black male journalist. He went to nearby Waukegan, Illinois, a couple of summers ago to work on a story about a murderer who was born there. Mistaking the reporter for the killer, police hauled him from his car at gunpoint and but for his press credentials would probably have tried to book him. Such episodes are not uncommon. Black men trade tales like this all the time.

12   In "My Negro Problem—And Ours," Podhoretz writes that the hatred he feels for blacks makes itself known to him through a variety of avenues—one being his discomfort with that "special brand of paranoid touchiness" to which he says blacks are prone. No doubt he is speaking here of black men. In time, I learned to smother the rage I felt at so often being taken for a criminal. Not to do so would surely have led to madness—via that special "paranoid touchiness" that so annoyed Podhoretz at the time he wrote the essay.

13 I began to take precautions to make myself less threatening. I move about with care, particularly late in the evening. I give a wide berth to nervous people on subway platforms during the wee hours, particularly when I have exchanged business clothes for jeans. If I happen to be entering a building behind some people who appear skittish, I may walk by, letting them clear the lobby before I return, so as not to seem to be following them. I have been calm and extremely congenial on those rare occasions when I've been pulled over by the police.

14 And on late-evening constitutionals along streets less traveled by, I employ what has proved to be an excellent tension-reducing measure: I whistle melodies from Beethoven and Vivaldi and the more popular classical composers. Even steely New Yorkers hunching toward nighttime destinations seem to relax, and occasionally they even join in the tune. Virtually everybody seems to sense that a mugger wouldn't be warbling bright, sunny selections from Vivaldi's *Four Seasons*. It is my equivalent of the cowbell that hikers wear when they know they are in bear country.

Considering Ideas

1. When Staples walks at night, what effect does he have on people? What do people do when they see him?
2. Although Staples is often viewed as a threat, he is the one at risk. Why? That is, how is Staples affected by being perceived as dangerous?
3. Staples explains that his effect on people—particularly women—is understandable. Why does he think so?
4. According to Staples, what causes a young man to become a thug? What do you think prompts a black male to become a thug? How did Staples escape becoming a thug?
5. In paragraphs 5 and 12, Staples refers to essays by Norman Podhoretz and Edward Hoagland. What point do you think Staples is trying to make with these references?
6. Staples's essay first appeared in *Ms.* and *Harper's*. Do you think the readers of these magazines make the best audience for the piece? Explain.

Considering Technique

1. What approach does Staples take to his introduction? Does the introduction engage your interest? Explain.
2. The essay is not about what the opening sentences lead you to believe it will be about. Is that a problem? Explain.
3. In your own words, write out the thesis of "Just Walk on By." Which sentence in the essay comes closest to expressing that idea?
4. Which paragraphs include brief narrations? What do they contribute to the essay?

5. What approach does Staples take to his conclusion? Do you think the conclusion brings the essay to a satisfying close? Why or why not?

6. Consult a dictionary if you are unsure of the meaning of any of these words: *affluent* (paragraph 1), *quarry* (paragraph 2), *stalking* (paragraph 2), *wayfarers* (paragraph 2), *foyer* (paragraph 2), *errant* (paragraph 2), *avid* (paragraph 4), *taut* (paragraph 4), *extols* (paragraph 5), *warrenlike* (paragraph 6), *bandolier* (paragraph 6), *lethality* (paragraph 7), *flailings* (paragraph 8), *cowered* (paragraph 8), *bravado* (paragraph 9), *ad hoc* (paragraph 10), *labyrinthine* (paragraph 10), *cursory* (paragraph 11), *constitutionals* (paragraph 14).

For Group Consideration

With two or three classmates, discuss whether your experience confirms or contradicts Staples's thesis that young, black males are perceived as threats.

Journal Entry

Although we admit that appearances can be deceiving, we often are influenced by the way others look. To what extent are you influenced by the way people look? How do appearances affect who you speak to and interact with? How do appearances affect the judgments you make about people?

Essay Assignments

1. How safe do you feel walking alone on your campus or in your neighborhood? Explain why you feel the way you do and the effects of your feeling of security or insecurity.

2. Describe how you think you are perceived by others and explain why you think you are perceived that way. Consider how one or more factors such as your size, gender, skin color, age, manner of dress, and degree of attractiveness affect how people judge your social class, economic level, degree of intelligence, occupation, and such. Then go on to explain how you are affected by the way you are perceived.

3. If you have ever been perceived as a threat or if you have perceived someone else as a threat, explain what caused the perception and what its effects were.

4. Pick one of the following and explain how the person is typically perceived, as well as the effect the perception has on the person. If you do not have firsthand knowledge, you can interview the appropriate people to get your information.

a very attractive person	a very tall person
a male with long hair	a very short person

a male with an earring   a very muscular person
a physically disabled person   an elderly person

Considering Thematic Issues

1. In paragraph 8, Staples comments on men and power: "It is, after all, only manly to embrace the power to frighten and intimidate." Do you agree that our concept of manliness is linked to the sense of power and the ability to intimidate? If so, explain how men and women are affected by this concept of manliness. If not, explain why you disagree.

2. Using your own experience and observation, along with information in "Just Walk on By" and "Untouchables" (page 159), explain how people react to those they perceive as "different." Also explain why you think people react the way they do.

NO KICK FROM CHAMPAGNE
Harold Saltzman

◆

"The bias against singles begins at the earliest stages of planning a wedding," says Harold Saltzman, who writes to persuade his reader that unmarried people are social outcasts at weddings. To inform and share, the author explains the effects of weddings on single people. Saltzman wrote this essay for Newsweek's *"My Turn" column (June 24, 1990). As you read it, consider the author's points in light of weddings you have attended.*

◆

1   I received a wedding invitation from a friend the other day. After the initial touch of anger at having been invited as a *single* (no guest, please) I began experiencing some old unsettled feelings about being a divorced male in a married world. It's not that I didn't realize long ago that hosting these lavish catered affairs is a game invented by Mr. & Mrs. America to perpetuate, symbolize and elevate a chosen lifestyle. What has continued to trouble me since that first invitation as a single nearly 15 years ago isn't the game itself, but the way the game treats unmarrieds as outcasts.

2   In my post-married life, it has always felt a little strange to attend these celebrations without a date. Occasionally it was fun. More often uncomfortable. And sometimes excruciatingly painful to be alone in a sea of couples. But I'd tough it out, present my gift and leave at the earliest opportunity with the feeble excuse of having another pressing engagement.

3   Maybe getting upset about not having the option to bring a date was "my hang-up," as some friends suggested. Still, is discrimination based on marital status any less wrong than the dismissal of a female employee who refuses to wear makeup? These days, I refuse to attend any affair as a single unless it happens to be my preference. At long last I can say, "No thank you," and send a check.

4   The bias against singles begins at the earliest stage of planning a wedding. First, the betrothed and prospective in-laws parry over who gets to invite how many guests and who will pay for what—the ballroom, ceremony, music, flowers, menu, picture albums and videos. Quickly they realize that a consensus must be reached on how to reduce costs. Obviously the guest list will need to be trimmed. The first casualties are second cousins, teenagers and anyone who omitted the hosts from a guest list, gave less than a generous gift in the past or made a mildly disparaging remark about the bride's mother 25 years ago. Next come the singles, sitting ducks for the paring knife. If lucky (or unlucky) enough to survive the cut, they'll be invited as *single only*—escorts not welcome!

5   Let's examine why this is unfair:

6   First, a married person is always invited as part of a couple. It's automatic, a cardinal rule of the wedding game, accepted by all and inflexible. "Mr. and Mrs." the envelope reads, although the hosts may not know one of the spouses from an extraterrestrial. Or that spouse may be detested by all civilized beings, a blooming idiot, bigot, child molester or thief. Never mind. The spouse is invited. Case closed.

7   Another rule, a little more complex, is that a single person *may* be accorded the special privilege of bringing an escort if, and only if, that person is currently involved in an "ongoing and serious relationship." Naturally, it's the hosts who make the determination as to what qualifies as "ongoing and serious." There are tests. For example: "Didn't they break up twice this year?" Or, "Hasn't she started dating other men?"

8   In the eyes of the married, you see, to qualify under the "ongoing and serious" doctrine, the relationship must: (a) be monogamous, (b) hold out the prospect for marriage and (c) appear to be moving swiftly in that direction. If the couple in question are simply lovers, platonic friends or, God forbid, gay or lesbian, well that's too bad. That's not a real relationship in the eyes of the about-to-be-married—sorry, no escort!

9   **Disfavored Minority.**   The last rule may be the most insidious of all. It's cleverly concocted by Married America to reduce the ranks of the unwed, the millions of us who by fate or design are widowed, separated, divorced or never-married. For all but the most enlightened of married folk, the inescapable truth is that singles are, at best, a disfavored minority about whom hosts feel at least some guilt. One way or another, that guilt must be assuaged. So what do hosts do? They become matchmakers, of course, telling their single invites how they'll have this lovely table by the dance floor all to themselves, and that there's this extra-special person of the opposite sex who is also coming solo and "is just dying to meet you."

10   So there are the singles, conspicuous by their presence, seated at their own table, at an affair which by nature and intent exalts and pays tribute to the world of couples in general and marriage in particular. And at the end of the evening, the coup de grâce that somehow says it all—the ritual herding of all the single females on to the dance floor to see which of them will be lucky enough to find a husband by catching the bride's bouquet. So much for feminism in the '90s.

11   Of course, when there aren't enough singles to fill a table, odd-person-out seating is arranged. When the dance band starts playing, the single person is generally left sitting alone. At one wedding, I recall making frequent and prolonged visits to the men's room whenever the dancing began; embarrassed, I gave the attendant increasingly extravagant tips. Table-hopping was another useful refuge, but real relief didn't come until one young fellow who'd been sopping up the booze all night passed out, affording me the opportunity to administer first aid by applying ice packs to his neck and forehead on a lobby couch.

12   So this time I will reluctantly tell my friend that I'll miss seeing her in bridal splendor, walking down the aisle, embarking on a new and exciting life. I'll remember the endless hours we spent talking about her taking the risk, going for it all, getting what she truly wanted in life. I'll wish her happiness and joy in my own way and will remain her friend if she wants it. But I'm staying home on the wedding day. Pride, foolishness perhaps, prevents me from asking permission to bring a guest. Having to ask is demeaning. As in Robert Browning's "My Last Duchess," she should have known.

Considering Ideas

1. What specific effects does Saltzman experience as a result of being an outcast at weddings?
2. Why does Saltzman think that wedding invitations are unfair if they do not allow singles to bring a friend or date?
3. Do you agree with Saltzman that wedding invitations represent a bias against single people? Explain.
4. In paragraph 1, Saltzman says that "hosting these lavish catered affairs is a game invented by Mr. & Mrs. America to perpetuate, symbolize and elevate a chosen lifestyle." What do you think Saltzman means by this statement?
5. In your opinion, what is the significance of the title of the essay, and what does the title contribute to the piece?
6. Saltzman's essay first appeared in *Newsweek*. Do you think the readers of this magazine make a suitable audience for the essay? Explain.

Considering Technique

1. What sentence presents the thesis of "No Kick from Champagne"?
2. Paragraph 1 is the introduction. What approach does Saltzman take to that introduction?
3. In which paragraph does Saltzman use process analysis to help establish his point? (Process analysis, discussed in Chapter 7, explains how something is made or done.)
4. In which paragraph does Saltzman use examples to help establish his point?
5. What approach does Saltzman take to his conclusion?
6. Consult a dictionary if you are unsure of the meaning of any of these words: *perpetuate* (paragraph 1), *excruciatingly* (paragraph 2), *feeble* (paragraph 2), *betrothed* (paragraph 4), *prospective* (paragraph 4), *parry* (paragraph 4), *disparaging* (paragraph 4), *extraterrestrial* (paragraph 6), *monogamous* (paragraph 8), *platonic* (paragraph 8), *insidious* (paragraph 9), *assuaged* (paragraph 9), *exalts* (paragraph 10), *coup de grâce* (paragraph 10), *demeaning* (paragraph 12).

For Group Consideration

With two or three classmates, discuss whether Saltzman has identified a legitimate form of bias or whether he is making a big deal out of nothing. If you think he has identified a legitimate form of bias, decide what you think should be done about it. If you think he is making a big deal out of nothing, decide on a response to Saltzman's claim.

Journal Entry

Tell about the last wedding you attended. Explain whether you were comfortable or uncomfortable and why.

Essay Assignments

1. Saltzman tells about a social situation that angers him and makes him feel uncomfortable. Pick a social situation (or use weddings, as Saltzman does) and explain how you feel when you are in that situation. To establish a cause-and-effect pattern, explain why the situation causes you to feel the way you do and/or the specific effects the situation causes.
2. Saltzman calls weddings "lavish catered affairs [that are games] invented by Mr. & Mrs. America to perpetuate, symbolize and elevate a chosen lifestyle." Select another life-cycle event, (for example, graduation, confirmation, bar mitzvah, first communion, or baptism) and show how the effects of the ritual work to perpetuate and symbolize a particular lifestyle. Like Saltzman, establish a persuasive purpose and indicate whether the event's impact is positive or negative.
3. Pick a social situation (for example, a wedding, a dance, dating, or eating in a restaurant) and, like Saltzman, show how it discriminates against a particular group of people (teenagers, unmarried people, the elderly, women, childless couples, single parents, the disabled, and so on).

Considering Thematic Issues

1. Saltzman's view is that American society is weighted heavily in favor of married people and that "singles are, at best, a disfavored minority." To what extent (if at all) do you think that social forces (media messages, social conventions, religious doctrine, government regulations, and so on) pressure people to marry? Explain your view.
2. Read "Don't Just Stand There" (page 182), and "The Ways of Meeting Oppression" (page 332). Then describe the strategies you think Cole and King would recommend for dealing with discrimination based on marital status.

COMPLEXION
Richard Rodriguez

◆

Author Richard Rodriguez is a first-generation Mexican-American who writes frequently of his heritage. An editor at Pacific News Service, he has written several books, as well as articles for such magazines as Harper's *and* The American Scholar. *In the following excerpt from his autobiographical work* Hunger of Memory *(1981), Rodriguez combines contrast, narration, and description to share the effects his skin color had on his self-concept and to inform the reader about the Mexican-American experience. As you read, you may be reminded of your own adolescent struggle to feel at ease with your physical appearance.*

◆

1   Complexion. My first conscious experience of sexual excitement concerns my complexion. One summer weekend, when I was around seven years old, I was at a public swimming pool with the whole family. I remember sitting on the damp pavement next to the pool and seeing my mother, in the spectators' bleachers, holding my younger sister on her lap. My mother, I noticed, was watching my father as he stood on a diving board, waving to her. I watched her wave back. Then saw her radiant, bashful, astonishing smile. In that second I sensed that my mother and father had a relationship I knew nothing about. A nervous excitement encircled my stomach as I saw my mother's eyes follow my father's figure curving into the water. A second or two later, he emerged. I heard him call out. Smiling, his voice sounded, buoyant, calling me to swim to him. But turning to see him, I caught my mother's eye. I heard her shout over to me. In Spanish she called through the crowd: 'Put a towel on over your shoulders.' In public, she didn't want to say why. I knew.

2   That incident anticipates the shame and sexual inferiority I was to feel in later years because of my dark complexion. I was to grow up an ugly child. Or one who thought himself ugly. (*Feo.*) One night when I was eleven or twelve years old, I locked myself in the bathroom and carefully regarded my reflection in the mirror over the sink. Without any pleasure I studied my skin. I turned on the faucet. (In my mind I heard the swirling voices of aunts, and even my mother's voice, whispering, whispering incessantly about lemon juice solutions and dark, *feo* children.) With a bar of soap, I fashioned a thick ball of lather. I began soaping my arms. I took my father's straight razor out of the medicine cabinet. Slowly, with steady deliberateness, I put the blade against my flesh, pressed it as close as I could without cutting, and moved it up and down across my skin to see if I could get out, somehow lessen, the dark. All I succeeded in doing, however, was in shaving my arms bare of their hair. For as I noted with disappointment, the dark would not come out. It remained. Trapped. Deep in the cells of my skin.

3   Throughout adolescence, I felt myself mysteriously marked. Nothing else about my appearance would concern me so much as the fact that my complexion was dark. My mother would say how sorry she was that there was not money enough to get braces to straighten my teeth. But I never bothered about my teeth. In three-way mirrors at department stores, I'd see my profile dramatically defined by a long nose, but it was really only the color of my skin that caught my attention.

4   I wasn't afraid that I would become a menial laborer because of my skin. Nor did my complexion make me feel especially vulnerable to racial abuse. (I didn't really consider my dark skin to be a racial characteristic. I would have been only too happy to look as Mexican as my light-skinned older brother.) Simply, I judged myself ugly. And, since the women in my family had been the ones who discussed it in such worried tones, I felt my dark skin made me unattractive to women.

5   Thirteen years old. Fourteen. In a grammar school art class, when the assignment was to draw a self-portrait, I tried and I tried but could not bring myself to shade in the face on the paper to anything like my actual tone. With disgust then I would come face to face with myself in mirrors. With disappointment I located myself in class photographs—my dark face undefined by the camera which had clearly described the white faces of classmates. Or I'd see my dark wrist against my long-sleeved white shirt.

6   I grew divorced from my body. Insecure, overweight, listless. On hot summer days when my rubber-soled shoes soaked up the heat from the sidewalk, I kept my head down. Or walked in the shade. My mother didn't need anymore to tell me to watch out for the sun. I denied myself a sensational life. The normal, extraordinary, animal excitement of feeling my body alive—riding shirtless on a bicycle in the warm wind created by furious self-propelled motion—the sensations that first had excited in me a sense of my maleness, I denied. I was too ashamed of my body. I wanted to forget that I had a body because I had a brown body. I was grateful that none of my classmates ever mentioned the fact.

7   I continued to see the *braceros,** those men I resembled in one way and, in another way, didn't resemble at all. On the watery horizon of a Valley afternoon, I'd see them. And though I feared looking like them, it was with silent envy that I regarded them still. I envied them their physical lives, their freedom to violate the taboo of the sun. Closer to home I would notice the shirtless construction workers, the roofers, the sweating men tarring the street in front of the house. And I'd see the Mexican gardeners. I was unwilling to admit the attraction of their lives. I tried to deny it by looking away. But what was denied became strongly desired.

*Mexican laborers admitted into the country temporarily to do seasonal work, such as harvesting crops.

8   In high school physical education classes, I withdrew, in the regular company of five or six classmates, to a distant corner of a football field where we smoked and talked. Our company was composed of bodies too short or too tall, all graceless and all—except mine—pale. Our conversation was usually witty. (In fact we were intelligent.) If we referred to the athletic contests around us, it was with sarcasm. With savage scorn I'd refer to the 'animals' playing football or baseball. It would have been important for me to have joined them. Or for me to have taken off my shirt, to have let the sun burn dark on my skin, and to have run barefoot on the warm wet grass. It would have been very important. Too important. It would have been too telling a gesture—to admit the desire for sensation, the body, my body.

9   Fifteen, sixteen. I was a teenager shy in the presence of girls. Never dated. Barely could talk to a girl without stammering. In high school I went to several dances, but I never managed to ask a girl to dance. So I stopped going. I cannot remember high school years now with the parade of typical images: bright drive-ins or gliding blue shadows of a Junior Prom. At home most weekend nights, I would pass evenings reading. Like those hidden, precocious adolescents who have no real-life sexual experiences, I read a great deal of romantic fiction. 'You won't find it in your books,' my brother would playfully taunt me as he prepared to go to a party by freezing the crest of the wave in his hair with sticky pomade. Through my reading, however, I developed a fabulous and sophisticated sexual imagination. At seventeen, I may not have known how to engage a girl in small talk, but I had read *Lady Chatterley's Lover*.

10   It annoyed me to hear my father's teasing: that I would never know what 'real work' is; that my hands were so soft. I think I knew it was his way of admitting pleasure and pride in my academic success. But I didn't smile. My mother said she was glad her children were getting their educations and would not be pushed around like *los pobres*.* I heard the remark ironically as a reminder of my separation from *los braceros*. As such times I suspected that education was making me effeminate. The odd thing, however, was that I did not judge my classmates so harshly. Nor did I consider my male teachers in high school effeminate. It was only myself I judged against some shadowy, mythical Mexican laborer—dark like me, yet very different.

Considering Ideas

1. What effects did the color of Rodriguez's complexion have on him?

2. In what ways did the women in Rodriguez's family make him feel self-conscious and inferior?

*The poor ones.

3. Why do you think that Rodriguez was so attracted to the lives of the Mexican gardeners and construction workers?
4. Why did Rodriguez read so much? Why do you think he was afraid that reading and education would make him effeminate?
5. Using the information in the essay for clues, explain the author's idea of masculinity.
6. "Complexion" came from Rodriguez's autobiographical book. What kind of reader do you think would benefit most from reading about his life?

Considering Technique

1. In which paragraphs does Rodriguez use narration to help develop the cause-and-effect relationship in his piece?
2. In which paragraph does Rodriguez indicate what is *not* an effect of his reaction to his complexion?
3. With what people does Rodriguez contrast himself? What does that element of contrast contribute to the essay?
4. Cite an example of descriptive language and explain what the description contributes to the piece.
5. In what order are the effects arranged? What are the clues to this arrangement?
6. Consult a dictionary if you are unsure of the meaning of any of these words: *buoyant* (paragraph 1), *incessantly* (paragraph 2), *menial* (paragraph 4), *listless* (paragraph 6), *taboo* (paragraph 7), *precocious* (paragraph 9), *pomade* (paragraph 9), *effeminate* (paragraph 10).

For Group Consideration

With three or four classmates, consider the things that shape a person's self-concept. Discuss the influence of family, friends, teachers, coaches, television, advertisements, and anything else you can think of. Share your conclusions with the rest of the class.

Journal Entry

Rodriguez tells about feeling very self-conscious because of his skin color. Write about some aspect of your physical appearance that makes or made you self-conscious. Also, explain why you feel or felt self-conscious. As an alternative, write about some feature of your appearance that you are proud of.

Essay Assignments

1. Pick one aspect of your physical appearance (your height, weight, nose, skin color, hair, and so on) and explain what effect or effects that feature has had on you. (Your journal entry may give you some ideas to include.)

2. In paragraph 1, Rodriguez tells about his realization that his parents had a sexual relationship. Tell about a time when you came to understand something about one or both of your parents (or other caregiver) that you did not realize before. Explain what caused the insight and how that awareness affected you. As an alternative, use another adult who figured significantly in your life (for example, a coach, clergy member, teacher, or grandparent).

3. Things that happen to us in childhood and adolescence have the power to influence us long into adulthood. Tell about something that happened in your youth that has an effect on you today. Explain why you think the event continues to affect you.

4. Think about your high school years and settle on one experience (band, football, dating, grades, exams, homecoming, and so on). Then write an essay that explains the effects this experience had on you.

Considering Thematic Issues

1. Rodriguez tells the reader a little about what high school was like for him. Explain what high school was like for you and how that experience affected you then and now.

2. School has a great impact on the self-concept of young people. Consider "Complexion," "The Water-Faucet Vision" (page 118), and "By Any Other Name" (page 111), and explain school's potential to affect the way we view ourselves. If you like, you may also draw on your own experience and observation.

Additional Essay Assignments

1. If you have been the victim of sexual harassment, or if you have witnessed sexual harassment, write about the causes and/or effects of this problem. If you have not been a victim or witness, gather information by interviewing people who have been victims or witnesses or by visiting your campus affirmative action office or human resources office.

2. Analyze the causes or effects of stress in college or high school students.

3. If you have difficulty with a particular subject (English, math, science, etc.), explain why the subject causes you problems and/or the effect of having difficulty with that subject.

4. Explain the effects of an illness or disability on you or someone you know.

5. Explain why you chose the particular school you attend and the effects attendance at this school has had on your life. Your purpose can be to share or, if you want to use humor, to entertain.

6. Select a bad habit you have (for example, procrastinating, smoking, over-eating, or nail biting) and explain its causes and effects.

7. Tell about the effects of something that happened to you in school (for example, getting cut from the basketball team, being elected class president, becoming homecoming queen, or failing a course).

8. Discuss the effects of a technological advance (for example, the compact disc, the VCR, the camcorder, the microwave oven, or the word processor). You can be serious or use humor to make the piece funny.

9. Select a problem on your campus (for example, poor student housing, high tuition, degree requirements, or unpopular social events) and analyze the effects on students to persuade those in authority to remedy the problem.

10. Analyze how the neighborhood in which you grew up affected you.

11. Explain why students cheat and the effects cheating has on students.

12. If you have a particular fear (of heights, of math, of failure, and so on), share with your reader by explaining the causes and/or effects of that fear.

13. If you ever moved to a new town, explain how the move affected you.

14. If you have children, explain the effects of becoming a parent. If you want, you can make this essay humorous.

15. If you are an international student, explain how you have been affected by living and attending school in this country.

16. Explain why football (or baseball or basketball) is so popular in this country and how the sport affects American culture.

17. Explain the effects of the movement to achieve gender equality (or deseg-regation, or gay rights or, affirmative action).

18. Explain the techniques television commercials (or magazine ads) use to influence us. As an alternative, explain the effects of commercials (or magazine ads) on us.

19. People in the U.S. value youth. Analyze the effects of this youth orientation.

20. Select a person who has had a significant impact on you (for example, a coach, a minister, a teacher, or a friend) and explain the effects this individual has had on you.

CLASSIFICATION-DIVISION

The Purpose of Classification-Division
Selecting a Principle for Classification-Division
Selecting Detail
Structuring Classification-Division
Suggestions for Writing Classification-Division
Annotated Student Essay: Strictly Speaking

Wait Divisions—Tom Bodett *(classification-division to entertain)*
White Lies—Sissela Bok *(classification-division to inform and persuade)*
Country Codes—Noel Perrin *(classification-division to entertain, share, and inform)*
* *College Pressures*—William Zinsser *(classification-division to inform and persuade)*
The Ways of Meeting Oppression—Martin Luther King, Jr. *(classification-division to inform and persuade)*
* *Shades of Black*—Mary E. Mebane *(classification-division to inform and share)*

Additional Essay Assignments

---

* To fulfill the author's purpose, classification-division is combined with one or more other patterns.

Both classification and division are methods of grouping and ordering. *Classification* takes a number of items and groups them into categories, and *division* takes one entity and breaks it down into its parts. Consider your college, for example. It orders courses in the catalog by placing them into groups according to the departments that offer those courses (English, biology, mathematics, and so on); this is classifying. In addition, your college organizes itself by breaking into components (the School of Education, the School of Arts and Sciences, the School of Engineering, and so on); this is division.

Sometimes division and classification are each performed by itself, but more often they are companion operations performed together for a specific purpose. For example, let's say that you are the manager of a video store and you want to organize all the tapes so customers can locate titles easily. First, you would use *division* to establish a breakdown into groupings, such as westerns, musicals, science fiction, romance, horror films, and adventure movies. Then you would use *classification to sort the videos into the appropriate categories*— *Star Wars* into the science fiction area, *Friday the 13th* into the horror movie area, and so on. Similarly, when you write, you will often find yourself dividing and then classifying.

Classification and division are so much a part of our lives, that you do not have to look very far to find examples of them: the yellow pages of your phone book groups telephone numbers according to kinds of businesses; your biology text orders animals according to whether they are mammals, birds, reptiles, and so on; your local supermarket arranges items in aisles according to whether they are fruits, vegetables, meats, canned goods, cleaning products, and so on. Classification and division are common because they help us order items or pieces of information to study them easier, retrieve them faster, or deal with them more efficiently. Imagine, for a moment, a world without groupings. How hard would it be to find what you need in the grocery store or to locate a book in the library?

THE PURPOSE OF CLASSIFICATION-DIVISION

A writer can classify or divide in order to *inform* the reader. Sometimes a writer wants to inform the reader of the relative merits of the items grouped so the reader can choose one wisely. For example, you might group various CD and tape clubs according to expense and variety of selections so the reader can decide which club to join. Sometimes a writer classifies or divides to give the reader a fresh appreciation of the familiar. In "Whites Lies" (page 313), Sissela Bok groups white lies, something we all know about, in order to help us better understand them and their significance. Sometimes a classification-division helps the reader understand something he or she is not familiar with. For example, the groupings in "Country Codes" (page 317) can inform a city dweller about codes of conduct in rural New England.

A classification-division can also allow the writer to *share*. In "Country Codes," for example, the author shares the experiences he had learning the different categories of behavior in rural New England. Similarly, you could share the various Halloween celebrations you have enjoyed by grouping ways to celebrate that holiday.

Very often, a classification-division has a *persuasive purpose*, as is the case with "The Ways of Meeting Oppression" (page 332). In this essay, Dr. Martin Luther King, Jr., groups the ways to deal with oppression in order to convince the reader that one of those ways is better than the rest and should be employed.

Finally, classification-division can *entertain* the reader. For example, to amuse your audience, you could group all your eccentric relatives according to their amusing traits and behaviors.

 ## SELECTING A PRINCIPLE FOR CLASSIFICATION-DIVISION

Most things can be classified or divided more than one way, depending on the ordering principle used. For example, you could group colleges according to their cost, their location, the degrees they offer, their faculty, or prestige. Cost, location, degrees offered, faculty, prestige—each of these is an *ordering principle*.

Obviously, you must decide which principle you will use to group the items under consideration. When you do so, keep your purpose in mind and choose a principle compatible with that purpose. For example, if you were classifying white lies to entertain your reader, your ordering principle would not be the degree of hurtfulness of the lies; however, it might be the degree of inventiveness of the lies. If your purpose were to inform, then degree of hurtfulness would be an acceptable ordering principle.

When you establish your ordering principle, be sure to pick something that allows for at least three groups. If you have only two groups, then you are really comparing and contrasting, rather than classifying or dividing.

 ## SELECTING DETAIL

When you select detail, do not omit any groupings, or your classification-division will be incomplete. Let's say, for example, that you are grouping the forms of financial aid to inform students of ways to get help paying for college. You could include these groupings: loans, grants, and scholarships. However, by omitting work-study programs, your essay is less helpful than it could—and should—be.

On the other hand, you should avoid including groups that are not compatible with your ordering principle. For example, if you are classifying coaches according to how important winning is to them, you might have these groupings: coaches who think winning is everything; coaches who think winning is less important than learning and having fun; coaches who think winning is completely unimportant. In such a classification, you could not include coaches who are inexperienced, because that group is unrelated to the ordering principle.

In general, classification-division will include an explanation of what the groupings are and what elements are in each. Beyond that, your supporting detail can include a wide range of patterns of development meant to explain the characteristics of each grouping. Let's say, for example, that you are classifying Halloween celebrations into three types: the sedate, the jolly, and the scary. You could use *examples* to illustrate the kinds of harmless pranks people play for a jolly celebration; you could *describe* the frightening costumes people wear for a scary celebration; you could *narrate* the story of your last Halloween celebration, which was sedate. In addition, you could use *process analysis* to tell how to prepare for a scary Halloween celebration; you could use *cause-and-effect analysis* to explain the effects of the pranks played during the jolly celebration; you could use *definition* to explain the meaning of a sedate celebration; you could use *comparison and contrast* to show the similarities and differences among the three kinds of celebrations. Of course, you will not use all these patterns in a single essay, but they are all available for your consideration as ways to develop your details.

 ## STRUCTURING CLASSIFICATION-DIVISION

The thesis for classification-division can be handled a variety of ways. First, you can indicate what you are classifying or dividing and the ordering principle you will use, like this:

> The current crop of television talk shows can be classified according to the kinds of guests that appear. (Television talk shows will be classified; the ordering principle is the guests that appear.)

Another way to handle the thesis is to indicate what you are classifying or dividing, without mentioning the ordering principle. Here's an example:

Although more talk shows are on television than ever before, all of these shows are one of three types. (The thesis makes it clear that television talk shows will be grouped, but the ordering principle is not given.)

A third way to handle the thesis is to indicate what will be classified or divided, along with the specific groupings that will be discussed, like this:

Television talk shows can be distinguished according to whether the guests are primarily entertainers, politicians, or oddballs. (The thesis indicates that television talk shows will be grouped, and the groupings will be those with guests who are entertainers, those with guests who are politicians, and those with guests who are oddballs.)

Organizing a classification-division essay can be easier when topic sentences introduce the discussion of each grouping. For example, the classification of talk shows might have topic sentences like these:

The most common variety of talk show has entertainers for guests. (A discussion of talk shows with entertainers as guests would follow.)

Although more intellectual than the first type, another frequently seen talk show has politicians for guests. (A discussion of talk shows with politicians as guests would follow.)

Increasingly popular is the talk show that showcases oddballs. (A discussion of talk shows with oddballs as guests would follow.)

To move smoothly from one grouping to another, you can include transitional phrases in your topic sentences, phrases like these:

Another category . . .

A more significant group . . .

A more common kind . . .

A second division of . . .

When you order your details, consider your thesis. If it notes your groupings, then you should present those groupings in the same order they appear in the thesis. Otherwise, order is not much of an issue, unless your purpose is persuasive. Then you are likely to present the recommended grouping last. This is the case in "The Ways of Meeting Oppression," when Dr. Martin Luther King, Jr., presents last the method he wants people to adopt.

When you are discussing the same characteristics for each grouping, you should present those characteristics in the same order each time. Thus, if you group Halloween celebrations and discuss decorations, costumes, and degree of scariness for each kind of celebration, then you should discuss these features in the same order for each grouping.

SUGGESTIONS FOR WRITING CLASSIFICATION-DIVISION

1. To help order your draft, try writing your ordering principle at the top of a page. Then below that, write each of your groupings at the top of a column. Three groupings will give you three columns, four groupings will give you four columns, and so on. Under each column write out the elements in the grouping. Number the columns in the order you want to treat them. You now have a form of outline for your draft.
2. To discover methods for developing your points, ask yourself the following questions of every element in your columns. You can make notes on your outline, if you like.
   a. Can I narrate a story to develop this point?
   b. Can I describe something to develop this point?
   c. Can I analyze a process to develop this point?
   d. Can I analyze causes and/or effects to develop this point?
   e. Can I provide an example to develop this point?
   f. Can I define something to develop this point?
   g. Can I compare and/or contrast something to develop this point?
3. Using your outline as a guide, write your draft in one sitting without worrying about grammar, spelling, punctuation, or anything else.
4. When you revise, consider the following:
   a. Do you have at least three groupings?
   b. Have you included all relevant groupings?
   c. Have you omitted groups unrelated to your ordering principle?
   d. Does your thesis indicate that you are classifying or dividing? Should it indicate your ordering principle?
   e. Have you used transitional words to move from grouping to grouping?
   f. If you have discussed the same characteristics for each grouping, do they appear in the same order each time?

ANNOTATED STUDENT ESSAY

Student author David Wolfe uses classification to inform his reader about the origins of some common expressions. As you read, notice how the author uses examples to help make his point.

STRICTLY SPEAKING

Paragraph 1
This is the introduction. The thesis (the last sentence) indicates that classification will occur, and it gives the categories that will be used.

1   Expressions derived from outdoor life are so ingrained in everyday English that we fail to notice them or consider their origins. However, it is interesting to pause and think about these terms, and one way to do so is to look at three basic categories of expressions: those derived from the use of firearms, those derived from hunting, and those derived from the characteristics of wildlife or game.

Paragraph 2
The first sentence is the topic sentence. It presents the first category. The supporting detail is examples of expressions in the category.

2   Some common sayings come directly from the use of firearms. For example, if we buy something "lock, stock, and barrel," we have purchased the whole object or believed the whole story. This expression originally meant to buy the whole gun by purchasing its three parts: the "lock" as in the flintlock, the wooden "stock," and the metal "barrel." We also talk about "going off half-cocked," which means taking action or setting out without being fully prepared. This expression goes back to having a gun on "half cock." In the half-cocked position, the hammer is between the relaxed position and the fully cocked position, which means the gun is halfway between unready and fully ready for firing. Often we say we had our "sights set on" something or had a goal "in our sights." Both of these expressions refer to aiming a gun at something. Also, we can be "primed and ready," or fully prepared, as when a flintlock rifle is fully primed or prepared and ready to fire.

Paragraph 3
The topic sentence is the first sentence. It presents the second category. Supporting details are examples. Note the transition provided by *a second group, for example, another example,* and *similarly.*

3   A second group of expressions is derived from hunting. For example, the word "hello" has its origins there. It comes from hunters calling out "hulloa" or "haloo" when they saw other hunters in the woods, in order to attract attention and avoid being accidentally hurt. "Stop beating around the bush" is another example of a hunting expression. It comes from the European practice of using "beaters" or people to drive game out of the brush for the hunter to shoot at. To do the job properly, beaters had to get into the middle of the bush where the game was. Otherwise, they were not getting the job done because they were beating around the bush. If we "make tracks," we hurry. Originally, this expression referred to an animal going in a hurry and thus leaving behind a set of tracks that were easy to follow. Being on "the right trail" refers to doing something properly or going in the right direction, but its original meaning referred to a hunter being on the right trail while tracking game. Similarly, if we are "barking up the wrong tree," we are as mistaken as the hunting dogs that are howling up one tree when the raccoon is out on the limb of a different tree.

Paragraph 4
The first sentence is the topic sentence. It includes the transition *also* and presents the next category. The supporting details are examples.

Paragraph 5
The conclusion repeats the idea in the introduction that these expressions are ingrained in English.

4   Sayings related to wildlife or game are also interesting. We brag about saving money when we are "feathering our nests" or "building up our nest eggs," the way a bird does in the spring. We may be called "owl-eyed" for wearing glasses or be "wise as an owl" for knowing the right answers. If we are "blind as a bat," we can't see very well, just as a bat has poor vision. If we have a bad disposition, we are "grouchy as a bear" or told "don't be such a bear," since bears have angry temperaments. In addition, there are two ways we can get "skunked." We can actually get sprayed by a skunk, or we can lose a game of some kind very badly—in either case, we lose.

5   Expressions from the outdoors are so common that even those of us who never hunt, shoot, or get close to animals will find ourselves drawing on vocabulary derived from these sources, a fact you may be more aware of from now on.

WAIT DIVISIONS
Tom Bodett

◆

Humorist Tom Bodett has been heard locally on Alaskan radio and nationally on National Public Radio. In the following essay, which is from his 1987 book Small Comforts, *Bodett classifies for only one reason—to amuse his audience. As you read, pay close attention to the ways Bodett achieves his humorous effects.*

◆

1   I read somewhere that we spend a full third of our lives waiting. I've also read where we spend a third of our lives sleeping, a third working, and a third at our leisure. Now either somebody's lying, or we're spending all our leisure time waiting to go to work or sleep. That can't be true or league softball and Winnebagos never would have caught on.

2   So where are we doing all of this waiting and what does it mean to an impatient society like ours? Could this unseen waiting be the source of all our problems? A shrinking economy? The staggering deficit? Declining mental health and moral apathy? Probably not, but let's take a look at some of the more classic "waits" anyway.

3   The very purest form of waiting is what we'll call the *Watched-Pot Wait*. This type of wait is without a doubt the most annoying of all. Take filling up the kitchen sink. There is absolutely nothing you can do while this is going on but keep both eyes glued to the sink until it's full. If you try to cram in some extracurricular activity, you're asking for it. So you stand there, your hands on the faucets, and wait. A temporary suspension of duties. During these waits it's common for your eyes to lapse out of focus. The brain disengages from the body and wanders around the imagination in search of distraction. It finds none and springs back into action only when the water runs over the edge of the counter and onto your socks.

4   The phrase "A watched pot never boils" comes of this experience. Pots don't care whether they are watched or not; the problem is that nobody has ever seen a pot actually come to a boil. While they are waiting, their brains turn off.

5   Other forms of the Watched-Pot Wait would include waiting for your drier to quit at the laundromat, waiting for your toast to pop out of the toaster, or waiting for a decent idea to come to mind at a typewriter. What they all have in common is that they render the waiter helpless and mindless.

6   A cousin to the Watched-Pot Wait is the *Forced Wait*. Not for the weak of will, this one requires a bit of discipline. The classic Forced Wait is starting your car in the winter and letting it slowly idle up to temperature before engaging the clutch. This is every bit as uninteresting as watching a pot, but with one big difference. You have a choice. There is nothing keeping you from racing to

work behind a stone-cold engine save the thought of the early demise of several thousand dollars' worth of equipment you haven't paid for yet. Thoughts like that will help you get through a Forced Wait.

7   Properly preparing packaged soup mixes also requires a Forced Wait. Directions are very specific on these mixes. "Bring three cups water to boil, add mix, simmer three minutes, remove from heat, let stand five minutes." I have my doubts that anyone has ever actually done this. I'm fairly spineless when it comes to instant soups and usually just boil the bejeezus out of them until the noodles sink. Some things just aren't worth a Forced Wait.

8   All in all Forced Waiting requires a lot of a thing called *patience*, which is a virtue. Once we get into virtues I'm out of my element, and can't expound on the virtues of virtue, or even lie about them. So let's move on to some of the more far-reaching varieties of waiting.

9   The *Payday Wait* is certainly a leader in the long-term anticipation field. The problem with waits that last more than a few minutes is that you have to actually do other things in the meantime. Like go to work. By far the most aggravating feature of the Payday Wait is that even though you must keep functioning in the interludes, there is less and less you are able to do as the big day draws near. For some of us the last few days are best spent alone in a dark room for fear we'll accidentally do something that costs money. With the Payday Wait comes a certain amount of hope that we'll make it, and faith that everything will be all right once we do.

10   With the introduction of faith and hope, I've ushered in the most potent wait class of all, the *Lucky-Break Wait*, or the *Wait for One's Ship to Come In*. This type of wait is unusual in that it is for the most part voluntary. Unlike the Forced Wait, which is also voluntary, waiting for your lucky break does not necessarily mean that it will happen.

11   Turning one's life into a waiting game of these proportions requires gobs of the aforementioned faith and hope, and is strictly for the optimists among us. For these people life is the thing that happens to them while they're waiting for something to happen to them. On the surface it seems as ridiculous as following the directions on soup mixes, but the Lucky-Break Wait performs an outstanding service to those who take it upon themselves to do it. As long as one doesn't come to rely on it, wishing for a few good things to happen never hurt anybody.

12   In the end it is obvious that we certainly do spend a good deal of our time waiting. The person who said we do it a third of the time may have been going easy on us. It makes a guy wonder how anything at all gets done around here. But things do get done, people grow old, and time boils on whether you watch it or not.

13   The next time you're standing at the sink waiting for it to fill while cooking soup mix that you'll have to eat until payday or until a large bag of cash falls out of the sky, don't despair. You're probably just as busy as the next guy.

Considering Ideas

1. Bodett does not specifically state his ordering principle; yet there is a logic to his groupings. What do you think his ordering principle is?
2. According to Bodett, why is his classification important?
3. What kind of reader do you think "Wait Divisions" would appeal to? How do you know?
4. How does the Watched-Pot Wait differ from the Forced Wait? How does the Forced Wait differ from the Lucky-Break Wait?
5. Why do you think we find waiting so annoying?

Considering Technique

1. Which sentence is the thesis of "Wait Divisions"?
2. Bodett introduces each of his groupings in a topic sentence. What are these topic sentences?
3. In what kind of order does Bodett present his groupings?
4. Bodett uses examples in paragraphs 3, 6, and 7. How do these examples help him develop his classification?
5. How does Bodett relate his conclusion (paragraphs 12 and 13) to the rest of his essay?
6. Consult a dictionary if you are unsure of the meaning of any of these words: *Winnebagos* (paragraph 1), *apathy* (paragraph 2), *render* (paragraph 5), *demise* (paragraph 6), *potent* (paragraph 10), *aforementioned* (paragraph 11).

For Group Consideration

With three or four classmates, identify the aspects of the essay that you find the most amusing. What techniques does Bodett employ to create the humor?

Journal Entry

Think back to recent times when you were forced to wait (in a traffic jam, in a checkout line, in a doctor's office, and so on). Explain how you felt while you were waiting and what you did to pass the time. Do you need to alter what you think, feel, and do when you must wait?

Essay Assignments

1. Like Bodett, write a humorous classification of some annoying aspect of life: poor driving practices, annoying shoppers in supermarkets, annoying tele-

phone calls, frustrating salesclerks, and so on. If you like, use some of the humorous techniques in "Wait Divisions."

2. Just as there are many times when we find ourselves waiting, there are many times when we find ourselves hurrying up. With that in mind, write a humorous classification called "Rush Divisions."

3. Using a different ordering principle and therefore different groupings, write your own classification of the kinds of waiting people engage in. As an alternative, write a classification of the kinds of waiting students engage in.

4. Write a humorous classification of some aspect of college life: teachers, students, study techniques, ways to take examinations, roommates, advisers, and so on.

Considering Thematic Issues

1. For many people, stress is a troublesome fact of life, and waiting can contribute to that stress. Discuss other sources of stress that people must cope with on a routine basis. If you like, you can consider these questions: What are the effects of that stress? How does it affect the quality of life? Is stress the inevitable price we pay for certain lifestyles? Is the price worth it?

2. In "Country Codes" (page 317), Noel Perrin describes codes of conduct in rural New England. Write your own "waiting codes" to dictate the desired behavior of people in each of the wait divisions that Bodett describes.

WHITE LIES
Sissela Bok

◆

A frequent writer on ethics, Sissela Bok won the Orwell Award in 1976 for the book Lying: Moral Choice in Private and Public Life, *from which "White Lies" is taken. The author informs her reader of the kinds of white lies, and she makes a persuasive point about the harm these lies cause. As you read, consider how often you tell white lies.*

◆

1   White lies are at the other end of the spectrum of deception from lies in a serious crisis. They are the most common and the most trivial forms that duplicity can take. The fact that they are so common provides their protective coloring. And their very triviality, when compared to more threatening lies, makes it seem unnecessary or even absurd to condemn them. Some consider *all* well-intentioned lies, however momentous, to be white; in this book, I shall adhere to the narrower usage: a white lie, in this sense, is a falsehood not meant to injure anyone, and of little moral import. I want to ask whether there *are* such lies; and if there are, whether their cumulative consequences are still without harm; and, finally, whether many lies are not defended as "white" which are in fact harmful in their own right.

2   Many small subterfuges may not even be intended to mislead. They are only "white lies" in the most marginal sense. Take, for example, the many social exchanges: "How nice to see you!" or "Cordially Yours." These and a thousand other polite expressions are so much taken for granted that if someone decided, in the name of total honesty, not to employ them, he might well give the impression of an indifference he did not possess. The justification for continuing to use such accepted formulations is that they deceive no one, except possibly those unfamiliar with the language.

3   A social practice more clearly deceptive is that of giving a false excuse so as not to hurt the feelings of someone making an invitation or request: to say one "can't" do what in reality one may not *want* to do. Once again, the false excuse may prevent unwarranted inferences of greater hostility to the undertaking than one may well feel. Merely to say that one can't do something, moreover, is not deceptive in the sense that an elaborately concocted story can be.

4   Still other white lies are told in an effort to flatter, to throw a cheerful interpretation on depressing circumstances, or to show gratitude for unwanted gifts. In the eyes of many, such white lies do no harm, provide needed support and cheer, and help dispel gloom and boredom. They preserve the equilibrium and often the humaneness of social relationships, and are usually accepted as excusable so long as they do not become excessive. Many argue, moreover, that such deception is so helpful and at times so necessary that it must be tolerated as an exception to a general policy against lying. Thus Bacon observed:

Doth any man doubt, that if there were taken out of men's minds vain opinions, flattering hopes, false valuations, imaginations as one would, and the like, but it would leave the minds of a number of men poor shrunken things, full of melancholy and indisposition, and unpleasing to themselves?

5   Another kind of lie may actually be advocated as bringing a more substantial benefit, or avoiding a real harm, while seeming quite innocuous to those who tell the lies. Such are the placebos given for innumerable common ailments, and the pervasive use of inflated grades and recommendations for employment and promotion.

6   A large number of lies without such redeeming features are nevertheless often regarded as so trivial that they should be grouped with white lies. They are the lies told on the spur of the moment, for want of reflection, or to get out of a scrape, or even simply to pass the time. Such are the lies told to boast or exaggerate, or on the contrary to deprecate and understate; the many lies told or repeated in gossip; Rousseau's[*] lies told simply "in order to say something"; the embroidering on facts that seem too tedious in their own right; and the substitution of a quick lie for the lengthy explanations one might otherwise have to provide for something not worth spending time on.

7   Utilitarians often cite white lies as the *kind* of deception where their theory shows the benefits of common sense and clear thinking. A white lie, they hold, is trivial; it is either completely harmless, or so marginally harmful that the cost of detecting and evaluating the harm is much greater than the minute harm itself. In addition, the white lie can often actually be beneficial, thus further tipping the scales of utility. In a world with so many difficult problems, utilitarians might ask: Why take the time to weigh the minute pros and cons in telling someone that his tie is attractive when it is an abomination, or of saying to a guest that a broken vase was worthless? Why bother even to define such insignificant distortions or make mountains out of molehills by seeking to justify them?

8   Triviality surely does set limits to when moral inquiry is reasonable. But when we look more closely at practices such as placebo-giving, it becomes clear that all lies defended as "white" cannot be so easily dismissed. In the first place, the harmlessness of lies is notoriously disputable. What the liar perceives as harmless or even beneficial may not be so in the eyes of the deceived. Second, the failure to look at an entire practice rather than at their own isolated case often blinds liars to cumulative harm and expanding deceptive activities. Those who begin with white lies can come to resort to more frequent and more serious ones. Where some tell a few white lies, others may tell more. Because lines are so hard to draw, the indiscriminate use of such lies can lead to other deceptive practices. The aggregate harm from a large number of marginally harmful instances may, therefore, be highly undesirable in the end—for liars, those deceived, and honesty and trust more generally.

[*] Jean-Jacques Rousseau (1712–1778)—a French philosopher and author.

Considering Ideas

1. What do you think Bok means when she says in paragraph 1, "The fact that [white lies] are so common provides their protective coloring"?
2. What kinds of white lies does Bok classify? What are the justifications for each of these kinds of white lies?
3. Who are the utilitarians that Bok refers to in paragraph 7? What is their view of white lies?
4. What is Bok's view of the white lie?

Considering Technique

1. What is Bok's ordering principle?
2. In what kind of order does Bok arrange her groupings?
3. Bok introduces her groupings with topic sentences. What are those topic sentences? What transitions appear in the topic sentences in paragraphs 4 and 5? What purpose do these transitions serve?
4. What approach does Bok take to the introduction? What approach does she take to the conclusion?
5. In paragraph 2, Bok gives examples of items in one of her groupings. What purpose do these examples serve? Would any other paragraphs benefit from the addition of examples? Explain.
6. How does Bok use cause-and-effect analysis? (Cause-and-effect analysis, discussed in Chapter 9, explains the causes and/or effects of something.)
7. Consult a dictionary if you are unsure of the meaning of any of these words: *spectrum* (paragraph 1), *duplicity* (paragraph 1), *inferences* (paragraph 3), *innocuous* (paragraph 5), *placebos* (paragraph 5), *utilitarians* (paragraph 7), *abomination* (paragraph 7), *indiscriminate* (paragraph 8), *aggregate* (paragraph 8).

For Group Consideration

Describe what day-to-day living would be like if people never told white lies. After considering your description, decide if some kinds of lies would be missed more than others. Also decide whether or not white lies are largely a positive or negative force in communication and interpersonal relationships.

Journal Entry

In a page or two, respond to these questions: How often do you tell white lies? What kinds of white lies do you usually tell? Have you ever told a white lie that has hurt someone? Have you ever been hurt by a white lie?

Essay Assignments

1. Rather than focus on white lies as Bok does, write a classification of all lies. Explain the causes and effects of the lies. As an alternative, use division to break down the lie into its components. Then evaluate its causes and effects.
2. Classify the lies told in some specific context: in school, on a date, at family gatherings, in the workplace, and so on. Evaluate the degree of harm that the lies cause.
3. Classify the lies parents tell their children or the lies that teenagers tell their parents. Explain the causes and effects of these lies.
4. Write a classification of the types of some form of undesirable behavior: cheating, procrastination, disloyalty, and so on. Evaluate the degree of harm that the behaviors cause. As an alternative, use division to break down one form of undesirable behavior into its components and evaluate its degree of harm.

Considering Thematic Issues

1. Overall, do you agree with the utilitarian evaluation of white lies, or do you agree with Bok's evaluation? Write an essay that supports your view.
2. Read "Talk in the Intimate Relationship: His and Hers" (page 252), which describes the ways men and women communicate with each other. Drawing on your own experience and observation, explain what role white lies play in the communication between men and women.

COUNTRY CODES
Noel Perrin

Noel Perrin is a former city dweller who was transplanted to the country, where he is a college instructor. In "Country Codes," he classifies codes of conduct of rural New Englanders to entertain his audience and to inform the reader about the proper way to act in the country. At the same time, Perrin shares a bit of his own experience. As you read, think about to what extent codes of conduct dictate your own behavior.

1   Robert Frost once wrote a poem about a "townbred" farmer who was getting his hay in with the help of two hired men, both locals. As they're working, the sky clouds over, and it begins to look like rain. The farmer instructs the two hired men to start making the haycocks especially carefully, so that they'll shed water. About half an hour later (it still isn't raining), one of them abruptly shoves his pitchfork in the ground and walks off. He has quit.

2   The farmer is utterly baffled. The hired man who stays explains to him that what he said was a major insult.

> "He thought you meant to find fault with his work,
> That's what the average farmer would have meant."

This hired man goes on to say that he would have quit, too—if the order had been issued by a regular farmer. But seeing as it was a city fellow, he made allowances.

> "I know you don't understand our ways.
> You were just talking what was in your mind.
> What was in all our minds, and you weren't hinting."

Frost called that poem "The Code." He published it in 1914.

3   Sixty-four years later, the country code is still going strong, and it is still making trouble for town-bred people who live in rural areas. Only I think the code is even more complicated than Frost had room to describe in his poem. In fact there isn't just one country code, there are at least three. What they all have in common is that instead of saying things out plainly, the way you do in the city, you approach them indirectly. You hint.

4   I am going to call these three the Power Code, the Non-Reciprocity Code, and the Stoic's Code. These are not their recognized names; they don't *have* recognized names. Part of the code is that you never speak of the code, and I am showing my own town-bredness in writing this exposition. (As Frost showed his in writing the poem. He was a city kid in San Francisco before he was a farmer in New Hampshire.)

5   In Frost's poem, it was the Power Code that the townie violated. Under the rules of the Power Code, you *never* give peremptory orders, and you ordinarily don't even make demands. You make requests. What the code says is that everybody is to be treated as an equal, even when financially or educationally, or whatever, they're not. Treat them as either inferiors or superiors, and you can expect trouble.

6   Just recently, for example, a young city doctor moved to our town, and began violating the Power Code right and left. Take the way he treated the boss of the town road crew. The house the doctor was renting has a gravel driveway that tends to wash out after storms. It washed out maybe a month after he had moved in. He is said to have called the road commissioner and given him a brisk order. "I want a culvert installed, and I want it done by this weekend."

7   Now in the city that would be a quite sensible approach. You're calling some faceless bureaucrat, and you use standard negotiating technique. You make an outrageous demand; you throw your weight around, if you have any; and you figure on getting part of what you ask for. You're not surprised when the bureaucrat screams, "*This week!* Listen, we got a hunnert and sixty-two jobs aheada you right now. If you're lucky, we'll get to you in October." You scream back and threaten to call the mayor's office. Then you finally compromise on August.

8   But it doesn't work that way in the country. The code doesn't encourage throwing your weight around. Our road commissioner had been given an order, and he instantly rejected it. "Tain't the town's job to look after folks' driveways. If you want a culvert, you can buy one down to Write River Junction."

9   I happened to hear what the road commissioner told some friends later. The doctor had actually called at a good time. The town had several used culverts lying around—road culverts they had replaced, which were still good enough to go at the end of a driveway. "If he'd asked decent, we'd have been glad to put one in for him, some day when work was slack." If he'd used the code, that is.

10   That's nothing, though, compared with the way the young doctor handled one of our retired farmers. When the doctor decided to live in our town—it meant a fifteen-mile drive to the hospital where he worked—it was because he had gotten interested in country things. He wanted to have a garden, burn wood, learn how to scythe a patch of grass, all those things. During his first spring and summer in town, he probably asked the old farmer a hundred questions. He got free lessons in scything. He consulted on fencing problems. Learned how thick to plant peas.

11   Then one day the farmer asked *him* a question. "I understand you know suthin' about arthritis," the farmer said. "Well, my wife's is actin' up." And he went on to ask a question about medication.

12   The young doctor's answer was quick and smooth. "I'll be glad to see her in office hours," he said.

13   Again, normal city practice. You've got to protect yourself against all the people at cocktail parties who want free medical advice. Furthermore, you probably really should examine a patient before you do any prescribing. All the same, what he was saying loud and clear in the country code was, "My time is worth more than yours; I am more important than you are. So I can ask you free questions, but you must pay for any you ask me." Not very polite. What he should have done was put down the scythe and say, "Let's go have a look at her."

14   Actually, if he had done that, he probably would have muffed it anyway. Because then he would have come up against the Non-Reciprocity Code, and he didn't understand that, either. The Non-Reciprocity Code says that you never take any favors for granted (or call in your debts, as city politicians say). Instead, you always pretend that each favor done you is a brand-new one. In the case of the young doctor, suppose he *had* stopped his free scythe lesson and gone to examine the farmer's wife. When he was ready to leave, the farmer would have said to him, 'What do I owe you?' And then one of two things would have happened. Old habits would have asserted themselves, and he would have said smoothly, "That will be twenty-five dollars, please." Or else, a little cross with the farmer for not recognizing his generous motive (does the old fool think I make *house calls*?), he would have said that it was free, in a sort of huffy, look-what-a-favor-I'm-doing-you voice.

15   Both answers would have been wrong. The correct response would be to act as if the farmer was doing *you* a favor in letting you not charge. Something like, "Come on, if you can teach me to scythe, and how to plant peas, I guess there's no harm in my taking a look at your wife."

16   One of the funniest instances in which you see the Non-Reciprocity Code operating is after people get their trucks stuck, which during mud season in Vermont is constantly. You're driving along in your pickup, and there's your neighbor with two wheels in the ditch, unable to budge. You stop, get out your logging chain, hook on, and pull him out. "How much will that be?" he asks, as if his cousin Donald hadn't just pulled you out the week before. In a way it's a ritual question. He would be surprised out of his mind if you thought a minute and said, "Oh, I guess five dollars would be about right."

17   But it's not entirely ritual. He would be surprised. But he would hand over the five dollars. The point of the question is to establish that you don't *have* to pull him out just because he's a friend and will someday pull you out. It's treated as an act of free will, a part of New England independence.

18   The third code, the Stoic's Code, is sometimes confused with machismo, but really has no connection with it. Country people of both sexes practice it with equal fervency. Basically, it consists of seeing who can go without complaining longest.

19   I first became aware of the Stoic's Code when I was helping two people put hay bales into a barn loft about fifteen years ago. It was a hot day in late

June, with the humidity running at least ninety percent. I function badly in hot weather. Within ten minutes I was pouring sweat—as were my coworkers. The difference was that I kept bitching about it. Finally, after three-quarters of an hour, I flopped down and announced I'd have to cool off before I touched another bale.

20 To me this just seemed common sense. We had no special deadline to meet in loading that hay. What I really thought was that all three of us should go take a dip in the river.

21 But the Stoic's Code doesn't stress common sense. It stresses endurance. Maybe that's because to survive at all as a farmer in New England you need endurance. In any case, the other two flicked me one quick scornful look and kept on working. One of them has never really respected me again to this day. The other, like the second hired man in Frost's poem, made allowances for my background and forgave me. We have since become fast friends. I have never dared to ask, but I think he thinks I have made real progress in learning to shut my mouth and keep working.

22 I could never be a stoic on the true native level, though. Consider the story of Hayden Clark and Rodney Palmer, as Rodney tells it. A good many years ago, before there were any paved roads in town, Hayden ran a garage. (Rodney runs it now.) He also sold cordwood.

23 One day when there wasn't much doing at the garage, Hayden was sawing cordwood just across the road, where he could keep an eye on the gas pumps. If you saw with a circular saw, and do it right, it takes three men. One person lifts up the logs, one does the actual cutting, and one throws the cut pieces into a pile. The three jobs are called putting on, sawing, and taking off. In all three you are doing dangerous work at very high speed.

24 On this day a man named Charlie Raynes was putting on, Hayden was sawing, and young Rodney was taking off. Hayden kept the wood coming so fast that Rodney was always a beat behind. He never paused a second to let Rodney catch up, and this torture went on for nearly an hour. No one spoke. (Not that you could hear over a buzz saw, anyway.)

25 Then finally a customer pulled in for gas. Hayden left the other two sawing, and went over to pump it. Charlie continued to put on, and Rodney sawed in Hayden's place.

26 Rather than interrupt their rhythm when he came back. Hayden began to take off. Rodney and Charlie exchanged a quick glance, and began putting the wood to Hayden so fast that *he* was off balance the whole time, and not infrequently in some danger of getting an arm cut off. At this speed and in this way they finished the entire pile. It was Rodney's revenge, and as he told me about it, his eyes gleamed.

27 It was only a year or two ago that Rodney told me the story. In the very act of telling it, he included me as one who knew the code. But I instantly betrayed

it. My city background is too strong. I'm too verbal, too used to crowing over triumphs.

28   "After you were done sawing, Hayden never said anything about it?" I asked.

29   "Oh, *no,*" Rodney answered, looking really shocked. "Any more than I'd have said anything to him."

30   So, next time you're in a country store and you get a sense that the locals are avoiding you as if you had the worst case of B.O. in the county, you can be pretty sure of the reason. You've probably just said some dreadful thing in code.

Considering Ideas

1. What do all the country codes have in common? Why do you think city people have trouble adhering to these codes?
2. What is the difference between the way city people and the way country people make requests of bureaucrats?
3. Perrin opens by telling about a Robert Frost poem called "The Code." What do this poem and Perrin's essay have in common?
4. When Perrin asked if Hayden said anything, Perrin broke a code. In what way did he do so? How was his error typical of a city person?

Considering Technique

1. What does Perrin classify? What is his ordering principle? What are his groupings?
2. Which sentence is the thesis of "Country Codes"?
3. Paragraphs 1 through 4 form the introduction of the essay. What combination of approaches does Perrin take to the introduction?
4. Perrin includes several examples in his classification. Which paragraphs include examples, and how do these examples help develop the classification?
5. How does the author use narration (storytelling) to help develop his classification? (Narration is discussed in Chapter 5.) How does he use definition? (Definition, explaining what something means, is discussed in Chapter 11). How does he use cause-and-effect analysis? (Cause-and-effect analysis, discussed in Chapter 9, gives the cause and/or effects of something.)
6. What approach does Perrin take to the conclusion?
7. Consult a dictionary if you are unsure of the meaning of any of these words: *haycocks* (paragraph 1), *exposition* (paragraph 4), *reciprocity* (paragraph 4), *stoic* (paragraph 4), *peremptory* (paragraph 5), *culvert* (paragraph 6), *machismo* (paragraph 18), *fervency* (paragraph 18), *cordwood* (paragraph 22).

For Group Consideration

Codes of conduct are an integral part of life. They dictate our behavior in the classroom, in the workplace, at athletic events, in places of worship, on dates, and so on. Make a list of situations that are governed by codes of conduct. What purpose do these codes serve, and what would life be like without them? What happens when people violate a code?

Journal Entry

What do you think of the Power Code, the Non-Reciprocity Code, and the Stoic's Code? Are they sensible, appealing codes of conduct, are they illogical and troublesome, or are they a little of each? Explain.

Essay Assignments

1. Classify codes of conduct for students in the classroom, using examples and/ or narration to clarify the nature of your groupings, as Perrin does. Be sure to select your principle of classification carefully.
2. Write a humorous essay that classifies codes of conduct for people on a first date or for people meeting their in-laws for the first time.
3. Write an essay with the title "City Codes," in which you classify the behavior of city people based on their tendency to speak directly and say whatever is on their minds. Like Perrin, use examples and/or narration to clarify the nature of your groupings.
4. Classify codes of conduct for people where you live or where you have lived in the past (your dorm, on the coast, in the mountains, in a farming community, in an industrial area, in a large area, on a military base, and so on). Be sure to choose your principle of classification carefully.

Considering Thematic Issues

1. Do codes of conduct facilitate interaction among people, restrict interaction, or both? Support your view with specific examples. (Some ideas for this essay may come from the preceding group activity.)
2. Using the information in "Country Codes," "Salvation" (page 89), and "India: A Widow's Devastating Choice" (page 278), along with your own ideas, experience, and observation, write an essay that explains what happens when people violate the expectations of others.

COLLEGE PRESSURES
William Zinsser

William Zinsser has been a journalist, an English teacher at Yale, and editor of the Book-of-the-Month Club. He has also written a number of books on writing and American culture. In "College Pressures," Zinsser combines classification, examples, and cause-and-effect analysis to inform his reader of the nature and extent of the pressures Yale students face. In addition, he has a persuasive purpose: he argues that students, themselves, must eliminate college pressures. As you read, decide whether Zinsser's points about Yale students in 1979 are true today of college students in general.

◆

1   Dear Carlos: I desperately need a dean's excuse for my chem midterm which will begin in about 1 hour. All I can say is that I totally blew it this week. I've fallen incredibly, inconceivably behind.

2   Carlos: Help! I'm anxious to hear from you. I'll be in my room and won't leave it until I hear from you. Tomorrow is the last day for. . . .

3   Carlos: I left town because I started bugging out again. I stayed up all night to finish a take home make-up exam & am typing it to hand in on the 10th. It was due on the 5th. P.S. I'm going to the dentist. Pain is pretty bad.

4   Carlos: Probably by Friday I'll be able to get back to my studies. Right now I'm going to take a long walk. This whole thing has taken a lot out of me.

5   Carlos: I'm really up the proverbial creek. The problem is I really *bombed* the history final. Since I need that course for my major. . . .

6   Carlos: Here follows a tale of woe. I went home this weekend, had to help my Mom, & caught a fever so didn't have much time to study. My professor. . . .

7   Carlos: Aargh! Nothing original but everything's piling up at once. To be brief, my job interview. . . .

8   Hey Carlos, good news! I've got mononucleosis.

9   Who are these wretched supplicants, scribbling notes so laden with anxiety, seeking such miracles of postponement and balm? They are men and women who belong to Bradford College, one of the twelve residential colleges at Yale University, and the messages are just a few of the hundreds that they left for their dean, Carlos Hortas—often slipped under his door at 4 A.M.—last year.

10   But students like the ones who wrote those notes can also be found on campuses from coast to coast—especially in New England and at many other private colleges across the country that have high academic standards and highly motivated students. Nobody could doubt that the notes are real. In their urgency and their gallows humor they are authentic voices of a generation that is panicky to succeed.

11   My own connection with the message writers is that I am master of Branford College. I live in its Gothic quadrangle and know the students well. (We have 485 of them.) I am privy to their hopes and fears—and also to their stereo music and their piercing cries in the dead of night ("Does anybody *ca-a-are?*"). If they went to Carlos to ask how to get through tomorrow, they come to me to ask how to get through the rest of their lives.

12   Mainly I try to remind them that the road ahead is a long one and that it will have more unexpected turns than they think. There will be plenty of time to change jobs, change careers, change whole attitudes and approaches. They don't want to hear such liberating news. They want a map—right now—that they can follow unswervingly to career security, financial security, Social Security and, presumably, a prepaid grave.

13   What I wish for all students is some release from the clammy grip of the future. I wish them a chance to savor each segment of their education as an experience in itself and not as a grim preparation for the next step. I wish them the right to experiment, to trip and fall, to learn that defeat is as instructive as victory and is not the end of the world.

14   My wish, of course, is naive. One of the few rights that America does not proclaim is the right to fail. Achievement is the national god, venerated in our media—the million-dollar athlete, the wealthy executive—and glorified in our praise of possessions. In the presence of such a potent state religion, the young are growing up old.

15   I see four kinds of pressure working on college students today; economic pressure, parental pressure, peer pressure, and self-induced pressure. It is easy to look around for villains—to blame the colleges for charging too much money, the professors for assigning too much work, the parents for pushing their children too far, the students for driving themselves too hard. But there are no villains, only victims.

16   "In the late 1960s," one dean told me, "the typical question that I got from students was 'Why is there so much suffering in the world?' or 'How can I make a contribution?' Today it's 'Do you think it would look better for getting into law school if I did a double major in history and political science, or just majored in one of them?'" Many other deans confirmed this pattern. One said: "They're trying to find an edge—the intangible something that will look better on paper if two students are about equal."

17   Note the emphasis on looking better. The transcript has become a sacred document, the passport to security. How one appears on paper is more important than how one appears in person. *A* is for Admirable and *B* is for Borderline, even though, in Yale's official system of grading, *A* means "excellent" and *B* means "very good." Today, looking very good is no longer good enough, especially for students who hope to go on to law school or medical school. They know that entrance into the better schools will be an entrance into the better law firms and better medical practices where they will make a lot of money. They also know that the odds are harsh. Yale Law School for instance,

matriculates 170 students from an applicant pool of 3,700; Harvard enrolls 550 from a pool of 7,000.

18   It's all very well for those of us who write letters of recommendation for our students to stress the qualities of humanity that will make them good lawyers or doctors. And it's nice to think that admission officers are really reading our letters and looking for the extra dimension of commitment or concern. Still, it would be hard for a student not to visualize these officers shuffling so many transcripts studded with As that they regard a B as positively shameful.

19   The pressure is almost as heavy on students who just want to graduate and get a job. Long gone are the days of the "gentleman's C," when students journeyed through college with a certain relaxation, sampling a wide variety of courses—music, art, philosophy, classics, anthropology, poetry, religion—that would send them out as liberally educated men and women. If I were an employer I would rather employ graduates who have this range and curiosity than those who narrowly pursued safe subjects and high grades. I know countless students whose inquiring minds exhilarate me. I like to hear the play of their ideas. I don't know if they are getting As or Cs, and I don't care. I also like them as people. The country needs them, and they will find satisfying jobs. I tell them to relax. They can't.

20   Nor can I blame them. They live in a brutal economy. Tuition, room, and board at most private colleges now comes to at least $7,000, not counting books and fees. This might seem to suggest that the colleges are getting rich. But they are equally battered by inflation. Tuition covers only 60 percent of what it costs to educate a student, and ordinarily the remainder comes from what colleges receive in endowments, grants, and gifts. Now the remainder keeps being swallowed by the cruel costs—higher every year—of just opening the doors. Heating oil is up. Insurance is up. Postage is up. Health-premium costs are up. Everything is up. Deficits are up. We are witnessing in America the creation of a brotherhood of paupers—colleges, parents, and students, joined by the common bond of debt.

21   Today it is not unusual for a student, even if he works part time at college and full time during the summer, to accrue $5,000 in loans after four years— loans that he must start to repay within one year after graduation. Exhorted at commencement to go forth into the world, he is already behind as he goes forth. How could he not feel under pressure throughout college to prepare for this day of reckoning? I have used "he," incidentally, only for brevity. Women at Yale are under no less pressure to justify their expensive education to themselves, their parents, and society. In fact, they are probably under more pressure. For although they leave college superbly equipped to bring fresh leadership to traditionally male jobs, society hasn't yet caught up with this fact.

22   Along with economic pressure goes parental pressure. Inevitably, the two are deeply intertwined.

23   I see many students taking pre-medical courses with joyless tenacity. They

go off to their labs as if they were going to the dentist. It saddens me because I know them in other corners of their life as cheerful people.

24   "Do you want to go to medical school?" I ask them.

25   "I guess so," they say, without conviction, or "Not really."

26   "Then why are you going?"

27   "Well, my parents want me to be a doctor. They're paying all this money and . . ."

28   Poor students, poor parents. They are caught in one of the oldest webs of love and duty and guilt. The parents mean well; they are trying to steer their sons and daughters toward a secure future. But the sons and daughters want to major in history or classics or philosophy—subjects with no "practical" value. Where's the payoff on the humanities? It's not easy to persuade such loving parents that the humanities do indeed pay off. The intellectual faculties developed by studying subjects like history and classics—an ability to synthesize and relate, to weigh cause and effect, to see events in perspective—are just the faculties that make creative leaders in business or almost any general field. Still, many fathers would rather put their money on courses that point toward a specific profession—courses that are pre-law, pre-medical, pre-business, or, as I sometimes heard it put, "pre-rich."

29   But the pressure on students is severe. They are truly torn. One part of them feels obligated to fulfill their parents' expectations, after all, their parents are older and presumably wiser. Another part tells them that the expectations that are right for their parents are not right for them.

30   I know a student who wants to be an artist. She is very obviously an artist and will be a good one—she has already had several modest exhibits. Meanwhile she is growing as a well-rounded person and taking humanistic subjects that will enrich the inner resources out of which her art will grow. But her father is strongly opposed. He thinks that an artist is a "dumb" thing to be. The student vacillates and tries to please everybody. She keeps up with her art somewhat furtively and takes some of the "dumb" courses her father wants her to take—at least they are dumb courses for her. She is a free spirit on a campus of tense students—no small achievement in itself—and she deserves to follow her muse.

31   Peer pressure and self-induced pressure are also intertwined, and they begin almost at the beginning of freshman year.

32   "I had a freshman student I'll call Linda," one dean told me, "who came in and said she was under terrible pressure because her roommate, Barbara, was much brighter and studied all the time. I couldn't tell her that Barbara had come in two hours earlier to say the same thing about Linda."

33   The story is almost funny—except that it's not. It's symptomatic of all the pressure put together. When every student thinks every other student is working harder and doing better, the only solution is to study harder still. I see students going off to the library every night after dinner and coming back when it closes at midnight. I wish they could sometimes forget about their peers and

go to a movie. I hear the clacking of typewriters in the hours before dawn. I see the tension in their eyes when exams are approaching and papers are due: *"Will I get everything done?"*

34   Probably they won't. They will get sick. They will get "blocked." They will sleep. They will oversleep. They will bug out. *Hey Carlos, help!*

35   Part of the problem is that they do more than they are expected to do. A professor will assign five-page papers. Several students will start writing ten-page papers to impress him. Then more students will write ten-page papers, and a few will raise the ante to fifteen. Pity the poor student who is still just doing the assignment.

36   "Once you have twenty or thirty percent of the student population deliberately overexerting," one dean points out, "it's bad for everybody. When a teacher gets more and more effort from his class, the student who is doing normal work can be perceived as not doing well. The tactic works, psychologically."

37   Why can't the professor just cut back and not accept longer papers? He can, and he probably will. But by then the term will be half over and the damage done. Grade fever is highly contagious and not easily reversed. Besides, the professor's main concern is with his course. He knows his students only in relation to the course and doesn't know that they are also overexerting in their other courses. Nor is it really his business. He didn't sign up for dealing with the student as a whole person and with all the emotional baggage the student brought along from home. That's what deans, masters, chaplains, and psychiatrists are for.

38   To some extent this is nothing new: a certain number of professors have always been self-contained islands of scholarship and shyness, more comfortable with books than with people. But the new pauperism has widened the gap still further, for professors who actually like to spend time with students don't have as much time to spend. They also are overexerting. If they are young, they are busy trying to publish in order not to perish, hanging by their fingernails onto a shrinking profession. If they are old and tenured, they are buried under the duties of administering departments—as departmental chairmen or members of committees—that have been thinned out by the budgetary axe.

39   Ultimately it will be the students' own business to break the circles in which they are trapped. They are too young to be prisoners of their parents' dreams and their classmates' fears. They must be jolted into believing in themselves as unique men and women who have the power to shape their own future.

40   "Violence is being done to the undergraduate experience," says Carlos Hortas. "College should be open-ended: at the end it should open many, many roads. Instead, students are choosing their goal in advance, and their choices narrow as they go along. It's almost as if they think that the country has been codified in the type of jobs that exist—that they've got to fit into certain slots. Therefore, fit into the best-paying slot.

41   "They ought to take chances. Not taking chances will lead to a life of colorless mediocrity. They'll be comfortable. But something in the spirit will be missing."

42   I have painted too drab a portrait of today's students, making them seem a solemn lot. That is only half of their story; if they were so dreary I wouldn't so thoroughly enjoy their company. The other half is that they are easy to like. They are quick to laugh and to offer friendship. They are not introverts. They are usually kind and are more considerate of one another than any student generation I have known.

43   Nor are they so obsessed with their studies that they avoid sports and extracurricular activities. On the contrary, they juggle their crowded hours to play on a variety of teams, perform with musical and dramatic groups, and write for campus publications. But this in turn is one more cause of anxiety. There are too many choices. Academically, they have 1,300 courses to select from; outside class they have to decide how much spare time they can spare and how to spend it.

44   This means that they engage in fewer extracurricular pursuits than their predecessors did. If they want to row on the crew and play in the symphony they will eliminate one; in the '60s they would have done both. They also tend to choose activities that are self-limiting. Drama, for instance, is flourishing in all twelve of Yale's residential colleges as it never has before. Students hurl themselves into these productions—as actors, directors, carpenters, and technicians—with a dedication to create the best possible play, knowing that the day will come when the run will end and they can get back to their studies.

45   They also can't afford to be the willing slave of organizations like the *Yale Daily News*. Last spring at the one-hundredth anniversary banquet of that paper—whose past chairmen include such once and future kings as Potter Stewart, Kingman Brewster, and William F. Buckley, Jr.*—much was made of the fact that the editorial staff used to be small and totally committed and that "newsies" routinely worked fifty hours a week. In effect they belonged to a club; Newsies is how they defined themselves at Yale. Today's student will write one or two articles a week, when he can, and he defines himself as a student. I've never heard the word Newsie except at the banquet.

46   If I have described the modern undergraduate primarily as a driven creature who is largely ignoring the blithe spirit inside who keeps trying to come out and play, it's because that's where the crunch is, not only at Yale but throughout American education. It's why I think we should all be worried about the values that are nurturing a generation so fearful of risk and so goal-obsessed at such an early age.

47   I tell students that there is no one "right" way to get ahead—that each of them is a different person, starting from a different point and bound for a

*Ed. note: Stewart is a former U.S. Supreme Court Justice; Brewster is a former president of Yale; and Buckley is a conservative editor and columnist.

different destination. I tell them that change is a tonic and that all the slots are not codified nor the frontiers closed. One of my ways of telling them is to invite men and women who have achieved success outside the academic world to come and talk informally with my students during the year. They are heads of companies or ad agencies, editors of magazines, politicians, public officials, television magnates, labor leaders, business executives, Broadway producers, artists, writers, economists, photographers, scientists, historians—a mixed bag of achievers.

48   I ask them to say a few words about how they got started. The students assume that they started in their present profession and knew all along that it was what they wanted to do. Luckily for me, most of them got into their field by a circuitous route, to their surprise, after many detours. The students are startled. They can hardly conceive of a career that was not pre-planned. They can hardly imagine allowing the hand of God or chance to nudge them down some unforeseen trail.

Considering Ideas

1. According to Zinsser, what factors cause the pressure that college students experience?
2. Make a list of at least five words or phrases that describe the college student Zinsser writes about.
3. In a sentence or two, summarize Zinsser's advice to college students. What do you think of this advice?
4. According to Zinsser, how can college pressures be eliminated?
5. Do you think that the author's description of Yale students and his classification of the pressures they face is representative of students and their pressures in general? Explain.
6. In paragraph 39, Zinsser tells of inviting people to speak to his students. Do you think these classroom visits changed the attitudes of many students? Why or why not?

Considering Technique

1. In your own words, write out Zinsser's thesis.
2. In which paragraph does Zinsser's classification begin and in which paragraph does it end? What is he classifying? What does the classification contribute to the essay?
3. What element of cause-and-effect analysis appears in the essay? (Cause-and-effect analysis, discussed in Chapter 9, presents the causes and/or effects of something.) What does the analysis contribute to the essay?
4. What is the purpose of the opening examples of notes written to Carlos Hortas?

5. Zinsser uses *he* to refer to both college students and professors. He says, however, in paragraph 21 that he uses this pronoun for "brevity"; he recognizes that women, too, are under pressure. Do you think Zinsser should have been more careful to use language that includes women? Explain.

6. Consult a dictionary if you are unsure of the meaning of any of these words: *supplicants* (paragraph 9), *gallows humor* (paragraph 10), *privy* (paragraph 11), *venerated* (paragraph 14), *matriculates* (paragraph 17), *endowments* (paragraph 20), *accrue* (paragraph 21), *exhorted* (paragraph 21), *tenacity* (paragraph 23), *muse* (paragraph 30), *blithe spirit* (paragraph 46), *circuitous* (paragraph 48).

For Group Consideration

In paragraph 13, Zinsser expresses his wish for students. Do you share his wish? How likely is it that his wish can come true? What changes would have to occur in order for it to come true? Consider these questions with two or three classmates.

Journal Entry

In two or three pages, describe the kinds and amount of pressure you experience as a college student. Then explain the effects this pressure has on you.

Essay Assignments

1. In paragraph 12, Zinsser says that students "want a map—right now—that they can follow unswervingly to career security, financial security, Social Security and, presumably, a prepaid grave." If you disagree with Zinsser, or if you think students want more than a map, classify the things that students want and explain why they want what they do.

2. If you disagree with Zinsser's assertion that college students in general are pressured, stressed, and overly competitive, write a classification that informs your reader of what you think the various kinds of college students are. Try to use examples from your own experience and observation to illustrate your groupings. As an alternative, use division to explain the aspects of a typical college student.

3. Write an essay that classifies the pressures in some nonacademic setting. You could classify the pressures of parenthood, being an only child, working as a table server, being a housewife or househusband, or being a lifeguard. Like Zinsser, offer some advice for overcoming the pressures and/or explain the cause and effect of those pressures.

4. If you disagree with Zinsser's classification of college pressures, write your own classification of these pressures. Like Zinsser, explain the causes and effects of the pressures and use examples to illustrate their nature.

Considering Thematic Issues

1. In paragraph 14, Zinsser says, "One of the few rights that America does not proclaim is the right to fail." Do you think that Americans fear failure and therefore feel pressured to succeed? Cite examples to support your view.
2. "University Days" (page 146) was published in 1933, and "College Pressures" was published in 1979. Study these essays, then write about what has changed and what has stayed the same from 1933 to 1979 to the present.

THE WAYS OF MEETING OPPRESSION
Martin Luther King, Jr.

◆

The winner of the Nobel Peace Prize in 1964, Dr. Martin Luther King, Jr., was a Baptist minister and the most prominent civil rights leader of the 1950s and 1960s. In "The Ways of Meeting Oppression," King classifies ways to respond to oppression in order to inform his reader of the options oppressed people have. He then works to persuade his reader that nonviolent resistance is the best way to oppose oppression. As you read, notice that the thesis and topic sentences provide a clear organizational framework for King's classification.

◆

1   Oppressed people deal with their oppression in three characteristic ways. One way is acquiescence: the oppressed resign themselves to their doom. They tacitly adjust themselves to oppression, and thereby become conditioned to it. In every movement toward freedom some of the oppressed prefer to remain oppressed. Almost 2800 years ago Moses set out to lead the children of Israel from the slavery of Egypt to the freedom of the promised land. He soon discovered that slaves do not always welcome their deliverers. They become accustomed to being slaves. They would rather bear those ills they have, as Shakespeare pointed out, than flee to others that they know not of. They prefer the "fleshpots of Egypt" to the ordeals of emancipation.

2   There is such a thing as the freedom of exhaustion. Some people are so worn down by the yoke of oppression that they give up. A few years ago in the slum areas of Atlanta, a Negro guitarist used to sing almost daily: "Been down so long that down don't bother me." This is the type of negative freedom and resignation that often engulfs the life of the oppressed.

3   But this is not the way out. To accept passively an unjust system is to cooperate with that system; thereby the oppressed become as evil as the oppressor. Noncooperation with evil is as much a moral obligation as is cooperation with good. The oppressed must never allow the conscience of the oppressor to slumber. Religion reminds every man that he is his brother's keeper. To accept injustice or segregation passively is to say to the oppressor that his actions are morally right. It is a way of allowing his conscience to fall asleep. At this moment the oppressed fails to be his brother's keeper. So acquiescence—while often the easier way—is not the moral way. It is the way of the coward. The Negro cannot win the respect of his oppressor by acquiescing; he merely increases the oppressor's arrogance and contempt. Acquiescence is interpreted as proof of the Negro's inferiority. The Negro cannot win the respect of the white people of the South or the peoples of the world if he is willing to sell the future of his children for his personal and immediate comfort and safety.

4　　A second way that oppressed people sometimes deal with oppression is to resort to physical violence and corroding hatred. Violence often brings about momentary results. Nations have frequently won their independence in battle. But in spite of temporary victories, violence never brings permanent peace. It solves no social problem; it merely creates new and more complicated ones.

5　　Violence as a way of achieving racial justice is both impractical and immoral. It is impractical because it is a descending spiral ending in destruction for all. The old law of an eye for an eye leaves everybody blind. It is immoral because it seeks to humiliate the opponent rather than win his understanding; it seeks to annihilate rather than to convert. Violence is immoral because it thrives on hatred rather than love. It destroys community and makes brotherhood impossible. It leaves society in monologue rather than dialogue. Violence ends by defeating itself. It creates bitterness in the survivors and brutality in the destroyers. A voice echoes through time saying to every potential Peter, "Put up your sword."* History is cluttered with the wreckage of nations that failed to follow this command.

6　　If the American Negro and other victims of oppression succumb to the temptation of using violence in the struggle for freedom, future generations will be the recipients of a desolate night of bitterness, and our chief legacy to them will be an endless reign of meaningless chaos. Violence is not the way.

7　　The third way open to oppressed people in their quest for freedom is the way of nonviolent resistance. Like the synthesis in Hegelian philosophy, the principle of nonviolent resistance seeks to reconcile the truths of two opposites—the acquiescence and violence—while avoiding the extremes and immoralities of both. The nonviolent resister agrees with the person who acquiesces that one should not be physically aggressive toward his opponent; but he balances the equation by agreeing with the person of violence that evil must be resisted. He avoids the nonresistance of the former and the violent resistance of the latter. With nonviolent resistance, no individual or group need submit to any wrong, nor need anyone resort to violence in order to right a wrong.

8　　It seems to me that this is the method that must guide the actions of the Negro in the present crisis in race relations. Through nonviolent resistance the Negro will be able to rise to the noble height of opposing the unjust system while loving the perpetrators of the system. The Negro must work passionately and unrelentingly for full stature as a citizen, but he must not use inferior methods to gain it. He must never come to terms with falsehood, malice, hate, or destruction.

9　　Nonviolent resistance makes it possible for the Negro to remain in the South and struggle for his rights. The Negro's problem will not be solved by

---

*The apostle Peter had drawn his sword to defend Christ from arrest. The voice was Christ's, who surrendered himself for trial and crucifixion (John 18:11).

running away. He cannot listen to the glib suggestion of those who would urge him to migrate en masse to other sections of the country. By grasping his great opportunity in the South he can make a lasting contribution to the moral strength of the nation and set a sublime example of courage for generations yet unborn.

10　　By nonviolent resistance, the Negro can also enlist all men of good will in his struggle for equality. The problem is not a purely racial one, with Negroes set against whites. In the end, it is not a struggle between people at all, but a tension between justice and injustice. Nonviolent resistance is not aimed against oppressors but against oppression. Under its banner consciences, not racial groups, are enlisted.

Considering Ideas

1. According to King, what are the problems with acquiescence? With physical violence?
2. In paragraph 2, King refers to the "freedom of exhaustion." What do you think this phrase means?
3. In paragraph 1, King says that some "would rather bear those ills they have . . . than flee to others they know not of." What do you think King means by this? Why do you think that he makes this point?
4. According to King, how does nonviolent resistance balance the approaches of those who acquiesce and those who engage in physical violence?
5. Why does King advocate nonviolent resistance?

Considering Technique

1. What ordering principle does King use? What are his groupings?
2. Which sentence is the thesis of "The Ways of Meeting Oppression"?
3. King presents his groupings in topic sentences. What are those topic sentences?
4. Cause-and-effect analysis appears in paragraphs 5 and 6 and 8 through 10. (Cause-and-effect analysis, the explanation of the causes or the effects of something, is discussed in Chapter 9.) How does the analysis help advance the classification?
5. Which paragraph includes definition? (Definition, an explanation of what something means, is discussed in Chapter 11.) What purpose does that definition serve? What paragraphs include examples? What purpose do those examples serve?
6. Where in the essay does King make his persuasive purpose clear? Why do you think he waits so long to establish his persuasive point?
7. In what order does King arrange his details?
8. Consult a dictionary if you are unsure of the meaning of any of these words: *acquiescence* (paragraph 1), *tacitly* (paragraph 1), *fleshpots* (paragraph 1),

annihilate (paragraph 5), *succumb* (paragraph 6), *desolate* (paragraph 6), *legacy* (paragraph 6), *perpetrators* (paragraph 8), *glib* (paragraph 9), *en masse* (paragraph 9).

For Group Consideration

How much oppression exists in contemporary life? With two or three class-mates, make a list of all the examples of oppression that you can think of, drawing on what you read in newspapers and magazines, what you see on television, and what you know from your own experience and observation. Then select one of the examples and decide how effective nonviolent resistance would be in combating that oppression.

Journal Entry

Write about a time when you witnessed, experienced, or heard about some form of oppression or discrimination. Tell what the incident was and how it made you feel.

Essay Assignments

1. Classify the ways to deal with a bully, being sure to present the chief advantages and/or disadvantages of each way. Explain the effects of each technique.
2. Classify the ways to respond to snobs, being sure to present the chief advantages and/or disadvantages of each way. Also, explain the effects of each technique.
3. Classify the ways to deal with either stress or depression, being sure to present the chief advantages and/or disadvantages of each way. Also, explain the effects of each technique.
4. Classify the ways to deal with sex discrimination or sexual harassment. Indicate which of the ways is best and work to persuade your reader of that fact.

Considering Thematic Issues

1. Tell about a time when you witnessed, experienced, or heard about an instance of discrimination or oppression. Explain what happened and how you reacted. Also explain whether or not you have changed your thinking or behavior as a result of the incident. (Your journal entry may help you with ideas for this essay.)
2. Read "Untouchables" on page 159 and write an essay that explains to what extent the homeless are victims of oppression. Indicate whether or not you think King's policy of nonviolent resistance would help the homeless and explain why you believe as you do.

SHADES OF BLACK
Mary E. Mebane

Mary Mebane, who has a Ph.D. in English, is a teacher who has written two autobiographical books. "Shades of Black" is taken from one of those books. In the essay, Mebane informs her reader about color discrimination among blacks and its effects on black women. In the process of informing her reader, Mebane also shares her own experiences as a victim of discrimination. As you read, notice that Mebane establishes two separate classifications.

1   During my first week of classes as a freshman, I was stopped one day in the hall by the chairman's wife, who was indistinguishable in color from a white woman. She wanted to see me, she said.

2   This woman had no official position on the faculty, except that she was an instructor in English; nevertheless, her summons had to be obeyed. In the segregated world there were (and remain) gross abuses of authority because those at the pinnacle, and even their spouses, felt that the people "under" them had no recourse except to submit—and they were right except that sometimes a black who got sick and tired of it would go to the whites and complain. This course of action was severely condemned by the blacks, but an interesting thing happened—such action always got positive results. Power was thought of in negative terms: I can deny someone something, I can strike at someone who can't strike back, I can ride someone down; that proves I am powerful. The concept of power as a force for good, for affirmative response to people or situations, was not in evidence.

3   When I went to her office, she greeted me with a big smile. "You know," she said, "you made the highest mark on the verbal part of the examination." She was referring to the examination that the entire freshman class took upon entering the college. I looked at her but I didn't feel warmth, for in spite of her smile her eyes and tone of voice were saying, "How could this black-skinned girl score higher on the verbal than some of the students who've had more advantages than she? It must be some sort of fluke. Let me talk to her." I felt it, but I managed to smile my thanks and back off. For here at North Carolina College at Durham, as it had been since the beginning, social class and color were the primary criteria used in determining status on the campus.

4   First came the children of doctors, lawyers, and college teachers. Next came the children of public-school teachers, businessmen, and anybody else who had access to more money than the poor black working class. After that came the bulk of the student population, the children of the working class, most of whom were the first in their families to go beyond high school. The attitude toward them was: You're here because we need the numbers, but in all other things defer to your betters.

5   The faculty assumed that light-skinned students were more intelligent, and they were always a bit nonplussed when a dark-skinned student did well, especially if she was a girl. They had reason to be appalled when they discovered that I planned to do not only well but better than my light-skinned peers.

6   I don't know whether African men recently transported to the New World considered themselves handsome or, more important, whether they considered African women beautiful in comparison with Native American Indian women or immigrant European women. It is a question that I have never heard raised or seen research on. If African men considered African women beautiful, just when their shift in interest away from black black women occurred might prove to be an interesting topic for researchers. But one thing I know for sure: by the twentieth century, really black skin on a woman was considered ugly in this country. This was particularly true among those who were exposed to college.

7   Hazel, who was light brown, used to say to me, "You are *dark*, but not *too* dark." The saved commiserating with the damned. I had the feeling that if nature had painted one more brushstroke on me, I'd have had to kill myself.

8   Black skin was to be disguised at all costs. Since a black face is rather hard to disguise, many women took refuge in ludicrous makeup. Mrs. Burry, one of my teachers in elementary school, used white face powder. But she neglected to powder her neck and arms, and even the black on her face gleamed through the white, giving her an eerie appearance. But she did the best she could.

9   I observed all through elementary and high school that for various entertainments the girls were placed on the stage in order of color. And very black ones didn't get into the front row. If they were past caramel-brown, to the back row they would go. And nobody questioned the justice of these decisions—neither the students nor the teachers.

10   One of the teachers at Wildwood School, who was from the Deep South and was just as black as she could be, had been a strict enforcer of these standards. That was another irony—that someone who had been judged outside the realm of beauty herself because of her skin tones should have adopted them so wholeheartedly and applied them herself without question.

11   One girl stymied that teacher, though. Ruby, a black cherry of a girl, not only got off the back row but off the front row as well, to stand alone at stage center. She could outsing, outdance, and outdeclaim everyone else, and talent proved triumphant over pigmentation. But the May Queen and her Court (and in high school, Miss Wildwood) were always chosen from among the lighter ones.

12   When I was a freshman in high school, it became clear that a light-skinned sophomore girl named Rose was going to get the "best girl scholar" prize for the next three years, and there was nothing I could do about it, even though I knew I was the better. Rose was caramel-colored and had shoulder-length hair. She was highly favored by the science and math teacher, who figured the averages. I wasn't. There was only one prize. Therefore, Rose would get it until she

graduated. I was one year behind her, and I would not get it until after she graduated.

13 To be held in such low esteem was painful. It was difficult not to feel that I had been cheated out of the medal, which I felt that, in a fair competition, I perhaps would have won. Being unable to protest or do anything about it was a traumatic experience for me. From then on I instinctively tended to avoid the college-exposed dark-skinned male, knowing that when he looked at me he saw himself and, most of the time, his mother and sister as well, and since he had rejected his blackness, he had rejected theirs and mine.

14 Oddly enough, the lighter-skinned black male did not seem to feel so much prejudice toward the black black woman. It was no accident, I felt, that Mr. Harrison, the eighth-grade teacher, who was reddish-yellow himself, once protested to the science and math teacher about the fact that he always assigned sweeping duties to Doris and Ruby Lee, two black black girls. Mr. Harrison said to them one day, right in the other teacher's presence, "You must be some bad girls. Every day I come down here ya'll are sweeping." The science and math teacher got the point and didn't ask them to sweep anymore.

15 Uneducated black males, too, sometimes related very well to the black black woman. They had been less firmly indoctrinated by the white society around them and were more securely rooted in their own culture.

16 Because of the stigma attached to having dark skin, a black black woman had to do many things to find a place for herself. One possibility was to attach herself to a light-skinned woman, hoping that some of the magic would rub off on her. A second was to make herself sexually available, hoping to attract a mate. Third, she could resign herself to a more chaste life-style—either (for the professional woman) teaching and work in established churches or (for the uneducated woman) domestic work and zealous service in the Holy and Sanctified churches.

17 Even as a young girl, Lucy had chosen the first route. Lucy was short, skinny, short-haired, and black black, and thus unacceptable. So she made her choice. She selected Patricia, the lightest-skinned girl in the school, as her friend, and followed her around. Patricia and her friends barely tolerated Lucy, but Lucy smiled and doggedly hung on, hoping that some who noticed Patricia might notice her, too. Though I felt shame for her behavior, even then I understood.

18 As is often the case of the victim agreeing with and adopting the attitudes of oppressor, so I have seen it with black black women. I have seen them adopt the oppressor's attitude that they are nothing but "sex machines," and their supposedly superior sexual performance becomes their sole reason for being and for esteeming themselves. Such women learn early that in order to make themselves attractive to men they have somehow to shift the emphasis from physical beauty to some other area—usually sexual performance. Their constant talk is of their desirability and their ability to gratify a man sexually.

19 I knew two such women well—both of them black black. To hear their

endless talk of sexual conquests was very sad. I have never seen the category that these women fall into described anywhere. It is not that of promiscuity or nymphomania. It is the category of total self-rejection: "Since I am black, I am ugly, I am nobody. I will perform on the level that they have assigned to me." Such women are the pitiful results of what not only white America but also, and more important, black America has done to them.

20   Some, not taking the sexuality route but still accepting black society's view of their worthlessness, swing all the way across to intense religiosity. Some are staunch, fervent workers in the more traditional Southern churches—Baptist and Methodist—and others are leaders and ministers in the lower status, more evangelical Holiness sects.

21   Another avenue open to the black black woman is excellence in a career. Since in the South the field most accessible to such women is education, a great many of them prepared to become teachers. But here, too, the black black woman had problems. Grades weren't given to her lightly in school, nor were promotions on the job. Consequently, she had to prepare especially well. She had to pass examinations with flying colors or be left behind; she knew that she would receive no special consideration. She had to be overqualified for a job because otherwise she didn't stand a chance of getting it—and she was competing only with other blacks. She had to have something to back her up: not charm, not personality—but training.

22   The black black woman's training would pay off in the 1970's. With the arrival of integration the black black woman would find, paradoxically enough, that her skin color in an integrated situation was not the handicap it had been in an all-black situation. But it wasn't until the middle and late 1960s, when the post-1945 generation of black males arrived on college campuses, that I noticed any change in the situation at all. *He* wore an afro and *she* wore an afro, and sometimes the only way you could tell them apart was when his afro was taller than hers. Black had become beautiful, and the really black girl was often selected as queen of various campus activities. It was then that the dread I felt at dealing with the college-educated black male began to ease. Even now, though, when I have occasion to engage in any type of transaction with a college-educated black man, I gauge his age. If I guess he was born after 1945, I feel confident that the transaction will turn out all right. If he probably was born before 1945, my stomach tightens, I find myself taking shallow breaths, and I try to state my business and escape as soon as possible.

Considering Ideas

1. What is the primary point about discrimination that Mebane makes in "Shades of Black"?

2. Why is Mebane careful to note that she was challenged by a woman "who was indistinguishable in color from a white woman" (paragraph 1)?

3. How does Mebane define power in the segregated world?

4. Why did uneducated black men relate better to black black women than did educated black men?

5. How did the mid-1960s and 1970s mark a turning point for the black black woman?

6. Explain what you think Mebane's attitude is toward the light- and dark-skinned blacks she writes about and the discrimination she describes.

Considering Technique

1. Which sentence best presents the thesis of "Shades of Black"?

2. Paragraphs 1 through 3 present a narration. What point does that narration make? What does it contribute to the essay?

3. "Shades of Black" has two distinct classifications. In each case, what is classified and what is the ordering principle?

4. Mebane uses a number of examples. What do the examples in paragraphs 10 and 11, 12, 14, and 17 contribute to the essay?

5. What elements of cause-and-effect analysis appear? (Cause-and-effect analysis, discussed in Chapter 9, explains the causes or effects of something.) What does this cause and effect analysis contribute to the essay?

6. Consult a dictionary if you are unsure of the meaning of any of these words: *pinnacle* (paragraph 2), *fluke* (paragraph 3), *commiserating* (paragraph 7), *ludicrous* (paragraph 8), *irony* (paragraph 10), *stymied* (paragraph 11), *declaim* (paragraph 11), *stigma* (paragraph 16), *chaste* (paragraph 16), *doggedly* (paragraph 17), *nymphomania* (paragraph 19), *staunch* (paragraph 20).

For Group Consideration

Were you surprised to learn that members of a group are capable of discriminating against other members of that same group? Explain why or why not. What do you think accounted for the discrimination of lighter-skinned blacks against darker-skinned blacks? Discuss these questions with two or three classmates.

Journal Entry

Mebane tells about times in school when she was treated unfairly. If you have been treated unfairly in school (by a teacher, by a coach, or by a student), or if you have witnessed unfair treatment, tell what happened in a page or two.

Essay Assignments

1. Mebane explains that black women were classified according to the shade of their skin color. Write a classification that shows another way that we group

people (by attractiveness, intelligence, wealth, and so on). Indicate whether or not the tendency to classify in this way is discriminatory and why or why not. If you like, you can also indicate the effects the classification has on the people in the groupings.

2. Mebane classifies the way black black women made their way in the world. Select another group of people who are stigmatized (for example, the disabled, the overweight, the very tall or very short, or the unattractive) and classify the ways they make their way in the world and/or the ways they respond to their stigma.

3. Students in high school are often classified into groups, with members of some groups treated better than members of others. Write an essay that presents the ways students in your high school were grouped, as well as the discrimination members of one or more of these groups experienced.

Considering Thematic Issues

1. Write an essay that notes what our most frequently occurring prejudices are. Explain why you think we have these prejudices and what we can do to counteract them.

2. Compare and contrast the attitudes toward skin color in "Shades of Black" and "Complexion" (page 295). (Comparison and contrast are discussed in Chapter 8). Also consider to what extent our appearance affects the way others judge us and to what extent it shapes our perception of ourselves.

Additional Essay Assignments

1. Write a classification of popular music to inform people who do not know much about this variety of music.
2. Write a classification of either television talk shows or situation comedies to explain the nature of these forms of entertainment. As an alternative, use division to break down one of these shows into its various parts.
3. To share with your reader, classify teachers you have had.
4. Classify baseball pitchers, football quarterbacks, basketball forwards, or others who play a particular position on an athletic team.
5. Classify movie superstars to explain what their appeal is. As an alternative, use division to break down the typical superstar into his or her components.
6. To share with your reader, classify your friends, past and present.
7. Classify either radio disc jockeys or television newscasters.
8. Classify babysitters or divide them into their components. If you like, you can make this one humorous.
9. To inform or entertain, classify fast-food restaurants.
10. Classify types of inner strength or types of courage.
11. To help explain their appeal, classify horror movies or break them down into their various parts.
12. Classify parenting styles. If you wish, your purpose can be to persuade your reader that a particular style is the best.
13. Classify types of drivers. If you like, your purpose can be to entertain.
14. Classify beer advertisements on television or cigarette advertisements in magazines to inform your reader of the persuasive strategies that are employed.
15. To inform, share, and/or entertain, classify the kinds of parties college students attend. As an alternative, use division to present the various aspects of a college party.
16. Classify football, baseball, or basketball fans.
17. Classify the kinds of neighbors people can have.
18. Write a classification of the kinds of good luck or bad luck.
19. Classify the different kinds of theme parks or roller coasters. Try to convince your reader which kind is the most enjoyable.
20. Write a classification of the kinds of success.

DEFINITION

The Purpose of Definition
Supporting Details
Structuring Definition
Suggestions for Writing Definition
Annotated Student Essay: Autumn

What Is Poverty?—Jo Goodwin Parker *(definition to inform and persuade)*
*The Holocaust—Bruno Bettelheim *(definition to persuade and inform)*
Good Souls—Dorothy Parker *(definition to entertain and persuade)*
I Want a Wife—Judy Brady *(definition to inform and persuade)*
*The View from 80—Malcolm Cowley *(definition to inform and share)*
Lists—Jeanine Larmoth *(definition to entertain, share, and inform)*

Additional Essay Assignments

* To fulfill the author's purpose, definition is combined with one or more other patterns.

A dictionary will tell you what a word means. However, sometimes a writer wants to go beyond a word's literal dictionary meaning in order to explain the significance, associations, private meanings, and personal experiences associated with the word. This information can only come from an *extended definition,* the kind of essay this chapter treats. For example, consider the word *sled.* A dictionary will tell a reader that it is a vehicle on runners used for coasting on snow. However, an extended definition can tell the reader that a sled contributed to the happiest times you shared with your brother and father. Now consider the word *prejudice,* which can mean different things to different people. An extended definition of the word allows you to explain the meaning and significance *you* ascribe to the word. Thus, an extended definition affords a writer the opportunity to go beyond literal meaning to express feelings, opinions, knowledge, unusual views, and personal experiences associated with a word.

 ## THE PURPOSE OF DEFINITION

More often than not, an extended definition informs. Sometimes the writer informs by clarifying something that is complex. For example, an essay that defines *freedom* can help the reader understand this very difficult concept. A definition can also inform by bringing the reader to a fresh appreciation of something familiar or taken for granted. For example, if you think that Americans do not sufficiently appreciate free speech, you could define *free speech* to help readers renew their appreciation for this important liberty. A definition can also bring a reader to an understanding of something unfamiliar. In "What Is Poverty?" (page 349), for example, the author defines poverty for an audience who has not experienced it and hence does not fully understand what it means.

In addition to informing, an extended definition can allow a writer to share experience. For example, you could define *teenager* by explaining what your own teenage years were like and in this way share part of your experience with adolescence. Similarly, in "The View from 80" (page 370) author Malcolm Cowley shares by including his experience as an octogenarian to clarify his definition of aging.

A definition can also entertain, as when you write a humorous definition of *freshman,* to amuse your reader. Dorothy Parker's "Good Souls" (page 360) is an example of a definition that entertains.

Finally, an extended definition can serve a persuasive purpose. This is particularly true when the definition points to a conclusion about a controversial issue. For example, Jo Goodwin Parker presents a powerful, graphic definition of *poverty* in "What Is Poverty?" in order to move the reader to take steps to end this social condition. Similarly, Judy Brady defines *wife* in "I Want a Wife" (page 366) to convince the reader that the traditional wifely role is unfair to women.

SUPPORTING DETAILS

In general, a definition essay presents the characteristics of what is being defined. Often when you present these characteristics, you rely on other patterns. For example, if you wanted to define *sinus headache* to share your own experiences with this misery, you could *describe* the pain. If you wanted to define *math anxiety* to inform the reader of what this condition is like, part of your essay could *narrate* an account of a time you experienced this anxiety. If you wanted to define *a good teacher* to inform your reader of what a teacher should be like, you could, in part, *illustrate* with examples of good teachers from your past. If you wanted to define *maturity* to clarify this difficult concept, you could include a *contrast* of maturity with immaturity. If you wanted to define *sexual harassment* to convince people to take action against this practice, part of your piece could *analyze the causes and effects* of sexual harassment to show why it is such a problem.

Sometimes it makes sense to explain what your subject is not, especially if you need to correct a misconception. For example, if you were defining *poverty,* you could note that poverty is not something that people can escape if they just try hard enough.

Finally, when you write your definition, you should avoid stating the obvious and using a dictionary style. If you state the obvious, you will bore your reader. Thus, if you are defining *mother,* you need not state that a mother is a female parent. Similarly, a dictionary style is likely to bore a reader because it is stiff and unlike your own natural style. Thus, avoid defining *teenager* as "a person in that developmental period of hormonal and social change marking the transition from childhood to adulthood"—unless, of course, you want to put your reader to sleep.

 STRUCTURING DEFINITION

The thesis for an extended definition can state what will be defined and your view of what will be defined, like this:

Adolescence is not the happy time many people remember it to be.

This thesis allows you to define *adolescence* and show that it can be a difficult period.

You can also shape a thesis by noting what will be defined and why it is important to understand the term, like this:

If we do not understand the meaning of free speech, we will be in danger of losing it.

To create interest in your essay, your introduction can explain the significance of the definition. Thus, if you are defining *homelessness,* you can note the extent of homelessness in this country to show why an understanding is important. You can also tell a story related to what you are defining. In addition, if the meaning of your term has changed over the years, you can explain what your term used to mean before going on to give a current definition. For example, if you are defining *dating,* you could open by noting that dating used to mean sitting in the parlor with a girl's parents or attending a church social.

Since definition often includes other patterns, the order of details will be influenced by these patterns. Thus, narrations will use chronological order, cause-and-effect analysis will reproduce causal chains, and so on. Purpose, too, can influence order. Thus, if your purpose is persuasive, you may want to place the characteristics of what you are defining in a progressive order to save the most important points for last.

SUGGESTIONS FOR WRITING DEFINITION

1. If you need help with topic selection, consider the roles you play in your life and the aspects of those roles. For example, if you are an athlete, you can define *student athlete* or *competition.* If you select a topic this way, you can draw on your own experience for detail. Another way to find a topic is to consider the emotions and moods you have been experiencing lately. In this way, you might settle on defining something like *anger, anxiety, jealousy, anticipation,* or *satisfaction,* using recent personal experience as detail.
2. To generate details, make a list of all the characteristics of what you are defining. Then go back and circle the ones you want to treat.
3. For each characteristic you circled, ask yourself the following to come up with ideas for development:
   a. Is there a story I can tell to reveal or illustrate the characteristic?
   b. Are there examples I can provide to illustrate the characteristic?
   c. Can I describe the characteristic?
   d. Can I compare the characteristic with something?
   e. Can I contrast the characteristic with something?
   f. What causes the characteristic?
   g. What are the effects of the characteristic?
4. Decide if you need to clear up any misconceptions by explaining what your subject is *not.*
5. Write out a statement of the significance of your term and why it is important to define it. You can use a version of this for your introduction, thesis, or conclusion.
6. Using the ideas you generated, develop an outline.
7. In one sitting, write a draft from your outline. Just get your ideas down the

best way you can without worrying about grammar, punctuation, spelling, or anything else.

8. When you revise, consider the following:
   a. Have you avoided stating the obvious?
   b. Have you avoided a dictionary style?
   c. Do all your details help you achieve your purpose?
   d. Are all the characteristics of your term adequately developed?
   e. Is the significance of your definition clearly stated or strongly implied?

 ## ANNOTATED STUDENT ESSAY

Student writer Julie Cummins defines fall to give her reader a fresh appreciation of the familiar. To achieve her purpose, she shares her impressions of this time of year, relying heavily on vivid description.

AUTUMN

Paragraph 1
The introduction explains that the definition is important because most people's definition is inadequate. The thesis (the last sentence) specifies the three characteristics on which the definition will focus.

1 Autumn is a unique time of year. Most people define it as the season that comes between summer and winter, when the trees lose their leaves. While this definition is accurate, it is also inadequate. Autumn is a seasonal mirror, a reminder of the pleasant days of summer vacation and a glimpse into the approaching winter chill. However, fall is more than just varying temperatures and weather conditions. Fall is more than trees losing their leaves. To reflect on fall is to reflect on a specific look, flavor, and mood.

Paragraph 2
The first sentence is the topic sentence. It presents the first characteristic of what is being defined. The supporting details are descriptive to convey the warm look of fall.

2 The fall look is warm. All of autumn's colors are friendly hues of russet and amber. There is nothing so lovely as the sharp contrast of a hill exploding with crimson and bronze against a pale afternoon sky. A brisk afternoon walk along a sun-dappled lane affords occasional glimpses of bright marigolds, the last holdouts from summer's glory. The sunsets of fall are spectacular, as the sky becomes streaked with lilac when the brilliant red orb sinks slowly in the west. Autumn is also the season for the warm orange of pumpkins, whether they are in pies, cookies, or on the front porch sporting huge, toothless grins.

Paragraph 3
The paragraph begins with a topic sentence that presents the second characteristic of what is being defined. The supporting details are description to convey the flavor of fall.

3 The fall flavor is crisp. A cool fall evening is perfect for sitting in front of a crackling fire, enjoying the crunch of a tawny apple eaten with a handful of freshly popped popcorn. And what better way to wash them down than with the tart bite of apple cider? Even if one could get this pungent drink during any other season, it would not taste as good as it does in the fall.

Paragraph 4
The paragraph begins with a topic sentence to present the third characteristic of what is being defined. *Finally* provides transition. The supporting details are examples of revitalization.

Paragraph 5
The conclusion leaves the reader with a final impression of fall. For closure, the last sentence harkens to an idea in introduction by explaining what fall is not (just the time when trees lose their leaves).

4   Finally, the mood of fall is revitalizing. As summer ends and the apples ripen on the trees, one knows that pie and cider are not far behind. Nonetheless, the fall mood always comes as an invigorating surprise. One does not expect to feel so dramatically different in autumn, but still it happens. People seem to wake up to fall, refreshed as after a relaxing nap on a warm day. They return from vacation renewed; they return to school recharged; they return to their "real" lives reenergized. Fall's mood can be captured in the excited smile of a child with a scrubbed face, waiting eagerly for a bus on the first day of school. During autumn, the air crackles with excitement. Everyone and everything seems filled with restless energy. The warm, sunny afternoons and cold evenings lend themselves to busyness and productivity and then rest. Shedding their summer languor, animals are friskier, more playful. Yard work that has been a chore for months suddenly becomes a game as parents struggle valiantly to rake leaves into piles that children insist on jumping into and scattering. Youngsters who have been complaining of boredom all summer now have something to do, with pickup football games being played in every yard and vacant lot.

5   During fall, everything seems sharper, more in focus. It is as if all the animals and plants are giving life one last effort before they go to sleep for the winter. Even people seem to act and react differently in the fall. Yes, fall is when the leaves drop from the trees, but it is so much more.

WHAT IS POVERTY?

Jo Goodwin Parker

◆

When George Henderson was gathering material for his book America's Other Children: Public Schools Outside Suburbia *(1971), the following essay was mailed to him with the name Jo Goodwin Parker on it. We do not know for sure whether Ms. Parker is writing of herself or others. Either way, unless you have experienced poverty yourself, her definition will be an eye-opener for you. In addition to informing her audience about the nature of poverty, the definition attempts to persuade the reader to help solve the problem. As you read, consider how Parker's description helps her fulfill her purposes.*

◆

1   You ask me what is poverty? Listen to me. Here I am, dirty, smelly, and with no "proper" underwear on and with the stench of my rotting teeth near you. I will tell you. Listen to me. Listen without pity. I cannot use your pity. Listen with understanding. Put yourself in my dirty, worn out, ill-fitting shoes, and hear me.

2   Poverty is getting up every morning from a dirt- and illness-stained mattress. The sheets have long since been used for diapers. Poverty is living in a smell that never leaves. This is a smell of urine, sour milk, and spoiling food sometimes joined with the strong smell of long-cooked onions. Onions are cheap. If you have smelled this smell, you did not know how it came. It is the smell of the outdoor privy. It is the smell of young children who cannot walk the long dark way in the night. It is the smell of the mattresses where years of "accidents" have happened. It is the smell of the milk which has gone sour because the refrigerator long has not worked, and it costs money to get it fixed. It is the smell of rotting garbage. I could bury it, but where is the shovel? Shovels cost money.

3   Poverty is being tired. I have always been tired. They told me at the hospital when the last baby came that I had chronic anemia caused from poor diet, a bad case of worms, and that I needed a corrective operation. I listened politely—the poor are always polite. The poor always listen. They don't say that there is no money for iron pills, or better food, or worm medicine. The idea of an operation is frightening and costs so much that, if I had dared, I would have laughed. Who takes care of my children? Recovery from an operation takes a long time. I have three children. When I left them with "Granny" the last time I had a job, I came home to find the baby covered with fly specks, and a diaper that had not been changed since I left. When the dried diaper came off, bits of my baby's flesh came with it. My other child was playing with a sharp bit of broken glass, and my oldest was playing alone at the edge of a lake. I made

twenty-two dollars a week, and a good nursery school costs twenty dollars a week for my three children. I quit my job.

4   Poverty is dirt. You say in your clean clothes coming from your clean house, "Anybody can be clean." Let me explain about housekeeping with no money. For breakfast I give my children grits with no oleo or cornbread without eggs and oleo. This does not use up many dishes. What dishes there are, I wash in cold water and with no soap. Even the cheapest soap has to be saved for the baby's diapers. Look at my hands, so cracked and red. Once I saved for two months to buy a jar of Vaseline for my hands and the baby's diaper rash. When I had saved enough, I went to buy it and the price had gone up two cents. The baby and I suffered on. I have to decide every day if I can bear to put my cracked, sore hands into the cold water and strong soap. But you ask, why not hot water? Fuel costs money. If you have a wood fire it costs money. If you burn electricity, it costs money. Hot water is a luxury. I do not have luxuries. I know you will be surprised when I tell you how young I am. I look so much older. My back has been bent over the wash tubs for so long, I cannot remember when I ever did anything else. Every night I wash every stitch my school-age child has on and just hope her clothes will be dry by morning.

5   Poverty is staying up all night on cold nights to watch the fire, knowing one spark on the newspaper covering the walls means your sleeping children die in flames. In summer poverty is watching gnats and flies devour your baby's tears when he cries. The screens are torn and you pay so little rent you know they will never be fixed. Poverty means insects in your food, in your nose, in your eyes, and crawling over you when you sleep. Poverty is hoping it never rains because diapers won't dry when it rains and soon you are using newspapers. Poverty is seeing your children forever with runny noses. Paper handkerchiefs cost money and all your rags you need for other things. Even more costly are antihistamines. Poverty is cooking without food and cleaning without soap.

6   Poverty is asking for help. Have you ever had to ask for help, knowing your children will suffer unless you get it? Think about asking for a loan from a relative, if this is the only way you can imagine asking for help. I will tell you how it feels. You find out where the office is that you are supposed to visit. You circle that block four or five times. Thinking of your children, you go in. Everybody is very busy. Finally, someone comes out and you tell her that you need help. That never is the person you need to see. You go see another person, and after spilling the whole shame of your poverty all over the desk between you, you find that this isn't the right office after all—you must repeat the whole process, and it never is any easier at the next place.

7   You have asked for help, and after all it has a cost. You are again told to wait. You are told why, but you don't really hear because of the red cloud of shame and the rising black cloud of despair.

8   Poverty is remembering. It is remembering quitting school in junior high

because "nice" children had been so cruel about my clothes and my smell. The attendance officer came. My mother told him I was pregnant. I wasn't, but she thought that I could get a job and help out. I had jobs off and on, but never long enough to learn anything. Mostly I remember being married. I was so young then. I am still young. For a time, we had all the things you have. There was a little house in another town, with hot water and everything. Then my husband lost his job. There was unemployment insurance for a while and what few jobs I could get. Soon, all our nice things were repossessed and we moved back here. I was pregnant then. This house didn't look so bad when we first moved in. Every week it gets worse. Nothing is ever fixed. We now had no money. There were a few odd jobs for my husband, but everything went for food then, as it does now. I don't know how we lived through three years and three babies, but we did. I'll tell you something, after the last baby I destroyed my marriage. It had been a good one, but could you keep on bringing children in this dirt? Did you ever think how much it costs for any kind of birth control? I knew my husband was leaving the day he left, but there were no good-byes between us. I hope he has been able to climb out of this mess somewhere. He never could hope with us to drag him down.

9   That's when I asked for help. When I got it, you know how much it was? It was, and is, seventy-eight dollars a month for the four of us; that is all I ever can get. Now you know why there is no soap, no needles and thread, no hot water, no aspirin, no worm medicine, no hand cream, no shampoo. None of these things forever and ever and ever. So that you can see clearly, I pay twenty dollars a month rent, and most of the rest goes for food. For grits and cornmeal, and rice and milk and beans. I try my best to use only the minimum electricity. If I use more, there is that much less for food.

10   Poverty is looking into a black future. Your children won't play with my boys. They will turn to other boys who steal to get what they want. I can already see them behind the bars of their prison instead of behind the bars of my poverty. Or they will turn to the freedom of alcohol or drugs, and find them-selves enslaved. And my daughter? At best, there is for her a life like mine.

11   But you say to me, there are schools. Yes, there are schools. My children have no extra books, no magazines, no extra pencils, or crayons, or paper and the most important of all, they do not have health. They have worms, they have infections, they have pink-eye all summer. They do not sleep well on the floor, or with me in my one bed. They do not suffer from hunger, my seventy-eight dollars keeps us alive, but they do suffer from malnutrition. Oh yes, I do remember what I was taught about health in school. It doesn't do much good. In some places there is a surplus commodities program. Not here. The county said it cost too much. There is a school lunch program. But I have two children who will already be damaged by the time they get to school.

12   But, you say to me, there are health clinics. Yes, there are health clinics and they are in the towns. I live out here eight miles from town. I can walk that far (even if it is sixteen miles both ways), but can my little children? My neighbor

will take me when he goes; but he expects to get paid, *one way or another.* I bet you know my neighbor. He is that large man who spends his time at the gas station, the barbershop, and the corner store complaining about the government spending money on the immoral mothers of illegitimate children.

13   Poverty is an acid that drips on pride until all pride is worn away. Poverty is a chisel that chips on honor until honor is worn away. Some of you say that you would do *something* in my situation, and maybe you would, for the first week or the first month, but for year after year after year?

14   Even the poor can dream. A dream of a time when there is money. Money for the right kinds of food, for worm medicine, for iron pills, for toothbrushes, for hand cream, for a hammer and nails and a bit of screening, for a shovel, for a bit of paint, for some sheeting, for needles and thread. Money to pay *in money* for a trip to town. And, oh, money for hot water and money for soap. A dream of when asking for help does not eat away the last bit of pride. When the office you visit is as nice as the offices of other governmental agencies, when there are enough workers to help you quickly, when workers do not quit in defeat and despair. When you have to tell your story to only one person, and that person can send you for other help and you don't have to prove your poverty over and over and over again.

15   I have come out of my despair to tell you this. Remember I did not come from another place or another time. Others like me are all around you. Look at us with an angry heart, anger that will help you help me. Anger that will let you tell of me. The poor are always silent. Can you be silent too?

Considering Ideas

1. According to Parker, what are the chief characteristics of poverty?
2. What are the effects of poverty on children?
3. According to the author, why doesn't education provide a way out of poverty for children?
4. In paragraphs 11, 12, and 13, Parker addresses people who say that schools, health clinics, and the poor themselves can help alleviate poverty. How does she counter the argument these people make? Why does she bother to address this argument?
5. Paragraph 8 describes a vicious cycle that is part of poverty. What other vicious cycles can you detect as a result of reading the essay?
6. What kind of audience do you think is appropriate for "What Is Poverty?"

Considering Technique

1. Parker uses a great deal of description in her essay. Is this description objective or expressive? (See page 43 on objective and expressive details.) What does the descriptive detail contribute to the essay?

2. Many of Parker's paragraphs begin with the words "Poverty is . . ." Do you think that this technique is effective? Explain.
3. In which paragraph does Parker use examples? What do these examples contribute?
4. In which paragraphs does Parker use cause-and-effect analysis? (Cause-and-effect analysis, discussed in Chapter 9, explains the causes and/or effects of something.) What does the analysis contribute to the essay?
5. What approach does Parker take to the introduction?
6. What approach does Parker take to the conclusion?
7. Consult a dictionary if you are unsure of the meaning of any of these words: *privy* (paragraph 2), *chronic anemia* (paragraph 3), *oleo* (paragraph 4), *antihistamines* (paragraph 5), *repossessed* (paragraph 8).

For Group Consideration

With two or three classmates, decide which of Parker's descriptions best help her fulfill her purpose. Then explain why the description functions so effectively.

Journal Entry

Compare and contrast your understanding of poverty before and after you read "What Is Poverty?" What, if anything, did you learn as a result of reading the essay?

Essay Assignments

1. Define a problem that you have firsthand knowledge of (drug use, alcohol use, peer pressure, pressure faced by adolescents, sexual experimentation, materialism, sexism, racism, apathy, sexual harassment, and so on). Like Parker, try to arouse your audience to take action to solve the problem.
2. Define a school problem (for example, pressure for grades, competition, cheating, exam anxiety, or math anxiety). Like Parker, use description and/or exemplification.
3. Define one of the following: fear, ambition, pride, jealousy, hunger, or depression. Draw on personal experience for clarifying examples.

Considering Thematic Issues

1. Compare and contrast the stereotype of the poor with the description of the poor in "What Is Poverty?"
2. Using information from "What Is Poverty?" and "Untouchables" (page 159), write an essay to persuade legislators to increase their efforts to aid the poor and homeless. If you like, you can also include information gathered from newspapers and magazines like *Time, Newsweek,* and *U.S. News and World Report,* along with your own ideas. (See the appendix for information on how to handle material borrowed from sources.)

THE HOLOCAUST
Bruno Bettelheim

Born in Austria and trained as a psychologist in Freud's Vienna, Bruno Bettelheim was in two Nazi concentration camps. He has written about the experiences of those in the camps, as well as about children. The following selection is an excerpt from a longer essay published in Surviving and Other Essays *(1974). In the piece, he combines definition, cause-and-effect analysis, and process analysis to argue that the Holocaust and its victims are misnamed. In addition, Bettelheim informs the reader about the nature of Nazi crimes against humanity and our reaction to them. As you read, ask yourself how our perception of reality is influenced by the words we use to name things.*

♦

1 To begin with, it was not the hapless victims of the Nazis who named their incomprehensible and totally unmasterable fate the "holocaust." It was the Americans who applied this artificial and highly technical term to the Nazi extermination of the European Jews. But while the event when named as mass murder most foul evokes the most immediate, most powerful revulsion, when it is designated by a rare technical term, we must first in our minds translate it back into emotionally meaningful language. Using technical or specially created terms instead of words form our common vocabulary is one of the best-known and most widely used distancing devices, separating the intellectual from the emotional experience. Talking about "the holocaust" permits us to manage it intellectually where the raw facts, when given their ordinary names, would overwhelm us emotionally—because it was catastrophe beyond comprehension, beyond the limits of our imagination, unless we force ourselves against our desire to extend it to encompass these terrible events.

2 This linguistic circumlocution began while it all was only in the planning stage. Even the Nazis—usually given to grossness in language and action—shied away from facing openly what they were up to and called this vile mass murder "the final solution of the Jewish problem." After all, solving a problem can be made to appear like an honorable enterprise, as long as we are not forced to recognize that the solution we are about to embark on consists of the completely unprovoked, vicious murder of millions of helpless men, women, and children. The Nuremberg judges of these Nazi criminals followed their example of circumlocution by coining a neologism out of one Greek and one Latin root: genocide. These artificially created technical terms fail to connect with our strongest feelings. The horror of murder is part of our most common human heritage. From earliest infancy on, it arouses violent abhorrence in us. Therefore in whatever form it appears we should give such an act its true designation and not hide it behind polite, erudite terms created out of classical words.

3   To call this vile mass murder "the holocaust" is not to give it a special name emphasizing its uniqueness which would permit, over time, the word becoming invested with feelings germane to the event it refers to. The correct definition of *holocaust* is "burnt offering." As such, it is part of the language of the psalmist, a meaningful word to all who have some acquaintance with the Bible, full of the richest emotional connotations. By using the term "holocaust," entirely false associations are established through conscious and unconscious connotations between the most vicious of mass murders and ancient rituals of a deeply religious nature.

4   Using a word with such strong unconscious religious connotations when speaking of the murder of millions of Jews robs the victims of this abominable mass murder of the only thing left to them: their uniqueness. Calling the most callous, most brutal, most horrid, most heinous mass murder a burnt offering is a sacrilege, a profanation of God and man.

5   Martyrdom is part of our religious heritage. A martyr, burned at the stake, is a burnt offering to his god. And it is true that after the Jews were asphyxiated, the victims' corpses were burned. But I believe we fool ourselves if we think we are honoring the victims of systematic murder by using this term, which has the highest moral connotations. By doing so, we connect for our own psychological reasons what happened in the extermination camps with historical events we deeply regret, but also greatly admire. We do so because this makes it easier for us to cope; only in doing so we cope with our distorted image of what happened, not with the events the way they did happen.

6   By calling the victims of the Nazis martyrs, we falsify their fate. The true meaning of *martyr* is: "One who voluntarily undergoes the penalty of death for refusing to renounce his faith" (*Oxford English Dictionary*). The Nazis made sure that nobody could mistakenly think that their victims were murdered for their religious beliefs. Renouncing their faith would have saved none of them. Those who had converted to Christianity were gassed, as were those who were atheists, and those who were deeply religious Jews. They did not die for any conviction, and certainly not out of choice.

7   Millions of Jews were systematically slaughtered, as were untold other "undesirables," not for any convictions of theirs, but only because they stood in the way of the realization of an illusion. They neither died for their convictions, nor were they slaughtered because of their convictions, but only in consequence of the Nazis' delusional belief about what was required to protect the purity of their assumed superior racial endowment, and what they thought necessary to guarantee them the living space they believed they needed and were entitled to. Thus while these millions were slaughtered for an idea, they did not die for one.

8   Millions—men, women, and children—were processed after they had been utterly brutalized, their humanity destroyed, their clothes torn from their bodies. Naked, they were sorted into those who were destined to be murdered immediately, and those others who had a short-term usefulness as slave labor. But after a brief interval they, too, were to be herded into the same gas

chambers into which the others were immediately piled, there to be asphyxiated so that, in their last moments, they could not prevent themselves from fighting each other in vain for a last breath of air.

9   To call these most wretched victims of a murderous delusion, of destructive drives run rampant, martyrs or a burnt offering is a distortion invented for our comfort, small as it may be. It pretends that this most vicious of mass murders had some deeper meaning; that in some fashion the victims either offered themselves or at least became sacrifices to a higher cause. It robs them of the last recognition which could be theirs, denies them the last dignity we could accord them; to face and accept what their death was all about, not embellishing it for the small psychological relief this may give us.

10   We could feel so much better if the victims had acted out of choice. For our emotional relief, therefore, we dwell on the tiny minority who did exercise some choice: the resistance fighters of the Warsaw ghetto, for example, and others like them. We are ready to overlook the fact that these people fought back only at a time when everything was lost, when the overwhelming majority of those who had been forced into the ghettos had already been exterminated without resisting. Certainly those few who finally fought for their survival and their convictions, risking and losing their lives in doing so, deserve our admiration; their deeds give us a moral lift. But the more we dwell on these few, the more unfair are we to the memory of the millions who were slaughtered—who gave in, did not fight back—because we deny them the only thing which up to the very end remained uniquely their own: their fate.

Considering Ideas

1. What is Bettelheim's objection to the term *holocaust*?
2. According to Bettelheim, what purpose is served when we misname the Nazi mass murders the *holocaust* and when we misname its victims *martyrs*?
3. Why does the author think it is inaccurate to view Jewish victims of the Nazis as martyrs?
4. According to Bettelheim, why did the Nazis murder millions of people they considered "undesirable"?
5. What kind of reader do you think makes the best audience for "The Holocaust"?
6. Do you agree with Bettelheim that *holocaust* is an unsuitable term for the mass murder of six million Jews? Explain why or why not.

Considering Technique

1. Which sentence best expresses the thesis of "The Holocaust"?
2. To what extent does Bettelheim explain what something is not? What does this technique contribute to the essay?

3. As explained on page 345, a dictionary style is not often the best choice for an extended definition. In paragraph 6, however, Bettelheim uses a dictionary definition. Is this a problem? Explain why or why not.
4. Paragraph 8 is developed with process analysis. (Process analysis, an explanation of how something is made or done, is discussed in Chapter 7.) What does the analysis contribute to the essay?
5. What cause-and-effect analysis appears in the essay? What is the purpose of the analysis? (Cause-and-effect analysis, discussed in Chapter 9, explains the causes and/or effects of something.)
6. Consult a dictionary if you are unsure of the meaning of any of these words: *hapless* (paragraph 1), *revulsion* (paragraph 1), *encompass* (paragraph 1), *circumlocution* (paragraph 2), *neologism* (paragraph 2), *abhorrence* (paragraph 2), *erudite* (paragraph 2), *germane* (paragraph 3), *heinous* (paragraph 4), *profanation* (paragraph 4), *asphyxiation* (paragraph 5), *delusional* (paragraph 7), *endowment* (paragraph 7), *rampant* (paragraph 9).

For Group Consideration

What alternative names can you think of to replace *holocaust* as the term for the murder of millions of people? With two or three classmates, consider possibilities and decide which, if any, are suitable and why. If you think *holocaust* is the best term, explain why.

Journal Entry

When you think of the Holocaust, what do you think of? Respond in a page or two.

Essay Assignments

1. Select something that you think has been misnamed (*deficit spending* for spending after the money is gone, *passed away* for died, *adult entertainment* for pornography, and so on). Like Bettelheim, define the reality and argue for a change in the term to something that better reflects that reality.
2. If you know anyone who lived through the Holocaust, interview that person; then write your own definition of the term. As an alternative, do some research in your campus library before writing the definition. (See the appendix on how to handle material taken from sources.)
3. Write a definition of another historical event or concept (for example, manifest destiny, the Trail of Tears, the Bataan Death March, the Age of Chivalry, the cold war, the Renaissance, the Crusades, states' rights, or Federalism). If necessary, research the subject in your campus library, and consult the appendix on how to handle material taken from sources.

Considering Thematic Issues

1. Decide what it is about human nature that makes possible the mass murder of millions of people judged "undesirable" because of their religion. Then recommend something schools can do to educate people about this aspect of human nature so it can be kept in check.

2. A *euphemism* is a word that makes an unpleasant reality seem more pleasant. For example, a euphemism for garbage collector is *sanitary engineer;* a euphemism for old person is *senior citizen*. Using the information in "The Holocaust" and "Behind the Formaldehyde Curtain" (page 198), explain why we use euphemisms and how they affect our perception of reality. Then go on to explain whether or not you think euphemisms are a problem and why or why not.

GOOD SOULS
Dorothy Parker

◆

Dorothy Parker (1893–1967) was a humorist known for her satire. She wrote for Vogue *and* Vanity Fair *and was a book reviewer for* The New Yorker. *Eventually she moved to Hollywood and coauthored screenplays with her husband. In "Good Souls," published in 1919, Parker defines with her usual satiric wit to entertain her audience. However, as you read, ask yourself whether she writes solely to amuse, or whether she also has a serious point to make.*

◆

1   All about us, living in our very families, it may be, there exists a race of curious creatures. Outwardly, they possess no marked peculiarities; in fact, at a hasty glance, they may be readily mistaken for regular human beings. They are built after the popular design; they have the usual number of features, arranged in the conventional manner; they offer no variations on the general run of things in their habits of dressing, eating, and carrying on their business.

2   Yet, between them and the rest of the civilized world, there stretches an impassable barrier. Though they live in the very thick of the human race, they are forever isolated from it. They are fated to go through life, congenital pariahs. They live out their little lives, mingling with the world, yet never a part of it.

3   They are, in short, Good Souls.

4   And the piteous thing about them is that they are wholly unconscious of their condition. A Good Soul thinks he is just like anyone else. Nothing could convince him otherwise. It is heartrending to see him, going cheerfully about, even whistling or humming as he goes, all unconscious of his terrible plight. The utmost he can receive from the world is an attitude of good-humored patience, a perfunctory word of approbation, a praising with faint damns, so to speak—yet he firmly believes that everything is all right with him.

5   There is no accounting for Good Souls.

6   They spring up anywhere. They will suddenly appear in families which, for generations, have had no slightest stigma attached to them. Possibly they are throw-backs. There is scarcely a family without at least one Good Soul some-where in it at the present moment—maybe in the form of an elderly aunt, an unmarried sister, an unsuccessful brother, an indigent cousin. No household is complete without one.

7   The Good Soul begins early; he will show signs of his condition in extreme youth. Go now to the nearest window, and look out on the little children playing so happily below. Any group of youngsters that you may happen to see will do perfectly. Do you observe the child whom all the other little dears make "it" in their merry games? Do you follow the child from whom the other little ones snatch the cherished candy, to consume it before his

streaming eyes? Can you get a good look at the child whose precious toys are borrowed for indefinite periods by the other playful youngsters, and are returned to him in fragments? Do you see the child upon whom all the other kiddies play their complete repertory of childhood's winsome pranks— throwing bags of water on him, running away and hiding from him, shouting his name in quaint rhymes, chalking coarse legends on his unsuspecting back?

8 Mark that child well. He is going to be a Good Soul when he grows up.

9 Thus does the doomed child go through early youth and adolescence. So does he progress towards the fulfillment of his destiny. And then, some day, when he is under discussion, someone will say of him, "Well, he means well, anyway." That settles it. For him, that is the end. Those words have branded him with the indelible mark of his pariahdom. He has come into his majority; he is a full-fledged Good Soul.

10 The activities of the adult of the species are familiar to us all. When you are ill, who is it that hastens to your bedside bearing molds of blancmange, which, from infancy, you have hated with unspeakable loathing? As usual, you are way ahead of me, gentle reader—it is indeed the Good Soul. It is the Good Souls who efficiently smooth out your pillow when you have just worked it into the comfortable shape, who creak about the room on noisy tiptoe, who tenderly lay on your fevered brow damp cloths which drip ceaselessly down your neck. It is they who ask, every other minute, if there isn't something that they can do for you. It is they who, at great personal sacrifice, spend long hours sitting beside your bed, reading aloud the continued stories in the *Woman's Home Companion,* or chatting cozily on the increase in the city's death rate.

11 In health, as in illness, they are always right there, ready to befriend you. No sooner do you sit down, than they exclaim that they can see you aren't comfortable in that chair, and insist on your changing places with them. It is the Good Souls who just *know* that you don't like your tea that way, and who bear it masterfully away from you to alter it with cream and sugar until it is a complete stranger to you. At the table, it is they who always feel that their grapefruit is better than yours and who have to be restrained almost forcibly from exchanging with you. In a restaurant the waiter invariably makes a mistake and brings them something which they did not order—and which they refuse to have changed, choking it down with a wistful smile. It is they who cause traffic blocks, by standing in subway entrances arguing altruistically as to who is to pay the fare.

12 At the theater, should they be members of a box-party, it is the Good Souls who insist on occupying the rear chairs; if the seats are in the orchestra, they worry audibly, all through the performance, about their being able to see better than you, until finally in desperation you grant their plea and change seats with them. If, by so doing, they can bring a little discomfort on themselves—sit in a draught, say, or behind a pillar—then their happiness is complete. To feel the genial glow of martyrdom—that is all they ask of life. . . .

13 The lives of Good Souls are crowded with Occasions, each with its own

ritual which must be solemnly followed. On Mother's Day, Good Souls conscientiously wear carnations; on St. Patrick's Day, they faithfully don boutonnieres of shamrocks; on Columbus Day, they carefully pin on miniature Italian flags. Every feast must be celebrated by the sending out of cards—Valentine's Day, Arbor [Day], Groundhog Day, and all the other important festivals, each is duly observed. They have a perfect genius for discovering appropriate cards of greeting for the event. It must take hours of research.

14   If it's too long a time between holidays, then the Good Soul will send little cards or little mementoes, just by way of surprises. He is strong on surprises, anyway. It delights him to drop in unexpectedly on his friends. Who has not known the joy of those evenings when some Good Soul just runs in, as a surprise? It is particularly effective when a chosen company of other guests happens to be present—enough for two tables of bridge, say. This means that the Good Soul must sit wistfully by, patiently watching the progress of the rubber, or else must cut in at intervals, volubly voicing his desolation at causing so much inconvenience, and apologizing constantly during the evening.

15   His conversation, admirable though it is, never receives its just due of attention and appreciation. He is one of those who believe and frequently quote the exemplary precept that there is good in everybody; hanging in his bed-chamber is the whimsically phrased, yet vital, statement, done in burned leather—"There is so much good in the worst of us and so much bad in the best of us that it hardly behooves any of us to talk about the rest of us." This, too, he archly quotes on appropriate occasions. Two or three may be gathered together, intimately discussing some mutual acquaintance. It is just getting really absorbing, when comes the Good Soul, to utter his dutiful, "We mustn't judge harshly—after all, we must always remember that many times our own actions may be misconstrued." Somehow, after several of these little reminders, there seems to be a general waning of interest; the little gathering breaks up, inventing quaint excuses to get away and discuss the thing more fully, adding a few really good details, some place where the Good Soul will not follow. While the Good Soul pitifully ignorant of their evil purpose glows with the warmth of conscious virtue, and settles himself to read the Contributors' Club, in the *Atlantic Monthly,* with a sense of duty well done. . . .

16   Good Souls are no mean humorists. They have a time-honored formula of fun-making, which must be faithfully followed. Certain words or phrases must be whimsically distorted every time they are used. "Over the river," they dutifully say, whenever they take their leave. "Don't you cast any asparagus on me," they warn, archly; and they never fail to speak of "three times in concus-sion." According to their ritual, these screaming phrases must be repeated several times, for the most telling effect, and are invariably followed by hearty laughter from the speaker, to whom they seem eternally new.

17   Perhaps the most congenial role of the Good Soul is that of advice-giver. He loves to take people aside and have serious little personal talks, all for their own good. He thinks it only right to point out faults or bad habits which are,

perhaps unconsciously, growing on them. He goes home and laboriously writes long, intricate letters, invariably beginning, "Although you may feel that this is no affair of mine, I think that you really ought to know," and so on, indefinitely. In his desire to help, he reminds one irresistibly of Marcelline, who used to try so pathetically and so fruitlessly to be of some assistance in arranging the circus arena, and who brought such misfortunes on his own innocent person thereby.

18   The Good Souls will, doubtless, gain their reward in Heaven; on this earth, certainly, theirs is what is technically known as a rough deal. The most hideous outrages are perpetrated on them. "Oh, he won't mind," people say, "He's a Good Soul." And then they proceed to heap the rankest impositions upon him. When Good Souls give a party, people who have accepted weeks in advance call up at the last second and refuse, without the shadow of an excuse save that of a subsequent engagement. Other people are invited to all sorts of entertaining affairs; the Good Soul, unasked, waves them a cheery good-bye and hopes wistfully that they will have a good time. His is the uncomfortable seat in the motor; he is the one to ride backwards in the train; he is the one who is always chosen to solicit subscriptions and make up deficits. People borrow his money, steal his servants, lose his golf balls, use him as a sort of errand boy, leave him flat whenever something more attractive offers—and carry it all off with their cheerful slogan, "Oh, he won't mind—he's a Good Soul."

19   And that's just it—Good Souls never do mind. After each fresh atrocity they are more cheerful, forgiving and virtuous, if possible, than they were before. There is simply no keeping them down—back they come, with their little gifts, and their little words of advice, and their little endeavors to be of service, always anxious for more.

20   Yes, there can be no doubt about it—their reward will come to them in the next world.

21   Would that they were even now enjoying it!

Considering Ideas

1. Make a list of five or more of the characteristics of Good Souls mentioned in the essay.
2. What do you think Parker's attitude toward Good Souls is? Would she like to have one for a friend? How do you know?
3. Do you think most people share Parker's view? Explain.
4. One of the differences between comedy and satire is that comedy seeks only to amuse, but satire seeks to arouse the reader's contempt for its subject. Would you say that "Good Souls" is a form of comedy or satire? Explain.
5. "Good Souls" includes references common in 1919, when it was written—references like *Woman's Home Companion* in paragraph 10 and "box-party" in paragraph 12. Do such references hopelessly date the essay, or do you think the modern reader can still enjoy the piece? Explain.

Considering Technique

1. *Irony* is a contrast between what is said and what is meant. For example, in paragraph 4, Parker says, "It is heartrending to see him [the Good Soul] going cheerfully about. . . ." However, she really means the opposite, for she has no pity for the Good Soul. Cite two other examples of irony in the essay and explain what the irony contributes.
2. The introduction of the essay is paragraphs 1 through 3. What approach does Parker take to the introduction?
3. Paragraphs 3 and 21 are each a single sentence. What is the effect of these one-sentence paragraphs?
4. In general, in what order are Parker's details arranged? What are the clues to this order?
5. What approach does Parker take to the conclusion?
6. Consult a dictionary if you are unsure of the meanings of any of these words: *congenital* (paragraph 2), *pariahs* (paragraph 2), *perfunctory* (paragraph 4), *approbation* (paragraph 4), *stigma* (paragraph 6), *throw-backs* (paragraph 6), *indigent* (paragraph 6), *repertory* (paragraph 7), *winsome* (paragraph 7), *blancmange* (paragraph 10), *wistful* (paragraph 11), *altruistically* (paragraph 11), *volubly* (paragraph 14), *precept* (paragraph 15), *behooves* (paragraph 15), *congenial* (paragraph 17).

For Group Consideration

Parker's essay was published in 1919. Do Good Souls, like the ones she describes, still exist today? If so, what do you think causes them to act the way they do? What effect do they have on people?

Journal Entry

Are you a Good Soul or a "regular human being"? (See paragraph 1). Provide evidence of your own behavior to support your evaluation.

Essay Assignments

1. Today, we might call the Good Soul a "nerd." Write a definition of *nerd,* using satire and irony if you care to.
2. Write a definition of some unpleasant "type" (for example, the practical joker, the heartbreaker, the sports nut, the workaholic, the overachiever, the wimp, or the health nut). Use satire and irony, if you like.
3. In paragraph 1, Parker contrasts Good Souls with "regular human beings." Write a definition of *regular human beings.*

Considering Thematic Issues

1. Explain why you think Good Souls behave as they do. Explore possible internal motivation (their needs, their goals, their insecurities, and so on) and possible external motivation (social pressures, family practice, and so on). Then go on to discuss the way people react to Good Souls and why they react in that way. (The preceding group activity may give you some ideas.)
2. Read "White Lies" (page 313) and tell to what extent Good Souls tell white lies and to what extent they engage in other forms of dishonesty.

I WANT A WIFE
Judy Brady

◆

Freelance writer, feminist, and political activist Judy Brady published "I Want a Wife" in Ms. *in 1972, and it quickly became a classic of feminist literature. In the essay, Brady informs the reader of the servile nature of the traditional wifely role, and she works to persuade the reader of the fundamental injustice of that role. As you read, decide how much of what the author says is still true today.*

◆

1   I belong to that classification of people known as wives. I am A Wife. And, not altogether incidentally, I am a mother.

2   Not too long ago a male friend appeared on the scene from the Midwest fresh from a recent divorce. He had one child, who is, of course, with his ex-wife. He is obviously looking for another wife. As I thought about him while I was ironing one evening, it suddenly occurred to me that I, too, would like to have a wife. Why do I want a wife?

3   I would like to go back to school so that I can become economically independent, support myself, and, if need be, support those dependent upon me. I want a wife who will work and send me to school. And while I am going to school I want a wife to take care of my children. I want a wife to keep track of the children's doctor and dentist appointments. And to keep track of mine, too. I want a wife to make sure my children eat properly and are kept clean. I want a wife who will wash the children's clothes and keep them mended. I want a wife who is a good nurturant attendant to my children, arranges for their schooling, makes sure that they have an adequate social life with their peers, takes them to the park, the zoo, etc. I want a wife who takes care of the children when they are sick, a wife who arranges to be around when the children need special care, because, of course, I cannot miss classes at school. My wife must arrange to lose time at work and not lose the job. It may mean a small cut in my wife's income from time to time, but I guess I can tolerate that. Needless to say, my wife will arrange and pay for the care of the children while my wife is working.

4   I want a wife who will take care of *my* physical needs. I want a wife who will keep my house clean. A wife who will pick up after my children, a wife who will pick up after me. I want a wife who will keep my clothes clean, ironed, mended, replaced when need be, and who will see to it that my personal things are kept in their proper place so that I can find what I need the minute I need it. I want a wife who cooks the meals, a wife who is a *good* cook. I want a wife who will plan the menus, do the necessary grocery shopping, prepare the meals, serve them pleasantly, and then do the cleaning up while I do my studying. I want a wife who will care for me when I am sick and sympathize with my pain and loss of time from school. I want a wife to go along

when our family takes a vacation so that someone can continue to care for me and my children when I need a rest and a change of scene.

5   I want a wife who will not bother me with rambling complaints about a wife's duties. But I want a wife who will listen to me when I feel the need to explain a rather difficult point I have come across in my course of studies. And I want a wife who will type my papers for me when I have written them.

6   I want a wife who will take care of the details of my social life. When my wife and I are invited out by my friends, I want a wife who will take care of the babysitting arrangements. When I meet people at school that I like and want to entertain, I want a wife who will have the house clean, will prepare a special meal, serve it to me and my friends, and not interrupt when I talk about the things that interest me and my friends. I want a wife who will have arranged that the children are fed and ready for bed before my guests arrive so that the children do not bother us. I want a wife who takes care of the needs of my guests so that they feel comfortable, who makes sure that they have an ashtray, that they are passed the hors d'oeuvres, that they are offered a second helping of the food, that their wine glasses are replenished when necessary, that their coffee is served to them as they like it. And I want a wife who knows that sometimes I need a night out by myself.

7   I want a wife who is sensitive to my sexual needs, a wife who makes love passionately and eagerly when I feel like it, a wife who makes sure that I am satisfied. And, of course, I want a wife who will not demand sexual attention when I am not in the mood for it. I want a wife who assumes the complete responsibility for birth control, because I do not want more children. I want a wife who will remain sexually faithful to me so that I do not have to clutter up my intellectual life with jealousies. And I want a wife who understands that *my* sexual needs may entail more than strict adherence to monogamy. I must, after all, be able to relate to people as fully as possible.

8   If, by chance, I find another person more suitable as a wife than the wife I already have, I want the liberty to replace my present wife with another one. Naturally, I will expect a fresh, new life; my wife will take the children and be solely responsible for them so that I am left free.

9   When I am through with school and have acquired a job, I want my wife to quit working and remain at home so that my wife can more fully and completely take care of a wife's duties.

10   My God, who *wouldn't* want a wife?

Considering Ideas

1. What is Brady's attitude toward the wifely role she depicts in the essay?
2. What view of men does Brady present in her essay? Do you think she is being fair to men? Explain.
3. Why does Brady say she wants a wife? Do you think there is more to it than what she says? Explain.

4. What kind of woman would enjoy being the wife Brady describes?
5. Is "I Want a Wife" as pertinent today as it was when it was first published in 1972? Explain.

Considering Technique

1. Paragraphs 1 and 2 form the introduction of "I Want a Wife." What approach does Brady take to that introduction?
2. In your own words, write out the thesis of "I Want a Wife."
3. Brady frequently repeats the words "I want." What does this repetition contribute?
4. Brady uses classification-division to help develop her definition. (Classification-division, discussed in Chapter 10, sorts items into categories.) What categories does Brady establish for the wife's duties?
5. A *rhetorical question* is one for which no answer is expected. Brady closes "I Want a Wife" with a rhetorical question. Do you think this creates an effective conclusion? Explain.
6. Consult a dictionary if you are unsure of the meaning of any of these words: *nurturant* (paragraph 3), *hors d'oeuvres* (paragraph 6), *entail* (paragraph 7), *monogamy* (paragraph 7).

For Group Consideration

"I Want a Wife" originally appeared in *Ms.* in 1972. If the essay were to be published today, in what magazines do you think it could appropriately appear? Develop a list with two or three classmates, and explain why you have chosen the magazines on your list.

Journal Entry

Write a description of your ideal spouse. To what extent does your description conform to the stereotype of the ideal wife or husband?

Essay Assignments

1. Write an essay entitled "I Want a _____." Fill in the blank with some family role (husband, child, older brother, younger sister, mother, father, grandmother, grandfather, and so on.) Define the role and point out its difficulty and/or unfairness. If you like, you can borrow Brady's technique and repeat the words "I want a _____ who."
2. Write an essay that defines what you think the role of *wife* should be. As an alternative, define what you think the role of *husband* should be.

3. Write a definition of one of the roles you currently play or have played in the past: wife, husband, mother, father, child, friend, soldier, student, track star, musician, younger brother, older sister, student athlete, nontraditional student, international student, coach, and so on. Like Brady, let your definition convey how you feel about the role.

4. Define the role of someone who has traditionally been exploited: a table server, a nurse, a babysitter, a cleaning person, and so on.

Considering Thematic Issues

1. Brady presents the stereotype of the ideal wife, as it existed in 1972. What is the current stereotype of the ideal wife or husband? Describe that stereotype and explain what factors are responsible for that stereotype (television, movies, the women's movement, advertisements, and so on).

2. Drawing on the information in "I Want a Wife," "My Mother Never Worked" (page 93) and "What I've Learned from Men" (page 153), describe the traditional view of women. Then, using women you know as examples, explain to what extent women today conform to and/or depart from the view.

THE VIEW FROM 80
Malcolm Cowley

Malcolm Cowley (1898–1989) was a literary historian, critic, and poet. In 1929, he became the associate editor of the New Republic. In "The View from 80," Cowley blends description, pointed examples, cause-and-effect analysis, and narration to define old age and thereby inform the reader of what it is really like to be old. As he tells of his journey to "the country of age," the author also shares the joy and the sadness of this stage of life. As you read, decide how Cowley feels about being old.

◆

1   They gave me a party on my 80th birthday in August 1978. First there were cards, letters, telegrams, even a cable of congratulation or condolence; then there were gifts, mostly bottles; there was catered food and finally a big cake with, for some reason, two candles (had I gone back to very early childhood?). I blew the candles out a little unsteadily. Amid the applause and clatter I thought about a former custom of the Northern Ojibwas when they lived on the shores of Lake Winnipeg. They were kind to their old people, who remembered and enforced the ancient customs of the tribe, but when an old person became decrepit, it was time for him to go. Sometimes he was simply abandoned, with a little food, on an island in the lake. If he deserved special honor, they held a tribal feast for him. The old man sang a death song and danced, if he could. While he was still singing, his son came from behind and brained him with a tomahawk.

2   That was quick, it was dignified, and I wonder whether it was any more cruel, essentially, than some of our civilized customs or inadvertencies in disposing of the aged. I believe in rites and ceremonies. I believe in big parties for special occasions such as an 80th birthday. It was a sort of belated bar mitzvah, since the 80-year-old, like a Jewish adolescent, is entering a new stage of life; let him (or her) undergo a *rite de passage,* with toasts and a cantor. Seventy-year-olds, or septuas, have the illusion of being middle-aged, even if they have been pushed back on a shelf. The 80-year-old, the octo, looks at the double-dumpling figure and admits that he is old. The last act has begun, and it will be the test of the play.

3   To enter the country of age is a new experience, different from what you supposed it to be. Nobody, man or woman, knows the country until he has lived in it and has taken out his citizenship papers. Here is my own report, submitted as a road map and guide to some of the principal monuments.

4   The new octogenarian feels as strong as ever when he is sitting back in a comfortable chair. He ruminates, he dreams, he remembers. He doesn't want to be disturbed by others. It seems to him that old age is only a costume assumed for those others; the true, the essential self is ageless. In a moment he will rise

and go for a ramble in the woods, taking a gun along, or a fishing rod, if it is spring. Then he creaks to his feet, bending forward to keep his balance, and realizes that he will do nothing of the sort. The body and its surroundings have their messages for him, or only one message: "You are old." Here are some of the occasions on which he receives the message:

- when it becomes an achievement to do thoughtfully, step by step, what he once did instinctively
- when his bones ache
- when there are more and more little bottles in the medicine cabinet, with instructions for taking four times a day
- when he fumbles and drops his toothbrush (butterfingers)
- when his face has bumps and wrinkles, so that he cuts himself while shaving (blood on the towel)
- when year by year his feet seem farther from his hands
- when he can't stand on one leg and has trouble pulling on his pants
- when he hesitates on the landing before walking down a flight of stairs
- when he spends more time looking for things misplaced than he spends using them after he (or more often his wife) has found them
- when he falls asleep in the afternoon
- when it becomes harder to bear in mind two things at once
- when a pretty girl passes him in the street and he doesn't turn his head
- when he forgets names, even of people he saw last month ("Now I'm beginning to forget nouns," the poet Conrad Aiken said at 80)
- when he listens hard to jokes and catches everything but the snapper
- when he decides not to drive at night anymore
- when everything takes longer to do—bathing, shaving, getting dressed or undressed—but when time passes quickly, as if he were gathering speed while coasting downhill. The year from 79 to 80 is like a week when he was a boy.

5   Those are some of the intimate messages. "Put cotton in your ears and pebbles in your shoes," said a gerontologist, a member of that new profession dedicated to alleviating all maladies of old people except the passage of years. "Pull on rubber gloves. Smear Vaseline over your glasses, and there you have it: instant aging." Not quite. His formula omits the messages from the social world, which are louder, in most cases, than those from within. We start by growing old in other people's eyes, then slowly we come to share their judgment.

6   I remember a morning many years ago when I was backing out of the parking lot near the railroad station in Brewster, New York. There was a near collision. The driver of the other car jumped out and started to abuse me; he had his fists ready. Then he looked hard at me and said, "Why, you're an old man." He got back into his car, slammed the door, and drove away, while I stood there fuming. "I'm only 65," I thought. "He wasn't driving carefully. I can still take care of myself in a car, or in a fight, for that matter."

7   My hair was whiter—it may have been in 1974—when a young woman rose and offered me a seat in a Madison Avenue bus. That message was kind and also devastating. "Can't I even stand up?" I thought as I thanked her and declined the seat. But the same thing happened twice the following year, and the second time I gratefully accepted the offer, though with a sense of having diminished myself. "People are right about me," I thought while wondering why all those kind gestures were made by women. Do men now regard themselves as the weaker sex, not called upon to show consideration? All the same it was a relief to sit down and relax.

8   A few days later I wrote a poem, "The Red Wagon," that belongs in the record of aging:

For his birthday they gave him a red express wagon
with a driver's high seat and a handle that steered.
His mother pulled him around the yard.
"Giddyap," he said, but she laughed and went off
to wash the breakfast dishes.

"I wanta ride too," his sister said,
and he pulled her to the edge of a hill.
"Now, sister, go home and wait for me,
but first give a push to the wagon."
He climbed again to the high seat,
this time grasping that handle-that-steered.
The red wagon rolled slowly down the slope,
then faster as it passed the schoolhouse
and faster as it passed the store,
the road still dropping away.
Oh, it was fun.

But would it ever stop?
Would the road always go downhill?

The red wagon rolled faster.
Now it was in strange country.
It passed a white house he must have dreamed about,
deep woods he had never seen,
a graveyard where, something told him, his sister
was buried.

Far below
the sun was sinking into a broad plain.

The red wagon rolled faster.
Now he was clutching the seat, not even trying to steer.
Sweat clouded his heavy spectacles.
His white hair streamed in the wind.

9   Even before he or she is 80, the aging person may undergo another identity crisis like that of adolescence. Perhaps there had also been a middle-aged crisis, the male or the female menopause, but the rest of adult life he had

taken himself for granted, with his capabilities and failings. Now, when he looks in the mirror, he asks himself, "Is this really me?"—or he avoids the mirror out of distress at what it reveals, those bags and wrinkles. In his new makeup he is called upon to play a new role in a play that must be improvised. André Gide, that longlived man of letters, wrote in his journal, "My heart has remained so young that I have the continual feeling of playing a part, the part of the 70-year-old that I certainly am; and the infirmities and weaknesses that remind me of my age act like a prompter, reminding me of my lines when I tend to stray. Then, like the good actor I want to be, I go back into my role, and I pride myself on playing it well."

10   In his new role the old person will find that he is tempted by new vices, that he receives new compensations (not so widely known), and that he may possibly achieve new virtues. Chief among these is the heroic or merely obstinate refusal to surrender in the face of time. One admires the ships that go down with all flags flying and the captain on the bridge.

11   Among the vices of age are avarice, untidiness, and vanity, which last takes the form of a craving to be loved or simply admired. Avarice is the worst of those three. Why do so many old persons, men and women alike, insist on hoarding money when they have no prospect of using it and even when they have no heirs? They eat the cheapest food, buy no clothes, and live in a single room when they could afford better lodging. It may be that they regard money as a form of power; there is a comfort in watching it accumulate while other powers are dwindling away. How often we read of an old person found dead in a hovel, on a mattress partly stuffed with bankbooks and stock certificates! The bankbook syndrome, we call it in our family, which has never succumbed.

12   Untidiness we call the Langley Collyer syndrome. To explain, Langley Collyer was a former concert pianist who lived alone with his 70-year-old brother in a brownstone house on upper Fifth Avenue. The once fashionable neighborhood had become part of Harlem. Homer, the brother, had been an admiralty lawyer, but was now blind and partly paralyzed; Langley played for him and fed him on buns and oranges, which he thought would restore Homer's sight. He never threw away a daily paper because Homer, he said, might want to read them all. He saved other things as well and the house became filled with rubbish from roof to basement. The halls were lined on both sides with bundled newspapers, leaving narrow passageways in which Langley had devised booby traps to catch intruders.

13   On March 21, 1947, some unnamed person telephoned the police to report that there was a dead body in the Collyer house. The police broke down the front door and found the hall impassable; then they hoisted a ladder to a second-story window. Behind it Homer was lying on the floor in a bathrobe; he had starved to death. Langley had disappeared. After some delay, the police broke into the basement, chopped a hole in the roof, and began throwing junk out of the house, top and bottom. It was 18 days before they found Langley's body, gnawed by rats. Caught in one of his own booby traps, he had died in a

hallway just outside Homer's door. By that time the police had collected, and the Department of Sanitation had hauled away, 120 tons of rubbish, including, besides the newspapers, 14 grand pianos and the parts of a dismantled Model T Ford.

14   Why do so many old people accumulate junk, not on the scale of Langley Collyer, but still in a dismaying fashion? Their tables are piled high with it, their bureau drawers are stuffed with it, their closet rods bend with the weight of clothes not worn for years. I suppose that the piling up is partly from lethargy and partly from feeling that everything once useful, including their own bodies, should be preserved. Others, though not so many, have such a fear of becoming Langley Collyers that they strive to be painfully neat. Every tool they own is in its place, though it will never be used again; every scrap of paper is filed away in alphabetical order. At last their immoderate neatness becomes another vice of age, if a milder one.

15   The vanity of older people is an easier weakness to explain, and to condone. With less to look forward to, they yearn for recognition of what they have been: the reigning beauty, the athlete, the soldier, the scholar. It is the beauties who have the hardest time. A portrait of themselves at twenty hangs on the wall, and they try to resemble it by making an extravagant use of creams, powders, and dyes. Being young at heart, they think they are merely revealing their essential persons. The athletes find shelves for their silver trophies, which are polished once a year. Perhaps a letter sweater lies wrapped in a bureau drawer. I remember one evening when a no-longer athlete had guests for dinner and tried to find his sweater. "Oh, that old thing," his wife said. "The moths got into it and I threw it away." The athlete sulked and his guests went home early.

16   But there are also pleasures of the body, or the mind, that are enjoyed by a greater number of older persons. Those pleasures include some that younger people find hard to appreciate. One of them is simply sitting still, like a snake on a sun-warmed stone, with a delicious feeling of indolence that was seldom attained in earlier years. A leaf flutters down; a cloud moves by inches across the horizon. At such moments the older person, completely relaxed, has become a part of nature—and a living part, with blood coursing through his veins. The future does not exist for him. He thinks, if he thinks at all, that life for younger persons is still a battle royal of each against each, but that now he has nothing more to win or lose. He is not so much above as outside the battle, as if he had assumed the uniform of some small neutral country, perhaps Liechtenstein or Andorra. From a distance he notes that some of the combatants, men or women, are jostling ahead—but why do they fight so hard when the most they can hope for is a longer obituary? He can watch the scrounging and gouging, he can hear the shouts of exultation, the moans of the gravely wounded, and meanwhile he feels secure; nobody will attack him from ambush.

17   Age has other physical compensations besides the nirvana of dozing in

the sun. A few of the simplest needs become a pleasure to satisfy. When an old woman in a nursing home was asked what she really liked to do, she answered in one word: "Eat." She might have been speaking for many of her fellows. Meals in a nursing home, however badly cooked, serve as climactic moments of the day. The physical essence of the pensioners is being renewed at an appointed hour; now they can go back to meditating or to watching TV while looking forward to the next meal. They can also look forward to sleep, which has become a definite pleasure, not the mere interruption it once had been.

18   Here I am thinking of old persons under nursing care. Others ferociously guard their independence, and some of them suffer less than one might expect from being lonely and impoverished. They can be rejoiced by visits and meetings, but they also have company inside their heads. Some of them are busiest when their hands are still. What passes through the minds of many is a stream of persons, images, phrases, and familiar tunes. For some that stream has continued since childhood, but now it is deeper; it is their present and their past combined. At times they conduct silent dialogues with a vanished friend, and these are less tiring—often more rewarding—than spoken conversations. If inner resources are lacking, old persons living alone may seek comfort and a kind of companionship in the bottle. I should judge from the gossip of various neighborhoods that the outer suburbs from Boston to San Diego are full of secretly alcoholic widows. One of these widows, an old friend, was moved from her apartment into a retirement home. She left behind her a closet in which the floor was covered wall to wall with whiskey bottles. "Oh, those empty bottles!" she explained. "They were left by a former tenant!"

19   Not whiskey or cooking sherry but simply giving up is the greatest temptation of age. It is something different from a stoical acceptance of infirmities, which is something to be admired.

20   The givers-up see no reason for working. Sometimes they lie in bed all day when moving about would still be possible, if difficult. I had a friend, a distinguished poet, who surrendered in that fashion. The doctors tried to stir him to action, but he refused to leave his room. Another friend, once a successful artist, stopped painting when his eyes began to fail. His doctor made the mistake of telling him that he suffered from a fatal disease. He then lost interest in everything except the splendid Rolls-Royce, acquired in his prosperous days, that stood in the garage. Daily he wiped the dust from its hood. He couldn't drive it on the road any longer, but he used to sit in the driver's seat, start the motor, then back the Rolls out of the garage and drive it in again, back twenty feet and forward twenty feet; that was his only distraction.

21   I haven't the right to blame those who surrender, not being able to put myself inside their minds or bodies. Often they must have compelling reasons, physical or moral. Not only do they suffer from a variety of ailments, but also they are made to feel that they no longer have a function in the community. Their families and neighbors don't ask them for advice, don't really listen when

they speak, don't call on them for efforts. One notes that there are not a few recoveries from apparent senility when that situation changes. If it doesn't change, old persons may decide that efforts are useless. I sympathize with their problems, but the men and women I envy are those who accept old age as a series of challenges.

22   For such persons, every new infirmity is an enemy to be outwitted, an obstacle to be overcome by force of will. They enjoy each little victory over themselves, and sometimes they win a major success. Renoir was one of them. He continued painting, and magnificently, for years after he was crippled by arthritis; the brush had to be strapped to his arm. "You don't need your hand to paint," he said. Goya was another of the unvanquished. At 72 he retired as an official painter of the Spanish court and decided to work only for himself. His later years were those of the famous "black paintings" in which he let his imagination run (and also of the lithographs, then a new technique). At 78 he escaped a reign of terror in Spain by fleeing to Bordeaux. He was deaf and his eyes were failing; in order to work he had to wear several pairs of spectacles, one over another, and then use a magnifying glass; but he was producing splendid work in a totally new style. At 80 he drew an ancient man propped on two sticks, with a mass of white hair and beard hiding his face and with the inscription "I am still learning."

23   "Eighty years old!" the great Catholic poet Paul Claudel wrote in his journal. "No eyes left, no ears, no teeth, no legs, no wind! And when all is said and done, how astonishingly well one does without them!"

Considering Ideas

1. How would you describe Cowley's attitude toward old age and the elderly? Overall, would you say that his attitude toward old age is positive or negative? Explain.
2. Why does Cowley tell about the Ojibwa's customs for dealing with their aged (see paragraph 1)? Does he find the customs cruel, or does he think they have something to recommend them? Explain.
3. According to Cowley, what are some of the positive characteristics of being old? What are the negative characteristics?
4. In literature, a *symbol* is a situation, character, or thing that stands for something else. In Cowley's poem "The Red Wagon," what do you think the red wagon symbolizes? What is the strange country that the wagon rolls through? Why does the wagon roll faster and faster?
5. According to Cowley, what causes each of the vices of old age: avarice, untidiness, and vanity?
6. According to Cowley, why do some of the elderly just give up? Do you blame these people for not trying any longer? Explain.

Considering Technique

1. Where in the essay does Cowley present his thesis?
2. Cowley often uses a descriptive comparison called a *metaphor* (see page 45). For example, in paragraph 3, old age is compared to a country, and in the poem in paragraph 8, time is described as a red express wagon. Mention two other descriptive metaphors that are part of the definition. What purpose do these metaphors serve?
3. Cowley uses a considerable number of examples as part of his definition. Cite three paragraphs that include examples, and explain what the examples contribute to the definition.
4. Cause-and-effect analysis explains the causes and/or effects of something (see Chapter 9 for a full discussion). What elements of cause-and-effect analysis appear in paragraphs 11 through 15? In paragraphs 20 and 21?
5. Narration is storytelling (see Chapter 5 for a full discussion). What is the purpose of the narration in paragraphs 12 and 13?
6. In paragraph 4, Cowley includes a lengthy list of the evidence of old age. Do you think listing is a suitable technique here?
7. Consult a dictionary if you are unsure of the meaning of any of these words: *Ojibwas* (paragraph 1), *decrepit* (paragraph 1), *inadvertencies* (paragraph 2), *rite de passage* (paragraph 2), *cantor* (paragraph 2), *ruminates* (paragraph 4), *gerontologist* (paragraph 5), *hovel* (paragraph 11), *lethargy* (paragraph 14), *condone* (paragraph 15), *indolence* (paragraph 16), *nirvana* (paragraph 17), *stoical* (paragraph 1), *unvanquished* (paragraph 22), *lithographs* (paragraph 22).

For Group Consideration

With two or three classmates, answer these questions:

1. How do we treat the elderly in this country?
2. Is our treatment of the elderly more or less dignified and cruel than the practices of the Ojibwas mentioned in paragraph 1?

Journal Entry

What do you think old age will be like for you? Are there aspects you dread? Are there aspects you look forward to? Have any of your feelings been influenced by Cowley's essay?

Essay Assignments

1. Write an essay called "The View from _____ " (fill in the blank with your age). Using definition and any other patterns you wish, explain what it

is like to be your age. If you like, you may include a list, as Cowley does in paragraph 4.

2. In paragraph 9, Cowley refers to identity crises and mentions that a person may have one during adolescence, one during middle age, and one during old age. If you have ever had an identity crisis, write a definition of this phenomenon and explain the causes and/or effects of the crisis.

3. Cowley explains that three of the vices of old age are avarice, untidiness, and vanity. Write a definition of one of these vices. If you like, use examples and/ or narration to illustrate your points. Also, try to explain the causes and/or effects of the vice.

4. If you are familiar with old age as a result of spending time with an elderly friend, relative, or neighbor, write your own definition of *old age*.

Considering Thematic Issues

1. At what point do you think you will be old? Answer that question and go on to explain in detail what you think old age will be like for you. Consider such things as your health, social life, activities, place of residence, or anything else you think is pertinent. If you already consider yourself old, compare and contrast the reality of your old age with what you thought it would be like. As an alternative, describe the vices of adolescence the way Cowley describes the vices of old age (beginning in paragraph 11).

2. Using the information in "The View from 80," "The Endless Streetcar Ride into the Night" (page 98), and "Complexion" (page 295), along with your own experience and observation, compare and/or contrast the joys and difficulties of adolescence and old age. (Comparison-contrast is discussed in Chapter 8.)

LISTS
Jeanine Larmoth

◆

Are you a list maker? If so, the following essay, from Town and Country *(Nov. 1989), may give you a fresh view of those lists you make. Even if you are not a list maker, you will probably enjoy "Lists" because it entertains at the same time it shares something of the role lists play in the author's life. As you read, notice what a skillful wordsmith Jeanine Larmoth is.*

◆

1   My mother's way of reviewing a movie, in the days when we often went, was simple. If she found she was going over her lists in her head while Gable nibbled on Colbert's ear, the movie was poor. A good movie could make you forget even your lists.

2   Oh, the pleasure of lists, endless, ongoing lists. Lists of things that must be done, places to go, people to see, wines to try, courses to take, plays to applaud, restaurants to avoid, hotels to discover, books to read on a desert island. Shopping lists, laundry lists, Christmas card lists, lists of resolutions, lists scratched on the back of old envelopes, lists scrawled on a chalkboard in the kitchen. Lists no bigger than a postage stamp, stuck in a wallet. Lists like a friend of mine's, which unroll from his pocket like the Dead Sea Scrolls. Lists of lists.

3   Lists offer a wonderful way to confine the nearly insuperable demands of the chaotic, freewheeling world to the possible, of turning abstracts into specifics, cutting experience into bite sizes. I can do it. Only three more to go. With every scoring of the pen, a sense of achievement. Like Ariadne's thread, lists unwind to show us the way out of the maze of everyday life. They are maps of the earthworks of ennui—the duties, responsibilities, appointments and chores so ready to suffocate us in the mundane. Lists are a strategy, a declaration of intent to overtake rather than be overtaken; to clump and conquer. They even make it possible to go to the dentist in a neat, orderly fashion, as if it were a reasonable thing to do. Something more to be crossed off. Another triumph.

4   The danger, of course, is that, like many other laborsaving devices, the lists may enslave the list maker. The mob of waiting exigencies is kept at bay, to be sure, but suddenly a small scrap of paper, not the things to be done, becomes the despot. You're so busy checking your list, you don't notice life going by on the streets outside the bus or train window. Rather than enjoying the view from the Bridge of Sighs, what's more important is ticking it off the list of sights. The mere pleasure of going down the list, eliminating things done, becomes more rewarding than doing even agreeable things. Instead of leading you out of the maze, the thread is actually entangling your feet.

5   The best way around a list is to lose it; or drop it in a puddle, splatter it with olive oil or glob it with butter (because you're going over it during lunch),

and thus have to toss it away; to use it, when no other scrap of paper is handy, to mash a threatening mosquito on the bedroom wall; or just to throw the still-current one out under the delusion that it's an old, superseded list.

6   Somewhat craftier ways to avoid a list are to mislay your glasses so you can't read it, leave it in another pocket or pocketbook, or just plain forget to look at it. Such omissions strike at the very heart of the problem, since forgetfulness is a great reason lists exist. The failure of memory, so frightening and frequent in these days of overloaded minds, is part of why you keep them (or so lists would have you believe). Often, however, what we're afraid of overlooking might *well* be overlooked.

7   Any assurance from the cocky non-list keeper (with a knowing wink at Freud) that we will remember only what we want to remember causes the list keeper to pause briefly, like a startled hare, then go on scribbling. The true list maker is well aware that knowing what one wants is a matter of such complexity that quite a few people spend a lifetime pondering it without arriving at clear-cut answers. Such an assurance teeters on the twin fallacies that we know what we want, from moment to moment, and that we can act on this knowledge—when, in fact, we will forget the ice cream but remember the toothpaste, buy a special birthday card for a dear friend a year in advance, and then forget to send it in time for the actual birth date.

8   But, generally, lists are indestructible. You're more likely to let a dollar bill fall in the gutter than a list, spill drops of olive oil on a silk skirt or linen trousers, throw away a divine love letter, let travelers' checks go through the wash, mash the mosquito with a long-awaited rare book just received from the bookseller. The list will keep on being there, insisting, like the mosquito—missed—on the bedroom wall after you've turned out the light and are trying to suffocate yourself beneath the sheet (by God, he won't get you alive!).

9   In their tenacity, lists are like one of my favorites from the symbol-making days of childhood: the toy with a weighted bottom. Made of papier-mâché and standing about a foot high, the toy was introduced to me as a London bobby. Properly pear-shaped, he had a blue uniform, black belt and black helmet, rather prominent eyes and a bushy black mustache. As with all such toys whose mission is to give early lessons in frustration, he had the rebounding power of a rubber ball, and bounced back up with an irritatingly cheerful jingle. I disliked the toy intensely, as I was surely meant to do, and probably tried a variety of strategies to get him down, once and for all: sneaking up behind him, and then alternating a slow shove and a fast push, for example. Useless. He is still going strong.

10   Even were one to forgo the tyranny of a personal list, lists are like an ever-encroaching dragnet. There are lists of best-dressed men and women, worst-dressed men and women, lists of bestsellers, leading stocks, the richest men in America, the most wanted criminals in America, the world's endangered species, the wonders of the ancient world, world's records. Real estate pages are lists, as are want ads. Television guides are lists. The Academy Award ceremo-

nies televised every spring are nothing but illustrated lists; the running of the Kentucky Derby, a list in motion.

11   Whole industries have sprung up around lists. To jolly up the lists covering the refrigerator door, there are the cunning magnets shaped like lollipops, daisies, teddy bears in paper bags. 3M cleverly sells small pads of stick-'em-backed bits of yellow paper so that lists may be scattered with the profligacy of autumn leaves—everywhere, at all times and for all reasons. They might be called notes, but add them together and they are lists. What do computers do, basically, but make lists, lists that talk to lists, lists that answer lists with lists of their own?

12   From time to time, as well, attempts have been made to formulate ready-made lists to cash in on the compulsion. I once discovered a chic set of back-to-back lists, one simply headed "Town" and the other "Country," useful for those whose real reason for having a weekend house is to carry things back and forth. The laundry lists that are found in hotel rooms must be fairly satisfactory, since they are supplied as customarily as little soaps, shampoos and bath hats. Room-service order lists, on the other hand, hint at one reason ready-made lists never quite make it. The blank space on the order for special instructions doesn't stay blank. Not with me, in any case. Take ordering breakfast in Italy: a relatively straightforward procedure, it would seem. The choices could hardly be simpler: type of fruit juice, way the coffee should be prepared, time the breakfast should be brought. The pastry goes without saying, unless there's a blank. If there is, I jot down my preference for plain Italian bread rolls, not the Italian, sweet-doughed variations on a French theme. If there's not, room service has to be called. It would be simpler to call in the first place.

13   Occasionally, someone comes out with a ready-made shopping list for groceries. All well and good for the eggs-milk-butter-and-bread person. But then, hardly necessary, since the stops for such persons would be automatic. For people who need grocery lists, what should be on them are the items not regularly stocked in the kitchen and liable to be overlooked in the store: the anchovy paste in a tube that's half hidden by tins of salmon, the artichoke hearts that are kept on a shelf well above eye level. Yet no printed list that aspired to be shorter than my friend's scrolls could include all the possibilities. Grocery stores would have to provide rest stops where people could consult their lists and chart their next moves.

14   Undoubtedly, the theory behind ready-made lists is that people will be enormously relieved only to have to check the appropriate boxes. Not a bit of it. Lists, at the simplest level, give us an opportunity to use one of our first real skills: writing. Few of us, even those with indifferent-to-illegible handwriting, are immune to a childlike sense of satisfaction at seeing black ink impress white paper. More important, the composition of the list—headings, subheadings, order in which the must-do's appear, underlinings, exclamation points, asterisks, different colored inks—is part of the art. It requires a measure of clarity to compose a list, a sorting out of importances. There is even a sense that a well-

assembled list might almost take care of itself; that by recognizing what has to be done, you're partway to getting it done. In making the list, you have foreseen the problems that can arise, with the result that some items may seem ripe for immediate crossing off, others must be attacked at a run, and still others you may dozily decide to put off—which very often proves the best resolution of all.

15   Perhaps it's due to this dependence on composition that lists are often seen as a substitute for poetry or prose—with mixed results. A public speaker, having gotten off the requisite, feeble joke, can launch immediately into lists— thus slips the hour away. I have listened, trying not to, more than once to a priest whose sermons are nothing but lists, lists of stirring adjectives, superbly modulated, resonantly recited, which give the effect of something having been said, when nothing has been. Books, too, may be largely compilations of lists and statistics—space-sopping, page-gnawing lists—lists that, like the priest's, convince the reader he is acquiring something of substance or, at the very least, additional material for lists of his own.

16   A reliance on lists is not, however, automatically a sign of intellectual poverty. Just as a telephone directory recited by a well-schooled actor is said to be riveting, so the list flowing from the pen of an artist is a splendid tool. Lists, such as those quoted from an anonymous recorder by Vita Sackville-West in the introduction to the diary of Lady Anne Clifford, pile up images that bring a scene to exotic life. Before our eyes, a harbor's rim expands, piled high with the revealing magnificence of plunder brought back from the Azores for Queen Elizabeth I.

17   As Sackville-West quotes the unidentified scribe, "They unladed and discharged about five millions of silver all in pieces of eight or ten pound great, so that the whole quay lay covered with plates and chests of sil-ver. . . . Elephants teeth, porcelain, vessels of china, coconuts, hides, ebon wood as black as jet, bedsteads of the same; cloth of the rinds of trees very strange for the matter and artificial in workmanship."

18   Sackville-West concludes: "All this and more was trundled out on to English quays, together with ropes, corn, bacon, copper, all in great store, Negroes, monkeys, and Spanish prisoners, dark seamen with silver rings in their ears, herded together, sullen and aloof."

19   Used to quite different purpose is a list of Montaigne's cataloging the polarities in his own soul. "All contradictions are to be found in me in some shape or manner," he wrote. "Bashful, insolent; chaste, lustful; talkative, tac-iturn; tough, delicate; ingenious, stupid; morose, affable; lying, truthful; learned, ignorant; and liberal, and miserly, and prodigal: I find all this in myself, more or less, as I turn myself about; and whoever studies himself very attentively finds in himself, yes, even in his judgment, this mutability and discord."

20   Though the ordinary list cannot aspire to these literary heights, it nonethe-less plays its part in the dream of eternity, for not only does a list control life, it prolongs it. However goaded by his lists the list maker is, he is comforted by the confidence that he can never die: his list isn't finished. There will always be

petunias that need planting, a letter-to-the-editor to be dashed off, the birdbath to be waterproofed, stamps to be bought, a friend who's not been telephoned for a while. In short, the list maker is just too busy—though thanks awfully for the invitation.

21   Delighted as I am by the prospect of poetic lists, or failing that, immortality, I am, however, convinced that the only way to approach the simplification of life and true freedom that lists delude us into supposing they promote is to destroy them.

22   Unfortunately, mine don't allow me a moment to figure out how.

Considering Ideas

1. According to Larmoth, what purpose do lists serve?
2. How is it that lists, meant to help the list maker, can actually enslave him or her?
3. According to Larmoth, what are the chief characteristics of lists?
4. Why does list making appeal to people?
5. Using the information in the essay for clues, explain what you think Larmoth's view of list making is. Is there a paragraph that best expresses that view? If so, which one?
6. How serious do you think Larmoth is in her essay?

Considering Technique

1. Larmoth's essay on lists often includes lists of its own. For example, paragraph 2 includes a list of different kinds of lists. Cite one other example of lists in the essay. What do you think these lists contribute?
2. Larmoth uses many examples in her essay. Cite two such examples. What do the examples contribute to the definition?
3. Part of the pleasure of reading "Lists" comes from Larmoth's specific word choice. For example, in paragraph 15, she refers to "space-sopping, page-gnawing lists." Cite two examples of phrases or sentences that appeal to you because of the specific word choice. (See page 44 on specific word choice.)
4. Which paragraph makes use of comparison to explain a characteristic? (Comparison, discussed in Chapter 8, notes similarities.) Which paragraphs make use of cause-and-effect analysis? (Cause-and-effect analysis, discussed in Chapter 9, notes the causes and/or effects of something.)
5. Paragraphs 21 and 22 form the conclusion of the essay. Do those paragraphs bring the essay to a satisfying close? Explain.
6. Consult a dictionary if you are unsure of the meaning of any of these words: *Dead Sea Scrolls* (paragraph 1), *insuperable* (paragraph 2), *scoring* (para-

graph 2), *Ariadne's Head* (paragraph 3), *earthworks* (paragraph 3), *ennui* (paragraph 3), *mundane* (paragraph 3), *exigencies* (paragraph 4), *Bridge of Sighs* (paragraph 4), *tenacity* (paragraph 9), *papier-mâché* (paragraph 9), *encroaching* (paragraph 10), *dragnet* (paragraph 10), *profligacy* (paragraph 11), *compulsion* (paragraph 12), *chic* (paragraph 12), *quays* (paragraph 18).

For Group Consideration

Using the information and clues in "Lists," list the chief characteristics of the list maker.

Journal Entry

Are you a list maker? If so, explain why you make lists and their advantages and/or disadvantages. If not, explain why not and how you keep your life ordered without them.

Essay Assignments

1. Define something that helps you simplify your life: an answering machine, a microwave oven, a computer, and so on.
2. Pick something that tyrannizes or enslaves you, the way lists tyrannize and enslave Larmoth (for example, aerobics, running, weight training, vegetarianism, making the dean's list, dressing for success, video games, or a hobby). Then write a definition to share with or to entertain your reader. Either way, try to show how you are enslaved by what you define.
3. Write a definition of *list maker* or *lists* based on your own experience and understanding. Feel free to disagree with Larmoth's definition. (The preceding group activity may help you.)

Considering Thematic Issues

1. Summarize the kinds of lists and their purposes, using the information in "Lists" (and your own ideas, if you wish). Then go on to explain what the need to make lists says about modern life.
2. In paragraph 4, Larmoth explains that while the purpose of lists is ostensibly to order life and keep it manageable, lists may really interfere with the full enjoyment of life. Using your own experience and observation, along with the information in "Talk in the Intimate Relationship" (page 252), "White Lies" (page 313), and "Country Codes" (page 317), discuss what else is ostensibly meant to facilitate things but, in fact, has the potential to hinder in some way.

Additional Essay Assignments

1. To help your reader understand something complex, define one of the following: *fear, beauty,* or *loyalty.*
2. To give your reader a fresh appreciation for the familiar, define one of the following: *friend, family,* or *the ideal teacher.*
3. To help your reader appreciate its value, define *freedom of the press* or *freedom of religion.*
4. To persuade your reader that it is either good or bad, define *censorship.*
5. Define *racism, sexism,* or *homophobia.*
6. Define *horror movie* to help your reader appreciate the genre more.
7. Define *situation comedy* in a way that indicates your view of the quality of the genre.
8. Define *leisure* in a way that entertains your reader.
9. Define and illustrate *politically correct* to help your reader better understand its significance.
10. Define one of the following: *police officer, lifeguard, camp counselor, doctor,* or *nurse.*
11. To help your reader understand something complex, define *integrity.*
12. Define *peer pressure* to help your reader understand what a potent force it is.
13. Define *gossip* to inform and/or to entertain.
14. To clarify something not well understood, define *creativity.*
15. To entertain and/or to inform, define *style.*
16. To entertain and/or to inform, define *tacky.*
17. To share your own thoughts and feelings, define *Christmas spirit.*
18. To share your own experiences and observations, define *frustration.* If you want to make the piece amusing, your purpose can be to entertain.
19. Define *writer's block* to share and/or to inform.
20. If you are a member of an ethnic group, define some ethnic term (*chutzpah, gringo,* and so on) so someone who is not a member of your group will understand it.

A CASEBOOK FOR ARGUMENTATION-PERSUASION: THE CHANGING FAMILY

The Purpose of Argumentation-Persuasion
Argumentative Detail
Avoiding Errors in Logic
Persuasive Detail
Raising and Countering Objections
Organizing Argumentation-Persuasion
Suggestions for Writing Argumentation-Persuasion
Annotated Student Essay: Who Should Decide

Marriage Is a Fundamental Right—Thomas Stoddard
Reserve Marriage for Heterosexuals—Bruce Fein
I Wish They'd Do It Right—Jane Doe
Cohousing and the American Dream—Kathryn McCamant
    and Charles Durrett
Families—Jane Howard
Needed: A Policy for Children When Parents Go to Work—
    Maxine Phillips
Homemaking—William Raspberry
Self-Help—A Black Tradition—Dorothy Height

Additional Essay Assignments

Both *argumentation* and *persuasion* try to move the reader to adopt a particular view or to take a particular action. However, argumentation relies on sound reasoning and logic to move the reader, while persuasion employs appeals to emotion, values, and beliefs.

Argumentation will be a considerable part of your college work. As you read, you will analyze information, consider points of view, and then draw your own conclusions, which your instructors will ask you to present and defend in coolly logical, argumentative pieces.

Persuasion, too, will be an important part of your repertoire as a writer. For example, to convince your reader to act on behalf of the homeless, you might use emotionally charged language to describe living conditions and thereby cause your reader to feel sympathy and take action as a result.

Although argumentation and persuasion are slightly different, writers often combine the two because a balanced mix of reason and emotional appeal can be very convincing. Thus, this chapter will deal with both. In addition to an explanation of techniques of argumentation and persuasion, the chapter includes a number of readings that serve as examples of argumentation-persuasion and that provide information you can include in your own argumentative and persuasive essays.

THE PURPOSE OF ARGUMENTATION-PERSUASION

Argumentation persuasion works to convince the reader to think or act a particular way. For example, a newspaper editorial argues that the city's layoff of municipal employees is unnecessary in order to convince readers to think a particular way. Campaign literature extols the virtues of a candidate to convince people to vote a particular way.

Sometimes, however, you have no hope of convincing your reader, so you must establish a less ambitious goal, such as softening your reader's objection or convincing your reader that your view has some merit. Let's say, for example, that you are arguing that the governor should increase the sales tax to support public education. If your reader has children in school, you can reasonably aim to convince your audience to agree with you. However, if your reader is a retired person on a fixed income, expecting agreement may be unreasonable. In this case, a more suitable goal is to convince your reader that there are some good reasons to raise the sales tax—even if he or she does not fully support the idea. Perhaps you are wondering what good it is to soften a reader's objection or convince that person that your view has some merit. The answer is that if you can lessen a reader's resistance to your view, he or she may come around to your thinking eventually or work less hard to oppose you.

ARGUMENTATIVE DETAIL

For the most part, your argumentative detail will be the reasons you hold your view. Thus, if you want to convince your reader that the federal government should pay day-care expenses for working parents, you would give all the reasons this is a good idea. However, supplying reasons for your stand is not enough; you must also back up those reasons with support. Let's say you argue that the family unit is in trouble and you give the high divorce rate as one reason to support your view. You must then go on to back up this reason, perhaps by giving a statistic on how high the divorce rate is and by explaining the specific negative effects of divorce on the family.

To back up your reasons, you can rely on a number of strategies, including personal experience and observation, facts and statistics, quotations and paraphrases, and interviews.

Personal Experience and Observation

Let's say, for example, that you are in favor of federally funded day care, and you cite as one reason the fact that children of working parents do not always get satisfactory care without it. To back up this claim, you could rely on observation by telling about your neighbor, who cannot afford decent care for her child while she is at work. If your own experience as a working parent supports the point, you could also write about that experience to back up your claim.

Facts and Statistics

Let's say that you favor federally funded day care, and as one reason you mention the large number of working mothers. You could support that point by citing Maxine Phillips's claim in "Needed: A Policy for Children When Parents Go to Work" (page 423) that half of the mothers of children under a year old go to work. If you do use facts and statistics taken from sources, be sure to document this information according to the conventions explained in the appendix.

Quotations and Paraphrases

To support the point that we needed federally funded day care to assist the poor, you could quote or paraphrase Maxine Phillips, who says on page 423 that "we have far too few publicly funded day-care slots limited to poverty-level families." If you do use quotations or paraphrases, be sure to follow the guidelines given in the appendix.

Interviews

Let's say that to support the idea of federally funded day care you note that the tuition is too high for some individuals. To support this reason, you can interview the owners of local day-care centers to learn the cost of enrollment. If the figures are high, you could report them and note that many people cannot afford the tuition.

Sometimes you can shape an effective argument by explaining the good that would result if your view were adopted or the bad that would result if your view were not adopted. Say, for example, that you were arguing that homosexual couples should be allowed to marry. You could note that if homosexual marriages were allowed, more people would know the satisfactions of marriage. As an alternative, you could argue that if homosexual marriages were not allowed, then many people would be denied the financial advantages afforded to spouses.

To explain and back up the reasons for your stand, you can use any of the patterns discussed in this book. If, for instance, you want to convince your reader that couples should marry rather than just live together, you can *narrate* an account of what happened when your brother and his girlfriend lived together. You can also *provide examples* of the problems couples face when they do not marry. You can *contrast* the benefits of marriage with the drawbacks of living together. You can *classify* the benefits of marriage; you can *describe* the embarrassment of older relatives of the unmarried couple, and so on.

 ## AVOIDING ERRORS IN LOGIC

Convincing argumentation is the product of careful reasoning. Thus, to be convincing, you must avoid the errors in logic described below, or you will weaken your argument.

1. Avoid overgeneralizing. Very little is true all of the time.

example: The only reason people live together without marrying is to avoid real commitment. (This may be true for some, but not for all.)

2. Avoid oversimplifying. Most issues worth arguing are complex.

example: The day-care problem could be solved if women would just stay home to care for their children. (It's not that simple. Many women must work in order to feed their children.)

3. Avoid begging the question. "Begging the question" is basing an argument on an unproven point.

example: Immature couples who live together without marrying do not deserve spousal rights. (Where is the proof that people who live together are immature?)

4. Avoid name calling. Attack or defend issues, not the people who believe in them.

example: People who favor homosexual marriages are bleeding-heart liberals who will destroy this country. (The pros and cons of homosexual marriages are unrelated to the people who favor them.)

5. Avoid either-or reasoning. Usually more than two alternatives exist.

example: Either we provide federally funded day care, or we will have a child-care crisis on our hands. (What about other alternatives, such as privately funded day care or paying mothers to care for their children?)

6. Avoid the assumption that one event causes another because it occurred first.

example: Ever since homosexual characters began appearing in movies and on television, people have begun considering homosexual marriage. (The first event did not necessarily cause the second.)

7. Avoid attacking or defending an issue on the basis of what was believed or done in the past. That kind of argument would have prevented women from voting, for example.

example: If our grandparents managed without federally funded day care, then so can we. (Our grandparents lived in a different world.)

8. Avoid assuming that what is true for one person is true for everybody.

example: My cousin and his girlfriend live together without the benefit of marriage, and they are just fine. Obviously, marriage is not that important. (What is true for the cousin may not be true for others.)

9. Avoid the "as any fool can see" approach. It insults readers who disagree, so you risk putting distance between you and your audience.

examples: It is apparent to everyone that federally funded day care would solve many problems. (No, it is not apparent to everyone or your essay would not be necessary.)

As anyone can see, federally funded day care would solve many problems. ("As anyone can see" is an unfair overstatement.)

PERSUASIVE DETAIL

In addition to appealing to your reader's intellect with sound reasons, you can be convincing by appealing to your reader's emotions, needs, values, beliefs, and concerns. For example, to convince your reader that homosexual couples should be able to marry, you can move the reader to compassion by describing the heartache one such couple feels because they cannot legally commit to each other. Similarly, to convince your reader that the federal government should fund day care, you can stir up the reader's emotions with a graphic explanation of the substandard care the child next door is getting. Persuasive detail, then, uses emotionally charged language to move a reader to a particular view or action.

While appealing to your reader's emotions is a valid technique, you must be careful not to overdo. Emotional appeal should be restrained. It is fine to move your reader's emotions by arousing compassion for a homosexual couple who wants to marry, but it is unfair to charge that tens of thousands of people are despondent and totally unfulfilled because they cannot marry. Further, the number of emotional appeals should be reasonable. They should appear *in addition to* logical reasons—not *instead of* them. Thus, rely mostly on sound reasons, and supplement those reasons with emotional appeal when appropriate.

 RAISING AND COUNTERING OBJECTIONS

Regardless of what stand you take on an issue, some reasonable people will disagree with you, and those people will have valid points to support their view. While it is tempting to ignore this opposition, doing so will weaken your argumentation or persuasion because you will not come across as someone who has carefully examined both sides before arriving at a position. Furthermore, even if you ignore the opposition, your reader will not. Your audience will be thinking about the points that work against your view, and if you do not deal with those points, you may fail to convince your reader. Thus, you must recognize the opposing arguments and find a way to diffuse them. Recognizing and diffusing opposition points is called *raising and countering objections.*

To raise and counter objections, you first acknowledge the objection to your stand by stating it. This is *raising the objection.* Then you make the objection less compelling. This is *countering the objection.* In general, you can raise and counter objections three ways, as illustrated below.

1. State that the opposition has a point, but so do you.

Many people are concerned because federally funded day care will raise taxes [objection raised]. However, children who are currently given substandard care because we lack a comprehensive, federally funded program will not thrive. Children who do not thrive fail to realize their potential or they develop problems, both of which end up costing society money anyway [objection countered].

2. State that the opposition has a point, but your point is better.

Although some are concerned about the cost of federally funded day care [objection raised], we cannot put a price tag on the well-being of our children because they are our hope for a better future [objection countered].

3. State that the opposition's point is untrue.

There are those who maintain that we do not really need federally funded day care [objection raised]. However, as Maxine Phillips points out in "Needed: A Policy for Children When Parents Go to Work," "An estimated 9.5 million preschoolers have mothers who work outside the home." Phillips also notes that many of these working mothers are the sole support of their children, and could not stay home if they wanted to (p. 423) [objection countered].

Raising and countering objections helps strengthen your argumentation-persuasion, but you need not deal with every opposition view. Instead, identify the most compelling objections and deal with those.

 ## ORGANIZING ARGUMENTATION-PERSUASION

The introduction of an argumentative or persuasive essay can be handled many ways. Explaining why the issue is important can be effective because it helps the reader understand the seriousness of your purpose. Thus, if you are arguing that high schools should have day-care centers for teenage mothers, your introduction can note the large number of teen mothers who drop out of school because they have no child care. This figure should help your reader appreciate the urgency of the issue. If your reader needs certain background information in order to appreciate your argument, the introduction can be a good place to provide that information. Thus, if you are arguing the need to return to the extended family, you should explain what an extended family is if your reader is not likely to know.

Regardless of the approach it takes, your introduction should make clear what you are trying to convince your reader to think or do. To accomplish this, your thesis should state the issue and your stand on that issue, like one of the following:

> **This country desperately needs federally funded day care.** (*issue*: federally funded day care; *stand*: in favor of it)

> **Federally funded cay care would create more problems than it solves.** (*issue*: federally funded day care; *stand*: against it)

Be sure that the issue you are arguing is genuinely debatable. There is no reason to argue that parents should love their children because no one will disagree with you. Similarly, avoid matters of taste. For example, arguing that basketball is a better sport than football is not productive because the issue is a matter of personal preference.

In general, arranging your points in a progressive order (from least to most compelling) is effective. This way, you can save your most convincing arguments for the end so your reader leaves your essay with them fresh in mind. Or you can place your strongest arguments first and last for a big opening and finish. Remember, the points at the end of an essay are in the most emphatic position and therefore likely to have the biggest impact.

You will probably find topic sentences helpful when you structure argumentation-persuasion. You can place each reason for your view in its own topic sentence and follow each topic sentence with the appropriate support. Thus, an essay arguing that mothers should be paid for raising their children could have these topic sentences:

> **Paying mothers to raise their children would reduce the number of mothers who work outside the home.**

> **Another reason to pay mothers is to improve the status of stay-at-home moms.**

> **Finally, paying mothers would increase the paid workforce and improve the economy.**

If you raise and counter objections, you can do this throughout the essay, wherever a point to be countered logically emerges. However, if you are dealing with very few objections, you can raise and counter them together in one or two paragraphs at the beginning or end of the essay.

To conclude argumentation-persuasion, you can reaffirm your position for emphasis, summarize your chief arguments if your reader would appreciate the reminder, or present your most persuasive point. In addition, you can call your audience to action by explaining what you want your reader to do. Or you can recommend a particular solution to a problem. Finally, explaining what would happen if your view were or were not adopted can be an effective closing.

SUGGESTIONS FOR WRITING ARGUMENTATION-PERSUASION

1. If you have trouble thinking of a topic, review the essays in this book for ideas. You can also review local and campus newspapers to learn about issues of current importance.
2. Another way to come up with a topic is to fill in the blank in one of these sentences:
   a. It is unfair that _____.
   b. It makes me angry that _____.
   c. I disagree with people who believe that _____.
3. List every reason you can think of to support your view.
4. If any readings in this book deal with your issue, check them for facts, statistics, paraphrases, and quotations you can use.
5. For additional details, answer these questions:
   a. Why is the issue important?
   b. What would happen if my view were adopted?
   c. What would happen if my view were not adopted?
   d. What are the chief objections to my view?
   e. How can these objections be countered?
   f. Who can I interview for information?
   g. How can I appeal to my reader's emotions?
6. Draft a thesis that presents the issue and your stand.
7. Write an outline and then a first draft.
8. When you revise, answer these questions:
   a. Are details in a progressive or other suitable order?
   b. Are paraphrases and quotations documented? (See the appendix.)
   c. Does the introduction provide background, explain why the topic is important, or otherwise engage interest?
   d. Does the thesis present the issue and your stand on that issue?
   e. Are all points clarified and supported?
   f. Have you avoided problems with logic?
   g. Have you raised and countered compelling objections?
   h. Does the conclusion bring the essay to a satisfying close?

ANNOTATED STUDENT ESSAY

Student author Laurel Mahoney uses techniques of both argumentation and persuasion to convince the reader that the unwed teenage mother should decide the fate of her child.

WHO SHOULD DECIDE?

Paragraphs 1 and 2
This section forms the introduction. Paragraph 1 is a narration with emotional content. Paragraph 2 provides background information. The last sentence of paragraph 2 is the thesis, which presents the issue (who decides the fate of the teen's baby) and the writer's stand (the teen should).

Paragraph 3
The topic sentence (the first sentence) presents the first reason to support the writer's view (biological responsibility). An objection is raised (parents will be financially responsible) and countered (the pregnant teen *is* her parents' responsibility and the burden will be temporary).

Paragraph 4
The topic sen-

1   Sherry was sixteen, and she thought she was in love. Her boyfriend, a smooth talker, used every line imaginable to get what he wanted from Sherry. He promised to love and care for her forever, and so one night in the back seat of his car, Sherry became pregnant. Soon the guy who promised to love and care for her was gone, and Sherry's life was forever altered.

2   Should Sherry have known better? Of course. Was she to blame? Certainly. However, it's not a new story. In fact, teen pregnancy is more of a problem than ever, despite all the sex education in schools. The problem and its solutions are well publicized, so everyone knows the pregnant teen's options: adoption, abortion, or motherhood at a ridiculously early age. What most people have not considered, however, is who should make the decision: the teenage girl or her parents. By law, the teen is entitled to make the decision, and that is just how it should be.

3   The most obvious reason that the teenage mother should decide is that she is the biological parent and hence the responsible party. In the purest physiological sense, the decision is hers to make. Many parents argue, however, that while the girl may make the decision, it is the parents who will bear the responsibility because they will have to house the girl and her child, as well as provide financial support. Parents looking forward to the end of the bulk of their own parenting responsibilities may feel particularly burdened by continued support of their daughter and grandchild. That is certainly unfortunate, but two things must be remembered. Parenthood has no ending date, so the daughter—pregnant or not—remains the parents' responsibility. They are thus obligated to care for the girl and her child. Also, the financial burden and crowded house will be temporary. Once the girl graduates from school and gets a job, she can move out and be more self-supporting. True, she may still need some help, but her need should gradually lessen.

4   In addition to the financial aspect, the emotional aspect must be considered. If parents force their daughter to give up or abort her child when she does not want to, the decision will haunt

tence (the first sentence) presents the next reason supporting the writer's view (the emotional aspect). The paragraph makes an emotional appeal. Detail is cause-and-effect analysis.

Paragraph 5
The topic sentence (the first sentence) presents an objection, and the rest of the paragraph counters that objection.

Paragraph 6
The topic sentence (the first sentence) presents the last reason. The transition *finally* indicates a progressive order.

Paragraph 7
The conclusion provides closure by suggesting a course of action.

her the rest of her life, filling her with pain and regret from which she may never recover. Imagine the poor girl spending her life wondering about the child she never knew and hating herself and her parents. What kind of life would that be?

5   Many parents would argue that the teenager lacks sufficient maturity to make such a decision. No one will argue that a teenager is mature enough to fully appreciate the ramifications of her decisions. However, parents, her doctor, and counselors can provide her with information, and she will have to make the best decision she can with that information. Then she will have to live with that decision. Even adults are forced to make important decisions before they are ready, and they do the same thing: they get information, make the best decision they can at the time, and live with it. That part of life never changes, regardless of age.

6   Finally, the most important reason the teenage girl should be allowed to make the decision is that she probably knows in her heart what is best for her and the child. Her parents may *think* they know, but the girl is the better judge. Furthermore, the parents may decide according to what is best for them rather than their daughter.

7   Teenage pregnancy is a serious, ongoing problem for both the girl and her parents. The best way to deal with the decision about the baby is to provide the girl with all the information possible about her options and their consequences. Counseling by social workers, religious leaders, and psychologists can help. During this process, the parents should provide love, support, and acceptance. Then they must stand back and let their daughter make the decision.

MARRIAGE IS A FUNDAMENTAL RIGHT
Thomas Stoddard

◆

Attorney Thomas Stoddard is the executive director of the Lambda Legal Defense and Education Fund, which is a gay rights organization. In the following essay, Stoddard argues that people of the same gender should have the legal right to marry. As you read, notice how the opening example is used.

◆

1   "In sickness and in health, 'til death do us part." With those words, millions of people each year are married, a public affirmation of a private bond that both society and the newlyweds hope will endure. Yet for nearly four years, Karen Thompson was denied the company of the one person to whom she had pledged life-long devotion.

2   Her partner is a woman, Sharon Kowalski, and their home state of Minnesota, like every other in the United States, refuses to permit same-sex marriages.

3   Karen Thompson and Sharon Kowalski are spouses in every respect except the legal. They exchanged vows and rings. They lived together until November 13, 1983—when Kowalski, as the result of an automobile accident, was rendered unable to walk and barely able to speak.

4   Thompson sought a ruling granting her guardianship over her partner, but Kowalski's parents opposed the petition and obtained sole guardianship. They then moved Kowalski to a nursing home 300 miles away from Thompson and forbade all visits between the two women.

5   In February 1989, in the wake of a reevaluation of Kowalski's mental competence, Thompson was permitted to visit her partner again. But the prolonged injustice and anguish inflicted on both women hold a moral for everyone.

6   Marriage, the Supreme Court declared in 1967 in *Loving v. Virginia*, is "one of the basic civil rights of man" (and, presumably, of woman as well). The freedom to marry, said the Court, is "essential to the orderly pursuit of happiness."

7   Marriage is far more than a symbolic state. It can be the key to survival—emotional and financial. Marriage triggers a universe of rights, privileges and presumptions. In every jurisdiction in this country, a married person can share in a spouse's estate even when there is no will. She typically has access to the group insurance and pension programs offered by the spouse's employer, and she enjoys tax advantages.

8   **Individual Decision.**   The decision whether or not to marry belongs properly to individuals, not to the government. While marriage historically has required a male and a female partner, history alone cannot sanctify injustice.

9   If tradition were the only measure, most states still would limit matrimony to partners of the same race. As recently as 1967, before the Supreme Court declared in *Loving* that miscegenation statutes are unconstitutional, 16 states still prohibited marriages between a white person and a black person. When all the excuses were stripped away, it was clear that the only purpose of those laws was to maintain white supremacy.

10   Those who argue against reforming the marriage statutes because they believe that same-sex marriage would be "anti-family" overlook the obvious: Marriage creates families and promotes social stability. In an increasingly love-less world, those who wish to commit themselves to a relationship founded upon devotion should be encouraged, not scorned. Government has no legiti-mate interest in how that love is expressed.

11   And it can no longer be argued—if it ever could—that marriage is fundamentally a procreative unit. Otherwise, states would forbid marriage between those who, by reason of age or infertility, cannot have children, as well as those who elect not to.

12   The case of Sharon Kowalski and Karen Thompson demonstrates that sanctimonious illusions can lead directly to the suffering of others. Denied the right to marry, these women were left to the whims and prejudices of others, and of the law.

13   It is time for the marriage statutes to incorporate fully the concept of equal protection of the law by extending to the many millions of gay Americans the right to marry.

Considering Ideas

1. What reasons does Stoddard give to support his view that people of the same sex should be allowed to marry?
2. What objections to his view does Stoddard raise? How does he counter these objections?
3. Are there any objections that Stoddard should have raised and countered but did not?
4. Stoddard does not say anything about children, although many homosexual couples have children from previous heterosexual relationships. Would Stoddard's argument have been more or less convincing if he had dealt with children living with same-sex couples?
5. Stoddard compares laws against homosexual marriage to laws against inter-racial marriage. Do you think this is a valid comparison? Explain.

Considering Technique

1. Which sentence do you think best expresses Stoddard's thesis? What does the thesis present as the issue and Stoddard's stand on that issue?
2. What example does the author use to help make his point?

3. How does Stoddard's example work to convince the reader?

4. What element of emotional appeal appears in the essay?

5. In paragraphs 8, 9, 10, and 11, Stoddard raises and counters objections to his view. How does this technique help convince the reader?

6. Consult a dictionary if you are unsure of the meaning of any of these words: *affirmation* (paragraph 1), *rendered* (paragraph 3), *sanctify* (paragraph 8), *matrimony* (paragraph 9), *miscegenation* (paragraph 9), *statutes* (paragraph 9), *procreative* (paragraph 11), *sanctimonious* (paragraph 12).

For Group Consideration

With the members of your group, make a list of the social, emotional, and financial benefits a legal spouse enjoys that are likely to be denied to a same-sex partner.

Journal Entry

Explain how you feel about marriage between members of the same sex and try to account for why you feel the way you do.

Essay Assignments

1. Who do you think should have been granted guardianship over Kowalski: Thompson or Kowalski's parents? Argue your position by appealing to both your reader's intellect and emotions.

2. Do you think companies should offer health and life insurance benefits to employees' homosexual partners? Argue your view, being careful to raise and counter compelling objections.

RESERVE MARRIAGE FOR HETEROSEXUALS
Bruce Fein

◆

Attorney Bruce Fein has written for American Legion Magazine *and* National Review. *He is also the author of* Significant Decisions of the Supreme Court, 1979–1980. *In "Reserve Marriage for Heterosexuals," Fein argues against legalizing homosexual marriages. As you read, notice that he argues his position on grounds different from those Stoddard uses in the preceding essay.*

◆

1   Authorizing the marriage of homosexuals, like sanctioning polygamy, would be unenlightened social policy. The law should reserve the celebration of marriage vows of monogamous male-female attachments to further the goal of psychologically, emotionally and educationally balanced offspring.

2   As Justice Oliver Wendell Holmes noted, the life of the law has not been logic, it has been experience. Experience confirms that child development is skewed, scarred or retarded when either a father or mother is absent in the household.

3   In the area of adoption, married couples are favored over singles. The recent preferences for joint child-custody decrees in divorce proceedings tacitly acknowledges the desirability of child intimacies with both a mother and father.

4   As Supreme Court Justice Byron White recognized in *Taylor v. Louisiana* (1975): "[T]he two sexes are not fungible; a community made up exclusively of one is different from a community of both; the subtle interplay of influence one on the other is among the imponderables" (quoting from *Ballard v. United States*).

5   A child receives incalculable benefits in the maturing process by the joint instruction, consolation, oversight and love of a father and mother—benefits that are unavailable in homosexual households. The child enjoys the opportunity to understand and respect both sexes in a uniquely intimate climate. The likelihood of gender prejudice is thus reduced, an exceptionally worthy social objective.

6   **Protect Children.**   The law should encourage male-female marriage vows over homosexual attachments in the interests of physically, mentally, and psychologically healthy children, the nation's most valuable asset.

7   Crowning homosexual relationships with the solemnity of legal marriage would wrongly send social cues that male-female marriages are not preferable. And there is no constitutional right to homosexual marriage since homosexual sodomy can be criminalized. See *Bowers v. Hardwick* (1986).

8   The fact that some traditional marriages end in fractious divorce, yield no offspring, or result in families with mistreated children does not discredit

limiting marriage to monogamous female-male relationships. Anti-polygamy laws are instructive. They seek to discourage female docility, male autocracy, and intra-family rancor and jealousies that are promoted by polygamous marriages. That some might not exhibit such deplorable characteristics is no reason for their repeal or a finding of constitutional infirmity.

9   To deny the right of homosexual marriage is not an argument for limiting other rights to gays, because of community animosity or vengeance. These are unacceptable policy motivations if law is to be civilized.

10   Several states and localities protect homosexuals against discrimination in employment or housing. In New York, a state law confers on a homosexual the rent-control benefits of a deceased partner. Other jurisdictions have eschewed special legal rights for homosexuals, and the military excludes them. Experience will adjudge which of the varied legal approaches to homosexual rights have been the most enlightened.

11   Sober debate over homosexual rights is in short supply. The subject challenges deep-rooted and passionately held images of manhood, womanhood and parenthood, and evokes sublimated fears of community ostracism or degradation.

12   Each legal issue regarding homosexuality should be examined discretely with the recognition that time has upset many fighting faiths and with the goal of balancing individual liberty against community interests. With regard to homosexual marriage, that balance is negative.

Considering Ideas

1. Why does Fein believe we should not legalize homosexual marriages?
2. Do you think that Fein supports his contention that homosexual marriages do not "further the goal of psychologically, emotionally, and educationally balanced offspring"?
3. What do you think Justice Oliver Wendell Holmes meant when he said that experience, not logic, is "the life of the law" (paragraph 2)?
4. What objections does Fein raise? How does he counter these objections? Do you think that his counters are effective? Explain.
5. Do you think that Fein's argument is convincing? Explain.

Considering Technique

1. Which sentence serves as Fein's thesis? What issue and stand does the thesis present?
2. Fein compares legalizing homosexual marriage to other issues. What comparisons does he make? What purpose do these comparisons serve?
3. Fein quotes Supreme Court justices in paragraphs 2 and 4. What purpose do these quotations serve?
4. Are there any elements of emotional appeal in the essay?

5. Consult a dictionary if you are unsure of the meanings of any of these words: *sanctioning* (paragraph 1), *polygamy* (paragraph 1), *monogamous* (paragraph 1), *skewed* (paragraph 2), *tacitly* (paragraph 3), *fungible* (paragraph 4), *imponderables* (paragraph 4), *sodomy* (paragraph 7), *fractious* (paragraph 8), *docility* (paragraph 8), *autocracy* (paragraph 8), *rancor* (paragraph 8), *eschewed* (paragraph 10), *sublimated* (paragraph 11), *ostracism* (paragraph 11), *discretely* (paragraph 12).

For Group Consideration

In paragraphs 1 and 8, Fein compares laws against same-sex marriages to laws against polygamy. In paragraph 3, he compares laws against same-sex marriages to adoption policies that favor married people over singles. Discuss whether or not these comparisons are valid and report your findings to the class.

Journal Entry

In paragraph 11, Fein says that the issue of homosexual marriage "challenges the deep-rooted and passionately held images of manhood, womanhood and parenthood." Describe your own images of manhood, womanhood, and parenthood.

Essay Assignments

1. Fein's argument is based on the welfare of children, and Stoddard's argument in "Marriage Is a Fundamental Right" (page 397) is based on individual freedom and rights. Which do you think is the better basis for an argument on whether or not to legalize homosexual marriage? Defend your view.

2. In paragraph 10, Fein refers to the then-current policy of excluding homosexuals from the military. Since he wrote that essay, the military's policy has changed somewhat. Now recruits cannot be asked if they are homosexuals, but they can be denied admission if they volunteer the information that they are. Support or attack this new policy, taking care to raise and counter compelling objections.

3. Agree or disagree with Fein's statement in paragraph 7 that "crowning homosexual relationships with the solemnity of legal marriage would wrongly send social cues that male-female marriages are not preferable."

I WISH THEY'D DO IT RIGHT
Jane Doe

◆

In the following essay, first published in the New York Times, *the author argues that her son should marry the mother of his child, rather than merely live with her. Because the author wished to remain anonymous, the piece is attributed to "Jane Doe." As you read, ask yourself why "Jane Doe" wanted to keep her identity a secret.*

◆

1   My son and his wife are not married. They have lived together for seven years without benefit of license. Though occasionally marriage has been a subject of conjecture, it did not seem important until the day they announced, jubilantly, that they were going to have a child. It was happy news. I was ready and eager to become a grandmother. Now, I thought, they will take the final step and make their relationship legal.

2   I was apprised of the Lamaze method of natural childbirth. I was prepared by Leboyer for birth without violence. I admired the expectant mother's discipline. She ate only organic foods, abstained from alcohol, avoided insecticides, smog and trauma. Every precaution was taken to insure the arrival of a healthy, happy infant. No royal birth had been prepared for more auspiciously. All that was lacking was legitimacy.

3   Finally, when my grandson was two weeks old, I dared to question their intentions.

4   "We don't believe in marriage," was all that was volunteered.

5   "Not even for your son's sake?" I asked. "Maybe he will."

6   Their eyes were impenetrable, their faces stiffened to masks. "You wouldn't understand," I was told.

7   And I don't. Surely they cannot believe they are pioneering, making revolutionary changes in society. That frontier has long been tamed. Today marriage offers all the options. Books and talk shows have surfeited us with the freedom offered in open marriage. Lawyers, psychologists and marriage counselors are growing rich executing marriage contracts. And divorce, should it come to that, is in most states easy and inexpensive.

8   On the other hand, living together out of wedlock can be economically impractical as well as socially awkward. How do I present her—as my son's roommate? his spouse? his spice, as one facetious friend suggested? Even my son flounders in these waters. Recently, I heard him refer to her as his girl friend. I cannot believe that that description will be endearing to their son when he is able to understand.

9   I have resolved that problem for myself, bypassing their omission, introducing her as she is, as my daughter-in-law. But my son, in militant support of

his ideology, refutes any assumptions, however casual, that they have taken vows.

10   There are economic benefits which they are denying themselves. When they applied for housing in the married-students dormitory of the university where he is seeking his doctorate, they were asked for their marriage certificate. Not having one, they were forced to find other, more expensive quarters off campus. Her medical insurance, provided by the company where she was employed, was denied him. He is not her husband. There have been and will be other inconveniences they have elected to endure.

11   Their son will not enjoy the luxury of choice about the inconveniences and scurrility to which he will be subject from those of his peers and elders who dislike and fear society's nonconformists.

12   And if in the future, his parents should decide to separate, will he not suffer greater damage than the child of divorce, who may find comfort in the knowledge that his parents once believed they could live happily ever after, and committed themselves to that idea? The child of unwed parents has no sanctuary. His mother and father have assiduously avoided a pledge of permanency, leaving him drifting and insecure.

13   I know my son is motivated by idealism and honesty in his reluctance to concede to what he considers mere ceremony. But he is wise enough to know that no one individual can fight all of society's foibles and frauds. Why does he persist in this, a battle already lost? Because though he rejects marriage, California, his residence, has declared that while couples living together in imitation of marriage are no longer under the jurisdiction of the family court, their relationship is viewed by the state as an implicit contract somewhat like a business agreement. This position was mandated when equal property rights were granted a woman who had been abandoned by the man she had lived with for a number of years.

14   Finally, the couple's adamancy has been depriving to all the rest of the family. There has been no celebration of wedding or anniversaries. There has been concealment from certain family elders who could not cope with the situation. Its irregularity has put constraint on the grandparents, who are stifled by one another's possible embarrassment or hurt.

15   I hope that one day very soon my son and his wife will acknowledge their cohabitation with a license. The rest of us will not love them any more for it. We love and support them as much as possible now. But it will be easier and happier for us knowing that our grandson will be spared the continued explanation and harassment, the doubts and anxieties of being a child of unmarried parents.

Considering Ideas

1. In the opening sentence, the author refers to her grandchild's mother as her son's "wife." Why do you think she uses "wife"?

2. In paragraph 7, the author argues in favor of marriage by saying that "today marriage offers all the options." What do you think she means?
3. What reasons does Jane Doe give to support her view that her son should marry the mother of his child? Do you find these reasons convincing? Why or why not?
4. What objections to her view does Jane Doe raise? How does she counter them?
5. Why do you think the author did not want to reveal her identity?

Considering Technique

1. What issue is the author treating, and what is her stand on that issue?
2. Paragraphs 1 through 6 form the introduction of "I Wish They'd Do It Right." What approach does the author take to that introduction?
3. To what extent does the author speculate on what will happen if her view is not adopted? Where does she speculate on what will happen if her view is adopted?
4. What elements of emotional appeal appear in the essay? Are they sufficiently fair and restrained? Do they add to the convincing quality of the essay?
5. What reasons for her view does the author back up with examples?
6. What approach does Jane Doe take to her conclusion?
7. Consult a dictionary if you are unsure of the meaning of any of these words: *conjecture* (paragraph 1), *apprised* (paragraph 2), *Lamaze* (Paragraph 2), *Leboyer* (paragraph 2), *organic* (paragraph 2), *auspiciously* (paragraph 2), *impenetrable* (paragraph 6), *surfeited* (paragraph 7), *facetious* (paragraph 8), *militant* (paragraph 9), *scurrility* (paragraph 11), *assiduously* (paragraph 12), *foibles* (paragraph 13), *adamancy* (paragraph 14).

For Group Consideration

Consider the reasons Jane Doe gives for her view, along with her emotional appeals and counters to objections. What facet of her argumentation-persuasion is the most convincing? Why?

Journal Entry

Do you think couples should live together before they marry? Should they live together instead of marrying? Express your views in one or two pages.

Essay Assignments

1. Use argumentation-persuasion to convince Jane Doe that her son's living arrangement has its advantages. Try to counter one or more of the points Doe makes in her essay.

2. Paragraph 7 refers to a number of relatively recent innovations in the marriage institution: open marriage (which does not require spouses to be monogamous), marriage contracts, and easy, cheap divorces. Select one of these innovations and argue that it is or is not an improvement in marriage.
3. In paragraph 10, the author notes two economic drawbacks her son faced because he was not married to his partner: denial of admission to married students' housing and denial of coverage by his partner's medical insurance. Do you think these denials were a form of discrimination? Argue your view, being sure to raise and counter compelling objections.

COHOUSING AND THE AMERICAN DREAM
Kathryn McCamant and Charles Durrett

◆

Architects Kathryn McCamant and Charles Durrett researched the alternative housing concept, cohousing, in Scandinavia and the Netherlands before writing their book Cohousing: A Contemporary Approach to Housing Ourselves. *"Cohousing and the American Dream" is an excerpt from that book. The essay explains why traditional housing no longer meets the needs of many people and argues for the alternative cohousing form. As you read, decide whether or not you find cohousing appealing.*

◆

1   Traditional housing no longer addresses the needs of many people. Dramatic demographic and economic changes are taking place in our society, and most of us feel the effects of these trends in our lives. Things that people once took for granted—family, community, a sense of belonging—must now be actively sought out. Many people are mishoused, ill-housed, or unhoused because of the lack of appropriate options. This article introduces a new housing model that addresses such changes. Pioneered primarily in Denmark and now being adapted in other countries, the cohousing concept reestablishes many of the advantages of traditional villages within the context of late twentieth-century life.

2   Several years ago, as a young married couple, we began to think about where we were going to raise our children. What kind of setting would allow us to best combine our professional careers with child rearing? Already our lives were hectic. Often we would come home from work exhausted and hungry, only to find the refrigerator empty. Between our jobs and housekeeping, when would we find the time to spend with our kids? Relatives lived in distant cities, and even our friends lived across town. Just to get together for coffee we had to make arrangements two weeks in advance. Most young parents we knew seemed to spend most of their time shuttling their children to and from day care and playmates' homes, leaving little opportunity for anything else.

3   So many people we knew seemed to be living in places that did not accommodate their most basic needs; they always had to drive somewhere to do anything sociable. We dreamed of a better solution: an affordable neighborhood where children would have playmates and we would have friends nearby; a place with people of all ages, young and old, where neighbors knew and helped each other.

4   As architects, we had both designed different types of housing. We had been amazed at the conservatism of most architects and housing professionals, and at the lack of consideration given to people's changing personal needs.

Single-family houses, apartments, and condominiums might change in price and occasionally in style, but otherwise they were designed to function pretty much as they had for the last 40 years. Perhaps our own frustrations were indicative of a larger problem: a diverse population attempting to fit into housing that is simply no longer appropriate for them.

5   Contemporary post-industrial societies such as the United States and Western Europe are undergoing a multitude of changes that affect our housing needs. The modern single-family detached home, which makes up 67 percent of American housing, was designed for a nuclear family consisting of a bread-winning father, a homemaking mother, and two to four children. Today, less than one-quarter of the United States population lives in such households. Rather, the family with two working parents predominates, while the single-parent household is the fastest growing family type. Almost one-quarter of the population lives alone, and this proportion is predicted to grow as the number of Americans over the age of 60 increases. At the same time, the surge in housing costs and the increasing mobility of the population combine to break down traditional community ties and place more demands on individual house-holds. These factors call for a thorough reexamination of household and community needs, and the way we house ourselves.

6   As we searched for more desirable living situations, we kept thinking about the housing developments we had visited while studying architecture in Denmark several years earlier.

7   In Denmark, people frustrated by the available housing options developed a new kind of housing that redefines the concept of neighborhood to fit contemporary life-styles. Tired of the isolation and impracticalities of single-family houses and apartment units, they built or developed out of existing neighborhoods new housing that combines the autonomy of private dwellings with the advantages of community living. Each household has a private residence, but also shares extensive common facilities with the larger group, such as a kitchen and dining hall, children's playrooms, workshops, guest rooms, and a laundry. Although individual dwellings are designed to function independently and each has its own kitchen, the common facilities, and particularly common dinners, are an important aspect of community life.

8   As of last year, 67 of these communities had been built in Denmark, and another 38 were planned. They range in size from six to 80 households, with the majority between 15 and 33 residences. These communities are called *bofoellesskaber* in Danish ("living communities"), for which we have coined the term "cohousing." First built in the early 1970s, cohousing developments have quadrupled in number in the last five years. The Netherlands now features 30 cohousing communities and similar projects are being built in Sweden, France, Norway, and Germany.

9   Imagine . . . It's five o'clock in the evening, and Anne is glad the workday is over. As she pulls into her driveway, she begins to unwind at last. Some neighborhood kids dart through the trees, playing a mysterious game at the

edge of the gravel parking lot. Her daughter yells, 'Hi Mom!" as she runs by with three other children.

10   Instead of frantically trying to put together a nutritious dinner, Anne can relax now, spend some time with her children, and then eat with her family in the common house. Walking through the common house on her way home, she stops to chat with the evening's cooks, two of her neighbors, who are busy preparing dinner—broiled chicken with mushroom sauce—in the kitchen. Several children are setting the tables. Outside on the patio, some neighbors share a pot of tea in the late afternoon sun. Anne waves hello and continues down the lane to her own house.

11   After dropping off her things at home, Anne walks through the birch trees behind the houses to the child-care center where she picks up her four-year-old son, Peter. She will have some time to read Peter a story before dinner, she thinks to herself.

12   Anne and her husband, Eric, live with their two children in a housing development they helped design. Not that either of them is an architect or builder; Anne works at the county administration office, and Eric is an engineer. Six years ago they joined a group of families who were looking for a realistic housing alternative. At that time, they owned their own home, had a three-year-old daughter, and were contemplating having another child—partly so that their daughter would have a playmate in their predominantly adult neighborhood.

13   Responding to a newspaper ad, Anne and Eric discovered a group of people who expressed similar frustrations about their existing housing situations. The group's goal was to build a housing development with a lively and positive social environment.

14   In the months that followed, the group further defined its goals and began the long, difficult process of turning its dream into reality. Some people dropped out, and others joined. Two and a half years later, Anne and Eric moved into their new home—a community of clustered houses that share a large common house. By working together, these people had created the kind of neighborhood they wanted to live in— a cohousing community.

15   Today Tina, Anne and Eric's eight-year-old daughter, never lacks for playmates. She walks home from school with the other kids in the community. Her mother is usually at work, so Tina goes up to the common house, where one of the adults makes tea and toast for the kids and any adults who are around. Tina liked her family's old house, but this place is much more interesting. There's so much to do; she can play outside all day, and, as long as she doesn't leave the community, her mother doesn't worry about her.

16   John and Karen moved into the same community a few years after it was built. Their kids were grown and had left home. Now they enjoy the peacefulness of having a house to themselves; they have time to take classes in the evenings, visit art museums, and attend an occasional play in town. John teaches children with learning disabilities and plans to retire in a few years.

Karen administers a senior citizens' housing complex and nursing home. They lead full and active lives, but worry about getting older. How long will their health hold out? Will one die, leaving the other alone? Such considerations, combined with the desire to be part of an active community while maintaining their independence, led John and Karen to buy a one-bedroom home in this community. Here they feel secure knowing their neighbors care about them. If John gets sick, people will be there to help Karen with the groceries or join her at the theater. Common dinners relieve them of preparing a meal every night, and their children and grandchildren can stay in the community's guest rooms when they visit. John and Karen enjoy a house with no children, but it's still refreshing to see kids playing outside.

17   Cohousing is a grass-roots movement that grew directly out of people's dissatisfaction with existing housing choices. Its initiators draw inspiration from the increasing popularity of shared households, in which several unrelated people share a house, and from the cooperative movement in general. Yet cohousing is distinctive in that each family or household has a separate dwelling and chooses how much they want to participate in community activities.

18   Cohousing also differs from most of the communes and intentional communities we know in the United States, which are often organized around strong ideological beliefs and may depend on a charismatic leader to establish the direction of the community and hold the group together. Based on democratic principles, cohousing developments espouse no ideology other than the desire for a more practical and social home environment. Cohousing communities are organized, planned, and managed by their residents. The great variety in community size, ownership structure, and design illustrates the many diverse applications of the concept.

19   In many respects, cohousing is not a new idea. In the past, most people lived in villages or tightly knit urban neighborhoods. Even today, people in less industrialized regions typically live in small communities. Members of such communities know one another for many years; they are familiar with one another's families and histories, talents and weaknesses. This kind of relationship demands accountability, but in return provides security and a sense of belonging.

20   In previous centuries, households were made of at least six people. In addition to having many children, families often shared their homes with farmhands, servants, boarders, and relatives. A typical household might include a family with four children, a grandmother or an uncle, and one or more boarders who might also work in the family business. Relatives usually lived nearby. These large households provided both children and adults with a diverse intergenerational network of relationships in the home environment. The idea that the nuclear family should live on its own without the support and assistance of the extended family or surrounding community is relatively new, even in the United States.

21   To expect that today's small households, as likely to be single parents or

single adults as nuclear families, should be self-sufficient and without community support is not only unrealistic but absurd. Each household is expected to prepare its own meals, do its own shopping, and so far as finances permit, own a vacuum cleaner, washing machine, clothes dryer, and other household implements, regardless of whether the household consists of two people or six, and whether there is a full-time homemaker or not.

22   People need community at least as much as they need privacy. We must reestablish ways compatible with contemporary American lifestyles to accommodate this need. Cohousing offers a new model for recreating a sense of place and neighborhood, while responding to today's needs for a less constraining environment.

Considering Ideas

1. How would you explain the cohousing concept to someone who has never heard of it?
2. Who do you think would find cohousing an attractive alternative?
3. What changes in the American family make traditional housing arrangements less attractive than they once were?
4. In paragraph 22, McCamant and Durrett say that "people need community at least as much as they need privacy." What do you think the authors mean? How does cohousing address the need for both privacy and community?
5. Do you think cohousing would be popular in your hometown? Explain why or why not.
6. If you have ever lived in a residence hall, explain the similarities and differences between residence hall living and the cohousing concept.

Considering Technique

1. Which sentence is the thesis of "Cohousing and the American Dream"? What does that thesis present as the issue and the authors' stand on that issue?
2. In which paragraphs do the authors rely on personal experience and observation for their details?
3. What purpose do paragraphs 2 through 7 serve?
4. How do the examples in paragraphs 9 through 15 and in paragraph 16 help support the authors' argument? How does the contrast in paragraphs 17 and 18 help support the argument? What about the facts and statistics in paragraph 5?
5. The authors do not raise and counter objections. Would the essay have been more convincing if they had? Explain.
6. Consult a dictionary if you are unsure of the meaning of any of these words from the essay: *demographic* (paragraph 1), *condominiums* (paragraph 4), *nuclear family* (paragraph 5), *autonomy* (paragraph 7), *initiators* (para-

graph 17), *communes* (paragraph 18), *ideological* (paragraph 18), *charismatic* (paragraph 18), *espouse* (paragraph 18), *accountability* (paragraph 19).

For Group Consideration

McCamant and Durrett do not mention any of the problems that could be associated with cohousing. For example, they do not discuss how to determine who does the communal cooking or what happens if someone does not do his or her job. With two or three classmates, make a list of other problems associated with cohousing.

Journal Entry

In a page or so, consider whether or not you would be happy living in a cohousing community set up the way McCamant and Durrett describe it. Explain why or why not.

Essay Assignments

1. If you think cohousing is far less attractive than McCamant and Durrett say it is, argue against the idea by refuting some of their claims and noting your own criticisms of the concept.
2. In paragraph 5, McCamant and Durrett say that fewer than 25 percent of the United States lives in families with a "breadwinning father, a homemaking mother, and two to four children." Pick one problem created by the shifting character of the American family and devise a solution for that problem. Then argue for the implementation of your solution.
3. Cohousing is likely to involve multigenerational environments, as the young and old share communal living areas. Argue whether or not such multigenerational environments are an improvement over the nuclear unit.

FAMILIES
Jane Howard

◆

A reporter, editor, writer, and teacher, Jane Howard has written several books, including Families *(1978), from which the following excerpt is taken. Howard explains the characteristics of good families and notes that such families need not be biological—they can be formed from friends as well as relatives. As you read, decide what point Howard is arguing.*

◆

1   Call it a clan, call it a network, call it a tribe, call it a family. Whatever you call it, whoever you are, you need one. You need one because you are human. You didn't come from nowhere. Before you, around you, and presumably after you, too, there are others. Some of these others must matter a lot—to you, and if you are very lucky, to one another. Their welfare must be nearly as important to you as your own. Even if you live alone, even if your solitude is elected and ebullient, you still cannot do without a clan or a tribe.

2   The trouble with the clans and tribes many of us were born into is not that they consist of meddlesome ogres but that they are too far away. In emergencies we rush across continents and if need be oceans to their sides, as they do to ours. Maybe we even make a habit of seeing them, once or twice a year, for the sheer pleasure of it. But blood ties seldom dictate our addresses. Our blood kin are often too remote to ease us from our Tuesdays to our Wednesdays. For this we must rely on our families of friends. If our relatives are not, do not wish to be, or for whatever reasons cannot be our friends, then by some complex alchemy we must try to transform our friends into our relatives. If blood and roots don't do the job, then we must look to water and branches, and sort ourselves into new constellations, new families.

3   These new families, to borrow the terminology of an African tribe (the Bangwa of the Cameroons), may consist either of friends of the road, ascribed by chance, or friends of the heart, achieved by choice. Ascribed friends are those we happen to go to school with, work with, or live near. They know where we went last weekend and whether we still have a cold. Just being around gives them a provisional importance in our lives, and us in theirs. Maybe they will still matter to us when we or they move away; quite likely they won't. Six months or two years will probably erase us from each other's thoughts, unless by some chance they and we have become friends of the heart.

4   Wishing to be friends, as Aristotle wrote, is quick work, but friendship is a slowly ripening fruit. An ancient proverb he quotes in his *Ethics* had it that you cannot know a man until you and he together have eaten a peck of salt. Now a peck, a quarter of a bushel, is quite a lot of salt—more, perhaps, than most pairs of people ever have occasion to share. We must try though. We must sit

together at as many tables as we can. We must steer each other through enough seasons and weathers so that sooner or later it crosses our minds that one of us, God knows which or with what sorrow, must one day mourn the other.

5   We must devise new ways, or revive old ones, to equip outselves with kinfolk. Maybe such an impulse prompted whoever ordered the cake I saw in my neighborhood bakery to have it frosted to say "HAPPY BIRTHDAY SURRO-GATE." I like to think that this cake was decorated not for a judge but for someone's surrogate mother or surrogate brother: Loathsome jargon, but admirable sentiment. If you didn't conceive me or if we didn't grow up in the same house, we can still be related, if we decide we ought to be. It is never too late, I like to hope, to augment our families in ways nature neglected to do. It is never too late to choose new clans.

6   The best-chosen clans, like the best friendships and the best blood families, endure by accumulating a history solid enough to suggest a future. But clans that don't last have merit too. We can lament them but we shouldn't deride them. Better an ephemeral clan or tribe than none at all. A few of my life's most tribally joyous times, in fact, have been spent with people whom I have yet to see again. This saddens me, as it may them too, but dwelling overlong on such sadness does no good. A more fertile exercise is to think back on those times and try to figure out what made them, for all their brevity, so stirring. What can such times teach us about forming new and more lasting tribes in the future?

7   New tribes and clans can no more be willed into existence, of course, than any other good thing can. We keep trying, though. To try, with gritted teeth and girded loins, is after all American. That is what the two Helens and I were talking about the day we had lunch in a room up in a high-rise motel near the Kansas City airport. We had lunch there at the end of a two-day conference on families. The two Helens were social scientists, but I liked them even so, among other reasons because they both objected to that motel's coffee shop even more than I did. One of the Helens, from Virginia, disliked it so much that she had brought along homemade whole wheat bread, sesame butter, and honey from her parents' farm in South Dakota, where she had visited before the conference. Her picnic was the best thing that happened, to me at least, those whole two days.

8   "If you're voluntarily childless and alone," said the other Helen, who was from Pennsylvania by way of Puerto Rico, "it gets harder and harder with the passage of time. It's stressful. That's why you need support systems." I had been hearing quite a bit of talk about "support systems." The term is not among my favorites, but I can understand its currency. Whatever "support systems" may be, the need for them is clearly urgent, and not just in this country. Are there not thriving "megafamilies" of as many as three hundred people in Scandinavia? Have not the Japanese for years had an honored, enduring—if perhaps by our standards rather rigid—custom of adopting nonrelatives to fill gaps in their families? Should we not applaud and maybe imitate such ingenuity?

9   And consider our own Unitarians. From Santa Barbara to Boston they have been earnestly dividing their congregations into arbitrary "extended families" whose members are bound to act like each other's relatives. Kurt Vonnegut, Jr., plays with a similar train of thought in his fictional *Slapstick*. In that book every newborn baby is assigned a randomly chosen middle name, like Uranium or Daffodil or Raspberry. These middle names are connected with hyphens to numbers between one and twenty, and any two people who have the same middle name are automatically related. This is all to the good, the author thinks, because "human beings need all the relatives they can get—as possible donors or receivers not of love but of common decency." He envisions these extended families as "one of the four greatest inventions by Americans," the others being *Robert's Rules of Order*, the Bill of Rights, and the principles of Alcoholics Anonymous.

10   This charming notion might even work, if it weren't so arbitrary. Already each of us is born into one family not of our choosing. If we're going to devise new ones, we might as well have the luxury of picking the members ourselves. Clever picking might result in new families whose benefits would surpass or at least equal those of the old. As a member in reasonable standing of six or seven tribes in addition to the one I was born to, I have been trying to figure which characteristics are common to both kinds of families.

11   1. Good families have a chief, or a heroine, or a founder—someone around whom others cluster, whose achievements, as the Yiddish word has it, let them *kvell*,[1] and whose example spurs them on to like feats. Some blood dynasties produce such figures regularly; others languish for as many as five generations between demigods, wondering with each new pregnancy whether this, at last, might be the messianic baby who will redeem them. Look, is there not something gubernatorial about her footstep, or musical about the way he bangs with his spoon on his cup? All clans, of all kinds, need such a figure now and then. Sometimes clans based on water rather than blood harbor several such personages at one time. The Boomsbury Group[2] in London six decades ago was not much hampered by its lack of a temporal history.

12   2. Good families have a switchboard operator—someone who cannot help but keep track of what all the others are up to, who plays Houston Mission Control to everyone else's Apollo. This role is assumed rather than assigned. The person who volunteers for it often has the instincts of an archivist, and feels driven to keep scrapbooks and photograph albums up to date, so that the clan can see proof of its own continuity.

13   3. Good families are much to all their members, but everything to none. Good families are fortresses with many windows and doors to the outer world. The blood clans I feel most drawn to were founded by parents who are nearly

[1] Gush with pride.

[2] An informal group of intellectuals living in the Bloomsbury district.

as devoted to what they do outside as they are to each other and their children. Their curiosity and passion are contagious. Everybody, where they live, is busy. Paint is spattered on eyeglasses. Mud lurks under fingernails. Person-to-person calls come in the middle of the night from Tokyo and Brussels. Catcher's mitts, ballet slippers, overdue library books, and other signs of extrafamilial concerns are everywhere.

14   4. Good families are hospitable. Knowing that hosts need guests as much as guests need hosts, they are generous with honorary memberships for friends, whom they urge to come early and often and to stay late. Such clans exude a vivid sense of surrounding rings of relatives, neighbors, teachers, students, and godparents, any of whom at any time might break or slide into the inner circle. Inside that circle a wholesome, tacit emotional feudalism develops: you give me protection, I'll give you fealty. Such pacts begin with, but soon go far beyond, the jolly exchange of pie at Thanksgiving or cake on a birthday. They mean that you can ask me to supervise your children for the fortnight you will be in the hospital, and that however inconvenient this might be for me, I shall manage to do so. It means I can phone you on what for me is a dreary, wretched Sunday afternoon and for you is the eve of a deadline, knowing you will tell me to come right over, if only to watch you type. It means we need not dissemble. ("To yield to seeming," as Martin Buber wrote, "is man's essential cowardice, to resist it is his essential courage . . . one must at times pay dearly for life lived from the being, but it is never too dear.")

15   5. Good families deal squarely with direness. Pity the tribe that doesn't have, and cherish, at least one flamboyant eccentric. Pity too the one that supposes it can avoid for long the woes to which all flesh is heir. Lunacy, bankruptcy, suicide, and other unthinkable fates sooner or later afflict the noblest of clans with an undertow of gloom. Family life is a set of givens, someone once told me, and it takes courage to see certain givens as blessings rather than as curses. It surely does. Contradictions and inconsistencies are givens, too. So is the battle against what the Oregon patriarch Kenneth Babbs calls malarkey. "There's always malarkey lurking, bubbles in the cesspool, fetid bubbles that pop and smell. But I don't put up with malarkey, between my stepkids and my natural ones or anywhere else in the family."

16   6. Good families prize their rituals. Nothing welds a family more than these. Rituals are vital especially for clans without histories, because they evoke a past, imply a future, and hint at continuity. No line in the seder service at Passover reassures more than the last: "Next year in Jerusalem!" A clan becomes more of a clan each time it gathers to observe a fixed ritual (Christmas, birthdays, Thanksgiving, and so on), grieves at a funeral (anyone may come to most funerals; those who do declare their tribalness), and devises a new rite of its own. Equinox breakfasts can be at least as welding as Memorial Day parades. Several of my colleagues and I used to meet for lunch every Pearl Harbor Day, preferably to eat some politically neutral fare like smorgasbord, to "forgive" our only ancestrally Japanese friend, Irene Kubota

Neves. For that and other things we became, and remain, a sort of family.

17   "Rituals," a California friend of mind said, "aren't just externals and holidays. They are the performances of our lives. They are a kind of shorthand. They can't be decreed. My mother used to try to decree them. She'd make such a goddamn fuss over what we talked about at dinner, aiming at Topics of Common Interest, topics that celebrated our cohesion as a family. These performances were always hollow, because the phenomenology of the moment got sacrificed for the *idea* of the moment. Real rituals are discovered in retrospect. They emerge around constitutive moments, moments that only happen once, around whose memory meanings cluster. You don't choose those moments. They choose themselves." A lucky clan includes a born mythologizer, like my blood sister, who has the gift for apprehending such a moment when she sees it, and who cannot help but invent new rituals everywhere she goes.

18   7. Good families are affectionate. This of course is a matter of style. I know clans whose members greet each other with gingerly handshakes or, in what pass for kisses, with hurried brushes of jawbones, as if the object were to touch not the lips but the ears. I don't see how such people manage. "The tribe that does not hug," as someone who has been part of many *ad hoc* families recently wrote to me, "is no tribe at all. More and more I realize that everybody, regardless of age, needs to be hugged and comforted in a brotherly or sisterly way now and then. Preferably now."

19   8. Good families have a sense of place, which these days is not achieved easily. As Susanne Langer wrote in 1957, "Most people have no home that is a symbol of their childhood, not even a definite memory of one place to serve that purpose . . . all the old symbols are gone." Once I asked a roomful of supper guests if anyone felt a strong pull to any certain spot on the face of the earth. Everyone was silent, except for a visitor from Bavaria. The rest of us seemed to know all too well what Walker Percy means in *The Moviegoer* when he tells of the "genie-soul of a place, which every place has or else is not a place [and which] wherever you go, you must meet and master or else be met and mastered." All that meeting and mastering saps plenty of strength. It also underscores our need for tribal bases of the sort which soaring real estate taxes and splintering families have made all but obsolete.

20   So what are we to do, those of us whose habit and pleasure and doom is our tendency, as a Georgia lady put it, to "fly off at every other whipstich"? Think in terms of movable feasts, that's what. Live here, wherever here may be, as if we were going to belong here for the rest of our lives. Learn to hallow whatever ground we happen to stand on or land on. Like medieval knights who took their tapestries along on Crusades, like modern Afghanis with their yurts, we must pack such totems and icons as we can to make short-term quarters feel like home. Pillows, small rugs, watercolors can dispel much of the chilling anonymity of a motel room or sublet apartment. When we can, we should live in rooms with stoves and fireplaces or at least candelight. The ancient saying is still true: Extinguished hearth, extinguished family.

21   Round tables help too, and as a friend of mine once put it, so do "too many comfortable chairs, with surfaces to put feet on, arranged so as to encourage a maximum of eye contact." Such rooms inspire good talk, of which good clans can never have enough.

22   9. Good families, not just the blood kind, find some way to connect with posterity. "To forge a link in the humble chain of being, encircling heirs to ancestors," as Michael Novak has written, "is to walk within a circle of magic as primitive as humans knew in caves." He is talking of course about babies, feeling them leap in wombs, giving them suck. Parenthood, however, is a state which some miss by chance and others by design, and a vocation to which not all are called. Some of us, like the novelist Richard P. Brickner, look on as others "name their children and their children in turn name their own lives, devising their own flags from their parents' cloth." What are we who lack children to do? Build houses? Plant trees? Write books or symphonies or laws? Perhaps, but even if we do these things, there should be children on the sidelines if not at the center of our lives.

23   It is a sadly impoverished tribe that does not allow access to, and make much of, some children. Not too much, of course; it has truly been said that never in history have so many educated people devoted so much attention to so few children. Attention, in excess, can turn to fawning, which isn't much better than neglect. Still, if we don't regularly see and talk to and laugh with people who can expect to outlive us by twenty years or so, we had better get busy and find some.

24   10. Good families also honor their elders. The wider the age range, the stronger the tribe. Jean-Paul Sartre and Margaret Mead, to name two spectacularly confident former children, have both remarked on the central importance of grandparents in their own early lives. Grandparents are now in much more abundant supply than they were a generation or two ago, when old age was more rare. If actual grandparents are not at hand, no family should have too hard a time finding substitute ones to whom to pay unfeigned homage. The Soviet Union's enchantment with day-care centers, I have heard, stems at least in part from the state's eagerness to keep children away from their presumably subversive grandparents. Let that be a lesson to clans based on interest as well as to those based on genes.

25   Of course there are elders and elders. Most people in America, as David T. Bazelon has written, haven't the slightest idea of what to do with the extra thirty years they have been given to live. Few are as briskly secure as Alice Roosevelt Longworth, who once, when I visited her for tea, showed a recent photograph and asked whether I didn't think it made her look like "a malevolent Eurasian concubine—an *aged* malevolent Eurasian concubine." I admitted that it did, which was just what she wanted to hear. But those of us whose fathers weren't Presidents may not grow old, if at all, with such style.

26   Sad stories abound. The mother of one friend of mine languished for years, never far from a coma, in a nursing home. Only when her husband and

children sang one of her favorite old songs, such as "Lord Jeffrey Amherst," would a smile fleet across her face. But a man I know of in New Jersey, who couldn't stand the state of Iowa or babies, changed his mind on both counts when his daughter, who lived in Iowa, had a baby. Suddenly he took to inventing business trips to St. Louis, by way of Cedar Rapids, phoning to say he would be at the airport there at 11:31 P.M., and "Be sure to bring Jake!" That cheers me. So did part of a talk I had with a woman in Albuquerque, whom I hadn't seen since a trip some years before to the Soviet Union.

27   "Honey," she said when I phoned her during a short stopover and asked how she was, "if I were any better I'd blow up and *bust*. I can't *tell* you how *neat* it is to put some age on! A lot of it, of course, has to do with going to the shrink, getting uncorked, and of course it doesn't hurt to have money—no, we *don't* have a ranch; it's only 900 acres, so we call it a farm. But every year, as far as age is concerned, I seem to get better, doing more and more stuff I love to do. The only thing I've ever wanted and don't have is a good marriage. Nothing I do ever pleases the men I marry. The only reason I'm still married now is it's too much trouble not to be. But my girls are growing up to be just *neat* humans, and the men they're sharing their lives with are too. They pick nice guys, my girls. I wish I could say the same. But I'm a lot better off than many women my age. I go to parties where sixty-year-olds with blue bouffant hairdos are still telling the same jokes they told twenty-five or thirty years ago. Complacent? No, that's not it, exactly. What they are is sad—sad as the dickens. They don't seem to be *connected*."

28   Some days my handwriting resembles my mother's, slanting hopefully and a bit extravagantly eastward. Other days it looks more like my father's: resolute, vertical, guardedly free of loops. Both my parents will remain in my nerves and muscles and mind until the day I die, and so will my sister, but they aren't the only ones. If I were to die tomorrow, the obituary would note that my father and sister survived me. True, but not true enough. Like most official lists of survivors, this one would be incomplete.

29   Several of the most affecting relationships I have ever known of, or been part of, have sprung not from genes or contracts but from serendipitous, uncanny bonds of choice. I don't think enough can be said for the fierce tenderness such bonds can generate. Maybe the best thing to say is nothing at all, or very little. Midwestern preachers used to hold that "a heavy rain doesn't seep into the ground but rolls off—when you preach to farmers, your sermon should be a drizzle instead of a downpour." So too with any cause that matters: shouting and lapel-grabbing and institutionalizing can do more harm than good. A quiet approach works better.

30   "I wish it would hurry up and get colder," I said one warm afternoon several Octobers ago to a black man with whom I was walking in a park.
31   "Don't worry," he told me. "Like my grandmother used to say when I was a boy, 'Hawk'll be here soon enough.'"
32   "What did she mean by 'hawk'?"

33   "Hawk meant winter, cold, trouble. And she was right: the hawk always came."

34   With regard to families, many would say that the hawk has long been here, hovering. "I'd rather put up with being lonely now than have to put up with being still more lonely in the future," says a character in Natsume Soseki's novel *Kokoro*. "We live in an age of freedom, independence, and the self, and I imagine this loneliness is the price we have to pay for it." Seven decades earlier, in *Either/Or*, Sören Kierkegaard had written, "Our age has lost all the substantial categories of family, state, and race. It must leave the individual entirely to himself, so that in a stricter sense he becomes his own creator."

35   If it is true that we must create ourselves, maybe while we are about it we can also devise some new kinds of families, new connections to supplement the old ones. The second verse of a hymn by James Russell Lowell says,

> New occasions bring new duties;
> Time makes ancient good uncouth.

Surely one outworn "good" is the maxim that blood relatives are the only ones who can or should greatly matter. Or look at it another way: go back six generations, and each one of us has sixty-four direct ancestors. Go back twenty—only four or five centuries, not such a big chunk of human history—and we each have more than a million. Does it not stand to reason, since the world population was then so much smaller, that we all have a lot more cousins—though admittedly distant ones—than we were brought up to suspect? And don't these cousins deserve our attention?

36   One day after lunch at a friend's apartment I waited in his lobby while he collected his mail. Out of the elevator came two nurses supporting a wizened, staring woman who couldn't have weighed much more than seventy pounds. It was all the woman could do to make her way down the three steps to the sidewalk and the curb where a car was waiting. Those steps must have been to that woman what a steep mountain trail would be to me. The nurses guided her down them with infinite patience.

37   "Easy, darlin'," one nurse said to the woman.

38   "That's a good girl," said the other. The woman, my friend's doorman told us, was ninety. That morning she had fallen and hurt herself. On her forehead was something which, had it not been a bruise, we might have thought beautiful: a marvel of mauve and lavender and magenta. This woman, who was then being taken to a nursing home, had lived in my friend's apartment building for forty years. All her relatives were dead, and her few surviving friends no longer chose to see her.

39   "But how can that be?" I asked my friend. "*We* could never be that alone, could we?"

40   "Don't be so sure," said my friend, who knows more of such matters than I do. "Even if we were to end up in the same nursing home, if I was in markedly worse shape than you were, you might not want to see me, either."

41   "But I can't imagine not wanting to see you."

42   "It happens," my friend said.

43   Maybe we can keep it from happening. Maybe the hawk can be kept at bay, if we give more thought to our tribes and our clans and our several kinds of families. No aim seems to me more urgent, nor any achievement more worthy of a psalm. So *hosanna in excelsis*, and blest be the tie that binds. And please pass the salt.

Considering Ideas

1. What does Howard mean when she refers to "families of friends"? Why are families of friends important?
2. What are the two kinds of friends who become family?
3. What do you think of Howard's assertion in paragraph 5 that "we must devise new ways, or revive old ones, to equip ourselves with kinfolk"?
4. In paragraph 6, Howard says, "The best-chosen clans, like the best friendships and the best blood families, endure by accumulating a history solid enough to suggest a future." What do you think Howard means by this?
5. How important does Howard think families are? How do you know?
6. Howard explains ten characteristics of good families. Are there any characteristics that you think should be added or deleted? Explain.

Considering Technique

1. What arguable point prompts Howard's definition of a good family?
2. Does Howard attempt to prove that we can choose our own families? Why or why not?
3. What purpose does the narration in paragraphs 7 and 8 serve? What purpose does the narration in paragraphs 36 through 42 serve?
4. Which paragraphs include examples, and what purpose do the examples serve?
5. Each paragraph introducing a characteristic of good families begins with the words "good families." What is the purpose of this repetition?
6. Consult your dictionary if you do not know the meaning of any of these words from the selection: *ebullient* (paragraph 1), *alchemy* (paragraph 2), *ascribed* (paragraph 3), *surrogate* (paragraph 5), *deride* (paragraph 6), *ephemeral* (paragraph 6), *Yiddish* (paragraph 11), *demigods* (paragraph 11), *archivist* (paragraph 12), *exude* (paragraph 14), *tacit* (paragraph 14), *fealty* (paragraph 14), *dissemble* (paragraph 14), *direness* (paragraph 15), *feted* (paragraph 15), *seder* (paragraph 16), *phenomenology* (paragraph 17), *ad hoc* (paragraph 18), *yurts* (paragraph 20), *totems* (paragraph 20), *icons* (paragraph 20), *malevolent* (paragraph 25), *concubine* (paragraph 25), *serendipitous* (paragraph 29), *wizened* (paragraph 36).

For Group Consideration

Identify and illustrate the characteristics of the "families" that college students form with each other.

Journal Entry

Write about one or more friends you have had who qualify as family, and explain how they became part of your family. As an alternative, if you do not have friends who qualify as family, explain why not.

Essay Assignments

1. Argue that your family is or is not a "good family," based on Howard's definition of what a good family is.
2. Howard explains that friends can become our family when our biological relatives are unable or unwilling to be. If the concept of choosing your own family appeals to you, devise a plan whereby people, at a certain age, can "divorce" their family members and choose new ones. Also argue for the adoption of your plan.
3. In paragraph 1, Howard says that all people need families. Agree or disagree with her.

NEEDED: A POLICY FOR CHILDREN WHEN PARENTS GO TO WORK
Maxine Phillips

◆

Maxine Phillips argues that because "decent child care is now an issue that cuts across political and class lines," we need a national child-care policy. When you read her explanation of this policy, decide if you would like your tax dollars spent in the way she describes.

◆

1   Opponents of day care still call for women to return to home and hearth, but the battle is really over. Now the question is: Will day care continue to be inadequately funded and poorly regulated, or will public policy begin to put into place a system that rightly treats children as our most valuable national resource?

2   More than 50% of the mothers of young children are in the work force before the child's first birthday. An estimated 9.5 million preschoolers have mothers who work outside the home. Most women, like most men, are working to put food on the table. Many are the sole support of their families. They are economically unable to stay at home, although many would prefer to do so.

3   Decent child care is now an issue that cuts across political and class lines. But this reality has not yet caught up with public policy. Conservative Sen. Orrin G. Hatch (R-Utah) is sponsoring a bill that would authorize $325 million in child-care costs for poor children. Liberal Sen. Christopher J. Dodd (D-Conn.) has just introduced a $2.5 billion bill for better child care, a far-reaching piece of legislation backed by 20 other senators and more than 100 members of the House. The Dodd measure would be a big improvement over current legislation, carrying provisions for information and referral, for standards and for monitoring that would have an impact on all children. But because eligible families could not earn more than 115% of a state's median income, the greatest impact would be on children of the working poor.

4   As long as public policy treats day care as a service for the poor, it will be vulnerable to . . . [having its] funds [cut] . . . .

5   Thus at one end of the spectrum we have far too few publicly funded day-care slots limited to poverty-level families. At the other are high-quality non-profit centers available to the well-to-do. For the vast majority, in what *Business Week* calls the "day-care crisis of the middle-class," there is a crazy quilt of arrangements with neighbors, relatives and poorly staffed centers.

6   A barrage of negative day-care information assaults the working mother, claiming that her children will not bond properly with her, will suffer emotionally and intellectually and will be exposed to deadly diseases.

7   True, many women rightly feel uncomfortable about leaving children in many situations available. Day-care workers' salaries are in the lowest 10%.

Shoddy licensing statutes often allow one person to care for as many as six or eight infants. Unlicensed centers abound because working parents cannot pay the fees for the better ones. About 500,000 children are in scandalously unfit profit-making centers, which spend 45% less per child than federally funded nonprofit centers.

8   The average day-care cost is $60 per week—often as much as 30% of a working mother's salary. Quality day care costs about three times as much in urban situations, clearly beyond the reach of most families.

9   My family was among the lucky ones. When our daughter was 9 months old we enrolled her in a wonderful place where she has consistent, well-trained, loving caretakers, play equipment we could never afford at home and the intellectual stimulation that comes from being with other children overseen by concerned adults. Two years later, her verbal ability and social skills confirm the choice we made. I sometimes worry that her days at home are not as rich as her days at the center.

10   Yet this kind of care, considered a societal responsibility in such countries as France or Sweden, is available here only to the lucky or the privileged few.

11   Today, when most Americans will need child care at some time in their lives, day care should be a service universally available regardless of income. Then, as with public schools, parents can choose whether or not to use it.

12   This is what a national child-care policy would look like:

13   It would start with a family-leave law. If we seriously believe, as do most parents and other experts, that children should be with their parents in the early months when bonding is so important, why does society make it economically impossible? Unlike Canada, Italy, Sweden and many other nations, the United States has no national system of parental leave. Many women must return to work within a week or two of giving birth or risk losing their jobs. Yet a proposal in Congress this year to allow 16 weeks of unpaid parental leave met such resistance from the business community that it is almost dead.

14   Second, good policy would include neighborhood nonprofit day-care facilities open to everyone. These places would have parents involved, on the board and in the center. They would accommodate a variety of work schedules, with extra staff available for deployment to the homes of sick children whose parents could not make other arrangements.

15   Initial costs would be high (conservative estimates start at $30 billion) but must be measured against the lost tax revenues from people who would work—or work more productively—if reliable day care were available, not to mention the societal costs of children poorly cared for early in life.

16   Third, it would include after-school care for older children. Latch-key youngsters are a concern for all working parents; their lack of supervision poses a danger to them and to society.

17   These are the building blocks of a national system but the foundation must be a true commitment to the family unit.

18   This means prenatal care, nutrition, health care for both adults and chil-

dren, decent welfare benefits to allow parents to feed, shelter and clothe their children—plus assurances that both mothers and fathers can find work at wages that allow them to live decent family lives. These programs are expensive but no more so than programs already in place to pick up the wreckage caused by their absence. As long as America approaches child care in piecemeal fashion—as part of a welfare package or as a service only for children at poverty levels—we perpetuate the belief that this is an individual problem. We no longer believe that about education. In the current reality, why do we continue to believe it about child care?

19   Are these proposals utopian? No. Large parts are in place in every Western industrial society but our own.

20   We look most frequently to the public schools and Social Security as examples of entitlement accepted by the general society but I find added inspiration from a courageous group of parents who have already led the way in sensitizing the nation's conscience. Parents of developmentally disabled children, faced with a lifetime of caring for their youngsters and fears of what will happen after the parents die, organized to campaign for special funds and services. The results—including mandated education for all handicapped children—are far from perfect but demonstrate how parents can help society accept responsibility for some children. Now parents must help society accept responsibility for all of them.

Considering Ideas

1. What objection does Phillips have to the proposed child-care legislation she mentions?
2. According to the essay, who seems to be suffering the most as a result of the current child-care situation?
3. What does Phillips think we can learn from the parents of developmentally disabled children?
4. Why does Phillips think we need a national child-care policy?
5. What are the characteristics of the policy Phillips recommends?

Considering Technique

1. Which sentence do you think best serves as the thesis of the essay? What issue and stand does the thesis present?
2. What purpose do the statistics in paragraph 2 serve? What purpose do the statistics in paragraphs 7 and 8 serve?
3. Which paragraph includes the author's personal experience? What does her personal experience contribute to the essay?
4. Which paragraphs include contrast? What purpose does the contrast serve? (Contrast is discussed in Chapter 8.)

5. Which paragraphs raise and counter objections? What objections are raised and how are they countered?
6. What approach does Phillips take to her conclusion?
7. Consult a dictionary if you are unsure of the meaning of any of these words: *sole* (paragraph 2), *barrage* (paragraph 6), *bond* (paragraph 6), *shoddy* (paragraph 7), *deployment* (paragraph 14), *latch-key* (paragraph 16), *prenatal* (paragraph 18), *piecemeal* (paragraph 18), *utopian* (paragraph 19), *entitlement* (paragraph 20), *mandated* (paragraph 20).

For Group Consideration

If you have children, explain how you now or in the past have juggled work (or school) and parenthood. If you plan to have children, explain how you will juggle work (or school) and parenthood. What services do you, did you, or will you count on being available? Summarize the responses and report them to the class.

Journal Entry

If your mother worked outside the home, tell what it was like growing up with a working mother. Did your life have any special advantages or disadvantages that children without working mothers did not experience? If your mother did not work outside the home, tell what your childhood was like and whether you experienced any advantages or disadvantages that children with working mothers did not experience.

Essay Assignments

1. Write a letter to your representative or senator, arguing for or against the national child-care policy Phillips describes. Be sure to raise and counter important objections to your stand.
2. Interview several working mothers and use that information, along with the information in the essay and your own experience and observation, to summarize the pressures and problems that working mothers face as a result of juggling their working and family lives. Then describe a particular child-care policy that will address those problems and pressures and argue for its passage.
3. Construct a model for a national child-care policy and argue for its passage by Congress. Be sure to raise and counter compelling objections to your plan. The preceding group activity may give you ideas.

HOMEMAKING
William Raspberry

Syndicated columnist William Raspberry has been a journalism instructor, a television commentator, and a contributing editor of the ABC-TV Evening News. In 1982, he was nominated for a Pulitzer Prize. In "Homemaking," Raspberry explains why homemaking is devalued and, at the same time, argues that it should not be. The essay was written in 1977, so as you read, decide how much of what Raspberry says is still true today.

1   Since my wife was out of town last weekend—leaving me to look after our children and the house—I suppose I could make the case that I now have a better appreciation of what homemaking is about.

2   Well, if I do, it isn't because of what I had to do in her absence but because of what I didn't have to do. I had to cook and make sure that the little ones were warmly clothed, that they spent some time playing outside, that they got baths, picked up after themselves, and so on. In short, I took over a series of chores, many of which I would have performed even if my wife had been home.

3   But I didn't have to plan anything, schedule anything or fit anything into an overall design. I didn't have to see to my children's overall nutrition; I only had to see that they weren't too bored and didn't tear the house down. What I did was episodic, a combination of housework and babysitting. What my wife does is part of an ongoing enterprise: homemaking. Here is an executive role, though neither she nor I had ever thought to describe it as such.

4   I strongly suspect that the failure to make the distinction between homemaking and chores is one of the chief reasons why homemaking has fallen into such disrepute of late. As Jinx Melia, founder and director of the Martha Movement,[*] observed in a recent interview, "ethnic" homemakers, as a rule, have managed to retain a higher sense of respect for their calling, partly, she suspects, because their husbands may be somewhat more likely to work at blue-collar jobs that hold no attraction for their wives.

5   A larger part, though, may be that "traditional" husbands—whatever jobs they work at—are likelier to be ignorant (perhaps deliberately so) of homemaking skills. Homemaking may involve as much a sense of mystique for these husbands as outside work holds for their wives. Men of all classes are increasingly likely these days to help out with the chores, or even take over for a spell, as I did last weekend. And if we aren't careful, we come to believe that we can do easily everything our wives do—if we can only survive the boredom of it.

[*] This movement was founded to give a voice to homemakers in the United States.

The result is that we lose respect for what they do. Think of homemaking as a series of more or less unpleasant chores and the disrespect is virtually automatic.

6 Well, most jobs are a series of more or less unpleasant chores. But it doesn't follow that that's all they are. Looking up cases and precedents, trying to draw information out of a client who doesn't quite understand what you need to know, keeping records, writing "boiler-plate" contracts—all these things are routine, and a bright high school graduate could quickly learn to do them all. The chores are a drag; but lawyering is a fascinating career. Reducing a career to a series of chores creates this additional problem of perspective: Any time not spent on one or another of the chores is viewed as time wasted.

7 As Melia also pointed out, the men who work at professions spend an enormous amount of time doing the mirror image of what their non-career wives may be chided or even openly criticized for doing. They talk on the phone a lot (perhaps about business, but they often aren't doing business). They hold staff meetings or unit meetings that are hardly different from coffee klatches. A business lunch with a client you've already sold (or for whom you have no specific proposal at the moment) is not vastly different from a gathering of homemakers in somebody's kitchenette.

8 The main difference is that a man gets to call all these things "work." One reason for the difference is that the details of homemaking are far more visible (to the spouse) than the details of work done outside. As a result, husbands often not only devalue their wives' work but also feel perfectly free to question the wisdom of what they do as part of that work. Wives generally know too little about their husbands' work to question any aspect of it. They are more likely to magnify its importance.

9 None of this should be taken as a proposal that women be kept out of the labor market. There are women whose talents are so removed from home and hearth that it would be criminal to encourage them to become homemakers. There are women who need to earn income, for reasons ranging from fiscal to psychic. Women who choose careers outside the home, or who have no choice but to pursue careers, ought to be free to do so without any discrimination of any sort.

10 But there are also women who seek outside work primarily because they know their homemaking role is undervalued, by their husbands and by themselves. There is nothing intrinsic about producing income, on the one hand, or nurturing children and managing a household, on the other, that would lead to a natural conclusion that income-production is of greater value. The opposite conclusion would appear likelier, as in the distinction between worker and queen bees, for instance. But worker bees don't claim sole ownership and discretion over what they produce; they work for the hive. It would go a long way toward changing the onerous working conditions of homemakers if we could learn to think of family income as belonging to the family, not primarily to the person who happens to bring it home.

11   Maybe there is a logical reason why the marriage partner who doesn't produce income should be the fiscal dependent of the one who does. Off hand, I can't think what it might be.

Considering Ideas

1. According to Raspberry, what is our prevailing attitude toward homemaking?
2. How does Raspberry explain the fact that homemaking is not a valued occupation?
3. What do you think Raspberry means when he says that "the failure to make the distinction between homemaking and chores is one of the chief reasons why homemaking has fallen into disrepute of late"?
4. Why does Raspberry think that ethnic homemakers have more respect for homemaking? Do you agree with this assessment?
5. From what source does Raspberry get his information about homemaking?
6. What persuasive point is Raspberry making? Did he succeed in convincing you? Why or why not?
7. "Homemaking" originally appeared in 1977 in the *Washington Post*. Do you think today's readers of that newspaper would be any harder to convince than Raspberry's original audience? Explain.

Considering Technique

1. Which sentence do you think functions as Raspberry's thesis?
2. How does Raspberry make use of contrast in his essay? How does he make use of comparison? (Comparison-contrast is discussed in Chapter 8.)
3. Which paragraphs include cause-and-effect analysis? What purpose does that analysis serve? (Cause-and-effect analysis is discussed in Chapter 9.)
4. In which paragraph does Raspberry counter a possible objection to his view?
5. What approach does Raspberry take to his conclusion?
6. Consult a dictionary if you are unsure of the meaning of any of these words: *episodic* (paragraph 3), *disrepute* (paragraph 4), *mystique* (paragraph 5), *precedents* (paragraph 6), *boiler-plate contracts* (paragraph 6), *chided* (paragraph 7), *coffee klatches* (paragraph 7), *fiscal* (paragraph 9), *intrinsic* (paragraph 10), *onerous* (paragraph 10).

For Group Consideration

Assume you must design a public relations campaign to improve the image of homemakers. Explain how you would use the media to achieve your goal.

Journal Entry

"Homemaking" first appeared in 1977. Consider whether much has changed since then. What is society's current attitude toward homemaking? What is your own attitude?

Essay Assignments

1. Detail the responsibilities and skills of today's homemakers and carefully explain what they contribute to family life. Then argue that homemakers should be valued more than they are. If you need information for your essay, interview several homemakers.
2. Some people have argued that homemakers should be paid for their work, either with money or with credits that can be applied toward school tuition after the children are grown. If this idea appeals to you, explain how the plan could work and argue in its favor. If you do not like the idea, argue against it, explaining what problems it would create.

SELF-HELP—A BLACK TRADITION
Dorothy Height

◆

Dorothy Height is a social activist who has been the director of the Center for Racial Justice, the president of the National Council of Negro Women, Inc., a consultant on African Affairs to the Secretary of State, and a member of the President's Commission on the Status of Women. In "Self-Help—A Black Tradition," Height details the strengths of the black family and argues that its tradition of self-help should be extended to form caring communities. As you read, notice that Height also argues a second point.

◆

It is our task to make plain to ourselves the great story of our rise in America from "less than dust" to the heights of sound achievement. . . . The situation we face must be defined, reflected and evaluated.

—Mary McLeod Bethune, 1937

1   Recent negative portrayals of the black family have made it painfully clear to most African-Americans that although much has changed in the national life, much remains the same. The incessant emphasis on the dysfunctioning of black people is simply one more attempt to show that African-Americans do not really fit into the society—that we are "overdependent" and predominantly welfare-oriented. Quite overlooked in this equation is the fact that most black Americans are, on the contrary, overwhelmingly among the *working* poor.

2   Equally overlooked when the disingenuous topic of the supposed lack of black "self-help" is conjured up, is a fundamental truth: that the major energies of black people in America historically have had to be directed to attaining the most elementary human freedoms (such as owning one's own body and the fruits thereof) that our white sisters and brothers take for granted. The civil rights movement of the 1950s and 1960s was perhaps the most extraordinary example of a mass "self-help" movement in American history: self-help mounted under grave conditions to throw off the yoke of American apartheid. Yet it was not a new event so much as the continuation of an old tradition. Since the end of the slave era black people have had to provide services for one another in every conceivable way: feeding and clothing the destitute; tending the sick; caring for orphaned children and the aged; establishing insurance companies, burial societies, travelers' accommodations when hotels were segregated—the list goes on.

3   In 1909, almost fifty years before the modern civil rights movement emerged, the National Association for the Advancement of Colored People (preceded by the Du Bois–organized Niagara Movement) was founded following the lynching of a black man in Springfield, Illinois. Its first major undertaking was the fight against the hundreds of such atrocities then occurring

annually. The Urban League was founded the next year to advance economic self-help.

4   Eighteen years earlier, a fearless journalist named Ida B. Wells began a crusade against lynching, by lecturing, organizing and compiling the first documentation of the social, political and economic facts behind the atrocities. In 1895, the National Association of Colored Women's Clubs was formed to bring to bear the collective strength of women in ameliorating the desperate conditions in which our people lived.

5   What is clear to us in the current era of ever mounting disparagement of the black family—and the internalizing by our young people of the negativism thrust upon them daily—is that we need a movement that will retrieve and build upon the value system of the traditional extended family, the strong sense of kinship ties that goes back to the days of the trans-Atlantic slave trade, when it was up to us either to forge ties of mutual support or perish as a people. Those unbreakable bonds sent people searching for one another after the forced separations of slavery. They are still evident in our custom of calling one another brother and sister—and mother, aunt and uncle—even when there is no blood relationship. There's an entire history behind these interactions that is precious to our sense of self-worth and identity as a people. Those who attempt to supplant our conception of ourselves with their own are either ignorant of this proud history or, worse, bent on concealing or eradicating it.

6   The history of self-help among blacks offers models that will be useful in the search for innovative approaches to current problems. For instance, I recall that in 1939, when I worked in the Harlem Y.W.C.A., the Florence Crittendon Homes took in unmarried white mothers, but there was not a bed in the city for unwed black mothers. The only help available to them was in the limited facilities the Y.W.C.A. could provide. To supplement these we found some black women who belonged to an organization called Club Caroline and who were able to acquire a small house to shelter unwed mothers. Their example was followed by black women's clubs all over the country, whose members formed a national network of assistance, keeping registers of people who were willing to take in a young mother. Economic realities today make it impossible for black people to set up enough small homes to accommodate the large numbers of single mothers, drug addicts, the jobless and homeless, and the thousands of unclaimed black infants languishing in hospitals and foster homes.

7   Nevertheless, we can learn something from the methods used by the traditional black extended family in which adults possessed the authority to look out for the young, whether or not they were blood relatives. We may not be able to restore entirely the old concept of the extended family, given the present complex (and chaotic) social, political and economic conditions in the large urban centers. But enough of it survives to draw upon in encouraging more caring communities in which neighbors look around them to see what's happening and set up networks for alerting others to impending threats. It is important for our young people to know that our past holds valuable traditions.

Black sociologists have not been alone in pointing out that instead of constantly focusing on the problems of black families, their white counterparts should examine its historic strengths: the respect for older people, the communal nurturing of children, the ability to feed an entire family on next to nothing, the unceasing toil of parents (often assisted by the community) to send their children through college, the black entrepreneurs who built up businesses to serve our needs after others refused to. In short, our endless coping skills.

8   We have always stressed the work ethic. We have never been a lazy people; hard work has killed a great number of us. A. Philip Randolph, president of the Brotherhood of Sleeping Car Porters, used to say that what black folk needed was not more work but more pay for the work that they do, and they could manage the rest. It is only recently in the cities, where higher skills are required and the quality of education has deteriorated, that unemployment and the grimmest kind of poverty have become constants and whole generations are growing up in neighborhoods where few people have jobs.

9   Some social analysts are correct when they say that public policies had a great deal to do with producing this state of affairs, but they refuse to acknowledge the impact of racial discrimination on education and employment. They define a "family" as a social/economic/political unit with a man at its head, and they continue to insist on this definition even at a time when divorce rates and serial marriages, resulting in merged families and increasing numbers of female-headed households, reveal how archaic it is.

10   For black people, this definition has never applied. Black traditions of the extended family grew out of the primary need to survive, an urgency that for the most part made gender differentials largely irrelevant. So did the grim economic realities that traditionally necessitated that both black men and women work in order to earn a decent living for their families—or, for that matter, to make their way at all. That throughout history many black women have had to accomplish these things without male partners consistently at our sides is much more the result of the racism that limits—and frequently destroys—black males than of "immorality" (as white scholars could discern, if they ever deigned to do research in this area).

11   Blacks have never said to a child, "Unless you have a mother, father, sister, brother, you don't have a family." I think that the wrongheaded emphasis on the nuclear family has led to the demoralization of young people, both white and black. Because of it, a child who is not part of a nuclear family—or whose family does not behave in the manner of the model—may well say, "I'm nobody."

12   **The N.C.N.W. and the Black 'Family Celebrations'.**   For fifty-four years the National Council of Negro Women—composed of civic, church, educational, labor, community and professional organizations uniting 4 million members—has carried on the tradition of black self-help. We at the N.C.N.W., following in the footsteps of our founder, the indefatigable educator Mary McLeod Bethune, have focused attention on the concerns of black women and

their families. On behalf of young black people, the N.C.N.W. has taken counteractions aimed at restoring or bolstering collective self-esteem in order to lift the morale of the people in coping with the problems they face, whether related to drugs, education, teen-age pregnancy, employability, health problems or whatever they might be.

13   In recent years we at the N.C.N.W. have built on the special tradition of black "family celebrations" to bring people together. In 1986 we sponsored the first Black Family Reunion Celebration, held on the Washington Mall with almost 200,000 people in attendance. In 1987 three others followed, in Washington, Los Angeles, and Detroit. In 1988 a coming-together was celebrated in Philadelphia and again on the Washington Mall in what had become a national movement.

14   So far, nearly 2 million African-Americans have flocked to the black family celebrations, a turnout that attests to the hunger of our people to hear something other than the constant negativism that is directed our way, to gain strength and inspiration from one another and, in many cases, to secure advice or help from someone we can trust. We have used these occasions to stress black history and the tradition of helping one another, qualified by our awareness that we now live in a society and world that is vastly different from the simpler times in which our sense of community—whatever threatened us— was intact.

15   In these celebrations, the N.C.N.W. stresses what we consider to be genuine family values. Coretta Scott King shared what it has meant to be a single mother for all the years since her husband's assassination. She spoke not as the wife of a martyred leader but as the mother of children whom she had to bring up alone. We regularly have Masons come to talk about their early history and how they have contributed to the building of their communities. We have celebrities galore, but we also have young people rapping about teen-age pregnancy, drugs or whatever is their most urgent concern. And we also provide allied services. In Washington, when the D.C. Drugmobile was brought to the Mall, the lines before it were as long as those before the black film festival. The impact of our offerings has been felt in the public schools, where teachers report that in the week following the reunion celebration, children flock to school eager to make reports on their activities. All because we have a children's pavilion with black history puppets and African and African-American storytelling.

16   The N.C.N.W. also offers health checks. At the very first celebration, 20,000 people were tested for cholesterol levels and untold numbers for high blood pressure. Many had never had checkups of any kind before. And children waited patiently in line to get their teeth examined at facilities provided by the Howard University College of Dentistry.

17   Long lines also formed before our education booths. A young woman taxi driver told me recently that until she and her husband attended the Black Family Reunion Celebration she did not know that someone could earn a high-

school diploma without going back to the classroom. Subsequently, they decided that they were too young to be included in the numbers of unskilled blacks predicted for the year 2000. Both took extra jobs and were studying for the General Education Development test.

18   I was sobered by the realization that this young woman might have lived near an adult education center and never dreamed that it was meant for her. The N.C.N.W. is helping people understand that they can be active on their own behalf. At the Family Celebration in Atlanta we disseminated information from the Summer Youth Employment Training Program about jobs that were going begging for lack of applicants. When the young people in attendance discovered that the opportunities were not limited to those with special qualifications, they promptly got on the telephone to call their friends. As a result, there were applicants for almost all the jobs before the celebration ended.

19   There are many such stories growing out of our reunions. Of course, some may say the victories are small compared with the breadth of the problem. But activities in which a million people participate cannot be taken lightly. We at the N.C.N.W. and other black self-help organizations have no intention of spending our time lamenting the inadequacies of a society that has failed to develop the means to make every member aware that he or she belongs. The N.C.N.W. has a wide range of programs to serve African-American women and their families in the United States and an international division to assist women and their families in African countries. Currently, we are working to make a difference in all of the critical areas of human suffering enumerated here. Our first priority, as exemplified by our Black Family Reunion Celebrations, is to make clear that ours is a caring community and to inspire others, particularly our young, to press on in various ways, both to advance themselves and to further the larger struggle of our people.

20   One lesson is plain as we proceed: that public officials can establish all kinds of public programs thought up by people removed from the problems, and most will not work because the people for whom the programs are intended have been permitted no input in defining the problems as they actually know them to be, or in recommending the solutions. Skilled black professionals (and sensitive others) trusted by the community because they have contributed to its well-being can play a vital role in contributing to the formulation of wiser public policies—if only we can get decision-makers to listen.

Considering Ideas

1. How would you define the traditional black extended family?
2. What historical forces led to the creation of the traditional black extended family?
3. What does Height see as the chief strengths of the black family?

4. White society in the United States emphasizes the nuclear family (mother, father, and children). What effect does this emphasis have on blacks and whites?
5. What is it about the black extended family that Height celebrates?
6. What does the National Council of Negro Women have in common with the traditional black extended family?
7. What additional point does Height argue in her conclusion?

Considering Technique

1. Which sentence presents the thesis of the essay? What issue and stand does the thesis present?
2. Height's thesis is delayed until paragraph 5. What purpose do the four paragraphs before the thesis serve?
3. Which paragraphs include examples? What purpose do these examples serve?
4. What elements of contrast appear in the essay?
5. What do you think the purpose of Height's essay is?
6. Consult a dictionary if you are unsure of the meaning of any of these words: *incessant* (paragraph 1), *dysfunctioning* (paragraph 1), *disingenuous* (paragraph 2), *apartheid* (paragraph 2), *ameliorating* (paragraph 4), *disparagement* (paragraph 5), *languishing* (paragraph 6), *communal* (paragraph 7), *archaic* (paragraph 9), *indefatigable* (paragraph 12), *Masons* (paragraph 15), *disseminated* (paragraph 18).

For Group Consideration

With the members of your group, select a social problem and explore how the self-help concept described in the essay could be applied to help solve the problem.

Journal Entry

In about two pages, describe your own extended family and explain to what extent its members help each other.

Essay Assignments

1. Construct a model based on the National Council of Negro Women to deal with some current social problem. Explain how your model would work, tell how it could be implemented, and argue for its adoption. (The preceding group activity may give you some ideas.)

2. Height opens with this statement: "Recent negative portrayals of the black family have made it painfully clear to most African-Americans that although much has changed in the national life, much remains the same." Agree or disagree with this statement, citing specific examples to back up your stand.

Additional Essay Assignments

To respond to the assignments below, you can draw on the essays in this chapter, as well as these selections that treat family matters:

"My Backyard," page 65
"My Mother Never Worked," page 93
"The Water-Faucet Vision," page 118
"Untouchables," page 159
"Am I Blue?" page 240
"India: A Widow's Devastating Choice," page 278
"Complexion," page 295
"What Is Poverty?" page 349
"I Want a Wife," page 366

The information on summary, synthesis, paraphrasing, and quoting in the appendix may also be helpful.

1. In "Families," Jane Howard explains the characteristics of a good family. In "Needed: A Policy for Children When Parents Go to Work," Maxine Phillips comments on the large number of working mothers. Explain whether or not you think we can have good families with so many working mothers and why you think as you do. Also note what business, government, and parents can do to improve the family unit.

2. Do you think that tax dollars should be spent on paying people to stay home and take care of their children and/or on child care outside the home? Use your own ideas, along with those in "Homemaking" and "Needed: A Policy for Children When Parents Go to Work" to support your view and to raise and counter objections.

3. Argue for or against allowing same-sex marriages. In addition to your own ideas, draw on Stoddard's and Fein's essays as support for your view and/ or as objections to raise and counter.

4. Identify the argumentative-persuasive techniques used in "Marriage Is a Fundamental Right" and in "Reserve Marriage for Heterosexuals" and argue which author writes the more convincing piece. You are not to argue which author has the better position; you are to argue which one presents his position more convincingly.

5. Read "Self-Help—A Black Tradition," "Families," and "Needed: A Policy for Children When Parents Go to Work." Then construct a model for solving the child-care dilemma based on the principles of the extended family and self-help and argue for implementation of that model.

6. Use the information in "The Water-Faucet Vision," along with your own experience and observation, to attack or defend the idea that couples who do not get along should stay together for the sake of the children.

7. Identify what you think the greatest problem facing the American family is. Then offer a solution to that problem and argue for implementation of that solution. You may draw on any of the essays in this text for ideas.

8. Explain what special challenges you think children face and how you think families, society, or the government should address those challenges. Argue for adoption of your view. You may draw on any essays in this text.

9. Select one or more of the problems apparent in "What Is Poverty?" "Untouchables," and/or "India: A Widow's Devastating Choice," then argue that the extended family and self-help concepts explained in "Self-Help—A Black Tradition" could help solve the problem(s). As an alternative, argue that the cohousing concept described in "Cohousing and the American Dream" could help solve the problem(s).

10. Drawing on "My Mother Never Worked," "I Want a Wife," and "Homemaking," attack or defend the existing perception of the homemaker.

WRITING PARAPHRASES, QUOTATIONS, SUMMARIES, AND SYNTHESES

Writers frequently draw on the work of other writers. For example, you may use an idea from someone's essay to back up one of your points, or another writer's idea may prompt you to write an essay of your own. That's one of the exciting things about writing—writers engage in an ongoing conversation by responding to each other's ideas and using them for support or departure points. However, to be a part of this conversation, you must learn its rules, and that is what this appendix is all about. Here you will learn how writers can fairly and responsibly draw on the work of others.

 PARAPHRASING

To *paraphrase*, you restate another author's ideas, using your own writing style and wording. Paraphrasing is helpful because it allows you to incorporate brief excerpts from different sources into your essays to support your own ideas. (The sample synthesis on page 450 shows how paraphrases of different sources can be brought together.)

When you paraphrase, you must follow specific rules. These rules are illustrated with paraphrases of the following excerpt from "Self-Help—A Black Tradition" by Dorothy Height (page 431):

> One lesson is plain as we proceed: that public officials can establish all kinds of public programs thought up by people removed from the problems, and most will not work because the people for whom the programs are intended have been permitted no input in defining the problems as they actually know them to be, or in recommending the solutions (435).

1. Introduce the paraphrase with the author and/or source and a present tense verb; after the paraphrase place in parentheses the page number the paraphrase was taken from.

yes: In "Self-Help—A Black Tradition," Dorothy Height cautions that unless people who experience the problems help design the programs to solve them,
the programs probably will not work (435).

2. Do not add or alter meaning.

no: In "Self-Help—A Black Tradition," Dorothy Height says that the federal
government has not designed viable programs to solve problems because
they do not know how to (435). (Height does not specify the federal
government; she says "public officials," so meaning is altered. She does not
specifically say that officials do not know what they are doing, so meaning is
added.)

3. Alter style and wording.

no: Dorothy Height says in "Self-Help—A Black Tradition" that most public
programs designed by people removed from the problems will not work
(435). (*Public programs designed by people removed from the problems* is
almost identical to the source.)

◆ *Note:* Do not paraphrase by substituting synonyms, or you will have something that sounds stilted and unnatural, like this:

One moral is obvious as we go forward: that people who work in public
capacities can bring into being all manner of nonprivate programming con-
ceived by people distanced from the difficulties, and the majority will not work
because the folks for whom the programming is meant have been allowed no
opportunity to create definitions of the difficulties as they really recognize them to
exist, or in suggesting remedies (435).

Rather than plug in synonyms, explain the material in your own words to
achieve a more natural style.

 QUOTING

To *quote*, you reproduce an author's exact words. Like paraphrasing, quoting is
useful for bringing together ideas from one or more sources and for using
another author's ideas to support your own point. However, you should limit
the amount of quoting you do because if you quote too much, your writing will
lack your distinctive style. As a general guide, limit your quoting to those times
when paraphrase proves difficult or when something is so well expressed that
you want to preserve the original wording.

A number of conventions govern the use of quotations. Several of these are illustrated below, using material from "Reserve Marriage for Heterosexuals" (page 400) as examples.

1. Introduce the quotation with a statement of the author and/or source and a present tense verb. After the quotation, place the page number the quotation was taken from in parentheses. Be sure to preserve the words and punctuation in the original, and punctuate and capitalize correctly.

source: In the area of adoption, married couples are favored over singles.

quotation: Bruce Fein says, "In the area of adoption, married couples are favored over singles" (400).

2. When the introduction to the quotation has a direct object, use a colon instead of a comma before the quotation.

source: See number 1.

quotation: Bruce Fein notes a common bias toward married people: "In the area of adoption, married couples are favored over singles" (400).

3. Omit the comma and capital letter when the quotation follows an introduction with *that* in it.

source: See number 1.

quotation: Bruce Fein says that "in the area of adoption, married couples are favored over singles" (400).

4. Use ellipses (three spaced dots) to indicate that something has been left out.

source: Each legal issue regarding homosexuality should be examined discretely with the recognition that time has upset many fighting faiths and with the goal of balancing individual liberty against community interests.

quotation: Fein notes that "each legal issue regarding homosexuality should be examined discretely . . . with the goal of balancing individual liberty against community interests" (401).

5. Use brackets to add clarification or to make changes to work the quotation into your sentence.

source: To deny the right of homosexual marriage is not an argument for limiting other rights to gays, because of community animosity or vengeance.

quotation: Fein explains, "To deny the right of homosexual marriage is not an argument for limiting other rights [in housing, employment, school admissions, and so forth] to gays, because of community animosity or vengeance" (401).

6. For a quotation within a quotation, use single quotation marks where double quotation marks appear in the source.

source: As Supreme Court Justice Byron White recognized in *Taylor v. Louisiana* (1975): "[T]he two sexes are not fungible; a community made up exclusively of one is different from a community of both; the subtle interplay of influence one on the other is among the imponderables" (quoting from *Ballard v. United States*).

quotation: Fein tells us that Supreme Court Justice Byron White explains, " '[T]he two sexes are not fungible; a community made up exclusively of one is different from a community of both; the subtle interplay of influence one on the other is among the imponderables' " (400).

7. Underline to indicate that something appeared in italics in the source. See number 6.

quotation: Fein tells us that "Supreme Court Justice Byron White recognized in <u>Taylor v. Louisiana</u> (1975): '[T]he two sexes are not fungible' " (400).

 ## DOCUMENTING BORROWED MATERIAL

You probably know that taking another person's work and passing it off as your own is a form of academic dishonesty called *plagiarism*. However, another form of plagiarism, which is often unintentional but nonetheless serious, occurs when you paraphrase or quote and neglect to *document* the material by crediting its source.

If you use the words or ideas from sources in this text, you can document the borrowed material according to the conventions of the Modern Language Association (MLA). These conventions will be described below. However, different disciplines and different instructors will favor different conventions. In the social sciences, for example, the conventions of the American Psychological Association (APA) are often preferred. When in doubt, check with your instructor to learn which conventions you should follow.

When you paraphrase or quote, MLA documentation dictates that you credit the source material in two ways: with an introduction and with a parenthetical citation. The introduction states who the borrowing should be attributed to, and the parenthetical citation gives the page number where the borrowing can be found. Here are examples of the possibilities, taken from the sample synthesis that appears on page 450.

1. The first time you use a source, introduce it with the author's full name and the title of the source:

According to Maxine Phillips in "Needed: A Policy for Children When Parents Go to Work," more than half of all mothers go to work before their children are a year old (423).

◆ *Note:* The page number where the borrowed idea can be found appears in parentheses; the period goes outside those parentheses.

2. After the first time you use a source, you can introduce with either the author's last name or the title of the source; you do not need both.

As Fein says, "Experience confirms that child development is skewed, scarred or retarded when either a father or mother is absent in the household" (400).

◆ *Note:* Exact words appear in quotation marks; the page number appears in parentheses; the period goes outside those parentheses. Notice that the verb in the introduction is in the present tense.

3. If the name of the author or the title of the source does not appear in the introduction to the borrowing, place the author's name in the parenthetical citation.

According to Justice Byron White, " 'The subtle interplay of influence one on the other is among the imponderables' " (Fein 400).

◆ *Note:* The borrowing is introduced with the name of the speaker of the quotation, but that person is not the author of the essay the quotation appears in. The name of the essay author appears in parentheses.

4. Proper documentation requires you to follow your writing with an alphabetical listing of your sources. This listing is called the *Works Cited page*, and its purpose is to note all the information a reader needs to locate your sources. If you use sources that do not appear in this book, consult a handbook, a research paper guide, or your instructor for the correct format for entries on your Works Cited page. If your sources are essays in this book, your instructor may still require a Works Cited page. In that case, your format will be for a "work in an anthology," and it will look like this:

Stoddard, Thomas. "Marriage Is a Fundamental Right." *Patterns for a Purpose*. Ed. Barbara Fine Clouse. New York: McGraw-Hill, 1994. 397–398.

For examples of a Works Cited page, see pages 447 and 451.

SUMMARIZING

To *summarize*, you restate the main ideas of a piece, using your own style and wording. You may not interpret the author's ideas, evaluate them, or in any way add points that did not appear in the original. Thus, a summary is the distillation of what you see as the author's most important points. Because a summary includes only the highlights, it will be shorter than the original.

The Purpose of Summaries

College provides many opportunities to summarize. For one thing, summarizing is a valuable study technique because writing out the main points of material gives you a study guide and helps you learn information.

You may also write summaries for a grade. For example, instructors may ask you to summarize material so they can determine if you have read and understood assignments. On midterms and finals, they may also ask you to summarize reading assignments so they can check your comprehension and retention.

In addition, summaries are frequent components of other kinds of writing. If you are writing a research paper, for example, you will summarize information you discover in the library. If you are writing an argumentative-persuasive essay, you can summarize the main points in something you have read, and go on to disagree with those points. If you read something that helps explain a point you want to make in an essay, you can summarize what you read and use it as part of your supporting detail.

Suggestions for Writing a Summary

Step 1. Read the material over as many times as necessary in order to understand it. Look up unfamiliar words and get help with anything you do not understand. (You cannot summarize material you do not understand.)

Step 2. Identify the main points and underline them in the text or list them on a piece of paper. You can omit examples, description, repetition, or explanation that supports main points.

Step 3. Draft an opening sentence that mentions the author's name, the title of the piece you are summarizing, and one, two, or three of the following: the thesis, the author's purpose, the author's point of view. Here are some examples:

author, title,
   and thesis: In "I Wish They'd Do It Right," Jane Doe expresses her belief that her son is wrong not to marry the mother of his child.

author, title,	
and purpose:	"I Wish They'd Do It Right" is Jane Doe's attempt to convince people, including her son, that marriage is preferable to living together.
author, title,	
point of view:	In "I Wish They'd Do It Right," Jane Doe examines the issue of cohabitation from a parent's perspective.

◆ *Note:* Use a present tense verb with the author's name because the words "live on" into the present: Jane Doe *says, notes, expresses, believes* (not *noted, expressed, believed*).

Step 4.   Following your opening statement, draft your summary by writing out the main points you underlined or listed. Be sure to express these points in your own distinctive style by using your own wording and sentence structure. If you have trouble rewording a phrase or sentence, you can use the original if you place the borrowed words in quotation marks. Just be careful to use quotations sparingly.

◆ *Note:* If you have trouble expressing the author's ideas in a different way, imagine yourself explaining each idea to a friend. Then write each point the way you would explain it.

◆ *Note:* To keep your summary flowing smoothly, use transitions to show how ideas relate to each other. In addition, repeat the author's name with a present tense verb as a transitional device, like this:

Smith explains
Smith further believes
The author goes on to note

Step 5.   Revise by checking every point to be sure you have not added or altered meaning in any way. Also be sure that you have used your own wording and style and that you have placed borrowed words and phrases in quotation marks. Then read your summary out loud and listen for any gaps or abrupt shifts that signal the need to add transitions.

A Sample Summary

The following is a summary of "Needed: A Policy for Children When Parents Go to Work," which appears on page 423. The annotations in the margin call your attention to some of the summary's key features.

SUMMARY OF
NEEDED: A POLICY FOR CHILDREN
WHEN PARENTS GO TO WORK
Maxine Phillips

¹ Summary opens with a statement that gives the author, title, and thesis of material summarized.

² Verb is in the present tense.

³ First main point is given.

⁴ Borrowed words appear in quotation marks.

⁵ Transition is achieved with repetition of author's name. Note present tense.

⁶ Next main point is given.

⁷ Borrowed words appear in quotation marks.

⁸ Transitional word eases the flow.

⁹ Next main point is given.

¹⁰ Words quoted in the source appear in single quotation marks.

¹¹ Transitional word.

¹² Next main point.

¹³ Transition is achieved with repetition of the author's name. Note the present tense.

¹⁴ Borrowed words appear in quotation marks.

¹⁵ Transitional word.

¹⁶ The last main point is given.

¹⁷ In your summary, the "Works Cited" page should begin on a separate page.

In "Needed: A Policy for Children When Parents Go to Work," Maxine Phillips argues that we need a national child-care policy. She explains that day care is currently "inadequately funded and poorly regulated," so a new system is needed.

Phillips goes on to note that over 50 percent of mothers are working before their children are a year old. Because these mothers come from all strata, the child-care issue "cuts across political and class lines." However, current policy and legislation view day care as a service that only the poor need. As a result, funding will be subject to cuts. Particularly hard hit are the middle class, who face what *Business Week* calls " 'the day-care crisis of the middle-class.' " Furthermore, because of negative publicity and imperfect situations, many women are uncomfortable with existing centers, but better quality care is often not affordable.

To solve the problem, Phillips advocates a family leave law so parents can take time off following the birth of their children, "neighborhood nonprofit day-care facilities open to everyone," and after-school day care for school age children of working parents. She also calls for funding for prenatal care, nutrition, health care, and welfare to bolster the family unit. To secure these benefits, Phillips suggests that parents lobby for them.

Work Cited

Phillips, Maxine. "Needed: A Policy for Children When Parents Go to Work." *Patterns for a Purpose*. Ed. Barbara Fine Clouse. New York: McGraw-Hill, 1995. 423-425.

SYNTHESIZING

Synthesizing involves bringing material from two or more sources together in one essay. When you synthesize, you may evaluate the material you are working with and form judgments about it; you may draw conclusions from the material; you may use the material to support the thesis of your essay; or you may use the material to back up one or more of your points.

The Purpose of Synthesis

Synthesis can have an informational purpose. For example, to inform your reader about the effects of televised violence on children, you could mention all the effects discussed in a number of essays and books on the subject. Synthesis can also allow a writer to inform by presenting an overview of a topic. For example, if authorities disagree on how children are affected by televised violence, you could synthesize these views to inform your reader of current thinking on the subject.

Writers can use information from two or more sources to back up points in support of a thesis. In this case, the synthesis often serves a persuasive purpose. For example, to argue that televised violence is harmful to children, you could bring together the statements made in different sources about the ways televised violence is thought to hurt younger viewers.

Detail in a Synthesis

Sometimes a synthesis includes only the information from your sources. For example, you could present an overview of the pressures facing the family just by drawing on the information in the essays in Chapter 12. Other times, a synthesis blends source material and your own ideas. Thus, you could present an overview of the pressures facing the family by drawing on your own experience and observation, as well as the information in Chapter 12's essays.

Sometimes you evaluate your synthesized material and draw a conclusion. For example, you could present all the information from the essays in Chapter 12 about the pressures on the American family, and then you could conclude that the traditional family will not survive in its current form. Other times, you can use synthesized material to support your own points. For example, you could argue that the family is in no danger of extinction by using points in Chapter 12 for support.

An essay with synthesized material can take a number of forms. You can agree or disagree with information in sources. You can also show areas of agreement and disagreement between different sources, or you can show how the ideas in one source prove or disprove the ideas in another. You can even show how the ideas in one source serve as an example of points in another. Even these do not exhaust all the possibilities, for what you do with the material from sources is limited only by the conclusions you draw and the relationships you see among ideas.

Suggestions for Synthesizing Information

Step 1. Be sure you understand everything in all the sources you are dealing with. If necessary, look up words and ask your instructor for clarification.

Step 2. Underline or list the main ideas in each source.

Step 3. Review the main ideas and determine how they relate to each other. Answering these five questions can help:

1. Do the ideas in the sources support each other or contradict each other?
2. Do the ideas in the sources form a cause-and-effect relationship?
3. Do the ideas in one source explain or exemplify the ideas in another source?
4. Do the ideas in one source pick up where the ideas in another source end?
5. Do the sources examine the same topic from different perspectives?

Step 4. Decide how you want to use the material in the sources. Answering these five questions can help:

1. Can I use the information to explain something?
2. Can I use the information to prove something?
3. Can I show how the sources contradict each other or present different perspectives?
4. Can I explain the significance of the information?
5. Can I use the information to support my own experience or observation?

Step 5. Write some form of outline and a thesis that makes clear what point your essay makes.

Step 6. Write a draft from your outline.

Step 7.   When you revise, check the accuracy of your paraphrases and quotations, and be sure you have properly documented your sources with introductions and parenthetical citations. (See page 443 on documentation.)

A Sample Synthesis

The following essay shows how ideas from two sources ("Marriage Is a Fundamental Right" on page 397 and "Reserve Marriage for Heterosexuals" on page 400) can be synthesized. The notes in the margin call your attention to some of the key features of the synthesis.

THE CONTROVERSY SURROUNDING SAME-SEX MARRIAGES

[1] The writer's own background and evaluation lead in to the synthesis.

[2] The introduction credits source. It includes the author's full name and the title of the essay, since this is the first use of the source.

[3] Direct quotation of sentence 1.

[4] Parenthetical citation to credit the source.

[5] The thesis.

[6] Introduction includes full name and title since this is first use of source.

[7] Borrowing includes paraphrase and quotation from paragraph 6.

[8] The writer draws a conclusion.

[9] Only last name is used because full name used previously.

[10] Paraphrase of paragraph 7.

[11] Parenthetical citation.

[12] The topic sentence is the writer's evaluation.

[1] No one will deny that the makeup of the American family has changed dramatically in recent years. Whereas once the "normal" family consisted of a biological mother, a biological father, and children, now we are accustomed to families headed by unwed mothers, divorced fathers, grandparents, and stepparents. Half-brothers and -sisters may live with step-brothers and -sisters in configurations as diverse as the populace. All of this is now "normal." Despite this redefinition of family structures to encompass considerable diversity, we draw the line at one point: We seem unwilling to accept marriage among people of the same gender. Perhaps the legalization of same-sex marriages will occur in the future, but for now many people feel like Bruce Fein,[2] who says, in "Reserve Marriage for Heterosexuals," that "authorizing[3] the marriage of homosexuals, like sanctioning polygamy, would be unenlightened social policy" (400).[4] I[5] believe that this view is misguided.

[6]Marriage should be allowed between consenting adults, regardless of their gender. As Thomas Stoddard[6] explains in "Marriage Is a Fundamental Right," the[7] Supreme Court has ruled that our pursuit of happiness encompasses "the freedom to marry" (397). However,[8] marriage involves more than the constitutionally guaranteed right to the pursuit of happiness. It also figures significantly into the well-being of people. As Stoddard[9] points out, marriage is[10] a critical factor in emotional and financial survival (397).[11]

[12]If the issue were only the pursuit of happiness or emotional and financial survival, I doubt that people would object as strenuously as they currently do. People seem most opposed because of fears about how same-sex marriages

[13] Borrowing is introduced with last name because full name given previously.

[14] Quotation is from paragraph 7.

[15] Writer counters the objection.

[16] Idea is the writer's.

[17] Introduction with the author's last name because full name given previously. Note the present tense.

[18] Quotation is from paragraph 10.

[19] The conclusion, which is the author's idea, looks to the future.

will affect our children. Fein,[13] for example, fears that homosexual marriages "would[14] wrongly send social cues that male-female marriages are not preferable" (400). Such an[15] argument is spurious, for sanctioning same-sex marriages is more likely to teach acceptance and love for all people— ideals we should never fear.

Particularly[16] pertinent is the fact that heterosexual marriages have not been faring well lately. Divorce rates are alarmingly high, and children suffer from the breakup of their families. This instability can be partly offset by homosexual marriage, which Stoddard[17] notes "promotes social[18] stability" (398).

Change[19] is often hard to accept, but we have already accepted considerable change in the nature of the family. Eventually, we will accept one more: the legalization of same-sex marriages.

[20] In your synthesis, the "Works Cited" page should begin on a new page.

Works Cited[20]

Fein, Bruce. "Reserve Marriage for Heterosexuals." *Patterns for a Purpose*. Ed. Barbara Fine Clouse. New York: McGraw-Hill, 1995. 400-401.

Stoddard, Thomas. "Marriage Is a Fundamental Right." *Patterns for a Purpose*. Ed. Barbara Fine Clouse. New York: McGraw-Hill, 1995. 397-398.

ACKNOWLEDGMENTS

"America Has Gone on a Trip Out of Tune" by Dave Barry from MIAMI HERALD, July 14, 1991. Reprinted by permission of Tribune Media Services.

"Class Acts" by John Berendt from ESQUIRE, April 1991. Reprinted by permission of the author.

Excerpt from "The Holocaust" from SURVIVING AND OTHER ESSAYS by Bruno Bettelheim. Copyright © 1979 by Bruno Bettelheim and Trude Bettelheim as Trustees. Reprinted by permission of Alfred A. Knopf, Inc.

"The Unbearable Lightness of Air Travel" from NOW, WHERE WERE WE by Roy Blount, Jr. Copyright © 1989 by Roy Blount, Jr. Reprinted by permission of Villard Books, a division of Random House, Inc.

"Wait Division" (pp. 53–56) from SMALL COMFORTS by Tom Bodett. Copyright © 1987 by Tom Bodett. Reprinted by permission of Addison-Wesley Publishing Company, Inc.

"White Lies" from LYING: MORAL CHOICES IN PUBLIC AND PRIVATE LIVES by Sissela Bok. Copyright © 1978 by Sissela Bok. Reprinted by permission of Pantheon Books, a division of Random House, Inc.

"Why I Want a Wife" by Judy Brady from Ms. Magazine, December 1971. Copyright © 1971 by Ms. Magazine. Reprinted by permission of Ms. Magazine.

"Neat People vs. Sloppy People" from SHOW AND TELL by Suzanne Britt. Copyright © 1982 by Suzanne Britt. Reprinted by permission of the author.

"Grant and Lee: A Study in Contrasts" from THE AMERICAN STORY by Bruce Catton, published by U.S. Historical Society. Reprinted by permission of William B. Catton.

"Dawn Watch" from MANNER OF SPEAKING by John Ciardi. Copyright © 1972 by John Ciardi. Reprinted by permission of The Ciardi Family.

"Don't Just Stand There" by Diana Cole from A WORLD OF DIFFERENCE section of The New York Times, 4/16/89. Reprinted by permission of the author.

" 'Why' Is Worse Than 'What' " by George E. Condon from THE PLAIN DEALER, 1975. Reprinted by permission of The Plain Dealer.

Excerpt from THE VIEW FROM 80 by Malcolm Cowley. Copyright © 1976, 1978, 1980 by Malcolm Cowley. Used by permission of Viking Penguin, a division of Penguin Books USA Inc.

"The Deer at Providencia" from TEACHING A STONE TO TALK by Annie Dillard. Copyright 1982 by Annie Dillard. Reprinted by permission of HarperCollins Publishers, Inc.

"I Wish They'd Do It Right" by Jane Doe from THE NEW YORK TIMES, September 23, 1977. Copyright © 1977 by The New York Times Company. Reprinted by permission.

"What I've Learned From Men: Lessons For A Full-Grown Feminist" by Barbara Ehrenreich from Ms. Magazine, August 1985. Copyright © 1985 by Ms. Magazine. Reprinted by permission of Ms. Magazine.

"Reserve Marriage for Heterosexuals" by Bruce Fein from AMERICAN BAR ASSOCIATION JOURNAL, January 1990. Copyright © 1990 by American Bar Association. Reprinted by permission of the ABA Journal.

"On Holidays and How to Make Them Work" from SACRED COWS AND OTHER EDIBLES by Nikki Giovanni. Copyright (1988) Nikki Giovanni. Reprinted by permission of William Morrow & Co. Inc.

"Family and Community: Self-Help—A Black Tradition" by Dorothy Height from *The Nation*, July 31, 1989 issue. Copyright © The Nation Company, Inc. Reprinted by permission of *The Nation* magazine.

Excerpt from FAMILIES by Jane Howard. Copyright © 1978 by Jane Howard. Reprinted by permission of Simon & Schuster, Inc.

"Salvation" from THE BIG SEA by Langston Hughes. Copyright © 1940 by Langston Hughes, renewed © 1968 by George Houston Bass and Arna Bontemps. Reprinted by permission of Hill & Wang, a division of Farrar, Straus & Giroux, Inc.

"Brains and Computers" from THE ENCHANTED LOOM by Robert Jastrow. Copyright © 1981 by Reader's Library, Inc. Reprinted by permission of Simon & Schuster, Inc.

"The Water-Faucet Vision" by Gish Jen. Copyright 1987 by Gish Jen. First published in *Nimrod*. Reprinted by permission of the author.

Excerpt from "The Block and Beyond" in A WALKER IN THE CITY by Alfred Kazin. Copyright 1951 and renewed 1979 by Alfred Kazin. Reprinted by permission of Harcourt Brace & Company.

"The Way of Meeting Oppression" from STRIDE TOWARD FREEDOM by Martin Luther King, Jr. Copyright 1958 by Martin Luther King, Jr., copyright renewed 1986 by Coretta Scott King. Reprinted by arrangement with The Heirs to the Estate of Martin Luther King, Jr., c/o Joan Daves Agency as agent for the proprietor.

"Why We Crave Horror Movies" by Stephen King. Reprinted by permission of Arthur B. Greene for the author.

"Untouchables" from RACHEL AND HER CHILDREN: HOMELESS FAMILIES IN AMERICA by Jonathan Kozol. Copyright © 1988 by Jonathan Kozol. Reprinted by permission of Crown Publishers.

"Lists" by Jeanine Larmoth from TOWN & COUNTRY, November 1989. Reprinted by permission of the author.

"What Sort of Car-Rt-Sort Am I?" by Erik Larson from Harper's Magazine, July 1989. Reprinted by permission of Harper's Magazine.

"Cohousing and the American Dream" excerpted from *Cohousing: A Contemporary Approach to Housing Ourselves* by Kathryn McCamant and Charles Durrett. Copyright © 1988 by Kathryn McCamant and Charles Durrett. Used by permission of Ten Speed Press, P.O. Box 7123, Berkeley, CA 94707.

"My Backyard (Chapter 1)" and "Shades of Black" from MARY by Mary Mebane. Copyright © 1981 by Mary Elizabeth Mebane. Used by permission of Viking Penguin, a division of Penguin Books USA Inc.

INDEX

Active reading, 18–25
Adequate detail, 5–6
"Am I Blue," 240–245
"America Has Gone on a Trip Out of Tune," 270–273
"Americanization Is Tough on 'Macho,'" 21–24
Argumentation-persuasion, 386–439
  annotated student essay, 395–396
  emotional appeals, 391
  logic, 389–390
  organizing, 392–394
  purpose of, 387
  raising and countering objections, 391–392
  suggestions for writing, 394
  supporting detail, 388–394
  thesis, 393
  topic sentences, 393
Audience, 4, 31, 32
"Autumn," 347–348

Barry, Dave, "America Has Gone on a Trip Out of Tune," 270–273
"Behind the Formaldehyde Curtain," 198–206
Benedict, Carl, "Why Athletes Use Steroids," 267–269
Berendt, John, "Class Acts," 139–142
Bettelheim, Bruno, "The Holocaust," 355–359
Blount, Roy Jr., "The Unbearable Lightness of Air Travel," 177–181
Bodett, Tom, "Wait Division," 309–312
Body paragraphs, 8–9
Bok, Sissella, "White Lies," 313–316
Brady, Judy, "I Want a Wife," 366–369
"Brains and Computers," 246–251
Britt, Suzanne, "Neat People vs. Sloppy People," 228–231

"By Any Other Name," 111–117

Catton, Bruce, "Grant and Lee: A Study in Contrasts," 235–239
Cause-and-effect analysis, 263–300
  annotated student essay, 267
  organizing, 265–266
  purpose of, 264
  suggestions for writing, 266–267
  supporting detail, 264–266
  thesis, 266
Chronological order, 9, 85, 132, 174, 265
Ciardi, John, "Dawn Watch," 49–53
"Class Acts," 139–142
Classification-division, 301–343
  annotated student essay, 306–308
  organizing, 304–306
  principle for, 303
  purpose of, 302–303
  suggestions for writing, 306
  supporting details, 303–304
  thesis, 304–305
  topic sentences, 305
  transitions, 305
Clustering, 30
"Cohousing and the American Dream," 407–412
Cole, Diane, "Don't Just Stand There," 182–188
"College Pressures," 323–331
Comparison and contrast, 220–262
  annotated student essay, 220–262
  organizing, 223–224
  purpose of, 221
  suggestions for writing, 225
  supporting details, 222–224
  thesis, 223–224
"Complexion," 295–299
Conclusion, 13–15, 86, 393–394

Condon, George E., " 'Why' Is Worse Than 'What,' " 135–138
"Controversy Surrounding Same-Sex Marriages, The," 450–451
Conversation, 84
"Country Codes," 317–322
Cowley, Malcolm, "The View from 80," 370–378
Cummins, Julie, "Autumn," 347–348
Cummins, Julie, "In Chelsea's Room," 48

"Dawn Watch," 49–53
"Deer at Providencia, The," 76–80
Definition, 343–385
  annotated student essay, 347–348
  introduction, 346
  organizing, 345–346
  purpose of, 344
  suggestions for writing, 346–347
  supporting details, 345–346
  thesis, 345
Description, 42–81, 83
  annotated student essay, 47–48
  descriptive words, 45
  dominant impression, 46
  metaphors, 45
  objective and expressive details, 43, 44–45
  organizing, 46–47
  purpose of, 42
  sensory details, 43
  simile, 45
  specific words, 44–45
  suggestions for writing, 47
  supporting details, 46–47
  thesis, 46–47
Diction, 3, 4–5
  descriptive words, 43–45
  metaphors, 45
  similes, 45
  specific words, 44–45
Dillard, Annie, "The Deer at Providencia," 76–80
Division (see Classification-division)
Documenting borrowed material, 443–444
"Don't Just Stand There," 182–188

Drafting, 36–37
Durrett, Charles and Kathryn McCamant, "Cohousing and the American Dream," 407–412

Editing, 40
Ehrenreich, Barbara, "What I've Learned from Men," 153–158
Emotional appeal, 391
"Endless Streetcar Ride into the Night and the Tinfoil Noose, The," 98–104
Exemplification, 128–169
  annotated student essay, 133–134
  organizing, 130–132
  purpose of, 129, 130–133
  suggestions for writing, 132
  supporting details, 130–132
  thesis, 131
  transitions, 131
Expressive details, 443, 44–45

"Families," 413–422
"Family Reunion Revisited, The," 87–88
Fein, Bruce, "Reserve Marriage for Heterosexuals," 400–402
Formal outline, 35–36
Freewriting, 28

Giovanni, Nikki, "On Holidays and How to Make Them Work," 143–145
"Good Souls," 360–365
"Grant and Lee: A Study in Contrasts," 235–239
Guibault, Rose Del Castillo, "Americanization Is Tough on 'Macho,' " 21–24

"Hanging, A," 105–110
Height, Dorothy, "Self-Help—A Black Tradition," 431–437
"Holocaust, The," 355–359
"Homemaking," 427–430
"How I'll Become an American," 189–192
Howard, Jane, "Families," 413–422
Hughes, Langston, "Salvation," 89–92

"I Want a Wife," 366–369
"I Wish They'd Do It Right," 403–406
Idea generation, 26–31
"In Chelsea's Room," 48
"India: A Widow's Devastating Choice,"
 278–284
Informal outline, 33
Introduction, 11–13, 86, 346, 392–393
"Is Today's Athlete a Good Sport?"
 16–17

Jastrow, Robert, "Brains and
 Computers," 246–251
Jen, Gish, "The Water-Faucet Vision,"
 118–126
"Just Walk on By: A Black Man Ponders
 His Power to Alter Public Space,"
 285–290

Kazin, Alfred, "My Neighborhood,"
 71–75
King, Martin Luther, Jr., "The Ways of
 Meeting Oppression," 332–335
"Knife, The," 193–197
Kozol, Jonathan, "Untouchables,"
 159–160

Larmoth, Jeanine, "Lists," 379–384
Larson, Erik, "What Sort of Car-Rt-Sort
 Am I?" 207–217
"Lists," 379–384
Logic, 389–390

Mahoney, Laurel, "Who Should
 Decide?" 395–396
"Man's Game, A," 133–134
"Marriage Is a Fundamental Right,"
 397–399
McCamant, Kathryn and Charles
 Durrett, "Cohousing and the
 American Dream," 407–412
Mebane, Mary E., "My Backyard,"
 65–70
Mebane, Mary E., "Shades of Black,"
 336–341
Metaphors, 45
Mitford, Jessica, "Behind the Formal-
 dehyde Curtain," 198–206

"My Backyard," 65–70
"My Mother Never Worked," 93–97
"My Neighborhood," 71–75

Narration, 82–127
 annotated student essay, 87–88
 conversation in, 84
 description in, 83
 organizing, 84–86
 purpose of, 83
 suggestions for writing, 86
 supporting details, 83–86
 thesis, 86
 transitions, 85
"Neat People vs. Sloppy People,"
 228–231
"Needed: A Policy for Children When
 Parents Go to Work," 423–426
"No Kick from Champagne," 291–294

Objective and expressive details, 43,
 44–45
Objective details, 43
"On Holidays and How to Make Them
 Work," 143–145
"Once More to the Lake," 58–64
"Opposites Attract," 225–227
Organization:
 alternating, 224
 of argumentation-persuasion,
  392–394
 block, 223–224
 body pargraphs, 8–9
 of cause-and-effect analysis, 265–266
 chronological order 85, 132, 174–175,
  265
 of classification, 304–306
 of comparison and contrast, 223–224
 conclusion, 13–15, 86
 of definition, 345–346
 of description, 46–47
 of exemplification, 130–132
 introduction, 11–13, 86, 392–393
 of narration, 84–86
 ordering details, 9
 of process analysis, 173–174
 progressive order, 131, 265, 393
 sample student essay, 16–17

Organization (*Cont.*):
  supporting details, 5–11
  thesis, 1–3, 11–12, 46–47, 86, 131,
      173, 266, 304–305, 345, 393
  topic sentence, 8, 11, 266, 393
  transitions, 9–11, 85, 131, 174, 266
Orwell, George, "A Hanging," 105–110
Outline tree, 33–34
Outline worksheet, 34–35
Outlining, 31–36
  formal outline, 35–36
  informal outline, 33
  outline tree, 33–34
  scratch outline, 31–33
  outline worksheet, 34–35

Paraphrasing, 440–441
Parker, Dorothy, "Good Souls,"
    360–365
Parker, Jo Goodwin, "What Is Poverty?"
    349–354
Patterns of development, 7–8
  cause-and-effect analysis, 263–300
  classification-division, 301–343
  comparison-contrast, 220–262
  definition, 343–385
  description, 42–81
  exemplification, 128–169
  narration, 82–127
  process analysis, 170–176
Perrin, Noel, "Country Codes," 317–322
Persuasion (*see* Argumentation-
    persuasion)
Phillips, Maxine, "Needed: A Policy for
    Children When Parents Go to
    Work," 423–426
Plagiarism, 443
Prewriting (*see* Idea generation)
Process analysis, 170–176
  annotated student essay, 175–176
  organizing, 173–174
  purpose of, 171–172
  suggestions for writing, 174–175
  supporting details, 172–174
  thesis, 173
Progressive order, 9, 131, 265, 393
Proofreading, 40–41
Purpose, 3, 31, 32

Purpose (*Cont.*):
  of argumentation-persuasion, 387
  of cause-and-effect analysis, 264
  of classification-division, 302–303
  of comparison-contrast, 221
  of definition, 344
  of description, 42
  of exemplification, 129–130
  of narration, 83
  of process analysis, 171–172

Quoting, 441–443

Raising and countering objections,
    391–392
Raspberry, William, "Homemaking,"
    427–430
Rau, Santha Rama, "By Any Other
    Name," 111–117
Relevant detail, 6–7
"Reserve Marriage for Heterosexuals,"
    400–402
Revising, 38–39, 40
Revision checklist, 39
Rodriguez, Richard, "Complexion,"
    295–299
Role, writer's, 4, 31, 32

Saltzman, Harold, "No Kick from
    Champagne," 291–294
"Salvation," 89–92
Scratch outline, 31–33
"Self-Help—A Black Tradition,"
    431–437
Selzer, Richard, "The Knife," 193–197
Sensory details, 43
"Shades of Black," 336–341
Shepherd, Jean, "The Endless Streetcar
    Ride into the Night and the Tinfoil
    Noose," 98–104
Similes, 45
Smith-Yackel, Bonnie, "My Mother
    Never Worked," 93–97
"Sounds of the City, The," 54–57
Spatial order, 9
Specific words, 44–45
Stangl, Juthica, "India: A Widow's
    Devastating Choice," 278–284

Staples, Brent, "Just Walk on By: A Black Man Ponders His Power to Alter Public Space," 285–290

Stoddard, Thomas, "Marriage Is a Fundamental Right," 397–399

"Strictly Speaking," 306–308

Summarizing, 445–447

Supporting details, 5–11
   adequate detail, 5–6
   for argumentation-persuasion, 388–394
   body paragraphs, 8–9
   for cause-and-effect analysis, 264–266
   for classification-division, 303–304
   for comparison and contrast, 222–224
   for definition, 345–346
   for description, 46–47
   for exemplification, 130–132
   for narration, 83–86
   objective and expressive details, 43
   organizing, 8–9
   patterns of development, 7–8
   for process analysis, 172–174
   relevant detail, 6–7
   source of, 7–8
   topic sentence, 8, 11, 46, 266, 305
   transitions, 9–11

Synthesizing, 448–451

"Talk in the Intimate Relationship: His and Hers," 252–260

Tannen, Deborah, "Talk in the Intimate Relationship: His and Hers," 252–260

Thesis, 1–3, 11–12
   for cause-and-effect analysis, 266
   for classification-division, 304–305
   for comparison and contrast, 223–224
   for definition, 345
   for description, 46–47
   for exemplification, 131
   for narration, 86
   for process analysis, 173

Thurber, James, "University Days," 146–152

Titles, 15

Tone, 4–5, 31, 32

Topic Selection, 27–29

Topic sentence, 8, 11, 46, 266, 305

Transitions, 9–11, 85, 131, 174, 266, 305

Tuite, James, "The Sounds of the City," 54–57

Twain, Mark, "Two Views of the Mississippi," 232–234

"Two Views of the Mississippi," 232–234

"Unbearable Lightness of Air Travel, The," 177–181

"University Days," 146–152

"Untouchables," 159–168

Vámos, Miklós, "How I'll Become an American," 189–192

"View from 80, The," 370–378

"Wait Division," 309–312

Walker, Alice, "Am I Blue?" 240–245

Ware, Rhonda, "Your Basic Blast," 175–176

Warnock, Robbie, "The Family Reunion Revisited," 87–88

"Water-Faucet Vision, The," 118–126

"Ways of Meeting Oppression, The," 332–335

"What Is Poverty?" 349–354

"What I've Learned from Men," 153–158

"What Sort of Car-Rt-Sort Am I?" 207–217

White, E. B., "Once More to the Lake," 58–64

"White Lies," 313–316

"Why Athletes Use Steroids," 267–269

"Why We Crave Horror Movies," 274–277

" 'Why' Is Worse Than 'What,' " 135–138

Wolfe, David, "Strictly Speaking," 306–308

Word choice (*see* Diction)

Works cited page, 444, 447, 451

"Your Basic Blast," 175–176

Zinsser, William, "College Pressures," 323–331